PUBLIC RELATIONS
STRATEGIES AND TACTICS

PUBLIC

STRATEGIES

DENNIS L. WILCOX
San Jose State University

PHILLIP H. AULT
South Bend *Tribune*

WARREN K. AGEE
University of Georgia

RELATIONS

AND TACTICS

1817

HARPER & ROW, PUBLISHERS, NEW YORK

Cambridge, Philadelphia, San Francisco,
London, Mexico City, São Paulo, Singapore, Sydney

Sponsoring Editor: Phillip Leininger
Editorial Production Manager: Nora Helfgott
Text and Cover Design: Betty Binns Graphics/Martin Lubin
Text Art: Vantage Art, Inc.
Photo Research: Mira Schachne
Production Manager: Jeanie Berke
Compositor: Ruttle, Shaw & Wetherill, Inc.
Printer and Binder: R. R. Donnelley & Sons Company

Public Relations: Strategies and Tactics

Library of Congress Cataloging-in-Publication Data

Wilcox, Dennis, L.
  Public relations.

  Bibliography: p.
  Includes index.
  1. Public relations. I. Ault, Phillip H.,
1914–   .   II. Agee, Warren Kendall.   III. Title.
HM263.W49 1986   659.2   85-16384
ISBN 0-06-040176-1

86 87 88 9 8 7 6 5 4 3 2

BRIEF CONTENTS

DETAILED CONTENTS

PART ONE: **ROLE** 1

viii

x

PART FOUR: **APPLICATION**

FOREWORD

by Edward L. Bernays

I gave the first course in public relations ever offered at a university at New York University in 1923.*

One of the basic attributes of a profession is that it have a literature of its own. In 1923 I wrote a book, *Crystalizing Public Opinion,* published by Boni and Liveright. It defined the principles and practices of the new profession of public relations and laid down the principles of ethics by which it should be governed.

Today over 16,000 items exist in the bibliography of public relations. Every new volume of note that takes up and discusses the old and new problems the profession faces should be welcomed.

With the increasing complexity of our society, the professional public relations practitioner, an applied social science technician, must gain new and old knowledge from books before he or she can practice the profession effectively. That is the pattern pursued consistently by lawyers, medical doctors, and other professionals.

With people power the most dominant force in society today, it is essential that the professional public relations practitioner have the broadest understanding possible of the profession. This book meets that need.

The past is prelude to the future. That is why the historical treatment of public relations set forth in this volume is so important. Historical perspective provides proof why people must be given such serious consideration. Every activity depends on people for its survival, whether profit or nonprofit. By taking up the various steps to pursue in various fields, this book provides basic approaches for teacher, student, and practitioner.

I have found in my professional practice of 73 years that books have been my greatest and most valuable resource.

Many people in public relations, as in other fields, like to think of themselves as Columbuses and Magellans in tackling their problems, as if they were the first to ever burst upon a particular issue. But there are also those people who are the real Columbuses and Magellans. They read a book

---

* New York University commemorated the sixty-second anniversary of the teaching of public relations at a ceremony in 1985, during which NYU President John Brademas presented Dr. Bernays with a presidential citation.

like this and then proceed. That is why I urge young practitioners and older practitioners, too, to use books like this one as their greatest resource in the practice of their profession.

Yet there are serious problems concerning public relations that readers of this book must face if the profession is to survive. The words *public relations* are in the public domain. Unlike most other professions, public relations as a field has not been defined by law. And in the American language, words may have the stability of soap bubbles. Anyone can misuse the term *public relations*. And many people unfitted by education, experience, or ethics do use the term to mean almost anything.

I noted in one directory of a public relations association 14 different appellations, with none of them giving the least indication of an individual's education, experience, or ethics. Today any car salesperson or paperhanger can assume the title "public relations practitioner." I have seen help-wanted advertisements for tourist-guide public relations practitioners who are required to "love people." It is in the interest of all the readers of this book to maintain and strengthen the status of public relations as a profession.

Public relations is an art applied to a science—social science in which the public interest rather than financial motivation is the primary consideration. A professional practitioner in public relations would turn down Somoza, Franco, and Hitler as clients, as I did.

Public relations today has all the characteristics of a profession except one. Public relations lacks the final characteristic of a profession: licensing and registration by the state.

The public relations profession has its literature, an earmark of a profession. With over 16,000 items published as of this writing, the literature grows as every year *Public Relations Review* adds to the bibliography.

Public relations has its educational courses, another earmark of a profession. In this and most other countries, instruction is offered in public relations. But what is actually taught as public relations often differs from school to school. Obviously, education would be standardized if licensing and registration were adopted in public relations, as is currently the case with legal and medical instruction.

Public relations has its professional associations. They not only exist in this country but internationally as well. There is an International Public Relations Association, with members in more than 66 countries. In the corporate world, association members guard their secrets. In professional associations, knowledge is shared.

Ethics is still another earmark of a profession. The public relations societies have their codes of ethics. In the case of licensed and registered professions, these codes of ethics are enforced by law. In public relations, there are no legal sanctions.

Steps are now being taken by a group of practitioners to bring needed change about. A committee calling for registration and licensing with legal sanctions has been established, with Ted Baron, former president of the New York chapter of the Public Relations Society, and myself as cochairpersons. This change will not only preserve and codify the standards of the profession but also will prevent unqualified individuals from calling themselves public relations practitioners. It would also standardize the teaching of public relations in the United States.

In my judgment, degrees in public relations should be given upon completion of a liberal arts program. In the two years following, M.S. degree candidates in public relations would study all of the social science disciplines, including economics and history. Additionally, universities could set up a double-degree program for students who plan a career in a specific area of public relations; for example, degrees in medicine and public relations for a career in medical public relations.

In sum, this book promises to be a good preparation for life.

EDWARD L. BERNAYS
Cambridge, Mass.

We recognize that diversity exists in the teaching of an introductory course in public relations. At some colleges and universities, the course is offered as an overview of the entire field, covering theories, strategies, and on-the-job tactics. Other universities concentrate on theory and strategy, teaching the tactical applications in public relations writing courses.

This book has been organized for use under both methods. It is divided into five parts:

Part One	Role
Part Two	Process
Part Three	Strategy
Part Four	Application
Part Five	Tactics

The first four parts examine the principles, theories, and strategies of public relations in a natural teaching sequence. The fifth part explains the techniques of day-by-day public relations practice—such assignments as preparing a news release, writing a speech, coaching a client for a television appearance, and staging a press party. Instructors who do not include tactical applications in their introductory courses may simply omit Part Five.

The book is designed for public relations majors but also may be used by business students, speech communication specialists, and indeed by anyone, from nursing students to recreation directors, whose career will profit from a knowledge of public relations.

Readers will find the book anecdotal, written in an easy, informal style. To help them understand the realities of daily public relations practice, as well as its theoretical basis, we have included abundant case studies and examples drawn from recent professional experience.

Because public relations has taken on so many new dimensions, we have covered an unusually broad range of topics, some of which have recently gained increased emphasis as essential elements of the specialist's work.

These include the following:

Issues management

Crisis public relations

Ethics

International public relations

Legal ramifications

Also, we have brought fresh insights to an understanding of entertainment and sports publicity, internal corporate communication, and community affairs. A comprehensive history chapter explains how public relations developed.

The explosion of electronic techniques, through computer applications and transmission by satellite, is changing the face of public relations. We have discussed their use, impact, and implications for the future in the chapter "Public Relations and New Technologies."

Finally, for the reader's convenience, we have grouped the many techniques used in public relations practice into three categories, with a chapter on each: "Written Tactics," "Spoken Tactics," and "Visual Tactics."

Supplementing the body of the text are a glossary of public relations terms and a comprehensive bibliography prepared by the Public Relations Society of America. Study questions appear at the end of each chapter.

Acknowledgments

A textbook of such scope as this one could not have been written without the assistance of many academic and professional advisers and consultants. We particularly want to thank the following academics who read drafts of the manuscript and provided many helpful suggestions: Robert L. Bishop, University of Georgia; Michael B. Hesse, University of Alabama; Robert L. Kendall, University of Florida; Norman R. Nager, California State University at Fullerton; Walt Seifert, Ohio State University; Judy VanSlyke Turk, University of Oklahoma; and Albert Walker, Northern Illinois University.

We also wish to express our gratitude to the following individuals and organizations that provided illustrations and information:

INDIVIDUALS John E. Bennett, vice-president, Council for Advancement and Support of Education, Washington, D.C.

Leroy J. Bieringer, executive vice-president and general manager, Fleishman-Hillard, Inc., New York.

Marlene Bryan, coordinator of public relations, Clarke County School System, Athens, Georgia.

John F. Budd, Jr., vice-president of corporate relations, Emhart Corporation, Hartford, Connecticut.

Carolyn Campion, director of public affairs, Nestlé Nutrition Center, Washington, D.C.

Deborah Chism, editor, *Between Branches,* Avco Financial Services, Newport Beach, California.

James Christensen, director of public relations, Goodwill Industries of Santa Clara County, California.

Lenore Cooney, senior vice-president, Dudley-Anderson-Yutzy Public Relations, New York.

Clara Degan, director of educational affairs, International Association of Business Communicators, San Francisco.

David Drobis, president, Ketchum Public Relations, New York.

Lawrence G. Foster, vice-president of public relations, Johnson & Johnson, New Brunswick, New Jersey.

Larry Gavrich, editor, *J. C. Penney Today,* New York.

James E. Grunig, College of Journalism, University of Maryland, College Park.

Irene Hannon, Anheuser-Busch, Inc., St. Louis.

Carol Heyn, director of public relations, Parkview Memorial Hospital, Fort Wayne, Indiana.

Barbara Kessel, Marian Medical Center, Santa Maria, California.

Don Levin, senior vice-president, Hill and Knowlton, New York.

Lorry I. Lokey, general manager, Business Wire, San Francisco.

Richard L. Manning, vice-president for public relations, San Diego Gas & Electric Company.

Cliff McGoon, editor, *Communication World,* International Association of Business Communicators, San Francisco.

Randall Murray, professor, California Polytechnic State University, San Luis Obispo, California.

Doyle Peck, director of public relations, Braille Institute, Los Angeles.

A. Lee Rogers, special assistant to the president, Lockheed-Georgia Corporation, Marietta, Georgia.

David M. Schneer, head of secondary reseaarch, Regis McKenna Public Relations, Palo Alto, California.

Ralph "Casey" Shawhan, Los Angeles.

Paul Snodgrass, editor, *NSP news,* Northern States Power Company, Minneapolis.

Donald Sweeney, Santa Barbara, California.

Paul Weeks, director of public relations, Rand Corporation, Santa Monica, California.

Harry B. Williams, president, Georgia School Public Relations Association, Athens.

R. Barry Wood, assistant vice-president of development and public relations, University of Georgia, Athens.

Helen M. Wynn, director of communications, Connecticut General Life Insurance Company, Hartford.

We express special gratitude to Edward L. Bernays for writing the Foreword to this textbook and to Loet A. Velmans, Chairman, President, and Chief Executive Officer of Hill and Knowlton, Inc., for contributing the Afterword. Also, we thank Phillip Leininger, senior editor, and the staff of Harper & Row, for their numerous valuable suggestions.

ORGANIZATIONS   American Bankers Association

American Management Association

Chartmasters

The Hannaford Company

International Association of Business Communicators

International Paper Company

Public Relations Society of America

Sports Illustrated

DENNIS L. WILCOX
PHILLIP H. AULT
WARREN K. AGEE

Part one

ROLE

CHAPTER ONE

What Is Public Relations?

People frequently talk about public relations without knowing exactly what it is. Because the field has many aspects—some obvious, some subtle—they may apprehend only one element of an intricate activity.

Public relations is essential in today's complex world, to smooth the process of communication and understanding. It involves research and analysis, policy formation, programming, communication, and feedback from the publics affected. Its practitioners operate on two distinct levels: as advisers to their clients or to a company's management, and as technicians performing a multiplicity of functions.

Numerous definitions of public relations exist, because the field is so many-faceted that its wide range of functions cannot be captured easily in a few words. In this chapter many definitions are examined; having seen them in such variety, readers can formulate their own definitions based on common threads that run through all those listed.

It is evident that a person who works in public relations must be versatile. As the following pages explain, a practitioner needs ability and training to write well, create projects and events, handle the technical aspects of dealing with the news media, advise clients and employers, assess the public mood, detect and analyze problems, and make delicate decisions.

The Challenge of Public Relations

Humanity has at its disposal tools of communication so swift, so abundant, and so pervasive that their potential is not yet fully comprehended. Messages are flashed around the world by satellite within seconds. Computers produce almost instantaneous calculations, operate machinery, and pour out information at the rate of thousands of words a minute. Immense warehouses of information stored in electronic data banks are available at the touch of a fingertip to a keyboard.

Today's generation also has at its command an understanding of human behavior far greater than ever before. Research and analysis have provided knowledge of the motivation behind individual behavior, the dynamics of group conduct, and the psychological and sociological factors that create interest blocs. We know that "public opinion" is not monolithic—that the population consists of many "publics," whose interests, desires, and attitudes differ.

Yet, ironically, misunderstanding, lack of comprehension, and antagonism abound in the world. Our tools and accumulations of knowledge far surpass our ability to use them. Time after time, a crisis or conflict is caused by failure to communicate effectively.

The world needs a group of communicators and interpreters to fill this void—skilled men and women who can explain the goals and methods of organizations, individuals, and governments to others in a socially responsible manner. Equally, these interpreters must provide their employers with knowledge of what others are thinking, to guide them in setting their policies wisely for the common good. This two-way responsibility is a challenging aspect of the public relations practitioner's role.

Those who fill this role are in the challenging field of public relations. And, in the United States, a study by Professor Robert L. Kendall, University of Florida, indicated that in 1984, 384,000 people were public relations managers, representatives, or specialists. He added, "When the more obvious public relations job titles are included—lobbyists, fund raisers, and a reasonable proportion of those in communication, promotion, industrial or labor relations, and advertising (determined by the proportion in a sample of the Public Relations Society of America [PRSA] membership)—the totals are between 422,689 and 539,496."

This textbook discusses what public relations is, what it does, and how its practitioners achieve their goals. In the process, mention will be made of how the field is developing rapidly, with the Bureau of Labor Statistics projecting a growth rate for public relations occupations at between 36 and 57 percent until 1990. The opportunities awaiting those who enter the field will also be emphasized.

A Plethora of Definitions

Formulating a definition of public relations is a game any number may play. Pioneer public relations educator Rex Harlow once compiled about 500 definitions from almost as many sources.

Harlow found definitions ranging from simple to complex. Some are:

Good performance, publicly appreciated.

PR stands for *Performance* and then *Recognition*.

Doing good and getting credit for it.

Actions taken to promote a favorable relationship with the public.

An organization's efforts to win the cooperation of groups of people.

Public relations is relations with the public.

Other educators have their own definitions. Doug Newsom and Alan Scott, for example, declare that, "ideally, public relations is not just a matter of saying good things, but of doing good as well." Scott M. Cutlip and Allen H. Center state in *Effective Public Relations,* Fifth Edition, that public relations is "the planned effort to influence opinion through socially responsible and acceptable performance, based on mutually satisfactory two way communication."

National and international public relations organizations also have formulated definitions, broad enough to apply anywhere in the world, including the following:

"Public relations is the deliberate, planned, and sustained effort to establish and maintain mutual understanding between an organization and its publics." (British Institute of Public Opinion, whose definition has also been adopted in a number of Commonwealth nations.)

"Public relations is the conscious and legitimate effort to achieve understanding and the establishment and maintenance of trust among the public on the basis of systematic research." (Deutsche Public Relations Gesellschaft of the Federal Republic of Germany—note that there is no term equivalent to *public relations* in the German language.)

"Public relations is the sustained and systematic managerial effort through which private and public organizations seek to establish understanding, sympathy, and support in those public circles with whom they have or expect to obtain contact." (Dansk Public Relations Klub of Denmark, which also uses the English term.)

"Public relations practice is the art and social science of analyzing trends, predicting their consequences, counseling organization leaders, and implementing planned programs of action which serve both the organization's and the public's interest." (A definition approved at the World Assembly of Public Relations in Mexico City in 1978 and endorsed by 34 national public relations organizations.)

Careful study of these explanations should enable anyone to formulate his or her own definition of public relations; committing any single one to memory is unnecessary. The key words to remember in defining public relations are as follows:

Deliberate. Public relations activity is intentional: It is designed to influence, gain understanding, provide information, and obtain *feedback* (reaction from those affected by the activity).

Planned. Public relations activity is organized. Solutions to problems are discovered and logistics are thought out, with the activity taking place over a period of time. It is systematic, requiring research and analysis.

Performance. Effective public relations is based on the actual policies and performance of an individual or organization. No amount of public relations can generate good will and support if an organization is a poor employer or unresponsive to community concerns. To use the old saw, "You cannot make a silk purse out of a sow's ear."

Public interest. The rationale for any public relations activity is to serve the public interest, and not simply to achieve benefits for the organization. Ideally, public relations activity is mutually beneficial to the organization and the public; it is the alignment of the organization's self-interests with the public's concerns and interests. For example, the Atlantic Richfield Company sponsors quality programming on public television because it enhances the company's image; by the same token, the public benefits from the availability of such programming.

Two-way communication. Dictionary definitions often give the impression that public relations consists only of the dissemination of informational materials. It is equally important, however, that the definition include feedback from audiences. The ability to listen is an essential part of communication expertise.

Management function. Public relations is most effective when it is part of the decision-making of top management. Public relations involves counseling and problem-solving at high levels, not just the releasing of information after a decision has been made. Public relations is defined by Denny Griswold, founder and owner of *PR News,* as "the management function which evaluates public attitudes, identifies the policies and procedures of an organization with the public interest, and executes a program of action (and communication) to earn public understanding and acceptance."

To summarize, a person can grasp the essential elements of public relations by remembering 10 words: deliberate . . . planned . . . performance . . . public interest . . . two-way communication . . . management function.

In his own definition, based on the interpretations of public relations that he assembled, Rex Harlow strongly emphasized the role of management:

Public relations is a distinctive management function which helps establish and maintain mutual lines of communication, understanding, acceptance, and cooperation between an organization and its publics; involves the management of problems or issues; helps management to keep informed on and responsive to public opinion; defines and emphasizes the responsibility of management to serve the public interest; helps management keep abreast of and effectively utilize change, serving as an early warning system to help anticipate trends; and uses research and ethical communication techniques as its principal tools.

Other definitions stress the importance of counseling management. As public relations pioneer Edward L. Bernays explained to the World Assembly of Public Relations in 1976, professional counsel advises management on attitudes and actions to gain social objectives. He added:

The public relations counsel first ascertains adjustments and maladjustments between the principals and the publics. He then gives the principal advice to modify indicated attitudes and actions. He then advises on how to inform and persuade relevant publics on services, products or ideas. Counseling covers adjustment, information and persuasion.

The Versatile Role of the Practitioner

Public relations practitioners play a dual role. On one level, they serve as advisers and counselors to management. On another level, they often function as technicians using a tool bag of communication techniques (news releases, slide presentations, special events, and so forth) to tell the public about management actions and decisions. People working in the field often define public relations by the activities they perform on a regular basis. Public relations people, for example, do the following:

Advise management on policy

Participate in policy decisions

Plan public relations programs

Sell programs to top management

Get cooperation of middle management

Get cooperation from other employees

Listen to speeches

Make speeches

Write speeches for others

Obtain speakers for organizational meetings

Place speakers on radio and television programs

Attend meetings

Plan and conduct meetings

Prepare publicity items

Talk to editors and reporters

Hold press conferences

Write feature articles

Research public opinion

Plan and manage events

Conduct tours

Write letters

Plan and write booklets, leaflets, reports, and bulletins

Edit employee newsletters

Supervise bulletin boards

Design posters

Plan films and videotapes

Plan and prepare slide presentations

Plan and produce exhibits

Take pictures or supervise photographers

Make awards

Greet visitors

Screen charity requests

Evaluate public relations programs

Figure 1.1 demonstrates the role of the news conference as a basic public relations tool.

In 1982 the Public Relations Society of America (PRSA), after several years of deliberation, issued an official statement describing the functions of public relations in the United States. It is reprinted on pages 10–11.

These activities are elaborated on throughout this book, especially in Chapters 2 and 5. At least two of the functions of public relations practitioners—working with employees and planning films and videotapes—are represented in Figure 1.2.

Public Relations As a Process

Public relations can also be defined as a *process*—that is, as a series of actions, changes, or functions that bring about a result. One popular way to describe the process, and to remember its components, is to use the RACE acronym, first articulated by John Marston in his 1963 book, *The Nature of*

FIGURE 1.1

Geraldine Ferraro made skillful use of news conferences during her 1984 campaign as the first woman to run on a major party ticket for vice-president of the United States. (Photo courtesy of Grace, Sygma.)

FIGURE 1.2

An organization's employees form an audience its public relations efforts must serve. Burlington Industries, Inc., produces a filmed year-end report for its workers. Here an employee is interviewed on camera for a sequence in an annual report. (Photo courtesy of Burlington Industries, Inc.)

Official Statement on Public Relations
(FORMALLY ADOPTED BY PRSA ASSEMBLY, NOVEMBER 6, 1982.)

Public relations helps our complex, pluralistic society to reach decisions and function more effectively by contributing to mutual understanding among groups and institutions. It serves to bring private and public policies into harmony.

Public relations serves a wide variety of institutions in society such as businesses, trade unions, government agencies, voluntary associations, foundations, hospitals and educational and religious institutions. To achieve their goals, these institutions must develop effective relationships with many different audiences or publics such as employees, members, customers, local communities, shareholders and other institutions, and with society at large.

The managements of institutions need to understand the attitudes and values of their publics in order to achieve institutional goals. The goals themselves are shaped by the external environment. The public relations practitioner acts as a counselor to management, and as a mediator, helping to translate private aims into reasonable, publicly acceptable policy and action.

As a management function, public relations encompasses the following:

Anticipating, analyzing and interpreting public opinion, attitudes and issues which might impact, for good or ill, the operations and plans of the organization.

Counseling management at all levels in the organization with regard to

Public Relations. Essentially, this means that public relations activity consists of four key elements:

*R*esearch—What is the problem?

*A*ction and Planning—What is going to be done about it?

*C*ommunication—How will the public be told?

*E*valuation—Was the audience reached and what was the effect?

Part Two of the text discusses this key four-step process.

Another approach is to think of the process as a never-ending cycle in which six components are links in a chain. Figure 1.3 shows the process.

policy decisions, courses of action and communication, taking into account their public ramifications and the organization's social or citizenship responsibilities.

Researching, conducting and evaluating, on a continuing basis, programs of action and communication to achieve informed public understanding necessary to the success of an organization's aims. These may include marketing, financial, fund raising, employee, community or government relations and other programs.

Planning and implementing the organization's efforts to influence or change public policy.

Setting objectives, planning, budgeting, recruiting and training staff, developing facilities—in short, *managing* the resources needed to perform all of the above.

Examples of the knowledge that may be required in the professional practice of public relations include communication arts, psychology, social psychology, sociology, political science, economics and the principles of management and ethics. Technical knowledge and skills are required for opinion research, public issues analysis, media relations, direct mail, institutional advertising, publications, film/video productions, special events, speeches and presentations.

In helping to define and implement policy, the public relations practitioner utilizes a variety of professional communication skills and plays an integrative role both within the organization and between the organization and the external environment.

The public relations process also may be conceptualized as follows:

A. Public relations personnel obtain insights into the problem from numerous sources.

B. Public relations personnel analyze these inputs and make recommendations to management.

LEVEL 1 ↑
LEVEL 2 ↓

C. Management makes policy and action decisions.

D. Public relations personnel execute a program of action.

E. Public relations personnel evaluate the effectiveness of the action.

FIGURE 1.3

In the conceptualization of public relations as a cyclical process, feedback—or audience response—leads to assessment of the program, which then becomes an essential element in the development of another public relations project.

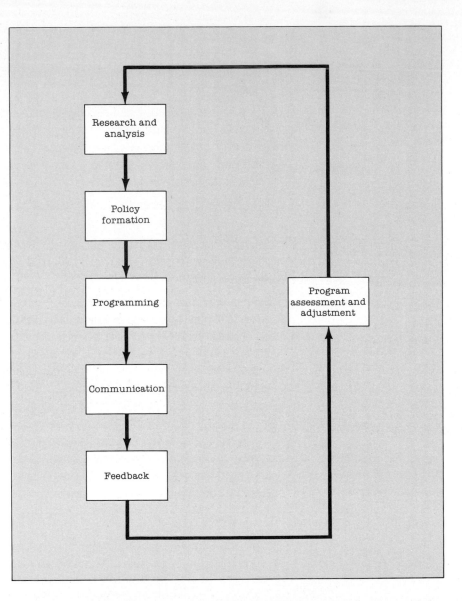

Step A consists of inputs that determine the nature and extent of the public relations problem. These may include feedback from the public, media reporting and editorial comment, analysis of trend data, other forms of research, personal experience, and government pressures and regulations.

In step B, public relations personnel assess these inputs, establish objectives and an agenda of activity, and convey their recommendations to management. As previously noted, this is the adviser role of public relations.

After management makes its decisions, in step C, public relations personnel execute the action program in step D through such means as news releases, publications, speeches, and community relations programs. In step E, the effect of these efforts is measured by feedback from the same components that made up step A. The cycle then is repeated to solve related aspects of the problem that may require additional decision-making and action.

Note that public relations plays two distinct roles in this process, thus serving as a "middle ground" or "linking agent." On level 1, public relations interacts directly with external sources of information, including the public, media, and government, and relays these inputs to management along with recommendations. On level 2, public relations becomes the vehicle through which management reaches the public with assorted messages. Veteran public relations counselor Philip Lesly explains:

Public relations people have the role of being always in the middle—pivoted between their clients/employers and the public. They must be attuned to the thinking and needs of the organizations they serve or they cannot serve well. They must be attuned to the dynamics and needs of the publics so they interpret the publics to the clients, as well as interpret the clients to the publics.

Diffusion of knowledge theorists call public relations people "linking agents." Sociologists refer to them as "boundary spanners." This means that public relations people act to transfer information between two systems. As the last lines of the official statement on public relations by the Public Relations Society of America note: " . . . the public relations practitioner utilizes a variety of professional communication skills and plays an integrative role within the organization and between the organization and the external environment."

Other Names for Public Relations

Because, through improper practices, the term *public relations* has fallen into some disrepute among the news media and the public, the activity sometimes is referred to by other titles.

Many of America's largest companies, for example, prefer the term *corporate communications*. According to the 1983 *O'Dwyer's Directory of Corporate Communications,* the phrase *corporate communications* is used by 108 companies in *Fortune* magazine's list of America's 500 largest corporations. The term is a handy umbrella to cover all types of communication within a company, such as advertising, employee publications, news bureau, speech writing, community relations, government affairs, and consumer hotlines.

The term *public affairs* is another popular substitute. *O'Dwyer's* reports that 63 companies in the *Fortune* 500 use the term *public affairs,* particularly oil companies that are among the 25 largest U.S. corporations. According to the Washington-based Public Affairs Council, most public affairs specialists work in the areas of government and community relations, but others engage in such activities as corporate contributions, media relations, financial relations, advertising, consumer affairs, and graphics. The term is also widely used in military circles.

Many corporations prefer the term *marketing communications.* This activity consists largely of product publicity and promotion. According to an article in the *Harvard Business Review,* product publicity is "the activity of securing editorial space, as divorced from paid advertising space, for the specific purpose of assisting in the meeting of sales goals."

Public information is the term most widely used by social service agencies, universities, and government agencies. The implication is that only information is being disseminated, in contrast to persuasive communication, generally viewed as the purpose of public relations. According to most state and federal legislation, government entities are only supposed to provide information and not advocate any particular idea or program. In reality, a great deal of hairsplitting must be done, because information, in itself, can be persuasive.

Figure 1.4 illustrates how a major national health organization has used public relations to broadcast a message of concern to everyone.

The term *public relations* is also too broad for some specialized activities. A *publicist,* for example, works in only one area of public relations—the preparation and dissemination of informational materials in the news media. A *press agent* also is a specialist, operating within a subcategory of public relations that concentrates on planning events that attract media attention, such as a stunt by an aspiring Hollywood actor or a planned demonstration to protest nuclear weapons.

News reporters who have contact only with publicists and press agents often have the distorted view that their activities are the sum and substance of what is called public relations. And journalists' impressions sometimes are not very favorable. A favorite pejorative term for a publicist or a press agent is *flack.* Norman R. Nager of the California State University at Fullerton has likened *flack* to the derogatory terms *quack* for physicians, *shyster* for lawyers, and *hack* for bad writers. Anything that comes under suspicion is labeled a "PR gimmick." For example, a writer on a California daily newspaper, describing the visit of an 11-year-old Maine girl to the Soviet Union at the invitation of Soviet president Yuri Andropov, wove into the news story the statement that the visit was a "Russian PR gimmick," organized by Kremlin "flacks." Another California daily headlined a feature article about a Hollywood press agent with "Flack Master Steals Space and Time."

Professional public relations personnel are tired of such stereotyping by the news media; hence the adoption of the several terms listed here. In

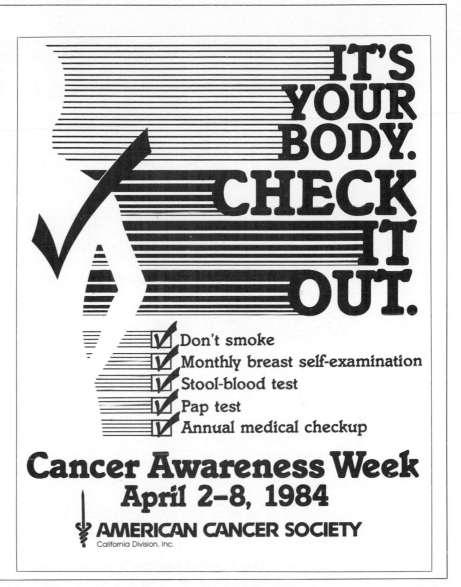

addition, some practitioners are seeking to discourage further use of the popular term "PR" to describe the occupation. In 1980 the Task Force on the Stature and Role of Public Relations, under auspices of the Public Relations Society of America, reported as follows:

Even in the easy familiarity common to Americans, nicknames are often in conflict with the aura of respect. Doctors do not call each other "Doc" and lawyers do not employ the terms "legal beagle" or "mouthpiece." The field cannot prevent others from using the nickname, but the nickname contributes to the field's image as a breezy, rules-breaking calling when it uses the nickname itself. And its own use of the nickname stimulates others to use it with growing frequency.

The task force has a point, but others wonder if too much time is being spent on definitions and consternation about the media's and the public's perceptions of public relations. Frank W. Wylie, former national president of PRSA and recipient of the society's 1982 Gold Anvil award for outstanding contributions to public relations, urges: "Let us now cease the 'Holy Grail' search for the ultimate definition of public relations, and spend more time publicizing the good works that public relations practitioners are already doing."

How Public Relations Differs from Advertising

Just as many people mistakenly equate publicity with public relations, there is also some confusion between publicity (one area of public relations) and advertising.

Publicity, or information about an event, an individual or group, or a product, is disseminated through the news media and other channels to attract favorable public notice. The practitioner who prepares and distributes the information is often called a *publicist.*

Advertising is paid space and time in print, including billboards, and in electronic media. Organizations and individuals contract to purchase space and time, and an advertisement is almost always broadcast or printed exactly as the purchaser has prepared it.

One Way to Describe Public Relations

The following anecdote by Margaret Norman is reprinted with permission from the July 1982 issue of *Reader's Digest*:

When I accepted a position in public relations, a friend remarked that the job would be a breeze for me with my advertising/promotion background. I explained that the areas are quite different, and I illustrated my point with this example. "If the circus is coming to town and you paint a sign saying, 'Circus coming to fairground Saturday,' that's advertising. If you put the sign on the back of an elephant and walk him through town, that's promotion. And if the elephant walks through the mayor's flower bed, that's publicity."

"And," he chimed in, "if you can get the mayor to laugh about it, that's public relations."

Publicity, on the other hand, appears in broadcast news programs and in newspaper and magazine stories. The prepared copy is sent to the news department (not the advertising department) and *gatekeepers* (reporters and editors) modify the material according to news requirements. In other words, there is no guarantee that an organization's news release will be used or will appear in the form in which it was prepared.

There are other differences between public relations activities and advertising. Here are some of them:

Advertising deals with the selling of goods and services; public relations generates public understanding and fosters good will for an organization.

Advertising works almost exclusively through mass media outlets; publicity relies on a number of communication tools—brochures, slide presentations, special events, speeches, news releases, feature stories, and the like.

Advertising is addressed to external audiences—primarily consumers of goods and services; public relations presents its message to specialized external audiences (stockholders, vendors, community leaders, environmental groups, and so on), and internal publics (employees).

Advertising is readily identified as a specialized communication function; public relations is broader in scope—dealing with the policies and performance of the entire organization, from the morale of employees to the way telephone operators respond to calls.

Advertising often is used as a communication tool in public relations and public relations activity often supports advertising campaigns. Advertising's function is to sell goods and services; the public relations function is to create an environment in which the organization can thrive. This calls for dealing with economic, social, and political factors that can affect the organization.

The Values of Public Relations

This chapter has defined public relations within the context of definitions, activities, and process. Perhaps a good summarizing statement is one prepared by PRSA's Task Force on the Stature and Role of Public Relations:

Public relations is a means for the public to have its desires and interests felt by the institutions in our society. It interprets and speaks for the public to otherwise unresponsive organizations, as well as speaking for those organizations to the public.

Public relations is a means to achieve mutual adjustment between institutions and groups, establishing smoother relationships that benefit the public.

Public relations is a safety valve for freedom. By providing means of working out accommodations, it makes arbitrary action or coercion less likely.

Public relations is an essential element in the communications system that enables individuals to be informed on many aspects of subjects that affect their lives.

Public relations personnel can help activate the organization's social conscience.

Public relations (either systematic or unconscious) is a universal activity. It functions in all aspects of life. Everyone practices principles of public relations in seeking acceptance, cooperation, or affection of others. Public relations professionals practice public relations as an occupation.

QUESTIONS FOR REVIEW AND DISCUSSION

1. Is *monolithic* a suitable adjective to use in describing public opinion? Explain your answer.

2. Chapter 1 lists numerous definitions of public relations. From these, select the one that you find most satisfying and be prepared to discuss your choice.

3. Discuss the meaning and importance of *feedback* in public relations.

4. What 10 words characterize the essential elements of public relations?

5. Public relations practitioners play a dual role. Identify and describe the two roles.

6. Name 10 activities in which public relations practitioners frequently are engaged.

7. The RACE acronym is a popular way of describing the public relations process. For what procedure does each initial stand?

8. Public relations people have been called "linking agents." What does this mean?

9. List two terms sometimes used as substitutes for *public relations.* Why do some practitioners prefer to use such substitute terminology?

10. Discuss the differences between public relations and advertising.

CHAPTER TWO

Types of Public Relations Work

Chapter 1 examined definitions of public relations and its basic principles and purposes. Now it is time to discuss the specifics of contemporary practice, to learn where and how these concepts are applied. Just what do public relations practitioners do? To what aspects of business, education, government, and nonprofit organizations do these specialists devote their skills?

Although the same principles apply in all areas of public relations, practitioners work in diverse fields and aim at hundreds of different targets. The tasks they perform are almost infinite in variety. One practitioner might seek to increase public awareness of a major health danger such as heart disease, while another's job may be to inform consumers about a new product on the market. Others may work in corporate employee communications, recruit volunteers for a community fund drive, or even publicize the winning streak of a major league football team.

Virtually all commercial and noncommercial organizations that deal with the public, from computer manufacturers to hospitals to art museums, need public relations guidance and service. Public relations practitioners apply their skills across a richly varied spectrum. The quick sweep of the field in this chapter will reveal its scope and variety.

This "door-opening" chapter gives a concise summary of the principal types of public relations work. With this broad picture in mind, the reader will examine each type in detail later in the book.

Corporations

A substantial majority of public relations professionals work to further the well-being of profit-earning organizations. They do so either as members of a corporate public relations department or as staff members of a counseling firm employed by the corporation. Especially in large companies, public relations programs have many facets, each of which requires development of specialized knowledge and techniques.

The primary areas of corporate public relations work are the following:

1. *Reputation—protection and enhancement.* This involves building good will for a company by demonstrating to the public that the firm is an efficient producer of well-made products, an honest seller of goods or services, and a responsible corporate citizen. Among the aspects of this function are:

a. Protecting the company against attacks

b. Telling its story well when controversy arises

c. Initiating programs to explain company goals and policies

d. Displaying company concern for environmental problems

e. Showing that the company cares for the welfare of its employees and the communities in which its facilities are situated

This role sometimes is called image-building. "Image" in this sense means the character projected to the public by someone or something. Some public relations experts dislike the term, because they sense in it a disparaging undertone wrongly suggesting deceptive manipulation. Image alone indeed is empty and potentially false; behind it must be substance.

2. *Information service.* Public relations representatives must take the initiative in building a company's reputation; they also must fill the more passive role of supplying information in response to queries from the public and the news media. Judgments of companies often result from the manner in which inquiries are answered. Prompt, comprehensive, and gracious responses build friends. Perceived "brushoffs" make enemies and lose customers. Reporters for publications and broadcasting stations soon learn which public relations representatives are cooperative in answering questions and arranging interviews with company executives, and which ones are not. Although reporters are supposed to keep personal feelings out of their work, the attitude a public relations representative projects toward them often subtly influences their feeling toward the company.

3. *Product publicity.* Introduction of new products, and campaigns to put fresh life into the sales of established products, are important functions. In this role, the public relations practitioners work closely with the marketing department.

Closely, and unhappily, linked with product publicity is *product recall.* Companies face this problem when a belatedly discovered defect requires recall of a product from the market for repair or replacement. Recalls by automobile manufacturers are the most widely known examples. Urgent action becomes necessary if danger exists for users of a defective product. When a recall is required, public relations representatives use a wide range of techniques to disseminate the recall notice.

4. *Investor relations.* A major function is to provide information to the stockholders about a company's financial achievements, operations, and plans. Corporate managements stay in office at the pleasure of the stockholders, as represented by the board of directors. Elaborate annual reports, quarterly reports mailed with dividend checks, and other printed materials are sent to stockholders. A public annual meeting is held at which stockholders may ask questions of management and voice complaints. If a proxy fight develops, or one company attempts the forced takeover of another, public relations personnel often are called upon to mount a campaign among stockholders, the investment community, employees, and various governmental regulatory agencies. A good job of organizing opposition and eventually defeating an unfriendly takeover bid was done by Marathon Oil of Ohio (1981). The company was headquartered in a small community and was able to mobilize employees as well as community residents to oppose a takeover by an outside company.

5. *Financial community relations.* A parallel function is to provide extensive information to the financial community. Security analysts at brokerage houses, large banks, and similar institutions weigh the information and make judgments on a company's financial strength and prospects. These judgments heavily influence the decisions of potential investors about purchasing a company's stock and bonds. When new stock offerings are planned, a detailed prospectus prepared in accordance with Securities and Exchange Commission rules must be published. In this role, the public relations department works with the financial officers of the company.

6. *Employee relations.* An open flow of information from management to employees, and from employees to management, is recognized as essential by most corporations. To achieve this, the public relations department works closely with the personnel or industrial relations department. Among the functions it performs are (1) the publication of an employee magazine or newspaper, (2) the writing of brochures for employees explaining company policies, (3) the preparation of audiovisual materials for training and policy-transmission purposes, (4) the scheduling of staff meetings and seminars, and (5) the training of speakers among top management and lower-echelon supervisors who serve as communicators to employees (see Figure 2.1).

FIGURE 2.1

As a gesture of appreciation for their company's excellent personnel relations, employees of Delta Air Lines presented the corporation with a $30 million gift of a new Boeing 767 aircraft. (Photo courtesy of Delta Air Lines.)

7. *Recruiting.* Closely allied to employee relations is the continuing task of recruiting new employees, particularly in specialized fields. Here again, public relations practitioners help the personnel department through preparation of materials portraying the advantages of working for the company.

8. *Public affairs.* Some companies involve themselves actively in the political process. Working through public affairs executives, they seek to influence legislation by contact with legislators. Their representatives in Washington, commonly called *lobbyists,* provide members of Congress, the administration, and government departments with information that helps them understand corporate and industrywide needs and concerns. Usually the public affairs section of a corporation is a part of, or closely affiliated with, the public relations department.

9. *Feedback.* Public relations representatives form a sensitive listening post for company management. The chief executive officer looks to them for information about public and employee attitudes, political developments, social trends, and economic indications that may affect the company's position. Using their training in sensing and measuring the moods of individuals, groups, and the media, public relations specialists should detect potential trouble for the company and sound a warning. Equally, they should be alert for opportunities the company might pursue to improve its profitability and

A Reference List

Among the principal areas in which public relations practitioners work are the following:

CORPORATIONS

Reputation—protection and enhancement
Information service
Product publicity
Investor relations
Financial community relations
Employee relations
Recruiting
Public affairs
Feedback

ASSOCIATIONS

Trade associations
Labor unions
Professional and cultural societies
"Cause" organizations

SOCIAL AND RELIGIOUS AGENCIES

PERSONAL AND ENTERTAINMENT PUBLICITY

PUBLIC AFFAIRS, THE MILITARY, AND POLITICS

EDUCATION

strengthen its reputation in the eyes of the public, employees, and investors. They must be two-way communicators. Before management can make wise decisions in response to public issues it faces, it needs good reporting and astute judgments from its public relations staff.

Associations

Significant among the communication channels that tie contemporary society together are organizations made up of individuals sharing a strong interest—financial, professional, social, cultural, or intellectual. Usually these organizations exist to provide a service, not to sell a product directly. Public relations has a vital role in their success. Without effective communication with members and with the public, an organization will deteriorate. The major types of nonprofit organizations include the following:

TRADE ASSOCIATIONS A *trade association* consists of members who produce the same type of product or provide similar services. Although they may compete for the consumer's dollar, they band together in an association to further common interests. Their association promotes or opposes legislation, informs the public about the industry it represents, and does statistical and other research for the benefit of its members. Examples of powerful trade associations are the National Association of Manufacturers, the American Farm Bureau Federation, and the American Bankers Association.

LABOR UNIONS To serve members and build favorable public recognition, labor organizations must rely on public relations extensively. Union leadership administers pension plans, insurance programs, and the like; the members must be kept informed about how these programs may benefit them. Grievance procedures must be explained to members. New members must be sought and new locals formed. Before contract negotiations, union leadership must learn what the members desire and in turn keep them informed about negotiating strategy. Just as in corporate structures, two-way communication is essential.

If a breakdown in negotiations leads to a strike, or threatens to do so, unions must outline their positions and enlist public support. Since the public often is inconvenienced by strikes, unions must find ways to explain the justness of their cause. When agreement is reached, union leadership must present the contract provisions to the members in order to obtain ratification.

Labor organizations participate heavily in political affairs, from the federal to the local level, by endorsing and financing candidates and taking strong positions on issues. Union leadership urges members to vote according to its recommendations. Less evident, but continuous, is the task of developing and publicizing activities for members and their families, and of participating in community affairs as part of the union's efforts to be a constructive organizational citizen. Political participation and community affairs both require a wide variety of public relations activities.

PROFESSIONAL AND CULTURAL SOCIETIES Members of a profession band together in associations for their mutual benefit, including the exchange of information, just as trade associations do. The public relations work of professional societies includes (1) legislative campaigns, (2) advocacy of professional standards, (3) publication of information at both the skilled professional and general readership levels, (4) membership recruitment, and (5) general work to strengthen the profession's stature in the public mind. Associations of health professionals such as the American Medical Association and the American Dental Association, for instance, conduct vigorous campaigns to promote good health practices. Other representative professional societies are the American Bar Association and the American Chemical Society.

Cultural societies resemble professional societies, except that the common bond of members is interest in a cultural cause rather than career enhancement. The Metropolitan Museum of Art, the Chicago Historical Society, and the New Orleans Symphony Orchestra are examples. All use public relations practitioners to (1) publicize their programs, (2) produce their publications, (3) arrange speaking engagements, (4) enlarge their membership, and (5) present their purposes to the public.

"CAUSE" ORGANIZATIONS

Still another group of organizations seeking to influence the public and to serve their members are those that advance a wide spectrum of special causes. Their public relations needs resemble those of professional and cultural societies. Representative of this category are the National Safety Council, the National Wildlife Federation, the American Association of Retired Persons, and the American Civil Liberties Union (see Figure 2.2).

FIGURE 2.2

Nonprofit institutions frequently publish brochures explaining their purposes and listing the names of their leaders, in order to increase the public's understanding of their role and significance. This example was issued by a major research organization. (Courtesy of The Rand Corporation.)

The Rand Corporation • 1700 Main Street, Santa Monica, Calif. 90406 • (213) 393-0411

Rand

FACT SHEET

The Rand Corporation is a private, nonprofit institution engaged in research and analysis of matters affecting national security and the public welfare and in the operation of educational programs. Rand conducts its work with support from federal, state and local governments; from foundations and other private philanthropic sources; and from its own funds drawn from fees earned.

For further information contact Paul Weeks, Director of Public Information
January 1982

Social and Religious Agencies

Nonprofit organizations that serve social welfare, health, and religious needs call extensively upon their staffs of public relations specialists. They must alert the public to the services offered and raise funds to finance those services. As a group, these agencies have inherent public approval because of the obviously valuable work they do. However, this abstract approval must be translated into tangible support.

Social service and religious agencies have four areas in which public relations techniques are essential:

1. Role promotion—stimulating public awareness of their work and demonstrating what can be accomplished through their services

2. Client services—making these services known to the public and convincing individuals to use them

3. Fund-raising

4. Enlistment of volunteers

The Salvation Army and Goodwill Industries are examples of social service agencies. So are the American Red Cross and the Visiting Nurse Association. On a different level are such health organizations as the American Heart Association and the American Cancer Society, which warn the public about the dangers of the diseases they combat. Hospital public relations is a rapidly expanding field as these institutions enlarge their work in preventive medicine and add ancillary services.

Religious organizations on state and national levels use public relations practices in much the same way that social service agencies do. Some of these organizations are denominational; others are interdenominational, including the National Council of Churches and the Religious Public Relations Council. Their concerns are to increase the role of religion in contemporary life and to provide related social services.

Personal and Entertainment Publicity

Publicizing individuals and promoting entertainment constitute the aspect of contemporary public relations practice that comes closest to the traditional mantle of *press agentry.* This work requires intense contact with the media, by telephone and mail and in person. Name recognition is its primary goal.

The impact of television on the field of personality promotion is immense. An unknown person who appears on a nationally distributed television show may become an almost instant celebrity. Public relations agencies specializing in personality buildup have staffs who book clients—show-business people, politicians, sports figures, and authors of promotional-type books in particular—for TV and radio talk shows in a highly organized manner. Distribution of news items about personalities to print media columnists and electronic media commentators, and the scheduling of interviews with newspapers and magazines, also are major functions. So are public relations tours for film and television stars.

Promotion of entertainment events is a many-faceted activity, intensely competitive because many events compete for the consumer's time and money. Exposure in the print and electronic media is fundamental. The success of theatrical engagements, fairs and exhibitions, and entertainment centers such as Disney World depends upon their public relations and publicity programs.

Professional and big-time college sports is another category in which energetic public relations efforts are necessary. Every professional team has its public relations specialist, and athletic departments of large universities have their sports information directors.

Public Affairs, the Military, and Politics

Many men and women pursue public relations careers by working for government agencies, the military services, and political figures.

The massive administrative and legislative structure of federal, state, and local governments needs to explain its work to the taxpayers who support it and to help them obtain the services it provides. This work is done by thousands of specialists, usually called *public information officers* or *public affairs officers*. Best known of these is the presidential press secretary at the White House, who has a sizable staff of assistants. Every government department and agency in Washington has its public information office. Similar but less elaborate establishments do the same work for state governments, large municipalities, and assorted other agencies such as regional water authorities.

The military services have an elaborate public information service network. Its principal functions are to (1) provide information about military policies and operations, (2) encourage recruiting, (3) maintain good relationships between military installations and their surrounding communities, and (4) distribute news about individuals in the service (see Figure 2.3, pp. 28–29).

National political leaders frequently have personal public relations aides, although the functions of these assistants may be obscured by such a title as "administrative assistant." Governors and large-city mayors have them, too. Image-building is a constant preoccupation for politicians, who seek to give the impression that they are energetic practitioners of good government, working hard to help the people who elected them.

When a politician runs for major office, the press secretary is a key figure on the candidate's staff. Often a candidate hires a public relations firm that specializes in political campaigns to help plan strategy. Voter opinion polls help to form the strategy. Spot television commercials have become a primary campaign tool.

Education

Public relations programs are essential to the well-being of universities and colleges. Practitioners on campus either conduct or assist in several important functions that further the school's cause among students, alumni, and the public. In large universities, the public relations staffs needed to perform these functions are substantial in size.

Among the areas in which collegiate public relations practitioners may be involved are:

FIGURE 2.3

Creation of persuasive recruiting literature is among the functions
of military public information work.

1. News releases—distribution to the news media of information about campus events and personalities.

2. Publications—preparation of periodicals, brochures, and catalogues.

3. Alumni contact work—various activities, including campus tours for returning alumni and other visitors.

4. Relations with federal, state, and local governments.

5. Fund-raising—solicitation of donations from foundations, alumni, federal and state governments, and special interest groups. This work is vital to privately operated universities and colleges and also of great importance to tax-supported institutions.

6. Student recruitment.

7. Internal public relations with faculty and staff.

In urban areas, elementary and high school districts frequently have public relations officers to assist the news media and to work with parents and school groups. More information on educational relations can be found in Chapter 19.

QUESTIONS FOR REVIEW AND DISCUSSION

1. Protecting and enhancing a corporation's reputation comprise an important role for a public relations practitioner. Name three ways in which this function may be carried out.

2. Why do some public relations experts dislike the term *image-building?*

3. Why is urgent action required in certain cases of product recall?

4. Maintenance of good employee relations is an assignment given to most corporate and institutional public relations departments. What are some of the ways to carry out this task?

5. Describe the principal functions of a trade association.

6. Why do labor unions need public relations programs?

7. Name three nationally known professional and cultural societies or "cause" organizations.

8. As public relations director of a social service organization such as the Visiting Nurse Association, you would be involved in four principal areas of effort. Name them.

9. Which of the mass media is especially important to a publicist in promoting a "personality"?

10. Universities need strong public relations departments. List the principal functions of such a department.

CHAPTER THREE

History of Public Relations: The Evolving Functions

Practitioners who lack an understanding of how public relations developed cannot consider themselves professionals. Knowledge of the history of the field is essential if today's practitioners are to benefit from the ideas generated by their predecessors. Every society, and every craft, owes a distinct debt to the past.

This chapter explores some of the opinion-influencing practices of past centuries, including the press agentry of the nineteenth century. It also explains how modern counseling and other public relations activities evolved out of simple publicity at the beginning of the twentieth century, when public relations began to emerge as a social force. In the process some interesting, imaginative people will be introduced: Phineas T. Barnum, Ivy Ledbetter Lee, Edward L. Bernays, Henry Ford, Paul W. Garrett, Carl O. Byoir, and others—individuals who have helped shape the course of public relations over the last 100 years.

The Roots of Public Relations

Public relations is a twentieth-century phenomenon whose roots extend deep into history; in a sense it is as old as human communication itself. In succeeding civilizations, such as those of Babylonia, Greece, and Rome, people were persuaded to accept the authority of government and religion through techniques that are still used: interpersonal communication, speeches, art, literature, staged events, publicity, and other such devices. None of these endeavors was called public relations, of course, but their purpose and their effect were the same as those of similar activities today.

The following remarks of Peter G. Osgood, president of Carl Byoir & Associates, provide a few examples of the early practice of the art of public relations:

> The art has many roots. For example, the practice of dispatching teams to prepare the way for a traveling dignitary or politician was not invented by Harry Truman or Richard Nixon. Their political ancestors in Babylonia, Greece, and Rome were quite adept at it.
>
> St. John the Baptist himself did superb advance work for Jesus of Nazareth.
>
> Publicity, community relations, speech writing, positioning, government relations, issues analysis, employee relations, even investor relations: when you think about these activities in terms of the skills needed to practice them, it's plain they have deep historical roots.
>
> Generating publicity for the Olympics in ancient Athens, for example, demanded the same skills as it did [in 1984] in Los Angeles.
>
> Speech writing in Plato's time meant the same thing as it does today at Byoir: you must know the composition of your audience, never talk down to them, and impart information that will enlighten their ignorance, change their opinion, or confirm their own good judgments.
>
> Businesses in the Republic of Venice in the latter half of the Fifteenth Century practiced as fine an art of investor relations as IBM does in the United States in the latter half of the Twentieth Century: perhaps even finer since it was practiced one-on-one, face-to-face, every day on the Rialto, just as it was under the spreading elm tree on Wall Street in the early days of the Stock Exchange.

Other examples abound. In the eleventh century, throughout the far-flung hierarchy of the Roman Catholic Church, Pope Urban II persuaded thousands of followers to serve God and gain forgiveness of their sins by engaging in the Holy Crusades against the Muslims. Six centuries later, the church was among the first to use the word *propaganda,* with the establishment by Pope Gregory XV of the College of Propaganda to supervise foreign missions and train priests to propagate the faith.

One of the most famous staged events of all times, as related by Doug Newsom and Alan Scott in *This is PR: The Realities of Public Relations,* occurred when Lady Godiva rode a horse nude through the streets of

Coventry, England, in a successful attempt to persuade her husband to lower taxes. The stories that Spanish explorers publicized of the never-discovered Seven Cities of Gold, and even the fabled Fountain of Youth, induced others to travel to the New World. Some of the explorers probably believed those stories themselves. More blatant deceptions—examples of actions unacceptable to public relations people today—occurred when Eric the Red, in A.D. 1000, discovered a land of ice and rock and, to attract settlers, named it Greenland; and when Sir Walter Raleigh in 1584 sent back glowing accounts of what was actually a swamp-filled Roanoke Island, to persuade other settlers to travel to America. It is clear, then, that the idea of using all forms of human communication—drama and storytelling among them—to influence the behavior of other people is nothing new.

The Evolving Functions

An excellent way to understand what public relations is all about today is to examine the evolution of its principal functions—press agentry, publicity, and counseling—along with the methods used to carry out those functions.

PRESS AGENTRY

"Hyping"—the promotion of movie and television stars, books, magazines, and the like, through shrewd use of the media and other devices—is an increasingly lively phenomenon in today's public relations world. At the center of hyping is the press agent, whom the *American College Dictionary* defines as "a person employed to attend to the advertising of a theater, performer, etc., through advertisements and notices to the press."

This work is simply an extension of the activities of those who, in ancient civilizations, promoted athletic events such as the Olympic games and built an aura of mythology around emperors and heroes. Its modern expression may be found in the press agentry that, during the nineteenth century in America, promoted circuses and exhibitions; glorified Davy Crockett as a frontier hero in order to draw political support from Andrew Jackson; attracted thousands to the touring shows of Buffalo Bill and his sharpshooter Annie Oakley; made a legend of frontiersman Daniel Boone; and promoted hundreds of other personalities, politicians, and theatrical performers with remarkable success.

The oldtime press agents and the show people they most often represented played upon the credulity of the public in its longing to be entertained, whether deceived or not. Advertisements and press releases were exaggerated to the point of being outright lies. Doing advance work for an attraction, the press agent dropped a sheaf of tickets on the desk of a newspaper city editor along with the announcements. Voluminous publicity generally resulted, and reporters, editors, and their families flocked to their free entertainment with scant regard for the ethical constraints that largely prohibit such practices today.

Small wonder then that today's public relations practitioner, exercising the highly sophisticated skills of evaluation, counseling, communication, and influencing management policies, shudders at the suggestion that public relations grew out of press agentry. And yet some aspects of modern public relations have their roots in the practice.

Phineas T. Barnum, the great American showman of the ninteenth century, for example, was the master of the pseudoevent, the planned happening that occurs primarily for the purpose of being reported—a part of today's public relations activities.

Barnum, who was born in Connecticut in 1810, was also a hardheaded businessman, devoted to his family, a generous contributor to charities, a nondrinker, an accumulator of property, imaginative and energetic, a man whose primary love in staging his circus performances was to make children smile. Beyond that, however, most of today's public relations people would like to part company—for Barnum used deception, hoax, and humbugging in his operations and in his advertising and publicity. Even so, a public hungry for entertainment accepted his exaggerations, perhaps because they were audacious, and thrilled to the wonders that he presented:

Joice Heath was a slave who said she was 161 years old and claimed to have been George Washington's nurse. Barnum even produced a stained birth certificate, but an autopsy disclosed she was far younger.

Tom Thumb became one of the sensations of the century. Barnum discovered Charles S. Stratton in Connecticut when Stratton was 5 years old, only an inch over 2 feet in stature, and weighing 15 pounds. Barnum made a public relations event of "General" Tom Thumb's marriage to another midget. After triumphal tours of the United States, where Tom Thumb entertained audiences with singing, dancing, and comedy monologues, Barnum took his attraction to England. But Europeans were already familiar with midgets—their use as entertainment dated back to the royal courts of the Middle Ages—so Barnum had to come up with something that made Tom Thumb special. A small-size carriage and ponies helped to attract public attention, but Barnum decided that the best way to get public acceptance was first to involve the opinion leaders. Consequently, he invited London society leaders to his townhouse, where they met the quick-witted Tom Thumb. This resulted in an invitation to the palace. Having entertained royalty, Tom Thumb drew full houses every night. Barnum, even in his day, knew the value of third-party endorsement.

Jenny Lind, the "Swedish Nightingale," was one of Europe's most famous singers but was virtually unknown in the United States. Consequently, Barnum launched an unprecedented press campaign to acquaint the American public with her well-loved voice. He obtained full houses on opening nights in each community by donating part of the proceeds to charity. As a civic activity, the event attracted many of the town's opinion leaders, whereupon the general public flocked to attend succeeding performances—a device still employed today. Barnum also capitalized on the idea, current at the time, that anything from Europe must be culturally superior.

The American Museum in New York City, filled with a mixture of art and curiosities, by 1851 had become the most popular institution of its kind in the country. Many people regarded attendance at plays as wicked, but Barnum presented shows in his museum theater that even the clergy could attend.

The Feejee Mermaid was a contrived 3-foot object bearing the body of a fish and the head and hands of a monkey. Barnum mounted this exhibit at the height of public debate on evolution, and he encouraged the press to question the authenticity of the mermaid. He knew, as many public relations personnel and social activists realize today, that basic news values include conflict and controversy. The resulting press coverage encouraged thousands of people to visit the exhibit to "see for themselves." Museum receipts almost tripled.

Jumbo, the world's largest elephant, was brought by Barnum from England with enormous publicity. Posters and pamphlets featuring exaggerated woodcuts and inflated prose trumpeted the animal's size.

The Barnum & Bailey Circus, with its 3 rings, 2 stands, and 800 employees, was proclaimed "The Greatest Show on Earth." Neil Harris, in his book, *Humbug: The Art of P. T. Barnum,* describes the circus as the showman's "one enduring monument to fame; the legacy lies in his name left for the future."

Barnum owed much of his success to a corps of press agents headed by Richard F. "Tody" Hamilton. A famous circus clown, "Uncle" Bob Sherwood, described Hamilton as a verbal conjuror whose language was so polysyllabic that "an Oxford professor would have found it difficult to understand."

Upon Barnum's death, in 1891, the London *Times* joined in almost universal acclaim of his life with the eulogy: "His death removes an almost classic figure, and his name is a proverb already, and a proverb it will continue until mankind has ceased to find pleasure in the comedy of the showman and his patrons—the comedy of the harmless deceiver and the willingly deceived."

PUBLICITY   EARLY DEVELOPMENT   Publicity, which consists mainly of the issuing of news releases to the media about the activities of an organization or an individual, is one of the earliest forms of public relations. It has been used for virtually every purpose. Signs such as "Vote for Cicero. He is a good man" have been found by archeologists in ruins of ancient civilizations. In 59 B.C. Julius Caesar ordered the posting of a news sheet, *Acta Diurna,* outside the Forum to inform citizens of actions of Roman legislators; Caesar's *Commentaries* were published largely to aggrandize the achievements of the emperor.

THE COLONIAL ERA   In 1620, broadsides were distributed in Europe by the Virginia Company offering 50 acres of free land to those bringing settlers to America by 1625. In 1641, Harvard College published a fund-raising brochure, and in 1758, Kings College (now Columbia University) issued its first press release, announcing commencement exercises.

Mainly through the use of newspapers and pamphlets, a staged event (the Boston Tea Party), and wide publicity accorded the so-called Boston Massacre, fiery Samuel Adams and the Boston Radicals achieved a propaganda triumph in helping persuade the American colonists to revolt against Great Britain. Also highly instrumental in bringing lukewarm citizens into the Revolutionary movement was Tom Paine's *Common Sense;* more than 120,000 copies of the pamphlet were sold in three months. Influencing public opinion both in the colonies and in England were the *Federalist Papers,* comprised of 85 letters written by Alexander Hamilton, James Madison, and John Jay, and a series of articles by John Dickinson titled "Letters from a Farmer in Pennsylvania." Benjamin Franklin lent his journalistic skills to the American cause too (see Figure 3.1).

NINETEENTH CENTURY   Public affairs were controlled mainly by the aristocratic, propertied class until the revolt of the so-called common man placed rough-hewn Andrew Jackson in the White House in 1828. Amos Kendall, a former Kentucky newspaper editor, became an intimate member of Jackson's "kitchen cabinet" as probably the first presidential press secretary. The appointment demonstrated for the first time that public relations is integral to political policy-making and management.

Jackson's campaign and presidency represented the first attempt in American political life to gain broad-based support for a presidential candidate. Kendall sampled public opinion on issues, advised Jackson, and skillfully interpreted his rough ideas, putting them into presentable form as speeches and news releases. He served as Jackson's advance man on trips, wrote glowing articles which he sent to supportive newspapers, and was probably the first to use newspaper reprints in public relations: almost every complimentary news story or editorial about Jackson was reprinted and circulated.

After the Jacksonian era, American politicians increasingly used press releases, pamphlets, posters, and emblems to win favor. The effort reached a nineteenth-century crescendo during the presidential campaigns of William Jennings Bryan and William McKinley in 1896.

Throughout the century, publicity techniques helped populate Western lands. Newly sprung-up villages competed to attract printers, whose news-

FIGURE 3.1

This famous cartoon was published in 1754 in Benjamin Franklin's *Pennsylvania Gazette* as part of the campaign to create unity among the American colonies.

paper copies and pamphlets describing almost every community as "the garden spot of the West" were sent back East to induce increased settlement. Many settlers were lured to Illinois, for example, by gazettes that extolled the fertile land. Henry W. Ellsworth's *Valley of the Upper Wabash,* in the 1830s, and another publication, *Illinois in 1837,* were subsidized by speculators seeking to lure land-buyers. One critic of the time called these gazettes downright puffery, "full of exaggerated statements, and high-wrought and false-colored descriptions."

In addition, the supporters of such causes as antislavery, antivivisectionism, women's rights, and prohibition employed publicity to maximum effect throughout the century. One of the most influential publicity ventures for the abolition of slavery was the publication of Harriet Beecher Stowe's *Uncle Tom's Cabin.*

A wave of industrialization, mechanization, and urbanization swept the nation after the Civil War. Concentrations of wealth developed throughout manufacturing and trade. Amid the questioning of business practices, the Mutual Life Insurance Company in 1888 hired newspaperman Charles J. Smith to write press releases designed to improve its image. In 1889 Westinghouse Corporation established what is said to be the first in-house publicity department, with a former newspaper reporter, E. H. Heinrichs, as manager. In 1897 the term *public relations* was used by the Association of American Railroads in a company listing.

TWENTIETH CENTURY   As the use of publicity gained increased acceptance, the first publicity agency, known as the Publicity Bureau, was established in Boston in 1900. Harvard College was its most prestigious client. George F. Parker and Ivy Lee opened a publicity office in New York City in 1904. Parker remained in the publicity field, but Lee became an adviser to companies and individuals, as will be discussed in the section that follows. In Washington, D.C., William Wolf Smith established a firm to provide publicity to influence legislators.

A second Boston publicity business was opened in 1906 by James D. Ellsworth, who later joined the staff of the American Telephone & Telegraph Company. Theodore N. Vail greatly expanded the press and customer relations operations at AT&T after becoming its president in 1907. In 1909 another pioneer, Pendleton Dudley, established a public relations office in New York.

The Chicago Edison Company broke new ground in public relations techniques under the skillful leadership of its president, Samuel Insull. Well aware of the special need of a public utility to maintain a sound relationship with its customers, Insull established an external magazine, *Chicago, The Electric City,* in 1903; used press releases extensively; was the first business-man to use films for public relations purposes, in 1909; and started the "bill stuffer" idea in 1912 by inserting company information into customer bills.

Another businessman, Henry Ford, probably was the first major industrialist to utilize thoroughly two basic public relations concepts. The first was the notion of *positioning*—the idea that credit and publicity always go to those who do something first—and the second idea was ready accessibility to the press. Joseph Epstein, author of *Ambition,* says, "He may have been an even greater publicist than mechanic."

In 1900 Ford obtained coverage of the prototype Model T by demonstrating it to a reporter from the Detroit *Tribune*. By 1903 Ford achieved widespread publicity by racing his cars—a practice that is still carried out today by auto makers. Ford hired Barney Oldfield, a champion bicycle racer and a popular personality, to drive a Ford car at a record speed of 1:06 minutes per mile, or a bit less than 60 miles per hour. The publicity from these speed runs gave Ford financial backing and a ready market for the regular production of cars.

Ford also positioned himself as the champion of the common person and was the first auto maker to envision that a car should be affordable for everyone. To this end, he produced his first Model T in 1908 for $850 and, by 1915–1916, was able to reduce its selling price to $360. Such price reductions made Ford dominant in the auto industry and on the front pages of the nation's newspapers. He garnered further publicity and became the hero of working men and women by being the first auto maker to double his workers' wages to $5 per day.

Ford became a household word because the manufacturer was willing to be interviewed by the press on almost any subject, including the gold standard, evolution, alcohol, foreign affairs, and even capital punishment. His comments, not always based on informed knowledge, were pithy and easily quotable. A populist by nature, he once said, "Business is a service, not a bonanza," an idea reiterated by many of today's top corporate executives who believe business has a social responsibility.

Although Ford was the first major industrialist to hire blacks in large numbers, he also wrote a number of anti-Semitic articles. In the 1930s, his earlier image as the champion of the working class was shattered by his resistance to organized labor, which led to several violent confrontations as the United Automobile Workers attempted to organize Ford workers.

In politics, President Theodore Roosevelt proved himself a master in generating publicity. Roosevelt was the first president to make extensive use of press conferences and interviews in drumming up support for his projects. He knew the value of the presidential tour for publicity purposes. On a trip to what became Yosemite, designed to publicize the idea of national parks, Roosevelt was accompanied by a bevy of reporters and photographers who wrote glowing articles about the need to preserve the area for public recreational use.

Not-for-profit organizations joined the publicity bandwagon in the century's first decade. The American Red Cross and the National Tuberculosis Association began extensive publicity programs soon after their formation in 1908. Two other nonprofit organizations, the Knights of Columbus and the National Lutheran Council, opened press offices in 1918.

COUNSELING

INDUSTRIALISTS AND MUCKRAKERS   In the latter part of the nineteenth century, the United States was transformed by mighty economic and social forces. Industrialization moved forward on a major scale; cities swelled with even more immigrants; production was rapidly being mechanized; and business firms grew through the use of vastly improved transportation and communication facilities, along with new interlocking corporate structures and financing methods.

It was the era of the so-called robber barons, exploiters of natural resources and labor, known in less accusatory terms as founders of great American industries. Heavy concentrations of power were held by John D. Rockefeller, Sr., in oil; Andrew Carnegie in steel; J. Pierpont Morgan, Cornelius Vanderbilt, and Jay Gould in finance; Leland Stanford, Collis P. Huntington, James J. Hill, and George Pullman in railroading; Gustavus F. Swift and Philip D. Armour in meat packing; and other industrial leaders. Labor strife intensified, and the government, upon the urging of populist and progressive forces, began to challenge big business with the enactment of such measures as the Interstate Commerce Act and the Sherman Antitrust Act.

Within the dozen years after 1900, several magazines developed a literature of exposure that Theodore Roosevelt called the work of "muckrakers." He was comparing the more sensational writers to the Man with the Muckrake in the seventeenth-century work *Pilgrim's Progress*—a character who did not look up to see the celestial crown but continued to rake the filth. These writers posed a serious threat to business. They were led by Ida M. Tarbell, who wrote a series of articles published by *McClure's* in 1903 titled "History of the Standard Oil Company," an attack on the corruption and unfair practices of the Rockefeller oil monopoly. Other noted muckrakers included Upton Sinclair, who exposed unsanitary and fraudulent practices of the meat packers in his 1906 book, *The Jungle*.

THE FIRST PUBLIC RELATIONS COUNSEL The combination of stubborn management attitudes and improper actions, labor strife, and widespread public criticism produced the first public relations counselor, Ivy Ledbetter Lee. Although, as previously noted, this Princeton graduate and former business reporter for the New York *World* began his private practice as a publicist, he shortly expanded that role to become the first public relations counsel.

The emergence of modern public relations can be dated from 1906, when Lee was hired by the anthracite coal industry, then embroiled in a strike. Lee discovered that, although the miners' leader, John Mitchell, was supplying reporters with all the facts they requested, by contrast the leader of the coal proprietors, George F. Baer, had refused to talk to the press or even to President Theodore Roosevelt, seeking to arbitrate the dispute. Lee persuaded Baer and his associates to change their policy. He issued a press notice signed by Baer and the other leading proprietors that began: "The anthracite coal operators, realizing the general public interest in conditions in the mining regions, have arranged to supply the press with all possible information. . . ."

Lee issued a "Declaration of Principles," which signaled the end of the "public-be-damned" attitude of business and the beginning of the "public-be-informed" era. Eric Goldman said the declaration "marks the emergence of a second stage of public relations. The public was no longer to be ignored, in the traditional manner of business, nor fooled, in the continuing manner of the press agent." The declaration reads:

This is not a secret press bureau. All our work is done in the open. We aim to supply news. This is not an advertising agency; if you think any of our matter ought properly to go to your business office, do not use it. Our matter is accurate. Further details on any subject treated will be supplied promptly, and any editor will be assisted most cheerfully in verifying directly any statement of fact. . . . In brief, our plan is, frankly and openly, in behalf of business concerns and public institutions, to supply to the press and the public of the United States prompt and accurate information concerning subjects which it is of value and interest of the public to know about.

FIGURE 3.2

Ivy Ledbetter Lee won recognition early in the twentieth century as the first public relations counsel. (Courtesy of UPI/Bettmann Archive.)

The continuance of Lee's policy of providing accurate information about corporate and institutional activities has saved American news media millions of dollars in reporter salaries during the intervening eight decades. Despite some misleading information given out by some public relations people, news releases quickly became extremely valuable, even a necessity, to the media (see Figure 3.2).

Railroads at the time also were seeking to operate secretly in their dealings with the press. Retained by the Pennsylvania Railroad Company to handle press relations after a major rail disaster, Lee persuaded the president to alter his policy. Lee provided press facilities, released all available information, and enabled reporters to view the disaster scene. Although such action appeared to the conservative railway directors to constitute reckless indiscretion, they later acknowledged that the company had received fairer press comment than on any previous such occasion.

In 1914, John D. Rockefeller, Jr., hired Lee in the wake of the vicious strike-breaking activities known as the Ludlow Massacre at the Rockefeller family's Colorado Fuel and Iron Company plant. Lee went to Colorado and talked to both sides. He also persuaded Rockefeller to talk with the miners and their families. Lee made sure that the press was there to record Rockefeller's eating in the workers' dining hall, swinging a pick ax in the mine,

FIGURE 3.3

John D. Rockefeller, Sr., handed out dimes to strangers during the 1920s in a public relations effort to give the aged millionaire a more benign image. Here he presents a coin to William Gebele, Jr., after a church service at Lakewood, New Jersey. (Courtesy of AP/Wide World Photos.)

and having a beer with the workers after hours. The press portrayed Rockefeller as seriously concerned about the plight of the workers, thus increasing his popularity with the striking miners. Meanwhile, Lee distributed a factsheet giving management's view of the strike and even convinced the governor of Colorado to write an article supporting the position taken by the company.

Rockefeller's visits with the miners led to policy changes and more worker benefits, but the company also prevented the United Mine Workers from gaining a foothold. According to former South Dakota Senator George McGovern, who wrote his doctoral dissertation on the Ludlow Massacre, "It was the first time in any American labor struggle where you had an organized effort to use what has become modern public relations to sell one side of a strike to the American people."

Lee's success in transforming a labor dispute into a positive situation (and public image) for the Rockefeller family was based on the fact, according to Gordon M. Sears, president of T. J. Ross and Associates, that "Lee tried to solve the problem or at least establish the proper course toward solution before turning to communications." Lee's achievement led the Rockefeller family to hire him for a full-scale renovation of the Rockefeller name, badly damaged by the muckrakers who often pictured John D. Rockefeller, Sr., as an exploiter and the king of the greedy capitalists (see Figure 3.3). Lee advised the Rockefellers to announce publicly the millions of dollars that they gave to charitable institutions. He also convinced John, Sr., to allow reporters and photographers to record his golf playing and socializing with family and friends. When John, Sr., died in 1937, he was mourned worldwide as a kindly old man and a great humanitarian and philanthropist.

In 1933 Ivy Lee assessed his contribution to the Rockefeller family: "It might interest you to know that in the 18 years I have been associated with Mr. Rockefeller, the only thing that has been done has been to assist Mr. Rockefeller in his interest in the development of sound policies and to let the public find out about those policies in a natural way."

Lee's public relations firm became Lee, Harris, and Lee in 1916. Three years later he was joined by Thomas J. Ross in the firm of Ivy Lee and T. J. Ross and Associates. Among other counseling activities, Lee advised the American Tobacco Company to initiate a profit-sharing plan, the Pennsylvania Railroad to beautify its stations, and the movie industry to stop inflated advertising and form a voluntary code of censorship.

Lee lost a measure of public trust by advocating diplomatic recognition and trade with the Bolsheviks in the 1920s. He defended his stand by arguing that such action was necessary to resolve differences between the United States and the Soviet Union. His reputation was damaged further when he represented a German chemical firm in the 1930s and was accused of being a Nazi sympathizer. Lee said he counseled the firm to oppose Hitler as a means of obtaining good will and product sales in this country.

Lee died in 1934. He is remembered for four important contributions to public relations: (1) advancing the concept that business and industry should align themselves with the public interest, and not vice versa; (2) dealing with top executives and carrying out no program unless it had the active support and personal contribution of management; (3) maintaining open communication with the news media; and (4) emphasizing the necessity of humanizing business and bringing its public relations down to the community level of employees, customers, and neighbors.

WARTIME COUNSEL TO GOVERNMENT   Both world wars saw a tremendous upsurge in the role of public relations on behalf of the government—especially the Creel Committee during World War I and the Office of War Information during World War II.

The Creel Committee. "Literally public relations counselors to the United States Government" during World War I is the description given to members of the Committee on Public Information by James O. Mock and Cedric Larson in their book, *Words That Won the War.* President Wilson called upon George Creel, a former newspaper reporter, to organize a comprehensive public relations effort to advise him and his cabinet, to carry out programs, and to influence United States and world opinion. Wrote Mock and Larson:

> Mr. Creel assembled as brilliant and talented a group of journalists, scholars, press agents, editors, artists, and other manipulators of the symbols of public opinion

as America had ever seen united for a single purpose. It was a gargantuan advertising agency, the like of which the country had never known, and the breathtaking scope of its activities was not to be equalled until the rise of the totalitarian dictatorship after the war. George Creel, Carl Byoir, Edgar Sisson, Harvey O'Higgins, Guy Stanton Ford, and their famous associates were literally public relations counselors to the United States Government, carrying first to the citizens of this country and then to those in distant lands, the ideas which gave motive power to the stupendous undertaking of 1917–1918.

Among numerous other activities, the committee persuaded newspapers and magazines to contribute volumes of news and advertising space to encourage Americans to save food and to invest heavily in Liberty Bonds, which more than 10 million people purchased. Thousands of businesses set up their own groups of publicity people to expand the effort. Wilson accepted Creel's advice that hatred of the Germans should be played down and loyalty and confidence in the government should be emphasized. The committee publicized the war aims and ideals of Woodrow Wilson—to make the world safe for democracy and to make World War I the war to end all wars. The American Red Cross, operating in cooperation with the committee, enrolled more than 19 million new members and received over $400 million in contributions during the period.

The massive effort had a profound effect upon the development of public relations by demonstrating the success of these full-blown techniques (see Figure 3.4). It also awakened an awareness in Americans of the power of

FIGURE 3.4

James Montgomery Flagg's posters inspired civilians during World War I. He also created the famous "Uncle Sam Wants You" poster.

FIGURE 3.5

Walter Lippmann's writings provided a basis for research into the formation of public opinion. (Courtesy New York Herald Tribune.)

persuasive approaches, which, coupled with postwar analysis of British propaganda devices alleged to have helped get the nation into the war, resulted in a number of scholarly books and college courses on the subject. Among the books was Walter Lippmann's classic *Public Opinion,* in which he pointed out how people are moved to action by "the pictures in our minds" (see Figure 3.5).

Another legacy was the training received by the noted public relations practitioners Carl Byoir, associate chairman of the committee, and Edward L. Bernays. Byoir in 1930 founded a company that today is one of the five largest public relations firms in the United States. Bernays's contributions to public relations will be discussed shortly.

Office of War Information (OWI). To head this vital operation during World War II, President Franklin Roosevelt turned to Elmer Davis, an Indiana-born journalist and a Rhodes Scholar (see Figure 3.6). Davis had spent 15 years as a novelist and free-lance writer, 10 years as a New York *Times* reporter, and 3 years as a radio commentator for the Columbia Broadcasting System.

Profiting by knowledge of the techniques so successful in World War I, Davis orchestrated an even larger public relations effort during World War II. His job was exceptionally difficult because his office had to coordinate information from the military and numerous government agencies, wrestle

FIGURE 3.6

As director of the Office of War Information, Elmer Davis led the United States government public relations program in World War II. (Courtesy ABC.)

for funds each year with a Congress suspicious that the OWI would become Roosevelt's personal propaganda vehicle, and overcome opposition from a large segment of the press that resented having to do business with an official spokesperson.

As in World War I, the OWI's campaigns were extremely successful in promoting the sale of war bonds and in obtaining press and broadcast support for other wartime necessities. These included food, clothing, and gasoline rationing; more "victory gardens"; higher productivity and less absenteeism; and secrecy regarding troop movements and weaponry development.

The OWI news bureau had 250 full-time employees, and 300 reporters and correspondents used its facilities. Davis established a Domestic Branch, which, according to the director, "did not withhold news because we did not like it, nor delay it to produce a greater effect." His Overseas Branch also provided news to foreign peoples but with selective timing and emphasis. The OWI worked harmoniously and effectively with the Office of Censorship.

Of the domestic operation, Davis declared: "It is the job of OWI not only to tell the American people how the war is going, but where it is going and where it came from—its nature and origins, how our government is conducting it, and what (besides national survival) our government hopes to get out of victory."

The Voice of America, established by the Department of State in 1942, carried news of the war to all parts of the world. The film industry provided support through such means as Frank Capra's documentary film for the U.S. Signal Corps, designed to build patriotism; bond-selling tours by film stars; and the production of commercial movies glorifying U.S. fighting forces.

The OWI was the forerunner of the United States Information Agency, established in 1953 under President Eisenhower to "tell America's story abroad." A number of the people who worked with Davis became public relations leaders during ensuing decades.

FURTHER DEVELOPMENT OF THE COUNSELING FUNCTION   The role of the public relations practitioner as an adviser to corporate and institutional managements grew in significance as the American economy expanded during the 1920s. The man most responsible for defining this function and drawing public attention to it was Edward L. Bernays.

The Concept Explained. "In wrting this book I have tried to set down the broad principles that govern the new profession of public relations counsel." With this opening sentence of *Crystallizing Public Opinion,* published in 1923, Bernays coined a term to describe a function that was to become the core of public relations. Writing in collaboration with his wife and partner, Doris E. Fleischman, former assistant editor of the New York *Tribune,* Bernays illuminated the scope and function, methods and techniques, and social responsibilities of public relations. Following by a year Walter Lippmann's insightful treatise on public opinion, the book attracted much attention, and Bernays was invited by New York University to offer the first public relations course in the nation.

Even so, the name and definition that Bernays gave to the scope and function of public relations failed for years to gain acceptance by editors and scholars, most of whom equated the new business with press agentry. Stanley Walker, famed city editor of the New York *Herald Tribune,* wrote later:

Bernays has taken the sideshow barker and given him a philosophy and a new and awesome language. ... He is no primitive drum-beater. ... He is devoid of swank and does not visit newspaper offices [as did the circus advance agents]; and yet, the more thoughtful newspaper editors, who have their own moments of worry about the mass mind and commercialism, regard Bernays as a possible menace, and warn their colleagues of his machinations.

This antipathy toward public relations still lingers among journalists.

In 1955 Bernays refined his approach to public relations and, in a book entitled *The Engineering of Consent,* he gave the field a new name. To many people, the word *engineering* implied manipulation through propaganda and other devices. Bernays, who himself later railed at use of the word *image* to mean reputation-building, defended his terminology and concept:

The term engineering was used advisedly. In our society, with its myriads of group interests, interest groups, and media, only an engineering approach to the problems of adjustment, information, and persuasion could bring effective results. . . .

Public relations practiced as a profession is an art applied to a science, in which the public interest and not pecuniary motivation is the primary consideration. The engineering of consent in this sense assumes a constructive social role. Regrettably, public relations, like other professions, can be abused and used for anti-social purposes. I have tried to make the profession socially responsible as well as economically viable.

Early Examples of Counseling. The following examples illustrate how effectively Bernays performed his public relations work:

When, in the 1910s, the actor Richard Bennett wanted to produce *Damaged Goods,* a play about sex education, Bernays blunted the anticipated criticism of moralists, and possibly avoided a police raid, by organizing the Sociological Fund of the *Medical Review of Reviews* journal, with contributors paying $4 each to attend the play as an educational event.

To help Procter & Gamble sell Ivory soap, Bernays attracted the attention of children and their parents to cleanliness by developing a nationwide interest in soap sculpture.

In an effort to humanize President Coolidge, described by one person as "weaned on a pickle," Bernays arranged a breakfast at the White House during which Al Jolson, the Dolly Sisters, and other celebrities performed. The unprecedented event brought nationwide publicity.

To help Cheney Brothers, a New England silk manufacturer, establish its style leadership, Bernays initiated activities to stress art in industry, a new concept at the time, by arranging for the Luxembourg Museum in Paris to hold an exhibition of Cheney silks.

In behalf of *Good Housekeeping* magazine, Bernays's firm built public support for one of the first congressional bills for prenatal maternal care, the Shepherd-Towner Act.

To demonstrate the safety of radium when properly handled and to gain acceptance of radium in therapy for cancer and for use in luminous gauges, Bernays, in behalf of the U.S. Radium Corporation, carried a gram of the substance by rail to a state hospital in Buffalo.

At a time when public opinion and some legislation kept women from smoking in public, Bernays was hired by George Washington Hill, president of the American Tobacco Company, to expand sales of Lucky Strike cigarettes. Bernays consulted a psychoanalyst, who told him that cigarettes might be perceived as "torches of freedom" by women seeking equality with men. Bernays helped break the barrier by inducing 10 debutantes to "light up" while strolling in New York City's traditional Easter parade.

Later, when research showed that sales of Lucky Strike cigarettes to women were down because many felt that the green package clashed with their costumes, Bernays tried to persuade Hill to change the color. Unsuccessful in the effort, Bernays made green fashionable by arranging a prestigious socialites' ball with that color scheme; getting makers of accessories to promote green shoes, hosiery, and gloves; and arranging for green fashion displays on the covers of *Harper's Bazaar* and *Vogue* on the date of the ball. (Only during World War II, when an ingredient in the color became an industrial scarcity, did Hill relent, nevertheless reaping continued sales with the slogan, "Lucky Strike Green Has Gone to War.")

When the short-hair fashion introduced by dancer Irene Castle sharply reduced the sale of hairnets, Bernays, working for the Venida Company, emphasized the use of hairnets as a safety measure for women working with machinery, and laws were passed requiring the protective devices. The sanitary aspect of hairnets worn by cooks and waitresses also was heralded.

When book publishers became worried about sluggish sales, Bernays got world leaders to tell which books had been influential in their lives. He also lobbied contractors to include built-in bookshelves in new houses on the theory, which proved successful, that people would buy books to fill them up.

Perhaps the most spectacular example of Bernays's skill took place in 1929. To celebrate the fiftieth anniversary of Edison's invention of the electric light bulb, Bernays arranged the worldwide-attention-getting Light's Golden Jubilee. On October 21, many of the world's utilities shut off their power all at one time, for one minute, in honor of Edison. President Hoover and many other dignitaries attended a banquet climaxing the celebration. The event achieved such fame that the U.S. Post Office, on its own, issued a commemorative two-cent postage stamp.

Sociologist Leonard W. Doob described the jubilee as "one of the most lavish pieces of propaganda ever engineered in this country during peace time." Bernays, wrote Doob, was working "not for Edison or for Henry Ford, but for very important interests [General Electric and Westinghouse had hired Bernays] which saw this historic anniversary as an opportunity to publicize the uses of the electric light." Of course, the worldwide publicity and media attention also were helped by the fact that Thomas Edison was already widely heralded as the godhead of American science and ingenuity.

Light's Golden Jubilee is considered one of Bernays's major accomplishments. It showed, in 1929, the potential of effective public relations. And when television commentator Bill Moyers interviewed Bernays in 1984 on a Public Broadcasting System program about the early beginnings of public relations, Moyers said: "You know, you got Thomas Edison, Henry Ford, Herbert Hoover, and masses of Americans to do what you wanted them to

FIGURE 3.7

Edward L. Bernays became a legendary figure in public relations counseling during an exceptionally long and vigorous career. This photograph, taken in 1984, shows Bernays at 92. (Photograph by Helen M. Wynn, courtesy of *Communication World.*)

do. You got the whole world to turn off its lights at the same time. You got American women to smoke in public. That's not influence. That's power."

Replied Bernays: "But you see, I never thought of it as power. I never treated it as power. People want to go where they want to be led."

At age 93 in 1985, Bernays continues to do consulting, write, give interviews, and lecture about his favorite theme of public relations as a profession and an applied social science (see Figure 3.7). He wrote regularly for the *Public Relations Quarterly,* often on the theme of licensing as a way to remove incompetent and unethical practitioners from the field. He is widely acknowledged as the founder of modern public relations; one historian has even described him as "the first and doubtless the leading ideologist of public relations." Sigmund Freud, founder of psychoanalysis, must have been proud of his nephew.

Other Public Relations Pioneers. Benjamin Sonnenberg and Rex Harlow loom large in the list of other early, influential public relations counselors.

It was Sonnenberg who suggested that the Texaco Company sponsor performances of the Metropolitan Opera Company on national radio. The Saturday afternoon series, which began in the late 1930s, still continues. Sonnenberg, who believed that a brief mention of a client in the right context is better than a long-winded piece of flattery, proposed Texaco's sponsorship after some segments of the American public criticized the company for negotiating with Hitler on an oil deal in the mid-1930s. With time, Texaco emerged as a patron of the arts, and critics forgot about the dealings with Hitler before the outbreak of World War II.

Harlow, who was 92 years old in 1984, was probably the first full-time public relations educator. As a professor in Stanford University's School of Education, Harlow began teaching a public relations course on a regular basis in 1939. In that same year he founded the American Council on Public Relations (which eventually became the Public Relations Society of America), serving as its president for 8 years. He criss-crossed the country giving workshops and seminars for practitioners that continued for about 20 years. It is estimated that 10,000 people received their first formal instruction in public relations from this educator.

Harlow founded the *Social Science Reporter* in 1952, one of the first newsletters in the field. In it he actively sought to show practitioners and top management how social science research findings benefit the practice of public relations. Harlow, a prolific writer, produced many articles and seven books on public relations.

SERVING ON THE MANAGEMENT TEAM   Public relations counseling is at its best when it functions at the very top level of management. American corporate executives have been slow to accept this viewpoint. Its recognition in recent years has resulted mostly from the experiences of companies whose leaders understood much of what public relations is all about.

Arthur Page, who became vice-president of the American Telephone & Telegraph Company in 1927, helped shape today's practice by advocating the philosophy that public relations is a management function and that it should have an active voice in management. He also expressed the belief that a company's performance, not press agentry, comprises its basis for public approval.

Alfred P. Sloan, then president of General Motors Corporation, also was among the first executives to place great trust in public relations. In 1931, during the early years of the Great Depression when business was attacked widely for its failures, Sloan hired Paul W. Garrett as his first public relations employee (see Figure 3.8).

Garrett was charged with ascertaining public attitudes and executing a program to bring the company into full public approval. For one thing, the board of directors felt that favor might be gained by making the billion-dollar corporation appear small. Garrett considered that approach neither reasonable nor possible. Instead, he informed management that it must interpret itself by words and deeds that had meaning to those outside the company; that it must put the broad interests of the public first; that it must develop sound internal relationships with its employees; and that it must be

FIGURE 3.8

Paul Garrett developed an extensive and highly regarded public relations program for General Motors. (Courtesy General Motors Corp.)

frank and honest and explain the company's policies clearly and simply through every possible medium.

Garrett's program proved highly effective, and his speechmaking and other activities during a 25-year career with General Motors broadened the understanding of leaders of many other major organizations about the full-fledged public relations function. *Fortune* magazine, in a series of articles in 1938 and 1939, praised the GM program, along with those of Chrysler, Ford, and AT&T, and also lauded public relations itself as a valuable economic, social, and political function. No important magazine had previously reported on a corporation's public relations and described the function as a vital management responsibility.

Another example of high-level management counseling that won wide attention was that provided by Earl Newsom for Henry Ford II. When Ford took over the reins of the company, he was relatively unknown, because Edsel Ford had been groomed as the heir apparent. There was widespread conjecture as to whether Henry Ford II could lead the company properly. The grandson of the pioneer automobile maker employed Newsom in 1945 to advise him during a strike by the United Automobile Workers. Planning was Newsom's forte: he issued no news releases and held no press conferences. By preparing five major speeches for Ford II before major, influential audiences, Newsom achieved both public and press recognition for Ford's ability, along with much quotable copy.

Public Relations Comes of Age

The booming economy after World War II produced rapid growth in all areas of public relations. Companies opened public relations departments or expanded existing ones. Government staffs increased in size, as did those of nonprofit organizations such as educational institutions and health and welfare agencies. Television emerged in the late 1940s as a new challenge for public relations expertise. New firms sprang up in cities throughout the country, many discovering that they were required not only to sell their own services to potential clients but first to educate many managers on the value of public relations itself.

By 1950 an estimated 17,000 men and 2,000 women were employed as practitioners in public relations and publicity. Typical of the public relations programs of large corporations at midcentury was that of the Aluminum Company of America. Heading the operation was a vice-president for public relations-advertising, aided by an assistant public relations director and an advertising manager. Departments included community relations, product publicity, motion pictures and exhibits, employee publications, news bureau, and industrial economics (speechwriting and educational relations). *Alcoa News* magazine was published for all employees, as well as separate publications for those in 20 plants. The main broadcast effort was sponsorship of Edward R. Murrow's "See It Now" television program.

A British scholar, J. A. R. Pimlott, wrote in 1951: "Public relations is not a peculiarly American phenomenon, but it has nowhere flourished as in the United States. Nowhere else is it so widely practiced, so lucrative, so pretentious, so respectable and disreputable, so widely suspected and so extravagantly extolled."

Census-takers in 1960 counted 23,870 men and 7,271 women engaged in public relations, although some observers put the total figure at approximately 35,000. Most were employed in fields of manufacturing, business services, finance and insurance, religion and other nonprofit groups, public administration, and communications.

During the quarter century since 1960, the number of practitioners of public relations and its affiliated functions in the United States has risen to its present total of approximately 100,000, together with more than 1,500 counseling firms. Recent surveys have disclosed that 4 out of 5 large companies and trade associations conduct formalized public relations activities.

**Megatrends in
Public Relations**

John Naisbitt, in his best-selling book, *Megatrends*, pinpointed a number of trends that are transforming American society in the 1980s. If one reads between the lines, Naisbitt's ideas provide guideposts for the continued evolution of public relations. Here is a summary of major anticipations:

1. Workers will be retrained as smokestack America gives way to information and service industries.

2. Public relations firms will emphasize information-gathering and computer data searches for clients. Information will be a commodity with sales value.

3. Increased emphasis will be placed on issues management (monitoring the environment), proactive communications, and strategic planning.

4. Specialization in public relations will increase. These fields will include employee relations, government affairs, investor and financial relations, high technology product publicity, and international public relations.

5. Public relations activities and job opportunities will shift from so-called sunset industries such as steel, automobiles, textiles, and heavy industrial manufacturing to sunrise industries such as electronics, robotics, biology, and alternative energy sources.

6. Attention will increasingly focus on the ethnic diversity in the United States, with more specialized messages and communication tools for the growing Hispanic population. Public relations programs will be tailored to accommodate local and regional differences.

7. Public relations personnel will be knowledgeable about computers, data bases, word processing, teleconferencing, and satellite communications.

Public relations majors swelled classrooms in the nation's journalism and mass communication schools. From about 7,800 in 1975, the number of students majoring in the field increased to approximately 15,000 in 1983, according to surveys by Professor Albert Walker of Northern Illinois University. In 1983, public relations sequences ranked first or second in school enrollments at 60 percent of the institutions offering such a program of study. Chapters of the Public Relations Student Society of America increased to approximately 120, with about 5 new charters granted annually by PRSSA and its parent organization, the Public Relations Society of America. The International Association of Business Communicators vigorously expanded the number of its college chapters, from 16 in 1983 to 42 in 1984, offering out-of-classroom learning experiences for its student members. Professionals

8. Knowledge of the world's issues, geography, and cultures will be more important as a global economy and infrastructure become dominant. Such a perspective will be needed by public relations personnel in almost every business and industry.

9. Continuing education and professional development will be a necessity for the public relations practitioner.

10. Government public affairs will receive more emphasis as local and state governments assume more responsibilities and the number of grassroot political activities increases.

11. Job opportunities in public relations will increase more rapidly in new, start-up companies than in the large, well-established corporations.

12. There will be a new emphasis on employee citizenship rights and freedom of speech. Public relations personnel will be concerned with employee privacy, due process, whistle-blowing, sexual discrimination, and the employees' right to know. Two-way communication and advisory panels will be stressed.

13. Consumerism will stay at a high level, and corporate performance will remain under close scrutiny. Public relations personnel will engage in more conflict resolution with single-issue activist groups.

14. Increased specialization of the mass media, including magazines, broadcast narrowcasting, and cable networks, will require more sophisticated and knowledgeable public relations experts.

15. Interpersonal communication will remain one of the most effective ways to reach people alienated by a high technology society.

cooperated in innumerable ways, including the offering of thousands of internships.

Public relations has become essential in modern life because of a multiplicity of reasons, including the following: heavy, continuing population growth, especially in cities where individual citizens have scant direct contact with Big Business, Big Labor, Big Government, Big Institutions, and other powerful organizations influencing their lives; scientific and technological advances, including automation and computerization; the communications revolution; mergers and consolidations, with bottom-line financial considerations often replacing the more personalized decision-making of previous, more genteel times; and the increased interdependence of a complex world society.

The following list of national public relations organizations, with the dates of their founding, is based on a paper written by Kathleen S. Schoch, former president of the Public Relations Student Society of America, when she was a graduate student at the University of Georgia in 1982. The name changes of each organization are shown beneath each entry.

1915　Financial Advertising Association
　　　　Financial Public Relations Association (1947)
　　　　Bank Public Relations and Marketing Association (1966)
　　　　Bank Marketing Association (1970)

1917　American College News Bureaus
　　　　American College Publicity Association (1930)
　　　　American College Public Relations Association (1946)
　　　　Council for Advancement of Support for Education (1975)

1922　National Publicity Council for Health and Welfare Services

1929　Religious Publicity Council
　　　　National Religious Publicity Council (1949)
　　　　Religious Public Relations Council (1963)

1935　National Association for Educational Publicity
　　　　School Public Relations Association
　　　　National School Public Relations Association

1936　National Association of Accredited Publicity Directors
　　　　National Association of Publicity Directors (1941)
　　　　National Association of Public Relations Counsel (1944)

1938　American Association of Industrial Editors

1939　Library Public Relations Council

Many citizens feel alienated, bewildered by such rapid change, cut off from the sense of community that characterized the lives of previous generations. They seek power through innumerable pressure groups, focusing on causes such as environmentalism, human rights, and antinuclear campaigns. Public opinion, registered through continual polling, has become an increasingly powerful force in combatting or effecting change.

Both physically and psychologically separated from their publics, American business and industry have turned increasingly to public relations specialists for audience analysis, strategic planning, and issues management, among other functions. Corporate social responsibility has become the norm

1939   Institute of Public Relations
        American Institute of Public Relations (1939)
        American Council on Public Relations (1939)

1941   International Conference of Industrial Editors

1944   American Public Relations Association

1948   Public Relations Society of America (formed by merger of the American Council on Public Relations and the National Association of Public Relations Counsel; the American Public Relations Association merged with PRSA in 1951)

1949   Government Public Relations Association

1949   Association of Municipal Public Relations Officers

1952   Chemical Public Relations Association

1952   Railroad Public Relations Association

1952   Agricultural Relations Council

1964   American Society for Hospital Public Relations Directors
        American Society for Hospital Public Relations (1972)

1968   Public Relations Student Society of America (formed by PRSA)

1970   International Association of Business Communicators (formed by merger of American Association of Industrial Editors and International Conference of Industrial Editors; joined in 1974 by Canadian Industrial Editors Association)

Other, more recently formed national organizations include the National Investor Relations Institute, the Issues Management Association, the Public Utility Communicators Association, and the Society of Consumer Affairs Professionals. Foreign and world public relations organizations are discussed in Chapter 16.

and the expectation. One of the most important tasks of these specialists is that of environmental surveillance—serving, in effect, much like the periscope of a submarine. The continued growth of companies, if not survival itself, depends in large part upon the skills of public relations technicians.

Research has assumed an importance never before known. Back in 1853, Theodore N. Vail, founder of the American Telephone & Telegraph Company, had sensed its importance, sending letters to his customers seeking their opinions. In 1912, public relations-wise Henry Ford had asked 1000 customers why they had purchased his Model T car. These were among the forerunners of the social science research techniques that were developed after

World War I. In the 1930s, George Gallup, Elmo Roper, Claude Robinson, and others began to conduct modern public opinion and marketing surveys. They provided a tool by which public relations specialists and others could evaluate public attitudes quantitatively and obtain objective measurements to supplement personal estimates of public opinion. By the 1980s, aided by the computer, research had become invaluable as a means by which companies and institutions, through their public relations experts, could interact effectively with their many specialized publics.

Public relations continues to develop throughout the United States and the world, with press agentry, publicity, and counseling still important ingredients. Ivy Lee, Edward L. Bernays, Rex Harlow, and other pioneers built exceedingly well.

QUESTIONS FOR REVIEW AND DISCUSSION

1. The roots of public relations extend deep into history. What are some of the early antecedents of today's public relations practice?

2. What is meant by "hyping"?

3. Which practices of press agent Phineas T. Barnum should modern practitioners use? Which should they reject?

4. Describe briefly the publicity practices used by Henry Ford and by Theodore Roosevelt.

5. Ivy Lee made four important contributions to public relations. Can you identify them?

6. What effect did the Creel Committee of World War I have upon the development of public relations?

7. Identify three of the successful public relations campaigns conducted by Edward L. Bernays.

8. Public relations counseling is at its best when functioning at the very top level of management. Has much progress been made in the acceptance of that concept by the leaders of United States corporations?

9. What are some of the aspects of current American social and business life that make public relations essential?

10. Modern public opinion and marketing survey techniques are widely used by practitioners today. When and by whom were these techniques first developed?

CHAPTER FOUR

Public Relations Departments and Firms

The first three chapters have presented an introductory look at the many faces of public relations—the numerous types of activities that practitioners are involved in. This chapter will examine the operational structure of the industry. Two basic types of operations exist: the public relations department and the public relations counseling firm. The text describes how both are organized and how they perform their functions.

A substantial majority of practitioners work for public relations or communications departments of companies and nonprofit organizations. A recent survey found that 85 percent of the 1500 largest corporations in the United States have such a department. According to another survey, a 1983 study by the International Association of Business Communicators, nearly half its members work in a corporate setting. Another 10 percent are employed in public relations departments of not-for-profit organizations. And the Public Relations Society of America reports that 45 percent of its members work in business and industry, while another 25 percent are in public relations firms. The remaining 30 percent are employed in nonprofit agencies, associations, educational institutions, and government.

Public relations firms offer a wide range of services and expert advice to clients on a fee basis. Their clients primarily are organizations that have limited public relations staffs or seek specialized services.

The chapter takes a look at the advantages and disadvantages of public relations work in each type of setting, and explores some of the problems that each area faces. Students can thus gain an understanding of the operational setup of the industry, as seen in an examination of the two major branches.

Public Relations Departments

THE ROLE OF DEPARTMENTS

For nearly 100 years, public relations departments have served companies and organizations. George Westinghouse is reported to have created the first corporate department in 1889 when he hired two men to publicize his pet project, direct current electricity. Their work was relatively simple when compared to the melange of physical, sociological, and psychological elements that contemporary departments employ. Eventually Westinghouse lost to Thomas A. Edison's alternating current system, which became the standard in the United States. Westinghouse's public relations department concept, however, has grown into a basic part of today's electronic world.

For years public relations had the limited function of getting information into the mass media. Edmund T. Pratt, Jr., chairman of Pfizer, Inc., said, "The aim was to get your name around and get publicity for a new product and build a corporate reputation." Media relations and product publicity to a large extent still dominate the activities of many corporate public relations departments. Today's environment, though, is giving public relations an even larger and more influential role.

AN INCREASE IN PRESSURE ON BUSINESSES S. Bruce Smart, Jr., president of Continental Insurance Company, said that increasing social demands on business have created a need for public relations professionals to advise management in formulating overall strategies for an organization. As if to underline Smart's thought, 40 percent of the chief executives interviewed in a survey agreed that a public relations person should be a member of an organization's top policy-making group.

The continuing social pressures referred to by Smart were summarized in a special report on public relations in *Business Week* (January 22, 1979):

It [the corporation] is under siege from consumerists, environmentalists, women's liberation advocates, the civil rights movement and other activist groups. Their demands are steadily translated into an unprecedented wave of intervention by federal and state governments into the affairs of business.

These activist groups, of course, are exercising their democratic rights, a fact that public relations representatives should keep in mind. Instead of striking a defensive or belligerent posture, they can accomplish their goals better with programs emphasizing their corporations' role as good citizens, pointing out that corporations too have rights in a democracy, and seeking common ground for negotiation with those who condemn them.

Other factors also have stimulated a new appreciation of public relations. These include (1) increased competition by foreign firms; (2) unfriendly takeover attempts by other companies; and (3) closer scrutiny by the media, which have reemphasized the need for candor, honesty, and openness.

AN ACTIVIST STANCE   Indeed, some businesses no longer are remaining silent but are assuming activist roles themselves. Among the most aggressive is Mobil Oil. It has spent a decade producing advocacy advertisements and answering critics. When the corporation became frustrated by the way in which television networks reported oil company earnings, it prepared an advertisement showing the percentage of profit for the three commercial networks during the same period. Mobil ranked behind all three in percentage of profits. The networks refused to run the ad because, they claimed, it was controversial and fell under the equal time provisions of the Federal Communications Commission (FCC). The networks didn't relent even after Mobil volunteered to pay the costs of any rebuttal by other groups. As an alternative, Mobil took out full-page ads in many daily newspapers with the same information.

Bechtel Power Company, accused of CIA connections by the muckraking monthly *Mother Jones,* released a point-by-point rebuttal of the allegations and distributed it widely to the mass media. And Illinois Power Company even produced a 45-minute videotape rebutting a feature on CBS's "60 Minutes" about the cost of building nuclear power plants.

A corporate public relations department should correct the news media when they make mistakes about the company. Significant errors should be challenged with requests for publication or broadcast of corrections. Newspapers often have a space designated for this purpose. A letter to the editor is another method for setting the record straight. Regrettably, the broadcast networks have created no such mechanism.

In the environment of the 1980s, all organizations must formulate policies that serve the public interest and can be defended in the marketplace of public opinion. Management now recognizes that public relations is a tool for problem-solving as well as attention-getting. Public relations, if conducted in a dignified and intelligent fashion, can help the corporation function more effectively in a crisis-ridden environment.

EXPECTATIONS OF MANAGEMENT

Top management today expects much more from its public relations department than simply news releases and other forms of media contact. It wants the following:

1. *Information analysis.* Public relations staff members should function as information analysts and information brokers, says R. D. Lilley, president of the American Telephone & Telegraph Company. They must be able to interpret the world to the corporation and the corporation to the world.

2. *Issues management.* The public relations staff should monitor trends in society and pinpoint public concerns before they erupt into full-fledged controversies. Indeed, the Task Force on the Stature and Role of Public Relations, formed by PRSA in 1980, pointed out:

... [T]he greatest value of the public relations professional is in anticipating and shaping what is happening, not in reporting or coping with what has already been determined. By the time an organization is confronted with attitudes of its publics, it is usually too late for public relations thinking to have an effect on them. Dealing with existing attitudes is important, but helping to shape and direct future attitudes is far more valuable.

3. *Education.* The public relations staff has an important educational role in helping management understand how the mass media operate and what their role in society is. Indeed, IABC members report that management-administration is the prime audience for much of their efforts.

4. *Training.* Public relations personnel must counsel management on how to communicate the organization's position to the public effectively. Because of societal pressures, top management increasingly is spending more time on public affairs and in speaking to a variety of audiences. Peter Drucker, a management expert, estimates that top executives now spend up to 75 percent of their time on public affairs. Top executives also are less hesitant than previously to appear on television talk shows.

5. *Management expertise.* Public relations personnel—at least those who aspire to policy-making positions in an organization—must master the techniques of management. They must understand such concepts as management by objective (MBO), allocation of resources, supervision of personnel, and use of cost-effective communication tools. All public relations strategies and programs must relate directly to the organization's overall objectives. As the president of Quaker Oats stated: "The ones who don't move along are apt to be simply interested in the technical handling of issues and the communications involved. But they are unaware of its impact on the strategy of the company."

The change in the scope and structure of public relations departments has been summarized by *Business Week* as follows:

Public relations men [and women] are striving to give an intellectual substance to what they do. They are moving away from the seat-of-the-pants approach that has characterized their activities in the past and are trying to adopt long-range planning and other apparatus of modern management. In the process, new conceptions are evolving as to what PR is, extending beyond the traditional functions of media, community, employees and financial relations.

ORGANIZATION OF A DEPARTMENT

A public relations department is headed by a person most frequently titled "director of public relations." Especially in large corporations, the director may be a vice-president or perhaps hold the broader title "vice-president of corporate communications." In the latter case, responsibility may also include advertising and marketing supervision.

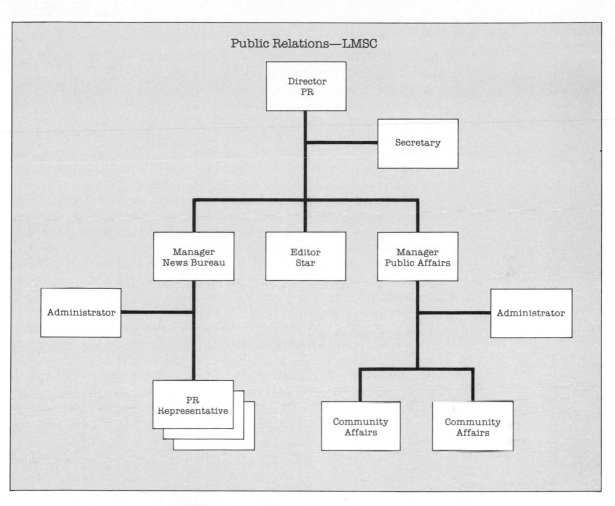

FIGURE 4.1

This chart shows how the public relations department of Lockheed Missiles & Space Company is organized. (Courtesy of Lockheed.)

Under its director, a department usually is divided into sections and even into subsections. Each section manager reports to the director. Each section has a specialized area of responsibility, such as press relations, investor relations, consumer affairs, employee relations, and community affairs.

A typical organizational chart for a public relations department is the one shown here from Lockheed Missiles & Space Company of Sunnyvale, California, with a staff of 14 (see Figure 4.1). The head of the department, called director of public relations, reports to the president. A secretary and three other persons report to the director. They are the manager of the news bureau (responsible for news releases and media relations), the editor of the Lockheed *Star* (employee newspaper), and the manager of public affairs (primarily government and community relations).

The news bureau manager has an administrative assistant and three public relations representatives who handle news and contribute articles to the *Star*. The public affairs manager has an administrative assistant and two persons who work directly in community affairs, covering the entire San Francisco Bay area.

One of the world's largest corporations, General Motors, has more than 300 public relations personnel and a wide range of job titles based on geography and operating divisions. Each division, such as Buick and the Saginaw Steering Gear Division, has its own director of public relations. General Electric, another corporate giant, has several hundred persons in various public relations functions.

These examples should not mislead the reader about the size of public relations departments in American companies. Multimillion-dollar corporations often have small departments. Most public relations people work in departments that have fewer than 10 on the staff.

Public relations personnel also may be dispersed throughout an organization in such a manner that an observer has difficulty in ascertaining the extent of public relations activity. Some may be housed under marketing communications in the marketing department. Others may be assigned to the personnel department as communication specialists producing newsletters and brochures. Still others may be in advertising, working exclusively on product publicity. Decentralization of the public relations function, and the frictions it causes, will be discussed a little later in the chapter.

LINE FUNCTION VERSUS STAFF FUNCTION

Traditional management theory divides an organization into *line* and *staff* functions. A line person—for example, a vice-president of manufacturing—is concerned with achievement of an organization's objectives, such as the manufacture and sale of personal computers. A line manager accomplishes this goal through the delegation of authority, the assignment of projects, and the supervision of others, such as assembly-line workers. A staff person, in contrast, indirectly influences the work of others through the use of suggestions, recommendations, and advice.

According to accepted management theory, public relations is a staff function. Public relations personnel are experts in communication. Line managers, including the president of the organization, rely on public relations people to utilize their skills in preparing and processing data, making recommendations, and executing communication programs to implement the organization's policies. Figure 4.2 shows a news release for a world-famous jewelry store.

Public relations staff members, for example, may find through a community survey that people have only a vague understanding of what the

FIGURE 4.2

Publicity for new products is a function of public relations departments and counseling firms. Cartier, the international jeweler, introduced its line of luxury eyewear at an invitational Hollywood studio dinner dance. The news release was accompanied by photographs of the products and a list of television and film stars scheduled to attend the "Evening With Cartier."

Cartier

FIFTH AVENUE AND 52ᴺᴰ STREET • NEW YORK, N.Y. 10022 • TEL. 212 PL 3-0111

TELEX: (710) 581-3909   CABLE: TIERCAR

FOR IMMEDIATE RELEASE   From: Fernanda K. Gilligan
                                           (212) 753-0111
May 3, 1984
                                              or

                                           Rupert Allan
                                           (213) 655-8970

                     EVENING WITH CARTIER

Cartier, the international jeweler, introduced their newest
product, "Eyewear by Cartier," on Wednesday, May 2nd at
Paramount Studios in Hollywood, California. The unique introduction featured a gourmet dinner, a multi-faceted show and
dancing in a tented and specially decorated sound stage which
was described as "the splendor of a golden vision."

Mr. and Mrs. Marvin Davis served as Honorary Chairmen.
Mr. Alain Dominique Perrin, President of Cartier International,
and Mr. Ralph Destino, President of Cartier USA, served as hosts
for the glamorous soiree. On behalf of the 400 guests, Cartier
made a contribution to the Barbara Davis Center for Childhood
Diabetes. The guests, by invitation only, were assembled from
the entertainment world, society and civic leaders.

                               More...

company manufactures. In order to improve community comprehension and create greater rapport, for instance, the public relations department may recommend to top management that a community open house be held at which product demonstrations, tours, and entertainment would be featured.

Notice that the department *recommends* this action. It would have no direct authority to decide arbitrarily on an open house and to order various departments within the company to cooperate. If top management approves the proposal, the department may take responsibility for organizing the event. Top management, as line managers, has the authority to direct all departments to cooperate in the activity.

Although public relations departments can function only with the approval of top management, there are varying levels of influence that departments may exert. These levels will be discussed shortly.

ACCESS TO MANAGEMENT The power and influence of a public relations department usually result from access to top management, which uses advice and recommendations to formulate policy. That is why public relations, as well as other staff functions, is located high in the organizational chart and is called upon by top management to make reports and recommendations on issues affecting the entire company. In today's environment, public acceptance or nonacceptance of a proposed policy is an important factor in decision-making—as important as costing and technological ability.

The organizational chart of General Motors, for example, shows public relations as a policy group reporting directly to the executive committee, consisting of the GM president and key board members. Other policy groups with the same status as public relations include engineering, marketing, personnel, and research—all of which have functions that affect every area of the corporation.

LEVELS OF INFLUENCE Management experts state that staff functions in an organization operate at various levels of influence and authority. On the lowest level, the staff function may be only *advisory:* line management has no obligation to take recommendations or even request them.

When public relations is purely advisory, often it is not effective. A good example involves the Metropolitan Edison Company and the Three Mile Island nuclear power plant crisis (see Chapter 14). Analysis showed that the utility's credibility suffered a major blow because the public relations function was low-level. Top management did not accept recommendations or perhaps even ask for them. After the initial damage had been done in terms of public confusion and misunderstanding, management brought in experts from the firm of Hill & Knowlton and took steps to implement the counseling firm's recommendations. The utility's own public relations staff was relegated to a minor role throughout the crisis.

Johnson & Johnson, on the other hand, gives its public relations staff function higher status. The Tylenol crisis, in which seven persons died after taking capsules containing cyanide, clearly showed that the company based much of its reaction and quick recall of the product on the advice of public relations staff. In this case, public relations was in a *compulsory advisory* position (see the case study on Tylenol in Chapter 14).

Under the compulsory advisory concept, organization policy requires that line managers (top management) at least listen to the appropriate staff experts before deciding on a strategy. Don Hellriegel and John Slocum, authors of the textbook *Management,* state: "Although such a procedure does not limit the manager's decision-making discretion, it ensures that the manager has made use of the specialized talents of the appropriate staff agency."

Another level of advisory relationship within an organization is called *concurring authority.* For instance, an operating division wishing to publish a brochure cannot do so unless the public relations department approves the copy and layout. If differences arise, the parties must agree before work can proceed. Many firms use this mode to prevent departments and divisions from disseminating materials not in conformity with company standards. In addition, the company must ascertain that its trademarks are used correctly to ensure continued protection (see Chapter 13).

Concurring authority, however, also may limit the freedom of the public relations department. Many companies have a policy that all employee magazine articles and external news releases must be reviewed by the legal staff before publication. The material cannot be disseminated until legal and public relations personnel have agreed upon what will be said. The situation is even more limiting on public relations when the legal department has *command authority* to change a news release with or without the consent of public relations. This is one reason that newspaper editors find some news releases so filled with "legalese" as to be almost unreadable.

Editors are likely to find news releases in the high technology field particularly difficult to follow, because the engineering staff has command authority to insert technical terms and jargon without the consent of the public relations staff. In such a case, the unfortunate public relations person usually reaps the criticism of the news media for giving out material that is useless for publication or broadcast.

SOURCES OF FRICTION

Invariably, frictions arise between line and staff people. This problem results from such factors as personality conflicts, orientation, and place in the organizational chart.

Surveys show that line people are generally oriented to the advancement of the company and that their future is heavily dependent upon being loyal to the organization. Staff people, on the other hand, tend to be oriented toward the advancement of their profession, whether it be engineering, scientific research, advertising, marketing, or public relations. Staff people identify highly with an occupation rather than with an organization. Physicians, for example, have more loyalty to the standards of the medical profession than to the particular hospital in which they practice.

A major cause of friction is the fact that staff units are higher in the organizational structure than line units and enjoy a direct reporting relationship with top management. Staff people often acquire informal authority by having the ear of management. Staff recommendations accepted by top management are effective in shaping policies that line managers must carry out.

Friction also occurs between staff units. The public relations function often intrudes on the staff functions of legal, personnel, advertising, and marketing.

The legal staff tends to be concerned about the possible effect of any public statement on present or impending lawsuits. Consequently, lawyers often frustrate public relations personnel by requiring revisions of news releases, sometimes excessively. The work of attorneys may take place in a court of law, while public relations people strive to represent the organization in what Professor Walt Seifert of Ohio State University has called "the court of public opinion." Composing a clear, succinct news release while satisfying the legal department's needs often tests a writer's skill.

Personnel departments (human resources) are often in a struggle with public relations departments over who should communicate with employees. Personnel administrators believe that they should control the flow of information. Public relations personnel contend that satisfactory external public relations cannot be achieved unless effective employee communications are conducted at the same time. Unfortunately, many personnel managers have poor communication skills and do not understand how a lack of information generates rumors and morale problems.

When Atari, the videogame manufacturer, dismissed 1700 workers, the human resources (personnel) department did not consider the layoff important enough for the employee newsletter. Employees had to read about the details in the local daily newspaper. Atari's employee newsletter, as a result, lost considerable credibility.

Advertising and public relations departments often collide because they compete for funds to communicate with external audiences. Advertising's approach to communications is, "Will it sell?" Public relations asks, "Will it make friends?" These differing orientations frequently cause breakdowns in coordination of overall strategy. Marketing departments also compete with public relations departments for funds; marketing's emphasis is on product publicity.

To avoid conflicts between departments, the following suggestions are made:

1. Representatives of departments should serve together on key committees to enable an exchange of information.

2. Heads of departments should be equals in job title. In this way, the autonomy of one executive is not subverted by another.

3. All department heads should report to the same superior, so that all viewpoints can be considered before an appropriate decision is made.

4. Informal, regular contacts with representatives in other departments can help create mutual trust and respect.

5. Written policies should be established to spell out the responsibilities of each department. Such policies are helpful in settling disputes as to which department has authority to communicate with employees or alter a news release.

PLACE IN OVERALL STRUCTURE

In any modern organization, public relations is a management function as well as a staff function. Its power and influence are directly related to two factors.

First, as noted earlier, public relations efforts can be effective only if the head of the department has direct access to top management and is represented on key policy-making committees. The desirable model is for the public relations department to have a *compulsory advisory* role.

Second, the head of public relations must be equal in status and rank to heads of other departments. It is important that all have the same title. If other department heads are at the vice-presidential level, for instance, the head of public relations should be, too.

Not all companies realize the value of this organizational model. In some, a director of public relations reports directly to a vice-president of marketing or advertising. This arrangement suggests that the organization narrowly defines the function of public relations. The department focuses on product publicity, to the detriment of other important activities.

Other large corporations have vice-presidents of corporate communications who supervise public relations, advertising, and marketing communications. This setup tends to work much better, because the managers or directors of the three departments have equal status and report to a centralized person, who then coordinates a total communications strategy after weighing the recommendations of all three.

Some models for the public relations function in an organizational chart are shown in Figure 4.3.

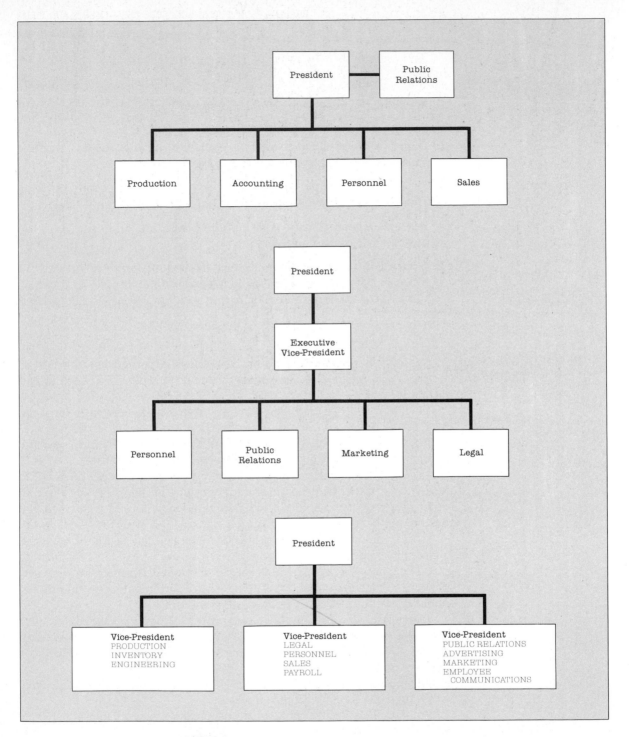

FIGURE 4.3

The chart depicts three examples of corporate management organization, showing the important position of public relations.

ADVANTAGES AND DISADVANTAGES OF WORKING IN A DEPARTMENT

Work in a public relations department can be invigorating and can offer staff members a sense of accomplishment as they help the organization achieve its objectives. The advantages of employment in a corporate setting are (1) generally good salaries, (2) extensive health and insurance benefits, (3) the opportunity to work with a group of professional peers, and (4) extensive resources. The disadvantages can be (1) a laborious approval process before production or dissemination of information, (2) lack of understanding by management of the public relations function, (3) lack of advancement opportunities in a small department, and (4) involvement in routine activities that change little over a period of time.

At the beginning of their careers, most public relations people perform at the technician level. Those who aspire to management positions at policy-making levels should have, in addition to technical skill, a good understanding of management methods and business in general.

Public Relations Firms

In size, public relations firms range from one- or two-person staffs to giants such as Burson-Marsteller, which employs more than 1500 people worldwide. The scope of services these firms provide to clients varies accordingly. Big or small, they have an identical purpose: to give counsel and, to the extent a client wishes, perform the technical services required to carry out an agreed-upon program. The counseling firm may operate as an adjunct to an organization's public relations department or, if no department exists, conduct the entire public relations effort.

These firms have proliferated in proportion to the growth of American business and industry. As American companies expanded after World War II into booming domestic and worldwide markets, many corporations felt a need for public relations firms that could provide them with professional expertise in communications.

Stimulating the growth of public relations firms were increased urbanization, expansion of government bureaucracy and regulation, more sophisticated mass media systems, the rise of consumerism, and demand for more information by the American people. Professionals were needed to maintain lines of communication in an increasingly complicated world and to provide much of the material to be distributed. Some experts, who point out that public relations services seem to grow best in an atmosphere of conflict, say that the number of firms multiplied as the American public placed less trust in large corporations and demanded more corporate responsibility in environmental and consumer matters.

THE SERVICES THEY PROVIDE

Counseling firms today offer services far more extensive than those provided by the nation's first firm, the Publicity Bureau, founded in 1900 in Boston. A full-fledged public relations firm provides these services:

Executive speech training. Top executives are coached on public affairs activities, including personal appearances.

Research and evaluation. Scientific surveys to measure public attitudes and perceptions are conducted.

Diversified communication tools. Slide presentations, videotapes, brochures, newsletters, and other materials are prepared and distributed.

Crisis communication. Management is counseled on what to say and do in an emergency such as an oil spill or recall of an unsafe product.

Media analysis. Appropriate media are examined for targeting specific messages to key audiences.

Community relations. Management is counseled on ways to achieve official and public support for such projects as building or expanding a factory.

Product promotion. Representatives are placed on radio and television talk shows; stories and artwork are provided for print media.

Events management. News conferences, anniversary celebrations, rallies, symposiums, and national conferences are planned and conducted.

Public affairs. Materials are prepared for government hearings, testimony before regulatory bodies, and background briefings.

Employee communications. Ways to motivate employees and raise productivity are discussed with management.

Positioning a company. Advice is given on corporate identity programs that establish a place in the market for the company and its products.

Financial relations. Management is counseled on ways to avoid takeover by another firm and effectively communicate with stockholders, security analysts, and institutional investors.

Increasingly, public relations firms emphasize the counseling aspect of their services. A number of executives now object to the idea that they operate public relations "agencies." They say that public relations is a management consulting function and cannot be delegated to others, as the term "agent" implies. On the contrary, many public relations practitioners say that a great number of public relations "agencies" do exist because they simply prepare and distribute publicity materials for clients. (In keeping with the niceties of nomenclature, advertising firms are called "agencies" because they buy time or space on behalf of a client, acting as the client's agent in such purchases.)

Public relations firms, large and small, tend to cluster in the major metropolitan centers of the United States. On the international level, American public relations firms or their affiliate agencies are found in most major world cities. Burson-Marsteller, for example, has offices in Toronto, Montreal, San Juan, Brussels, The Hague, Frankfurt, Geneva, London, Malmö, Milan, Paris, Hong Kong, Kuala Lumpur, Singapore, Tokyo, Melbourne, Sydney, and São Paulo.

A SUCCESS STORY: BURSON-MARSTELLER

The general ranking of the top 20 public relations firms does not change much from year to year, but the beginning of 1984 marked the advancement of Burson-Marsteller to the top position. The firm moved ahead of Hill & Knowlton, previously the largest firm since 1957.

Jack O'Dwyer's Newsletter, which annually reports on the growth and size of public relations firms, cites a number of reasons for Burson-Marsteller's success:

. . . **aggressive new business program; reputation for being able to counsel and execute; reputation for being innovative and results-oriented; businesslike way of charging clients (it does not use retainers or minimums, charging only for hours of service given); the best training program in PR at all levels; a loyal core of top executives; strong marketing orientation (ability to move products off the shelves), and B-M's worldwide integrated system of service.**

Burson-Marsteller's public relations work for high-technology firms began with the opening of an office in Silicon Valley at Santa Clara, California; its staff grew from one person in November 1982 to about 50 in 1985. Another firm in Silicon Valley, Regis McKenna Public Relations, Inc., of Palo Alto, deals exclusively with high-technology companies and is fifteenth in size on *O'Dwyer's* list.

ADVERTISING AND PUBLIC RELATIONS MERGERS

Until the late 1970s, the largest American public relations firms were independently owned by their principal officers or, in some cases, by employee stockholders. A significant change began in 1978 when Carl Byoir & Associates, the nation's third largest public relations company, was purchased by the advertising firm of Foote, Cone and Belding.

In rapid succession, Burson-Marsteller became part of the Young & Rubicam advertising conglomerate; Manning, Selvage & Lee into Benton & Bowles; and Doremus & Company into BBDO advertising. Finally, the largest of them all at the time, Hill & Knowlton, became part of J. Walter Thompson, Inc.

In all these cases, the public relations firms maintained their original names and continued to operate autonomously, with their own chief executives and separate staffs. The concept of advertising agencies' owning public relations firms, however, remains somewhat controversial.

Proponents contend that it is a natural evolution for public relations firms and advertising agencies to come under one roof. They hail the trend as

The Twenty Largest
Public Relations
Firms in the United
States

NAME	FEE INCOME	EMPLOYEES
Burson-Marsteller*	$84,258,000	1,541
Hill & Knowlton*	$69,400,000	1,210
Carl Byoir & Associates*	$30,950,469	573
Ruder Finn & Rotman	$19,240,000	350
Ogilvy & Mather Public Relations*	$16,300,000	300
Daniel J. Edelman	$14,240,194	281
Manning, Selvage & Lee*	$13,428,000	216
Fleishman-Hillard	$11,100,000	137
Brooke Communications Group	$10,923,670	137
Ketchum Public Relations*	$10,800,000	169
Doremus & Company*	$10,548,000	158
The Rowland Company	$10,362,000	138
Rogers & Cowan	$ 9,924,146	174
Gray and Co. Communications	$ 9,000,000	125
Regis McKenna, Inc.	$ 7,855,000	110
Creamer Dickson Basford*	$ 7,811,387	121
Robert Marston Associates	$ 7,013,000	74
Bozell & Jacobs Public Relations*	$ 5,000,000	70
Financial Relations Board	$ 4,460,770	66
Baron/Canning and Company	$ 4,150,000	45

* Denotes advertising agency subsidiary.
SOURCE: Copyright 1985 by J. R. O'Dwyer Co., Inc., New York, NY.

reflecting a new era that seeks to integrate various communication disciplines into "total communication networks." They maintain that no single-function agency is really equipped to handle complex marketing problems and that the combined resources of several functions can solve client needs more efficiently.

Critics of such mergers worry, however, that public relations will become a poor stepchild of the much larger advertising operation, and that all facets of public relations counseling will be subverted by the basic emphasis on advertising to sell goods. They also question the credibility of public relations representatives who deal with the news-editorial side of the mass media when reporters know that they work for an advertising agency.

These critics believe, too, that the total separation of the advertising and news departments of a newspaper should be maintained in public relations. Some public relations executives complain that advertising personnel think of public relations only as product publicity to supplement advertising.

Although 6 of the 10 largest public relations firms in the United States, including the top 3, are now associated with advertising agencies, the point is valid that 39 of the 50 largest firms remain independent. These firms control about half of all public relations billings. Many are adamant in their desire to keep their independence.

When advertising agencies offer public relations services as an adjunct to advertising, an especially dubious situation can exist. Advertising personnel in small agencies often wear two hats, attempting to write advertising copy one moment and a news release the next. Their news releases frequently are badly written product publicity that read like advertising copy. Some advertising agencies even throw in news releases free if a client is a good advertising customer. Many public relations people say, however, that the fears are exaggerated—that advertising agencies in recent years have become sophisticated enough to realize that public relations is not just product publicity.

STRUCTURE OF A COUNSELING FIRM

A small public relations firm may consist only of the owner (president) and an assistant (vice-president), supported by a secretary. Larger firms have a hierarchy something like this:

President

Executive vice-president

Vice-president

Account supervisor

Account executive

Assistant account executive

Secretarial-clerical staff

The chart of Ketchum Public Relations/San Francisco is fairly typical. The president is based in the New York office of Ketchum Public Relations, so the executive vice-president is the on-site director in San Francisco. A senior vice-president is associate director of operations. Next in line are several vice-presidents who primarily do account supervision or special projects.

An account supervisor is in charge of one major account or several smaller ones. An *account executive,* who reports to the supervisor, is in direct contact with the client and handles most of the day-by-day activity. At the bottom of the list is the assistant account executive, who does routine maintenance work compiling media lists, gathering information, and writing rough drafts of news releases.

A recent college graduate usually starts as an assistant account executive. Once he or she learns the firm's procedures and shows ability, promotion to account executive may occur within 6 to 18 months. After 2 or 3 years, it is not uncommon for an account executive to become an account supervisor.

Executives at or above the vice-presidential level usually are heavily involved in selling their firm's services. In order to prosper, a firm must continually seek new business and sell additional services to current clients. Consequently, the upper management of the firm calls on prospective clients, prepares proposals, and makes new business presentations. In this very competitive field, a firm not adept at selling itself frequently fails.

Firms frequently organize account teams, especially to serve a client whose program is multifaceted. One member of the team, for example, may set up a nationwide media tour in which an organization representative is booked on television talk shows. Another may supervise all materials going to the print media, including news stories, feature articles, background kits, and artwork. A third may concentrate on the trade press or perhaps arrange special events.

Another approach is to assemble a team with expertise in a particular field. Large firms make it a point to hire staff members with individual backgrounds in such fields as law, business, science, journalism, engineering, and marketing, so that the appropriate people can be selected for a team depending upon the client's needs.

A team of persons representing several backgrounds may have a better understanding of a client's total needs and develop more creative ideas. If a client is a computer manufacturing firm with a new product and seeking venture capital, an account team might consist of persons with engineering, legal, marketing, and journalism backgrounds. This is the approach of Regis McKenna Public Relations. One-third of its staff has electrical engineering degrees, while the other two-thirds are marketing and public relations specialists. In a modern public relations practice that emphasizes management counseling, problem-solving, and strategic positioning, the old idea that everyone should have a mass media background is increasingly passé.

WORKING IN A PUBLIC RELATIONS FIRM

To many, work in a public relations firm sounds glamorous. A person associates with a number of highly intelligent, creative people, and there is the stimulation of working on several exciting projects at any one time. One day may find the account executive at the opening of a plush restaurant, while the next finds the intrepid executive flying to New York or London to set up a press conference. Of course, there are the proverbial cocktail parties and the pleasure of learning that a well-written feature article has been picked up by 180 daily newspapers.

Although all these happenings do occur in public relations, they are less routine than one would suspect. On many days, an account person may sit in a small cubicle writing a standard news release about a new diesel engine and having a Big Mac for lunch. On other days, the person may spend fruitless hours on the phone trying to book a client's representative for radio and television interviews. It is not very exciting to write a brochure about the services of an engineering firm or to have a masterpiece of prose reduced to alphabet soup by a client's penchant for compound-complex sentences.

THE FRUSTRATIONS AND THE REWARDS Working for a public relations firm can be a source of both frustrations and rewards. Individuals often cite the following frustrations:

1. *Lack of privacy.* For their staff, most firms provide cubicles that are small, open at the top, and without doors. As one employee points out, "You have to think and work in a fish bowl."

2. *Constant documentation of work.* Great emphasis is placed on productivity, and account executives are expected to have 75 percent or more of their working hours billable to a client. Time sheets, accurate to the nearest 15 minutes and describing each activity in detail, must be recorded so that the firm may prepare the proper billings.

3. *Many demands on time.* An account executive usually works on several projects, and it is difficult to give each client the undivided attention that is often demanded.

4. *Client relationships.* Few clients have a good understanding of what public relations can or cannot accomplish. A firm's personnel must constantly educate clients about public relations.

5. *Extended workdays.* Many times an account person must attend night functions or work overtime to meet a deadline.

Despite these frustrations, many people thrive in a public relations firm. They enjoy the constant challenge of coming up with creative ideas—the psychic reward of observing their idea for a slogan become a household term or a planned special event achieve international publicity. Those who leave a public relations firm for jobs with corporations often miss the diversity of assignments. The news release in Figure 4.4 illustrates the kind of work a public relations firm might do for a client.

FIGURE 4.4

News release distributed
by a counseling firm on
behalf of a corporate
client.

ΠCO Holdings, Inc.

10880 Wilshire Boulevard, Los Angeles, California 90024
Telephone (213) 879-5252

Release Date: May 15, 1984

Subject: MCO HOLDINGS, INC. ANNOUNCES
1984 FIRST QUARTER RESULTS

Contact: MCO Holdings: Howard J. Bressler
(213) 879-5252

Burson-Marsteller: Mark P. Boyer
(213) 386-8776

MCO HOLDINGS, INC. REPORTS

1984 FIRST QUARTER RESULTS

LOS ANGELES -- MCO Holdings, Inc. ("MCO") today reported
net income of $2,576,000 or $0.33 per share assuming full dilution for the three months ended March 31, 1984, compared to
$2,391,000, or $0.25 per share assuming full dilution for the
same period in 1983. Revenues in the first quarter of 1984
were $45,652,000 compared with $39,937,000 in the first quarter
of 1983.

WHAT IT TAKES   What, then, does it take to work in a public relations firm? Harold Burson, chairman of Burson-Marsteller, once told a national convention of the Public Relations Student Society of America about the characteristics he seeks in a prospective employee.

First he asks a job applicant, "What do you read?" Burson wants individuals who are aware of the complex world around them. "If you want to pursue a career in public relations, learn to read—everything," he exhorts. Burson has the feeling that those who don't read can't write. And, he points out, in order to succeed in public relations a person must perfect his or her writing skills.

Burson also searches for people who have strong self-discipline. He says:

You are, to some considerable degree, able to do what you want to do and at your own pace. You can turn out a major feature article that sparkles or you can, in the same time frame, deliver up eight mundane news releases written to formula. You can go for a placement on the "Today" show or with the local town daily. You can take a day doing it—or two days. In most cases, you won't get much supervision. You're on your own for a lot of the work you do—almost regardless of who employs you.

Other public relations executives echo what Burson says about reading, writing, and self-discipline. They add such characteristics as the ability to (1) organize and plan; (2) juggle several projects at once without getting rattled; (3) give good, persuasive presentations; and (4) work well with others.

78

PROS AND CONS OF USING A PUBLIC RELATIONS FIRM

"Should we hire a public relations firm?" As they debate that question, executives of potential client organizations should weigh the services a firm can offer against disadvantages reported by some clients who employ such firms.

ON THE PLUS SIDE   Of advantage are the following services and capabilities:

1. *Objectivity.* The firm can analyze a client's need or problem from a new perspective and offer fresh insights.

2. *Variety of skills and expertise.* The firm has specialists who can address specific problems or do certain tasks, whether speechwriting or helping with proxy battles.

3. *Extensive resources.* The firm has abundant media contacts and works regularly with numerous suppliers of products and services. It has research materials, including data information banks, and experience in similar fields.

4. *Offices throughout the country.* A national public relations program requires coordination in major cities. Large firms have on-site staff or affiliate firms in many cities.

5. *Special problem-solving.* A firm may have extensive experience in desired areas such as investor relations, crisis communications, or new-product promotion.

6. *Credibility.* A successful public relations firm has a solid reputation for professional, ethical work. If represented by such a firm, a client likely will get more attention among opinion leaders in mass media, government, and the financial community. Such is the reputation, for example, of Regis McKenna Public Relations that an article in *Fortune* magazine stated, "Simply being a client of Regis McKenna Public Relations has become a kind of appointment for a high-tech business."

Following are two examples of how major corporations used the services of Burson-Marsteller. The programs not only fulfilled client objectives but won Silver Anvil awards in 1982 from the Public Relations Society of America.

General Electric. The assignment was to convince 2000 microwave oven dealers to carry the GE Dual Wave oven, which can prepare foods not normally recommended for microwave cooking. B-M mounted an extensive public relations campaign that included two press conferences during which editors ate elaborate meals prepared in the oven, a media tour featuring TV personality June Lockhart, and a microwave recipe contest co-promoted with major-market newspapers. The result: more than 4000 dealers ordered the Dual Wave Product.

A Cracker Jack Idea

The annual Cracker Jack Old Timers Baseball Classic demonstrates how a public relations firms can design a program tailored to the background and needs of a specific client.

Creation of an old timers' baseball game was proposed by Ketchum Public Relations because Cracker Jack was highly identified with Americana and had a nostalgic tie-in with baseball, popularized by the song "Take Me Out to the Ball Game." A five-inning game played by such former greats as Hank Aaron, Brooks Robinson, Warren Spahn, and Ernie Banks would attract baseball fans and the general public, who might purchase Cracker Jack.

The overall objective of the event was to stimulate grocery stores and other outlets to display Cracker Jack in special aisle exhibits. Research showed that the product was an impulse item that sold best when placed in highly visible positions in store aisles. The aisle displays featured consumer premiums such as baseball cards of former and current stars and also provided ballots so that fans could help choose the game's starting lineup.

The objectives of Ketchum Public Relations were (1) to create widespread awareness of the displays and (2) to maximize the media attention on Cracker Jack and the events leading to the game at R.F.K. Stadium in Washington, D.C. A number of communication tools were used, including:

1. *Announcement press conference.* The general manager of Cracker Jack, accompanied by several baseball stars, announced the forthcoming game. The press conference was covered by national media.

2. *News bureau.* During the year-long promotion of the game, news releases, photos, and other information were regularly sent to the press. The bureau also facilitated media interviews with players planning to participate.

3. *Media tour.* Hank Aaron, who had just been inducted into the Baseball Hall of Fame, appeared on numerous television talk shows and sports programs throughout the country.

4. *Trade dinners.* Receptions, and dinners, with former baseball greats as honored guests, were held in 13 markets.

Clark Equipment. The company decided to close four Michigan plants and write off enormous losses. B-M was asked to communicate the decision. A task force arranged analyst meetings; wrote speeches, press releases, and shareholder letters; conducted press conference training for plant managers; and scheduled newspaper interviews for Clark's chief executive officer.

5. *Special projects.* Former baseball players promoted the game by "barn-storming" the Washington and Baltimore area. Several weeks before the game, they appeared at shopping malls and on busy street corners, and gave local media interviews.

The public relations program was successful. Publicity generated more than 750 million consumer impressions (see Chapter 10 for explanation), and the game was seen by 30,000 fans. It was also broadcast on more than 4,000 ESPN cable affiliates. The client was pleased when A. C. Nielsen audits showed a 45-percent increase in Cracker Jack display activity compared with the same period a year earlier. In addition, 70,000 consumer premiums (collectors' baseball cards and major league ponchos) were redeemed.

SOURCE: Ketchum Public Relations, New York.

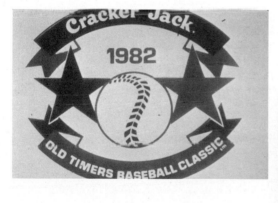

ON THE MINUS SIDE   Programs by public relations firms may fail to fulfill client goals, and problems may cause clients to drop a firm's services.

1. *Superficial grasp of a client's unique problems.* While objectivity is gained from an outsider's perspective, there is often a disadvantage in the public relations firm's not thoroughly understanding the client's business or needs.

2. *Lack of full-time commitment.* A public relations firm has many clients to service. Therefore, no single client can monopolize its personnel and other resources.

3. *Need for prolonged briefing period.* Some companies become frustrated because time and money are needed for a public relations firm to research the organization and make recommendations. Consequently, the actual start of a public relations program may take weeks or months.

4. *Resentment of internal staff.* The public relations staff members of a client organization may resent the use of outside counsel because of the inference that they lack the capability to do the job.

5. *Need for strong direction by top management.* High-level executives must take the time to brief outside counsel on specific objectives sought.

6. *Need for full information and confidence.* A client must be willing to share all information, including the skeletons in the closet, with outside counsel.

7. *Costs.* Outside counsel is expensive. In many situations, routine public relations work can be handled at lower cost by internal staff.

The problems often are two-way. Personnel in counseling firms complain at times that they cannot do a highly effective job for clients because (1) top corporate executives do not take time to define objectives and clarify what they want a public relations program to accomplish, (2) the clients fail to provide the information needed to tailor a program to the specific problem, and (3) clients often are penny-wise and pound-foolish in terms of not approving expenditures for key items.

Counselors also complain that clients often think of public relations as some sort of magical cure-all that can accomplish miracles. By the time counsel is called in, they say, the crisis has already occurred—and there really isn't much a public relations program can do. Public relations counsel must continually tell clients that they cannot (1) guarantee specified results, (2) change public perceptions or attitudes overnight, and (3) make any organization something that it is not.

FEES AND CHARGES   THE THREE METHODS OF CHARGING   A public relations firm charges for its services in several ways. The three most common methods are as follows:

1. *Basic hourly fee, plus out-of-pocket expenses.* The number of hours spent on a client's account is tabulated each month and billed to the client. Work by personnel in the counseling firm is billed at various hourly rates—for example, a secretary typing envelopes at $20 an hour and an account executive working at $85 an hour. Out-of-pocket expenses, such as cab fares, car rentals, airline tickets, and meals, also are billed to the client.

2. *Retainer fee.* A basic monthly charge billed to the client covers ordinary administrative and overhead expenses for maintaining the account and being "on call." Many retainer fees also specify the number of hours the counseling firm will spend on the account each month. Additional work is billed at normal hourly rates. Out-of-pocket expenses normally are billed separately.

3. *Fixed project fee.* The public relations firm agrees to do a specific project, such as an annual report, a newsletter, or a special event, for a fixed fee. For example, a counseling firm may write and produce a quarterly newsletter for $30,000 annually. The fixed fee is the least popular of the three methods because it is difficult to estimate accurately all work and expenses in advance.

The primary basis for all three methods is to estimate the number of hours that a particular project will take to plan, execute, and evaluate. The first method, the basic hourly fee, is the most flexible and most widely used among large firms. It is preferred by public relations people because they are paid for the exact number of hours spent on a project and because it is the only sound way that a fee can be determined intelligently. The retainer fee and the fixed project fee are based on an estimate of how many hours it will take to counsel a client.

Clients, however, like to have a fixed budget for their public relations expenses so that the proper allocation of funds can be made. Often a compromise agreement is reached as to the financial parameters of a program. The public relations firm estimates the number of staff members and hours a project will take, and this estimate then becomes the budget for the program. The counseling firm, for example, may estimate that a program will take 200 hours over 3 months at a cost of $10,500. The client signs an agreement to pay the firm $3,500 a month for 3 months. If the counseling firm finds that it is spending more time than estimated on the account, it has the choice of cutting back the number of hours during the next month or asking the client for permission to raise the established budget.

Most large public relations firms have sophisticated cost-accounting systems to keep track of hours and supplies spent on an account. Even use of the telephones and photocopying machines is programmed to produce a computer printout showing what calls or copying should be billed to what account number. As previously mentioned, anyone who works on the client account is required to keep detailed time sheets that are computer-tabulated on a weekly basis. This gives the counseling firm's management the ability to determine the status and profitability of an account at any given moment.

HOW ESTIMATES ARE MADE   A number of variables are considered when the public relations firm estimates the cost of a program. These may include the size and duration, geographical locations involved, number of personnel to be assigned to the project, and even the nature of the client. A major variable, of course, is billing the use of the firm's personnel to a client at the proper hourly rate.

The hourly billing rate of an employee depends on his or her experience, title, and salary level. An account executive who earns $30,000 annually would be making $15 per hour, based on his or her working 40 hours a week for 50 weeks a year—a total of 2,000 hours. The firm's management must also include such overhead expenses as office space, equipment, utilities, phone, insurance benefits, and pension plans. Another factor is the percentage of profit after all the bills are paid. In general, public relations firms try to operate on a profit level of between 18 and 22 percent.

Usually a public relations firm bills clients at three to five times a staff person's base hourly salary. The account executive in the example just cited would cost a client between $45 and $75 per hour. The principals of a counseling firm, because of their much higher salaries, often command $100 to $500 an hour.

The primary income of a public relations firm comes from the selling of staff time, but some additional income results from mark-ups on all production costs, such as printing, photography, and artwork. The standard in the trade is 17.65 percent of costs. Out-of-pocket expenses are billed to clients at net cost.

THE ETHICS OF BILLING   Ethical public relations firms charge clients only for their time and expertise. They avoid guarantees of specific results beyond their direct control. Thus, the firm will charge for the research, writing, and distribution of a news release but will not guarantee its use by the mass media. The counselor may give a company advice on how to avoid an unfriendly takeover but cannot guarantee that the recommended plan of action will succeed.

Some firms do charge on the basis of media placement. A Connecticut organization once advertised in the *Wall Street Journal* that a 4-inch story in a newspaper with a circulation above 500,000 would cost $500. The price for placing a client's representative on a network talk show was listed as $1000. Another firm advertises: "We guarantee you publicity."

Serious problems exist with this approach to public relations. First, no firm can really guarantee that a newspaper or broadcast news gatekeeper (reporter, editor, director) will use the client's material. Second, the approach usually stresses quantity instead of quality. A 4-inch story in the *Wall Street Journal* or New York *Times* may be worth more to the client (if it reaches the appropriate audience) than the same article in the Columbus (Ohio) *Dispatch* that may not reach the primary audience for the company's particular message.

Lorry I. Lokey, general manager of *Business Wire* in San Francisco, says: "To 'guarantee' results [broadcast time, inches of clippings] from publicity efforts is about as obnoxious as an attorney saying he wins 95 percent of his cases or a doctor claiming a 99 percent survival rate. If I were an editor evaluating a publicity effort by someone who guaranteed results, I would be inclined to wreck his batting average."

Professional public relations firms also avoid working on commission. In other words, firms do not make arrangements with clients for a percentage of the sales that might result from product publicity efforts, for two reasons:

1. Committing staff time and resources is risky because of numerous variables and unpredictable developments. Even with outstanding publicity a product may fail because it is overpriced or inferior to competing products. A counseling firm once developed an excellent campaign for an airline, but the pilots went on strike shortly after the campaign began.

2. A vested interest by the public relations firm in the success of a product or event can lead to overzealous and strong arm tactics to get favorable publicity, perhaps even attempted bribes of media gatekeepers.

Public relations firms are in the business of counseling management and providing specialized communication services to help clients achieve stated objectives. They are not simply publicity agents who are "hired guns" for anyone who wants to use their services. An ethical firm works only with clients who have legitimate objectives that serve the public interest.

QUESTIONS FOR REVIEW AND DISCUSSION

1. Who is credited with creating the first corporate public relations department? When?

2. Name three types of service that top management expects from a public relations department.

3. What is the difference between a line function and a staff function? To which function does public relations belong, and why?

4. Explain why a compulsory advisory role within an organization is a good one for a public relations department to have.

5. Work in a corporate public relations department has advantages and possible disadvantages. Name two of each.

6. Public relations counseling firms offer many services to their clients. List and explain five of these.

7. Do you regard the mergers of advertising agencies with public relations firms as a healthy or an unhealthy trend? Explain your opinion.

8. How does a counseling firm account team operate?

9. What are three reasons that some companies don't employ a public relations firm?

10. Discuss the methods that public relations firms use to charge clients for their services: basic hourly fee, retainer fee, and fixed project fee.

CHAPTER FIVE

The Individual in Public Relations

Earlier chapters have examined public relations as an institution; this chapter will alter the perspective and look at the field from a personal point of view: Where does the individual fit into public relations work? The pages that follow explain the mission of the public relations practitioner and discuss the talents and attitudes necessary for success in the field.

This chapter resembles an orientation tour. It opens the doors of public relations offices and shows what goes on inside. Students sit down at desks, figuratively, and learn answers to questions that every potential worker has about career opportunities, satisfactions, and rewards.

What should a newcomer expect to encounter on the job—what kind of assignments, what kind of pay, what kind of people? What career paths can the public relations practitioner follow, and toward what ultimate goals?

The importance of writing skill, research ability, and creativity are emphasized. So is the rapidly expanding role of women in public relations.

The Public Relations Role

HOW PUBLIC RELATIONS DIFFERS FROM REPORTING

Everyone entering public relations should understand its purpose and the role of the individual in carrying out that purpose. Although they may need many of the same skills as news reporters, public relations practitioners have an entirely different mission. The goal of reporters is to uncover the facts, to the fullest extent possible, on stories to which they have been assigned. Ideally, reporters should have no causes to promote nor vested interests to protect.

Public relations representatives, on the other hand, are by definition special pleaders. Their mission is to influence public opinion favorably toward the company, the cause, or the individual they represent. These practitioners develop ways to protect and enhance a client's reputation. Within an organization, they present management's views to employees and stockholders. They attempt to convey the views of various publics to management. As strongly as possible, they seek to shed a favorable light upon a client's reputation without violating ethical standards.

While carrying out their mission, some ultraprotective public relations representatives let reporters dig out unfavorable information on their own. They follow the dictum of King Charles I of England: "Never make a defense or an apology until you are accused." Wise public relations advisers do more than that. They practice preventive medicine. If they know that their clients are vulnerable to criticism for certain practices or attitudes, they work from within to remove the causes of the vulnerability before the public becomes aware of them. As they may remember, Charles I lost his head because he failed to correct his faults.

A CHANGING FOCUS IN PUBLIC RELATIONS

Traditionally, it was held widely that public relations practitioners should if possible have experience as reporters, to polish their writing skills and to learn first-hand how the media function. In an earlier era, a large percentage of public relations people did have newspaper or broadcast experience. For several reasons, this no longer is true. The field of public relations has broadened far beyond the media area. Writing skill and knowledge of the media are vital, but so is training in management, logistics, and planning—skills not usually acquired on a reporter's beat. In fact, former newspaper reporters often fail at public relations because they don't perceive the work as more than writing news releases and fail to conform as corporation-oriented team players.

Another factor limiting the number of graduates who acquire reporting experience before beginning public relations careers is the limited number of newspaper jobs. There are many more corporations and institutions with public relations departments than there are daily newspapers. Movement of well-educated graduates direct from the classroom into public relations jobs is well accepted today. Since good writing is so important in public relations, those who do not undergo the editing discipline of newspaper work should make a special effort on their own to polish their writing.

Many graduates choose public relations because they find the work at times to be stimulating and challenging, providing variety along with the routine. As the fictional hero in *Dazzle* by Elinor Klein and Dora Landey, a paperback novel about a public relations man, states: "As far as I know, it is the only profession left with infinite possibilities for learning everything from cereal to senators. . . . It allows me to keep in touch with all worlds and give up none." One day the young practitioner may prepare a news release; the next, work on a slide presentation; and the following, organize a conference. On a typical day, the practitioner may answer press inquiries, compile lists for mailing and for media contacts, escort visitors, read proof, write a brochure, scan incoming publications, help produce displays, select photographs, or compile questionnaires.

Although the reporter and the public relations representative have different functions and sometimes are in conflict, no reason ordinarily exists for antagonism between them. They need each other. The public relations representative should avoid displaying anger toward a reporter whose story causes a problem for a client. Nor should a reporter become upset with a public relations representative who does not provide complete information in a sensitive situation. Often, if given a free hand by management, the public relations person would tell more than he or she does. When each side understands the other's role, mutually satisfactory and pleasant relationships normally exist. In fact, in the bulk of their contacts, the public relations representative is free to give the reporter 100 percent cooperation because their interests coincide, with both sides desiring full disclosure of a situation.

Personal Qualifications and Attitudes

ERASING THE CLICHÉ IMAGE

From the outset, it is important to wipe out the cliché vision of public relations specialists as glad-handing *flacks*. Backslappers and armgrabbers still exist among public relations people today, as they do among accountants, gasoline station operators, and even schoolteachers. In public relations, they are found mostly among publicists of personalities and entertainment—a small minority, vastly outnumbered. The cliché image, carried over from the long-ago days of advance publicity agents for traveling circuses and theatrical troupes, lingers but is invalid and unrealistic (see Chapter 3).

In truth, no such thing as a public relations personality exists. Men and women of all types—extrovert or introvert, aggressive or a little shy, analytical or intuitive—can find satisfying positions in this multifaceted field.

A former public relations executive of a large oil corporation, Donald Sweeney, was asked his opinion about the attributes needed for success in public relations. He responded:

Unfortunately, too many people think a pleasing personality is the number one (and, often, only) qualification for public relations work. Except for a few jobs with a high increment of representational skills (read "glad hand"), personality has nothing to do with public relations work or success therein. I don't mean that boors and misfits should be preferred, but normal people with normal personalities who have the bundle of skills that often make good writers (information-gathering, analysis, idea formulation, idea presentation, articulateness, a will to persuade, a will to win) are the people I used to look for when I was hiring PR people.

I used to ask applicants a key question at the end of a long interview: "Why do you want to work in public relations?" Many would answer, "Because I like people." This was always a knockout factor with me. I'd offer to send their resumes to the sales department where liking people was a plus, explaining that PR people have to be strictly objective about people to succeed.

Sweeney's outlook was that of corporate operations. Another public relations executive who for many years directed Hollywood motion picture and television publicity programs, Ralph "Casey" Shawhan, answered the same question somewhat differently. His work involved promotion of shows and of personalities, many of whom are notoriously egocentric and unstable.

"Publicists must like the work and the people they are promoting, and be able to get along with them," Shawhan said. "No matter how good they are as writers and as creators of ideas, they will fail if they aren't congenial. I had to fire an excellent former newspaper reporter because he didn't like entertainment people and he let them see it."

These two views do not conflict; they merely emphasize the fact that public relations work has varying needs. Persons who make careers in the field eventually gravitate to the area they find most attractive. That former reporter who was dismissed from the entertainment job might have found exactly the right niche on the public relations staff of a large corporation.

A JOB-SEEKER'S QUALIFICATIONS

Asked to state the qualifications they regard as "very important" for job-seekers, a group of public relations directors and vice-presidents listed the following, in descending order:

1. Ability to write

2. Verbal skills

3. Professionalism

4. Maturity

5. Poise

6. Appearance

On the second level, rated as "important," the group gave these qualifi-

Evaluation Guide for
Public Relations
Work

To be an ideal public relations practitioner, an individual needs the following personal attributes, among others:

Ability to see things from another person's point of view

An eye for detail

Organizing ability

Ability to comprehend the views of top management in philosophical terms

Skill at expressing a viewpoint with clarity and succinctness

Willingness to perform anonymously behind the scenes

A person with the following tendencies is less likely to succeed in public relations:

Excessive independence; resistance to compromise

Inflated opinion of own writing ability, with reluctance to accept the necessary approval processes

Desire for a fixed routine

Unwillingness to accept frequent long and hectic workdays; preference for a 9-to-5 job

Preference for being highly visible rather than working behind the scenes

cations, in descending order: grade-point average, social graces, part-time work, college credit internship, recommendations, and work on campus media.

THREE ESSENTIAL TALENTS

Those who plan careers in public relations should develop three basic talents, no matter what area of work they enter. These are writing skill, research ability, and creative ingenuity.

1. *Writing skill.* Ability to put information and ideas onto paper clearly and concisely is essential. Good grammar and spelling are vital, not only to convey thoughts precisely but to make a favorable impression on those who receive the written material. Misspelled words and sloppy sentence structure make news releases, brochures, annual reports, and other material seem amateurish.

2. *Research ability.* Arguments for causes must have factual support. Speakers and writers need to cite specifics to bolster their generalities. Some facts are easily gathered; others must be dug out laboriously and often ingeniously from obscure sources. The amount of research behind an important publication or speech may be largely unrecognized by the audience. However, the researcher who spends hours developing facts that substantiate an important point feels a sense of personal satisfaction in the achievement, unsung though it may be.

3. *Creative ingenuity.* Some public relations people plod along a narrow track, handling problems and approaching new situations in routine, unimaginative ways. In identical circumstances, others see opportunities for innovative approaches and fresh ideas. Creativity cannot be toted up like a bank balance. Nevertheless, this extra ingredient spells the difference between a dull public relations program and a lively, attention-getting one. It does to a program what yeast does to a loaf of bread. Without this ingredient, both fall flat.

Certain persons are born with more imagination than others. Fortunate they are! But those not so well-endowed can achieve wonders by conscious, diligent efforts to look at old situations in fresh ways.

Some students may consider the following as belaboring the obvious, but personnel managers make the point frequently enough that it is worth stating: to succeed in public relations, as in any other business, an individual also needs self-confidence, suitably restrained; persistence; determination to succeed; and readiness to work hard.

What Kinds of Jobs?

Beginners in public relations usually find themselves with relatively simple assignments, to be performed under close supervision. They carry out details of programs conceived by others. As they accumulate experience they are given an opportunity to develop plans, working with clients as account executives in public relations counseling firms or handling planning assignments in public relations departments. Further years may bring advancement to manager of a public relations department or a supervising position in a counseling firm. After achieving this level, some men and women prefer to strike out as heads of their own small agencies, operating with one or two assistants until they build up their lists of clients. Often these small firms develop specialties, concentrating in a field such as politics or health service. On the other hand, those workers who make their careers in corporate departments may aspire eventually to the position of vice-president for public relations or corporate communications.

The following typical help-wanted advertisements show specifically what is involved in jobs the public relations worker may expect to hold at progressive career stages. The first three ads are for entry-level positions:

PUBLIC RELATIONS ASSISTANT

Metropolitan hospital seeks public relations assistant to join three-person staff. Duties include reporting and writing for hospital publications, bulletins, news releases; answering press inquiries about patients; some photography, graphics, and editorial work; assistance with layout and design for printed media; organization of some special events including the planning, publicity, supervision, and evaluation of results. Degree in public relations or journalism and some experience required. Successful applicant will have a people-oriented outlook, work well under pressure, have an excellent telephone personality, and be a self-starter requiring minimum supervision.

STAFF AIDE

Credit union seeks public relations aide to write and edit monthly newsletter, design and write brochure, and plan a variety of promotions for each quarter. Successful applicant must maintain rapport with members through publications as well as telephone and personal contact and assist various departments with public relations/promotion activities. Degree in public relations or journalism required. Candidate should be a self-starter with initiative to work independently, be able to work under pressure to meet deadlines, and accept constructive criticism without being offended.

STAFF WRITER

Electronics company has position open for staff writer to prepare releases and newsletters and work with printers. Requires a degree in journalism, public relations, or English. Interviewing, writing, editing, and layout skills plus expertise on in-house publications are a plus.

An individual who has gained several years' experience in a public relations job should be qualified to fill the following types of positions:

MANAGER OF COMMUNICATIONS PROGRAMS

A worldwide natural-resource company headquartered in San Francisco seeks a manager of communications. The successful candidate will have responsibilities for developing and administering corporate communications programs, including corporate publications, employee meetings, executive speeches, audiovisual aids, and presentations for corporate board meetings. The selected individual will have a degree in business, journalism, or public relations with more than five years' experience in corporate communications. Strong interpersonal, written, and oral communication skills are essential.

COMMUNICATIONS MANAGER

A dynamic medical facility in Portland, Oregon, is seeking a corporate-level communications manager for the newly created marketing department. If you are a creative communications manager with proven skills who enjoys a challenge and views the field from a marketing perspective, and if you have a minimum of five years' related experience supervising professionals in the areas of publications, brochures, direct mail, media relations, and graphics, please send resume. Advanced degree desirable.

MANAGER OF COMMUNICATIONS SERVICES

Large private utility company in the Pacific Northwest seeks a manager of communications services. In this highly visible position you will plan, organize, and coordinate the internal communication programs. The responsibility of managing the publications and audiovisual sections will also include overall supervision of 12 people. The successful applicant must have substantial management, administrative, and supervisory experience in corporate communications.

PUBLIC RELATIONS DIRECTOR

A comprehensive cancer center located in Philadelphia seeks an individual to direct the media/public relations function. Individual will be responsible for the creation of a long-range public relations program to include planning for multimedia exposure and resource development, arranging press interviews with scientific and clinical staff, and writing press releases and articles. The successful candidate must possess a bachelor's degree and a minimum of six years' experience in the public relations field. Excellent communication and writing skills required. Scientific background preferred.

Qualified practitioners may also find employment in more specialized fields of public relations. Here are two positions that require several years of experience.

INTERNATIONAL PUBLIC RELATIONS MANAGER

Career-minded international relations manager to assist director in a fast-paced, international corporate communications function for a top *Fortune* 500 company based in New England. Successful candidate will have college degree, 3–5 years as writer in journalism or public relations, and overseas work experience. Foreign language fluency a plus; job involves travel.

GOVERNMENT RELATIONS OFFICER

A California bank has an opening for a government relations officer. As an officer of a new, growing department, you will be responsible for monitoring and analyzing legislative and regulatory issues at all levels of government. You will coordinate the bank's political and contributions activities and act as the bank's liaison with government officials. The successful candidate will have up to four years' experience in government relations/public affairs. Strong writing and verbal skills are essential. Bachelor's degree required. Banking experience preferred.

Another example of an advertisement—this one for a writer-editor—appears in Figure 5.1.

WRITER-EDITOR
Corporate Communications

EXPLORE SOHIO

Our corporate public affairs staff in Cleveland needs a creative Writer-Editor who excels in hard news and business reporting, to write and produce Company communications for employees and external readers.

This is an excellent opportunity to become part of the exciting, fast-moving Standard Oil Company (Ohio) — one of the Fortune 500's top 20 firms.

We want a solid journalist who excels in breezy, yet hard-hitting copy — one who has corporate experience and knowledge of magazines, newspapers, brochures and audio-visual programming. And we want a person who can bring innovative ideas to our communications. If you're that person, here's your chance to hitch your wagon to a star.

Sohio's comprehensive relocation package for new hires includes all normal moving expenses. Homeowners also qualify for mortgage interest differential allowance, third party home purchase and other features typically restricted to internal transfers.

Please forward your resume, salary requirements and writing samples, in strict confidence to:

Ms. Sarah Steiner, Senior Executive Recruiter
THE STANDARD OIL COMPANY (Ohio)
1424 Midland Building — 579C • Cleveland, Ohio 44115
An Equal Opportunity Employer M/F/H/V
NO THIRD PARTY INQUIRIES OR PHONE CALLS, PLEASE.
"Help us Help to Assure America's Energy Future"

SOHIO

At the top level, a public relations executive must be able to formulate policy and organize campaigns to carry it out, as well as demonstrate polished administrative skills. The following advertisement describes such a high-echelon position:

95

VICE-PRESIDENT FOR UNIVERSITY RELATIONS

Has primary responsibility for assessing and advancing the university's relationship with its various publics and for promoting and directing the development activities of the university. The vice-president supervises the alumni office, institutional development, information services, and other administrative units as assigned, and the directors of such units have administrative responsibility to the vice-president for university relations.

An earned doctorate is preferred, with considerable experience in a university environment. The applicant should possess excellent interpersonal, speaking, and writing skills and exhibit evidence of ability to communicate with the various constituencies of a land-grant research university, as well as a demonstrated aptitude for working cooperatively and effectively with others and serving as a major officer of the institution in promoting the mission and goals of the university.

A comparison of the responsibilities in this vice-presidential position with those in the entry-level category illustrates how a successful career evolves.

Further specific information about the kinds of work practitioners may expect to do is found in a recent survey Ohio State University made of its graduates in full-time public relations practice. A questionnaire asked the respondents to rank their top 10 work functions in order. Professor Walt Seifert, writing in *Public Relations Journal,* reported this consensus:

News releases

Booklets and manuals

Newsletters

Meetings and conventions

Factsheets

Special events

Still photos

Product publicity

Magazine articles

Trade paper publicity

Seifert's survey emphasizes that, while the counseling and management role of public relations is growing in significance, most public relations personnel work at the specialist and technician level.

But systematic research does show that there is a hierarchy of roles in public relations practice. Bradford Sullivan, David Dozier, and Susan Hellweg of San Diego State University, in a paper presented to the public relations division of the Association for Education in Journalism and Mass Commu-

The Practitioner's Functions

Philip Lesly, president of the Philip Lesly Company, Chicago, has formulated a list of functions that today's public relations professional should be expected to perform. They are:

1. Counseling management on the attitudes, concerns, misunderstandings, and need for information among all publics that affect the organization.

2. Counseling management on the overall trends and general patterns of the human climate: What are the general concerns on people's minds, where are the trends of mass psychology and social intercourse headed, where will the target of public opinion be that we will expect to hit a couple of years from now?

3. Providing insight into where the various wheels of our social and economic structure mesh and how the organization can accommodate to them.

4. Helping in developing policies by providing sensitive judgment about human reactions, weighing the probable effects of various alternatives and expressing those policies for best effect.

5. Monitoring various plans and activities of the organization and providing judgment about their likely immediate and long-term effects.

6. Utilizing communication in all facets—including personal involvement to bring the organization into confluence with the attitudes of the public, rather than into conflict. That involves many skills, but the most vital one is skillful use of language. The importance of excellent writing cannot be overemphasized.

7. Dealing with misunderstandings and conflicts that arise between the organization and any of its publics by acting as a catalyst and intermediary, and then by directing communications to create the best mutual adjustments possible.

8. Planning, preparing and conducting all communications functions—usually arising out of these previous considerations—between the organization and all of its publics. Specific techniques of communication may be assigned elsewhere—such as product advertising—but their role in the total impact of the organization should be considered as part of the whole.

9. Tuning in to feedback resulting from all actions and communications of the organization, to assess what is happening to the human climate, to convey judgment on these developments to management and to help modify the process accordingly.

SOURCE: Adapted from a speech by Philip Lesly at Ball State University, Muncie, Indiana.

nication at its annual convention in 1984, found four empirically grounded organizational roles. They describe the four roles as follows:

Communication Managers. Practitioners playing this role are perceived by others as the organization's public relations experts. They make communication policy decisions and are held accountable by others and themselves for the success or failure of communication programs. They follow a systematic planning process.

Communication Liaisons. Practitioners playing this role represent the organization at public meetings and create opportunities for management to hear the views of priority publics. Predominantly communication facilitators, these practitioners also identify alternative solutions to organizational problems. Similar to *communication managers* in many respects, *communication liaisons* do not make policy decisions and are not held accountable for program success or failure.

Media Relations Specialists. Practitioners playing this role actively seek to place messages about the organization in the mass media. At the same time, they keep others in the organization informed of what is being said about the organization (and about issues important to the organization) in the media. They do not make policy, nor are they accountable for program outcomes.

Communication Technicians. Practitioners playing this role are responsible for producing communication products, implementing decisions made by others. They take photographs, assemble graphics; write brochures, pamphlets and news releases; and handle all aspects of production. They do not participate in policy decision-making, nor are they responsible for outcomes.

The San Diego research indicates that practitioners, as well as employers, perceive these role models and rate the communication manager at the top of the hierarchy in terms of prestige and salary levels. Although this hierarchy of roles can serve as a career ladder for aspiring public relations professionals, many practitioners continue to play lower-level organizational roles (technician or media relations specialist) even after years of professional experience.

It should also be noted that public relations, in an organizational structure, can be a training ground for wider responsibilities. For example, C. Lee Cox, a 1963 graduate of the public relations degree program at San Jose State University, eventually became vice-president of public relations for Pacific Bell. In 1984, he was named executive vice-president of operations for Pacific Bell, with responsibility for the activities of 55,000 employees.

Needed: An Understanding of Economics

In preparing themselves for public relations careers, students should obtain as solid a grounding in economics as possible. Once they are employed as professionals, they should study the financial aspects of their employers or clients. More and more, public relations involves distribution and interpretation of financial information. To handle this material well, the practitioner first must understand it.

After a few years of work, some public relations people return to the classroom to earn advanced degrees. The Master of Business Administration degree, commonly called the MBA, probably is the most frequently sought, but the list of master's and Ph.D. degrees held by public relations specialists ranges over many fields.

Students who plan to do corporate public relations work should remember the fundamental fact about American business: every company was created to earn a profit for those who risked their money to start it. Businesses can continue to exist only as long as they are profitable. The task of public relations in the business world is to help companies prosper. If college graduates enter corporate public relations with misunderstanding and mistrust of the profit motive, they will do poorly in their jobs. Unfortunately, many college students who plan public relations careers believe that American business makes excessive profits. This belief arises from a lack of comprehension of free enterprise economics.

A survey of public relations majors in 18 universities nationwide demonstrates this lack. Professor Richard Piland of Miami University (Ohio) analyzed the responses of 1052 public relations majors to the survey questionnaire. He found a disturbing misconception about the size of profits. He reported:

The estimated average after-tax profit on one dollar of sales was 31.7 cents, considerably higher than the actual figure of 4.8 cents. In fact, only one in five students had profit estimates within 5 cents of the actual average. More than half of the sample estimated company profits to be at least 25 cents above the actual figure. Tied to this exaggerated concept of business profits was the belief expressed by 38 percent of the respondents that most companies could easily raise wages without raising prices.

The students' opinions reflect a general public misunderstanding of profits. According to Opinion Research Corporation, Princeton, New Jersey, the public's latest estimate of the average manufacturer's after-tax profit margin was 37 percent. The reality for 1982: 3.8 percent.

Government Information Jobs

Nearly 1 in 10 of the students who participated in the Ohio State survey did public relations work for some division of government, from the local to the federal level. This percentage is quite common.

Usually those who work for the government are listed as "public information officers" or "public affairs officers." However, in order to disguise what some taxpayers perceive as an excess of "publicity people," their employers may call them by such euphemisms as "administrative assistant" and "director of constituent services."

A strong need exists for government to dispense information about itself to the public, which pays for it and to which it is responsible. The larger government becomes, especially at the federal level, the more pressing is this need. The most astute citizens may be baffled by the bureaucratic maze as they seek information or try to solve a problem involving the government. Public information officers can provide material and direct citizens to appropriate officials. They also help make the public aware of government agencies by issuing publications and producing radio and television programs and audiovisual material.

Although the profit motive is not a factor in government work, the scramble among government agencies for larger portions of the annual budget is ever-present. Protection and enhancement of vested interests—the space program, weapons procurement, agricultural subsidies, for example— are facts of life in government just as in business.

Practitioners usually find public information work for government agencies satisfying and pleasant. They enjoy serving as channels of communication between citizens and their government. They like the job security of civil service and the tightly structured work levels and salary scales most government agencies provide.

Some, however, find themselves engaged at times in promoting the careers of their superiors rather than in serving the public. Information officers may also be caught uncomfortably in agency in-fighting and "empire-building." Because of such problems, they may wish to switch to the private sector; some hesitate to do so, however, because of the uncertainties involved.

Professional Support Services

ORGANIZATIONS AND SOCIETIES

Public relations societies at the local, state, national, and international levels provide an important channel of communication for practitioners in all areas of the profession. Their meetings, publications, and other professional services help members keep up-to-date on developments in the field, share their experiences, and broaden their personal contacts.

With 11,700 members in 1984, the Public Relations Society of America is the largest national group of public relations people. PRSA was organized in 1948 with the merger of two groups—the National Association of Public Relations Counsel and the American Council on Public Relations—and in 1951 was joined by the American Public Relations Association. The society publishes the monthly magazine *Public Relations Journal* and is the parent organization of the Public Relations Student Society of America (discussed in the next section).

Based in the United States and expanding rapidly to other countries is the International Association of Business Communicators (IABC), whose membership in 1984 reached 12,000 worldwide. IABC describes itself as "a professional organization for writers, editors, audiovisual specialists, managers, and other business and organizational communicators." Approximately 1,500 of its members are in Canada, where the Toronto chapter, with 497 members, is IABC's second largest after New York's 551 members. Other chapters outside the United States in 1984 were in the United Kingdom and the Philippines. The association publishes the monthly magazine *Communication World*. (IABC is discussed further in Chapter 16.) Figures 5.2, 5.3, and 5.4 show the emblems of these three important professional organizations.

FIGURE 5.2

The emblem of the Public Relations Society of America is the insignia for the major American public relations organization in the United States. (Courtesy of PRSA.)

FIGURE 5.3

Membership in the Public Relations Student Society of America offers students an opportunity to participate in the field before they graduate. The society's emblem is shown here. (Courtesy of PRSSA.)

© Public Relations Student Society of America 1982

FIGURE 5.4

The International Association of Business Communicators, whose emblem is portrayed here, has chapters in North America, Europe, and elsewhere. (Courtesy of IABC.)

101

INTERNSHIPS A job-seeker whose resume includes practical work experience along with an academic record has an important advantage. Obtaining an internship offered by a public relations counseling firm, company department, or government agency is among the best ways to get this desired experience. The intern puts into practice the techniques learned in the classroom and gets first-hand knowledge of the way things are done in the professional world. In some cases, an internship in a firm leads to a full-time job there after graduation. An internship, for which students receive credit toward graduation, is required for communication majors in some universities.

Membership in the Public Relations Student Society of America provides training and professional exposure. The society has chapters at about 120 universities. In some chapters, members may work in student-run client agencies. Professional public relations practitioners assist chapters at seminars and in a student-professional pairing program. In addition, PRSSA operates a nationwide job referral network. Many public relations campaign classes operate as agencies, too, thus providing an in-house internship.

Another source of experience is work on student radio and television stations, as well as campus newspapers and magazines. Commercial radio and television stations in cities with colleges and universities frequently employ students as part-time help.

The Role of Women

Public relations is an attractive field for women, and they are entering it at an increasing rate. The doors are open. Because the field is relatively new and expanding rapidly, fewer vestiges of a "this-is-a-man's-job" attitude exist in public relations work than in some newspaper and broadcasting offices. Younger women have moved into public relations in force and have in many instances reached top-echelon positions, especially in smaller counseling firms and departments.

Membership rolls of four national public relations groups illustrate the large and growing role of women. The Public Relations Society of America has 38 percent female membership. The National Investor Relations Institute has 30 percent, the Society of Consumer Affairs Professionals 50 percent, and the International Association of Business Communicators 54 percent. Perhaps as a portent of things to come, membership of the Public Relations Student Society of America is 78 percent female.

The rise of women in management is emphasized even more forcefully in *O'Dwyer's Directory of Corporate Communications* (1983). Twenty percent of the 4100 chief public relations officers listed are female, up from 13.7 percent in 1979.

A survey of senior public relations executives of the *Fortune* 500 companies (the country's 500 largest companies, as compiled by *Fortune* magazine) by Matthew M. Miller provides an illuminating look at the status of female executives. Writing in *Public Relations Journal* at the end of 1982, Miller reported these findings:

Almost 50 percent of the younger public relations executives who responded—those 40 or younger—were female.

The top public relations positions in these corporations were still male-dominated—90 percent male to 10 percent female. The 10 percent figure is up from 2 percent in the 1960s.

The median salary for top corporate public relations executives was $59,300. Men earned considerably more money than women. Median income for men was $63,800, for women, $34,900.

Miller commented: "Possible explanations for the salary discrepancy: according to the research, females surveyed were named to their present jobs more recently, had been at their present companies for fewer years, and have had less public relations experience than male respondents."

Further evidence of the discrepancy between male and female salaries appeared in a survey taken by the International Association of Business Communicators in the early 1980s. The survey seems to indicate that the salaries of men increase rapidly with experience, while those of women do not move ahead at the same pace. The average salary shown for men up to age 29 was $19,300; for women in the same age group, $18,400. In the 30–39 age group, men advanced to $30,100 and women only to $22,600. In the 40–49 age group, men advanced to $35,600, while women reached only $23,300. Undoubtedly, pressure to correct this inequity will increase as women achieve greater stature as well as greater numbers in the field.

Thus, abundant evidence exists that women are a rising force in public relations as their numbers and experience grow. Advancement for women is faster in public relations than in newspaper work, in which the climb up the seniority ladder seems agonizingly slow to some.

A person attending the conventions of both the American Society of Newspaper Editors, whose membership is restricted to senior editors, and the Public Relations Society of America is struck by the difference in the convention delegations. Attendance at the editors' convention is overwhelmingly male. Speakers look out at a sea of dark business suits. At the public relations convention a substantial percentage of those attending and participating in the programs are female, many of them quite youthful. PRSA has recognized the importance of women in the field by electing them to its presidency. Judith Bogart and Barbara Hunter are two who have been honored recently. Another woman who has achieved success in the field—the head of the IABC—is featured in Figure 5.5.

In American universities substantially more than half the students en-

FIGURE 5.5

Myra L. Kruger, board chairman of the International Association of Business Communicators in 1984–1985, has qualified for the designation ABC (Accredited Business Communicator). Kruger typifies women who hold top professional positions in public relations. She also is regional manager of communication practice and a consultant in the Chicago office of Towers, Perrin, Forster & Crosby, international consulting firm. (Courtesy IABC.)

rolled in public relations sequences are women. Of the 1052 majors who responded to Professor Piland's survey, mentioned earlier in this chapter, 69 percent were female.

What Kind of Salaries?

Public relations work pays well. This is true from the entry level to the top, where a few high-echelon executives in the largest corporations may receive as much as $300,000 a year in salaries, bonuses, incentives, and benefits. The survey by Matthew M. Miller discussed above showed 11 percent of the public relations directors in *Fortune* 500 companies earning more than $100,000.

In the graduation-time hunt for employment, holders of college degrees find that beginning public relations jobs pay higher average salaries than those in advertising and newspapers. A Dow-Jones Newspaper Fund-Gallup survey of 17,700 journalism and communications graduates in 1983 showed median weekly starting pay in public relations to be about $255, in advertising about $245, and in newspapers about $215.

A recent report to the Public Relations Society of America by Larry Marshall, president of Larry Marshall Consultants, Inc., of New York, an executive search organization in the communications field, listed salary ranges during the first third of the 1980s as shown in Table 5.1.

TABLE 5.1   Public Relations Salary Ranges in Early 1980s

PUBLIC RELATIONS DEPARTMENTS

Corporate public relations directors	$60,000–$125,000
Corporate editorial directors	$45,000–$85,000
Staff members 5–10 years	$28,000–$60,000
Staff members 3–5 years	$22,000–$35,000

COUNSELING FIRMS

Managing supervisors, top agencies	$60,000–$125,000
Account supervisors	$35,000–$70,000
Account executives	$22,000–$60,000
Public relations starting salaries	$13,260*

*Newspaper Fund-Gallup survey.
SOURCE: Larry Marshall Consultants, Inc.

The financial rewards of a successful public relations career are generous. They are not the only consideration for job satisfaction, however; other factors also must be present. Marshall reported that in recruiting professionals, he had found them looking for what he called the "Five Cs" in a job: career growth, creativity, challenge, commitment, and compensation.

QUESTIONS FOR REVIEW AND DISCUSSION

1. Describe the mission of a public relations representative.

2. Is it sufficient for a public relations practitioner to follow the advice of King Charles I of England: "Never make a defense or an apology until you are accused"? Explain your answer.

3. Why do some former newspaper reporters fail in public relations work?

4. Those who plan careers in public relations should develop basic talents. What are they?

5. Is there a special type of personality most suited for public relations work?

6. List three specific work functions carried out by beginners in public relations.

7. Why should students of public relations have a solid grounding in economics?

8. When public relations practitioners return to school, what degree in particular do many of them seek?

9. Although the number of women in public relations is rising, the median income for male executives is much above that for women. What are some possible explanations for this discrepancy?

10. In addition to liberal salaries, what factors contribute to job satisfaction in public relations work?

CHAPTER SIX

Ethics

Sound ethical conduct is an important component of public relations. In the wake of Watergate, Koreagate, and other scandalous activities, including environmental pollution, the American public is demanding higher ethical practices of its business firms and institutions than in the past. These accelerating changes in public attitudes are reflected in legislation, in court decisions, in the views of professional commentators upon public affairs, and in public opinion as expressed in the news media.

These demands place a premium upon stellar performance by public relations specialists as they advise management executives about the probable effects of company and institutional decisions. Of equal importance to practitioners is the role of ethics in their own lives. In an effort to establish benchmarks of responsible conduct, they have enacted codes of ethics that are basic to the professionalism which they claim. Credibility, after all, is their chief stock-in-trade.

This chapter examines the role of ethics in public relations and explores some of the problems encountered when ethical decisions must be made.

Definition

Ethics refers to the value system by which a person determines what is right or wrong, fair or unfair, just or unjust. It is expressed through moral behavior in specific situations. An individual's conduct is measured not only against his or her own conscience but also against some norm of acceptability that has been societally, professionally, or organizationally determined. The difficulty in ascertaining whether an act is ethical lies in the fact that norms of behavior vary widely from individual to individual and from culture to culture.

Some people may make decisions and judge the actions of others based upon absolutist Judeo-Christian principles. Others may rely upon such ethical orientations as secular humanism (strong moral values with no religious commitment), utilitarianism (the case-by-case selection of the most effective choices), or positivism (social convention determines values). The range is broad, involving philosophical discussions not appropriate here. It is sufficient to point out that ethical considerations comprise a basic part of public relations.

Code of Ethics

THE PRSA'S CODE OF PROFESSIONAL STANDARDS

When the Public Relations Society of America was founded in 1948, one of its first concerns, according to the late Rea W. Smith, former executive vice-president, was "the development of an ethical code so that (1) its members would have behavioral guidelines, (2) managements would have a clear understanding of standards, and (3) professionals in public relations would be distinguished from shady promoters and ballyhoo advance men who, unfortunately, had been quick to appropriate the words 'public relations' to describe their operations."

The PRSA Code of Professional Standards for the Practice of Public Relations was adopted in 1954 and strengthened by revisions in 1959, 1963, and 1977. It is as follows:

DECLARATION OF PRINCIPLES

Members of the Public Relations Society of America base their professional principles on the fundamental value and dignity of the individual, holding that the free exercise of human rights, especially freedom of speech, freeedom of assembly and freedom of the press, is essential to the practice of public relations.

In serving the interests of clients and employers, we dedicate ourselves to the goals of better communication, understanding and cooperation among the diverse

108

individuals, groups and institutions of society, and of equal opportunity of employment in the public relations profession.

We pledge:

To conduct ourselves professionally, with truth, accuracy, fairness and responsibility to the public;

To improve our individual competence and advance the knowledge and proficiency of the profession through continuing research and education;

And to adhere to the articles of the Code of Professional Standards for the Practice of Public Relations as adopted by the governing Assembly of the Society.

ARTICLES OF THE CODE

These articles have been adopted by the Public Relations Society of America to promote and maintain high standards of public service and ethical conduct among its members.

1. A member shall deal fairly with clients or employers, past and present, with fellow practitioners and the general public.

2. A member shall conduct his or her professional life in accord with the public interest.

3. A member shall adhere to truth and accuracy and to generally accepted standards of good taste.

4. A member shall not represent conflicting or competing interests without the express consent of those involved, given after a full disclosure of the facts; nor place himself or herself in a position where the member's interest is or may be in conflict with a duty to a client, or others, without a full disclosure of such interests to all involved.

5. A member shall safeguard the confidences of both present and former clients or employers and shall not accept retainers or employment which may involve the disclosure or use of these confidences to the disadvantage or prejudice of such clients or employers.

6. A member shall not engage in any practice which tends to corrupt the integrity of channels of communication or the processes of government.

7. A member shall not intentionally communicate false or misleading information and is obligated to use care to avoid communication of false or misleading information.

8. A member shall be prepared to identify publicly the name of the client or employer on whose behalf any public communication is made.

9. A member shall not make use of any individual or organization purporting to serve or represent an announced cause, or purporting to be independent or unbiased, but actually serving an undisclosed special or private interest of a member, client, or employer.

10. A member shall not intentionally injure the professional reputation or practice of another practitioner. However, if a member has evidence that another member has been guilty of unethical, illegal or unfair practices, including those in violation of this Code, the member shall present the information promptly to the proper authorities of the Society for action in accordance with the procedure set forth in Article XIII of the Bylaws.

11. A member called as a witness in a proceeding for the enforcement of this Code shall be bound to appear, unless excused for sufficient reason by the Judicial Panel.

12. A member, in performing services for a client or employer, shall not accept fees, commissions or any other valuable consideration from anyone other than the client or employer in connection with those services without the express consent of the client or employer, given after a full disclosure of the facts.

13. A member shall not guarantee the achievement of specified results beyond the member's direct control.

14. A member shall, as soon as possible, sever relations with any organization or individual if such relationship requires conduct contrary to the articles of this Code.

Six-member grievance boards hear complaints of members filed in accordance with Article 10 of the code. Their findings are reviewed and final decisions made by the society's board of directors. PRSA may censure, suspend, or expel a member. However, the society has no legal authority to punish a member through publicity. Nor does the society have a legal right to condemn nonmembers of the organization for incompetent practice.

The most common complaints have concerned account piracy and job infringement. However, by 1983 the society had only warned two members, reprimanded three, censured three, suspended two, and expelled two, while six others resigned their membership before action was taken. In this respect the organization finds itself largely in the same position as the American Society of Newspaper Editors, which encountered so many legal and other difficulties in endeavoring to censure members soon after adoption of its code of ethics in 1923 that future efforts were not attempted.

Nevertheless, although discussions of ethics are seldom heard at PRSA meetings and enforcement seems to have been minimal, members increasingly hold the code in high regard because of the benchmarks for professional conduct that it embodies and its usefulness in informing managers and clients of practices that cannot be condoned.

Donald B. McCammond, chairman of PRSA's grievance board in 1983, wrote in the November 1983 issue of *Public Relations Journal:* "From recent correspondence it is increasingly obvious that the society's code of professional standards is becoming known outside the membership." Among the questions asked of the grievance board in 1983 (and the answers given) were:

1. Are communications between a public relations practitioner and a client or employer privileged? (Yes, but such communications are not privileged against disclosure in a court of law.)

2. Who legally owns the records in a practitioner–employer/client relationship? (In the absence of a contractual agreement, the client or employer legally owns the rights to papers or materials created for him or her.)

3. Are discount or complimentary rates to the media permissible? (They are permissible if for business use and available to all journalists. Discount rates should not be extended to journalists for personal use.)

4. Is it ethical to disclose a potential client's plans to a competitor? (No.)

5. Is it permissible to guarantee a specific number of media placements? (No.)

McCammond, in his report to the PRSA Assembly in 1983, also gave a list of issues raised with the grievance board. They included:

Lack of professional behavior with the media

Nonperformance of a practitioner under contract

Misrepresentation of a speaker's status at a press conference

Copyright infringement

The proper use of blind solicitation in seeking new business

The proper use of the designation *APR* (discussed below under "Accreditation")

Libel by one member of another

Misleading statements in speeches made for an employer

False statements in news releases

Members, however, are reluctant to criticize each other's public relations actions publicly. When some members dared to criticize the Firestone Tire Company's stonewalling of accurate information about defective radial tires and the conflicting statements released in behalf of officials during the Three Mile Island nuclear accident, they themselves were criticized. In fact, Denny Griswold, owner and editor of *PR News,* and Leo Northart, editor of *Public Relations Journal,* labeled Firestone's critics unprofessional. Yet many members and other observers feel that the nation's confidence in public relations will not be improved until PRSA takes an active, vocal role in enunciating standards relating to such situations. The public relations community needs a healthy, frank discussion of contemporary practice.

THE IABC'S CODE OF STANDARDS

The International Association of Business Communicators, comprised mainly of publications editors and information specialists, adopted a code of standards in 1976 as follows:

As a communicator concerned with maintaining the highest ideals of ethical performance among the members of IABC and others in the field, I agree to practice and promote the following professional objectives:

To achieve maximum credibility by communicating honestly—conveying information candidly.

To respect the individual's rights to privacy as well as protect confidential information and its sources.

By the practice and promotion of these basic objectives, I hope to foster improved ethical awareness and importance in business and other organizational communication.

The IABC code is extremely generalized and, as one member observed, "It simply tells us to go out and do good." To date, IABC has not set up any grievance procedure, and there is no formal way to file a complaint about a member. According to John Bailey, former president of IABC, the few letters about members mostly concerned plagiarism. In late 1984, IABC'S board of directors began work on a revised code of ethics and a method of enactment.

Professionalism, Licensing, and Accreditation

PROFESSIONALISM Among public relations practitioners there are considerable differences of opinion whether public relations is a craft, a skill, or a developing profession. Certainly, at its present level, public relations does not qualify as a profession in the same sense that medicine and law do. Public relations does not have prescribed standards of educational preparation, a mandatory period of apprenticeship, or state laws that govern admission.

On the other hand, there is an increasing body of literature about public relations—including this text and many others in the field. In addition, substantial progress is being made in developing theories of public relations, in conducting research, and in publishing scholarly journals.

There is also the idea, advanced by many professionals and PRSA itself, that the most important thing is for the individual to *act like a professional* in the field. This means that a practitioner should have:

1. A sense of independence.

2. A sense of responsibility to the society and the public interest.

3. Manifest concern for the competence and honor of the profession as a whole.

4. A higher loyalty to the standards of the profession and fellow professionals than to the employer of the moment. The reference point in all public relations activity must be the standards of the profession and not those of the client or the employer.

Unfortunately, a major barrier to professionalism is the attitude that many practitioners themselves have toward their work. As James Grunig and Todd Hunt state in their text *Managing Public Relations,* practitioners tend to hold more "careerist" values than professional values. In other words, they place higher importance on job security, prestige in the organization, salary level, and recognition from superiors.

On another level, many practitioners are limited in their professionalism by what might be termed a technician mentality. These people narrowly define professionalism as the ability to do a competent job of executing the mechanics of communicating (preparing news releases, brochures, newsletters, etc.) even if the information provided by management or a client is in bad taste, is misleading, lacks documentation, or is just plain wrong.

The *Wall Street Journal,* in its September 13, 1984, issue, highlighted the pitfalls of the technician mentality. The story described how Jartran, Inc., used the services of the Daniel J. Edelman, Inc., public relations firm to distribute a press packet to the media. The packet included a letter offering information about wheels falling off trucks owned by U-Haul, its archrival. When the newspaper reporter asked about the ethics of this approach, an Edelman junior account executive was quoted as saying, "It was their idea. We're merely the PR firm that represents them."

In other words, readers may get the impression that the public relations expertise of a firm is available to the highest bidder, regardless of professional values, fair play, and ultimately, the public interest. When public relations firms and departments take no responsibility for what is communicated—only *how* it is communicated in terms of techniques—it reinforces the perception that public relations is more flackery than profession.

Some practitioners defend the technician mentality, however, arguing that public relations people are like lawyers in the court of public opinion. Everyone is entitled to his or her viewpoint and, whether the public relations person agrees or not, the client or employer has a right to be heard. Thus, a public relations representative is a paid advocate, just as a lawyer is. The only flaw in this argument is that public relations people are not lawyers, nor are they in a court of law where judicial concepts determine the role of defendant and plaintiff. In addition, lawyers have been known to turn down clients or resign from a case because they doubted the client's story.

In Chapter 13, which concerns legal aspects of public relations, it is pointed out that courts increasingly are holding public relations firms accountable for information disseminated on behalf of a client. Thus, it is no longer acceptable to say, "The client told me to do it."

LICENSING

Proposals that public relations be licensed were discussed before PRSA was founded. Proponents, such as Edward L. Bernays, who was instrumental in formulating the modern concept of public relations (see Chapter 3), believe that licensing would protect the profession and the public from incompetent, shoddy opportunists who do not have the knowledge, talent, or ethics required. Thus, under licensing, only those individuals who pass rigid examinations and tests of personal integrity could call themselves "public relations" counselors. Those not licensed would have to call themselves "publicists" or adopt some other designation.

Although licensing has some attraction, particularly in view of the fact that there are many incompetent people who say they are in public relations, it does have certain drawbacks. Opponents to licensing list some of their reasons in question form:

1. Does licensing give automatic credibility to a profession? The public image of lawyers, for example, is not exactly ideal.

2. How can public relations be licensed when there is still considerable debate as to what constitutes a single definition of public relations or its connotative meaning? There is the additional problem of public relations activity being called "public information," "corporate communications," or "public affairs."

3. Do public relations professionals really want "big brother" government setting the standards and policing the profession?

4. Is it really feasible to set up a licensing procedure for the estimated 100,000 persons who call themselves public relations practitioners in this country? The administrative red tape and the bureaucracy needed to conduct licensing would not be worth the expense and time.

5. Would licensing be a violation of free speech and free press as outlined by the First Amendment? Does it mean that someone who wanted to write a news release or give a press conference would have to be licensed?

The Public Relations Society of America has commissioned studies about licensing on more than one occasion, but the ultimate conclusion, to date, has been no endorsement of licensing from the organization's governing Assembly of delegates.

ACCREDITATION The major effort to improve standards and professionalism in public relations has been related to establishing accreditation programs. PRSA, for example, began its accreditation program in 1965.

To become an accredited member of the society, with the designation *APR*, a person must have at least five years' experience in public relations practice or teaching, must have two sponsors who will testify as to integrity and ability, and must pass a one-day written examination and an oral exam as well. To date, about a third of PRSA's 11,700 members have earned the *APR* designation.

In recent years the society has also launched an information campaign to make the general public and potential employers aware of what the *APR* designation means. In this way, it is hoped that such a "seal of approval" will separate public relations professionals from those less qualified. It is a slow process, however, because many senior public relations practitioners do not feel the need to prove themselves through a "test." Another major obstacle is that few employers require accreditation as a prerequisite for top-level positions in public relations.

The International Association of Business Communicators also has an accreditation program for its membership. A member may use the designation *ABC (Accredited Business Communicator)* after submitting a portfolio for evaluation and passing written and oral examinations. At present, fewer than 5 percent of IABC's 12,000 members have an *ABC* designation.

OTHER STEPS TOWARD PROFESSIONALISM

In addition, PRSA, IABC, and the Association for Education in Journalism and Mass Communication have worked to improve and standardize the curricula for programs of public relations and organizational communications studies at the bachelor's and master's degree level. For example, it is now standard that a public relations sequence should have a minimum of three core courses—principles of public relations, case studies in public relations, and publicity techniques—plus a mandatory internship in the field. At present, about 30 public relations sequences in United States universities are accredited by the Accrediting Council on Education in Journalism and Mass Communications.

The Foundation for Public Relations Research and Education, which was established in 1956 with the support of PRSA but which is now independent, seeks to advance professionalism through grants for research studies, scholarships, an annual lecture by a distinguished public relations practitioner, and sponsorship of the scholarly quarterly *Public Relations Review.* The IABC Foundation, established in 1983, also encourages professionalism and study of the field through research grants. Figure 6.1 shows some of the periodicals that provide a forum for the exchange of ideas and information among public relations professionals.

Ethics in Individual Practice

Despite codes of professional practice and formalized accreditation, ethics in public relations boils down to deeply troubling questions for the individual practitioner: Will I lie for my employer? Will I rig a doorprize drawing so a favorite client can win? Will I deceive in order to gain information about another agency's clients? Will I cover up a hazardous condition? Will I issue a news release presenting only half the truth? Will I seek to bribe a reporter

FIGURE 6.1

Magazines edited for public relations professionals provide a forum for discussion of ethical issues. These periodicals include *Public Relations Review,* published by the Foundation for Public Relations Research and Education; *Public Relations Journal,* issued by the Public Relations Society of America; *Communication World,* produced by the International Association of Business Communicators; and *Public Relations Quarterly,* published by an independent firm. (Reprinted by permission of *Public Relations Review, Communication World,* and *Public Relations Quarterly. Public Relations Journal* cover reprinted with permission from the April 1984 issue of the *Public Relations Journal*; copyright 1984.)

| Burger's Four Lessons | Chester Burger, president of the New York management consulting firm of Chester Burger & Company, Inc., in a *Public Relations Journal* article on the ethics of public relations, summarized what he had learned during a newspaper reporting and public relations career spanning more than four decades: |

Lesson 1. Communicators must trust the common sense of their audience. More often than not, the public will justify our trust by seeing accurately the issues and the contenders and the motivations. Communicators should not use clever headlines, gimmicks, distortions, or lies to communicate effectively. Don't underestimate the public's perceptiveness.

Lesson 2. People generally will know or care very little about the issue that concerns you. You've got to inform, to clarify, to simplify issues in a truthful manner, and in ways that will relate to the self-interest of your audience.

Lesson 3. Don't compromise your own ethical standards for anyone. Don't take the easy way out. Don't say what you don't really believe, and don't do for the sake of expediency what you think is wrong. It ain't worth it. Ask yourself how your action would look if it were reported tomorrow on the front page of your local newspaper. Who would absolve you from the responsibility if you said you wrote it or said it or did it because your boss told you to?

Lesson 4. Choices for communicators between right and wrong are rarely black or white, yes or no. Questions of ethics involve degrees, nuances, differing viewpoints. Too many times in my life have I been wrong to feel sure that I know the right answer. A bit of uncertainty and humility sometimes is appropriate in considering ethical questions.

SOURCE: Reprinted with permission from the December 1982 issue of the *Public Relations Journal.* Copyright 1982.

or a legislator? Will I withhold some information in a news conference, and provide it only if a reporter asks a specific question? Will I quit my job rather than cooperate in a questionable activity? In other words, to what extent, if any, will I compromise my personal beliefs?

These and similar questions plague the lives of many public relations people, although a number hold such strong personal beliefs and/or work for such highly principled employers that they seldom need to compromise their personal values. If employers make a suggestion that involves questionable ethics, the public relations person often can talk them out of the idea by citing the possible consequences of such an action—adverse media publicity, for example.

"To thine own self be true," advised New York public relations executive Chester Burger, at a conference of the International Association of Business Communicators. A fellow panelist, Canadian politician and radio commentator Stephen Lewis, commented: "There is a tremendous jaundice on the part of the public about the way things are communicated. People have elevated superficiality to an art form. Look at the substance of what you have to convey, and the honesty used in conveying it." With the audience contributing suggestions, the panelists formulated the following list of commendable practices:

Be honest at all times.

Convey a sense of business ethics based on your own standards and those of society.

Respect the integrity and position of your opponents and audiences.

Develop trust by emphasizing substance over triviality.

Present both sides of an issue.

Strive for a balance between loyalty to the organization and duty to the public.

Don't sacrifice long-term objectives for short-term gains.

Adherence to professional standards of conduct—being truly independent—is the chief measure of a public relations person. Faced with such personal problems as a mortgage and children to educate, practitioners may be strongly tempted to become "yes men (or women)" and decline to express their views forcefully to an employer, or to resign. J. Kenneth Clark, vice-president for corporate communications, Duke Power Company, Charlotte, North Carolina, gave the following advice to an IABC audience in 1981:

If the boss says newspapers are no damn good, the yes man agrees.

If the boss says to tell a reporter "no comment," the yes man agrees.

If the boss says the company's employees get a paycheck and don't really need to be informed about anything else, the yes man agrees.

If the boss says the public has no right to pry into what's going on inside a company—even though that company is publicly held and is dependent upon public support and public sales—the yes man nods his head agreeably and starts work on the corporate version of a Berlin Wall.

The fate of the yes man is as inevitable as it is painful. Although your boss may think you're the greatest guy in the world for a while, you're going to lose your internal credibility because you never really state your professional opinions. And you're talking to a person who dotes on strong opinions and does not think highly of people who fail to offer them. . . .

Professor Allen H. Center of San Diego State University and a long-time corporate public relations executive has written: "Public relations has emerged more as an echo of an employer's standards and interests than that of a professional discipline applied to the employer's problems." Yet many a practitioner has resigned rather than submit to a compromising situation.

Told that his job at a company was "to turn excrement into applesauce" (the official used a less elegant word than *excrement*), one public relations man resigned. He pointed out later that "the attitude exemplified two things—the reality of the company at the top level, where policy is made, and the perception at that level of the role of public relations."

Another professional resigned after initial participation in ethically dubious practice by United Brands (formerly United Fruit) Company to manipulate press coverage, public opinion, and political and military action involving the Latin America republic where the company operates.

In some cases practitioners have been arbitrarily fired for refusing to write news releases that are false and misleading. This happened to an accredited PRSA member in the San Francisco Bay area. The company president wanted him, among other things, to write and send a news release giving a list of company clients when, in fact, none of the companies had signed a contract for services. When the practitioner refused, on the grounds that the PRSA code would be violated, he was fired. In turn, the practitioner sued the company for unlawful dismissal and received almost $100,000 in an out-of-court settlement.

Tommy Ross, pioneer public relations practitioner and partner of Ivy Lee before founding T. J. Ross and Associates, once told a *Fortune* magazine interviewer: "Unless you are willing to resign an account or a job over a matter of principle, it is no use to call yourself a member of the world's newest profession—for you are already a member of the world's oldest."

Thus, it can be readily seen that ethics in public relations really begins with the individual—and is directly related to his or her own value system as well as to the good of society. Although it is important to show loyalty to an employer, practitioners must never allow a client or an employer to rob them of their sense of self-esteem and self-worth.

Ethical Dealings with News Media

The most practical consideration facing a public relations specialist in his or her dealings with the news media is that anything less than total honesty will destroy credibility and, with it, the practitioner's usefulness to an employer. The news media depend upon public relations sources for much of the information they convey to readers and listeners. Although a number of public relations releases are used simply as tips on which to develop stories, many reporters and editors know that they can rely upon the accuracy and thoroughness of much public relations copy and use it with little change.

Achieving trust is the aim of all practitioners, and it can be achieved only through highly professional and ethical performance. It is for this reason that providing junkets with doubtful news value, extravagant parties, expensive gifts, and personal favors for media representatives should never be done. On occasion, an unethical journalist will ask favors, but the public relations professional will decline such requests tactfully.

Some other aspects of public relations–news media ethical relationships are discussed in "The Press Party" section of Chapter 23.

Rising Business Concern with Ethics

The job of the public relations practitioner has been made easier during the last decade or so because of the increased attention that many businesses are paying to the ethical dimensions of their operation. Much of the new consciousness can be traced directly to the effects of Watergate, Koreagate, and the 1975 corporate bribery scandals, during which dozens of United States companies were revealed to have made payments to government officials in foreign countries in exchange for lucrative overseas contracts. (The Lockheed Aircraft Corporation's involvement and public relations recovery will be discussed later in this chapter.) Opinion polls revealing that Americans consider only about 20 percent of business executives to have high ethical standards are another reason for the concern.

The Ethics Resource Center, a nonprofit organization that helps businesses and other groups write codes of ethics, surveyed 650 major American corporations in 1979 and found that 3 out of 4 of the companies had written codes of ethics, as well as a provision that violation constituted grounds for dismissal. In a variety of innovative programs, *Fortune* 500 companies and other firms are providing ethics training for their employees. Companies increasingly are using "angel's advocates"—outside consultants or panels—to examine systematically the social implications of impending decisions. An alternative is the use of an internal executive or ethics committee with the power to approve or veto major decisions.

Ethics and Laws Concerning Financial News

Public relations personnel working for publicly held companies have not only an ethical but also a legal obligation promptly to release news about dividends, earnings, new products, mergers, and any other developments that might affect security values or influence investment decisions of stockholders or the public. News must not be delayed so that insiders can derive financial benefit. The U.S. Securities and Exchange Commission and the individual stock exchanges strictly enforce these requirements.

Corporations also are prohibited from using public relations techniques in connection with the sale of new issues of securities. Publicity and advertising are permitted at other times, provided the statements are truthful (see Chapter 13).

Public relations personnel also must be thoroughly aware of Federal Trade Commission regulations regarding the promotion of a product or service. A company can get into trouble for such things as unsubstantiated claims, fraudulent testimonials, deceptive pricing, "independent" surveys that are not really independent, and rigged contests.

The Food and Drug Administration also has a list of regulations concerning the promotion and advertising of medicines and drugs.

A Case Study

LOCKHEED PUBLIC RELATIONS AT WORK

THE PROBLEM   The Lockheed Aircraft Corporation public relations office was confronted with an almost unparalleled problem in 1975 when the U.S. Securities and Exchange Commission charged that the company had made payments to foreign government officials, had used secret funds for that purpose, and had hidden those activities by falsifying its financial records and reports.

Through the years Lockheed, with 55,000 employees and officers and a worldwide market, had developed a reputation for scientific and technological excellence, highly important to the nation's economy and defense. Most of its planes, space vehicles, and other major products were sold to the United States government, and a private bank-loan guarantee approved by Congress in 1971 was partially responsible for the company's survival during difficult times.

As if it were not enough of an undertaking to report progress for such a huge company and to dispel recurring prophecies of the firm's imminent demise in the face of a series of setbacks, management and the public relations office were confronted with a grave crisis over the foreign payment disclosures.

Negative news media publicity was enormous, although, as the *Wall Street Journal* reported later, more than 400 other United States firms filed information with the Securities and Exchange Commission acknowledging similar overseas payments. Lockheed was the first "big name" company identified, and it received the lion's share of the adverse press coverage.

In early 1976, Lockheed's board of directors appointed a special committee of directors, with no company connections, to review the matter of commissions and other payments made in connection with foreign sales.

The committee exhaustively collected information in more than 70 countries in Europe, Africa, the Middle East, Southeast Asia, and Japan, and reviewed the work of Lockhead's auditors.

Among the committee's findings were the following:

The basic policy of certain members of Lockheed's senior management involved a double standard: one standard of propriety for sales in the United States (found to be spotless), but a quite different standard of propriety for sales in foreign countries (where local customs, standards, and practices often differed radically from those in the United States).

From 1970 through 1975 Lockheed paid more than 150 sales consultants in 50 foreign countries commissions and other fees of approximately $165 million. These payments amounted to 6.4 percent of total foreign sales of approximately $2.6 billion, with foreign sales representing 14.8 percent of the company's total receipts. Of the total $165 million paid, some $38 million was considered "questionable."

Diverse patterns of payment were followed, including both direct and indirect payments to, or for the benefit of, government and military officials and employees, and to consultants. These payments were hidden from disclosure, even to the company's board of directors.

Payments of this nature are "a way of life" in many countries, often the only method through which a company may remain competitive. "Admirable as are our [U.S.] legal and ethical standards, they have not yet engaged worldwide allegiance," the committee noted.

Lockheed's board of directors accepted the committee's recommendations. The board developed policies and objectives and made necessary changes in organization and procedures in order to establish a system of open and constructive communication. In 1977 the board adopted the following statement of principles of business conduct for Lockheed:

High principles of business conduct must underlie the policies of any corporation. We believe the management of Lockheed has an obligation to articulate the general principles which should guide and motivate the people of Lockheed. We are clearly stating them now as a mark of our determination to conduct the company's business on an ethical basis and as an imperative signal to every man and woman in the corporation that he or she must share these principles.

Lockheed will comply with the laws of the United States and will comply with foreign law in those countries in which we do business, making all reasonable effort to determine what laws are applicable to our operations in those countries. Beyond legal compliance, we will strive for integrity in every aspect of our work.

Lockheed's business will be fully recorded in the corporate records and open to appropriate inspection. Our people not only must scrupulously avoid any conflict of interest, but also must avoid even the appearance of such conflict.

Ethical conduct is the highest form of loyalty to Lockheed. For that reason, it is the responsibility of every man and woman in the corporation to know and accept these principles. It is the obligation of every manager, from the chief executive officer to all ranks of supervision, to understand the principles and the specific policies that govern the corporation and to see that they are understood by every person within his or her responsibility.

These principles governing ethical conduct will be distributed to Lockheed employees and will be enforced by management. These policies will be reviewed and modified as the need arises.

Two years after the charges against Lockheed were filed, Congress passed the Foreign Corrupt Practices Act. This act, for the first time, made it illegal under United States law for Americans to pay foreign government officials for business purposes. The act since has been drastically weakened. The Department of State entered into negotiations with other countries seeking parity for American industry in competing with other foreign firms in those nations.

THE PUBLIC RELATIONS RESPONSE   Lockheed public relations personnel made the best of what they had to work with during the two years in which the investigations were conducted. They could not, however, make much progress in stemming the flow of negative publicity on the payments issue. "The big PR problem was a classic one," an article in the April 1977 issue of *Lockheed Life* stated (see Figure 6.2). "If you want to reflect a good image, you have to have something solid to start with. What Lockheed had was superb technological achievement, but in the firestorm of criticism, technology seemed almost irrelevant. You can't make much headway in answering charges of bribery or rumors of financial collapse by pointing to all the great aircraft and space vehicles you build."

With the company's financial position strengthened through restructuring and new foreign business rolling in, Lockheed's management and public relations staff realized that a very persuasive story could be told about the "new Lockheed."

First, a high-level strategy committee was established. It included people from corporate public relations, legal, technical, and other areas, as well as the president of the public relations consulting firm of Earl Newsom. Actions in response to their suggestions included the following:

A series of corporate advertisements was run in major United States newspapers as well as in publications in Africa, Asia, Latin America, the Middle East, Australia, Canada, and Great Britain. Emphasized were company aircraft and other products, and the achievements of "the 55,000 people of Lockheed." Other such advertisements followed.

A review of the progress in financial and internal reform was added to the

FIGURE 6.2

The cover of the first issue of *Lockheed Life,* produced by the public relations department "for the people, worldwide, of Lockheed Aircraft Corporation," featured Robert W. Haack, interim chairman of the board of directors. The monthly publication was started to bolster morale after widespread publicity was given to charges that the company had made payments to foreign government officials. (Reprinted with permission of Lockheed-Georgia Company.)

LOCKHEED LIFE
April 1977

INSIDE:
PR: Speaking Up
Trident 3 Flies

What's Behind...What's Ahead?
An Interview with Robert Haack

technical achievement story in a "corporate statement" advertisement placed in 18 major United States newspapers.

External public relations efforts were increased in the company's various divisions, and stronger emphasis was placed on better internal communications—through films, posters, and other means—to improve morale and understanding of company operations.

The company commissioned the Gallup organization to conduct a public image survey.

Media contacts were expanded, and an official traveled throughout the country to acquaint newspapers, television stations, and editorial boards with Lockheed's growing financial strength, expanding markets, and changes in marketing policies.

Other activities included speeches by high-level officials to prominent civic groups, with reprints widely distributed; financial presentations to analysts and brokers; interviews on network television shows; and a stepped-up publicity and advertising campaign stressing science and technology, aimed at various target audiences.

That's how Lockheed public relations survived its greatest crisis. With the moral issue essentially laid to rest, public relations people returned to the job they love the best: informing the world about Lockheed's on-schedule, below-cost-estimate production and its other accomplishments in the fields of aircraft, space vehicles, shipbuilding, and electronics.

QUESTIONS FOR REVIEW AND DISCUSSION

1. Sound ethical practice is essential in public relations work. What is meant by *ethics?*

2. Review some of the main points of the PRSA Code of Professional Standards. What have been the most common types of complaints filed by members under this code? Why have relatively few members been warned, reprimanded, censured, suspended, or expelled by the PRSA board of directors?

3. In your opinion, should public relations practitioners criticize each other publicly? Why, or why not?

4. What is meant by the term *professionalism?* Does public relations qualify as a profession? Why, or why not?

5. Should public relations practitioners be licensed? What are some of the reasons pro and con?

6. What steps must a practitioner complete in order to gain official accreditation by PRSA? IABC? What should the designation *APR or ABC* mean to those who employ the services of a public relations counselor?

7. Ethics in public relations poses some troublesome questions for practitioners. Can you identify four situations in which a public relations person may be called upon to wrestle with his or her conscience? What are some of the precepts to follow in developing and maintaining a personal code of ethics?

8. How are some corporations sensitizing their employees to ethical problems?

9. What special ethical obligations are involved in the handling of financial news? What agencies enforce these requirements?

10. What steps did the Lockheed Corporation take to overcome some of the negative publicity that it received through discovery that some of its business dealings in foreign countries were improper?

Part two

PROCESS

CHAPTER SEVEN

Research

Effective public relations is a process, and this chapter is about the essential first step—research. "Research is where public relations starts," writes Professor Edgar Trotter of California State University at Fullerton. "You can't write if you don't have something to write about or know whom you're writing to," says Professor Frank Kalupa of the University of Alabama. And Professor Mark MacElreath of George Washington University states, "Research provides the baseline information you need to manage the resources of a large public relations program."

The importance of research as a valuable tool in public relations is probably best expressed by Professor William Baxter of Marquette University. He writes: "Most public relations practitioners consider research as important a tool to them as a stethoscope is to a doctor. Almost every communication problem or project calls for varying degrees of research: fact-finding, opinion assessment, message testing, planning, and evaluation."

This chapter deals with the value of research in public relations and takes a look at the kinds of research methods utilized. Two general types of research—informal and scientific sampling—are examined. The text stresses the importance, in scientific sampling, of selecting an adequate number of respondents and of wording the questions and answer categories objectively. Methods of obtaining responses—through the mail, by phone, or in personal interviews—are also discussed.

The Need for Research

Research is a form of listening. Before any public relations program can be undertaken, information must be gathered, data collected, and facts compiled. Only by performing this first step in the public relations process can an organization begin to map out policy decisions and strategies for effective communication programs.

WHAT RESEARCH CAN ACCOMPLISH

Research, or fact-gathering, can accomplish a number of objectives:

1. Help probe basic attitudes of groups so that pertinent messages can be structured.

2. Measure true opinions of various groups. A vocal minority may not represent the group's genuine feelings or beliefs.

3. Identify opinion leaders who can influence target publics.

4. Reduce costs by concentrating on valid objectives and key audiences.

5. Help pretest messages and proposed communication channels on a pilot basis before implementing an entire program.

6. Help determine the timing of a public relations program to take advantage of current public interests and concerns.

7. Achieve two-way communication. Feedback from audiences can fine-tune messages and choice of media.

8. Reveal trouble spots and public concerns before they become page-one news. Problems seldom just happen; they often begin as minor nuisances and then develop into full-scale explosions.

9. Achieve credibility with top management. Executives want facts, not guesses and hunches. Public relations practitioners get more support from top management if they can provide evidence to back up their recommendations.

WHY RESEARCH IS NECESSARY

Research is necessary in today's complex society for several reasons. One is the increasing fragmentation of audiences into groups that have specific interests and concerns. To communicate effectively, it is necessary to have a detailed knowledge of audiences. A practitioner who understands these audiences—their attitudes, hopes, fears, concerns, frustrations—will be better able to formulate messages that appeal specifically to them. In addition, self-interest is a strong motivating force. If communication can be tailored to the self-interest of audiences, there is a much greater chance of reaching them.

A second reason is the increasing isolation of top management from personal contact with the public. Top management and those in specialized professions tend to associate only with each other. Rarely does an executive, for example, get a chance to exchange views with an assembly-line worker.

In addition, executives rarely do their own shopping, so they have little idea how members of the public perceive the organization's products or services. The president of an automobile rental agency is never required to wait in line for a car at the airport; the insurance executive never has to argue with a local agent about coverage on a dented fender; nor does the president of a department store have to purchase goods from a gum-chewing salesclerk with little knowledge of the merchandise. Systematic and periodic research about customers and clients can help bridge this gap and give executives vital feedback.

Third, research can prevent organizations from wasting time, effort, and money in attacking problems that don't really exist. Several years ago, for example, American companies spent millions of dollars on advertising and public relations campaigns to make sure that Americans understood the benefits of the free-enterprise system. Survey research showed, however, that the American public was thoroughly sold on capitalism as an economic system; citizens were just unhappy with inflation and the overabundance of shoddy goods in the marketplace.

In another situation, the American Dairy Association some years ago was planning a multimillion dollar campaign to tell Americans that milk is not a major contributor to cholesterol in the diet—before survey research by a public relations firm showed that most Americans do not associate milk with high cholesterol. Research can save an organization from costly mistakes simply by ascertaining public perceptions rather than guessing at them.

A great deal of money and energy also is spent on public relations programs that do not interest the public. More than a few companies, for example, continue to flood the media with information about personnel changes or sophisticated new machines in which the general public is not interested. Companies and foreign governments also send piles of magazines, long reports, and background materials to media gatekeepers when, in actuality, few editors read them. Systematic monitoring of materials and their use (or nonuse) would eliminate many expensive brochures and the shotgun method of distributing them. In today's environment in which the cost of producing and disseminating messages is very high, bottom-line considerations require that all communications activity be cost-effective.

Fourth, research can provide the facts upon which a public relations program will be based. A good example is the way in which the petroleum industry successfully changed the public perception that oil companies are owned by a handful of of very wealthy individuals and families. This stereotype, of course, began in the days of John D. Rockefeller, Sr. Since there were no industrywide data on ownership, it was necessary to research the question. It was found that six of the largest oil companies had more than 2 million stockholders and more than 11,750,000 indirect stockholders (beneficiaries of pension plans that owned oil company stock). The dissemination of these data did a great deal to modify the public stereotype about ownership of oil companies (more details of this survey are provided in Chapter 8).

Fifth, surveys can generate publicity through dissemination of results. The National Personnel Associates organization, for example, conducted surveys of its members which formed the basis for a five-year public relations program. A number of news stories were generated from survey findings that showed, for example, that 87 percent of personnel consultants would advise a management job applicant not to smoke during the interview. Magic Pan Restaurants also achieved extensive media coverage with the results of a survey that polled professional women about the protocol of inviting a male business associate to lunch and picking up the tab. Media gatekeepers found the survey results of topical interest to their readers and viewers.

Informal Research Methods

Research is not comprised necessarily of scientific surveys and statistical tabulations. It can be as casual as telephoning a colleague to ask for some information he or she has. Or it may be a brief visit or call to the local library to confirm a fact. Research also takes place every day as a public relations person scans newspapers and clips articles of pertinent interest to the organization.

The research needed, therefore, depends on the subject and the situation. The following questions should be asked before formulating a research design:

1. What is the problem?

2. What kind of information is needed?

3. How will the results of research be used?

4. What specific public (or publics) should be researched?

5. What research techniques should be used (literature review, mail, telephone, personal interviews)?

6. Should there be open-ended (essay) or closed (multiple-choice) questions?

7. Should the organization do the research or hire an outside consultant?

8. How will the research data be analyzed, reported, and applied?

9. How soon are the results needed?

10. How much will it cost?

These questions will help the public relations practitioner determine the extent and nature of the research that is needed. Informal research may be all that is required, and there are a number of approaches.

ORGANIZATIONAL MATERIALS

All pertinent data relating to the problem or project at hand should be collected. The material may include business records, marketing studies, policy statements, summaries of objectives, market projections, annual financial reports, speeches by key executives, reports on past public relations efforts, pamphlets, newsletters, and news releases.

PERSONAL CONTACTS

Interviews should be conducted with individuals within the organization as well as with customers or clients. If the program affects the community, it is a good idea to talk with community leaders to get ideas and suggestions. Experts in particular fields may also be consulted.

NEWS ARTICLES

Newspapers, popular magazines, and trade publications often provide pertinent information about trends and issues. These publications should be systematically monitored and clipped for up-to-date information. A file on relevant, current issues is the first step in issues management.

REGIONAL AND NATIONAL POLLS

It is often not necessary for a public relations person to conduct a poll because public attitudes on various issues may have already been assessed by regional and national polling firms. The results of these surveys regularly appear in the news media. When reading the results of a poll in the newspaper, however, the public relations person should assess the information by ascertaining: (1) who paid for the poll, (2) when it was taken, (3) how the interviews were obtained, (4) how the questions were worded, (5) who was interviewed, and (6) how large the sample was. Figure 7.1 shows the results of a survey conducted by a professional polling organization on behalf of Atlantic Richfield. The data compiled might be of interest to other corporations as well.

TRADE GROUPS

Local, regional, and national trade groups, including professional societies, should be contacted. Many organizations maintain reference libraries and conduct periodic surveys and studies that are available to those interested.

FIGURE 7.1

A study of consumer concerns, sponsored by the Atlantic Richfield Company and conducted by Louis Harris and Associates, Inc., illustrates one form of public opinion research done by corporations. (Reprinted by permission of Atlantic Richfield Company.)

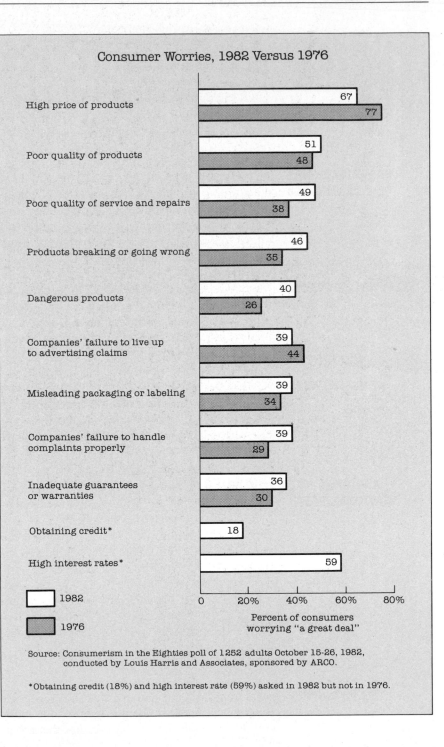

Consumer Worries, 1982 Versus 1976

High price of products — 67 / 77

Poor quality of products — 51 / 48

Poor quality of service and repairs — 49 / 38

Products breaking or going wrong — 46 / 35

Dangerous products — 40 / 26

Companies' failure to live up to advertising claims — 39 / 44

Misleading packaging or labeling — 39 / 34

Companies' failure to handle complaints properly — 39 / 29

Inadequate guarantees or warranties — 36 / 30

Obtaining credit* — 18

High interest rates* — 59

☐ 1982
▧ 1976

0   20%   40%   60%   80%

Percent of consumers worrying "a great deal"

Source: Consumerism in the Eighties poll of 1252 adults October 15-26, 1982, conducted by Louis Harris and Associates, sponsored by ARCO.

*Obtaining credit (18%) and high interest rate (59%) asked in 1982 but not in 1976.

LIBRARY RESEARCH   Reference books, other scholarly publications, and books and journals about particular subjects should be consulted. Government documents, particularly the *Statistical Abstract of the United States,* and other publications based on the 1980 census can provide a wealth of demographic data. Additional information may be gleaned from computer data banks (see Chapter 21). An estimated 200 firms in the United States provide information retrieval for a fee. One of the largest is FIND. This company subscribes to 800 periodicals and several thousand directories and reference books and rents access to 300 computer data banks.

ADVISORY PANELS, IDEA JURIES   Many organizations form advisory boards to generate recommendations and provide ideas about issues facing the organization. Most nonprofit groups, for example, have citizen advisory boards to provide feedback on how the agency is doing in terms of public support. A public relations advisory board usually consists of outstanding public relations professionals in the community.

MAIL AND TELEPHONE ANALYSIS   Letters and telephone calls from consumers or clients often provide good feedback about problems with the organization's policies and services. A pattern of letters and telephone calls that point out a defect in a product or the quality of service is evidence that something should be done.

FOCUS GROUPS   Focus groups are popular in advertising and are used now with increasingly regularity in public relations. Basically, the organization or an outside consultant gets 8 to 12 people together to discuss an organization's image or its products. In advertising, these people often give their impressions regarding the themes of proposed advertising campaigns. The focus groups should be representative of the audience that the organization wants to reach.

COPY TESTING   It is important that the target audience thoroughly understand the message. Consequently, several representatives of the target audience should read or view the material in draft form before it is mass-produced and distributed. A brochure about employee medical benefits or pension plans, for example, should be pretested with rank-and-file employees for comprehension. Executives and lawyers who must approve copy may understand the material, but a worker with an eighth-grade education might find it difficult to follow.

COMMUNICATION AUDITS   Many organizations periodically check what employees are reading in the company newsletter or magazine. Another form of communication audit is to have employees complete a questionnaire on topics they would like covered in company publications. Communication audits also can be done among editors of general-circulation and trade publications to determine if they are receiving information pertinent to their needs.

Sampling Public Opinion

The informal approaches to research methods just mentioned can provide good insight to public relations staff members and help them formulate effective programs. Practitioners must be sure, however, that the feedback is representative, so that decisions are made on the basis of information that is typical of general trends or majority views.

The number of people interviewed, for example, is a crucial factor. If not enough people are questioned, the results of the survey may be *skewed,* or distorted. When public relations practitioners want more dependable, systematic responses, they often utilize scientific sampling methods. These methods are based on established procedures that make it more likely that the results will be meaningful and useful.

THE PROBABILITY SAMPLE

For best results, a *probability sample* is taken. This means that everyone in the targeted audience (called the "universe") has an equal chance of being selected for the survey. This method contrasts with a nonprobability sample, in which everyone does not have an equal chance to be selected.

A nonprobability survey, for example, might consist of interviews with employees in the company cafeteria between 11:30 A.M. and noon. The interviewer using this time period, however, will miss completely employees from a division who have their lunch from noon to 12:30 P.M. The interviewer also will miss employees who work another shift. In other words, *any* survey of employees in the cafeteria between 11:30 A.M. and noon would be a nonprobability sample—not every employee in the organization would have an equal chance of being selected.

The survey would be more scientific if the interviewer remained in the cafeteria during the entire lunch period. Yet the results may continue to be skewed if a large number of employees did not use the cafeteria that day but ate lunch in nearby restaurants or brought their lunches from home and ate at their workplaces.

The best way to ensure that every employee has a chance of being surveyed is to select names from a master list of employees. The selection can be made by using a table of random numbers or simply drawing a number from a hat. If the number were 25, the researcher would then interview every twenty-fifth person on the master list.

THE QUOTA SAMPLE   Another common method to ensure representation is to draw a sample that matches the characteristics of the audience. This is called *quota sampling.* Personnel departments, for example, usually have breakdowns of employees by job classification, and it is relatively easy to proportion a sample accordingly. If 32 percent of the employees work on the assembly line, for instance, then 32 percent of the sample should be assembly-line workers. A quota sample can be drawn on any number of demographic factors—age, sex, religion, education, race, income—depending upon the purpose of the survey.

THE SIZE OF THE SAMPLE   In any probability study, there is always the question of sample size. National polling firms usually sample 1200 to 2000 persons and get a highly accurate idea of what the American adult population is thinking. The average national poll samples 1500 people, and the margin of error is within three percentage points 95 percent of the time. In other words, 19 out of 20 times that the same questionnaire is administered, the results should be within the same three percentage points and reflect the whole population accurately.

The three-percentage-points variance in poll results is important in predicting the outcome of an election. If 48 percent of the voters say they will support candidate A and 52 percent endorse candidate B, the election is too close to call. What the 3 percent variance means is that candidate A may actually receive 45 to 51 percent of the vote. Candidate B, on the other hand, may gather 49 to 55 percent of the vote. This means that, given the statistical accuracy of polls, either candidate could win.

In public relations the primary purpose of poll data is to get indications of attitudes and opinions, not to predict elections. Therefore, it is not usually necessary or practical to do a scientific sampling of 1500 people. A sample of 250 to 500 will give relatively accurate data—with a 5 or 6 percent variance—that will help determine general public attitudes and opinions. A sample of about 100 people, accurately drawn according to probability guidelines, will include about a 10 percent margin of error.

This percentage of error would be acceptable if a public relations person, for example, asked employees what they want to read in the company magazine. Sixty percent may indicate that they would like to see more news about opportunities for promotion. If only 100 employees were properly surveyed, it really doesn't matter if the actual percentage is 50 or 70 percent. The large percentage, in either case, would be sufficient to justify an increase in news stories about advancement opportunities.

This is also true in ascertaining community attitudes. If a survey of 100 or fewer citizens indicates that only 25 percent believe the organization is a good community citizen, it really doesn't matter whether the result is 15 or 40 percent. The main point is that the organization must take immediate steps to improve its image.

PURPOSIVE SAMPLING   Probability sampling, with the size of the sample varied as needed for accuracy, offers the most valid data to a public relations researcher. Nonprobability sampling, however, may be better for certain kinds of research. One kind of nonprobability research is called *purposive sampling*.

In use of this method, the people interviewed are selected because they are opinion leaders. Fund-raising firms, for example, conduct purposive sampling before advising a hospital, school, or other nonprofit organization on the potential success of a capital fund drive.

Crucial to the success of any major fund drive seeking $500,000 or more is the support of key community leaders and wealthy individuals, because about 90 percent of these funds come from 10 percent of the population. It is therefore necessary to interview influential people in a community to get their reaction to the proposed drive and, most important, their financial support. In such a situation, interviewing the average homemaker or the man or woman in the street will not generate the type of information nor the financial support needed to determine the feasibility of the project.

Questionnaire Design

Although correct sampling is important in gaining accurate results, pollsters generally acknowledge that sampling error may be far less important than the errors that result from poor question selection.

BIAS IN QUESTIONS   The wording of questions on a questionnaire is a time-consuming process; every attempt should be made to ensure that a question does not bias the respondent's answer. There is a difference between one question, "Is it a good idea to limit handguns?" and another, "Do you think registration of handguns will curtail crime?" On first glance, they seem to be asking the same thing. But, on closer examination, one can realize that a respondent could easily answer "yes" to the first question and "no" to the second.

The first question asks if the limiting of handguns is a good idea. The second asks if people think it will curtail crime. A third question that might elicit a different response would be, "Do you think laws curtailing the use of handguns would work?" Thus, the questions emphasize three different aspects of the problem. The first stresses the value of an idea, the second explores a possible effect, and the third examines the practicality of a proposed solution. Research shows that people often think something is a good idea, but do not think it would work. Another related problem is how respondents might interpret the words *limit* and *curtail*. To some, they may refer to a total ban on handguns, while others may think the words suggest that all guns should be kept away from people with criminal records.

Depending upon who is sponsoring the survey, questions can be loaded to elicit answers in conformity with the group's objectives. The Gun Owners of California once distributed a questionnaire that included the following:

1. Do you believe that federal and state governments have a right to confiscate firearms from law-abiding citizens?

2. Do you believe that Americans have the right to own firearms for hunting and self-defense?

3. Will you vote against legislators who have supported federal laws restricting the private ownership of firearms?

DOUBLE-BARRELED QUESTIONS

Questions can also be double-barreled by including two concepts in the same question. A double-barreled question might be: "Do you favor stricter laws about the ownership of handguns and hunting rifles?" This question poses a problem for the individual who favors stricter laws concerning handguns but who believes such laws should not affect the use of rifles by hunters.

"COURTESY BIAS"

Some survey questionnaires do not generate accurate answers because respondents choose the "correct" answer instead of the one that accurately reflects their feelings. Those conducting employee surveys often fall into this trap by posing such questions as, "How much of the employee newsletter do you read every issue?" or "How well do you like the column by the general manager?" Employees may never read the publication or may think the manager's column is ridiculous, but they know the "correct" answer should be that they read the "entire issue" and that the column is "excellent."

Less of this *courtesy bias* is obtained if the respondents are reasonably assured that their answers are confidential, that there is a mechanism for questionnaires to be filled out in such a way that no one (including the surveyor) will know who completed which questionnaire. Because employees usually consider the public relations department a part of management, many companies seeking candid feedback from employees hire an outside research firm to interview employees or process questionnaires. In any case, a survey of employee attitudes should guarantee anonymity to the respondent.

THE ANSWER CATEGORIES

Answer categories can skew a questionnaire. It is important that answer choices are provided to cover a range of opinions. A national polling organization several years ago asked the question "How much confidence do you have in business corporations?" but provided only the following answer categories: (A) a great deal, (B) only some, and (C) none at all. A large gap exists between a "great deal" and the next category, "only some." Such

Professional and Ethical Guidelines for the Conduct and Reporting of Public Opinion Research

The American Association for Public Opinion Research (AAPOR) has established a code of professional ethics for the conduct and reporting of public opinion research. The following is a selection of guidelines from the code that are particularly relevant to public relations personnel.

CONDUCT OF RESEARCH

1. Exercise due care in gathering and processing data, taking all reasonable steps to assure the accuracy of results.

2. Use only research tools which are well suited to the research at hand.

3. Do not make interpretations of research results that are inconsistent with the data available.

4. Do not mislead survey respondents or use methods which abuse, coerce, or humilate them.

5. Respect the confidentiality of respondents and do not disclose the names for nonresearch purposes.

RELEASE OF SURVEY RESEARCH FINDINGS IN NEWS RELEASES OR OTHER PUBLICITY MATERIALS

1. Identify who sponsored the survey.

2. Give exact wording of the questions asked.

3. Define the population actually sampled.

4. Give size of sample. For mail surveys, this should include the number of questionnaires mailed out and the number returned.

5. Tell what allowance should be made for sampling error.

6. Tell what results are based on parts of the sample, rather than on the whole sample.

7. Indicate whether interviewing was done personally, by telephone, or mail; at home or on street corners.

8. Give time of the interviewing in relation to relevant events.

SOURCE: Adapted from the code of professional ethics and practices, American Association for Public Opinion Research, Box 17, Princeton, New Jersey, 08540.

categories invariably skew the results to show very little confidence in business. A better list of answers might have been (A) a great deal, (B) quite a lot, (C) some, (D) very little, and (E) none. Perhaps an even better approach would be to provide the answer categories (A) above average, (B) average, and (C) below average. The psychological distance between the three choices is equal, and there is less room for respondent interpretation of what "quite a lot" means.

In general, "yes-or-no" questions are not very good for examining respondents' perceptions and attitudes. A "yes" or "no" answer provides little feedback on the strength or weakness of a respondent's opinion. A question such as, "Do you agree with the company's policy of investment in South Africa?" can be answered by "yes" or "no," but more useful information would be obtained by setting up a Likert-type scale—(A) Strongly agree, (B) Agree, (C) Undecided, (D) Disagree, (E) Strongly disagree. These types of answers enable the surveyor to probe the depth of feelings among respondents, and may serve as guidelines for management in making major changes or just fine-tuning the existing policy.

For statistical purposes many questionnaires give an assigned numerical score to the categories ranging from "Strongly disagree" to "Strongly agree." Such a scale might look like this:

___5___ Strongly disagree

___4___ Disagree

___3___ Neutral

___4___ Agree

___5___ Strongly agree

Another way of expressing a numerical scale in order to pinpoint a respondent's beliefs or attitudes is to use, for example, a 5-point scale. Such a scale might look like this:

QUESTION: How would you evaluate the company's efforts to keep you informed about job benefits? Please circle one of the following numbers ("1" being a low rating and "5" being a high rating).

ANSWER: 1   2   3   4   5

The advantage of numerical scales is that medians and means can be easily calculated. In the example above, the average from all respondents might be 4.25, which indicates that employees think the company does keep them informed about job benefits but that there is still room for communication improvement.

Another way to get at perceptions is to use the semantic differential technique. Essentially, this is a list of bipolar words; the respondent places a mark along a continuum. A semantic scale might look like this:

QUESTION: How would you evaluate the company magazine on the following criteria?

Unbiased	____	____	____	____	____	Biased
Trustworthy	____	____	____	____	____	Untrustworthy
Valuable	____	____	____	____	____	Worthless
Fair	____	____	____	____	____	Unfair
Interesting	____	____	____	____	____	Uninteresting

QUESTIONNAIRE GUIDELINES

Here are some general guidelines for the construction of questionnaires:

1. Decide what kinds of information are needed and in what detail.

2. State the objectives of the survey in writing.

3. Decide which group will receive the questionnaire.

4. Decide on the size of the sample.

5. State the purpose of the survey and guarantee anonymity.

6. Use closed-end (multiple-choice) answers as much as possible. Respondents find it easier and less time-consuming to check answers than to compose them in an open-end (essay) questionnaire.

7. Design the questionnaire so that it is easy to read; use simple-to-understand sentences and an orderly format.

8. Make the questionnaire 25 questions or fewer. Long questionnaires "put off" people and reduce the number of responses.

9. Pretest questions for understanding and possible bias. Representatives of the proposed sampling group should read the questionnaire and make comments for possible improvement.

10. Use categories when asking questions about education, age, and income. People are more willing to answer when a category is used. For example: What category best describes your age? (A) Under 25, (B) 26 to 40, (C) 41 to 55, and (D) 56 or above.

11. Provide space at the end of the questionnaire for respondents' comments and observations. This allows them to provide additional information or elaboration that may not have been covered in the main body of the questionnaire.

Ways of Reaching Respondents

MAIL QUESTIONNAIRES   Questionnaires may be used in a variety of settings. They may be handed out at a manufacturing plant, at a county fair, or even in a bank lobby. Most survey questionnaires, however, are mailed to respondents. There are several reasons for this:

1. Because the researchers have better control as to who receives the questionnaire, they can make sure the survey is representative.

2. Large geographical areas can be covered economically.

3. It is less expensive to administer them than to hire an interviewer to conduct personal interviews.

4. Large numbers of people can be included at minimal cost.

Mail questionnaires have some disadvantages. The biggest is lack of response rate. A mail questionnaire by a commercial firm to the general public usually produces a response rate of 1 to 2 percent. If the survey concerns issues affecting the general public, the response rate might be 5 to 20 percent. A much better response rate would be generated, however, if the questionnaire were mailed by an organization to its members. In this case, the response rate may be 30 to 80 percent. The more closely people identify with the organization and the questions, the better the response.

The response rate to a mail questionnaire can be increased, say the experts, if all the guidelines of questionnaire construction are followed. In addition, a researcher should keep the following suggestions in mind:

1. Include a stamped, self-addressed return envelope and a personally signed letter explaining the importance of participation.

2. Mail questionnaires by first-class mail. Some research shows that placing special issue stamps on the envelope attracts greater interest than simply using a postage meter.

3. Mail a reminder postcard three or four days later.

4. Do a second mailing (either to nonrespondents or to the entire sample) two or three weeks after the first mailing. Again, enclose a stamped, self-addressed return envelope and a cover letter explaining the crucial need for the recipient's participation.

A number of commercial firms are now enclosing token amounts of money with the questionnaire to generate a higher response rate. *Aviation Week*, for example, tucks a dollar in the envelope with the questionnaire. *Newsweek* promises to make a charitable donation in the subscriber's name if he or she returns the survey form. Other groups, if the questionnaire is short, enclose a quarter or a 50-cent piece.

Sending a dollar bill usually guarantees at least a 50 percent response, states an official of Erdos & Morgan, a New York market research firm. According to an article in the *Wall Street Journal,* enclosing money makes people feel guilty if they don't respond.

TELEPHONE SURVEYS

Surveys by telephone, particularly if the survey is locally based, are extensively used by research firms. The telephone survey has several advantages:

1. There is an immediate response or nonresponse. A researcher doesn't have to wait several weeks for responses to arrive by mail.

2. A telephone call is personal. It is effective communication, and it is much cheaper than a personal interview.

3. A phone call is less intrusive than going door-to-door and interviewing people. Surveys show that many people are willing to talk on the phone for up to 45 minutes but will not stand at a door for more than 5 or 10 minutes and are less willing to admit strangers to their homes.

4. The response rate, if the survey is properly composed and phone interviewers trained, can reach 80 to 90 percent.

One major disadvantage of phone interviewing is the difficulty in getting access to everyone's telephone number. In some cities, up to a third of households have unlisted telephone numbers. Although researchers can utilize a "reverse" telephone book that lists numbers according to street address, this method is not as effective as actually knowing who is being called. Another disadvantage is the negative connotation of a phone interview because so many salespeople have attempted to sell goods by posing as researchers.

PERSONAL INTERVIEWS

The personal interview is the most expensive form of research because it requires trained staff and travel. If travel within a city is involved, a trained interviewer often can interview only 8 or 10 people a day—and salaries and transportation costs make it expensive. There is also the need for considerable advance work in arranging interviews and appointments and, as previously pointed out, researchers encounter reluctance by residents to admit strangers to their homes.

Personal interviews, on the other hand, can be cost-effective and can generate a wealth of information if the setting is controlled. Many research firms conduct personal interviews at national conventions or trade shows, where there is a concentration of people with similar interests. An equipment company, for example, may hire a research firm to interview potential customers at a national trade show.

Interviewing at a trade show, however, can have its pitfalls. The *Wall Street Journal* reported that Owens-Corning Fiberglas Corporation commissioned a survey at a homebuilders' convention in Houston. Contrary to what most forecasters had expected, the survey showed that builders were planning a 30-percent increase in housing starts for the next year. Owens-Corning immediately scheduled a press conference with a panel of housing experts to analyze the survey results. According to the *Wall Street Journal,* "The star of the panel was Michael Sumichrast, chief economist for the National Association of Home Builders. When asked to interpret the surprising forecast, he quickly dismissed it: 'Well, it shows when you ask stupid questions, you get stupid answers."

Continued the newspaper, "He was referring to the poll's dubious methodology; it was taken only among builders at the convention, who tend to be the larger and more aggressive companies." In other words, it is essential for public relations personnel to know the limitations of research and not to make too many generalizations from it.

A Case Study

COORS RESEARCHES CBS's "60 MINUTES"

The chapter has emphasized that research can take many forms and serve a variety of public relations purposes. A good example of pragmatic research occurred when Adolph Coors Company was approached by the CBS-TV "60 Minutes" program to do a feature on the beer company's labor relations. Shirley Richards, director of corporate communications for Coors, told the annual meeting of the International Association of Business Communicators in Atlanta how her staff utilized informal research to prepare for reporter Mike Wallace and the network's film crew:

RESEARCH TO DECIDE IF APPEARING ON "60 MINUTES" WOULD BE GOOD FOR THE COMPANY:

1. Formal research showed that Coors' corporate image had slipped badly. A comprehensive public relations program was in effect to combat the problem, but progress being made to change attitudes was slow.

2. Thorough analysis of labor union charges and the boycott showed they were based on misunderstandings and falsehoods. An open-door policy with "60 Minutes" could set the record straight on a program with a national audience.

3. Research among distributors and employees showed morale was eroding because they believed Coors' management was not doing enough to combat the boycott.

4. Meetings with management led to the decision that cooperating with "60 Minutes" would be better than refusing to participate.

RESEARCH TO PREPARE FOR "60 MINUTES" VISIT:

1. Requested a letter from Mike Wallace stating the subject matter of his investigation.

2. Learned more about the internal workings of "60 Minutes" by travel to New York and talking with the producer, Allan Maraynes.

3. Obtained tapes of recent speeches and information about David Sickler, the AFL-CIO official who headed the Coors boycott.

4. Researched and gathered all facts surrounding every issue which could be brought up by Mike Wallace.

Coors, by doing its homework, was thoroughly prepared for Wallace. The result was a favorable and sympathetic feature on "60 Minutes" that accurately portrayed the company's viewpoint. How Coors evaluated the effect of the broadcast is discussed in Chapter 10.

QUESTIONS FOR REVIEW AND DISCUSSION

1. What kinds of objectives can be accomplished through public relations research?

2. Name four reasons why public relations personnel should use research in today's complex society.

3. How can survey research data be used as a publicity tool?

4. What questions should you ask yourself before formulating a research study?

5. Name at least seven informal research methods.

6. What is the difference between probability and nonprobability samples?

7. What percentage margin of error is associated with various size samples? What size samples are usually adequate for public relations research?

8. Name at least three pitfalls of questionnaire design that should be avoided.

9. Name at least five guidelines that should be followed when designing a survey questionnaire.

10. Compile a list of pros and cons of mail questionnaires, telephone interviews, and personal interviews.

CHAPTER EIGHT

Planning and Action

Chapter 7 examined the goals and methods of research, a fundamental step in the public relations process. The second phase, planning a program, embodies the results of the research effort.

A public relations program should not be a hit-or-miss action. When a problem arises, it is foolish to throw money at it haphazardly, in hopes of hitting the target. Rather, a successful campaign consists of a series of seven basic steps. Chapter 8 takes a close look at this well-established procedure.

The process begins with a definition of the problem and ends with an assessment of the results. The steps follow each other in logical progression so that waste is avoided. Setting the objectives of a campaign before the problem has been clearly defined, for example, can lead to muddled results.

In the first two steps the practitioner applies the research techniques explained in Chapter 7. Similarly, each element that follows evolves from the step taken just before it. The procedure offers guidance for both the beginner and the experienced practitioner in setting up a well-conducted campaign.

Elements of a Program

The fundamental steps of every successful public relations program are these:

1. Define the problem.

2. Research the facts.

3. Set objectives.

4. Define the audiences.

5. Plan the program.

6. Execute the program.

7. Assess the results.

The remaining sections of this chapter will examine the creation of a program step by step.

The Steps in Detail

DEFINE THE PROBLEM The initial step in formulating a public relations program is to determine the nature of the problem the practitioner is called upon to solve.

In corporate life recognition of public relations problems sometimes is more difficult than might be assumed. All too frequently a chief executive, deeply immersed in the immediate pressures of making the company return a satisfactory profit, is unaware that a public relations problem exists in the organization—a problem that in the long run may seriously threaten the very profitability for which the chief executive is striving.

Using sensitive antennae developed to detect the moods of the public and employees, a company's public relations director and/or a counseling firm should recognize a problem as it develops. Then the specialist must demonstrate to top management that a problem is emerging that requires prompt attention. Unless this attention-calling function is carried out successfully, the necessary funds for attacking the problem will not be forthcoming from management.

If an unexpected crisis occurs, the problem is urgently and painfully evident to everyone. When seven persons in Chicago died after taking capsules of Tylenol laced with cyanide, top management at Johnson & Johnson, makers of the headache remedy, knew instantly that a public relations crisis existed. The question was not "Should we do something?" but "What can we do right now?" (A detailed discussion of the Tylenol crisis appears in Chapter 14.)

When no dramatic event occurs to raise a danger flag, a public relations problem may be less readily recognized. The problem may be insidious, sneaking up over a long time or concealed beneath the surface of routine corporate or organizational life.

So numerous and so varied are the problems addressed by public relations practitioners that listing them all is impossible. They may be grouped, however, into three general categories. Each must be approached in a different way.

1. *Overcoming a negative perception of an organization or product.* Usually such perceptions develop slowly. A specific happening may jar management into recognizing the unfavorable trend and precipitate action. Here are a few types of negative perceptions that occur:

a. Resistance by the public to company products on the basis of price or quality—for example, word-of-mouth assertions that the body of a certain make of automobile is poorly made.

b. Belief expressed by security analysts that a manufacturing company's production equipment has become outdated, making the firm lose ground competitively.

c. Evidence that employees believe their company lacks concern for their interests.

d. Complaints from patients about what they perceive as excessively high hospital bills.

e. A decline in membership of a professional association.

2. *Conducting a specific, one-time project.* On most public relations assignments in this category the practitioner starts from a neutral position. No obvious negative perceptions exist to be overcome. If they do exist, they will come to light later in the program. Conversely, latent support for the program probably exists but has not been developed. The specialist given such an assignment is in the same position as a baseball hitter stepping to the plate: no balls or strikes have yet been called on the batter. To make a hit, the batter must study the pitcher's movements and "stuff"—that is, define the problem being faced. Here are typical problems in the one-time project category that a public relations specialist must define and attempt to solve:

a. Convince voters to approve a bond issue for a municipal auditorium.

b. Introduce a new product.

c. Conduct a fund drive for a hospital expansion.

d. Enlist employee input and support for a major revision of company medical benefits.

e. Obtain shareholder approval for acquisition of another company.

The American Meat Institute faced a vexing problem. Americans in the early 1980s consumed 18 percent less beef annually than they did years earlier. They had turned increasingly to chicken, fish, pasta, and cheese. Yet sirloin steaks and cuts of prime rib were as tasty as ever. What had happened to the market and what could be done about it?

To find the facts, the institute employed a research firm.

The researchers reported that beef still had high social status. A Gallup poll found that steak remained the first choice of people eating out so long as the price was no object.

The fact-finding project defined the beef producers' problem as three-fold: price, public worries about health, and changing social patterns. In the preceding decade, retail meat prices had risen 110 percent. Warnings about the health dangers of high cholesterol and fat caused many Americans to reduce their meat intake. In addition, the number of Americans living alone had grown substantially. Single persons, who depend extensively on convenience foods, consume less meat than family members.

After studying these findings, the National Live Stock and Meat Board counterattacked in two ways—paid advertising and promotion. It adopted a slogan, "Somehow, nothing satisfies like beef." This was designed to promote self-satisfaction as a motivation for buying meat. Television commercials showed individuals in various situations yearning for juicy cuts of beef.

Using public relations tools, the industry promoted National Barbecue Month and a national Beef Cook-Off. It created a beef recipe service for the food editors of newspapers and a library of filmstrips and teaching kits, all emphasizing the theme established by the slogan. Also, as marketing aids it created in-store beef promotions.

The objective of this multimillion-dollar campaign was set realistically: not to restore beef consumption to its highest level of the past, which seemed impractical, but to halt the decline and achieve limited improvement. A research organization was employed to evaluate the effect of the program. As is evident, the way in which the problem was identified and handled follows the fundamental pattern described in this chapter.

3. *Developing or expanding a continuing program.* Much public relations work is of an ongoing nature—the necessity to create or maintain a favorable situation. Although lacking the urgency of a crisis or the clearly drawn needs of a one-time project, this work is vital. It also contains the inherent danger of slipping into stagnant routine and losing effectiveness. The practitioner should watch for fresh techniques, especially the rapidly expanding use of computer technology, and should review the entire program periodically to determine whether it needs redefining. The following are common examples of continuing program objectives:

a. Maintain community confidence that a company is a good corporate citizen with a sense of social responsibility.

b. Satisfy employees that a company is a good place to work. Retention of trained employees is a constant management problem.

c. Convince members that a trade organization or a union represents them effectively.

d. Raise funds on an annual basis to keep human welfare programs like those of the American Red Cross or American Heart Association functioning.

e. Supply the media with a steady flow of newsworthy information about the employer and answer their requests promptly and openly.

To summarize, a public relations program usually is designed to correct a negative situation, achieve a well-defined, one-time objective, or maintain and improve an existing positive situation.

RESEARCH THE FACTS Assume that the public relations specialist has established that a problem exists. Its general outlines have been identified. Before an attempt to solve the problem can be made, however, detailed research must be done to determine its causes and extent. What are the facts? The practitioner, who has been an *intelligence agent* to identify the problem and a *salesperson* to demonstrate its existence to top management, now takes on a third role, that of *researcher*.

In researching a public relations problem, the fact-finder can begin effectively by focusing on four areas of concern: (1) cost, (2) quality of the product or service, (3) degree of attention to customer convenience, and (4) effectiveness of communication. Cost, quality, convenience, and communication are crucial issues in most public relations projects. Specific problems may have additional unique aspects; usually these will come to light as the researcher investigates the four basic areas.

Here are some examples of the hard-nosed fact-finding needed as a basis for remedial action.

THE PROBLEM A manufacturing company finds that customers are rejecting its most important product, an electric razor, because they believe it is poorly made and too expensive. Here are some of the questions for which the researcher should seek answers:

What is the specific nature of customer complaints?

Do parts of the product break easily?

Does it wear out too quickly?

Is the warranty inadequate?

Does the razor fail to shave as closely as the company claims it will?

Is it difficult to operate?

Does it look shoddy?

How many complaints has the company received?

How serious are these complaints—strong or only mildly critical?

Do they fall into a pattern, indicating one primary cause of dissatisfaction?

This is the time for candor. *Is* the product poorly made? How does it compare with competing products in objective tests?

It is also the time for open-minded listening. The researcher should not undertake the project with preconceived ideas about the problem and what should be done. How does the client or company management perceive the problem and its causes?

Surveys by questionnaires and personal interviews with a sampling of purchasers of the product, both those who have complained and those who have not, can yield valuable answers. So can surveys of merchants who sell the product and reports from company salespersons.

With answers in hand, management must make a decision. How can the product be redesigned so that a campaign projecting a positive new image may be instituted? Once that has been decided, the public relations, advertising, and marketing staffs can design programs to achieve this goal.

THE PROBLEM   Membership in a state teachers' association has fallen sharply, although the number of teachers in the state's schools has risen. Obviously something is wrong in this professional organization. What it it? Here are some of the questions an able public relations practitioner would ask in order to find the answer:

Do members believe that annual dues are too high?

That the association provides insufficient benefits such as insurance and purchasing discounts?

That it doesn't hold enough interesting meetings?

That its publications are poor and fail to deliver enough useful information?

Are members dissatisfied with the way the association has negotiated contracts with local school boards?

Do members believe that the association doesn't work hard enough in the state legislature to protect the profession's interests?

Do many teachers dislike having the association take partisan political positions?

To seek the answers, the first action public relations personnel must take is to *analyze membership statistics.* In what parts of the state is the membership decline especially bad—rural or urban? Are the nonmembers mostly new teachers or veterans? men or women? How does this association compare with other state associations in percentage of members to total certified teachers in the state?

The second step is to *conduct a membership audit.* Surveys by questionnaire should be undertaken so that members may indicate their opinions of listed association activities and policies and tell which ones they wish to see increased, decreased, or altered. A similar survey should be sent to former members, who may be a center of discontent. A third survey should go to active teachers who have never joined the association, to find out why. These surveys can be conducted directly from state headquarters or by association chapters in each school district. Results of the surveys may be supplemented and reinforced by in-depth personal interviews with a cross-section sampling in each of the categories (for a discussion of surveys, see Chapter 7).

A REAL-LIFE INSTANCE   The two problems described illustrate the way fact-finding is done. The following account describes how a major trade association actually developed a set of facts to offset a negative public perception.

At one point in the recurring American debate about energy supplies, extensive criticism arose that oil industry profits were excessive. A handful of wealthy individuals were frequently described as exploiting the American public through their supposed control of the oil companies. To counteract this perception, the American Petroleum Institute planned a public relations campaign to demonstrate that in fact ownership of the oil companies was spread widely among Americans and did not rest in the hands of a small number of rich families and individuals. But the institute encountered a problem. It discovered that statistical information about ownership of the oil industry had never been assembled. So it commissioned a research group to do the fact-finding. The result was a 56-page report titled "Shareownership of the Six Largest U.S. Oil Companies."

The companies turned over their stockholder lists to the research team. Using methods developed by the New York Stock Exchange Census of Shareownership, the researchers analyzed the lists, which provided evidence of direct ownership. Then the researchers turned to other financial sources for facts about indirect ownership—for example, individuals who had shares in a mutual fund that owned oil company stock, or were beneficiaries in pension plans that held such stock. By use of standard statistical methods, the researchers eliminated as much duplication of ownership as possible. Supplementing this process, the research team had a professional firm conduct detailed telephone interviews with a scientifically selected sample of 500 stockholders to gather information about other investments and personal facts such as extent of education.

The primary findings of the study were these: The shareholders of the six largest U.S. oil companies are estimated to number 2,300,000. In addition, more than 11,750,000 other people are indirect owners of these companies. The estimated total of both direct and indirect owners is 6.6 percent of the population of the United States. In addition, the study found that 91 colleges and universities, nearly 200 mutual funds, and almost 1000 charitable foundations owned shares in one or more of the six companies.

Using this carefully researched information, the American Petroleum Institute conducted an effective public relations campaign demonstrating the falsity of the perception that oil profits were enjoyed by only a few. Its message was this: when the oil industry earns profits, these profits are spread among approximately 14 million Americans. While emphasizing the breadth of ownership, of course, the campaign did not focus on the amounts of stock held by certain individuals and organizations.

SET OBJECTIVES

To conduct successful campaigns, practitioners should ask, "Precisely what do we wish to accomplish?" The more specifically they answer that question, the better is the prospect for success and the greater the potential for measuring results. A vague goal such as, "To get publicity for our new product," is relatively meaningless. The objective might be better stated: "To make people aware of our new product and induce them to buy it." The significant target is the number of units sold, not the size of the press clipping file.

THE TWO TYPES OF OBJECTIVES   Objectives are of two types—*informational* and *motivational*.

An *informational* campaign tells people about an event, introduces a product, or seeks to enhance the perception of a company. One difficulty with informational campaigns occurs in measuring how well the objective has been achieved.

Although difficult to accomplish, *motivational* objectives are easier to measure. They should be stated as succinctly as possible, such as, "Increase attendance at this year's concert by 25 percent," "Convince voters to approve the bond issue for the new municipal stadium," or "Improve the employees' understanding of the company's retirement program." (Evaluation of public relations campaigns is discussed in Chapter 10.)

If well planned and conducted, public relations projects can accomplish much, but they cannot achieve impractical goals. Objectives must be realistic.

They should be placed high, so participants must stretch to reach them, but not at an impossible level. If a goal is unattainable, despite determined and ingenious efforts to achieve it, the failure may cause frustration and disenchantment among those who work on a campaign. This creates a negative attitude toward future projects. If a public fund-raising goal is impossibly high and the drive fails by a wide margin, the campaign force is embarrassed and public support for the project may dwindle.

BUDGET CONSIDERATIONS   In setting objectives, practitioners must consider the amount of money available. Budget and achievement are not always directly related, of course. Under some circumstances a small budget judiciously spent may attain remarkable success. Nevertheless, large expenditures increase the prospect of success because they make possible the use of more extensive methods and staff. If the cost of a campaign exceeds the value of its objective, however, the effort cannot be called a success. When a charitable organization spends so much to conduct a fund drive that operating costs absorb an excessive portion of the donations, it is properly open to public criticism. (A discussion of fund-raising appears in Chapter 19.) And no matter how much money is spent and how much effort is made, a program cannot succeed if the product is poor or the objective unacceptable to the audience.

A management decision must be made, either to establish a large objective or a set of objectives and supply sufficient funds to permit success, or to allot a limited amount of money and set an objective attainable with such a sum. The public relations specialist should supply top management with well-informed opinions about what its money might achieve.

THE TIME FACTOR   Time is another factor to be considered in setting an objective. The amount of time to be spent on a campaign depends upon its purpose and its nature. Some programs should be quick, hard-driving, and completed within a relatively brief, specified period. Other projects—for instance, publicity for an event such as an exhibition—have a built-in time limit; by the close of the show they have either suceeded or failed. When a project is designed to correct a negative perception or to develop public acceptance of a new concept, a long period of time may be required. *Negative attitudes change slowly.* There is no quick fix for an unfavorable public perception. Objectives for such projects should be determined with this in mind; one-, two-, and three-year goals may be appropriate. Interim measurements of progress can be made, but everyone involved in creating the program must recognize the need for patience.

THE WRITTEN STATEMENT   Before planning a program, the practitioner should state its objective, or objectives, in writing. This helps to focus individual

| Supporting the Marketing Function | The introduction of a new product requires extensive planning of communication strategy at every stage of the marketing cycle. The following shows the kind of communication activity that must be planned: |

NEW PRODUCT DEVELOPMENT

Market research

Counseling

MANUFACTURING

Research

TESTING AND TEST MARKETING

Research (quantitative and qualitative)

Testing of themes, positioning through events, publicity, trade relations

INTRODUCTION TO SALES FORCE

Sales meeting presentations

Collateral material

INTRODUCTION TO DISTRIBUTION SYSTEM, DISTRIBUTORS

Audiovisual presentations

Trade publicity

Newsletters

Brochures, flyers

Contests, events

thinking and to prevent later misunderstanding with management. Depending upon the complexity of the program, the goal can be summarized in two or three sentences, perhaps in one.

In the American Petroleum Institute campaign cited earlier, the objective might be summarized as follows:

Promote public awareness that oil companies are owned by millions of shareholders who benefit from the profits the companies earn, and correct the misconception that the companies belong to a small number of extremely rich individuals.

INTRODUCTION TO RETAIL OUTLETS

Audiovisual presentations

Trade publicity

Newsletters

In-store events

Contests, events

How-to publicity kits

MERCHANDISING AND SALES PROMOTIONS

Collateral materials

In-store events

Contests, other selling ideas

Mall events

CONSUMER PROMOTION

Publicity

Contests, events

Direct mail

SOURCE: Hill & Knowlton, New York.

DEFINE THE AUDIENCES

Once the objective has been set, the practitioner should define the audience or audiences at which the campaign will be aimed. Precisely whom is the campaign intended to inform or motivate? The purpose of specifying an audience is simply to avoid wasted effort and dollars. Some campaigns can be aimed at the general public. Other campaigns should be directed at a smaller, more focused audience. Spending large sums of money to educate the public at large on issues in which it has no stake is nonproductive. Targeting the message to the appropriate audience is more likely to produce significant results.

Public relations programs fall into three general categories, aimed at the following groups: (1) *a broad general audience,* (2) *a target audience,* and (3) *an internal audience.*

In a broad-based project aimed at the *entire public,* the practitioner seeks to register as many impressions as possible on as many individuals as possible. The American Cancer Society, for example, uses a number of methods to warn every person it can reach about the seven danger signs of cancer. The more often that individuals read or hear about those signs, the more likely they are to check their bodies for symptoms. On a local level, sponsors of a citywide July 4 ethnic festival in a Midwestern city, trying to attract as many persons as possible to the event, spread the word through newspaper stories, radio and television shows, publicity photographs in newspapers of exotic foods to be sold, club meeting announcements, personal solicitation of ethnic groups to operate booths, and as many other methods as they had the time and money to employ.

In a campaign aimed at an external *target audience,* selection of public relations methods is more restricted. Impressions made upon individuals not concerned with an issue are wasted. Broadside use of radio and television, in particular, might be of scant value—if, indeed, the practitioners could convince news directors and program directors to use their material.

How is a target audience campaign conducted? As an example, consider the campaign run by motorcycle enthusiasts seeking repeal of a state law that requires them to wear helmets while riding. The issue is of minimal interest to the general public. The campaign must be aimed at two special audiences—state legislators, who will vote on the repeal proposal, and motorcycle users, whose opinions pro and con will influence their decision. Since the issue is nonpartisan and involves no expenditure of state money, two common concerns of legislators—party loyalty and the budget—are not involved.

Sharp differences of opinion exist among motorcyclists as to the wisdom of the repeal effort. Those who favor repeal maintain that the government has no right to tell them as citizens how they should dress—an emotional argument—and that helmets impair their peripheral vision—a physical one. They agree that the use of helmets reduces the danger of head injuries but argue that they should have freedom of choice about wearing them. Supporters of the law contend that helmets save lives and that the government has a duty to protect those motorcyclists who would be foolhardy enough to ride bareheaded unless forbidden by law.

The perimeters of the two target audiences are easily defined. There is a known number of legislators, approximately 100. The names and addresses of registered motorcycle owners and licensed riders can be obtained from the Department of Motor Vehicles. Motorcycle sales agencies, equipment stores, and repair shops are natural channels of repeal communication. So are motorcycle clubs.

The proponents of repeal ask club members to write to their legislators, using sample letters provided for them. Clubs are urged to adopt formal resolutions to be sent to the legislature. Repeal advocates testify before legislative committee hearings on the bill and hold face-to-face discussions with individual legislators, pressing their cause. They distribute pamphlets and information sheets urging repeal. They hand out bumper stickers with a catchy repeal slogan to their members and place piles of them in motorcycle shops for free distribution. They submit feature stories favoring repeal to motorcycle publications and request supporting editorials.

Safety organizations and motorcyclists who want the helmet law retained also mount a campaign, but with less fervor and money. They cite instances in which a motorcyclist's life was saved by a helmet and show the legislators graphs depicting the rise in motorcycle fatalities in states that have repealed the helmet law. However, their arguments are overpowered by the pile of letters, petitions, and resolutions favoring repeal that arrive on legislators' desks. Convinced that a majority of motorcyclists desire repeal, the legislators shrug, "If they want to risk their necks, let them," and pass the bill repealing the law.

The general public, meanwhile, hears little about the dispute, except for a few news stories by legislative reporters, a scattering of letters to newspaper editors, and passing glimpses of bumper stickers. Its awareness of the intense, tightly focused public relations campaign is almost nonexistent and its concern about the outcome is negligible.

The third type of campaign is aimed at an *internal audience*. This might be the employees of a company or members of a professional organization. This kind of campaign also relies upon specific types of public relations tools.

If a company plans to revise the stock-purchase plan it offers to employees, for instance, management should explain the changes and the reasons for them to employees. Failure to do so may produce confusion, rumors, and suspicious grumbling that management is attempting a trick that will harm employees financially. It is axiomatic that in any large group some people will resist change and suspect the motives for it. Although the issue is of intense concern to employees, the general public probably knows (or cares) nothing about it and has no influence in shaping the outcome. Thus distribution of the company's message to the public is pointless.

To tell its story to employees, management uses brochures illustrated with simple graphs and charts explaining how the revised plan will operate and how it will benefit the workforce. These are distributed at in-plant meetings or mailed to employees' homes. Top management officials address groups of employees, give audiovisual presentations, and answer questions. One issue of the employee magazine concentrates on the plan. If the company's plants are situated in several cities, the chief executive officer may, use a videoconference to address the staffs of all the plants simultaneously.

These actions constitute an intensive internal communications project, yet the only information the public may learn about it is from a news story on the financial pages reporting the proposal.

That is how public relations programs are planned for carefully analyzed audiences. A good program is designed to fit the need as carefully as a tailor measures a customer for an expensive suit.

PLAN THE PROGRAM   As indicated in the discussion of the ways in which audiences should be defined and addressed, a practitioner has numerous options available when planning the program.

The commercial media—written, spoken, and visual—provide ways to deliver the program's message. These media include newspapers, magazines, books, radio, television, and motion pictures. In addition, the message can be presented through speeches, meetings, and written and audiovisual material prepared by the public relations department or counseling firm conducting the program.

Here is a list of principal ways in which public relations messages can be delivered. Subsequent chapters will examine each of these methods in detail.

WRITTEN METHODS

News releases

Factsheets

Newspapers and
magazine feature articles

Newsletters

Brochures and handbooks

Company periodicals

Annual reports

Corporate advertising

Books

SPOKEN METHODS

Face-to-face discussions

Speeches

Radio newscasts

News conferences

Press parties

Interviews, printed and broadcast

Meetings

Word-of-mouth (the "grapevine")

VISUAL METHODS

Television newscasts

Television appearances

Videotapes

Motion pictures

Slides and filmstrips

Transparencies

160

Still photographs

Teleconferencing

Charts and graphs

Other graphics
(cartoons, paintings, logos)

Billboards

Truly a smorgasbord from which to choose! In most cases, an integrated program using several of these methods in a coordinated manner is best. Under certain circumstances, however, the practitioner might find it desirable or necessary to use only a single carefully chosen medium.

Figure 8.1 is an example of use of film to communicate a message.

**EXECUTE THE
PROGRAM**

Conducting a public relations project requires preparation time, efficient administration, and sufficient trained personnel. Temporary additions to the staff may be needed, along with the services of outside specialists.

An example of a well-run program occurred in Columbus, Ohio. The Area Chamber of Commerce conducted a combined campaign for passage of three proposals in a city election—a school tax increase, a County Children Services tax levy, and a municipal bond package to maintain and improve city services. It established a campaign budget of $225,000.

With this money it purchased $117,000 in radio and television advertising and $9,500 worth of newspaper advertising, and also designed and printed 450,000 pieces of literature. Much of its effort went toward providing the media with news stories. While the chamber paid nothing, of course, for the

FIGURE 8.1

Months of planning by United Technologies Corporation preceded its production of a 17-minute film titled *Count on It!* and starring Jonathan Winters, to explain company benefits to employees and families. The comedian played several roles in the film. (Reprinted by permission of United Technologies.)

ONE MONTH ACTION PLAN
PRECEDING
HOME ENERGY TOUR

Four Weeks Prior to Home Energy Tour:

·Set Final Dates
  - Editorial Boards
  - Community Advisory Meeting
  - Community Leader Meeting
  - Home Energy Tour

·Select and call 8 potential community leaders for Community Advisory Meeting
  to be scheduled in third week.

·Compile Community mailing list

·Begin coordinating format and informal editorial boards.

Three Weeks Prior to Home Energy Tour:

·Community Advisory Meeting

·Select Home for Home Energy Tour

·Select three community spokespeople from Advisory Committee Leader Meeting.

·Mail letters to community leaders inviting them to Community Leader Meeting
  scheduled for second week.

·Send thank you letters to Advisory Meeting attendees

ZIP: PG&E's Zero Interest Program
Ketchum Public Relations, 55 Union Street, San Francisco, CA 94109 (415) 781-9480

coverage it received through newspaper stories, radio and television news programs, and broadcast talk shows, substantial costs were incurred to hire professional market research and to prepare news releases, film clips, and similar material. Local companies assisted the project by lending professional talent and office equipment.

All three ballot measures were approved by the voters. For its successful campaign, described in *Public Relations Journal,* the chamber received a Silver Anvil award from the Public Relations Society of America.

When a crisis arises, a program in response must be executed quickly. Having a contingency plan ready for use in a foreseeable crisis speeds the response time, but some crises take unexpected form. In most projects,

JULY 1982

SUNDAY	MONDAY	TUESDAY	WEDNESDAY	THURSDAY	FRIDAY	SATURDAY
	Meeting w/RCS - Draft Complete Mayor's letter - Gov. Relations will deliver letter to Mayor - Comp. Mailing list for Comm. Leader Meeting on 7/3. - Select & Call 8 Community Advisors for meeting 7/1.	-Letter en route to Mayor - Tour Home to be selected		**1** Contractor's Meeting - Select Contractor for Energy Tour - Receive Mayor's Letter -Community Advisory Meeting – 6:00 p.m. San Jose PG&E *****************	**2**	**3**
4	**5** HOLIDAY	**6** -PG&E will mail Mayor's letter to Community Leader Meeting on July 13	**7** Call 3 Community Leaders from Advisory meeting 7/1 to speak at 7/13 meeting in support of ZIP.	**8** (Community Leaders to receive invitations to 7/13.)	**9**	**10**
11	**12**	**13** 6:00 COMMUNITY LEADER MEETING - PG&E Auditorium - Food/Refreshments - Introduce ZIP Program. *****************	**14** Send thank you letters to all attendees along with flier invitations to Home Energy Tour	**15** Editorial Boards including San Jose Mercury News - Bring Press packets - New Bureau Representatives will coordinate. *************************	**16**	**17**
18	**19** - Contractor will install Big 6. - Call speaking participants for 7/26(Comm. Leader, Mayor, Council Person, County Supervisor) (No more than 3 incl. PG&E spokersperson.	**20** - RCS will inspect installations - Call PG&E photographer to cover on 7/26.	**21** Send Press Advisories for Home Energy Tour 7/26.	**22** Walk through tour home with all participants.	**23** - Send Press Release. - Follow-up Media calls	**24**
25	**26** -Morning Press calls. -10:00 Home Energy Tour - Press Feeds *****************	**27**	**28** - Write Thank You letters to all participants. - Follow-up with any additional New Releases or pictures - Coordinate Community speakers Bureau - Deliver materials and Posters to community organizations - Start Follow-up activities	**29**	**30**	**31**

FIGURE 8.2

Deadlines and calendars are important in public relations programming. These two pages are excerpted from a program plan prepared by Ketchum Public Relations, San Francisco, for the Pacific Gas & Electric Company. The action plan details what should be done before an event. The calendar gives an overall view of what occurs on a day-to-day basis. (Courtesy of Ketchum Public Relations, San Francisco.)

however, crisis urgency is not involved. Sufficient time usually is available to prepare the materials and make the physical arrangements before the kickoff date. A program that starts, then bogs down because necessary materials are not ready or speakers are not available, is headed for failure.

Among the steps the director and staff of a campaign must take in order to execute the program efficiently are these:

Create a program calendar and maintain a checklist of progress. This prevents the possibility of deadlines being missed or of some aspects being overlooked. Figure 8.2 shows a typical calendar prepared by a public relations firm.

| Preparing | Writing a plan for a public relations activity is nothing more than preparing |
| a Program Plan | a blueprint of what is to be done and how it will be accomplished. By |

Writing a plan for a public relations activity is nothing more than preparing a blueprint of what is to be done and how it will be accomplished. By preparing such a plan, either as a brief outline or an extensive document, the practitioner can make sure that all elements have been properly considered and that everybody involved knows what the procedure is. Ketchum Public Relations, San Francisco, uses the following outline in preparing program plans for clients:

1. *Define the problem.* Valid objectives cannot be set without a clear understanding of the problem. To understand the problem, (1) discuss it with the client to find what the public relations effort is expected to accomplish, (2) do some initial research, and (3) evaluate ideas in the broader perspective of the client's long-term goals.

2. *Identify objectives.* Once the problem is understood, it should be easy to define the objective. A stated objective should be evaluated by asking (1) does it really solve the problem? (2) is it realistic and achievable? and (3) can success be measured in terms meaningful to the client?

3. *Identify audience.* Identify, as precisely as possible, the group of people who comprise the primary audience for the message. If there are several groups, list them according to what group would be most important in achieving the client's primary objectives.

4. *Develop strategy.* The strategy describes how, in concept, the objective is to be achieved. Strategy is a plan of action that provides guidelines and

Write the printed material and scripts.

Obtain management approval of program material.

Order the printing, after obtaining price bids and having specialists prepare attractive layouts.

Write the speeches to be delivered. These may include the "pattern" speech, a basic presentation that various speakers may adapt appropriately to fit individual situations.

Train the speakers and brief them thoroughly.

Arrange meeting dates and places, and schedule speakers.

Make contact with editors to propose feature stories in newspapers and magazines and supporting editorials if the campaign objective justifies them.

Offer articulate representatives for appearances on radio and television shows.

themes for the overall effort. There is usually one, and often several, strategies for each target audience. Strategies may be broad or narrow, depending on the objective and the audience.

5. *Specify tactics.* This is the body of the plan that describes, in sequence, the specific activities proposed to achieve each objective. In selecting communication tools—news releases, brochures, radio announcements, videotapes, special events, etc.—make sure the communication tools are appropriate for the designated audience.

6. *Develop calendar.* It is important to have a timetable, usually in chart form, that shows the start and completion of each project within the framework of the total program. Using a calendar enables practitioners to make sure that projects—such as brochures, slide presentations, newsletters, and invitations—are ready when they are needed.

7. *Ascertain budget.* How much will it cost to implement the public relations plan? Outline, in sequence, the exact costs of all activities. Budgets should include such details as postage, car mileage, labor to stuff envelopes, typesetting, office supplies, telephone, etc. About 10 percent of the budget should be allocated for contingencies.

8. *Specify evaluation procedures.* Determine what criteria will be used to evaluate the success of the public relations program. Evaluation criteria should be realistic, credible, specific, and in line with client expectations. When determining objectives, make sure that each of them can be adequately evaluated at the end of the program.

Send out invitations to news conferences, press parties, and meetings.

This list of steps, while comprehensive, is not all-inclusive. Each program has special requirements. The more that these can be anticipated, the better the results.

ASSESS THE RESULTS Every public relations campaign is an educational experience for those who conduct it as well as for those to whom it is directed. Assessment of the program's results, like the fact-finding step taken before it is planned, should be a time for candor and self-examination.

The results of some projects are easily determined. A fund drive either meets its announced goal or it does not. A campaign for passage of certain legislation either succeeds or fails. The crowds attending a state fair can be counted at the turnstiles. But measuring the effectiveness of campaigns with more abstract goals, such as reversing a negative perception, is more difficult because no obvious statistics are available as benchmarks.

QUESTIONS FOR REVIEW AND DISCUSSION

1. Name the first step in every successful public relations program.

2. Negative perceptions often develop about an organization. What are some danger signals for which a public relations director should watch?

3. List three examples of specific one-time projects a public relations specialist might be asked to conduct.

4. If assigned to research the reasons why a certain brand of bicycle sells poorly, what important questions would you ask?

5. Describe how you would try to determine why the number of volunteer workers at a hospital is decreasing and list ways to recruit new volunteers.

6. Why should the goal of a public fund drive be set at an attainable level?

7. Public relations objectives should be stated in writing. Prepare a one-sentence statement of objectives for a campaign to convince local residents that the local factory of a national company is a good community citizen.

8. What public relations methods are often used to reach an internal audience?

9. List five visual methods for delivering public relations messages.

10. A program calendar is a basic tool in a public relations campaign. Why is it so important?

CHAPTER NINE

Communication

The third step in the public relations process, after appropriate research and planning, is communication.

In a public relations program plan, as pointed out in Chapter 8, communication is the *implementation of a decision.* It may take the form of news releases, press conferences, special events, brochures, speeches, bumper stickers, newsletters, parades, posters, and the like. In a program plan, this stage is referred to as *strategies and tactics,* but it is also known as *outbound communication.*

The purpose of the communication process, of course, is to inform, persuade, and motivate people. To be an effective communicator, a person must have a thorough knowledge of what constitutes communication and of how people receive messages. An understanding of the way people adopt new ideas, and an awareness of the ever-present barriers that limit effective communication, also are needed.

This chapter explores these concepts and offers guidelines on the construction and dissemination of messages. Additional aspects of communication, from a persuasion standpoint, are discussed in Chapter 11.

The Nature of Communication

THE NEED FOR A COMMON GROUND

Communication is the act of transmitting information, ideas, and attitudes from one person to another. Communication can take place, however, only if the speaker and the listener (called the sender and the receiver) have a common understanding of the symbols being used.

Words are the most common symbols. The degree to which two people understand each other is heavily dependent upon their common knowledge of word symbols. Anyone who has traveled abroad can readily attest to the observation that very little communication occurs between two people who speak different languages. Gestures often provide a form of simple communication, but every traveler has his or her favorite stories of frustration and amusing misinterpretations.

Even if the sender and the receiver speak the same language, the effectiveness of the communication is highly dependent upon such factors as education, social class, regional differences, and cultural background. Most Americans, for example, would have difficulty understanding a South African who said it was somewhat "dicey" getting a "lift" in a "bakkie" at the "robot" because of some "cheeky" bystanders. Translated, the South African's words mean that it was risky getting a ride in a pickup truck at the stop light because of some rude and outspoken bystanders.

Occupational and bureaucratic jargon are also poor symbols for effective communication. Educational theorists say that communication occurs only when there is commonality, or shared experience, between the sender and the receiver. When a nuclear engineer at the Three Mile Island power plant told the press that "energetic disassembly" and "rapid oxidations" were impossible, he apparently did not realize that the majority of his listeners had no framework for such specialized terms. Thus, little communication and much misunderstanding occurred. The engineer should have said that it was impossible for the plant to explode or catch on fire.

FEEDBACK

An important aspect of communication is the opportunity for *feedback,* or response from the listener to the speaker. Feedback is just as important as the dissemination of the message itself, because it tells the sender whether he or she is being understood. Questions can clarify the meaning for the listener and also alert the sender that alternative words and examples should be used.

Most communication models, whether simple or complex, include feedback as an integral part. Social scientist David K. Berlo's model, for example, has four components—sender-source (encoder), message, channel, and receiver (decoder)—with a feedback line between the sender and the receiver (see Figure 9.1).

168

FIGURE 9.1

This simplified version of Berlo's communication model shows the vital role of feedback between sender and receiver.

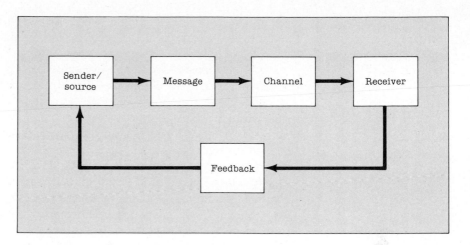

Feedback is also integral in all models showing the public relations process of research, planning, communication, and evaluation. Many public relations professionals view the process as a loop. Communication to internal and external audiences produces feedback that is taken into consideration during research, the first step, and evaluation, the fourth step. In this way, the structure and dissemination of messages are continually refined for maximum effectiveness.

Generally, *interpersonal* (two or more people talking together) is the most effective form of communication. It is effective because the message is fortified by gestures, facial expressions, intimacy, tone of voice, and the opportunity for instant feedback. If the listener asks a question or looks puzzled, the speaker has an instant cue and can rephrase the information or amplify a point.

This is also true of small-group meetings, but the barriers of effective communication tend to mount as one advances to large-group meetings and, ultimately, the mass media. In other words, mass media can multiply an audience many times over, but the psychological as well as the physical distance between the sender and the receiver is considerably lengthened. This causes less effective communication because the audience is no longer intimately involved with the speaker. No immediate feedback is possible, and the message can undergo distortion as it passes through media gate-keepers.

THE ROLE OF THE SENSES

The five senses—sight, hearing, smell, touch, and taste—play a vital role in communication. Television and film or videotape, for example, are the most effective of the mass media because the audience can engage the senses of both sight and hearing. In addition, there are the attractions of color and movement. Radio, on the other hand, relies on only one sense, that of hearing. Print media, although capable of communicating a large amount of information, rely only on sight.

Individuals learn through all five senses, but psychologists estimate that 83 percent of learning is accomplished through sight. Hearing accounts for 11 percent of learning, while only 3 percent of total information is gained from smell. Two percent of learning comes from the sense of touch and only 1 percent is through taste. Fifty percent of what individuals retain consists of what they see and hear.

These figures have obvious implications for the public relations practitioner. Any communication strategy should, if possible, include vehicles of communication that combine sound and sight. This is why it is a good idea for speakers to use graphs, charts, overhead transparencies, and slides to supplement their talks. It also means that a variety of communication tools—news releases, slide presentations, videotapes, billboards, newsletters, radio announcements, TV clips, and the like—should be used to communicate a message to selected audiences. This practice not only assists learning and retention but also provides repetition of the message in a variety of forms that facilitate audience understanding.

McLUHAN'S "HOT" AND "COOL" MEDIA AND MESSAGES

Another way of looking at multiple communication channels and the nature of communication is to take a page from the late Canadian philosopher-educator Marshall McLuhan. He theorized that media are either "hot" or "cool" depending upon their fidelity. Hot media are clear, distinct, and easy to understand; they require little physiological or sensory involvement, because the signals are complete messages. In his terminology, for example, books, newspapers, photos, movies, letters, and stereo music are "hot" media. They are "high relief" and make a strong impact.

"Cool" media, on the other hand, are low-fidelity forms and require the individual to convert incomplete signals into complete messages. McLuhan's idea of a "cool" medium is television, because electronic impulses form only part of a picture or audio message at any given instant. The television picture, for example, is made up of electronic dots; people connect the dots to form a complete picture in their minds.

McLuhan's theory also applies to "hot" and "cool" messages. "Hot" messages, with their highly understandable, specific content, are particularly good for disseminating information. Listings of dates and times of a theater performance, the declaration of a stock dividend, and the announcement of a new product on the market are all "hot" messages. When people read such items in the newspapers, for instance, there usually is little sensory involvement or even the need to think much about the message.

"Cool" messages, on the other hand, may be more appropriate if the objective is to have people internalize and retain the information. This follows the psychological concept that people learn and retain more if they actively interpret the message through high physiological and sensory participation. In addition, it has been found that "cool" messages are more likely to create a mood or a feeling that a person internalizes according to his or her particular predispositions.

IN POLITICAL AND COMMERCIAL ADVERTISEMENTS   "Image" politics and some forms of commercial advertising are a direct outgrowth of McLuhan's ideas. Political candidates who seem to catch audience attention, for example, are those who project an easygoing approach. As social scientist Charles Larson says, "They [the candidates] are abstract to the voter, not distinct." Advertisements for products on television also rely less on words and specific information than on the creation of a mood. "Viewers," says Larson, "can add to or subtract from what they watch to get a final meaning."

Put another way, low-fidelity (cool) messages are abstract and allow each member of the audience to interpret the message differently. This is an advantage to the political candidate who makes a vague statement such as, "Education must be the nation's No. 1 priority." Voters, in turn, interpret the message according to their own beliefs about educational reform, which may, for example, be to (1) allocate more money to education, (2) raise educational standards, (3) give merit pay to outstanding teachers, or (4) reduce federal involvement in education.

The net result is widespread voter support, because each person has perceived the candidate as championing his or her conception of the solution. In many cases, the low-fidelity approach may be more effective than a high-fidelity (hot) message—for instance, that the candidate specifically supports a major increase in taxes to support education. This strategy follows the psychological concept that people have more agreement on goals than on specific ways to achieve those goals.

Much product advertising takes the same approach as that for a political candidate. Advertisements create moods or feelings by disseminating abstract messages that the audience can interpret any number of ways. An advertisement for the gold MasterCard simply states, "Here's to over-achievement: the ultimate recognition from your banker." Or an advertisement for a men's fragrance says, "A cologne for the other man lurking inside you." Individuals fill in or add to the message according to their needs and conceptions of self-identity.

IN PUBLIC RELATIONS   Public relations often concerns itself with actions that can be interpreted on several levels. The management of a company making a substantial donation to a senior citizen center hopes that audiences will interpret the gift as an indication of the company's quality and excellent products. Texaco has sponsored Metropolitan Opera performances on radio every Saturday afternoon for more than 40 years, and surveys indicate that the oil company is perceived as "high-class" by opinion leaders. Mobil has achieved an image of social responsibility and of support for the arts in much the same way—by sponsoring countless series on public television.

Thus, it can be seen that individual public relations activities often are, in McLuhan's world, "cool" messages. Sponsoring the opera or PBS programming has nothing to do with selling gasoline products, but such endeavors create a mood or feeling about the company among key publics.

The Effects of Communication

AVOIDING THE WASTED MESSAGE

Sociologist Harold Lasswell, in the 1940s, defined the act of communication as, "Who says what, in which channel, to whom, with what effect." The process is shown graphically in Figure 9.2.

Although in public relations much emphasis is given to the formation and dissemination of messages, all this effort is wasted if the message has no effect on the intended audience. It is therefore important for a student of public relations to understand fully the axiom of Walt Seifert, professor of public relations at Ohio State University. He says, "Dissemination does not equal publication, and publication does not equal absorption and action." In other words, "All who receive it won't publish it, and all who read or hear it won't understand or act upon it."

Seifert, as well as social psychologists, recognizes that the majority of the audience—at any given time—is passive and not particularly interested in the message or in adopting the idea. Polling specialist Elmo Roper, in his analysis of how messages are received, says that only 5 to 10 percent of the population is "politically active." Others are politically "inert," adopting ideas only after opinion leaders (the politically active) have evaluated and adopted them.

Roper's hypothesis is a variation of sociologist Paul Lazarsfeld's two-step flow theory of communication. He postulated that people rely on interpersonal communication with friends and opinion leaders in making decisions or adopting new ideas. Messages in the mass media, therefore, have limited influence in changing attitudes or opinions. The two-step flow idea is discussed more fully in Chapter 11.

HOW NEW IDEAS AND PRODUCTS ARE ADOPTED

What all this research suggests, of course, is the concept that ideas (and their adoption) penetrate the public very slowly. A public relations person may disseminate messages efficiently, but the effect on the intended audience is dependent upon other processes at work.

THE FIVE-STAGE ADOPTION PROCESS   One key process is the way people adopt new ideas or accept new products. The adoption process idea, formulated in the 1930s, suggests five stages:

FIGURE 9.2

Six key elements in transmission of a message are illustrated in this drawing depicting Don Hill's model of congruent communications. (Courtesy of Don Hill, APR, and *Public Relations Journal.*)

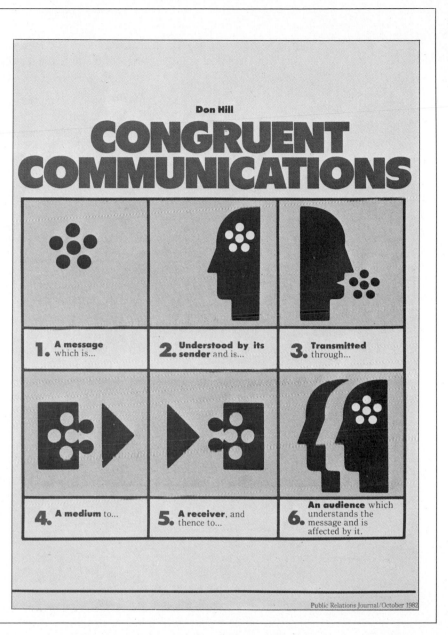

Don Hill

CONGRUENT COMMUNICATIONS

1. A message which is...

2. Understood by its sender and is...

3. Transmitted through...

4. A medium to...

5. A receiver, and thence to...

6. An audience which understands the message and is affected by it.

Public Relations Journal/October 1982

1. *Awareness.* A person becomes aware of an idea or a new product, often by means of an advertisement or a news story.

2. *Interest.* The person seeks more information about the idea or the product, perhaps by ordering a brochure, picking up a pamphlet, or reading an in-depth article in a newspaper or magazine.

3. *Evaluation.* The person evaluates the idea or the product on the basis of how it meets specific needs and wants. Feedback from friends is part of the process.

4. *Trial.* The person tries the product or the idea on an experimental basis, by using a sample, witnessing a demonstration, or making qualifying statements such as, "I read . . ." or "Senator Smith says . . . "

5. *Adoption.* The individual begins to use the product on a regular basis or integrates the idea into his or her belief system. The "Senator Smith says . . . " becomes "I think . . . " if peers provide support and reinforcement of the idea.

It is important to realize that a person does not necessarily go through all five steps in connection with any given idea or product. The process may be terminated after any one of the steps. A person, for example, may become *aware* of a plant open house or a new product by reading a newspaper but, for any number of reasons, may not continue to the *interest* step, in which more information is obtained. Or a person may gather brochures and other in-depth information at the *interest* stage and then decide in the *evaluation* or *trial* stage that the idea or product is not suitable to his or her needs.

THE TIME FACTOR   Another aspect that confuses people is the length of time it takes to adopt a new idea or product. Depending upon the individual, the entire adoption process may take only a few days. On the other hand, when major investments are involved, the adoption process may take months. Research also shows that some people are "early adopters" and others are "late adopters," depending upon personality characteristics and the amount of risk involved. A wealthy farmer, for example, can afford to be more innovative than a farmer with only a small plot of land. Marketing experts, for obvious reasons, spend much time and money attempting to identify "early adopters."

HOW DECISIONS ARE INFLUENCED   Of particular interest to public relations people is the primary source of information at each of the steps in the adoption process. Mass media—radio, television, newspapers, and magazines—are most influential at the preliminary *awareness* and *interest* stages. In other words, a newspaper article or a brochure may begin the process of possible adoption. That is why media publicity or fancy brochures in themselves often have little effect on motivating people to buy a product, accept a new idea, or take a course of action. (Media, however, can reinforce an individual's decision once it is made.)

In most cases, friends and relatives, as well as respected opinion leaders, ultimately determine the effect of a communication message. Evaluation, trial, and adoption steps are dependent upon group norms and opinions that influence and reinforce individual actions. A steelworker, for example, may be highly sold on purchasing a Japanese automobile after reading advertisements and product publicity in car magazines, but the unfavorable reaction of his union friends probably would deter him from buying the car. On the other hand, if everyone on the block has a foreign car, a person is a prime candidate for purchasing one even if he or she thinks American cars are as cheap and just as fuel-efficient.

THE PUBLIC RELATIONS OBJECTIVES

All of this gives perspective on exactly what a public relations person can hope to accomplish. James Grunig, professor of mass communications and public relations at the University of Maryland, has organized a typology of possible objectives for an information campaign. They are the following:

1. *Message exposure.* Public relations personnel provide materials to the mass media and disseminate other messages through controlled media such as newsletters and brochures. Intended audiences are exposed to the message in various forms.

2. *Accurate dissemination of the message.* The intended audience acknowledges the message and retains all or part of it.

3. *Acceptance of the message.* Based on its view of reality, the audience not only retains the message but accepts it as valid.

4. *Attitude change.* The audience not only believes the message but makes a verbal or mental commitment to change behavior as a result of the message.

5. *Change in overt behavior.* Members of the audience actually change their current behavior or begin a new behavior.

Grunig says that most public relations experts usually aim at the first two objectives—exposure to the message and accurate dissemination. The last three objectives—acceptance of the message, attitude change, and changes in overt behavior—are difficult to accomplish unless the audience is already highly interested and predisposed to accept the message in the first place. The first two objectives are also much easier to evaluate than attitude change.

A professional communicator, says Grunig, can better tailor messages and select appropriate communication channels if he or she understands the mental state of the intended audience. Grunig's model divides the audience into two modes—those who actively seek information and those who passively process information. As might be expected, it is much easier to accomplish communication objectives if the intended audience is actively seeking information. It wants to receive the message and will listen to or read it. The passive information processor, as explained earlier, is not seeking information and generally will do little to understand it.

Philip Lesly, president of the Philip Lesly Company, outlined some guidelines for effective communications. Lesly made his remarks during a lecture, sponsored by the Ball Corporation, at Ball State University. In Lesly's words these guidelines are as follows:

Approaching everything from the viewpoint of the audience's interest—what is on their minds, what is in it for them.

Giving the audience a sense of involvement in the communication process and in what is going on. Get them involved and you get their interest.

Making the subject matter part of the atmosphere the audience lives with— what they talk about, what they hear from others. That means getting the material adopted in their channels of communication.

Communicating with people, not at them. Communication that approaches the audience as a target makes people put their defenses up against it.

Localizing—getting the message conveyed as close to the individual's own milieu as possible.

Using a number of channels of communications, not just one or two. The impact is far greater when it reaches people in a number of different forms.

Maintaining consistency—so what is said on the subject is the same no matter which audience it's directed to or what the context is.

Still, tailor-making each message for the specific audience as much as possible.

Not propagandizing but making sure that you make your point. When a communicator draws conclusions in his [or her] summation of information, it is more effective than depending on the audience to draw its own conclusions.

Maintaining credibility—which is essential for all of these points to be effective.

Grunig goes on to say that the effective communicator will acknowledge the existence of both audiences, and structure messages accordingly. Passive audiences, for example, can be made aware of a message only through brief encounters—with the billboard glanced at on the way to work, the radio announcement heard in the car, the television advertisement broadcast before the show begins, and information available in a doctor's waiting room— in other words, with communication channels that can be utilized while the audience is doing little else.

In addition, passive audiences need messages that have style and creativity. The person must be lured, by photos, illustrations, and catchy slogans, into processing information. Press agentry, the dramatic picture, and even the scantily clad model can make passive audiences aware of the message. The objectives of the communication, therefore, are simply exposure to and accurate dissemination of the message. Changes in attitude or overt behavior rarely occur among passive audiences.

A communicator's approach to audiences actively seeking information may be different. These people are already at the *interest* stage of the adoption process and seek supplemental information. At any given time, of course, the intended audience has passive and active information-seekers in it. It is important, therefore, that multiple messages and a variety of communication channels be used in a full-fledged information campaign.

Two approaches can help the public relations practitioner determine appropriate strategies. First, research into audience attitudes can give insight into the extent of group interest in or apathy toward a new product or idea. Second, more efficient communication can be achieved if the intended audience is segmented as much as possible. If research shows that the audience is passive about the product or idea, the strategy calls for communication tools that include (1) billboards, (2) radio and television announcements, (3) posters, (4) catchy slogans, (5) dramatic pictures, (6) bumper stickers, (7) buttons, and (8) special events that emphasize entertainment. On the other hand, more sophisticated messages should be planned for those who have passed the *awareness* stage and are seeking more information. These tools might include (1) brochures, (2) in-depth newspaper and magazine articles, (3) slide presentations, (4) videotape demonstrations, (5) 30-minute movies, (6) symposiums and conferences, (7) major speeches before key groups, and (8) display booths at trade shows.

This book contains a number of case histories about public relations programs. The reader should note the diverse messages and media used in most of the campaigns to reach both passive and active audiences.

The Process of Communication

Communication among individuals, groups, or organizational entities is a complex process involving a number of variables.

SOURCE CREDIBILITY   One key variable, discussed more fully in Chapter 11, is *source credibility*. Do members of the audience perceive the source as knowledgeable and expert on the subject? Do they perceive the source as honest and objective or just representing a vested interest? Audiences, for example, ascribe lower credibility to an advertisement than to the same information contained in a news article. The perception is that news articles, selected by media gatekeepers, are more credible. Source credibility is the main reason that organizations use respected experts or celebrities as representatives to convey their messages.

**CONTEXT OF
THE MESSAGE**

A second variable is the *context* of the message. It has already been pointed out that action (performance) speaks louder than a stack of news releases. A bank may spend thousands of dollars on a promotion campaign with the slogan, "Your friendly bank—where service and courtesy count," but the effort is wasted if employees are not trained to be friendly and courteous. An industrial firm can position itself as deeply concerned about chemical wastes, but all the executive speeches in the world mean nothing if the company makes headlines after dumping toxic wastes into the local river.

**SYMBOLS, ACRONYMS,
AND SLOGANS**

Clarity and simplicity of message constitute another important variable. This is why symbols, acronyms, and slogans are used in public relations campaigns. Each is a form of shorthand that quickly conceptualizes ideas and travels through extended lines of communication.

The world is full of symbols, such as the Christian cross, the star of David, and the crusading sword of the American Cancer Society. Corporate symbols such as the Mercedes Benz star, the General Electric logo, the Chase Manhattan octagon, and the multicolored apple of Apple Computer are known throughout the world. Figure 9.3 shows the symbol devised for AT&T to help publicize its new corporate status after divestiture. On a national level, one of the most successful symbols ever used by the U.S. government is Smokey the Bear, who has reminded several generations of Americans about the danger of forest fires. In fact, Smokey's message was so successful that the U.S. Forest Service caused a public uproar when it began a policy of controlled burning.

FIGURE 9.3

The breakup of AT&T, in which the operating divisions were separated from other parts of the company, led to creation of this new symbol. Strong publicity efforts soon made it familiar to Americans nationwide. (Printed by permission of AT&T.)

A symbol should be unique, memorable, widely recognized, and appropriate. Organizations spend millions annually on searching for unique symbols that convey the essence of what they are or hope to be. Additional millions are spent on publicizing the symbols and creating meaning for them. The Mercedes star means nothing without the context of a reputation for precision engineering, fine craftsmanship, and expensive automobiles. The Mercedes symbol is a graphic, simple way of saying all this.

Acronyms also are shorthand for conveying information. An acronym is a word formed from the initial letters of other words. The Group Against Smoking Pollution goes by the acronym GASP. Juvenile Opportunities in Business become JOB. The National Organization for Women has the acronym NOW, which says a great deal about its political priorities. The Agency for International Development has an acronym for what it does—AID.

In many cases, the acronym—because it is short and simple—becomes the common name of the organization. Thus, the mass media continually use the term *NATO* instead of *North Atlantic Treaty Organization*. *FTC* and *SEC* are used instead of *Federal Trade Commission* and *Securities and Exchange Commission*. And *UNESCO* is easier to write and say than *United Nations Educational, Scientific and Cultural Organization*. *SWAT* is less cumbersome than *special weapons and tactics team*.

Public relations personnel, when involved in naming an organization, committee, or special event, should consider a title that provides a good acronym, especially if the official name is quite long. The acronym may succinctly convey what the organization does (such as *AID*), or it may simply be easy to say and memorable (such as *NATO*). Unfortunately, Richard Nixon did not think about acronyms when the Committee to Re-Elect the President was formed and the press immediately gave it the acronym of *CREEP*.

Slogans have been part of the American scene since "No Taxation Without Representation" and "Don't Tread on Me" were used during the American Revolution.

Slogans, like symbols or acronyms, also convey considerable information in short, memorable terms. They are easy to comprehend and suggest a number of meanings perceived by audiences according to basic needs and wants. Many slogans derive their meaning from the context of events. This is shown, for example, in slogans used during recent presidential elections:

1964   "A Great Society" (Lyndon Johnson)

1968   "Bring Us Together" (Richard Nixon)

1972   "Re-Elect the President" (Richard Nixon)

1976   "Leadership—For a Change" (Jimmy Carter)

1980   "Together—A New Beginning" (Ronald Reagan)

Public relations practitioners, of course, should not overlook color as an aid to communication effectiveness. Psychologists say that bold colors indicate strength: for instance, red is exciting and sensual. Blue can be icy and unfriendly, while green can suggest nature and even a "go-ahead" approach. Pastels and earth tones—ivory, tan, buff, orange, yellow—are good because they are "friendly," warm, and nonthreatening.

Although much has been written about the psychology of color to enhance a message, the main point is the appropriate use of color for the intended audience. In the United States, for example, a brochure for business executives is rarely printed in pink, purple, or red. Use of white on black, or of earth tones, is more neutral and acceptable. On the other hand, a brochure in red and yellow is appropriate in Hong Kong, where the Chinese value the colors for luck and success.

Writing for Clarity

A communicator should pretest messages on the intended audience. Do members of this audience understand what is being said? Do they have difficulty with word meanings? Can simple, one-syllable words be substituted for multisyllable ones? Are the writing level and sentence structure appropriate to the audience's educational level? These questions need answering, and they often are not, when experts within an organization write, approve, and send messages without considering the target audience.

AVOIDING JARGON One source of blocked communication is technical and bureaucratic jargon. Thus, the vice-president of engineering may understand perfectly a product news release that means nothing to the general public. A good example of a useless news release actually sent to business editors of daily newspapers is one that began with the following lead sentence:

Versatec, a Xerox Company, has introduced the Graphics Network Processor—SNA (Model 451). The processor, operating as a 377x RJE station, sends and receives EBCDIC or binary data in IBM System Network Architecture (SNA) networks using Synchronous Data Link Control (SDLC) protocol. . . .

Given this approach to communication, it is no wonder that media gatekeepers bitterly complain about the poorly written, jargon-ridden news releases that often blanket their desks in a single day. The major problem seems to be that public relations personnel in too many organizations have abdicated their responsibility to make sure that messages are clear, simply stated, and devoid of jargon.

To the general audience, jargon, pure and simple, is what social scientists call *semantic noise*. It interferes with the message and impedes the receiver's ability to comprehend it. The study of words, and how they are used and interpreted, is called *semantics*.

Company executives talk about "interfacing" with someone when they really mean "talking." Transit officials talk about "fare modifications" when they mean a fare increase. Educators talk about a child as having "motivational deprivation" when they think a student is lazy. The military talks about a "violence source" when it means a weapon.

FITTING THE LANGUAGE TO THE AUDIENCE

Public relations personnel should be on the alert for more than occupational and bureaucratic words. Words used by college-educated people are often quite different from those used by people with less education. One study, for example, suggested that the following words should be avoided when the primary audience consists of people with no more than a high school education. The left column shows the unacceptable word and the right column an appropriate substitute or substitutes.

accrue—pile up, collect

delete—cancel, remove

increment—raise, increase

generate—create, build, produce

jeopardy—danger

designate—name, appoint, select

inadequate—not enough

compensation—salary, wages

The advice, in other words, is: don't use a 25-cent word when a 5-cent word will do.

An institutional advertisement for United Technologies Corporation as a statement on clarity in writing appears in Figure 9.4.

UNDERSTANDING THE MEANINGS OF WORDS

The other aspect of semantic noise is the meaning of words. Words have *denotative* meanings—generally accepted dictionary definitions—and *connotative* meanings—what the word means to an individual or a group. A good example is the word *scheme*. The denotative definition is "a plan of work or action." The connotative definition, to most Americans, is something that is underhanded and dishonest. It is acceptable to have a "scheme" in England but it is better to have a "program" in the United States.

Keep It Simple

Strike three.
Get your hand off my knee.
You're overdrawn.
Your horse won.
Yes.
No.
You have the account.
Walk.
Don't walk.
Mother's dead.
Basic events
require simple language.
Idiosyncratically euphuistic
eccentricities are the
promulgators of
triturable obfuscation.
What did you do last night?
Enter into a meaningful
romantic involvement
or
fall in love?
What did you have for
breakfast this morning?
The upper part of a hog's
hind leg with two oval
bodies encased in a shell
laid by a female bird
or
ham and eggs?
David Belasco, the great
American theatrical producer,
once said, "If you can't
write your idea on the
back of my calling
card,
you don't have a clear idea."

Many other words have strong negative connotations for the majority of Americans. They include "socialist," "communist," "propaganda," and "terrorist." Of course, the difference between a "terrorist" and a "freedom fighter" depends on which side the person using the term supports. In Central America, for example, President Reagan called the Contra insurgents in Nicaragua freedom fighters comparable to the founding fathers of the United States, while supporters of the Nicaraguan government denounced them as terrorist rebels.

Public relations personnel should thoroughly understand connotations to make sure that favorable words are used to convey the intended message. At the same time, practitioners have an obligation to communicate with honesty and integrity. Using euphemistic words to hide information and mislead people is unacceptable ethical behavior.

A study conducted at Yale University has pinpointed words that seem to have the most persuasive power with an audience. They are the following:

Save	*Easy*
Money	*Safety*
You	*Love*
New	*Discovery*
Health	*Proven*
Results	*Guarantee*

AVOIDING DISCRIMINATORY LANGUAGE

In today's world, effective communication also means *nondiscriminatory* communication. Public relations personnel should double-check every message to eliminate sexual, racial, and ethnic connotations.

In regard to sex, it is unnecessary to write about something as being *manmade* when a word such as *synthetic* or *artificial* is just as good. Companies no longer have *manpower* but *employees* or *workers.* Airlines have *flight attendants* instead of *stewardesses,* even if all are women.

Writers also should be careful about descriptive phrases for women. A female executive doesn't like to be described as "trim and petite with flowing blonde hair" because her physical appearance has nothing to do with her professional responsibilities. Nor is it appropriate in professional settings to say that a woman is the wife of someone who is also well known. A female vice-president of a public relations firm in San Francisco, for example, cried foul when a local newsletter described her as the wife of a prominent local journalist. The newsletter editor, in a subsequent issue, apologized.

Messages should avoid any ethnic designations. It is unacceptable to say, "Juan Hernandez, an Hispanic, is employed. . . ." Persons using any racial reference should always ask whether the same sentence would sound awkward if the word *white* or *Anglo-Saxon* were substituted for *black, Hispanic, Asian,* and so on. (Chapter 13 discusses the possible legal consequences of racial slurs.) Ethnic designation was a complaint of Jesse Jackson when he was a presidential hopeful in the 1984 Democratic primaries. The media kept referring to him as the black candidate, but did not refer to Walter Mondale or Gary Hart as the white candidates. English usage experts are still arguing about the use of *Ms.* or *Mrs.* with Geraldine Ferraro, the vice-presidential nominee.

It is also unacceptable to have hidden stereotypes. Writing that "Juan Hernandez is an energetic and conscientious worker . . ." may imply that Hispanics usually are lazy and unmotivated.

Barriers to Communication

Despite the communicator's best efforts, a number of barriers may impede effective communication. A major obstacle is that no message is received in its pure form. The receiver may magnify, modify, misinterpret, or even ignore it. This is called *self-selection* and *self-perception*. As previously discussed, each person interprets messages through a complex array of social structures and belief systems.

Barriers also exist because the sender and the receiver, as discussed earlier, lack common backgrounds and shared levels of experience. This may include the following:

Divergent backgrounds of participants

Differences in education

Differences in interest about the message

Differences in intelligence level

Lack of mutual respect

Differences in age, sex, race, and class

Differences in language skills

Lack of skill on the part of the communicator

Lack of skill on the part of the listener

Lack of background information

Messages also undergo distortion as they are sent through long lines of communication. Paul Lazarsfeld, for example, says that a message undergoes sharpening and leveling as it is received, interpreted, summarized, and passed on to others. Other social scientists call this *message entropy*—a natural tendency for a message to dissipate (lose information) as it is disseminated.

A two-page news release often is published only as a one-paragraph story in the local daily. A complex social issue, because of perceived audience interest and media space requirements, is often portrayed in simplistic terms without any of the nuances that made it a complex issue in the first place.

George Gallup, the social scientist and pollster previously mentioned,

<table>
<tr><td>The Decline
of Message
Understanding</td><td>Messages tend to disintegrate as they pass through various levels of an organizational structure. E. Scannell, author of *Communication for Leadership* (McGraw-Hill, 1970), developed the following chart. It shows, in numerical terms, how much of the original message remains as it travels down the corporate hierarchy:</td></tr>
</table>

100 percent	Top management's understanding
66 percent	Vice-president's understanding
56 percent	General supervisor's understanding
40 percent	Plant manager's understanding
30 percent	Foreman's understanding
20 percent	Production line worker's understanding

Message entropy, coupled with various barriers to effective communication, is a problem that every professional communicator must overcome.

has compiled a list of seven regulators that, he says, restrict the absorption of new information and ideas. They are as follows:

1. *Complexity of the idea.* The more complex the idea, the less likely people will be to understand it and take action. Bankers, for example, say that the regulations for opening Individual Retirement Accounts (IRAs) are so complex that many Americans are not taking advantage of them.

2. *Difference from accustomed patterns.* People do not accept new ideas or products if they are radically different from what they know. Cable television companies are finding penetration of the market much slower than originally projected because, among other reasons, people are not accustomed to the idea of paying for television programming.

3. *Competition with prevailing ideas.* New ideas must compete in the marketplace with already accepted ideas. Tobacco companies have slowed the enactment of antismoking laws by capitalizing on the prevailing idea that such laws restrict individual freedom and generate more government bureaucracy.

4. *Necessity for demonstration and proof.* Ideas are more readily accepted if they can be demonstrated and proved. Achieving public support for additional taxes to fund local schools is difficult because it cannot be clearly demonstrated that the quality of teaching and learning would correspondingly improve.

5. *Strength of vested interests.* Vested interests may be strong enough to block innovative concepts. Unions, for example, have been highly successful in forestalling the use of robots in manufacturing plants. Millions of hunters and sportspeople effectively prevent major gun control legislation.

6. *Failure to meet a felt need.* President Reagan had trouble getting congressional support for his Central America policies because Congress was not enthusiastic about a "Vietnam style" of involvement.

7. *Frequency of reminders.* An idea or a product succeeds only if the public is constantly reminded of it. Advertising and public relations campaigns for a new product may cost millions of dollars and continue over a period of months. The Coca-Cola Company spent $12 million in six months to introduce Diet Coke.

A Checklist

The professional communicator considers a host of variables when planning a message on behalf of an employer or client.

Patrick Jackson, editor of *PR Reporter* and past national president of the Public Relations Society of America, says communicators should ask the following:

1. Is the communication appropriate?

    a. For the sender?

    b. For the recipient?

2. Is it meaningful?

    a. Does it stick to the subject?

    b. Is it geared to the recipient's interest, not the sender's?

3. Is it memorable?

    a. In phraseology or metaphor?

    b. Through the use of visual or aural devices?

4. Is it understandable?

    a. In both denotative and connotative language?

    b. Graphically or aurally?

5. Is it believable?

    a. Does the audience trust the spokesperson?

    b. Does the communication exhibit expertise in the subject matter?

"Many a wrongly directed or unnecessary communication has been corrected or dropped by using a screen like this," Jackson says. And after all, that is what effective communication is all about.

QUESTIONS
FOR REVIEW
AND DISCUSSION

1. Why is interpersonal communication the most effective form of communication?

2. Name some reasons why public relations personnel should use a variety of communication vehicles to reach an intended audience.

3. Name and describe the five stages of the process by which new ideas are adopted or new products accepted.

4. What is the role of the mass media in the adoption process? the role of friends and peer groups?

5. What communication methods would you use to reach passive audiences? active information-seeking audiences?

6. What makes a good symbol? a good slogan?

7. What is the difference between denotative and connotative word meanings?

8. What guidelines are suggested to avoid discriminatory communication and stereotyping?

9. Name six barriers to effective communication.

10. George Gallup says there are seven regulators that inhibit the absorption of new ideas. Name and describe them.

CHAPTER TEN

Evaluation

The final step in the public relations process is evaluation. It is the measurement of results against the established objectives set during the planning process discussed in Chapter 8.

Evaluation is well described by Frank W. Wylie, director of public affairs for California State University at Los Angeles and former president of the Public Relations Society of America. He wrote:

We are talking about an orderly evaluation of our progress in attaining the specific objectives of our public relations plan. We are learning what we did right, what we did wrong, how much progress we've made and, most importantly, how can we do it better next time.

The desire to do a better job next time is a major reason for evaluating public relations efforts, but another equally important reason is the widespread adoption of the management by objectives system by clients and employers of public relations personnel. They want to know if the money, time, and effort expended on public relations are well spent and contribute to the realization of organizational objectives—whether it is attendance at an open house, product sales, or increased public awareness of the organization's contributions to the local community.

The chapter examines the most widely used methods for evaluating a public relations campaign, including measurement of message exposure, message accuracy, audience acceptance, attitude change, and audience action. The merits and shortcomings of the techniques are discussed, to provide students with a means of determining the usefulness of a particular approach. The text stresses the fact that sheer numbers of press clippings, for example, do not necessarily indicate how well a message is getting across to the audience. Because the ultimate objective of any campaign is to create a particular response among readers and viewers, the most meaningful evaluation is measurement of audience action.

Objectives: A Prerequisite for Evaluation

Before any public relations program can be properly evaluated, it is important first to have a clearly established set of objectives. This should be part of the program plan, as discussed in Chapter 8, but some points need reviewing because, as Frank Wylie wrote, " . . . [I]t is relatively impractical to attempt to evaluate a program which has neither established goals or objectives."

Ketchum Public Relations, in a monograph on public relations programming, points out that a public relations person and management should jointly agree on the criteria that will be used to evaluate the success of attaining objectives. The criteria should be as follows:

1. Realistic (achievable)

2. Credible (the achievement was the result of public relations activity)

3. Specific (avoidance of vague promises)

4. Acceptable (in line with the client's expectations regarding public relations)

Objectives and evaluation criteria must be compatible. If an objective is *informational* such as, "Generate awareness of . . . ," "Enhance image of . . . ," "Educate consumers about . . . ," and "Inform audience that . . . ," measurement techniques must show how successfully information was communicated to target audiences. Such techniques go under the rubric of "dissemination of message," but they do not measure the effect on attitudes or overt behavior.

On the other hand, *motivational* objectives such as, "Increase sales of . . . ," "Stimulate trial of . . . ," "Increase attendance at . . . ," and "Change attitudes about . . ." are more difficult to accomplish. For example, if the objective is to increase sales, it is important to show that public relations efforts caused the increase rather than advertising, lower competitive prices, or other variables. Or, if the objective is to change attitudes, it is important that research be done both before and after the public relations activity, to measure differences in attitude.

In any event, a practitioner should carefully set up objectives in the program plan that can be measured in some way to evaluate the success of public relations activity. The Ketchum Public Relations monograph simply states: "Write the most precise, most results-oriented objectives you can that are realistic, credible, measurable, and compatible with the client's demands on public relations."

Obstacles to Measurement and Evaluation

A national sampling of public relations practitioners by Professor Mark McElreath of George Washington University indicated that no more than half of today's practitioners formally evaluate their public relations activities on a regular basis.

McElreath, however, did find considerable informal evaluation by practitioners, the "seat-of-the-pants" approach described by Professor David Dozier of San Diego State University in a similar research study.

Dozier found that many practitioners:

Prepared communications by drawing upon their own professional experience—instead of testing preliminary message strategies and formats on focus groups drawn from the publics involved, or by reviewing relevant public opinion surveys.

Monitored dissemination of messages through their close personal contacts among mass media professionals—instead of formal ongoing content analysis of items in the clipping file.

Checked impact by keeping eyes and ears open to the reactions obtained through personal and public contacts—instead of counting or tabulating public comments that came in by letter or phone, or through surveys of scientifically selected cross sections of major publics.

Other research studies have cited various reasons for the lack of systematic evaluation. They include the following:

1. Lack of expertise by public relations practitioners not trained in social science research methods

2. The time required for systematic research and evaluation

3. The hesitation of public relations practitioners and even management to spend money evaluating completed programs when such funds could be used for current or future public relations activity

Proponents of systematic evaluation, of course, find these reasons somewhat less than convincing. First, they say that not all systematic evaluation need be done by a person thoroughly skilled in research methods. Many techniques are relatively easy to incorporate in any ongoing evaluation of public relations efforts. The argument is also advanced that, unless a public relations practitioner is able to give top management credible evidence of accomplishing objectives, he or she is destined to occupy a low-level position at that organization. And finally, with the introduction of public relations courses at the university level, most graduates today have learned social science measurement methods.

It is true that systematic evaluation, particularly of attitude changes among target audiences, does take considerable time—but there are less exacting methods that can be incorporated into the time constraints.

As for the argument that evaluation takes money away from current or future public relations programs, it is pointed out that a primary purpose of evaluation is to provide feedback that can be used in planning more cost-efficient programs for the future. Frank Wylie wrote: "While it is true that evaluation measures what is happening and what has happened, its purpose is to study what was done so that it can and will be done better next time. That is where the cost saving comes in."

There really is no good reason, then, for evaluations not to be done. A variety of evaluation techniques exists if the practitioner is willing to use them. The following checklist contains the most important evaluating questions the practitioner should ask:

1. Was the activity or program adequately planned?

2. Did recipients of the message understand it?

3. How could the program strategy have been more effective?

4. Were all primary and secondary audiences reached?

5. Was the desired publicity achieved?

6. What unforeseen circumstances affected the success of the program or activity?

7. Did the program or activity fall within the budget set for it?

8. What steps can be taken to improve the success of similar future activities?

Measurement of Production

One elementary form of evaluation is simply to count how many news releases, feature stories, photos, letters, and the like are produced in a given period of time.

This kind of evaluation is supposed to give management an idea of a staff's productivity. Public relations professionals, however, do not believe that this evaluation is very meaningful because it emphasizes quantity instead of quality. It may be more cost-effective to write fewer news releases and spend more time on the few that really are newsworthy. It may, for example, be more important for a staff person to spend five weeks working on an article for the *Wall Street Journal* or *Fortune* than to write 29 routine personnel releases.

Another side of the production approach is to specify what the public relations person should accomplish in obtaining media coverage. One state trade association evaluated its director of media relations on the expectation that (1) four feature stories would be run in any of the 11 largest newspapers in the state and (2) news releases would be used by at least 20 newspapers, including 5 or more among the 50 largest.

Such evaluation criteria not only are unrealistic but almost impossible to guarantee because media gatekeepers—not the public relations person—make such decisions. The approach also violates the code of ethics of the Public Relations Society of America, which states, "A member shall not guarantee the achievement of specified results beyond the member's direct control."

Measurement of Distribution

Closely allied to the production of publicity materials is their distribution. Thus a public relations department might report, for instance, that a total of 756 news releases were sent to 819 daily newspapers, 250 weeklies, and 137 trade magazines within one year, or that 110,000 copies of the annual report were distributed to stockholders, security analysts, and business editors. Although such figures may be useful in evaluating how widely a particular piece of publicity was distributed, they do not answer the question of readership or, more important, of attitude change.

Measurement of Message Exposure

The most common way of evaluating coverage is to collect press clippings. Small public relations departments, which provide materials only to local media outlets, often have a secretary or clerk clip published articles regularly. Large companies with regional, national, or even international outreach usually hire one or more clipping services that scan large numbers of publications for mentions of the company.

The purpose of systematically gathering press clippings is to learn if news releases, background kits, and photographs have been used by the media. By so doing, it is common for a public relations department to compile a large scrapbook of clippings that, in the words of one practitioner, "show the results of my publicity efforts." Public relations people often circulate clippings on a weekly or monthly basis to top executives so management knows what is being said about the company.

Radio and television mentions of the company can also be compiled, but less reliably. Because of the fleeting nature of the audio or visual signal, the coverage must be monitored at the time it occurs. This is easy to do when a company knows in advance that a representative will appear on a local television or radio talk show or even on a national media tour. Again, as with press clipping services, professional monitoring firms can be hired to provide videotapes or transcripts of what was said on those occasions.

Compilation of press clippings and broadcast mentions, however, has its critics. Although the 7-inch-high scrapbook may look impressive, many skeptics say it measures only the acceptability of the organization's news releases to media gatekeepers. Press clippings do not indicate how many people actually read the stories and, more important, how many people absorbed or acted on the information.

GROSS IMPRESSIONS   One way to determine the number of people who may have been exposed to a message is to calculate gross impressions—that is, to compile statistics on the potential audience reached by a periodical or by a broadcast program.

If, for example, a story about the company appears in the local daily with a circulation of 130,000, the gross impressions figure is 130,000. By compiling the total circulation of all periodicals that used the news release (one paragraph or more), a public relations person may report to management that the company's message reached an audience of, say, 69 million people.

The same approach is done for mentions on radio and television stations. A report to management by the public relations department might be designed in the following manner:

RADIO	PLACEMENTS		GROSS IMPRESSIONS		TOTAL GROSS IMPRESSIONS
KGO-AM	6	×	109,000	=	654,000
KCBS-AM	1	×	60,000	=	60,000
KYA	2	×	30,000	=	60,000
KMEL-FM	10	×	35,000	=	350,000
Total Gross Impressions					1,124,000

Gross impressions tabulations commonly are used in advertising to illustrate the penetration of a particular message. The number of gross impressions, however, shows only that the company's message appeared in 130,000 copies of the newspaper, or that a radio announcement potentially reached 109,000 people. It is unlikely that all 130,000 readers of the newspaper or 109,000 listeners actually received the message.

DOLLAR VALUE   The numbers game is also played by converting publicity stories in the regular news columns or on the air into equivalent advertising costs. For example, if a 5-inch article about the company appeared in a publication that charges $100 per column inch for advertising, a public relations person might report to management that the article was worth $500 to the company. Indeed, one major electronics firm estimated that it had received $158,644 worth of exposure in a single year because of press mentions about the company and its products. In another example, a Creighton University professor was given a grant by the National Collegiate Athletic Association to estimate the financial benefit colleges get from newspaper coverage of their sports programs. The professor's methodology was to count the column inches of newspaper space devoted to the athletic teams of 15 universities. He then multiplied the total by the price charged advertisers per column inch. During one 4-month period, the researcher estimated the universities received publicity worth $2.46 million.

Converting space in newspaper columns or time on television talk shows to equivalent advertising rates, many public relations people say, quickly shows marketing executives and budget-conscious top management that publicity efforts are well worth the time and investment. After all, the coverage received has given the company "free advertising" that can be easily quantified in dollars.

This may be true, but converting news mentions to comparable advertising space is a bit like comparing apples and oranges. Advertising copy is directly controlled by the company or institution and can be oriented to specific objectives. News mentions, on the other hand, are determined by media gatekeepers and can be negative, neutral, or favorable.

Atari Corporation, for example, got a great deal of negative publicity when it fired 1700 employees without advance notice. It would be difficult to justify the statement that the company received comparable advertising space worth $100,000 from this kind of publicity. Or, in the case of a university, the press accounts of how a football team lost a crucial game would not likely be worth "thousands of dollars" to the university no matter what comparable advertising per column inch cost in the various publications. Thus, simply converting news space to advertising value makes no distinction among negative, neutral, and favorable publicity.

Another problem of measuring publicity by dollar value is deciding what exactly to include. Should an entire 15-inch story be counted if the company's name were mentioned only once along with those of six other firms? How can the cover of *Fortune* or *Time* be measured, since it is impossible to purchase the cover of these magazines?

On the other hand, there is an argument that a news story is worth more than a comparable advertisement. James B. Strenski notes, in *Public Relations Quarterly:*

This value equivalency rate for the publicity is actually a conservative figure. It reflects only the cost of the space or air-time. It has no direct one-to-one relationship with the actual value or exposure. It could easily be argued, for example, that the value of the publicity exposure is, in fact, far greater than the equivalent advertising value due to the higher credibility inherent in news and feature exposure.

An advertising executive, David Ogilvy, supports this contention. In his book *Ogilvy on Advertising,* he writes: "Roughly six times as many people read the average article as the average ad. Very few ads are read by more than one reader in ten."

This kind of argument, that news stories are more credible than advertisements, has led some public relations people to stretch further a suspect technique by factoring in a credibility index. If, for example, the newspaper article were worth $500 in comparable advertising space, then this amount should be multiplied by Ogilvy's "six times as many people read . . ." to get a value of $3000 for the article.

Such manipulation of figures is considered unprofessional by most public relations people, who believe there are more valid ways to evaluate public relations activity. Evaluation of effects, not exposure, will be discussed later in the chapter.

One final note: the equating of publicity with advertising rates for comparable space does not engender good media relations. The technique reinforces the opinion of many media gatekeepers that all news releases are just attempts to get "free advertising."

COST PER PERSON

Another way to evaluate exposure to the message is to find out how much it costs to reach each member of the audience.

The technique is commonly used in advertising in order to place costs in perspective. Although a 30-second commercial during a Super Bowl football game telecast may cost $525,000, advertisers feel it is well worth the price because an audience of more than 100 million people is reached. The advertiser has communicated a message to an audience for approximately a half-cent each—a relatively good bargain even if several million viewers take the opportunity to visit the refrigerator while the commercial is playing.

Cost effectiveness, as this technique is known, is used widely in public relations to evaluate collateral materials such as films, brochures, and newsletters. A film produced by Ford Motor Company, for example, may cost $50,000 but may reach 150,000 school children during its distribution period. It thus costs Ford 33 cents to reach each child. Cost effectiveness, of course, is increased if the film is shown to additional children.

Determining the cost effectiveness of public relations materials is very important, and it can help professionals control the price of message exposure. A division of a large corporation had only 500 employees but the monthly magazine cost $3500 to produce and distribute—at $7 per employee. The division quickly decided on a newspaper format that cost only $1 per employee to produce and distribute.

SYSTEMATIC TRACKING

As noted earlier, press clippings are often measured by sheer bulk. A more systematic analysis, however, can determine (1) exactly which news releases are most utilized by which periodicals and (2) whether releases are being used by the news media in key market areas.

A content analysis may show that 40 percent of a company's news releases consists of management and personnel stories, but that these releases account for only 5 percent of the stories published about the company. In contrast, stories about new product developments may constitute only 10 percent of the news releases but amount to 70 percent of potential press and broadcast coverage. Given these data, public relations personnel likely will decide to send out fewer personnel stories and more product development articles.

A systematic tracking system also can show which publications and broadcast media are using a company's news releases. This knowledge can be important in two ways.

First, a company's mailing list may include 300 periodicals, but it is learned that only half of these publications have a record of using company-provided material. It would thus be wise to save money by culling the mailing list. Ampex Corporation did such a systematic tracking and found that it could reduce its mailing list from 447 publications to 358.

Second, a company's news releases may not be penetrating its key markets. For cost effectiveness and even for product sales, it is more important that media in large urban areas use company publicity materials than that weekly newspapers in rural areas do so—unless, of course, the company is a farm equipment manufacturer.

PR Data Systems of Wilton, Connecticut, a pioneer in computer analysis of press clippings, can tell a company if the media in key urban markets are being reached effectively. Ketchum Public Relations, with headquarters in Pittsburgh, has also developed a computer tracking model that analyzes the amount of media exposure a company gets in the top 120 markets in the country and even computes a publicity value index, assessing the worth of the publicity. Such a computer profile shows a company whether its news releases are being published in prime market areas. If not, the public relations strategy needs restructuring.

A good example of how systematic tracking helped a company restructure its public relations efforts is the experience of Ampex Corporation. The public relations staff analyzed press clippings for a year and made the following recommendations to management:

1. Divisions should be discouraged from sending out releases about relatively small contracts obtained, because the media do not show much interest in such stories.

2. For new products, press conferences do not guarantee as much publicity as pre–trade show publicity.

3. There is slight media interest in stories about personnel promotions at the group manager or regional sales manager levels. In the interest of economy and effectiveness, such stories should be discouraged.

4. Because the company's second largest division is not getting its share of the firm's product publicity (only 17.5 percent), more news releases should be distributed about this division.

5. Media interviews with Ampex executives are given good coverage, so executives should be available for additional interviews.

COUPONS AND REQUESTS

Exposure to the message can also be determined by tabulating the number of letters or phone calls requesting more information. Many trade and specialized magazines have cards on which readers can request more information about a specific product by circling a number. If the information is disseminated in a newsletter or brochure, a self-addressed postcard often is enclosed so that more information may be requested.

A story in a newspaper frequently carries the name and address of the company so readers may request more information. This is often done in the travel and food sections of a newspaper. On broadcast media a product representative may give a demonstration and then tell listeners or viewers how they may receive a book of recipes or other information. The California Prune Board, for example, got 7000 requests for a booklet on exercise and nutrition after its representative appeared on a number of television shows.

Many companies also use toll-free 800 telephone numbers to measure message exposure. Logging and monitoring calls can show areas of the country that received the greatest message exposure, as well as what types of media have been most effective in communicating the information.

AUDIENCE ATTENDANCE

Attendance at a meeting is a relatively simple way of evaluating the number of people exposed to a message. Attendance figures also say something about the effectiveness of premeeting publicity.

Poor attendance at a meeting likely indicates that major exposure to the speaker's anticipated message has not been accomplished. Should the media cover the speech, however, exposure of the message is considerably enhanced; that is why public relations personnel work hard to get media coverage.

PILOT TESTS AND SPLIT MESSAGES

Evaluation is important even before a public relations effort is launched. If exposure to a message is to be maximized, it is wise to pretest it with a sample group from the targeted audience. Do its members easily understand the message? Do they accept the message? Does the message motivate them to adopt a new idea or product?

A variation of pretesting is the *pilot* test. Before going national with a public relations message, companies often test the message and key copy points in selected cities to learn how the media accept the message and how the public reacts. This approach is quite common in product marketing because it limits the costs and enables the company to revamp or fine-tune the message for maximum exposure. It also allows the company to switch channels of dissemination if original media channels are not exposing the message to the proper audiences.

The *split-message* approach is common in direct mail publicity campaigns. Two or three different appeals may be prepared by a charitable organization and sent to different audiences. The response rate is then monitored (perhaps the amount of donations is totaled) to learn what message and graphics seemed to be the most effective.

Measurement of Message Accuracy

The computer analysis of press clippings, which many large public relations firms and corporations now do routinely, is a valuable way to make sure that key copy points are being included in published stories or broadcast items. A company may wish to emphasize in all its publicity materials that it manufactures high-quality kitchen appliances and is a well-established firm with the largest share of the market. Analysis may show that 70 percent of the media stories mention the high quality of the products but that only 20 percent mention or give the impression that the company has the largest share of the market. This kind of evaluation helps the company restructure its news releases so the percentage of the market is given more emphasis.

IMPORTANCE OF OBJECTIVES

One way to determine whether the media are conveying the key copy points accurately is to measure how well the message supports the organization's objectives. If the objective of an organization is to raise $50,000 for charitable purposes, raise sales by 25 percent, get a political candidate elected, or change the attitudes of Americans about oil companies, effective evaluation must be based on achievement of these goals.

Ketchum Public Relations, for example, won a Silver Anvil award from the Public Relations Society of America by showing that its extensive publicity campaign for the California Prune Board resulted in a sales gain of 4 percent for the year (with no advertising involved) after more than five years of declining sales.

Ketchum's objective was to increase prune sales. The strategy was to generate positive awareness among women, from 25 to 49 years of age, through a campaign with the theme "Prunes . . . Just Plum Good." By using a credible representative and introducing prunes as a health snack food, Ketchum attained its objective by making sure that its publicity and key copy points were accurately disseminated by the media.

FIGURE 10.1

Techniques of computer-assisted telephone interviewing are explained to interviewers by Peter Finn, chairman of Research & Forecasts. (Courtesy of Research & Forecasts.)

AUDIENCE SURVEYS   The other approach to determining the accuracy of the message is to ascertain the knowledge base of potential audiences. This can be done in a variety of ways, and Chapter 7 has outlined such methods as focus groups, random personal or telephone interviews, and the more formalized use of a written questionnaire (see Figure 10.1).

The objective here is to measure comprehension, not necessarily to learn whether the audience agrees or disagrees with the message or plans to do anything about it. Multiple-choice items on a questionnaire may simply ask the person to match concepts and images with a specific organization. For example, Mobil Oil Company wants to be positioned as a strong supporter of the arts and the Public Broadcasting System. A multiple-choice question may ask:

What company sponsors "Masterpiece Theatre" on Public Television?

A. General Electric

B. Texaco Oil Company

C. Mobil Oil Company

D. Chrysler Corporation

E. Gulf Oil Company

If the majority of respondents select Mobil as the correct answer, the idea is supported that this particular message has been adequately understood.

On occasion, media gatekeepers are surveyed to ascertain their comprehension of what a company does or manufacturers. A multiple-choice question to electronic trade editors might ask:

Which of the following product lines do you associate with Millennium Systems?

A. Portable test instruments

B. Microprocessor development systems

C. Automatic test equipment

D. Microprocessor systems

E. Logic analyzers

F. Don't know

By questioning media gatekeepers or even purchasing agents, the company ascertains whether it is strongly identified with a product. Little recognition means that the company needs to expend more effort on public relations and advertising.

Open-ended questions in a survey or interview can also be used to determine what a person thinks is a company position on a particular issue. Political candidates often do this kind of questioning to learn if voters properly identify the candidates' positions on specific issues. Again, public confusion signals a need for more intensive communication efforts.

Measurement of Audience Acceptance

So far, techniques of measuring audience exposure and accurate dissemination of the message have been discussed. It is important, however, for the public relations person also to know if the target audience has accepted the message. Does the recipient agree with the information?

Audience acceptance of a message concerns the formation of attitudes rather than the acceptance of factual information. A person may easily identify Mobil Oil Company as the sponsor of "Masterpiece Theatre" on public television but may or may not agree that Mobil is a company that practices a high degree of social responsibility—the real message that Mobil wants to communicate through such sponsorship.

Again, surveys or interviews can be used to discover whether audiences agree or disagree with opinion statements. As noted in Chapter 7, the most commonly used is a Likert scale, in which respondents can indicate the extent of their agreement with an opinion statement. For example:

Mobil makes significant contributions to the arts in America and is a socially responsible company.

_____ Strongly agree

_____ Agree

_____ Undecided

_____ Disagree

_____ Strongly disagree

The National Association of Manufacturers (NAM) may conduct a survey after an extensive public relations campaign concentrating on the need for business profits to modernize plants and generate a high level of employment. In order to ascertain the degree of message acceptance, NAM could conduct a survey in which respondents would be asked to agree or disagree with a number of opinion statements. A sample statement to be tested:

Profits of large companies help make things better for everyone.

The answer categories would be the Likert scale of (A) Strongly agree, (B) Agree, (C) Undecided, (D) Disagree, and (E) Strongly disagree. Open-ended questions also can be used, but they are more difficult to quantify. The advantage of the Likert scale is its standardization and ability to record intensity of agreement or disagreement.

Depending on the results of such a survey, NAM may decide that more public relations efforts are needed in order to gain acceptance of its message among the American public. Or, if people do agree with the statement, only reinforcement of the message is needed.

On a more informal basis acceptance of the message can also be determined by noting about what critics of business continue to write or talk, proposed legislation restricting profit levels of companies, the nature of letters to the editor in magazines and newspapers, and the results of national opinion polls conducted by Gallup or Harris.

Measurement of Attitude Change

Public relations efforts designed to change a person's perceptions and opinions are even more difficult to evaluate than determining acceptance of the message.

Coors Evaluates Its
Appearance on CBS-
TV's "60 Minutes"

The Adolph Coors Company used informal and systematic evaluation techniques to assess the impact of a CBS-TV "60 Minutes" program about the company and its labor-related boycott.

The company already had a good idea of its corporate image as a result of a benchmark study conducted several years previously. The result of that survey showed that the company image had slipped. Coors hired a research firm to measure formally the program's impact on beer drinkers in Los Angeles and Denver. The first wave of interviews took place one week before the program's airing, thus providing another benchmark of attitudes. The second wave was taken one week after the broadcast.

The research revealed that one out of five beer drinkers had viewed the program. The change in attitudes among the minority who saw it was large enough to cause a notable shift in the total sample. Surveys disclosed that 90 percent of media gatekeepers in the cities had viewed the program. Both groups expressed belief that the story was positive for Coors. Significantly, the people with some of the strongest anti-Coors feelings six months earlier showed the largest change in attitude.

Coors also made the following evaluations:

1. *Audience exposure.* According to a Nielsen survey, the program received a 25.1 rating (42 share) that equated to 20.8 million households. It was the No. 2-rated show of the week.

2. *Accuracy of message.* A review of the script showed that all message objectives were communicated at least once.

3. *Audience acceptance.* Coors received more than 800 letters expressing viewers' thoughts about the program. Of these, only six were negative.

4. *Change in attitude action.* Many organizations, including Hispanic groups and colleges, as well as gay editors in San Francisco, lifted their boycotts as a result of the broadcast, and pro-Coors editorials appeared in several newspapers.

The research conducted by Coors to prepare for the "60 Minutes" interview is discussed in Chapter 7.

A major technique to determine attitude change is the *benchmark study.* Basically, it is a measurement of audience attitudes before and after a public relations campaign. This kind of study graphically shows the percentage difference in attitudes as a result of increased information and publicity. There are, of course, a number of possible intervening variables that may account for changes in attitude, but statistical analysis of variance can help pinpoint to what degree the attitude change is attributable to public relations efforts.

U.S. Steel some years ago did a benchmark study of its image among American business leaders and major educators. The company first surveyed a sample of the publics and found that there was little knowledge or recognition of U.S. Steel even though it was one of the largest producers.

The company then sent a number of speech reprints and other publications on a regular basis to a selected sample of these opinion leaders. At the same time, it made sure that a control group did not receive the materials. At the end of the year it was found that the group receiving company publications was considerably more positive than previously about U.S. Steel as a progressive and well-managed company that spoke on behalf of the steel industry. On the other hand, a survey of the control group that had not received any company materials found that its members retained their low-level image of the company. This is an excellent example of the impact of a public relations program.

Mobil Oil, General Electric, AT&T, and other *Fortune* 500 companies regularly utilize benchmark surveys to measure the effectiveness of public relations campaigns. Surveys before and after specific campaigns document to a great extent the impact of public relations efforts. Continuing surveys, for example, show that Mobil's sponsorship of "Masterpiece Theatre" on PBS has gained the company a reputation among opinion leaders for corporate leadership and social responsibility.

Changes in public opinion on political issues are constantly tracked by periodic surveys. In this way, organizations that advocate or oppose a particular issue monitor their success in persuading the electorate. Evaluation of survey data allows each side to fine-tune its public relations efforts and make midcourse corrections.

A statewide ballot proposition to limit handguns in California, for example, started out with two-thirds of those polled endorsing the idea. During the campaign, however, the National Rifle Association and other interest groups mounted an extensive information drive that ultimately reversed voter attitudes, and the proposition was soundly defeated. Figure 10.2 shows part of a survey conducted by a nonprofit organization to determine whether it was getting its message across to the public.

Measurement of Action

The ultimate objective of any public relations effort is to make something happen. This takes us back to the beginning portion of the chapter which pointed out that the purpose of public relations activity is to advance organizational objectives.

```
                    "ACS CALIFORNIA POLL" --
              CANCER AWARENESS WEEK SURVEY 1984

                 Thursday, April 5, 5 - 8 p.m.


    Introduction - "Hello.  Do you have 3 minutes to help me with an
                   American Cancer Society telephone survey that
                   we're doing tonight in California?  There are 5
                   short questions.

        TOTAL:                Completed calls -  742  (44%)
        (1,701 calls)         Incomplete calls - 959  (56%)

    Question #1a. -  Did you know that this week is Cancer Awareness
                     Week?"

        TOTAL:                Yes - 276  (37%)
        (742 respondents)     No  - 466  (63%)

        Area I:               Yes -  67  (35%)
        (193 respondents)     No  - 126  (65%)

        Area II               Yes -  36  (39%)
        (45 respondents)      No  -  57  (61%)

        Area III              Yes - 173  (38%)
        (456 respondents)     No  - 283  (62%)

    Question #1b. -  "Do you recall the subject of Cancer Awareness
                     Week?"

        TOTAL:                Yes -  96  (33%)
        (290 respondents)     No  - 194  (67%)

        Area I                Yes -  14  (20%)
        (70 respondents)      No  -  56  (80%)

        Area II               Yes -   9  (20%)
        (45 respondents)      No  -  36  (80%)

        Area III              Yes -  73  (42%)
        (175 respondents)     No  - 102  (58%)

    Question #1c.  If respondent answered "yes" to preceding question
    (#1b.), check all the subjects below which they mention.

        TOTALS:               Prevention        - 50  (28%)
        (177 responses)         Early detection - 57  (32%)
                              Dietary, nutrition - 37  (21%)
                              Specific sites    - 33  (19%)
```

The objective of the amateur theater group is not to get media publicity; the objective is to sell tickets. The objective of an environmental organization like Greenpeace is not to get editorials written in favor of whales, but to motivate the public (1) to write elected officials and (2) to send donations for its preservation efforts. The objective of a company is to sell its products, and the creation of good will through public relations is one method to accomplish this objective.

Thus it can be seen that public relations efforts are ultimately evaluated on how they help the organization achieve its objectives. The evidence may be as follows:

1. The increase in number or amount of donations to a charitable agency

2. Sales of the product or service

3. The number of letters written to members of Congress about a public issue

4. The election of a candidate

5. The defeat or passage of proposed legislation

6. Attendance at a conference or symposium

Other changes in behavior can be ascertained through surveys to determine if people have altered their personal patterns. Have they quit smoking? Have they decided to get an annual physical checkup? Have they reduced their alcohol consumption? Are they driving more carefully? How people answer often depends on the public relations efforts of organizations and groups interested in such matters.

Change can also be tracked by informal or formal observation of audience behavior. In recent years, utilities have launched extensive information campaigns about energy conservation. The success of such efforts can partly be noted in the reduced energy consumption per household, as shown on individual bills, or by observing thermostat settings during a door-to-door survey. In some ways, observation is more valid than survey data. People may state on a survey questionnaire that they have a commitment to energy conservation, but their actual behavior—leaving lights on and keeping the thermostat up—may negate their good intentions.

Measurement of Supplemental Activities

COMMUNICATION AUDIT

The entire communication activity of an organization should be evaluated at least once a year to make sure that every primary and secondary public is receiving appropriate messages.

David Hilton-Barber, past president of the Public Relations Institute of South Africa, has written:

The most important reasons for an audit are to help establish communication goals and objectives, to evaluate long-term programs, to identify strengths and weaknesses, and to point up any areas which require increased activity.

. . . A communications audit can be useful at any time, but is especially appropriate when a company changes direction—changes product/service emphasis, goes public, merges or acquires—or when there is a change in management. The audit is also useful when management senses that something is wrong with its communications efforts and wants to find out what it is—or when a communications function is being created or restructured.

A communication audit, as an assessment of an organization's entire communication program, could include the following:

1. Analysis of all communication activities—newsletters, memos, policy statements, brochures, annual reports, position papers, mailing lists, media contacts, personnel forms, graphics, logos, advertising, receptionist contacts, waiting lounges for visitors, and the like

2. Informal interviews with rank-and-file employees and middle management and top executives

3. Informal interviews with community leaders, media gatekeepers, consumers, distributors, and other influential persons in the industry

A number of research techniques, as outlined in Chapter 7, can be utilized during a communication audit—including mail and telephone surveys, focus groups, and so forth. The important point is that the communications of an organization should be analyzed from every possible angle, with the input of as many publics as possible. Security analysts may have something to say about the quality of the company's financial information; municipal leaders are best qualified to evaluate the company's efforts in community relations. Consumers, if given a chance, will make suggestions about quality of sales personnel and product instruction booklets.

After an audit is completed, a written set of recommendations should be made to top management suggesting better ways to communicate effectively.

MEETINGS AND EVENTS

It has already been pointed out that meetings can be evaluated to some degree by the level of attendance. Such data provide information about the number of people exposed to a message, but still don't answer the more crucial question of what they thought about the meeting.

Public relations people often get an informal sense of an audience's attitudes by its behavior. A standing ovation, spontaneous applause, complimentary remarks as people leave, and even the expressions on people's faces provide clues as to how a meeting was received. On the other hand, if people are not responsive, if they ask questions about subjects supposedly explained, if they express doubts or antagonism, the meeting can be considered only partly successful.

Public relations practitioners use a number of informal methods to evaluate the success of a meeting, but they also employ more systematic methods. The most common technique is an evaluation sheet that participants fill out at the end of the meeting.

A simple form asking people to rate such items as location, costs, facilities, and program on a 1-to-5 scale (one being the best) can be used. Other forms may ask people to rate aspects of a conference or meeting on the basis of (1) Excellent, (2) Good, (3) Average, and (4) Could be better. One organization, which conducted a workshop at a racetrack, tied in the setting by asking those attending to rate program elements by (1) Win, (2) Place, and (3) Show.

Evaluation forms also can ask how people heard about the program and what suggestions they would make for future meetings.

The systematic gathering of such information enables meeting planners to pinpoint problem areas and to recognize which aspects of the program went especially well. A better meeting then can be planned next time. The evaluation thus is not just an analysis of a past event but the start of planning for future activities.

NEWSLETTERS   Editors of newsletters should evaluate readership annually. Such an evaluation can help ascertain (1) reader perceptions, (2) the degree to which stories are balanced, (3) the kinds of stories that have high reader interest, (4) additional topics that should be covered, (5) credibility of the publication, and (6) the extent to which it is meeting organizational objectives.

Systematic evaluation, it should be emphasized, is not based on whether all the copies are distributed or picked up. This information doesn't tell the editor what the audience actually read, retained, or acted upon. A newsletter, newspaper, or even a brochure can be evaluated in a number of ways. The methods include (1) content analysis, (2) readership interest surveys, (3) readership recall of articles actually read, (4) application of readability formulas, and (5) use of advisory boards.

CONTENT ANALYSIS   From a representative sample of past issues stories may be categorized under general headings such as (1) management announcements, (2) new product developments, (3) new personnel and retirements, (4) features about employees, (5) corporate finances, (6) news of departments and divisions, and (7) job-related information.

Such a systematic analysis will show what percentage of the publication is devoted to each category. It may be found that one division rarely is covered in the employee newsletter or that management pronouncements tend to dominate the entire publication. Given the content-analysis findings, editors may wish to shift the content somewhat.

READERSHIP INTEREST SURVEYS   The purpose of these surveys is to get feedback about the types of stories employees are most interested in reading.

The most common method is simply to provide a long list of generic story topics and have employees rate each as (1) Important, (2) Somewhat important, or (3) Not important. The International Association of Business

Communicators conducted such a survey on behalf of several dozen companies and found that readers were not very interested in "personals" about other employees (birthdays, anniversaries, and the like).

A readership interest survey becomes even more valuable when it is compared to the content analysis of a publication. Substantial differences signal a possible need for changes in the editorial content.

ARTICLE RECALL   The best kind of readership survey occurs when trained interviewers ask a sampling of employees what they have read in the latest issue of the publication.

Employees are shown the publication page by page and asked to indicate which articles they have read. As a check on the tendency of employees to report that they have read everything, interviewers also ask them (1) how much of each article they have read and (2) what the articles were about. The results are then content-analyzed to determine which kinds of articles have the most readership.

A variation of the readership recall technique involves individual evaluation of selected articles for accuracy and clarity. For example, an article about a new production process may be sent before or after publication to the head of production for evaluation. On a form with a rating scale of excellent, good, fair, and deficient, the person may be asked to evaluate the article on the basis of such factors as (1) technical data provided, (2) organization, (3) length, (4) clarity of technical points, and (5) quality of illustrations.

READABILITY   It is important to ensure that employees understand the story even if it concerns technical data. Although the source of the article—a scientist or an engineer—thoroughly understands the multisyllabic words, workers on the assembly line may find the material over their heads. The use of jargon also creeps into publications unless there is constant monitoring. For effective communication, of course, it is necessary to write at the educational level of the organization's employees. (For a further discussion of jargon and word choice, see "Writing for Clarity" in Chapter 9.)

Readability can be assessed by using such common formulas as those of Rudolf Flesch and Robert Gunning, or the Cloze procedure. Basically these methods allow a researcher to determine the comprehension level of copy by determining the average length of sentences and the number of multisyllabic words used. Some methods also include the number of personal pronouns. In general, material is more readable if the sentences are simple and short, and there are many one- or two-syllable words.

One solution to the problem of producing a publication suitable for disparate groups is to prepare several periodicals or brochures. Scientists and engineers may get one newsletter and assembly-line workers another, and the results compared.

ADVISORY BOARDS Periodic feedback and evaluation can be provided by organizing an employee advisory board that meets several times a year to discuss the direction and content of the publication. This is a useful technique because it expands the editor's feedback network and elicits comments that employees might be hesitant to tell the editor face-to-face.

A variation of the advisory board method is periodically to invite a sampling of employees to meet to discuss the publication. This approach is more systematic than just soliciting comments from employees in the hallway or cafeteria.

QUESTIONS FOR REVIEW AND DISCUSSION

1. What is the role of stated objectives in evaluating public relations programs? What is the difference between informational and motivational objectives?

2. What are some reasons why systematic research and evaluation are not used more extensively in public relations?

3. Name some general guidelines that should be used when evaluating a public relations activity.

4. Name four ways that publicity activity is evaluated. What, if any, are the drawbacks to each method?

5. Name some systematic methods of evaluating whether public relations efforts helped accomplish organizational objectives.

6. How are pilot tests and split messages used to determine suitability of a message?

7. What evaluation methods can be used to determine if target audiences have changed their opinions or perceptions?

8. How did the Adolph Coors Company evaluate its appearance on the CBS-TV "60 Minutes" program?

9. What is a communication audit?

10. What methods could be used to evaluate the readership and effectiveness of an employee newsletter or magazine?

Part three

STRATEGY

CHAPTER ELEVEN

Public Opinion and Persuasion

"The public be damned" was the comment attributed to railroad tycoon William Vanderbilt in the 1880s. Earlier in the century, Sir Robert Peel wrote: "Public opinion is a compound of folly, weakness, prejudice, wrong feeling, right feeling, obstinacy, and newspaper paragraphs."

Neither man thought much of public opinion, but it has emerged as a powerful force in the late twentieth century. Scott Cutlip and Allen Center, authors of *Effective Public Relations,* for example, have written: "The power of public opinion must be faced, understood and dealt with. It provides the psychological environment in which organizations prosper or perish."

Public relations personnel in particular should know what constitutes public opinion and how this major force is formed. They are constantly engaged in interpreting shifts in public opinion and at the same time attempting to influence it through persuasive communications. They are active participants in the marketplace of ideas. As such, public relations people are an essential part of freedom of inquiry and expression that leads to democratic decision-making.

In its examination of public opinion, the chapter discusses the role of opinion leaders, both formal and informal. It outlines the methods that practitioners use in gauging public opinion. Factors in persuasion, including source credibility, audience analysis, and appeal to self-interest, are detailed. The chapter ends with a review of ethical guidelines for those who use persuasion in behalf of an employer or client.

What Is Public Opinion?

Americans talk about public opinion as if it were a monolithic entity over-shadowing the entire landscape. Editorial cartoonists, in contrast, humanize it in the form of John Q. (and sometimes Jane) Public, characters who symbolize what people think about any given issue. The reality is that public opinion is somewhat elusive and extremely difficult to measure at any given moment.

In fact, to continue the metaphor, public opinion is a number of mono-liths and John and Jane Publics all existing at the same time. Few issues create unanimity of thought among the population, and public opinion on any issue is split in several directions. It may also come as a surprise to note that only a small number of people, at any given time, take part in public opinion formation on a specific issue.

There are two reasons for this. First, psychologists have found that the public tends to be passive. Few issues generate an opinion or feeling on the part of an entire citizenry. It is often assumed that a small, vocal group represents the attitude of the public when, in reality, it is more accurate to say that the majority of the people—because the issue doesn't interest or affect them—are apathetic. Thus, "public" opposition to nuclear power plants is really the view of a small, but significant, number of Americans who are concerned about the issue.

Second, one issue may engage the attention of one part of the population while another arouses the interest of another segment. Parents in a com-munity, for example, may form public opinion on the need for improved secondary education, while senior citizens constitute the bulk of public opinion on the need for increased Social Security benefits.

These two examples illustrate the most common definition of public opinion: "Public opinion is the sum of individual opinions on an issue *affecting* those individuals." Another popular definition states: "Public opin-ion is a collection of views held by persons *interested* in the subject." Thus a person unaffected by or uninterested in (and perhaps unaware of) an issue does not contribute to public opinion on the subject.

Inherent in these definitions is the concept of self-interest. The following statements appear in the literature of public opinion:

1. Public opinion is the collective expression of opinion of many individuals bound into a group by common aims, aspirations, needs, and ideals.

2. People who are interested or who have a vested or *self-interest* in an issue—or who can be affected by the outcome of the issue—form public opinion on that particular item.

3. Psychologically, opinion basically is determined by *self-interest.* Events, words, or any other stimuli affect opinion only insofar as their relationship to self-interest or a general concern is apparent.

4. Opinion does not remain aroused for any long period of time unless people feel their *self-interest* is acutely involved or unless opinion—aroused by words—is sustained by events.

5. Once *self-interest* is involved, opinion is not easily changed.

How practitioners utilize the concept of self-interest in focusing their message to fit the audience is discussed under "Appeal to Self-Interest," later in the chapter.

The literature also emphasizes the importance of events in the formation of public opinion. Social scientists, for example, have made the following generalizations:

1. Opinion is highly sensitive to *events* that have an impact on the public at large or a particular segment of the public.

2. By and large, public opinion does not anticipate *events*. It only reacts to them.

3. *Events* trigger formation of public opinion. Unless people are aware of an issue, they are not likely to be concerned or have an opinion. Awareness and discussion lead to crystallizing of opinions and often a consensus among the public.

4. *Events* of unusual magnitude are likely to swing public opinion temporarily from one extreme to another. Opinion does not stabilize until the implication of the event is seen with some perspective.

It also has been found that people have more opinions and are able to form opinions more easily with respect to goals than with the methods necessary to reach those goals. Thus there is fairly strong public opinion, according to polls, in favor of improving the quality of the nation's schools. But there is not much agreement on how this goal should be accomplished. One group advocates higher salaries for "master" teachers, while another equally vocal group endorses substantial tax increases for school operations. A third group thinks more rigorous standards will solve the problem. All three groups, plus assorted other ones with still other solutions, make up public opinion on the subject.

Opinion Leaders as Catalysts

Public opinion on an issue may have its roots in self-interest or in events, but the primary catalyst is public discussion. Only in this way does opinion begin to crystallize, and pollsters can measure it.

Serving as catalysts for the formation of public opinion are people who are knowledgeable and articulate about specific issues. They are called *opinion leaders*. Sociologists describe them as (1) highly interested in the subject or issue, (2) better informed on the issue than the average person, (3) avid consumers of mass media, (4) early adopters of new ideas, and (5) good organizers who can get other people to take action.

TWO TYPES OF LEADERS
There are two kinds of opinion leaders. First, there are those who are *formal opinion leaders* because of their position and title. The mayor of a city, the president of the chamber of commerce, the chief executive officer of a major corporation, the chairperson of an environmental group—all are opinion leaders because they are heads of organizations. They often are asked by news reporters to make a statement when a specific issue relates to their area of responsibility.

Second, there are any number of *informal opinion leaders* at every level of society. The leader may be a co-worker on the plant assembly line, the neighbor next door, the homemaker down the street, or the young insurance agent. These people, of course, are not opinion leaders on every subject but they do exert considerable influence on their peer groups by being highly informed and credible on a particular issue.

An employee, for example, may be sought out by colleagues for an opinion on management's new benefits package. The neighbor next door is a car buff and becomes the expert resource on which automobile is the best buy. The homemaker is active in the League of Women Voters and her friends rely on her to make recommendations about political candidates. The insurance agent, who has learned a good deal about securities, influences the investment decisions of friends. Almost everyone, depending on his or her interest and perceived expertise, is an informal opinion leader for peers on one or several subjects.

THE FLOW OF OPINION
Sociologists Daniel Katz and Paul Lazarsfeld in the 1940s discovered the importance of opinion leaders during a study of how people chose candidates in an election. They found that the mass media had minimal influence on electoral choices, but voters did rely on person-to-person communication with formal and informal opinion leaders.

These findings became known as the two-step flow theory of communication. Although later research confirmed that it really was a multiple-step flow, the basic idea remained intact. Public opinion is really formed by the views of people who have taken the time to sift information, evaluate it, and form an opinion that is expressed to others.

The model is graphically illustrated by a series of concentric circles. In the epicenter of action are opinion-makers. They derive large amounts of information from the mass media and other sources and share that information with people in the adjoining concentric circle, who are labeled the "attentive public." These latter are interested in the issue but rely on opinion leaders to provide synthesized information and interpretation. The outer ring consists of the "inattentive public." They are unaware of or uninterested in the issue and remain outside the opinion-formation process. The multiple-step flow theory, however, means that some will eventually become interested in, or at least aware of, the issue.

THE MEDIA'S ROLE The mass media, of course, pervade all three concentric circles, but only opinion leaders actively use the information. An opinion leader on local politics, for example, avidly reads stories and editorial comment about the affairs of the city, while a member of the inattentive public may skip such reading in favor of the sports page. It should be noted, however, that the devoted sports-page reader may be an informal opinion leader among his or her friends about who is the best player in the league.

Lazarsfeld's and Katz's point is that the influence of the mass media is exaggerated. It is now generally accepted that the mass media serve the primary role of *agenda-setter*. They tell the public, through selection of stories and headlines, what to think about—but not what to think. For opinion leaders they are an information source but not (except for editorial comment) a source of ready-made opinions.

Although this understanding of mass media influence is generally valid, other research indicates that there are some exceptions. When people have no prior information or attitude disposition regarding a subject, the mass media do play a role in telling people what to think. Psychologist Carl Hovland says people tend to change their perceptions if the information and opinion provided (by mass media or other sources) are not ego-involving or contradictory to previous experiences. Thus a person who doesn't know much about the state budget tends to accept the newspaper's headline, "School Officials Call Budget a Disaster."

Not everyone is happy with the mass media as an agenda-setter. Critics say newspapers and television news shows are so oriented to generating an audience that any agenda for public discussion of substantive issues is drowned out by the latest sex scandal, ax murder, or spectacular accident. One social scientist complains: "The news is manipulated, selected, shaped and massaged to attract the largest share of the audience, to please the most and offend the fewest."

It is a complaint that has no real solution, since the media sell a product just like any other business. Individuals highly interested in a particular topic or issue will always be disappointed by general newspaper and television coverage. Consequently, opinion-makers tend to get their information not only from the mass media but from other highly specialized sources. The opinion leader on environmental problems, for example, reads various newsletters, government reports, and specialized magazines. He or she also attends meetings and conventions during which environmental topics are discussed.

Chapter 9, concerning the process of communication, has already pointed out that the mass media are most influential in making people aware of an issue or topic. Motivating and influencing people comprise a more complex process that requires thorough knowledge of formal and informal opinion leaders as receivers of communication and conduits of persuasion.

Public Opinion and Public Relations

Understanding public opinion and how it is formed is fundamental to public relations. Such knowledge enables the practitioner to (1) effectively monitor shifts in public opinion, (2) pinpoint formal and informal opinion leaders who should be reached with specific messages, and (3) understand that dissemination of information through the mass media can only create awareness, not tell people what to think.

Public relations people use a number of methods to monitor public opinion. They include the following:

1. *Personal contacts.* Friends, business associates, consultants, opinion leaders, customers, and employees.

2. *Media reports.* News stories, letters to the editor, op-ed (opposite the editorial page) articles, and editorials.

3. *Field reports.* Questions, inquiries, complaints, suggestions, and compliments expressed by salespeople and customers.

4. *Letters and telephone calls.* The tracking and monitoring of patterns that might indicate necessary changes in policies—communication messages.

5. *Advisory committees.* Citizen committees to provide feedback on proposed policies, ideas, and public relations programming.

6. *Staff meetings.* An opportunity to share knowledge gleaned from experience and informal research.

7. *Polling/sampling.* Systematic research on public attitudes and interests (see Chapter 7).

Failure to monitor public attitudes and consult opinion leaders can cause a number of problems for an organization.

The California battle against the invasion of the Mediterranean fruit fly during 1980–1982 is a good example. State and federal officials finally decided that aerial spraying of malathion over urban areas was necessary to eradicate the pest. Permission to spray, however, required the consent of 14 city councils in the San Francisco Bay area.

Medfly officials, without any monitoring of public concerns about spraying or even consulting with the key opinion leaders in government and citizen organizations, simply went to scheduled city council meetings and made a request. This caught city officials off-guard and without adequate background information. On the other hand, environmentalists, highly organized, testified against aerial spraying. Given the situation, each city council promptly voted against aerial spraying.

The ultimate result was a delay of several months while Medfly officials went back to square one and started the tedious process of building support for aerial spraying. The project lost valuable time simply because officials had failed to do their homework about the necessity of preselling aerial spraying to civic and community leaders before requesting permission. Background briefing sessions would have gone a long way in allaying public fears and answering the charges of environmental groups. Once key opinion leaders understood the necessity of aerial spraying, the two-step flow process was instrumental in getting community support.

In another situation, the campaign for the Equal Rights Amendment (ERA) stalled in the final months before the congressional deadline because advocates failed to recognize the necessity of reaching opinion leaders with an organized, well-planned campaign. ERA proponents got plenty of media coverage with pseudo-events (like spraying the doors of a state legislature in red paint and scolding legislators for being "chauvinist pigs"), but that approach just made the lawmakers more reluctant to pass the measure. After ERA's defeat, analysts concluded that proponents had failed to communicate effectively with the most important public of all—state legislators.

A contrast to the Medfly and ERA failures is the success of an electronics company that was successful in building a plant in a small Oregon community after other firms had failed to get city approval. The key to success was the effort by the company's public relations staff to contact local opinion leaders and civic officials before final plans were announced. Discussion of the company's projected plans gave local opinion leaders an opportunity to make suggestions and also to participate in the decision-making process. As a result they announced support of the new plant to their followers. This illustrates another aspect of public opinion. *People who participate in solving a problem are more likely to support its implementation.*

Persuasion: Pervasive in Our Lives

It is difficult to imagine any human activity in which *persuasion* does not exist. The process involves everybody from children convincing parents that bedtime should be delayed a half hour to a salesperson who makes a living persuading people to buy a product. Friends persuade each other when debating what movie to see. Employees try to persuade bosses that they deserve a raise.

The study of persuasion was central to the education of the Greeks. Aristotle was the first to set down the ideas of *ethos, logos,* and *pathos,* which roughly translate as "source credibility," "logical argument," and "emotional appeal."

DEFINITIONS OF PERSUASION

In the twentieth century Winston Brembeck and William Howell, two communication experts, described persuasion as "communication to influence choices." A longer description is, "any communication, intended or not, that causes a change in a receiver's attitude, belief, or action." Another definition is, "a process that changes attitudes, beliefs, opinions, or behaviors."

USES OF PERSUASION

The strategies of persuasion are used daily by public relations practitioners because their job is to engage in purposive communication—with the objective of influencing people in some way.

Persuasion is used to (1) change or neutralize hostile opinions, (2) crystallize latent opinions and positive attitudes, and (3) conserve favorable opinions.

The most difficult persuasion is to change hostile opinions into favorable ones. There is much truth to the adage "Don't confuse me with the facts; my mind is made up." Once people have decided, for instance, that oil companies are making excessive profits or that a nonprofit agency is wasting public donations, they tend to ignore or disbelieve any contradictory information. Everyone, as Walter Lippmann has described, has pictures in his or her head based on individual perception of reality. People generalize from personal experience and what peers tell them. For example, if a person has an encounter with a rude clerk, the inclination is to generalize that the entire department store chain is not very good. The self-perception of the audience is a barrier to communication that will be discussed later in this chapter.

The task of persuasion is much easier if the message is compatible with a person's general disposition about a subject. If a person tends to identify General Electric as a company with a good reputation, he or she may express this feeling by purchasing a GE appliance. Nonprofit agencies usually crystallize the public's latent inclination to aid the less fortunate by asking for a donation. Both examples illustrate the reason that organizations strive to have a good reputation—it is translated into sales and donations. The concept of message channeling will be discussed in more detail later in the chapter.

The easiest form of persuasion is communication that reinforces favorable opinions. Public relations people, by providing a steady stream of reinforcing messages, keep the reservoir of good will in sound condition. More than one organization has survived a major problem because public esteem for the organization tended to minimize current difficulties. Continual efforts to maintain the reservoir of good will is called *preventive public relations*—the most effective of all.

Factors in Persuasive Communication

A number of factors are involved in persuasive communication, and the public relations practitioner should be knowledgeable about each one. The following is a brief discussion of (1) audience analysis, (2) source credibility, (3) appeal to self-interest, (4) clarity of message, (5) timing and context, (6) audience participation, (7) suggestions for action, (8) content and structure of messages, and (9) persuasive speaking.

AUDIENCE ANALYSIS Energy conservation programs in the United States got off to a slow start during the early 1970s because the public was resistant. People were accustomed to big cars, cheap gasoline, and consumption of electric power in ever-increasing quantities. Energy was an inexhaustible resource, and the average American tended to ignore warnings until the OPEC cartel made its presence known with a vengeance.

The public attitude toward energy conservation illustrates two key points about persuasion. First, people are good at reacting to events but not at anticipating them. Second, any message (such as conservation) or suggested action (smaller cars) must be compatible with group values and beliefs. Energy conservation was not adopted until the public realized through long lines at the gas pump and high utility bills that conservation was in their economic self-interest.

The knowledge of group attitudes and beliefs is an essential part of persuasion because it helps the communicator to tailor messages that are salient, answer a felt need, and provide a logical course of action. Polling and census data, as well as pretesting of messages, can accomplish a great deal in structuring a message that builds upon group attitudes.

Tapping a group's attitudes is called *channeling*. It is the technique of recognizing a general audience belief and then suggesting a specific course of action. One common channeling tactic is the appeal to patriotism by politicians. Lyndon Johnson called on all patriotic Americans to "support our boys" in Vietnam, and Ronald Reagan urged support for his defense policies because, he said, America is the "hope of the free world."

Environmental groups such as the Wilderness Society or the Sierra Club channel messages that capitalize on the public's concern for the quality of life. If a person wants to preserve the forests and mountains for his or her children (and who doesn't?), isn't it worth a $20 membership?

Business, on the other hand, knows that consumers are concerned about prices. A number of companies launched national advertising and public relations campaigns, in 1979–1980, to tell consumers how excessive government regulation was significantly adding to the cost of goods and services. These campaigns, giving facts and figures about the cost of preparing government reports, hit a nerve with consumers and were a factor in the defeat of Jimmy Carter for re-election in 1980. This is a good example of how business aligned itself with consumer interests to roll back government regulation.

There are numerous other examples of how organizations tailor messages to group beliefs. The public has a distaste for exploitation, so unions talk about "workers as pawns of big business." Pro-gun organizations capitalize on the public's concern about crime and the need to protect one's family. The California Raisin Board takes advantage of the craze for physical fitness by depicting its product as a nutritious snack for the jogger.

SOURCE CREDIBILITY

A message is more believable to the intended audience if the source has *credibility.* This was Aristotle's concept of *ethos,* and it explains why organizations use a variety of spokespeople, depending upon the message and the audience.

The California Strawberry Advisory Board, for example, arranges for a home economist to appear on television talk shows to discuss nutrition and to demonstrate easy-to-follow strawberry recipes. The audience for these programs, primarily homemakers, not only identifies with the representative but perceives her as highly credible. By the same token, a manufacturer of sun-screen lotion uses a professor of pharmacology who is past president of the State Pharmacy Board to discuss the scientific merits of sun-screen versus suntan lotions. And, of course, Lee Iacocca has been the chief speaker in Chrysler Corporation advertisements because he is both articulate and chairman of the company.

THE THREE FACTORS   Source credibility is based upon three factors. One is *expertise.* Is the person perceived by the audience as being an expert on the subject? Companies, for instance, use engineers and scientists to answer news conference questions about how an engineering process works or whether a chemical waste dump is dangerous to human life.

The second component is *sincerity.* Does the person come across as believing what he or she is saying? Jane Fonda, for example, is not considered an expert on nuclear power but she does get high marks for sincerity in her feelings about its dangers.

The third component is even more elusive. It is *charisma.* Is the individual personable, self-assured, and articulate, projecting an image of competence and leadership? All contribute to source credibility.

Public relations personnel are well aware of the need for providing the

"Luminaries" Help Launch Apple's Macintosh

"Ninety percent of the world's views are controlled by the 10 percent who are opinion makers," says Regis McKenna, whose public relations firm handled product publicity for the introduction of Apple Computer's Macintosh.

As part of the overall strategy, Apple executives and staff from Regis McKenna, Inc., spent many months giving background briefings to key groups within the electronics industry—software designers, distributors, and computer dealers—before making any public announcement about the computer.

In addition, McKenna made sure that the "luminaries," or key opinion leaders in the electronics industry, knew about the Macintosh and its capabilities. He explains: "There are probably no more than 20 or 30 people in any one industry who have major impact on trends, standards, and a company's image or character."

McKenna also realizes that journalists rely on opinion leaders to provide objective judgments about the merits of a new product and the way it compares with the competition. Thus the strategy was to ensure that opinion leaders in the industry were cultivated and informed about the Macintosh before the media picked up the story and began interviewing their sources in the electronics field. Positive statements from such sources provided important third-party endorsement for the new product.

right person for an audience. They know that reporters prefer to talk with the person in the organization who is most directly involved in or knowledgeable about the subject. It may be the chief executive officer or the head of the research laboratory. It is also a good idea to use, say, a physicist or a biologist to address an audience of scientists, or a corporate treasurer to speak to a group of security analysts, because the audiences will accord them more credibility.

Celebrities also can present an organization's case when the audience is composed of consumers. Sports figures, for example, often are used to sell food products. Race car drivers become spokespersons for automobiles, gas, and oil. And doctors have been known to represent makers of patent medicines. The technique is one type of *transfer*—implying product credibility through the credibility of the speaker.

VISUAL SYMBOLS   Another aspect of credibility consists of the visual symbols surrounding the speaker. Political candidates pose for news photographers with the Liberty Bell or the Capitol behind them. A favorite backdrop of television correspondents is the White House. The speaker is another visual symbol. Audiences, in general, attribute credibility to a well-groomed person in business attire. There are, of course, exceptions, depending on the fame of the speaker or the message itself. The president of the United Farm Workers probably is more credible in jeans and a sport shirt than in a three-piece business suit.

APPEAL TO SELF-INTEREST

Self-interest was described during earlier discussion about the formation of public opinion. People get involved in issues or pay attention to messages that appeal to their psychic or economic needs.

The public relations person, when structuring an angle for a news release, brochure, or slide presentation, must think, first and foremost, about the nature of the audience and what it wants to know.

Publicity for a personal computer can serve as an example. A news release to the trade press serving the computer industry might focus on the technical proficiency of the equipment. The audience, of course, consists of engineers and computer programmers interested in the hardware. A brochure prepared for the public, however, may emphasize how the computer can (1) help people keep track of personal finances, (2) assist youngsters in becoming better students, (3) fit into a small space, and (4) offer good value. Consumers are less interested in technical details than in how the personal computer can make life easier for them.

Charitable organizations don't sell products, but they do need volunteers and donations. This is accomplished by careful structuring of messages that appeal to self-interest. This is not to say that altruism is dead. Thousands of people give freely of their time and money to charitable organizations, but they do receive something in return or they would not do it. The "something in return" may be (1) self-esteem, (2) the opportunity to make a contribution to society, (3) recognition from peers and the community, (4) a sense of belonging, (5) ego gratification, or even (6) a tax deduction. Public relations people understand psychic needs and rewards, and that is why there is constant recognition of volunteers in newsletters and award banquets. (Further discussion of volunteerism appears in Chapter 18.)

Appeals to self-interest are based on psychologist Abraham Maslow's *hierarchy of needs*. The first level involves basic needs such as food, water, shelter, and even transportation to and from work. The second level consists of security needs. People need to feel secure in their jobs, safe in their homes, and confident about their retirement. At the third level are "belonging" needs. People are social animals who seek association with others. This is why individuals join organizations. Depending on the person's need in this area, he or she may join only one club or up to 10 or 12.

"Love" needs comprise the fourth level in the hierarchy. Humans have a need to be wanted and loved—fulfilling the desire for self-esteem. At the fifth and highest level in Maslow's hierarchy are self-actualization needs.

Once the other four needs are met, Maslow says, people strive to achieve maximum personal potential. Thus successful executives may "self-actualize" by engaging in activities of high personal interest—perhaps taking a 21-day canoe trip in Nepal, becoming an expert on orchids, or even writing a book. These sorts of pursuits are denied to people who are still fulfilling more basic needs.

Public relations personnel, as persuaders, direct their messages toward audience needs. The promise or perhaps only the hint is that, by following the advice, individuals can fill or reduce a need. Charles Larson, author of the book *Persuasion,* writes that "success in persuasion largely depends upon the ability to assess need states accurately."

CLARITY OF MESSAGE

Many messages fail because the audience finds the language too complex or unclear as to what the communicator wants the receiver to do.

Public relations personnel should always ask two questions: "What do I want the audience to do with the message?" "Will the audience understand the message?"

It is an axiom of persuasion that people are more committed to a course of action if they draw their own conclusions. The reason for this is that they are forced to internalize the decision instead of merely accepting, with perhaps much mental effort, the conclusion of the speaker. Educational theory also says that students who are asked to draw conclusions from data retain classroom learning longer than if the conclusion is provided by the teacher.

There is danger, however, that the audience will draw the wrong conclusions and not understand what is expected of it. The story is told about a biology professor who, as a classroom experiment, dropped a worm into a beaker of water, where it continued to wiggle. The professor then dropped it into a beaker of alcohol and it immediately died. "What conclusion can we draw from this experiment?" asked the professor. A student in the back of the class replied, "If you don't want worms, drink alcohol."

A persuasive message should explicitly state what action an audience should take. Is it to buy the product, visit a showroom, write a member of Congress, make a $10 donation, or what?

TIMING AND CONTEXT

A message is more persuasive if environmental factors support the message or if the message is received within the context of other messages and situations with which the individual is familiar.

Information from a utility on how to conserve energy is more salient if the consumer has just received the January heating bill. A pamphlet on a new stock offering is more effective if it accompanies an investor's dividend check. A citizens' group lobbying for a stoplight gets more attention if a major accident has just occurred at the intersection.

Political candidates are highly aware of public concerns and avidly read polls to find out what issues are most salient with voters. If the polls indicate that high interest rates and high-quality secondary education are key issues, the candidate begins to use these issues—and to offer his or her proposals—in the campaign.

Timing and context also play an important role in achieving publicity in the mass media. Public relations personnel, as pointed out earlier, should read newspapers and watch television news programs to find out what media gatekeepers consider newsworthy. A manufacturer of a locking device for computer files got extensive media coverage about its product simply because it followed a rash of news stories about thieves' gaining access to bank accounts through computers. Media gatekeepers, ordinarily uninterested in security devices for computers, found the product newsworthy within the context of actual news events.

News events also provide the context for op-ed articles written by corporate executives, consultants, and organizational heads. A bank president got half a page in a metropolitan daily for an op-ed article about the future of banking. This topic, in itself, ordinarily is not very newsworthy—but it becomes newsworthy if Congress is considering major legislation affecting the banking industry.

The value of information and its newsworthiness are based on timing and context. Public relations professionals disseminate information at the time it is most highly valued.

AUDIENCE PARTICIPATION

A change in attitude or reinforcement of beliefs is enhanced by *audience involvement and participation.*

A company, for example, may have employees discuss productivity in a quality-control circle. Management may already have figured out what is needed, but if workers are involved in the problem-solving, they often come up with the same solution or even a better one. And, from a persuasion standpoint, the employees are more committed to making the solution work because it came from them—not as a policy or order handed down by higher management.

Participation can also take the form of samples. Many companies distribute product samples so the consumer can conveniently try them without expense. A consumer who samples the product and makes a judgment about its quality is more likely to purchase it.

Activist groups use participation as a way of helping people actualize their beliefs. Not only do rallies and demonstrations give people a sense of belonging, but the act of participation reinforces their beliefs. Asking people to do something—conserve energy, collect donations, or picket—activates a form of self-persuasion and commitment.

SUGGESTIONS FOR ACTION

A principle of persuasion is that people endorse ideas only if they are accompanied by a proposed action from the sponsor.

Recommendations for action must be clear. Public relations practitioners must not only ask people to conserve energy, for instance, but also furnish detailed data and ideas on how to do it.

A campaign conducted by Pacific Gas & Electric Company provides an example. The utility inaugurated a Zero Interest Program (ZIP) to offer customers a way to implement energy-saving ideas. The program involved several components:

Energy kit. A telephone hotline was established and widely publicized so interested customers could order an energy kit detailing what the average homeowner could do to reduce energy use.

Service bureau. The company, at no charge, sent representatives to homes to check the efficiency of water heaters and furnaces, measure the amount of insulation, and check doors and windows for drafts.

ZIP program. The cost of making a home more energy-efficient was funded by zero-interest loans to any qualified customer.

CONTENT AND STRUCTURE OF MESSAGES

A number of techniques can make a message more persuasive. Writers throughout history have emphasized some information while downplaying or omitting other pieces of information.

Expert communicators continue to use a number of devices, including (1) drama, (2) statistics, (3) examples, (4) testimonials, (5) mass media endorsements, and (6) emotional appeals.

DRAMA Because everyone likes a good story, the first task of a communicator is to get audience attention. This is often accomplished by graphically illustrating an event or situation. Newspapers often dramatize a story to get reader interest in an issue. Thus we read about the family evicted from its home as part of a story on the increase in bankruptcies; the old man who is starving because of red tape in the welfare office; or the worker who is now disabled because of toxic waste. In the news trade this is called humanizing an issue.

Dramatizing is also used in public relations. A relief organization knows that a story about the miserable life of a refugee family in Ethiopia or Cambodia will attract more donations than will the flat statement that four million people are starving. Individuals can relate to a family but not to four million people. Humanizing the problem is facilitated by illustrations. A photograph of a thin, sick woman cradling a baby with a distended belly reinforces the old saying that a picture is worth a thousand words.

A more common use of dramatizing is the so-called application story, sent to the trade press. This is sometimes called the case study technique, in which a manufacturer prepares an article on how an individual or a company is using the product. Apple Computer, for example, provides a number of application stories about the unique ways in which its product is being used.

STATISTICS   It is often said, perhaps with some reason, that Americans are awed by numbers. People tend to ascribe high credibility to government statistics and survey studies that support a claim. The use of percentages and totals can convey objectivity, bigness, and importance. Statistics, however, should be used sparingly. A news release crammed with figures tends to be boring and turns off the potential reader.

EXAMPLES   Statements of opinion have more credibility if the speaker or writer gives examples that back up the contention. A school board often can get substantial public support for a bond issue by citing examples of how the present facilities are inadequate for student needs.

TESTIMONIALS   This is another form of source credibility. A company receives more public attention if the mayor signs a proclamation or a widely known expert publicly endorses the company's product. Testimonials also may relate what writers or researchers say. For example, a book that cites a company for excellent employee communications constitutes a testimonial.

MASS MEDIA ENDORSEMENTS   When one of the mass media endorses a campaign, an individual, or a product, this action builds public support for the recipient. A newspaper or radio editorial urging contributions to a United Way campaign is an example; so is a newspaper's preelection marked ballot recommending votes for certain candidates. The testimonial as a propaganda device is discussed later in the chapter.

In its advertisement opposing the sale of weapons to Saudi Arabia, a nonprofit religious organization quoted two highly respected newspapers, the New York *Times* and the *Wall Street Journal,* as sources of information on the controversy (see Figure 11.1).

EMOTIONAL APPEALS   Emotional appeals have been used throughout history. Two masters of the technique in the twentieth century were Winston Churchill and Franklin D. Roosevelt. Their speeches, laden with emotional appeal, galvanized entire populations to fight for victory in World War II.

In a more current setting the Greenpeace organization sends out literature that constitutes strong emotional appeal to save Harp seals. The cover of a direct mail brochure shows a baby Harp seal—all fuzzy, with large liquid eyes—and the headline "Kiss This Baby Good-Bye." Inside, seal behavior is

Who'll Get Stung By Our Stingers?

It is time America stopped feeding Saudi Arabia's insatiable appetite for weapons.

The Saudi regime already has a huge arsenal of American arms: Redeye surface-to-air missiles, Hawkeye surface-to-air missiles, F-5 fighters, F-15 fighters, AWACS command planes and a vast array of other war materiel—$40 billion worth.

Four hundred Stinger antiaircraft missiles and 200 shoulder-held launchers are the newest addition to the Saudi military storehouse. Meanwhile, the feudal kingdom continues to frustrate American policy by providing $1 million a day to the terrorist PLO and by financing Syrian military purchases from the Soviet Union.

What "emergency" impelled the President to waive the rule requiring Congress to approve arms sales to foreign governments? The New York Times reports that even some Administration officials admit there was no intelligence information showing a likely Iranian air attack on Saudi oilfields. The Stingers, it turns out, were really sent "to reassure the Saudis, politically and psychologically."

A frightening risk.

Whatever the purpose, this sale poses a special peril. The Stinger is compact, lightweight, portable. You can bet the PLO is already attempting to get hold of it. That would not be the first time American arms have fallen into terrorist hands. Immense quantities of munitions we sold to the Saudis were part of the hoard of PLO weapons discovered by Israeli forces in Lebanon.

But this time the danger is especially grave. The Wall Street Journal calls the Stinger "a perfect weapon against civilian aircraft."

In catering to Saudi Arabia's unquenchable thirst for military hardware, the Administration has created a new and frightening risk.

We pray that our country and its allies are not stung by our own Stingers.

George Rothman Institute of the
Zionist Organization of America
Alleck A. Resnick, President • Alfred H. Kleiman, Chairman, Nat'l Exec. Comm.
• Ivan J. Novick, Chairman of the Board • Paul Flacks, Exec. Vice Pres.
4 East 34th St., New York, NY 10016

portrayed so the reader can identify the seal's fate with that of a human infant. Here is an excerpt:

At that tender and vulnerable age, with his mother at his side, he wiggles forward, waggling his whole backside. He goes to meet, in a curious, friendly, playful way, the first human being he has ever seen and is—by the same human—clubbed in the head and skinned on the spot—sometimes while he is still alive.

Such material, distributed in thousands of bulk mail letters, has been extremely successful in creating a groundswell of demand that the harvesting of seals be forbidden. The public outcry became so intense several years ago that the Canadian government hired a public relations firm in New York to present the industry's side of the story.

Emotional appeals can do much to galvanize the public into action, but they can also backfire. Such appeals raise ego defenses, and people don't like to be told that in some way they are responsible. A description of suffering makes many people uncomfortable, and, rather than take action, they may tune out the message. A relief organization runs full-page advertisements in magazines with the headline "You Can Help Maria Get Enough to Eat . . . Or You Can Turn the Page." Researchers say that most people, their ego defenses raised, turn the page and mentally refuse to acknowledge that they even saw the ad. In sum, emotional appeals that attempt to lay a guilt trip on the audience are not very successful.

Strong fear arousals also can cause people to tune out, especially if they feel that they can't do anything about the problem anyway. Research indicates, however, that a moderate fear arousal, accompanied by a relatively easy solution, is effective. A moderate fear arousal is: "What would happen if your child were thrown through the windshield in an accident?" The message concludes with the suggestion that a baby, for protection and safety, should be placed in a secured infant seat.

Psychologists say that the most effective emotional appeal is one coupled with facts and figures. The emotional appeal attracts audience interest, but logical arguments also are needed.

PERSUASIVE SPEAKING

Psychologists have found that speakers (and salespeople) use several persuasion techniques. These devices, and the advice given, are as follows:

1. *Yes-yes.* Start with points with which the audience agrees, to develop a pattern of "yes" answers. Getting agreement to a basic premise often means that the receiver will agree to the logically developed conclusion.

2. *Structured choice.* Give structured choices that require the audience to chose between A and B. Political candidates or cause-oriented organizations often use this technique. "Do you want four more years of inflation, or a new beginning?" "Will you work for wilderness preservation, or allow industrial exploitation?"

3. *Partial commitment.* Get a commitment for some action on the part of the receiver. This leaves the door open for commitment to other parts of the proposal at a later date. "You don't need to decide on the new insurance plan now, but please attend the employee orientation program on Thursday."

4. *Ask for more/settle for less.* Submit a complete public relations program to management, but be prepared to compromise by dropping certain parts of the program. It has become almost a cliché that a department asks for a larger budget than it expects to receive. Or, to put it another way, the entire sales field is built on the notion of setting prices that can be marked down.

Persuasive speeches require that the speaker give all sides of the issue. The only exceptions might be the partisan political rally or the company sales meeting.

By mentioning all sides of the argument, the speaker accomplishes three objectives. First, he or she is perceived as having objectivity. This translates into increased credibility and makes the audience less suspicious of motives. Second, by giving both sides, the speaker is treating the audience as mature, intelligent adults. Third, including counterarguments allows the speaker to control how these arguments are structured. It also deflates opponents in the audience who might challenge the speaker by saying, "But you didn't consider. . . ."

Panel discussions and debates present other problems. Psychologists say the last person to talk in a panel probably will be most effective in changing audience attitudes—or at least be longer remembered by the audience. But it has also been shown that the first speaker sets the standard and tone for the remainder of the discussion. Being first or last is better positioning than being between two presentations.

Propaganda

CONNOTATIONS AND DENOTATIONS OF THE WORD

No discussion of persuasion would be complete without a discussion of *propaganda* and its techniques.

The word *propaganda* generates a number of connotative definitions, mostly negative. Older Americans often equate it with the activities of the enemy during World War II. Germany and Japan were sending out propaganda while America and its allies were disseminating truth. Today the Soviet Union is accused of spreading propaganda, while the United States Information Agency and the Voice of America are said to provide accurate, truthful information. Propaganda, obviously, is in the eyes of the beholder.

The dictionary defines *propaganda* as "publicity intended to spread ideas or information that will persuade or convince people." Under this definition, advertising and public relations activity by IBM or the Sierra Club could be considered propaganda.

Yet in today's usage the word has taken on a more specific definition. A number of social scientists say that the word should be used only to denote activity that sells a belief system or constitutes political or ideological dogma. According to this definition, commercial advertising and public relations would not be propaganda. The experts also say that propaganda intentionally misleads an audience by concealing (1) the source of information, (2) the source's goal, (3) other sides of the story, and (4) the consequences if the message is adopted. A case could be made, therefore, that some advertising and public relations activities—those that utilize concealment—not only are unethical but have aspects of propaganda.

PROPAGANDA TECHNIQUES

Propaganda techniques are used today by many commercial and political organizations. The most common techniques are as follows:

1. *Plain folks.* An approach often used by politicians to show humble beginnings and an empathy with the average citizen. Jimmy Carter used the theme during his presidency by being photographed wearing jeans and playing softball in Plains, Georgia.

2. *Testimonial.* A frequently used device to achieve credibility, as earlier discussed. A well-known and supposedly expert source gives testimony about the value of a product or the wisdom of a decision.

3. *Bandwagon.* The implication or direct statement that everyone wants the product or that the idea has overwhelming support. "Volvo has become the No. 1 European import," or "Most major labor unions in the United States have endorsed Walter Mondale for president."

4. *Card stacking.* The selection of facts and data to build an overwhelming case on one side of the issue while concealing the other side. Environmental groups, for example, gave the impression that former Secretary of the Interior James Watt was the arch-villain in raping the country's wilderness areas.

5. *Transfer.* The technique of associating the person, product, or organization with individuals of high or low credibility, depending upon the intention of the message. A company, for example, may maintain that a product has high reliability because the National Aeronautics and Space Administration selected it for use by astronauts. On the negative side, opponents of a political candidate may spread the rumor that he or she has friends with known criminal connections.

6. *Glittering generalities.* The technique of associating a cause, product, or idea with favorable abstractions such as freedom, justice, the American way, integrity, and dedication.

7. *Name-calling.* The use of terms charged with negative meanings, such as kook, fellow traveler, pervert, radical, or warmonger, to refer to a person.

A WORD ABOUT ETHICS

A student of public relations should be aware of these techniques, if only to ensure that he or she doesn't unintentionally use them to advance a cause or an idea for an employer or client. There are ethical responsibilities in any form of purposive communication; guidelines are discussed at the end of the chapter.

Persuasion and Manipulation

On previous pages are discussions of a number of ways in which an individual can formulate persuasive messages. The ability to use this persuasive language often leads to charges that public relations people have great power to manipulate (a loaded word) people. For example, a book exposé is published about once a year supposedly telling the inside story of how advertising and public relations executives brainwash (another loaded word) the public into buying products they don't need or voting for a cardboard candidate created by Madison Avenue.

In reality, persuasion as an overwhelming influence is greatly exaggerated. Persuasion is not an exact science, and there is no sure-fire way to predict that people will be persuaded to act on a message, or even accept it. If persuasion techniques were as refined as the critics say, everyone might be driving the same car, using the same soap, and voting for the same political candidate.

Four factors limit the effectiveness of any persuasive message. They are (1) lack of message penetration, (2) competing messages, (3) self-selection, and (4) self-perception.

LACK OF MESSAGE PENETRATION

Diffusion of messages, despite modern communications technologies, is not pervasive. Not everyone, of course, listens to the same television programs or reads the same newspaper and magazines as another. Not everyone receives the same mail or attends the same meetings. Everyone the communicator wants to reach will not be in the audience eventually reached. There is also the problem of the distortion of messages as they pass through media gatekeepers.

COMPETING MESSAGES

Earlier in the century, before much was known about the complex process of communication, it was believed that people received information directly without any intervening variable. This was called the *hypodermic needle theory* of communication. Today communication experts realize that no message is received in a vacuum. Messages are filtered through a receiver's entire social structure and belief system. Nationality, race, religion, sex, cultural patterns, family, and friends are some of the variables that filter messages. In addition, people receive countless competing and conflicting messages daily. It is estimated, for example, that today's 18-year-old has viewed more than 20,000 hours of television programs, including several hundred commercials each week.

Social scientists say a person is rewarded for conforming to the standards of the group. Consequently, people are cautious about adopting new ideas or opinions without first testing them on their peers. For example, people may tell friends, " I read in *Time* that. . . ." If the idea proves acceptable to their friends, the statement then becomes "I think. . . ."

SELF-SELECTION The people most wanted in an audience are often the least likely to be there. As any minister attests, sinners don't go to church on a regular basis. Vehement supporters of a cause frequently ignore information provided by the other side. Asking a friend which magazines he or she subscribes to may reveal a good deal about that person's interests and political philosophy. In sum, people seek out information that is compatible with and reinforces their current dispositions and attitudes.

SELF-PERCEPTION Self-perception is the channel through which messages are interpreted. People will perceive the same information differently, depending upon predispositions and already-formulated opinions. Carl Rogers, a psychotherapist, says: "The greatest barrier to human communications is the tendency to form snap judgments about a person or what he or she is saying and then tune out." Thus, depending on a person's views, an action by a company may be considered a "great contribution to the community" or "a self-serving gimmick." A good story about self-perception is that of a United States senator who, upon hearing that Billy Jean King had soundly trounced Bobby Riggs in a widely promoted television tennis match, asked: "Isn't it just like a woman to lure an older man to a meeting at night, exhaust him physically, take his money, and humiliate him in front of his friends?"

The Ethics of Persuasion

Public relations people by definition are advocates of clients and employers. The emphasis is on persuasive communication to influence a particular public in some way. At the same time, as Chapter 6 pointed out, public relations practitioners must conduct their activities in an ethical manner.

The use of persuasive techniques, therefore, calls for some additional guidelines. Charles Larson, author of the book *Persuasion,* lists the following ethical criteria in using persuasive devices that should be kept in mind by every public relations professional:

1. Do not use false, fabricated, misrepresented, distorted, or irrelevant evidence to support arguments or claims.

2. Do not intentionally use specious, unsupported, or illogical reasoning.

3. Do not represent yourself as informed or as an "expert" on a subject when you are not.

Persuasion and Ethics	The strategies and tactics of persuasion, like all knowledge, can be used to subvert or benefit the public interest. Bill Moyers, host for a Public Broadcasting System program on the early beginnings of public relations ("A Walk Through the Twentieth Century"), wondered, in a concluding comment on the program, about the persuasive power of public relations. He said:

And where has public relations led us? To a world where just about everybody uses it and defends it. The people in the business say their aim is to inform as much as to persuade. And persuasion is no dirty word, they insist; it's the sound of democracy and free enterprise in action. That's a point. But it is hard to recognize Adam Smith's "rational buyers" or Jefferson's "enlightened voters" in a public bombarded with contrived events to make someone's point. Who's pulling the string and why? It's one thing when funny people in bathing suits celebrate Equal Potato Chips Week, another when the answer to some governmental breach of law, or violation of human rights, is a highly paid media consultant. Something else too when the remedy for shoddy merchandise is a new corporate logo or a press conference featuring a blizzard of facts from hired experts. In a world where the rich and powerful can hire more and better persuaders, who has the last word? So the challenge for those who use public relations is one of ethics. . . .

4. Do not use irrelevant appeals to divert attention or scrutiny from the issue at hand. Among the appeals that commonly serve such a purpose are "smear" attacks on an opponent's character, appeals to hatred and bigotry, innuendo, and "God" or "devil" terms that cause intense but unreflective positive or negative reactions.

5. Do not ask your audience to link your idea or proposal to emotion-laden values, motives, or goals to which it actually is not related.

6. Do not deceive your audience by concealing your real purpose, your self-interest, the group you represent, or your position as an advocate of a viewpoint.

7. Do not distort, hide, or misrepresent the number, scope, intensity, or undesirable features of consequences.

8. Do not use emotional appeals that lack a supporting basis of evidence or reasoning or that would not be accepted if the audience had time and opportunity to examine the subject itself.

9. Do not oversimplify complex situations into simplistic two-valued, either/or, polar views or choices.

10. Do not pretend certainty when tentativeness and degrees of probability would be more accurate.

11. Do not advocate something in which you do not believe yourself.

A Checklist

Successful public relations campaigns are built on a thorough knowledge of public opinion and the principles of persuasive communication. A practitioner should keep in mind the following points:

1. Convey a sense of credibility by utilizing sources who are expert and sincere in their beliefs.

2. Tailor messages to the prevailing climate of information and opinion. Events speak louder than words.

3. Direct messages to formal and informal opinion leaders. They, in turn, will help shape the opinions of their followers.

4. Build messages on the audience's beliefs, personal experiences, and self-interests.

5. Accept ethical responsibility by communicating with clarity and integrity.

QUESTIONS FOR REVIEW AND DISCUSSION

1. Public opinion is highly influenced by self-interest and events. Explain these concepts.

2. It is said that people can more easily agree on goals than on methods to solve a problem. Why do you think this is so?

3. Explain the importance of opinion leaders in the formation of public opinion.

4. What is the role of the mass media in public opinion formation?

5. Name several ways in which public relations people monitor public opinion.

6. Name the three objectives of persuasion in public relations work. What is the easiest form of persuasion in terms of effect on the audience? What is the most difficult kind of persuasion to accomplish?

7. The text lists nine factors involved in effective persuasion. Name and describe them.

8. Name three aspects of source credibility.

9. Why is audience involvement important in persuasion?

10. What are the pros and cons of using emotional appeals?

CHAPTER TWELVE

Reaching the Audience

Since communication lies at the heart of public relations, those who work in the field must know what the channels of communication are and how they function.

Selection of the most effective ways to communicate in a public relations program is a crucial part of strategy. Just as a general seeks the most advantageous terrain for battle, the director of a public relations campaign must decide which media are most suitable for reaching the desired audiences and attaining the objective.

This chapter explains how the organized media in our society operate, the special attributes of each, and the ways in which practitioners can use the various channels.

Like a highway map, the chapter shows major routes leading to the various audiences that public relations seeks to address. Later chapters will examine in detail how to deliver messages to these audiences once they have been reached.

Other methods of communication that supplement the organized media—public speaking, word of mouth, and slide presentations, to mention three—will be discussed in Part Five.

The Print Media

NEWSPAPERS Every edition of a newspaper contains hundreds of news stories and pieces of information, in much greater number than the largest news staff can gather by itself. More than most readers realize, and many editors care to admit, newspapers depend upon information brought to them voluntarily.

The *Columbia Journalism Review* noted in its March 1981 issue, for example, that in one edition the *Wall Street Journal* had obtained 45 percent of its 188 news items from news releases. Because of its specialized nature, the *Journal*'s use of news releases may be higher than that of general-interest daily newspapers.

Newspapers have a primary role in public relations work. They need, and indeed welcome, intelligent input from public relations sources. In return, they provide a channel through which public relations communicators can reach a broad general audience.

Approximately 1700 daily newspapers and 7600 weekly newspapers are published in the United States. Most cities today have only one daily newspaper, although competition between two newspapers, or more, exists in the metropolitan centers and in a few smaller cities. While some metropolitan newspapers have circulations as high as a million copies a day, approximately two-thirds of the daily newspapers have circulations of 20,000 or less.

Newspapers published for distribution in the late afternoon, called evening or P.M. papers, outnumber morning (A.M.) papers approximately four to one. Especially in larger cities, however, a substantial trend toward morning publication is in progress. Some cities have 24-hour newspapers; these publish several editions around the clock. Knowledge of a newspaper's hours of publication and the deadlines it enforces for submission of copy is essential for everyone who supplies material to the paper.

Approximately two-thirds of American daily newspapers are owned by newspaper groups. The publishers and editors of a group-owned newspaper have broad local autonomy but must adhere to certain operating standards and procedures laid down by the group headquarters.

A COMMERCIAL INSTITUTION In dealing with a newspaper, public relations people should remember that it is a commercial institution, created to earn a profit as a purveyor of news and advertising. Although newspapers often are so deeply rooted in a community that they seem like public institutions, they are not. Their publishers and editors as a whole genuinely seek to serve the public interest, and often succeed admirably in doing so, but like any other business a newspaper that does not earn a profit soon disappears. Therefore, in the long run and sometimes in the short run as well, management decisions about what appears in a newspaper must be made with the balance sheet in mind.

Mobil Boycotts *Wall Street Journal*	One sure way to alienate the press and negate any effective media relations is to throw a temper tantrum.

Mobil Oil Corporation, piqued at how the *Wall Street Journal* covered some stories about the company, announced in November 1984 that it would no longer answer questions by *Journal* reporters and would discontinue spending about $500,000 annually on advertising in the *Journal*.

Such a boycott, of course, doesn't mean that the newspaper will forgo coverage of Mobil Oil. Nor will the newspaper suffer seriously from the loss of advertising revenue, which is a fraction of its total advertising income.

Most public relations executives thought such a boycott would be ineffective because the *Wall Street Journal* would still have access to company reports required by the Securities and Exchange Commission. In addition, the newspaper would continue to pick up information from other news sources and financial news services.

Time magazine quoted Exxon representative Philip Wetz: "You have to communicate to have a chance of getting your point of view across." Mobil Oil, the experts predicted, would eventually realize this and reopen the door.

Newspapers receive about 70 percent of their income from advertising and about 30 percent from circulation sales. They cannot afford to publish press releases that are nothing more than commercial advertising; to do so would cut into their largest source of income. To be published, a release submitted to a newspaper must contain information that an editor regards as news of interest to a substantial number of readers. Every public relations representative who works with newspapers should keep this in mind and prepare material accordingly.

Since newspapers are protected by the First Amendment to the Constitution, they cannot be forced to publish any news story, nor need they receive permission from the government or anyone else to publish whatever they desire. Editors resist pressure on them to suppress material they consider to be newsworthy and, conversely, to print material they believe to be unnewsworthy. However, the definitions of newsworthiness are abstract and fluctuating. What one newspaper considers to be news, another will not. *Demanding that a newspaper publish a news release is the surest way to have it rejected.*

Nevertheless, editors do not enjoy the unfettered privilege of publishing whatever they desire. Two severe limitations hang over their decisions:

1. *The laws of libel and invasion of privacy.* Publication of material that, if challenged in court, is ruled to be libelous or an unreasonable invasion of privacy can cost a newspaper extremely heavy judgments and legal expenses.

The newspaper management is legally responsible for everything a news-paper publishes, including material submitted by outsiders. Even letters to the editor are covered by the law of libel.

2. *The interests and desires of their readers.* If a newspaper fails to publish news and features that readers find to be valuable or entertaining, its circulation will dwindle and it will perish. Alert editors, therefore, are receptive to fresh ideas. They recognize the need for community service and look for ways in which their newspapers can perform this function. Their doors are open to public relations representatives who supply ideas and information that help the papers to please and inform their readers and to carry out the newspapers' social responsibility.

ORGANIZATION OF A NEWSPAPER   Those who work with newspapers in any aspect of public relations should know how a newspaper staff is organized, so they can take story ideas or policy problems to the proper person. In the usual table of organization, the publisher is the director of all financial, mechanical, and administrative operations. Frequently the publisher also has ultimate responsibility for news and editorial matters; in many instances he or she carries the title of editor and publisher.

The editor heads the news and editorial department. The associate editor conducts the editorial and commentary pages and deals with the public concerning their content. The managing editor is the head of news opera-tions, to whom the city editor and the editors of sections such as sports, business, entertainment, and family living answer. Some newspapers have an executive editor above the managing editor. The city editor directs the local news staff of reporters. Some members of the city staff cover beats such as police and city hall; others are on general assignment, meaning that they are sent to cover any type of story the city editor deems to be potentially newsworthy.

SUBMISSION OF NEWS RELEASES   News releases normally are submitted to the city desk, unless they are clearly designed for specialized sections such as sports. Although these special sections and the city desk operate separately, some liaison is maintained among them under the eye of the managing editor to maintain balance and prevent duplication of effort.

A large daily newspaper receives hundreds of news releases each day, most of which end in a wastebasket. Vast numbers of news releases never have a chance of being published because they lack relevance in the news-paper's circulation area, arrive too late, or pertain to events either so minor or so blatantly commercial that an editor discards them immediately. Public relations persons should pinpoint the outlets for which each release is relevant, rather than depend automatically upon a standard media list for all releases. Selective distribution of news releases saves the sender delivery expense and saves the recipients time.

Other news releases with genuine news potential may not be published because they have been sent to the wrong desk at a large newspaper. Obviously, a release about new interior decorating color schemes should not go to the sports editor. But such blunders happen. Although most newspapers try to route potentially usable releases from the city desk to appropriate departments, the systems are far from foolproof. Practitioners should send special-interest material to the section most likely to use it. Another cause of nonpublication is submission of poorly written releases.

A news release addressed to an editor by name has a subtle advantage over one merely addressed to *City Editor* or *Business Editor.* This person-alized method should be used whenever possible. Mailing lists *must* be kept up to date. Staff changes on newspapers are relatively frequent, especially on weeklies and small dailies, and mail appears inefficiently handled if addressed to someone no longer on the job.

Newspapers frequently make up some inside pages the afternoon before publication and certain special sections even earlier. Persons submitting news releases should have them delivered well before the desired publication date, as much as a week or more on feature-type material and at least a day on stories involving a time element. A news release delivered within a few hours of a newspaper's final deadline has little chance of being used that day unless it contains important spot-news information.

WEEKLY NEWSPAPERS Weekly newspapers have a different focus from that of daily newspapers, and much smaller staffs. A daily newspaper concerns itself with the world, the nation, and its local community. The weekly newspaper concentrates exclusively upon its own community. Its target zone may be no more than one segment of a metropolitan area, which it attempts to cover in more depth than a daily newspaper can provide. An editor with two or three staff assistants may produce the entire contents of a weekly newspaper. In order to do so, weekly editors need the help of much volunteered material. Although weekly newspapers often are overlooked in public relations programs, they can be effective outlets for those who study how to meet their needs.

Large daily newspapers, to demonstrate editorial independence, often have a rule against publishing a news release exactly as received. Relatively few weekly newspapers have the staffs to enforce such a policy. The odds that a well-prepared news release may be published exactly as written are favorable in most weekly newspapers. Although the circulation total for each weekly newspaper may be small because of its limited distribution area, the intensity of readership is high and story exposure is good.

When a weekly newspaper is distributed free of charge to all homes in its locality, as happens often in areas of concentrated housing, its circulation may be large; however, its readership may be less intense than that of paid-subscription weeklies. Such free-delivery weeklies make their money entirely from advertising, usually being dependent upon large advertisements from chain grocery and department stores that demand saturation coverage of neighborhoods (papers received by every household). The majority of weekly newspapers are published on Wednesday or Thursday. Unless they involve late-breaking information, news releases should reach them by Monday morning at the latest.

PUBLIC RELATIONS OPPORTUNITIES IN NEWSPAPERS

Material for a newspaper should be submitted either as a news release ready for publication or as a factsheet from which a reporter can develop a feature story or interview. When an invitation to a news conference is sent to a newspaper, it should include a factsheet containing basic information. Frequently, the reporter to whom an editor assigns a news release for processing rewrites and expands it, developing additional story angles and background. When a public relations representative presents an important story idea in factsheet form rather than as a news release for publication, a personal conversation with the appropriate editor, if it can be arranged, helps to sell the concept and expand its potential. *Such personal calls on editors should last no longer than is necessary to explain the idea adequately.* Although some practitioners make a follow-up phone call shortly after the factsheet has arrived, this practice irritates many editors. They are busy and dislike being interrupted. (Preparation of news releases is discussed in Chapter 22.)

Emphasizing contemporary living styles, newspapers often publish special sections on home improvement, fashion and beauty, business, sports, and recreation. This trend creates additional opportunities for practitioners, because editors seek story ideas and well-developed releases for these sections.

A public relations representative wishing to discuss a large-scale project such as a communitywide fund drive should do so by appointment with the managing editor or city editor after the deadline hour has passed. A cooperative plan of publicity can be developed at such a session. A newspaper is more likely to give a major project sympathetic treatment if its editors receive background information before the first stories break. This allows them time to think about the ramifications of the project and plan coverage.

At times, an organization's representative or other individual needs to discuss a policy issue with the newspaper management—a complaint against perceived mistreatment by the newspaper, for example, or an attempt to obtain editorial support. Usually this is done by appointment with the editor or associate editor or, in the case of a news story, with the managing editor. Often problems arise from misunderstanding rather than from intent.

To cite an actual example, in a large city that has three hospitals the directors of the smallest believed that the newspaper was ignoring it while giving extensive coverage to the other two. They were disturbed because no story had been published about a recent enlargement of the hospital's outpatient treatment facilities. The hospital was planning an important addition to its building that would involve the moving of two adjacent Victorian-era homes. The directors feared opposition to the removal of these landmark houses if the community did not understand the benefits of having the new facilities.

The chairman of the hospital board called the newspaper's public relations director, a friend, who arranged a three-way luncheon with the associate editor. As the editor and the hospital executive discussed the problem, it became apparent that the hospital administrator had failed to notify the newspaper about the enlargement of the outpatient facilities. He had assumed that the newspaper staff knew about the project, which it did not. It is a common error to assume that a newspaper automatically knows about everything that is happening.

Later, the associate editor explained the situation to the city editor, who assigned a reporter to do a story about the hospital's major expansion plans. The published story included a photograph of the architect's drawing and a detailed explanation of the additional beds and treatment facilities the new addition would provide. The neighborhood welcomed the addition as a civic improvement, and no protest was made about moving the historic houses. When the new wing opened, the newspaper published an extensive story about the dedication. The hospital's directors were pleased and the newspaper's reputation for thoroughness in its local coverage was enhanced. The lesson here is simple: when you have news to announce, tell the newspaper; don't wait for the paper to come to you.

CREATING NEWS EVENTS

Some news stories *happen*. Other stories must be *created*. Successful public relations practitioners must do more than produce competent, accurate news releases about routine occurrences in the affairs of their clients or employers. They must use ingenuity and organizing ability to create events that attract coverage in the news media. This extra dimension of creativity is the difference between acting to make news and merely reacting to news that happens. We are not speaking here of feeding phony stories to the media or doing anything else unethical. We are talking about causing something to occur. A good example is Light's Golden Jubilee, which was organized by Edward Bernays (see Chapter 3).

Here are some of the routine, semiautomatic events in a company's affairs about which a public relations representative should send news releases to the newspapers and other media:

Speeches by executives

Awards to employees

Staff promotions

Annual reports

Groundbreaking for new facilities

Corporate changes and mergers

Company anniversaries, such as the fiftieth and one hundredth

New products

Receipt of large orders

Unusual uses of company products

Much more than this can be done to improve the public's impression of the company. Recipe contests in newspapers and other media are a popular attraction, since readers and viewers are invited to share their cooking expertise (see Figure 12.1). These are a few of the *created* news events that can be publicized by news releases and feature story ideas suggested to editors:

Plant tours and open houses

Art shows by local artists in company headquarters, with wine and cheese served

Scholarship programs

Sponsorship of an important motion picture opening, with proceeds going to a local charity

Seminars at which guest speakers discuss significant issues

Halloween party for children of employees

Sponsorship of sporting events, such as a local long-distance run and tennis or golf clinics for teenagers

The recipes in this booklet are winners—as proclaimed by a panel of nationally-recognized food authorities judging a recent Kraft Marshmallow Creme "Easy Secret Ingredient" Recipe Contest. Your desserts will also be winners with family and friends when you know the "secret ingredient" for recipe success.

Kraft marshmallow creme has long been recognized as the "secret ingredient" for making creamy, smooth no-fail fudge and other candies. The contestants who submitted these prize-winning recipes know that it can also simplify baking and dessert-making.

Chilled treats have a mousse-like texture when prepared with marshmallow creme. It produces no-fail meringues—there is never any fear that the egg mixture will "fall" from overbeating. With marshmallow creme in the recipe, frozen creations are velvety-smooth without extra effort or specialized equipment. The wide-mouth jar makes for easy spooning of the Kraft marshmallow creme for use in recipes or served "as is" over ice cream, warm baked desserts or on hot beverages.

Use this collection of prize-winning recipes adapted by the Kraft Kitchens as a starting point. Then take a jar of Kraft marshmallow creme from the kitchen shelf and make your own winning creations with the "secret ingredient."

For starters, here are some tips and suggestions from the Kraft Kitchens:

- If a recipe calls for 2 cups of marshmallow creme, there's no need to measure. Use one 7 ounce jar or one-half of a 13 ounce jar. Recipes prepared with 1 cup marshmallow creme are successful when one-half of a 7 ounce jar is used.

- Marshmallow creme and marshmallows have different consistencies and characteristics, so a direct substitution in recipes between the two products is not possible.

- Thinned with a little water or another liquid, the Kraft marshmallow creme becomes a delicious sauce or simple dip for fruit. It can also be used as a change-of-pace "syrup" for serving over pancakes, waffles, or French toast.

Carmallow Apple Swirl

2 cups oatmeal cookie crumbs
⅓ cup Parkay margarine, melted
1 12-oz. jar Kraft caramel topping
2 7-oz. jars Kraft marshmallow creme
2 cups sour cream

1 8-oz. pkg. Philadelphia Brand cream cheese, softened
2 8-oz. containers (3 cups each) La Creme whipped topping with real cream, thawed
¾ cup apple butter
¼ cup chopped walnuts

Combine crumbs and margarine; press onto bottom of 9-inch springform pan.

Reserve ¼ cup caramel topping. Combine remaining caramel topping, marshmallow creme, sour cream and cream cheese, mixing at medium speed with an electric mixer until well blended. Fold in one 8-oz. container whipped topping. Add apple butter; cut through mixture with knife several times for marble effect. Pour over crust; freeze. Top with remaining whipped topping, reserved caramel topping and walnuts.

12 to 14 servings

Variation: Substitute 13 x 9-inch baking pan for springform pan.

Micky Kolar, Fountain Hills, AZ
1st PRIZE WINNER · Special Occasion Desserts

Caramel Pecan Cups

1 cup vanilla wafer crumbs
¼ cup Parkay margarine, melted
16 Kraft caramels
¼ cup milk

1 7-oz. jar Kraft marshmallow creme
1 cup chopped pecans, toasted
2 cups thawed La Creme whipped topping with real cream

Combine crumbs and margarine; reserve ¼ cup crumb mixture for topping. Press remaining crumb mixture onto bottom of paper-lined muffin cups.

Melt caramels with milk over low heat, stirring until smooth. Remove from heat; stir in marshmallow creme. Cool to room temperature. Stir in pecans; fold in whipped topping. Spoon caramel mixture into baking cups; sprinkle with reserved crumb mixture. Freeze.

12 servings

Gloria A. Shamanoff, Fort Wayne, IN
1st PRIZE WINNER · Make Ahead Treats

Yogurt Creme Sauce

1 8-oz. container plain yogurt
1 7-oz. jar Kraft marshmallow creme

1½ teaspoons lemon juice

Combine yogurt, marshmallow creme and juice, mixing with electric mixer or wire whisk until well blended. Chill. Serve with fruit or ice cream.

1¾ cups

Janet Koehlinger, Huntington, IN
1st PRIZE WINNER · Desserts For The Family

FIGURE 12.1

Food manufacturers focus much of their public relations effort on food sections of newspapers and magazines and homemaking programs on television. One method is to conduct recipe contests, such as this one by Kraft promoting its marshmallow creme.

Annual dinner for employees and families (if the company is small enough)

Endowment of a faculty position at the local university in the company's field of work

Every one of these events represents a legitimate news story that the local newspaper and other media might cover. But these stories exist only because a shrewd public relations adviser convinced the company to sponsor or conduct them. Once this decision is made, the practitioner must produce

1. Tie in with news events of the day.

2. Work with another publicity person.

3. Tie in with a newspaper or other medium on a mutual project.

4. Conduct a poll or survey.

5. Issue a report.

6. Arrange an interview with a celebrity.

7. Take part in a controversy.

8. Arrange for a testimonial.

9. Arrange for a speech.

10. Make an analysis or prediction.

11. Form and announce names for committees.

12. Hold an election.

13. Announce an appointment.

14. Celebrate an anniversary.

15. Issue a summary of facts.

16. Tie in with a holiday.

a flow of news releases with fresh angles, as well as use other techniques to build public interest.

Openings of stores and shopping centers, as well as groundbreakings, happen so frequently that the ingenuity of public relations representatives is challenged. Newspapers are weary of the traditional, rigidly posed group of men in dark business suits and incongruous hardhats lined up behind one man with a shovel. The same is true of ribbon-cuttings. Some newspapers refuse to publish these photographic clichés. However, fresh approaches can be found, especially if a little humor is employed.

In one small Southwestern town, a long-retired movie cowboy, who had won additional fame in early television Westerns, was a prominent resident. When a new shopping area was to be opened, he was invited to appear in a cowboy costume on a horse and cut the ribbon. Things didn't work out that way. His horse had died. He had grown too heavy to get into his cowboy pants. But clever thinking saved the situation for the community sponsors. The actor arrived at the scene in an automobile, wearing his cowboy hat and shirt. The gun he carried was a cap pistol. The broad red ribbon strung

17. Make a trip.

18. Make an award.

19. Hold a contest.

20. Pass a resolution.

21. Appear before public bodies.

22. Stage a special event.

23. Write a letter.

24. Release a letter you have received.

25. Adapt national reports and surveys for local use.

26. Stage a debate.

27. Tie into a well-known week or day.

28. Honor an institution.

29. Organize a tour.

30. Inspect a project.

31. Issue a commendation.

32. Issue a protest.

across the street had secretly been cut almost through the middle by the public relations specialist in charge.

At a signal, the rotund cowboy fired his toy pistol at the ribbon. At the popping sound, a slight tug by the ribbon-holders sent the red strand fluttering. Cameras clicked and everyone laughed. Although born of a practitioner's desperation, the tongue-in-cheek travesty drew more publicity than a routine ribbon-cutting would have done.

The year 1983 gave public relations people a good opportunity to mark a historic occasion—the one hundredth anniversary of the Brooklyn Bridge, an engineering landmark (see Figure 12.2).

MAGAZINES   Magazines differ markedly from newspapers in content, time element, and methods of operation. Therefore, they present different opportunities and problems to the public relations practitioner. In contrast to the daily newspaper with its hurry-up deadlines, magazines are published weekly, monthly, or sometimes quarterly. Because these publications usually deal with subjects

FIGURE 12.2

The centennial celebration of the opening of the Brooklyn Bridge exemplifies the successful created news event. A 1880s costume parade was part of the observance. Dudley-Anderson-Yutzy Public Relations, Inc., was hired to create awareness of the centennial. The well-attended celebration drew worldwide publicity. (Courtesy of Dudley-Anderson-Yutzy.)

in greater depth than newspapers do, magazine editors may allot months for development of an article. Those who seek to supply subject ideas or ready-to-publish material to them must plan much further ahead than is necessary with newspapers. Ideas for Christmas season stories, for example, should be submitted as much as 6 months in advance.

A newspaper is designed for family reading, with something for men, women, and children; its material is aimed at an audience of varying educational and economic levels. Its editors fire buckshot, to hit the reading interests of as many persons as possible. Magazine editors, on the other hand, in most instances aim carefully at special-interest audiences. They fire rifle bullets at limited, well-defined readership groups.

The approximately 5000 periodicals published in the United States may be classified in several ways. For purposes of this discussion, they are grouped into two broad categories, each in turn broken down into several subdivisions.

PERIODICALS FOR THE PUBLIC AT LARGE   Among the types in this category are the following:

General interest. In pretelevision days, general-interest magazines with audiences comparable to those of daily newspapers flourished, such as the

Saturday Evening Post and *Look*. Only a few national magazines with across-the-board appeal exist today. Prominent among them are *Reader's Digest,* enormously successful worldwide; *People,* which capitalizes on the contemporary interest in personalities; and *National Geographic,* whose simply written, splendidly illustrated articles provide a popular look at the world and its people.

News magazines. These high-circulation weekly publications report and interpret the news, adding background that daily newspapers lack time to develop. The biggest periodicals of this type are *Time, Newsweek,* and *U.S. News and World Report. Time* and *Newsweek* are tightly departmentalized, including sections devoted to the arts, science, business, and sports.

Women's interest. Magazines designed for women have a very large audience. They publish articles about fashions and beauty, cooking, home decorating, self-improvement, work and leisure, and personal relationships. Some include fiction carefully crafted for the same readership. Prominent in this group are *Ladies' Home Journal, Cosmopolitan, Ms., Better Homes and Gardens, Good Housekeeping, House and Garden,* and *Family Circle.*

Men's interest. Definition of this group is less clear than that of the women's group. Growing participation of women in athletics has increased female readership of sports magazines once regarded as almost exclusively for men. *Sports Illustrated* and *Field and Stream* are perhaps the best known of these magazines. With emphasis on sex and photographs of nude young women, *Playboy* and *Penthouse* aim primarily at the male audience but also draw substantial female readership. They publish long interviews with prominent persons, as well as material about such topics as stereo equipment and automobiles. Numerous other "skin" magazines, more blatantly sexual, also are found in the men's group.

The categories of magazines just listed, designed for the public as a whole or for large segments of it, offer public relations opportunities that pay large rewards in readership when successful. They are difficult markets to hit, however, except by highly experienced specialists well acquainted with the magazines' operating methods. Altogether, these magazines best known to the general public number no more than 50. Far more abundant opportunities for placing public relations material exist with the other 4900-plus periodicals, those aimed at more specific audiences.

PERIODICALS FOR SPECIFIC AUDIENCES   This group includes a wide array of publications, including the following:

Special-audience magazines. Hundreds of these prosper because they are carefully edited on single themes. Each attracts an audience with strong interest in its particular topic; this audience in turn draws advertisers whose products are especially relevant to these readers. A glance at the magazine rack in a supermarket gives an indication of the diversity of special-interest magazines—only an indication, however, because such periodicals are far too numerous for over-the-counter sale. Many are distributed primarily by subscription.

For example, one neighborhood market rack includes these narrow-target periodicals: *Dog World, Backpacker, High Fidelity, Stereo Review, Horse & Rider, Trailer Life, Creative Computing, Model Railroader, Road & Track, Car Craft, Dirt Bike, Skin Diver, Surfing, Private Pilot, Cycle World, Photography, Ski, Hot Rod,* and *Radio-Electronics.* Broader in appeal than many of these, but nevertheless aimed at a special-interest audience, are magazines about business, including *Fortune, Business Week, Forbes,* and *Barron's.*

Trade journals. Each of the special-audience magazines listed above appeals to a portion of the public that cares about its particular topic mostly as a hobby or a sport. Trade journals, on the other hand, are designed for persons who read them for business and professional reasons, not recreational ones. While virtually unknown to the public, these periodicals are vital channels of communication within various industries and professions. In their pages, readers learn about the activities of their competitors, new products and trends in their field of work, and the movement of individuals from one job to another. Often trade journals have the same intimacy in their respective fields as weekly newspapers do in their communities.

The following small sampling of trade journals indicates the extremely specialized nature of their contents: *American Christmas Tree Journal, Mini-Micro Systems, Fleet Owner, The Indian Trader, Insulation Outlook, The Internal Auditor, Journal of Micrographics, Modern Power Systems, National Mall Monitor, Nursing Homes, Electronic Design, Pest Control Magazine, Progressive Grocer, Wire Journal.*

Placement of material in trade journals is an essential assignment for many public relations representatives. A story about a new product published in an appropriate trade journal may be more valuable to the manufacturer of that product than a story about it in a large newspaper, because the information reaches a target audience containing potential purchasers. Products and specialized services offered by companies often are not publicized to a general audience, because it neither needs nor cares about them. If a manufacturer of coin-operated machines has a new product ready for release, its public relations representative should concentrate on placing announcement stories in such trade journals as *American Coin-Op, Coinamatic Age, Game Merchandising, Leisure Time Electronics, Play Meter Magazine,* and *Vending Times.* Similarly, the producer of a new kind of milking machine should seek an audience in *Butter-Fat, Dairy Goat Journal, Dairy Herd Management, The Dairyman,* and *Dairyman's Digest.*

Practitioners handling specialized products or services should scrutinize pertinent trade journals, to be certain that they are supplying these publications with effective news releases, story ideas, and illustrations. A one-year analysis of these journals will show how well a client and its competitors fared. With this analysis in hand, the publicist might find it desirable to submit more stories about large orders received by the client, for example, or stories about unusual uses of a product.

Company and organizational magazines. These are of two types:

1. *Internal,* designed for and distributed primarily to employees, retirees, influential outsiders who may have some interest in the organization, and often stockholders of the firm. (These are discussed in Chapter 22.)

2. *External,* distributed to selected portions of the public. Published by companies and organizations to promote public appreciation of the sponsor, and to form a psychological tie between sponsor and recipient, these usually are circulated among customers, stockholders, and users of the sponsor's services (see Figure 12.3). Editorial content of such external periodicals has general appeal—articles on travel, personalities, self-help, food, and the like—plus material about the issuing company. The magazines that airline travelers find in the seat pockets in front of them, such as *American Way* (American Airlines) and *TWA Ambassador* (Trans World Airlines), are prime examples of this group. Another is *Westways,* published by the Automobile Club of Southern California and sold by subscription to the club's very large membership. Mixed in with its elaborately illustrated articles on travel and California living is material about auto club tours. *Inland, The Magazine of the Middle West,* published by the Inland Steel Company, uses a formula in which half of each issue is on topics other than steel and is related to aspects of living in the Midwest.

Such external magazines offer a good target for the public relations specialist. Their audiences tend to be relatively affluent.

PUBLIC RELATIONS OPPORTUNITIES IN MAGAZINES

A study of the annual *Writer's Market* and the monthly periodicals *Writer's Digest* and *The Writer* will provide abundant information about individual magazines and the kind of material each publishes. Every magazine has its special formula.

Like newspapers, magazines are protected by the First Amendment. They may publish whatever they choose but are subject to the libel and invasion of privacy laws.

Operating with much smaller staffs than newspapers have, magazines are heavily dependent upon material submitted from outside their offices. Some, especially the smaller ones, are almost entirely staff-written. The staffs create ideas and cover some stories; they also process public relations material submitted to them. The more carefully the submitted material is tailored to the particular periodical's audience and written in a style the editor prefers,

the more likely it is to be published, with or without rewriting by the staff. Many magazines purchase part, or almost all, of their material from free-lance writers on a fee basis. An editor may buy a submitted article for publication if it fits the magazine's formula, or the editor may commission a writer to develop an idea into an article along specified lines.

Thus, a public relations practitioner has five principal approaches for getting material into a periodical:

1. Submit a story idea that would promote the practitioner's cause either directly or subtly and urge the editor to have a writer, free-lance or staff, develop the story on assignment.

2. Send a written query to the editor outlining an article idea and offering to submit the article in publishable form if the editor approves the idea.

3. Submit a completed article on a free-lance basis and hope that the editor will accept it for publication. (At many magazines, editors are more likely to accept an article if they have been queried about it first.)

4. Have a free-lance writer propose to an editor an article on a topic you have suggested to him or her. Then, if the editor expresses interest in publishing the article, assist the writer in the research and suggest angles that will be favorable to your interest.

5. For trade journals and other periodicals that use such material, submit news releases in ready-to-publish form.

The size and nature of each magazine determines its content. Most common is a formula of several major articles, one or two short articles, and special departments. These may be personal commentary, a compilation of news items in a specific category (short items about new products in a trade journal, for example), or chit-chat about personalities. Special departments offer excellent public relations opportunities. A favorable item in one of them need not be long to be effective. Within weeks after the Potpourri section of *Playboy* mentioned the existence of "No Bozo!" stickers, intended to criticize greedy or rude conduct by motorists, shoppers, and others, the small firm that created them sold a half-million stickers. A small international fad was born.

When a magazine has a by-lined columnist and the publicist has material suitable for that column, it may be sent directly to the columnist. The risk is that if the columnist rejects the item, he or she may throw it in the wastebasket when in fact it might be usable elsewhere in the magazine. When there is doubt, it is safer to submit such material to the editor. As with newspaper material, news releases and proposals should be addressed to the editor by name. Examination of a magazine's masthead will show the name of the proper editor to address.

BOOKS   Because their writing and publication is a time-consuming process, often involving years from the conception of an idea until appearance of the volume, books are not popularly recognized as public relations tools. Yet they can be. A book, especially a hard-cover one, has stature in the minds of readers. They read it with respect and give attention to the message it carries.

Books are promulgators of ideas. As channels of communication, they reach thoughtful audiences, including opinion leaders. Often publication of a book starts a trend or focuses national discussion on an issue. Historically, Harriet Beecher Stowe's *Uncle Tom's Cabin* was a catalyst for antislavery opinion just before the Civil War. In the 1950s Rudolf Flesch's *Why Johnny Can't Read* was tremendously successful because it expressed the public's uneasiness over contemporary teaching methods. And in the 1960s Rachel Carson's *Silent Spring* focused attention on harmful effects of some herbicides upon wildlife.

The standard method of book publishing is for an author and publisher to sign a contract describing the material the author will deliver to the publisher and the conditions under which the publisher will issue and sell the book. The publisher pays the cost of production and marketing. The author receives a royalty fee on each copy sold, usually 10 to 15 percent of the retail price. Publishers often make advance payments to authors against the royalties their books are expected to earn. Both parties take a risk; the author invests time and the cost of researching and writing the book, while the publisher invests substantial amounts of money to put the manuscript into book form and sell it.

A book published in hard covers often requires a year from acceptance of the manuscript to publication. Thus, a public relations effort made through publication of a hard-cover book must be long range in nature and aimed at the broad-stroke influencing of public opinion. The hard-cover book is not the tool for stirring up a new hulahoop fad or publicizing a video game.

The tremendous growth of paperback publishing has opened new avenues for use of books as public relations vehicles. Mass paperbacks are produced much more rapidly than hard-cover books and sell for lower prices. They are marketed much like magazines, appearing on thousands of sales racks in airports, drug stores, bus stations, shopping malls, and other locations with heavy foot traffic. The rack-life of paperback novels, in particular, is very short. Each month's new issues are heavily promoted and displayed, only to give way to the next month's crop. Some are kept on longer sale in bookstores.

Not all paperbacks are so ephemeral, of course. Hundreds of titles ranging from classical literature to how-to-do-it books on gardening, plumbing, and sex are on sale in bookstores. An examination of nonfiction titles on the paperback shelves will show the range of opportunity that exists to promote products, ideological movements, personalities, and fads.

The traditional royalty system of hard-cover books is also used for paperback books, but various forms of fee payments to authors are employed as well.

Literary agents have an influential role in the creation of books. An agent represents the author in dealings with publishers, urging a publishing house to accept a manuscript and negotiating contracts that include provisions for subsidiary rights, film rights, and other sources of income. For this assistance, the agent ordinarily receives 10 percent of the author's income from the literary property involved. Unless he or she is well acquainted with the publishing industry, a public relations representative seeking to publicize a client's cause through publication of a book is well advised to work through an agent rather than make a personal round of publishing houses. Competent agents know the financial angles and offer shrewd editorial advice as well.

Although the fact is seldom mentioned publicly, companies and nonprofit organizations sometimes pay subsidies to both hard-cover and paperback publishers to help defray production costs of a book they wish to see published. The subsidy may take the form of a guarantee to purchase a specific number of copies. A corporation, for example, might wish to commemorate its centennial with a company history and desire the prestige of a prominent publishing house behind it. Yet sales experience indicates that the book, although expertly and objectively written, will not sell enough copies for the publisher to break even. So a quiet subsidy arrangement is made. A handsome book results; it receives favorable reviews, the corporation gains prestige, the publisher makes some money, and the public's fund of knowledge is increased. The book must be an honest one, however, not a blatant "puff" job. It must report the bad with the good. If not, everyone involved loses respect instead of gaining it.

An example of an open tie-in book is *Cooking With a Food Processor,* which publicizes the uses of General Electric blenders. The book was published by Random House, with the General Electric name on the title page and a note stating that the recipes were tested in GE kitchens.

PUBLIC RELATIONS OPPORTUNITIES IN BOOKS

As indicated above, books as public relations tools, both hard-cover and paperback, usually are best suited to promote ideas and create a favorable state of mind. Political movements often are publicized through books by proponents. On a more mundane level, every book published about gardening indirectly helps the sale of garden tools. Although a specific brand of tools is not mentioned in such a book, it benefits from the book's existence. The manufacturer's public relations representative can help the company's cause by assisting the author in assembling material for the book. Public relations efforts need not be overt to be effective. Also, public relations benefits may occur without being planned. The cookbook *The Complete Dairy Foods Cookbook,* by E. Annie Proues and Lew Nichols, inevitably helped promote use of dairy products, while *The Joy of Chocolate,* by Judith Olney, must have made the chocolate manufacturers happy.

The following hypothetical but realistic example shows how the promotional underwriting system can work. A beautifully illustrated book about a New England state appears in the stores. How did the book come into being? Perhaps the publishing house conceived the idea and engaged an author and photographer; or a writer-photographer team might have proposed it to the publisher. Conceivably, the idea originated within the state tourist agency as a way to promote travel there. The tourist agency could have passed the idea along to an author whose work it respected. Or it might have proposed the book to the publisher, directly or through a literary agent, with an offer to underwrite part of the production cost. In any event, the tourist agency almost certainly would be brought into the project as a supplier of factual material and illustrations. An examination of acknowledgements and photographic credits in such books reveals how public relations agencies have a role in their creation.

From the point of view of publishers, publicity for books and their authors is an important public relations function. The public relations departments of publishing houses use news releases, prepublication endorsements, interviews, and other standard techniques to create awareness of a forthcoming book. If the book lends itself to heavy promotion and the author is articulate, the writer may be taken on a tour of major cities for an intensive series of radio and television appearances and newspaper interviews, plus autographing parties in bookstores.

DIRECT MAIL   The scene is repeated millions of times each day. A person brings in the handful of mail and sorts it into two stacks: the "important" mail, to be read immediately, and the "junk" mail, to be glanced at afterward or thrown away unopened. Considering how much of this unsolicited mail lands in the wastebasket, one might assume that the companies and organizations that send it are wasting millions of dollars in printing and postage. Quite the contrary is true.

Use of complex computer techniques to compile target mailing lists and produce letters, and psychological techniques to compose persuasive messages, makes direct mail productive and cost-efficient. Properly done, it is a very valuable method for certain types of campaigns. Fund-raising and opinion-molding are the two most important public relations uses of direct mail. Marketing departments employ it extensively for mail-order sale of merchandise. (Direct mail techniques for public relations purposes are discussed in Chapter 18.)

The Spoken Media

RADIO   Speed and mobility are the special attributes that make radio unique among the major media of communication. If urgency justifies such action, messages can be placed on the air by radio almost instantly upon their receipt at a

Pacific Bell, official sponsor of telecommunications for the 1984 Olympics in Los Angeles, provided a number of facilities and materials for visiting newspeople from around the world.

A basic fact kit on the Olympics and on how to use Pacific Bell's telecommunications facilities (including electronic mail) was printed in a number of languages including Japanese, Spanish, French, Italian, German, Chinese, Arabic, and even Russian. Each journalist who visited the Pacific Bell information center could also pick up a 50-page color "Olympic Guidebook" with maps, mileages, and photos of sites. And journalists who forgot to bring a toothbrush could pick up a complete grooming kit at the center.

Other booklets distributed to the press included "Media Telephone Directory and Guide," "1984 Directory for the News Media in Greater Los Angeles and Ventura Counties," and "News Numbers for News People." Supplemental information included fact cards on various athletes, a comic book illustrating how fiber optics helps the press cover the Olympics, a record single titled "LA . . . Here's Looking at Ya," and two books about California history.

radio station. They need not be delayed by the time-consuming production processes of print. Since radio programming is more loosely structured than television programming, interruption of a program for an urgent announcement can be done with less internal decision-making. Although most public relations material does not involve such urgency, moments of crisis do occur when quick on-the-air action helps a company or other organization get information to the public swiftly. A train wreck in which overturned cars of toxic material are leaking is an example. Although not at fault for the railroad's accident, the chemical company involved urgently wishes to distribute accurate information about the risk to persons living in the neighborhood.

Radio benefits, too, from its ability to go almost anywhere. Reporters working from mobile trucks can be broadcasting from the scene of a large fire within minutes after it has been discovered. They can hurry from a press conference to a luncheon speech, carrying only a small amount of equipment. A disc jockey can broadcast an afternoon program from a table in a neighborhood shopping center. Flexibility is ever-present.

So is flexibility among listeners. Radios in automobiles reach captive audiences, enhancing the popularity of drive-time disc jockeys. The tiny transistor radio brings programs to mail carriers on their routes, carpenters on construction sites, homeowners pulling weeds in their gardens.

Nearly 10,000 radio stations are on the air in the United States, ranging from low-powered outlets operated by a handful of staff members to large metropolitan stations audible for hundreds of miles. Slightly more than half of these stations are of the amplitude modulation (AM) type; the others use frequency modulation (FM), which has shorter range but generally clearer reception. Some AM stations aim at general audiences, using middle-of-the-road music, while others appeal to special listener interests. FM stations, with restricted listening areas, usually seek target audiences. This is especially true in metropolitan areas, where two dozen or more stations may be in competition. Both AM and FM stations attempt to develop distinctive "sounds" by specializing in one kind of music, such as hard rock or country-and-western. A public relations practitioner should study each station's format and submit material suitable to it. There is little sense in sending information about senior citizen recreational programs to the news director of a hard-rock station with an audience primarily of teenagers.

Radio programming hardly needs description here; virtually everyone has been exposed to it. Recorded music played in segments of approximately 3 minutes and interspersed with commercials forms the backbone. Frequent newscasts are a primary ingredient. For many stations, so is sports.

A radio station operates under license, renewable every 7 years, from the Federal Communications Commission. After several decades of strict FCC regulation, the radio industry was partially deregulated in 1981, thus obtaining greater flexibility in programming. No longer must a station devote part of its air time to nonentertainment programming or restrict the number of minutes in each hour devoted to commercials. Even with these restrictions removed, a station may encounter license renewal trouble if it cannot demonstrate reasonably well under challenge that it operates in the public interest, necessity, and convenience. All programs are subject to the laws of libel.

PUBLIC RELATIONS OPPORTUNITIES IN RADIO

Commercial radio is highly promotional in nature and provides innumerable opportunities for public relations specialists to further their causes over its facilities. Radio programs may be divided into two general categories, news programs and entertainment shows. A station's news director is responsible for the former, the program director for the latter.

Most stations have frequent newscasts, of which the 5-minute variety is the most common. If the station has a network affiliation, some newscasts it carries are national in content. Of much more interest to the public relations practitioner are the local newscasts. These have abundant public relations potential. News releases sent to a radio station should cover the same newsworthy topics as those sent to a newspaper; they should follow identical rules of accuracy and timeliness. The practitioner cannot expect to hear extended versions of these releases on the air. Brevity is fundamental on radio. A story that runs 400 words in a newspaper may be told in 75 words or less on radio. Lengthy news releases for radio stations are unnecessary, indeed unwise, unless portions of them are clearly identified as background information, in case the news director chooses to develop a story at greater length in a special feature broadcast.

Many stations broadcast a daily program called the "Community Bulletin Board" or with a similar title. This listing of coming events is an excellent place to circulate information about a program the practitioner is handling.

Radio news directors brighten their newscasts by including *actualities*. These are brief reports from scenes of action, either live or on tape. Public relations representatives may supply stations with actualities to be used on newscasts. If a high executive of a practitioner's client speaks at a luncheon, a brief taped highlight from that speech, if sent to a radio station, may find a place on a local newscast. So might a taped highlight from the dedication ceremony for a manufacturing plant. Radio stations tend to have small news staffs and cannot cover as many events as they desire. They welcome assistance if it is provided in an objective manner.

Another goal for public relations efforts is the radio talk show, on which a moderator and guests discuss issues. Placement of a client on a talk show provides exposure for the individual and for the cause being espoused. Talk shows may be news-oriented, such as a discussion of a controversial issue, and produced by the news director. Or they may be entertainment-oriented, controlled by the program director and handled by a staff producer. Mid-morning homemaker hours have numerous spots for guest appearances.

Larger radio stations, in particular, broadcast daily editorials, comparable to newspaper editorials. Usually these are delivered by the station manager. Public relations specialists may be able to persuade a station to carry an editorial of endorsement for their cause. They should stay alert, too, for editorials that condemn a cause they espouse. The representative should request equal time on the air for a rebuttal, usually given by a leading executive of the organization or cause under attack. Stations are required by the Federal Communications Commission to air rebuttals to their editorials.

On the entertainment side, disc jockeys in their programs of music and chit-chat frequently air material provided by public relations sources. The DJs conduct on-the-air contests and promotions, give away tickets to shows, discuss coming local events, offer trivia quizzes—whatever they can think of to make their programs distinctive and lively. A disc jockey talking on the air several hours a day devours large amounts of material. After studying a program's style, an able practitioner can supply items and ideas that the DJ welcomes, and thus promote the causes of public relations clients.

At times, radio stations sponsor community events such as outdoor concerts or long-distance runs. Repeated mention of such an event on the air for days or weeks usually turns out large crowds. Here, too, is an opportunity for the public relations person, either to convince a station to sponsor such an event or to develop tie-ins with it.

A close relationship exists between radio stations and the recording industry. Recording companies depend upon the stations to play their new releases; the stations in turn use those companies as the primary source for the music they play. This relationship has created a highly specialized form of public relations work by representatives of the record companies.

TELEVISION   Our lives feel the impact of television more than that of any other communications medium. Daily patterns of living are shaped around the broadcast
time of favorite programs. Perceptions of contemporary American life are
influenced by the settings and often highly contrived plots of situation comedy series. Television money dictates the starting hours of sporting events
and national political conventions. A high percentage of Americans regard
television as their primary source of news, although TV newscasts are essentially an illustrated headline service into which "show-biz" techniques have
been injected.

Approximately 1150 television stations are in operation, projecting over-
the-air visual programming. According to estimates provided by the A. C.
Nielsen Company, the major rating firm for national programming, more
than 84 million American households owned television sets in 1985. At that
time, according to Nielsen statistics, the average American family watched
television 7 hours and 8 minutes a day.

Little wonder that public relations specialists look upon television as an
enormous arena in which to tell their stories!

The fundamental factor that differentiates television from the other media
and gives it such pervasive impact is the visual element. Producers of entertainment shows, newscasts, and commercials regard movement on the screen
as essential. Something must happen to hold the viewer's attention. Persons
talking on the screen for more than a brief time without movement, or at
least a change of camera angle, are belittled as "talking heads."

Because of this visual impact, television emphasizes personality. Entertainment programs are built around stars; if persons little known to the
public appear on popular new programs, they soon become stars with instant
recognition in millions of homes. Only on television do news reporters
achieve "star quality"; although many anchor men and women on newscasts
are merely polished readers of the news, they become local and national
celebrities. When public relations people plan material for television, they
should remember the importance of visual impact and personality.

Television shows live and die by their ratings. Scorecard mentality dominates the selection of programs and program content, especially on the
networks. The viewing habits of a few thousand Americans, recorded by the
Nielsen and Arbitron rating services, determine what programs all television
watchers can see. The explanation is money. Networks and local stations
determine the prices they charge to show commercials by the estimated size
of the audience watching a program when the commercial is shown. Thus
the larger the audience, the higher the price for commercial time and the
higher the profit. Even nonprofit television stations keep a close watch on
the size of their audiences, because their income in part comes from the
grants corporations give them to show certain programs.

In addition to the traditional free over-the-air television, a tremendous
proliferation of delivery systems for television shows is taking place. Until

the early 1980s, reception by viewers was primarily from three national networks—American Broadcasting Company (ABC), Columbia Broadcasting System (CBS), and National Broadcasting Company (NBC)—through their owned and affiliated stations; from independent stations; and from public broadcast stations. All stations were either VHF (very high frequency) or the weaker UHF (ultra high frequency). Then the technological revolution exploded. Programs became available on the home screen from cable television channels, subscription television transmitted by a scrambling system on over-the-air channels, direct satellite reception, videodiscs, and videocassettes inserted into adapters connected to the TV set. Two-way cable systems in which viewers could reply to programs came into operation. The Federal Communications Commission authorized construction of low-power television transmitters with a range of about 15 to 20 miles.

A tremendous battle for admission to the home viewer's screen developed among the proprietors of the new forms, and between them and the traditional over-the-air stations and networks. In the mid-1970s, the three basic commercial networks were viewed by more than 90 percent of the audience during prime-time evening hours. This figure had diminished to 75 percent by the mid-1980s and continued to fall as the total television audience was fragmented.

This turmoil opened enormous new programming potential and a consequent increase in public relations opportunities. When a cable system offers up to 100 channels, as some are technically capable of doing, the demand for program material is voracious.

Although most television stations are on the air for 18 hours or more a day, only a few hours of programming originate in their studios—mostly newscasts, local talk shows, and midmorning homemaker programs with a host or hostess and guests. Because of the high costs involved, only rarely does a local station create an entertainment program. More of the day's programming consists of network "feeds," if the station has a network affiliation; reruns of movies and former network series episodes; and other programs purchased from syndicators. Development of satellite transmission (discussed in Chapter 21) has created numerous smaller networks that provide entertainment, news, and sports shows, giving independent stations new sources of programming.

PUBLIC RELATIONS OPPORTUNITIES IN TELEVISION

The possibilities for the public relations specialist to use television are so numerous that they are worth examining on two levels, network and local.

THE NETWORK LEVEL   These are the principal methods commonly used:

1. *Guest appearances on news and talk shows.* Placement of clients on such programs as the "Tonight Show" and "Today" allows them to give plugs to new products, books, films, and plays, and to advocate their causes. For entertainment personalities in particular, these interviews provide a setting in which to display their skills. National leaders are interviewed in depth on the Sunday discussion panel shows such as "Meet the Press." Guests on network interview shows must be articulate and poised, so they won't freeze up before the camera. Consequently, they are carefully screened by show production staffs before being granted an appearance. As an example of the promotional power of these shows, Eastman Kodak Company chose the ABC-TV "Good Morning America" program as the place to unveil its revolutionary disc camera, the kickoff of an intense global publicity campaign that is discussed in Chapter 18. Nationally syndicated talk programs such as the "Phil Donahue Show" and the "Merv Griffin Show," which are sold to individual stations, provide similar showcases.

Public relations people wishing to place guests on these programs should apply to the producers of the shows.

2. *News releases and story proposals to network news departments.* This process is identical to that followed with radio stations. If a story or an idea is accepted, the assignment editor gives it to a reporter for visual development. When a client is criticized in a controversial news situation or editorial, a representative should submit the client's response and urge that it be used on the air. If the response is submitted in concise videotape form, the likelihood of a quick airing is increased.

3. *Videotapes of unusual feature stories for use in news programs.* Medical research developments, as well as odd personalities and offbeat human interest events that can be told briefly as "kicker" stories to close newscasts, are especially useful.

4. *Program ideas.* The representative of an important cause may propose to a network that it build an episode in a dramatic or situation comedy series around this cause. A comedy star might join an antismoking campaign, only to suffer humorous withdrawal pangs, or a dramatic hour might be built around efforts of doctors to save a child from an often-fatal disease. Such programs do not make overt sales pitches for the treatment organizations, but the message is inherent in the story line. In one episode of "All in the Family," a renowned comedy series that broke much new ground on television, the father, Archie Bunker, suffered a heart attack, and the program showed what should be done in such circumstances. This was the message the American Heart Association sought to deliver. The public relations person can assist the program producer by supplying technical information.

5. *Silent publicity.* There are almost subliminal impacts in entertainment programs that quietly publicize a representative's cause. In a private detective show, for example, as the star chases the villain through an airport terminal, they are shown running past a TWA sign. Or the automobiles used by the

How to Place a Client on a TV Talk Show	Television stations are looking for interesting, articulate guests for their talk shows. The larger the station, the more stringent are its requirements for accepting a guest. This summary of needs and procedures for "AM/San Francisco," the morning show on KGO-TV, the ABC network outlet in San Francisco, is typical of those for metropolitan stations. The information is from an article published in *Bulldog,* a West Coast public relations newsletter.

The station wants guests "who will provide information that will help our viewers to save money and save time, helpful hints around the house, consumer-type things." The station also uses guests from the business community who can comment on money, taxes, the stock market, and similar topics.

KGO-TV defines the audience for this show as primarily nonworking women, 18 to 49, married, with at least one child. The show also attracts working viewers before they leave for their jobs.

Segments on the 1-hour show run from 6 to 10 minutes. The usual pattern is to open with a celebrity-entertainer, then offer two segments on consumer topics. Segments 4, 5, and 6 cover "more serious subjects."

The production staff normally will consider for appearance only those who have appeared on television previously. Usually it asks to see a video clip of a prior TV appearance; an effective clip is an important way to gain acceptance.

"TV is a visual medium and a lot of our audience isn't just sitting there watching. They're folding clothes or ironing, so we need a voice that will grab their attention."

The public relations practitioner should submit a brief written query to the show's producer—"a 1-page letter getting straight to the basics: who you're offering, what their experience is, exactly what their topic would be, what shows they've been on previously, a bio (biographical statement) and all other information available on the person, as well as clippings, copies of articles on the person or topic."

Staff members try to answer queries in about a week, perhaps sooner. The show is booked at least a week in advance but sometimes has last-minute openings.

---

lead characters during a show may be Ford products exclusively. Sometimes a program's credits include a mention such as, "Transportation provided by American Airlines." Another way to generate silent publicity, especially valuable for the tourist industry, is to convince network show producers to shoot their programs in a client's city or region, showing the scenery there.

The network series "Hawaii Five-O," "The Streets of San Francisco," and "WKRP in Cincinnati" provided those localities with immeasurable publicity.

6. *Public service commercials.* Announcements for important nonprofit causes are run occasionally by stations nationwide as public relations gestures. The Advertising Council often prepares materials for national nonprofit organizations as a public service.

THE LOCAL STATION LEVEL   The methods listed for network public relations apply just as effectively on the local level—indeed, even more so in some instances, because competition for time on local stations often is less intense. The more intimate nature of local programming increases public relations opportunities. Even a diaper-changing contest at a shopping mall can gain air time.

These are the most frequently used techniques:

1. *Guest appearances on local talk shows.* Visiting experts in such fields as homemaking crafts, sponsored by companies and trade associations, demonstrate their skills for moderator and audience. National public relations firms send such clients around well-established circuits of local television and radio shows in each city they visit.

2. *Protest demonstrations.* These are such a staple on some television stations in large cities as to be a visual cliché. A group supporting or opposing a cause notifies a station that it will march at a certain time and place. Carrying placards, the marchers parade before the camera and a representative is shown explaining their cause. Although, for fairness, stations should put on an advocate for the other side in the same sequence, some stations neglect this responsibility, and so the marching group's point of view dominates. Many group demonstrations are so much alike, however, that their impact is minimized. Stations use them primarily because they involve movement.

3. *Videotapes for news shows.* Smaller TV stations, in particular, lack enough staff to cover all potentially newsworthy events in their areas. Practitioners can fill the gaps by delivering videotapes of events they handle, for inclusion in newscasts. Excerpts from a local speech by a prominent client may be incorporated in an evening news show. Arrival or departure at the local airport of a client in the news might be used, too, if the person says something newsworthy on camera.

4. *General-interest films.* Local cable channels sometimes will show films of 15- or 20-minute duration produced by corporations in which the direct commercial message is nonexistent or muted. The purpose of such films is to strengthen a company's image as a good community citizen. Films explaining large civic programs by nonprofit organizations also may be used.

MOTION PICTURES   Mention of motion pictures brings to mind, first and inevitably, the commercial entertainment film turned out by that nebulous place called Hollywood. From a public relations point of view, possibilities for influencing the content of commercial motion pictures for client purposes are relatively limited. Practitioners who know their way through the labyrinth of Hollywood financing and production can make deals for silent publicity through use of brand-name merchandise; and in a broad sense, causes sometimes get a helping hand from the thrust of a plotline, perhaps inadvertently.

Public relations counselors and corporate departments serve occasionally as advisers on films that involve their areas of expertise. Filmmakers seek this advice to prevent embarrassing technical errors on the screen and to protect themselves from inadvertently angering a group that might retaliate by denouncing the picture. In terms of specific public relations results similar to those obtainable from the other mass media, however, commercial films are a minor channel.

SPONSORED FILMS   In other forms, the motion picture is an important public relations tool.

Corporations and nonprofit organizations use motion pictures for internal purposes as part of audiovisual programs to train and inform their employees, and for external purposes to inform and influence the public and the financial community.

Some films are effective for both internal and external audiences. The San Diego Gas and Electric Company, for example, won the Best of Show award at the Public Relations Society of America's 1982 national convention for its 20-minute film, "The Heartbeat of the City." The film was made for showing to new employees, explaining the company's operations and problems—a straightaway internal use. Because of its excellence and balanced approach, including footage in which San Diegans emotionally condemn the company for its high rates, "The Heartbeat of the City" also was shown to the general public on a cable television channel. A film of this nature is both an educational tool and a molder of public opinion. (For further discussion of how this company responded to a serious public relations problem, see Chapter 14.)

A second significant use of the motion picture in public relations is directly promotional. Although avoiding frontal-attack sales messages such as those in television commercials, these films seek to whet the interest of audience members who are potential purchasers of the sponsor's product or contributors to the sponsor's cause. For example, a travel agency shows members of an invited audience a film about a Caribbean cruise. Colorful photography with voice-over narration depicts the scenery cruise passengers will see. Shipboard activities, including a few humorous touches, are shown. So are the luxurious accommodations and the enormous buffet tables from which travelers select their meals (no passenger ever is seasick in such films,

FIGURE 12.4

Preparations are made for shooting a dramatic sequence in the Levi Strauss corporate film, *Quality Never Goes Out of Style,* at Old Tucson, Arizona. (Produced by Furman Films, directed by Will Furman, for Levi Strauss & Co.)

of course). An example of a corporate film made for external distribution is shown in Figure 12.4.

Similarly, a university president at a dinner meeting of alumni shows a film of the campus as it is today. The film is a carefully contrived balance of nostalgia and progress, with scenes of football games and students at work in the new science building. Having rekindled alumni interest in the old school, the film closes with a recital of the university's plans and aspirations. Usually these include the need for a new building and the payment for which the alumni are invited to contribute.

Motion pictures of the types just described usually are made on 16-millimeter film. Pictures to be shown to small audiences under limited projection conditions, such as on a portable screen or a white classroom wall, may be shot on 8-millimeter film.

(A discussion of filmmaking appears in Chapter 24.)

QUESTIONS FOR REVIEW AND DISCUSSION

1. On what basis do newspaper editors select the news releases they publish?

2. When a public relations practitioner desires to challenge and/or respond to a daily newspaper editorial, to whom should the material be addressed?

3. A good public relations person knows how to create news events. Why is this important?

4. What significant differences between magazines and newspapers must a public relations practitioner keep in mind when submitting material to them?

5. Why are special-audience magazines and trade journals such important objectives for many public relations people?

6. For what purpose can books be used effectively as public relations outlets?

7. What two special attributes make radio distinctive among the major media of mass communication?

8. Do local radio newscasts have a good potential as an outlet for news releases? If so, why?

9. Ratings determine which television programs survive and which die. Why do ratings have such power?

10. How should public relations representatives go about trying to place their clients on television interview shows?

CHAPTER THIRTEEN

Public Relations and the Law

The public relations professional, in order to do his or her job well, must be familiar with laws and government regulations that affect the content and distribution of messages.

A practitioner, for example, can be held liable (along with the organization's officers) for such malpractices as (1) using an employee's picture in a sales brochure without proper authorization, (2) writing a news release that makes false claims about a product, (3) saying that a labor union leader is associated with organized crime, (4) using a copyrighted article or cartoon without permission, or (5) even failing to take precautions to avoid injury to a participant at a special event.

The impact of what public relations people do or say is magnified many times because they are considered the official representatives of an organization. A practitioner's words are interpreted as reflecting management's viewpoint. And the courts have long held that certain types of public relations materials are subject to legal action if they are misleading, untruthful, or libelous.

This chapter provides a brief overview of legal concepts that must be kept in mind as members of a public relations staff go about their work. It covers the areas of (1) libel and slander, (2) employee rights, (3) photo releases, (4) ownership of ideas, (5) copyright, (6) trademarks, (7) the Federal Trade Commission (FTC) and the Securities and Exchange Commission (SEC), (8) meeting rooms, plant tours, and open houses, and (9) relationship with legal counsel.

A Sampling of Legal Problems

The law and its many ramifications are somewhat abstract to the average person. Many people may have difficulty imagining exactly how public relations personnel can run afoul of the law, or generate a suit, by simply communicating information.

To bring things down to earth, and to make this chapter more meaningful, we provide here a sampling of recent government regulatory agency cases and lawsuits that involved statements or materials prepared by public relations personnel:

The SEC suspended stock sales of ATI, Inc., after the company made the claim in a news release that one of its disinfectants kills one kind of herpes virus. The release also touted the spray as "newly developed" when in fact it was already being marketed under several other names. Government officials said the company's claims were misleading and caused unjustified interest in the company's stock.

The American distributor of Norelco shavers was sued for $50 million by Remington Products, a competitor, after the company made the claim in a news release that its electric shavers were preferred by astronauts on trips into space. The release also stated that NASA's decision to use Norelco shavers was based on "extensive research" when in fact NASA selected the shaver simply because it fit more conveniently than others in the astronauts' personal kits.

The Jos. Schlitz Brewing Company and its public relations firm were sued for $3.5 million by three former executives of the company who maintained that a news release had libeled them by implying that they were guilty of unethical and illegal conduct.

The United Way of America was sued for $100,000 by an 81-year-old man featured on a campaign poster. He charged that his picture had been used without permission.

Burroughs Corporation filed a $1.9 million suit against Quality Books, Inc., after the firm had placed advertisements and given news interviews criticizing the Burroughs computers as having fouled up its bookkeeping system. Burroughs, citing adverse publicity, charged that Quality Books had defamed the company and contributed to a loss in sales. An action in which a company is criticized in this manner is called "trade disparagement."

The Federal Communications Commission (FCC) renewed the license of a Las Vegas, Nevada, television station for only one year, instead of the customary three, after the station distributed misleading publicity about its sponsorship of a tennis tournament. The publicity proclaimed that it was a "winner-take-all" event when in fact all players received substantial payment.

The FTC fined the J. Walter Thompson Company for producing advertisements and product publicity releases that stated that a Sears dishwasher would clean dishes without the users' first rinsing or scraping them. Testing, said the FTC, did not substantiate such claims. The government agency also chastised the advertising because the agency's employees apparently had not read the instruction manual, which made no such claims.

A Los Angeles amusement park, Marineland, was fined by the attorney general of California for publicizing a "Winter Wonderland" that included, among other things, "the world's tallest Christmas tree"—actually an observation tower strung with lights. The state said the park's claims were false and misleading.

United Features Syndicate sued a senator from New York for using the famous cartoon character Snoopy on campaign literature with the quotation, "You're a good man, D'Amato." The syndicate claimed copyright and trademark infringement.

These examples provide some idea of the legal pitfalls that a public relations person may encounter in preparing materials for a client or employer. In many cases the suits are eventually dismissed or settled out of court, but the organization still pays dearly for the adverse publicity generated and the expense of defending itself.

Public relations personnel must also be aware that they can be held legally liable if they provide advice or tacitly support an illegal activity of a client or employer. This area of liability is called *conspiracy*. A public relations person can be named as a co-conspirator with other company officials if he or she:

1. Participates in an illegal action such as bribing a government official or covering up information of vital interest to the public health and safety.

2. Counsels and guides the policy behind an illegal action.

3. Takes a major personal part in the illegal action.

4. Helps establish a "front group" whereby the connection to the public relations firm or its client is kept hidden.

5. Cooperates in any other way to further an illegal action.

Libel and Slander

It is the responsibility of a public relations person to ensure that a company publication or speech does not defame anyone.

Defamation is a published or spoken false statement that damages a person's reputation. A written defamation constitutes *libel* and an oral defamation, *slander*. Because a person may be injured as greatly in a radio or television broadcast as in a printed publication, the courts have come to treat broadcast defamation as libel.

Most libel suits are directed against newspapers, magazines, and broadcast media when an individual feels that a false statement has damaged his or her reputation. Carol Burnett successfully sued the *National Enquirer* for printing a story that implied she was drunk and got into a loud argument with former Secretary of State Henry Kissinger in a Washington, D.C., restaurant. More recently, the president of the Mobil Corporation got a $2 million jury award from the Washington *Post* because a news story implied that he had used Mobil resources and influences to set up his son in the shipping business. A federal district judge denied the jury award, however, on the basis that the prosecution had not proved the story was published with malicious intent. Later the U.S. Court of Appeals reinstated the award.

SUITS AGAINST COMPANY OFFICIALS

There isn't much investigative reporting in public relations work, but libel and slander suits are filed against company officials when they send out news releases or make false statements that injure someone's reputation. More than one executive has been sorry that he or she lost control during a news conference and called the leaders of a labor union "a bunch of crooks and compulsive liars." Suits have also been filed for calling a news reporter "a pimp for all environmental groups" or charging that a dissident stockholder is "a closet Communist."

PROVING DAMAGE TO A CORPORATE REPUTATION

A corporate reputation also can be damaged, but it is difficult to prove it in a court of law. The corporation must show beyond all doubt that the damaging words applied to it and that the accusations are not true. Thus a corporation cannot do much when an environmental group names it among its annual "dirty dozen" of corporations that pollute. A utility company in Indiana recently sued a man who wrote a letter to the newspaper criticizing the utility for seeking a rate hike. The company maintained that the letter included "false and misleading comments" that damaged its reputation.

The judge threw out the case. He said that the rate increase was "a matter of public interest and concern" and that the utility is a "public figure." After this ruling, the letter writer sued the utility for harassment and was awarded $90,000 in damages. In general, corporations rarely sue individuals for damaging their reputations because the chances of success are minimal in relation to the amount of adverse publicity that might be generated. The issues the judge raised—that of public interest and concern (fair comment and criticism), and of "public figure"—are discussed in the next two sections.

FAIR COMMENT AND CRITICISM

An individual or even a company criticizing another corporate entity for shoddy products or poor service usually does so under the protection of what is termed *fair comment and criticism*. This is the same concept that theater and music critics use when they lambast a play or a concert. The term means that companies and individuals who voluntarily show their wares to the public for sale or consumption are subject to "fair comment," whether good or bad. Thus everyone has the right to comment on matters of public interest and concern, provided it is done with honest purpose and lack of malicious intent.

THE "PUBLIC FIGURE" CONCEPT

The other concept that public relations personnel should know about, from the standpoint of answering press inquiries, is what constitutes a *public figure*. Does the press, for example, have a right to publish information about the activities of the company's chief executive officer? Does a newspaper have a right to make judgments about the management decisions of a company executive? Can an executive who is the subject of such a newspaper article sue for invasion of privacy? The answers tend to vary somewhat depending upon how the courts continue to define "public figure." Recent court decisions, such as those concerning Carol Burnett and the president of Mobil, were somewhat contradictory on the matter.

Such persons as political candidates, government officeholders, actors, and athletes usually are considered public figures and they have trouble winning suits for libel, slander, and invasion of privacy. On the other hand, a corporate executive who has not sought the limelight is more likely to be considered a private citizen, with better odds for winning such a suit.

Public relations counselors have an obligation to keep up with the changing standard of what constitutes a public figure. They must also advise top executives that some of their immunity to press criticism and investigative reporting dissipates if they voluntarily step into debates on controversial issues. Immunity also is lessened if the company is involved in a major news event, such as the crash of a DC-10 or the Tylenol poisonings.

Rights of Employees

EMPLOYEE COMMUNICATIONS

The concepts of libel, defamation, and invasion of privacy must be kept in mind as public relations personnel write and edit materials that involve employees.

It is no longer true, if it ever was, that an organization has an unlimited right to publicize the activities of its employees. In fact, Morton J. Simon, a Philadelphia lawyer and author of *Public Relations Law* (1969), says, "It should not be assumed that a person's status as an employee waives his right to privacy." Simon correctly points out that a company newsletter or magazine does not enjoy the same First Amendment protection that the news media enjoy when they claim "newsworthiness" and "public interest." A number of court cases, he says, show that company newsletters are considered commercial tools of trade.

This distinction does not impede the effectiveness of newsletters, but it does indicate that they should try to keep employee stories organization-oriented. Indeed, most lawsuits and complaints are generated by "personal columns" that may invade privacy by telling everyone that Joe Doaks honeymooned in Hawaii or that Mary Worth is now a great-grandmother. This information in itself may not constitute an invasion of privacy but it is often compounded into possible defamation by "cutesy" editorial asides that are in poor taste. If there is any chance that the person will be embarrassed by what is printed, it is a good policy not to make the statement.

To avoid any embarrassment and possible lawsuits, many organizations have abandoned the "personals" column in their publications. Others continue the columns but require that all copy must be submitted in writing by the persons involved. Another method is to have those named initial the copy before it is sent to the printer.

The organization usually is on safe ground when it restricts employee information to on-the-job activities. Thus there is rarely any problem if an editor says in a story that an engineer has developed a new machine, or that the personnel director is starting a short course for employees.

The writer must be careful in such articles, however, to avoid stereotypical or racial comments. An employee can file a lawsuit or a complaint to the Equal Opportunity Employment Commission based on the way he or she is portrayed. For example, it would be poor practice to do a feature story about the organization's only black manager and write, "John, a black with amazing leadership abilities, is going places." This implies that blacks generally lack leadership abilities. Women are also unnecessarily stereotyped. A woman in the accounting department with an MBA degree doesn't like being described as "a beautiful redhead with laughing eyes who hides her petite figure behind a charcoal-gray business suit. . . ."

In sum, one should avoid anything that might subject an employee to ridicule by fellow employees. It is expensive and unpleasant for an organization to deal with a lawsuit of any kind, even one with no merit.

Here are some guidelines to remember when writing about employee activities:

1. Keep the focus on organization-related activities.

2. Have employees submit "personals" in writing.

3. Double-check all information for accuracy.

4. Ask, "Will this embarrass anyone or cause someone to be the butt of jokes?"

5. Have employees initial a draft copy of the story in which they are named.

6. Don't rely on second-hand information; confirm the facts with the person involved.

7. When photographing or writing about employees, tell them what the purpose of the photo or story is and how it will be used.

8. Have employees sign a blanket release that the organization may publicize their work activity in newsletters and news releases.

ADVERTISING CONSIDERATIONS

The information just given applies to employee newsletters and news releases. If an employee's photograph or comments are used in an advertisement or sales brochure, however, it is essential that a signed release be on file. As an added precaution it is better to give some financial compensation to make a more binding legal agreement.

Chemical Bank of New York, unfortunately, learned this lesson the hard way. The bank used pictures of 39 employees in various advertisements designed to "humanize" the bank's image, but the employees maintained that no one had requested permission to use their photos in advertisements. Another problem was that the pictures had been taken up to five years before they began appearing in the series of advertisements.

An attorney for the employees, who sued for $600,000 in damages, said, "The bank took the individuality of these employees and used that individuality to make a profit." The judge agreed and ruled that the bank had violated New York's privacy law. The action is called *misappropriation of personality*. Jerry Della Femina, an advertising executive, succinctly makes the point: get permission. "If I used my mother in an ad," he said, "I'd get her permission—and I almost trust her 100 percent."

Written permission should also be obtained if the employee's photograph is to appear in sales brochures or even in the corporate annual report. (In the case of outsiders, the same rule applies. If, for example, a corporation wants to show customers dining in one of its chain restaurants, permission must be given in writing.) To avoid any possible lawsuits, many companies use professional models as "customers." This avoids the problem of a person's agreeing orally at the time of the photo session but having second thoughts several months later when the picture is published. When a child appears in such a photo, it is essential that the parents sign a release.

PRESS INQUIRIES

Because press inquiries have the potential of invading an employee's right of privacy, public relations personnel should follow basic guidelines as to what information will be provided in the employee's behalf.

In general, employers should give a news reporter only basic information. This may include (1) confirmation that the person is an employee, (2) the person's title and job description, and (3) date of beginning employment, or, if applicable, date of termination.

Unless it is specified by law or permission is given by the employee, a public relations person should avoid providing information about an employee's (1) salary, (2) home address, (3) marital status, (4) number of children, (5) organizational memberships, and (6) job performance.

If a reporter does seek any of this information, because of the nature of the story, several methods may be followed.

First, a public relations person can volunteer to contact the employee and have the person speak directly with the reporter. What the employee chooses to tell the reporter is not then a company's responsibility. Second, many organizations do provide additional information to a reporter if it is included on an optional biographical sheet that the employee has filled out. In most cases, the form clearly states that the organization may use any of the information in answering press inquiries or writing its own news releases. A typical biographical form may have sections in which the employee can list his or her (1) honors and awards, (2) professional memberships, (3) marital status and names of any children, (4) previous employers, (5) educational background, and (6) hobbies or interests. This sheet should not be confused with the person's official employment application, which must remain confidential.

If an organization uses biographical sheets, it is important that they be dated and kept current. A sheet compiled by an employee five years previously may be hopelessly out of date. This is also true of *file photographs* taken at the time of a person's employment (see the section on "Photo Releases").

INFORMATION ABOUT EMPLOYEE BENEFITS

Recently enacted federal and state legislation makes it easier for employees to know what benefits they are entitled to. For one thing, regulations require that pension and insurance plans be written in such a way that employees can understand them. The rationale is that an employee should not be deprived of benefits simply because no one in the organization explained them in basic English. Suits can be filed against employers who have not complied with the law. Furthermore, employers must post information about health and safety regulations, workers' compensation guidelines, and the like. Public relations practitioners often work with the personnel office in making such information available to employees.

EMPLOYEE FREEDOM OF SPEECH

Employee free speech, according to Francis W. Steckmest in *Corporate Performance* (1982), has emerged as a major legal nettle in the 1980s.

Public relations executives, as well as high-level managers, must work to ensure that employees are not arbitrarily denied promotion or fired simply because they have criticized the organization. Employees, as citizens, have a right to express a point of view. Thus, many employee newsletters now carry "letters to the editor" from employees who question company policy. This not only breeds a healthy atmosphere of two-way communication but makes employee publications more credible.

Unfortunately too many executives still perceive employee questions and criticism as "disloyalty." Public relations personnel can do much to dispel this perception by educating managers about employee rights. A number of state and federal laws already protect the job rights of "whistle-blowers," and this area is rapidly expanding to prevent employees from being dismissed just because they express views not popular with the boss.

Photo Releases

A public relations department should have a central photographic file containing information readily available about (1) source of the picture and date taken, (2) copyright information, and (3) signed releases from subjects in photos.

Such information will ensure the proper use of photos and substantially reduce the threat of lawsuits. A notation of the date taken, for example, will help eliminate the use of pictures that are no longer appropriate for news releases or company brochures. It is embarrassing to publish a picture of a person who died three years ago, or to show in a new brochure a picture of a manufacturing facility that was sold last year.

Permission statements indicate whether the photo may be used in company brochures and advertising or whether it is strictly a file photo for use in the employee magazine. The copyrighting of a picture by a photographer may mean that the organization cannot use it again unless the photographer gives permission or receives payment. A photo release is important if a person protests that his or her picture was used without permission.

Ordinarily a public relations practitioner doesn't need to worry about getting a signed release if the person gives "implied consent" by posing for the picture and is told how it will be used. This is particularly true for "news" pictures to be published in internal newsletters or for materials accompanying a news release.

If it is not known in what specific ways the photo will ultimately be used, the best solution is to get a written release. Public relations personnel often accompany a photographer to (1) ensure that the names of all persons in a picture are properly recorded and (2) to have each sign a release.

Here is a Lockheed release form:

The undersigned, having previously consented to being photographed, does hereby authorize Lockheed Aircraft Corporation and Lockheed Missiles & Space Company, Inc. to use and reproduce the said photograph and copy for Lockheed publicity and promotional purposes.

Ninety-nine times out of a hundred, people are flattered to be photographed for publicity purposes. On occasion, however, people do have second thoughts. A hospital photographer, for an annual report, once took a picture of a patient after getting verbal consent. Some months later, when the report was published and the patient was back home, he found the picture showing him in a wrinkled hospital gown somewhat objectionable and claimed invasion of privacy. A written release would have solved some legal difficulties for the hospital.

Ownership of Ideas

The employee suggestion box and the submission of ideas from outside the organization require precautions if the public relations staff is to avoid several legal headaches.

The threat of lawsuit is most real when there is an attempt to solicit ideas that can save money or generate additional income for the company. Many organizations regularly encourage employees to submit ideas on how to conserve energy, improve production efficiency, or make a product more desirable.

In such cases the organization must clearly spell out the conditions under which an idea will be accepted and the extent of compensation that will be paid for an implemented idea. Thus many companies have suggestion forms that specifically state that all ideas become the property of the firm and that a set maximum amount will be paid for ideas judged outstanding. Such an approach tends to limit an organization's liability for an idea, but placing a maximum of a $500 award for an idea may not necessarily hold up in court if the plaintiff can prove that the company made a large sum on the idea. Sears Roebuck & Company, for example, was ordered to pay several hundred thousand dollars and a royalty to a former employee after he proved that the department store had made millions on his invention. In the vast majority of cases, however, the courts honor a company's policy to pay only a specific maximum amount.

Paying a specific amount for an idea is much better than utilizing a sliding percentage figure, as United Airlines discovered several years ago. United announced that it would give up to 10 percent of the savings incurred from any suggestion submitted by an employee. Two employees presented an idea, but later filed suit maintaining that United had not adequately compensated them. The major court argument revolved around the actual amount of savings that United had obtained from the idea. In addition, the airline contended that the idea was not new and had already been under consideration. A few more legal precautions in setting up the suggestion system would have saved the airline an expensive court battle.

The submission of ideas from the general public is another area of concern. Businesses often receive unsolicited advice on how to develop new products or improve existing ones, and the public relations department is frequently responsible for keeping track of these suggestions. It is important, then, to establish policies for handling submitted ideas.

Some companies totally reject all unsolicited ideas and have the public relations department return the communications with a polite letter. Others will consider an idea if the sender signs a release form that (1) the company is the sole arbitrator of how much the idea is worth, (2) no compensation whatsoever will be given, or (3) a specific maximum amount ($100 to $500) will be awarded if an idea is utilized. The latter, however, may not prevent a lawsuit if the value of the idea is worth more than a token amount of money.

Suggestions often are used as a way of generating audience involvement in a public relations program. Several years ago Atlantic Richfield ran full-page advertisements in various magazines requesting public ideas on mass transit and the nature of American life in the twenty-first century. All advertisements carried the following sentence: "Please note that all ideas submitted shall become public property without compensation." ARCO got thousands of suggestions from people and printed some of the ideas, along with the names of those who submitted them, in subsequent advertisements and brochures. Individuals chosen for publicity, however, still signed a release form giving permission for their names to be used.

Use of Copyright

Should a news release be copyrighted? How about a corporate annual report? Can a *New Yorker* cartoon be used in the company magazine without permission? What about reprinting an article from *Fortune* magazine and distributing it to the company's sales staff? Are government reports copyrighted? What constitutes copyright infringement?

These are some of the bothersome questions that a public relations professional should be able to answer. Knowledge of copyright law is important from two perspectives: (1) what organizational materials should be copyrighted and (2) how correctly to utilize the copyrighted materials of others.

Before going into these areas, however, it is important to know what copyright means. In very simple terms, *copyright* means protection of a creative work from unauthorized use. A section of the U.S. Copyright law of 1978 states: "Copyright protection subsists . . . in the original works of authorship fixed in any tangible medium of expression now known or later developed." The word *authorship* is defined in seven categories: (1) literary works; (2) musical works; (3) dramatic works; (4) pantomimes and choreographic works; (5) pictorial, graphic, or sculptural works; (6) motion pictures; and (7) sound recordings. The word *fixed* means that the work is sufficiently permanent or stable to permit it to be perceived, reproduced, or otherwise communicated.

Thus a copyright does not protect ideas, but only the specific ways in which those ideas are expressed. An idea for promoting a product, for example, cannot be copyrighted—but brochures, drawings, news features, animated cartoons, display booths, photographs, recordings, videotapes, corporate symbols, slogans, and the like that express a particular idea can be copyrighted.

Because much money, effort, time, and creative talent are spent on organizational materials, copyright protection is important. By copyrighting materials a company can prevent competitors from capitalizing on its creative work or producing a facsimile brochure that tends to mislead the public. A manufacturer of personal computers would be in serious legal difficulties if it began distributing sales brochures that tended to look just like ones from Apple Computer. The concept of trademark infringement (such as copying the Apple logo with slight changes) will be discussed in the section entitled "Trademarks."

The 1978 law, in a major change from the previous one, presumes that material produced in some tangible form is copyrighted from the moment it is created. This is particularly true if the material bears a copyright notice. One of the following methods may be employed:

1. Using the letter "c" in a circle (©), followed by the word *copyright*

2. Citing the year of copyright and the name of the owner

This presumption of copyright is often sufficient to discourage unauthorized use, and the writer or creator of the material has some legal protection if he or she can prove that the material was created before another person claims it.

A more formal step, providing full legal protection, is official registration of the copyrighted work within three months after creation. This is done by depositing two copies of the manuscript (it is not necessary that it has been published), recording, or artwork with the Copyright Office, Library of Congress, Washington, D.C. 20559. Copyright registration forms are available from U.S. post offices; the registration fee is $10. Registration is not a condition of copyright protection, but it is a prerequisite to an infringement action against unauthorized use by others.

Copyright protection of a work lasts for the life of the author plus 50 years, and no longer. Material copyrighted by a business or organization is protected for 75 years from the time the material is published. When a public relations writer creates materials as part of regular employment for an organization, the employer owns the material and has right of copyright. In legal terms, this situation is known as "work made for hire."

PHOTOGRAPHY AND ARTWORK

The copyright law makes it clear that free-lance and commercial photographers retain ownership of the image in a picture unless they specifically agree, in writing, to surrender that right. In other words, these photographers own all negatives, and they can negotiate with a business regarding the use of a picture.

Copyright ownership then primarily applies to free-lance photographers who do assignments for a number of companies. A staff photographer for a business firm, on the other hand, has no ownership rights because the employer possesses the copyright. The same situation applies to a public relations writer: all work produced is owned by the employer. Photographers and staff writers who want to sell photos or articles produced on company time must, legally, get permission.

Free-lance photographers generally charge for a picture on the basis of its use. If it is used only once, perhaps for an employee newsletter, the fee is low. If, however, the company wants to use the picture in the corporate annual report or on the company calendar mailed to 5000 people, the fee may be considerably higher. Consequently it is important for a public relations person to tell the photographer exactly how the picture will be used. Arrangements and fees then can be determined for (1) one-time use, (2) unlimited use, or (3) the payment of royalties every time the picture is used.

In practice there is much slippage in honoring a photographer's copyright—either because the client is unfamiliar with the copyright law or the photographer doesn't pursue the letter of the law. Nevertheless, responsible public relations practitioners strive to give adequate compensation and recognition for a photographer's creative work.

The guidelines discussed for photography also apply to created artwork. It is important to determine in writing exactly what rights the artist retains if he or she creates a new corporate logo or other artwork for an organization. A graduate student at San Jose State University, for example, sued the university because the logo he designed for the athletic teams was also given to commercial vendors. The student claimed that the university had the right to use the logo only on football helmets—and that he retained all commercial rights to the logo.

FAIR USE VERSUS INFRINGEMENT

Public relations people are in the business of gathering information from a variety of sources, so it is important to know where *fair use* ends and *infringement* begins.

Fair use means that part of a copyrighted article may be quoted directly, but the quoted material must be brief in relation to the length of the original article. It may be, for example, only one paragraph in a 750-word article and up to 300 words in a long article or in a book. Complete attribution of the source must be given regardless of the length of the quoted copy.

It is important to note, however, that fair use has distinct limitations when the material is to appear in a format outside the traditional scope of scholarship and critical review or analysis. If part of a copyright article is to be used by a corporate entity directly to influence sales and profits, permission is required. Thus the use of a selected quotation from an outside source in a sales brochure should be cleared with the source, whereas its use in a company magazine as part of a feature article does not require permission.

The extent of use is significant. Photocopying a *Business Week* article for distribution to 10 persons in a department could be considered fair use, but photocopying 250 for the entire sales staff likely would be considered unfair use and copyright infringement. *Business Week* might contend that the company, by reprinting the article in quantity, had violated copyright (all magazines and newspapers are copyrighted) and deprived the magazines of potential income. Quantity reprints should be ordered directly from the publisher.

Context of use is a factor. A public relations person must make sure that selected quotations from a copyrighted work are not taken out of context. Some years ago a tobacco company used three sentences from a book on health. The quotation, placed in advertisements and news releases, gave the impression that the author endorsed smoking. In the lawsuit that followed, the court ruled that (1) the company had failed to get the author's permission, (2) the sentences were taken out of context and distorted the author's beliefs, and (3) the company had used the work of another for commercial advantage.

Government documents (city, county, state, and federal) are in the public domain and cannot be copyrighted. Public relations personnel can freely use quotations and statistics from a government document, but care must be exercised to ensure that the material is in context and not misleading. The most common problem occurs when an organization uses a government report as a form of endorsement for its services or products. An airline, for example, may cite a government study showing that it provides the most service to customers but neglect to state the basis of comparison or other factors. Norelco, cited earlier in this chapter, got in trouble because the company implied that NASA had officially tested and endorsed the shaver.

Copyright infringement also extends to videotaping television documentaries or news programs. The Supreme Court has ruled that it is "fair use" to make a videotape of a television show for later personal viewing, but a public relations staff must get permission from the television producer if widespread use of the videotape is planned. Adolph A. Coors Company paid $40,000 to CBS-TV for the right to show a videotape throughout the country of a "60 Minutes" segment about the company (see Chapters 7 and 10).

Illinois Power Company, on the other hand, spliced segments of a "60 Minutes" feature about the nuclear power industry into a rebuttal tape but, to avoid a suit from CBS charging copyright infringement, made only one master tape. People interested in the power company's rebuttal were asked to submit a blank tape and the company made a copy for them free of charge. The rationale was that CBS would have trouble showing that the company used copyrighted material for commercial advantage by selling the videotape. This is one way around the problem, but it severely limited the company's distribution of the rebuttal and probably would have had dubious legal standing had CBS chosen to file suit.

Titles of books or plays cannot be copyrighted, but the principle of unfair competition is in effect. Lawyers counsel that a public relations staff should not copy anything if the intent is to capitalize on or take advantage of its current renown. The key to a suit is whether an organization in some way is obtaining commercial advantage by implying that a service or product has the endorsement of or is closely allied with the literary property. Thus a public relations staff should come up with a more creative information campaign than one using such a phrase as, "May the Force Be With You."

Some years ago TV talk show host Johnny Carson sued a company that provided portable toilets to construction sites. He claimed copyright infringement and charged that the company was capitalizing on his famous name by publicizing its toilets as "Here's Johnny." The court denied Carson's claim, stating that (1) there was no connection between his show and portable toilets, so the public was not confused; (2) the word *john* is commonly used in the construction industry for a toilet; and (3) there was no evidence that the company commercially gained from Carson's entry theme.

COPYRIGHT GUIDELINES

A number of points have been discussed about copyright. A public relations person should keep the following in mind:

1. Ideas cannot be copyrighted, but the expression of those ideas can be.

2. Major public relations materials (brochures, annual reports, videotapes, motion pictures, position papers, and the like) should be copyrighted if only to prevent unauthorized use by competitors.

3. Although there is a concept of *fair use,* any copyrighted material intended directly to advance the sales and profits of an organization should not be used unless permission is given.

4. Copyrighted material should not be taken out of context, particularly if it implies endorsement of the organization's services or products.

5. Quantity reprints of an article should be ordered from the publisher.

6. Permission is required to use segments of television programs or motion pictures.

7. Permission must be obtained to use segments of popular songs (written verses or sound recordings) from a recording company.

8. The purchaser should tell photographers how photos will be used.

9. Permission is always required to reprint cartoons and cartoon characters. Cartoons in magazines are copyrighted, as well as characters such as Snoopy and Donald Duck.

Trademarks

This section will discuss trademarks and the role that a public relations department plays in (1) selecting trademarks, (2) safeguarding their use, and (3) avoiding improper use of other registered trademarks. It also will briefly explain the significance of generic names.

A *trademark,* according to the *American Heritage Dictionary,* is a "name, symbol, or other device identifying a product, officially registered and legally restricted to the use of the owner or manufacturer."

SELECTING TRADEMARKS

To protect a trademark by law, a company registers its name, logo (identifying symbol), and product names. The registered trademark symbol is a superscript small-capital "R" in a circle—®. A "TM" in small capital letters indicates a trademark that isn't registered. It represents a company's common-law claim to a right of trademark, or a trademark for which registration is pending.

A service mark is like a trademark, but it designates a service rather than a product, or is a logo. An "SM" in small capitals in a circle—㏂—is the symbol for a registered service mark. If registration is pending, the "SM" should be used without the circle.

Businesses and industrial firms spend millions of dollars each year in the search for a distinctive name, slogan, or logo that can be used to symbolize the company in the minds of the American consumer. Additional millions are spent advertising and publicizing the trademark (see Figure 13.1).

SAFEGUARDING TRADEMARKS

A public relations practitioner must be thoroughly familiar with the registered trademarks of his or her employer so that the trademarks can be used correctly in news releases, brochures, background kits, videotapes, and the like. A registered trademark name, for example, is always capitalized. Failure to do so in company materials can lead to a loss of trademark status; if so, the word becomes generic, available for anyone's use.

The public relations department and legal counsel work to safeguard an organization's trademarks in several ways. They are:

1. Ensuring that company trademarks are capitalized in all organizational literature and graphics.

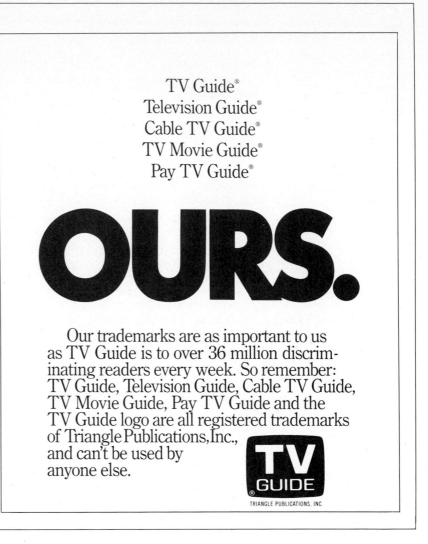

2. Ensuring that any graphics of the logo or phrases ("Reach Out and Touch Someone") indicate that they are trademarked by using®, TM, (SM), or SM next to the logo or phrase.

3. Distributing trademark manuals and brochures to editors and reporters and placing advertisements in trade publications, designating names to be capitalized.

4. Educating employees as to what the company's trademarks are and how to use them correctly.

5. Monitoring publications—newspapers, trade magazines, newsletters—to ensure that trademarks are capitalized. If not, a gentle reminder is sent.

6. Monitoring publications to ensure that other organizations are not infringing on a registered trademark. If they are, the legal department pursues the situation with letters and threats of injunctions or lawsuits.

7. Placing advertisements in journalism magazines and reviews reminding readers of trademark names. Johnson & Johnson does this for Band-Aids, Xerox reminds the press that there is no such thing as a "xerox"—only a Xerox copier—and Coca-Cola is adamant that *Coke* is always capitalized.

AVOIDING IMPROPER USE OF OTHER REGISTERED TRADEMARKS

Public relations personnel often work with the legal department and outside design consultants to come up with names, slogans, and logos for an organization. The first step is to conduct a brainstorming session for ideas, but the second step is to research a potential trademark to be sure it isn't already being used. This is usually done by specialty trademark search firms that make extensive use of the computer.

Today, when there are thousands of businesses and organizations, finding a name trademark not already in use is extremely difficult. The task is even more frustrating if a company wants to use a trademark on an international level.

It is not uncommon for a company to start with 150 possible names and, after a trademark search, be left with only two or three possible designations. The other choice a company has is to purchase rights to a name. First Interstate Bank, in 11 Western states, had to pay a small, rural Vermont bank $1 million because that bank owned the name First Inter-State Bank. By purchasing the name the bank's holding corporation now has its name registered in all 50 states.

The complexity of finding new names has invariably spawned a number of lawsuits claiming trademark infringement. Here are some examples:

General Mills, owner of the invented "Betty Crocker" name, was granted an injunction against a book publishing firm that wanted to name a bar guide *The Betty Crocker Crock Book for Drunks.*

The Washington *Post* sued a Madison, Wisconsin, restaurant for naming itself "Washington Post, Ltd."—despite the owner's claims that the facility was on Washington Street and featured "post and beam" construction.

McDonald's has registered "Quarter Pounder" as a trademark, so it sued a meat-packing company for publicizing its beef patties as "quarter pounders."

The Bank of America, which has "BofA" as a registered service mark, filed suit against a consulting firm that decided to call itself "B-A Associates."

Rolls Royce won an injunction against a Los Angeles public relations firm that adopted a logo almost an exact replica of the famous logo used by the auto company.

Mervyn's Department Stores agreed to pay $190,000 after the Los Angeles Olympic Organizing Committee filed a lawsuit charging the department store with unauthorized use of a logo, resembling the Games' trademarked symbol, on merchandise. In an out-of-court settlement Mervyn's was also required to turn over all advertising copy and signs publicizing the merchandise to the committee.

Phoenix Mutual Life Insurance Company sued Merrill Lynch Pierce Fenner & Smith, Inc., for naming and publicizing a mutual fund as the "Phoenix Fund."

In all these cases organizations filed lawsuits charging that their registered trademarks were being commercially exploited by profit-making entities. Some guidelines used by courts to determine if there has been trademark infringement are as follows:

1. Has the defendant used a name as a way of capitalizing on the reputation of another organization's trademark—and does the defendant benefit from the original organization's investment in popularizing its trademark?

2. Is there an intent (real or otherwise) to create confusion in the public mind? Is there an intent to imply a connection between the defendant's product and the item identified by trademark?

3. How similar are the two organizations? Are they providing the same kinds of products or services?

4. Has the original organization actively protected the trademark by publicizing it—and by actually continuing to use it in connection with its products or services?

5. Is the trademark unique? A company with a trademark that merely describes a common product might be in trouble.

Trademark infringement also can result from the concept of *right of publicity.* It is well known that permission must be given if a living celebrity's likeness is used in advertising and public relations materials. But the issue is more clouded regarding people who are deceased.

On occasion a public relations practitioner gets the bright idea to use movie stills from an old Marx Brothers or W. C. Fields movie to make a slide presentation or a brochure more interesting. At other times the advertising staff decides to use Laurel and Hardy look-alikes for a commercial.

These ideas are fine, but the practitioner must realize that the image or artistic work of a deceased celebrity may still be protected. Movie studios, for example, may own rights to stock photos of old movies. The heirs of a celebrity also may retain control over how a person's work or image is portrayed. For example, six heirs of W. C. Fields have formed a company exclusively for the purpose of licensing organizations that want to use representations of the famed comic in advertisements and publicity materials. Royalties and licensing fees must be paid. Licensing fees are also a bone of contention among colleges and universities that are now prosecuting manufacturers for using the school logo or the name of the football team on beer mugs, ashtrays, pennants, and the like without paying for the right.

The conclusion to draw is: don't use a famous cartoon figure, the pictures of a deceased celebrity, movie stills, or a college coat of arms in publicity materials unless a licensing fee has been negotiated.

GENERIC NAMES

Every company wants to publicize its trademarks to the point that they become household names, but there is a danger in doing so. A U.S. Court of Appeals has stated: "When the public takes unto itself a trade name word and substitutes it for the commodity, the manufacturer loses the exclusive right to the name."

Some trade names that have become generic include *aspirin, cellophane, thermos, escalator, raisin bran,* and *mimeograph.* This essentially means that any company can use these names to describe a product.

When a trade name becomes generic, the company suffers a tremendous loss; that is why corporations zealously guard the trademark from incorrect use. Coca-Cola, it is said, has a battery of 200 lawyers constantly monitoring how restaurants and the media use the name *Coke.* If a person orders a Coke in a restaurant and is served another kind of cola, Coca-Cola lawyers immediately file suit. Xerox spends several hundred thousand dollars annually making sure the public understands that *Xerox copy* and *photocopy* are not interchangeable words.

Federal Trade Commission

It is well known that the Federal Trade Commission (FTC) has jurisdiction over advertisements to determine that they are not deceptive or misleading, but it is less well known that the agency also has jurisdiction over product news releases.

In the eyes of the FTC both advertisements and product publicity materials are vehicles of commercial trade—and therefore subject to restriction. Thus a company cannot claim "freedom of speech" when the FTC moves to curb misleading news releases.

In general, the FTC monitors advertising and publicity by assigning one of the following labels to material it considers misleading:

1. Unsubstantiated claims

2. Ambiguous claims

3. Fraudulent testimonials

4. Puffery and exaggerated claims

5. Deceptive demonstrations

6. Deceptive pricing

7. Defamation of the competition

8. Fraudulent contests

9. Misuse of the word *free*

10. "Bait and switch" tactics

Public relations practitioners must be cognizant of these guidelines when writing product publicity. Such knowledge by the public relations staff at Norelco would have prevented the news release that implied that NASA endorsed its product for astronauts—and the resulting $50 million suit filed by Remington, a competitor.

The following guidelines should be taken into account when writing product publicity materials:

1. Make sure the information in the release is accurate and can be substantiated.

2. Don't make flat statements that are difficult to prove. Stick to the facts. Don't "hype" the product or service by using flowery, nonspecific adjectives.

3. Make sure that celebrities who endorse a product actually use it. They should not say anything about the product's properties that cannot be substantiated.

4. Don't use testimonials from satisfied consumers for publicity purposes unless the individuals give written permission.

5. Watch the language. Don't say "independent research study" when the research was done by the organization's staff.

6. If government findings are quoted, provide proper context. Government agencies do not endorse products.

7. Describe tests and surveys in sufficient detail so the consumer understands what was tested and under what conditions.

8. Describe prizes and awards accurately.

9. Remember that a product is not "new" if only the packaging has been changed.

Companies found in violation of FTC guidelines usually are given the opportunity to sign a consent order. This means that the company admits no wrongdoing but agrees to change its advertising and publicity claims.

A good example of a consent order has been summarized by *Alert,* a newsletter prepared by the legal staff of Ketchum Communications, Inc., Pittsburgh:

WATER PIK AGREES TO ORDER DEALING WITH "TREATMENT AND PREVENTION" CLAIMS

A consent order will require the maker of Water Pik and its advertising agency, J. Walter Thompson Company, to have a reasonable basis for claims about the effectiveness of the product in preventing gum disease. The company had been using a survey to base their claim that "four out of five dentists recommended the Water Pik."

They claimed approval by the American Dental Association, and claimed that the product "reduces the causes of gum diseases." The commission had charged that there was no substantiation that the product, either alone or used with other methods of dental care, played a significant role in the prevention of gum disease.

A consent order will require the company to substantiate any gum disease treatment or prevention claims with at least one long-term test conducted on human subjects. Further, the FTC's charge that their survey was not designed and conducted in accordance with accepted standards led to the order that the company will not misrepresent the content, results or conclusions of any survey, and will use accepted survey procedures.

Companies also may be fined by the FTC or ordered to engage in corrective advertising and publicity. Listerine makers and Firestone Tire Company in recent years have been ordered to do corrective advertising. If a product is defective and a hazard to public health, the FTC can order a product recall.

Securities and Exchange Commission

Product claims are handled by the FTC; information on the financial affairs of a company is closely monitored by the Securities and Exchange Commission (SEC).

Financial public relations and investor relations are high-paying fields for practitioners, but this is a complex area in which knowledge of accounting practices and government regulations is absolutely essential.

The SEC, for example, has a large number of regulations that specify everything from what a news release can say about a public stock offering to the size and type used in a corporate annual report. The agency is particularly concerned about the dissemination of misleading or fraudulent information that can affect the price of a company's stock.

Consequently, the three basic guidelines of the SEC are as follows:

1. Full information must be given on anything that might materially affect the company's stock.

2. Timely disclosure is essential. A company must act promptly to dispel or confirm rumors that result in unusual market activity or market variations.

3. Insider trading is illegal. The company should not provide information to selected people unless it willingly gives the same information to the press for publication.

Through the years there have been a number of cases in which companies have been heavily fined for not adhering to these guidelines. The major case setting the pattern for illegal insider trading occurred in 1965 involving Texas Gulf Sulphur. Company executives used inside information about an ore strike in Canada to buy up stock while at the same time issuing a news release tending to deny that a rich strike had been found.

Other situations since then have included the following:

Pig 'n Whistle (1971). This administrative proceeding established the concept that a company's public relations counsel can be named as a defendant if news releases contain false and misleading information. The court ruled that public relations firms must take prudent caution to ascertain the accuracy of information given them for release by either a client or an employer.

Memorex Corporation (1975). The corporation had to pay $3.6 million in an out-of-court settlement with persons who purchased the company's stock. The company was charged with artificially inflating the price of stock by issuing incorrect and misleading statements and news releases about the earnings of a subsidiary.

Bache & Co. (1976). The brokerage firm was ordered to return $900,000 to customers who bought shares of an insurance company shortly before the company announced an unexpectedly large loss. The brokerage firm in turn sued the insurance company, maintaining that the vice-president of investor relations had given analysts misleading and distorted information.

Apple Computer Inc. (1984). A group of stockholders filed a lawsuit against company executives, claiming that they sold 2.1 million shares of stock and received proceeds of $84.1 million by making "positive public statements" about the expected success of the Lisa when the executives knew about slow sales and production difficulties. The company said the lawsuit had no merit.

Wall Street Journal (1985). A former reporter was put on trial for conspiracy and fraud after the Securities and Exchange Commission charged him and his stockbroker friends with benefiting from advance knowledge of "Heard on the Street" columns in the newspaper. The reporter, the government charged, leaked market-sensitive information to friends prior to the column's being published.

These examples should make it clear that public relations staff and counsel are responsible for the full, accurate, and prompt disclosure of financial data. A public relations person is often privy to information affecting the price of stock before the press and the public know about it. Under SEC guidelines buying and selling a stock on the basis of inside information is illegal.

The SEC requires public relations personnel to disclose the following information about a company as soon as it is available:

1. Dividends or their deletion

2. Annual and quarterly earnings

3. Preliminary, but unaudited, interim earnings

4. Annual reports

5. Stock splits

6. Mergers or takeovers

7. Major management changes

8. Major product developments

9. Expansion plans

10. Change of business purpose

11. Defaults

12. Proxy materials

13. Disposition of major assets

14. Purchase of own stock

15. Announcements of major contracts or orders

At the same time the SEC frowns on a company's excessive eagerness to

FIGURE 13.2

The Securities and Exchange Commission was established in 1934 to protect investors. Its emblem is shown here.

announce information or its continual optimism. Therefore, it is necessary to avoid the following practices:

1. Unrealistic sales and earnings reports

2. Glowing descriptions of products in the experimental stage

3. Announcements of possible mergers or takeovers that are only in the speculation stage

4. Junkets for business reporters or offers of stock to financial analysts and columnists

5. Omission of unfavorable news and developments

6. Leaking of information to selected outsiders and financial columnists

Figure 13.2 shows the seal of the Securities and Exchange Commission.

Meeting Rooms, Plant Tours, and Open Houses

What is the responsibility of a firm if meeting rooms are made available to community groups? What about the legal ramifications of having plant tours or a community open house?

These are not idle questions to the public relations staff, who are often responsible for such activities. Providing a meeting room or having an open house is part of community relations. Plant tours also involve the public, and specialized audiences as well.

MEETING ROOMS

Every firm or organization that makes a meeting room available to community groups should have an established policy in writing that specifies what types of groups qualify. Some companies specify that only nonprofit groups associated with the United Way may use facilities. Other firms allow religious organizations, hobby clubs, and senior citizen groups if an employee of the company sponsors them.

A written policy provides clear-cut guidelines so a public relations person knows how to respond if, for example, a local rug merchant wants to use the room for a "private showing," or a group of unchaperoned young people want to hold a party.

Groups should submit a written request and perhaps sign a standard form that outlines their responsibilities in using the room. The standard form might clearly state that the company in no way officially endorses the activities of the group. Furthermore, standard agreement forms enable the organization to keep track of which groups have booked the room for which date. Also, from a legal standpoint, the company is less liable if the community group has formally requested such use.

Here are some other points to remember.

1. The room must be clean and well maintained so that there are no safety hazards such as worn rugs, frayed electrical cords, or flimsy chairs.

2. Instructions on how to operate the coffee maker or other electrical equipment must be clearly posted.

3. An employee of the company should be on the premises during the meeting in case of emergency.

4. Parking lots must be well lighted and easily accessible.

5. Icy sidewalks and other possible danger areas must be made safe before the meeting.

It is only good community relations to ensure that a community meeting room creates good will for the company, not antagonisms or even possible lawsuits because of negligence.

PLANT TOURS

Plant tours should not be undertaken lightly. They require detailed planning by the public relations staff to guarantee the safety and comfort of visitors. Consideration must be given to such factors as (1) logistics, (2) possible work disruptions as groups pass through the plant, (3) safety, and (4) amount of staffing required.

First, the public relations staff must establish the objective of having plant tours. Is it primarily to create community good will? Is it a sales method by which, at the end of the tour, visitors can buy the manufactured product? Or is it simply an opportunity to respond to public interest in seeing how things are made, as in the case of an automobile plant?

Once the objective is determined, the next question is the kind of tour that will best meet the objective. What parts of the plant should be shown? What areas should be off-limits because of trade secrets or safety? The tour route, of course, should be planned so there is a minimum of work disruption and a maximum of safety. It is not wise, for example, to have tour groups walk where there is water on the floor or where machinery is running. Many companies build catwalks that give visitors a good view of the operations but keep them relatively remote from possible danger.

A well-marked tour route is essential; it is equally important to have trained escort staff and tour guides. Guides should be well versed in company history and operations, and their comments should be somewhat standardized to make sure that key facts are conveyed. In addition, guides should be trained in first aid and thoroughly briefed on what to do in case of an accident or heart attack. At the beginning the guide should outline to the visitors what they will see, the amount of walking involved, the time required, and the number of stairs. This warning tells visitors with heart conditions or other physical handicaps what they can expect.

Such precautions will generate good will and limit the company's liability. It should be noted, however, that a plaintiff can still collect if negligence on the part of the company can be proved.

OPEN HOUSES   Many of the points about plant tours are applicable to open houses. The additional problem is having large numbers of people on the plant site at the same time. Moffett Field in California, for example, was host to 300,000 people on a Sunday when a Blue Angels precision-flying team performed. Such an event calls for special logistical planning by the public relations staff, possibly including the following measures:

1. The hiring of off-duty police to direct traffic

2. The chartering of shuttle buses

3. The availability of paramedics, and an ambulance on site

4. The rental of portable toilets

5. The briefing of employee volunteers who will be stationed throughout the facility

294

6. Provision for additional parking space

7. Contracts with catering firms for food

8. Special rest areas for those who get fatigued

9. A central location for lost-and-found children

10. Maps of the facility and a schedule of events

11. The building and staffing of displays and exhibits

12. Contracts with entertainment groups

13. Special permits for vendors selling souvenirs

14. Alternative arrangements in case of adverse weather

15. Provision for extra liability insurance

Each special event or open house has its own requirements. It is the responsibility of the public relations staff to ascertain exactly what is needed and to make appropriate plans. To do less is poor public relations and may result in legal problems.

Public Relations and Legal Counsel

Public relations and legal counsel are often at odds, as is pointed out in Chapter 4, but this is not an ideal situation.

A better relationship consists of a strong rapport between the two staffs so that their individual stores of expertise can complement each other. Public relations personnel are not lawyers, and they often need assistance in choosing the proper course of action about a matter that has clear legal ramifications. On the other hand, lawyers need to understand how important the court of public opinion is in determining the future of an organization. Respect and credibility must be maintained by both sides.

A number of steps can be taken by a company or organization to ensure that the public relations and legal staffs have a cordial, mutually supportive relationship:

1. The public relations and legal staffs should report to the same top executive, who can effectively listen to the viewpoints of both sides and decide on a course of action.

2. The organization should draft a clearly defined statement of responsibilities for each staff and its relationship to the other. Neither should dominate.

3. Both functions should be represented on key committees.

4. Public relations personnel and legal staff should get to know each other personally so a trusting relationship can be built.

5. Periodic consultations should be held during which materials and programs are reviewed.

6. The legal staff, as part of its duties, should brief public relations personnel on impending developments in litigation, so press inquiries can be answered in an appropriate manner.

7. Arrangements should be made for both staffs to forestall public relations and legal problems in connection with proxy battles; unfriendly takeover attempts; possible antitrust, consumer, and environmental legal action; and labor unrest.

Admittedly, the list is idealistic. But as laws and government regulations become more complex, it is essential that public relations and legal counsel work as equal partners in achieving organizational objectives.

QUESTIONS FOR REVIEW AND DISCUSSION

1. Name the five situations in which a public relations person, as the representative of an organization, can be named a co-conspirator with other company officials.

2. In what ways do libel and slander considerations affect the work of a public relations person?

3. What is the concept of *fair comment and privilege,* and what are the limitations?

4. What are some guidelines to follow in employee communications to avoid lawsuits?

5. What are some guidelines to follow if a news reporter inquires about an employee?

6. What is the concept of *implied consent* in the taking of photographs?

7. What legal precautions should an organization take if it actively solicits suggestions from employees and the public?

8. What are the basic guidelines of the 1978 copyright law about which public relations personnel should be familiar?

9. What constitutes "fair use" and "infringement" of copyrighted materials?

10. Why is it important for public relations personnel to know about trademarks?

11. Name at least five guidelines of the Federal Trade Commission that affect the way products can be publicized.

12. In what ways does the Securities and Exchange Commission regulate financial public relations activity? What kinds of information must be disclosed in a timely fashion?

13. What are some guidelines to remember if an organization is having an open house or a tour of a manufacturing facility?

14. What should be the relationship between the public relations and legal staffs of an organization?

Part four

APPLICATION

CHAPTER FOURTEEN

Corporations

All areas of endeavor in which public relations practitioners are engaged share basic operating methods. Yet each has its special needs and emphasis. The largest of these areas, in which approximately half of all professionals are involved, is public relations for corporations.

In corporate work, the task of public relations personnel is to interpret the goals, methods, products, and services of commerce and industry to the public and simultaneously to help their employers operate in a socially responsible manner. Such practitioners indeed function as bridges. On one side are managements whose legitimate profit-motivated goals suffer at times from their own insensitivity to the public's wishes and perceptions. On the other side, part of the public misunderstands the role of business in a free, competitive society and looks at corporations—especially the large ones—suspiciously.

Among the topics discussed in this chapter are the human factor in business, consumerism, the business-media relationship, the handling of crises, and issues management—the process whereby companies take the initiative in becoming involved in matters of public concern. The chapter also examines the specific problems several corporations faced. The discussions demonstrate how these firms handled difficult situations—with blunder and counterattack, or with openness and a concern for the public welfare—both in moments of crisis and in long-range campaigns to improve public perception of themselves.

The Corporate Role

This is an era of giantism in American business. Massive conglomerates control subsidiary companies that often produce a grab bag of seemingly unrelated products and services under the same corporate banner. These conglomerates must deal with government at many levels. Their operations affect the environment, control the employment of thousands, and have an impact on the financial and social well-being of millions. Truly, they have a compelling influence on contemporary life.

Bigness brings remoteness. The popular phrase "the faceless corporation" may be a cliché, but it represents a genuine distrust in the public mind—a distrust often based on lack of knowledge about a corporation rather than on actual unfavorable experiences.

When one oil company pays more than $13 billion to buy out a competitor, as Standard Oil of California did in 1984 to purchase the Gulf Corporation, the scope of the deal exceeds the comprehension of most citizens. They feel uneasy about the vast economic power of such a huge enterprise and suspect that it wields enormous backstage political influence. Beyond these broad, vague concerns they also see such a combination in

FIGURE 14.1

General Electric Company sees four factors that must be taken into consideration whenever a management decision is made. (1) Political—How do government regulations and other pressures affect the decision? (2) Technological—Do we have the engineering know-how to accomplish the goal? (3) Social—What is our responsibility to society? (4) Economic—Will we make a profit?

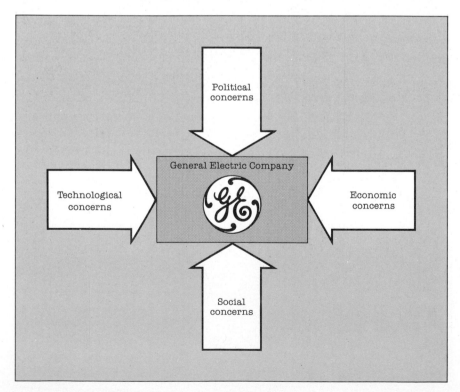

short-range personal perspective: "Will this force me to pay more for a gallon of gasoline?"

Since a corporation's impact on society is felt at so many levels, those who plan and conduct its public relations face a complex task. Even relatively small corporations need public relations programs that show them conducting their affairs, both external and internal, in a socially responsible manner.

Figure 14.1 presents, in schematic form, the way one company—General Electric—categorizes the various concerns it must take into consideration at every step of executive decision-making.

The Human Factor

THE PUBLIC PERCEPTION

The fundamental, irreplaceable element of every business is people—those who produce goods and services, those who consume them, and those inside and outside the companies whose lives and attitudes are influenced by how the companies act. What corporations *do* is not enough. The public's perception of their conduct also matters. A corporation may operate in a completely legal, technically sound, and financially efficient manner yet find itself viewed by segments of the public as cold, greedy, and heedless of cherished social values. The public relations practitioner's job is to see that this does not happen. The practitioner must work within the company to foster constructive, socially aware behavior, and outside the company to convince the public that the firm is a worthy, caring corporate citizen.

WHAT CAN HAPPEN WHEN BUSINESSES OVERLOOK THE HUMAN FACTOR

Businesses sometimes fail to recognize the human factor. They become so engrossed in computer technology, cash-flow charts, and management techniques that they overlook personal sensitivities. In a public relations blunder, the powerful Citibank of New York did precisely that. It announced that customers with accounts of less than $5000 at certain branches no longer would be served by human tellers but must use the bank's electronic teller machines. The efficiency experts forgot that "going to the bank" is a significant event in the lives of many people; that contact with a polite, cheerful teller gives the bank a personality in their minds. The arbitrary rule dehumanized the bank and created an atmosphere of class distinction based on money. Such loud complaints of "second-class-citizens!" arose that the bank was forced to abandon the rule.

Perception of business as a bully can occur in small firms as well as in corporate giants. During the Arab oil embargo of the early 1970s, the owner of a coffee shop in a small New Jersey community had an unexpected boom in business when motorists waiting in early-morning gasoline lines nearby came into his shop for refreshment. Business flourished so much that he added an employee. Then an ambitious 11-year-old boy named Billy appeared outside the shop, selling coffee and snacks from his small wagon. Billy drummed up trade by making derogatory remarks about the coffee shop's prices and food. Infuriated by the competition and juvenile insults, the coffee shop proprietor chased the boy away. Next, a local health inspector, a friend of the proprietor, told Billy that he could not sell food without a license.

The incident received national news coverage: the nasty monopolist against an enterprising 11-year-old boy. Customers shunned the coffee shop; phone callers denounced the owner. Business became so bad that he sold out and moved to another city.

Perception! The coffee shop proprietor had a history of working with youth groups. Citibank efficiency specialists made a plausible case that electronic teller machines are more economical than human teller service. Yet both proprietor and bank paid a price for their insensitivity.

The lesson is clear: before a company takes an action affecting the public, its management should attempt to view the move through the eyes of others. Providing management with these outside perceptions is the job of the public relations specialists. Their antennae should be as sensitive to public attitudes as cat's whiskers.

A contrast to these incidents: when thunderstorms knocked out electric service for a prolonged period during a July heat wave, the Baltimore Gas & Electric Company gave 7000 customers free dry ice to preserve their perishable foods. The result was a perception that the company cared about its customers.

COMPUTERS VERSUS HUMANS

As computer wizardry multiplies and increasingly ingenious automated voice equipment comes into service, companies are tempted to substitute this machinery for human contact with customers. This should be done with extreme caution. Unwise use of electronic response may alienate the very people the company needs to please. A dissatisfied customer who telephones to protest a billing error or shipping mistake resents being answered by a recording. Similarly, complaining letter-writers dislike receiving a computerized form-letter reply. Nor are customers placated by the cliché answer, "It was a computer error." They know that mistakes on computers result from errors committed by operators of the machines. Here is an area in which corporate public relations practitioners should exercise influence with management to maintain the human touch.

COURTESY PAYS

Too many corporations ignore opportunities to bind customers to them with small gestures such as thank-you letters. Although easily offended if they believe they are taken for granted, customers are impressed if someone in a supposedly remote corporation writes a note of appreciation. An example of the wrong way: a longtime customer of a mail-order house received in error two items worth $60 that she had not ordered. Because she was not billed for the items, she could have kept them without the company's knowing. Being honest, she returned the items to the company at considerable effort and postal expense, along with an explanatory note to the customer service representative whose name appeared on the company literature. She never received an acknowledgement for her effort and expense. Now she automatically throws into the wastebasket every catalogue she receives from the company and tells the story to her friends—a small but needless public relations failure.

Responding to customer inquiries and complaints is not only good public relations but good business. *Esquire* magazine (March 1984) carried the following item:

In a rare follow-up on complaints and inquiries from customers, Coca-Cola discovered that more than 30 percent of those who said they felt their complaints had not been resolved satisfactorily no longer buy company products and that 17 percent of those whose inquiries were satisfied buy more Coca-Cola products now. A company spokesperson reflected, "This study demonstrates that forward-looking management can turn the corporate response system into a high performance profit center."

Consumerism

The day when business could operate successfully on the Latin precept of *caveat emptor,* "Let the buyer beware," is long gone. In today's society, sellers are expected to deliver goods and services of safe, acceptable quality on honest terms, without misleading claims and deceptive financing practices. Consumers have rights protected by the federal government and enjoy the assistance of government and private agencies in enforcing those rights. Consumerism is a significant and growing force in the conduct of business. The manner in which public relations practitioners help to guide a company in handling the pressures of consumerism strongly affects the public's attitude toward that company.

THE DEVELOPMENT OF THE CONSUMER MOVEMENT

The consumer movement developed during the last quarter century because far too often business firms were caught either cheating their customers or carelessly giving them inferior products, then making it difficult for them to obtain adjustments. Public trust in business diminished. When the firm of Yankelovich, Skelly and White took a poll in 1967 to measure public trust, the result showed confidence in business at about 70 percent. In a similar poll in 1981, public confidence had plummeted to 19 percent. The troubles encountered by consumers contributed to this precipitous decline, which paralleled a loss of approval of most public institutions during that period.

Indicative of the public resentment was the creation in newspapers of "Action Line" columns, whose editors publish complaints from badly treated customers and try to solve their problems. In many instances a telephone call from "Action Line" to an offending business, with the implied threat of bad publicity, obtains results that the frustrated customer has been unable to achieve directly. Some television stations have similar consumer-service programs.

The high priest of the consumer movement during its growth stages was Ralph Nader, a youthful attorney in Washington, D.C. His book *Unsafe at Any Speed,* published in 1965, was a searing indictment of automobile safety standards. Nader organized study groups that published generally critical reports on other industries and dwelt heavily upon corporate responsibility to consumers.

Rising consumer protests coincided with a period of rapid expansion in the "watchdog" role of government. The power of federal regulatory agencies over business expanded in numerous directions. The Food and Drug Administration determines what medications can be sold to the public. The Federal Trade Commission regulates truth in advertising, and the Securities and Exchange Commission controls the financial conduct of corporations (see Chapter 13). The National Highway Traffic Safety Admnistration sets standards for automobile manufacture (the role of this agency in the Firestone tire crisis is discussed later in the chapter). The Consumer Product Safety Commission examines other manufactured goods. Other federal and state agencies have consumer-oriented policing powers in their domains.

CONSUMERISM IN THE 1980s

Although President Reagan's efforts to limit government regulation of business reduced government's role in several fields, public demand for government protection of consumers remained strong. A study taken by Louis Harris and Associates for Atlantic Richfield Company, released in 1983, showed public confidence in the consumer movement to be high. Strong sentiment was expressed favoring continued government regulation of safety, health, and truth in advertising, although opposition was voiced to regulation as a general concept (see Figure 7.1, in Chapter 7).

In the private sector, the nationwide network of Better Business Bureaus provides machinery through which wronged consumers may seek satisfaction. Nader's operations in Washington continue to publicize defective products and services. Other consumer organizations do similar work. *Consumer's Guide* is widely read.

Formation of the Society of Consumer Affairs Professionals in Business (SOCAB) provides an avenue for exchange of information among specialists in the field and a method for increasing corporate awareness of what can be accomplished in building good will.

Thus business and financial organizations function under extensive legal controls and unofficial pressures designed to give the public safe, reliable

FIGURE 14.2

The Alabama Power Company uses an animated figure called Louie the Lightning Bug in its television commercials to warn children against the dangers of electricity—an effective way to illustrate the company's sense of responsibility. (© 1984 Alabama Power Company.)

Louie the Lightning Bug.™

merchandise and honest services (see Figure 14.2). Whether a company meets the demands of consumers willingly or grudgingly—volunteering corrective action when the need is evident or fighting against having to do so—influences the public's perception of it.

PRODUCT RECALLS

Recall of a defective product from its purchasers is the most visible, and frequently very expensive, form of corporate response to consumer pressure. Millions of automobiles have been called back for correction of defects that might endanger the safety of riders. Some recalls by the auto makers are preventive and voluntary. Others have been done by agreement between manufacturer and the federal government. In certain instances, however, car makers have strenuously opposed government recall demands. Reaching the owners of defective automobiles is relatively easy, because of the state car registration laws. When other types of products are involved, especially those often purchased as gifts, the problem is more difficult.

Experience has shown that if a manufacturer recalls a defective product voluntarily, in a gracious manner that offers the owner suitable compensation, the company may generate enough good will to overcome the negative implications of the recall.

As an example, when Corning Glass Works belatedly discovered that 360,000 automatic percolators it made had handles bonded with epoxy that might deteriorate, it instituted a voluntary warning program, largely through the media. Among the methods Corning used were newspaper advertisements nationwide, advertisements in *Woman's Day* magazine, slide scripts to 300 television stations, audiocassettes to 400 radio stations, news releases, and information sheets to Corning dealers. Since local or factory repair of the defective percolators was impractical, and so was a one-for-one exchange of new for old, the company offered cash settlements, substitute products, free items, and merchandise from a specially prepared catalogue. Opinion surveys showed the Corning campaign to be effective in alerting the public. The number of percolators turned in was relatively small, however; many householders told survey-takers that the coffee makers were the only ones they owned and the handles on them had not broken. Corning's vigorous effort made a positive impression on the owners, as well as on nonowners who became aware of it.

The Business-Media Relationship

The performance and objectives of business become known to the public primarily through reporting by the news media. Far too frequently, however, misunderstandings and suspicions between the corporations and the media result in stories that business executives regard as inaccurate, incomplete, and biased against them. Editors and reporters reply that often they cannot publish or broadcast thorough, even-handed stories about business because many company executives, uncooperative and wary, erect barricades against them. They complain, too, that some business leaders don't understand the concept of objectivity and assume that any story involving unfavorable news about their company is intentionally biased.

Public relations practitioners serving business stand in the middle. They must interpret their companies to the media while showing their chief executive officers and other high officials how open, friendly press relations can serve their interests.

A RESEARCH STUDY OF THE RELATIONSHIP

Concerned about the misconceptions and distrust, the American Management Association commissioned a research study by David Finn, an eminent public relations counselor, the results of which were published in a booklet titled "The Business-Media Relationship." Its findings and recommendations are a valuable guide to all practitioners in the business field.

Finn conducted a series of detailed surveys. These are key findings as stated in the study:

AMA's surveys of public relations executives found that 73 percent believe reporters don't accurately research their topics, 62 percent believe reporters play on public emotion, and 72 percent see anti-business feelings and public sentiment as being on the side of the media. Most public relations executives (76 percent) consider the main problem of business reporting to be not necessarily bias but inaccuracies due to sloppiness.

AMA's companion survey of journalists found that 64 percent agreed that reporters don't accurately research their subjects, 58 percent attributed inaccuracies to sloppiness rather than bias, and 58 percent volunteered that media presentation is more important than factual reporting.

A majority of journalists (60 percent) feel that business executives are defensive and don't give reporters the chance to question them. A full 61 percent believe business people are not honest with their own public relations departments, and 36 percent think they often lie to reporters.[1]

[1] Reprinted, by permission of the publisher, from *The Business-Media Relationship: Countering Misconception and Distrust,* an AMA Research Study, by David Finn, pp. 10–13. © 1981 AMACOM, a division of American Management Associations, New York. All rights reserved.

RECOMMENDATIONS OF THE STUDY

Finn offers this set of recommendations to executives and reporters for achieving better reporting of business:

FOR EXECUTIVES

Arrange for direct contact between senior executives and reporters. Keep in touch with PR specialists and journalists on a continuing basis—not just when crises erupt. Do not, however, try to win favor of a reporter by giving confidences off the record or by offering gifts.

Provide means for executives to learn details of media practices, such as the need to attract readers and the importance of meeting deadlines.

Allow for the possibility that reporters may not be well acquainted with business practices, management techniques, economic principles, or the terminology of your industry.

Be well prepared on expected topics before meeting reporters. Where controversial issues are expected, consider drilling with colleagues beforehand: e.g., have them ask the twenty or so most likely questions, to be sure pertinent facts and explanations are at hand.

Study and practice specific techniques—e.g., using short sentences, repeating key phrases, avoiding "no comment" answers—that help to get ideas across in interviews.

Provide handouts or special memos to summarize key points, especially when complicated issues or financial data are involved.

Don't try to squelch a story by bringing pressure on higher-ups in the media.

Be aware of public concerns when commenting on issues involving corporate interests.

Have a third person present at interviews to listen objectively to what is said and to call inadvertent inaccuracies or oversights to the principal executive's attention.

Maintain a continuing good relationship between legal and PR counsel so that there will be a thoughtful balance between legal exposure and the amount of information volunteered.

Don't argue with a negative report in the media. To do so is to keep the issue before the public more than may be warranted.

In the event of a damaging story or series, make a long-range plan for constructive future actions.

FOR REPORTERS

Prepare for interviews by such means as studying pertinent company statements, position papers, and annual reports.

Become familiar with the fundamentals of finance, accounting, economics, and management practices.

Be aware of legitimate constraints—privacy laws, SEC rules, impending lawsuits, the value of certain facts to competitors—that limit the ability of executives to divulge certain information.

Be open with business executives. Be receptive in presentation materials and to the business point of view.

Be careful not to make the selling of news more important than the news itself.

Make certain that headlines reflect the content of the story. An effective, responsible story can be damaged by a misleading headline. [This is outside a reporter's realm, since copyeditors write headlines.]

Discourage off-the-record remarks by business executives.

Understand that business reactions to extensive, well-researched stories cannot always be immediate.

When possible, check quotes with source, in order to permit review.

When necessary, explain deadlines, off-the-record requirements, and other journalistic restrictions to executives.

Take advantage of business's willingness to review financial information.

Be wary of quoting disgruntled ex-employees exclusively.

In keeping with these guidelines, a corporate public relations department should serve as a door-opener for reporters within the corporation, as well as handle routine inquiries and provide background material. The public relations practitioners should make company executives realize that reporters are not automatically enemies out to get them. As William C. Adams, public relations manager of Phillips Petroleum Company, once said semi-facetiously, "The other side is not all 'commies.' We must educate management to this."

Crisis Public Relations

The most challenging test of public relations skill in corporate life arises in times of crisis. When an unexpected development involving a company embarrasses the organization or frightens the public—even in the worst instance creating the threat of death—the company's credibility and decency come under intense scrutiny. With the news media in hard pursuit of the facts, executives and public relations experts must act under severe pressure.

In a crisis, the first instinct of some companies is to "stonewall it": deny that a crisis exists, refuse to answer media questions, and resist involvement by appropriate government agencies. By behaving in this manner, managements suggest a "public-be-damned" attitude that harms their images severely.

A second course, followed by some, is to "manage" the news about the crisis by releasing partial, often inaccurate, and delayed information while concealing especially unfavorable facts. If these facts slip out anyway, as they frequently do through insider "leaks" and government inquiries, disclosure of a company's cover-up attempt shatters its credibility.

THE BEST COURSE TO FOLLOW

The third and best course is an open communication policy. The company keeps the media fully and promptly informed of the facts while providing background information to put the facts into perspective. A story candidly told, while perhaps embarrassing in its immediate impact, is less damaging than a cover-up version that generates rumors and suspicions much worse than reality.

Because crises may develop without warning, every corporation needs a well-prepared policy of emergency action. The plan should include advance selection of a qualified representative who will issue consistent, truthful information with an awareness of media deadlines. A management committee that meets frequently to assess the situation as it develops is an excellent way to identify and satisfy the public's concerns.

Other elements of an emergency plan should include these measures:

A manual of operations, distributed to all management personnel. The manual lists procedures to be followed in such emergencies as an earthquake, oil spill, product tampering, or other possibilities peculiar to the particular corporation

Arrangements for media facilities at a central location with telephones, typewriters, and electronic hookups

Selection and training of employees to handle the surge of telephone calls any emergency creates

Plans for notifying families of injured or dead workers

Arrangements with local hospitals and ambulance for handling casualties.

THREE MILE ISLAND

A classic case of public relations confusion in a life-and-death situation occurred when the Three Mile Island nuclear power plant near Harrisburg, Pennsylvania, suffered a series of breakdowns in its No. 2 reactor cooling system in 1979. A critical situation developed. A potentially disastrous meltdown of the reactor and a devastating explosion of hydrogen gas, with high loss of life from radiation, became a possibility.

During the weeklong crisis, the public received a baffling mixture of contradictory statements from Metropolitan Edison Company, the plant's owner; the Nuclear Regulatory Commission (NRC); and companies that had built portions of the nuclear system. Metropolitan Edison tended to issue statements minimizing the danger, while government representatives spoke in more alarming terms. The plant owners did not always keep the NRC and the public informed about their actions during the crisis—at a time when the nation, shaken by the realization of nuclear plant vulnerability and the fear of deadly release of radioactive material, deserved the fullest possible information. During several crucial moments public relations representatives of the company seemed ill-informed about what was happening.

At one point a Metropolitan Edison vice-president told a news conference, "I don't know why we need to tell you every step we take. We certainly feel a responsibility for people who live around our plant and we need to get on with our job." The rather brusque tone of this statement added to the generally poor impression made by the company's handling of the news.

Case studies of how two large corporations handled their public relations during crises—badly in one instance, excellently in the other—appear at the end of this chapter.

Issues Management

Corporations do not exist in a vacuum. Their creation of goods and services cannot be treated by management exclusively as a money-making operation. *Contemporary society expects a corporation also to exercise social responsibility.* A business should concern itself with the impact of its operations on the communities in which it is established and upon the nation as a whole, and with such problems as the environment, treatment of minorities, health, education, and equality of opportunity.

THE SOCIAL CONTRACT A corporation's set of responsibilities is known popularly as its *social contract*. The contract is unwritten and not clearly defined, although it is in part imposed by federal and state laws. Pressures from customers, the public, and groups of activist stockholders also stimulate corporate responsiveness. Wise managements do not merely react to governmental and economic pressures; they take the initiative to be good corporate citizens, and to let the world know that they are.

One obvious way to meet social responsibility is to give money. Corporate giving, as discussed more fully in Chapter 18, takes many forms, among them charitable contributions through the United Way, matching grants to institutions, and donations to organizations in which management and employees have an interest.

To emphasize their concern about education, companies award scholarships to outstanding students, either on the basis of merit and need or on academic merit alone, and as prizes in competitions. Scholarship competitions usually are in fields in which the donor companies have a special interest and identify talented young persons whom the sponsor might wish eventually to recruit as employees. The Westinghouse Science Talent Search gives a $10,000 first-place scholarship and 39 other awards annually; the top award has gone with increasing frequency to young women. The makers of Duracell batteries sponsor a scholarship competition with a $10,000 first prize going to the high school student who designs the best battery-powered device providing a practical function. The device must use Duracell batteries. At a less cerebral level, Atari has promoted its video games by awarding a $5,000 scholarship to the teenage winner of its International Atari Asteroids Championships.

Corporations cannot achieve social approval with money alone. They must strive for it in other ways. They need to focus on issues on which their work can achieve beneficial results for themselves and the public. While society benefits from these corporate efforts, it would be naive to claim that their endeavors are entirely altruistic. A company management alert to what goes on in the world outside its commercial boundaries can identify developing issues that may significantly affect its long-range corporate health. Then it can do something about them.

Issues management is the term applied to the process by which a corporation identifies the areas of public interest with which it chooses to become actively involved. The field of issues management has become an expanding one in public relations practice; it is partially political and partially socioeconomic. Much of this work involves persuading lawmakers to support or oppose legislation. Equally important are consultations with influential organizations that represent major policy concerns, such as the environment. An issues management approach to ecological problems is discussed in the next section.

ENVIRONMENTAL ISSUES

Among the most urgent issues many corporations face is the effect their operations have upon the environment. Factory owners once released dangerous chemicals into the air and pollution-laden discharges into the waterways with little thought about the resulting environmental damage. Rarely was this conduct questioned. The opposite is true today. Environmental activist groups, with strong public support, challenge every indication of industrial pollution they discover. And the federal Environmental Protection Agency has powers to create regulations affecting business and to enforce environmental controls.

At times environmental protesters may become excessively shrill and make assumptions of wrongdoing based on inadequate information, but they cannot be ignored. Companies that fight back by denouncing their environmental critics only heighten the antagonism. Nonactivist, but still skeptical, elements of the public tend to view the denunciations as a cover-up. Concern

Steps in Issues
Management

Here is a list of activities undertaken by the public relations department of Rexnord Corporation of Milwaukee when it began work in issues management:

Read periodicals on subject

List 100 or more issues of concern to the company

Seek out the concerns of other managers

Place selected issues in categories

Schedule information meetings to discuss issues

Start a central issue file

Determine which issues are relevant

Set priorities in each category

Circulate list to managers for comment

Compose and circulate a final list

Make a separate list of plans to support these actions

Determine need for formal public affairs activity

Prepare "white papers" on the most pressing issues

Present selected issues at appropriate meetings

Encourage issue-oriented executive speeches

Stimulate letters to employees, shareholders, retirees, customers

Discuss issues with elected officials

Learn what other industries are doing

Form a steering committee of those interested

Organize a speakers' bureau on issues

Write to community leaders for opinions on issues priorities

Evaluate the possibility of a company survey to gain support

Examine possibilities of an issues management seminar

Update issues list and priorities, using information gathered

Discuss possibility of president's letter to employees on issues of mutual interest about the finite limits of earth's air, water, and natural resources has become deeply embedded in the public consciousness, and any corporation that brushes aside environmentalist critics as "just a bunch of cranks" dangerously underestimates the strength of the movement.

The better course for corporations with an environmental problem is to seek common ground with their critics. Informal meetings between company executives and environmentalist leaders may help break down the barriers. Each group discovers that the other is human. The first steps in getting a point across to adversaries are to convince them to listen, and then to make them realize that the speaker has valid points to make. This is where the persuasive power of a public relations campaign comes into play. As mutual suspicions diminish through individual contacts, the opposing sides may be able to find certain points on which they agree and at least limited objectives toward which they can work together. At a minimum, this approach shows that the corporation recognizes its problem and desires to solve it (see Figure 14.3).

Typical of this progressive approach is a program by Texaco Inc. This energy giant established a constituency relations manager in its public relations and advertising department to work with third-party groups.

Texaco identified nationally more than a score of constituency groups, such as the National Association for the Advancement of Colored People (NAACP), that it desired to cultivate. After personal contacts were developed, Texaco set up communication workshops, refinery tours, a home-weatherization clinic, and alternative-energy dialogues with these groups. The company listened to their concerns and analyzed how they might affect its well-

FIGURE 14.3

DuPont & Company emphasized its concern for environmental issues by donating $50,000 to support the work of the Patuxent Wildlife Research Center in Maryland, where bald eagles are bred in captivity. Attending a news conference in Washington at which the gift was announced, Interior Secretary William Clark flinches as a bald eagle stretches its wings. (Courtesy UPI/Bettmann Archive.)

being. Emphasis was placed on long-term relationships, to prevent a feeling among the groups that Texaco was using them for quick, one-time purposes. One result has been instances in which Texaco and one or more of these constituency groups took joint positions on legislative matters. Texaco and the NAACP lobbied side by side in Congress on an issue involving credit practices in the petroleum industry. Texaco also supplied financial and editorial aid to an Hispanic organization that sought to establish a national office.

Using this network of contacts outside its own world of energy, Texaco broadens its awareness of the sociopolitical forces at work in the country, shows its intention to be a socially responsible corporation, and receives early warnings of emerging issues that it may need to face.

Publicity Efforts

Another aspect of public relations in business is image-making for products and publicity for company identity and trade names. This is part of the marketing function, and the extent to which a public relations department actually becomes involved in it varies from company to company.

The objectives can be achieved in many ways, as evidenced by this sampling of methods corporations have used:

Sponsorship of sporting events. By underwriting the cost of a competition, the company is permitted to attach its name to the event. Mention of the competition in newspaper, radio, and television news reports thus includes the corporate or brand name, a form of free institutional advertising. In addition, the company earns the appreciation of participants and others with strong interest in the event.

A few examples include the $250,000 Toyota Tennis Championships, the Kinney Invitational Track Meet (sponsored by Kinney Shoes), the Nabisco-Dinah Shore golf tournament, and the Virginia Slims tennis tournament for women. Although cigarette advertising is forbidden on television, Virginia Slims thus is able to have its brand name mentioned on the air.

Underwriting of cultural and civic events. Name exposure from these is less than from sporting events. Heavy use of brand-name sponsorship was a feature of the 1984 Olympic Games in Los Angeles.

Sponsorship of polls and research projects bearing a brand name. Again, the purpose is to obtain free mention of commercial names in news reports. The Philip Morris Company publicizes its Merit brand cigarettes by operating the Merit Report, a public opinion poll on a wide range of topics, in which voters use computerized machines in Merit trailers parked in public areas.

Public relations tours. Following up its entertaining television commercials featuring a monk, Brother Dominic, who declares its duplicating machine to be "a miracle," Xerox sent the "monk" on a personal-appearance tour. Comedian Jack Eagle, who played the role, visited hundreds of trade shows and Xerox branches nationwide.

Free entertainment. Coors beer sends its Coors Cowboy Band around the rodeo circuit, providing free music for the crowds. This ties in with the "macho" theme of Coors commercials.

Displays. Coca-Cola tethers a 20-foot-high plastic replica of a Coca-Cola can on the roof of a supermarket or other large sales outlet, to draw attention to its products. At Manchester, New Hampshire, pranksters apparently climbed a store roof at night, pulled down the display can, filled it with helium, and turned it loose. Air traffic controllers at a nearby airport reported the can floating off into the distance at 2000-foot altitude. For one brief, brave moment the Coca-Cola container was reminiscent of the Goodyear blimp that appears frequently above crowded football stadiums.

Gifts and prizes. Republic Airlines realized that it had an identity problem in Southern California after taking over a regional airline there. It created attention by holding four drawings, at each of which it gave away 150 free round-trip tickets. The promotion drew large crowds and news stories.

Financial Information

Maintenance of favorable relations with investors and security analysts, primarily by providing them with liberal amounts of financial information, is a vital part of corporate public relations. They form an easily defined target audience.

A corporation's annual report, issued in advance of its annual meeting, is the basic piece of printed information about its affairs. (The annual report is examined in Chapter 22.) Figure 14.4 presents the covers of typical annual reports. Brief quarterly reports and reports on what occurred at the annual meetings also are distributed. Another required piece of financial literature is a prospectus, issued by the company according to Securities and Exchange Commission guidelines at the time of any proposed sale of securities.

Annual meetings of corporations commonly are routine and dull, with everything going precisely as management has arranged it. Proxy votes obtained in advance assure management solid control of the voting. Managements often present slide and videotaped shows to illustrate their achievements, serve light refreshments, and in general try to create an atmosphere of competence and geniality. Behind the scenes, many hours of public relations department work have been spent in planning and preparing the meetings.

At times abrasive moments of controversy may arise if stockholders

FIGURE 14.4

Companies spend millions of dollars on annual reports for distribution to stockholders, financial analysts, and institutional investors. Often printed on glossy paper with colorful illustrations, the reports usually are written and coordinated by individuals specializing in financial public relations. These are examples of annual report covers. (Reproduced by permission of Potlatch Corporation; Varian Associates, Inc.; The Southern Company; and Bank of America. American President Companies' cover reproduced by permission of Mark Thompson, 1983 Annual Report, American President Companies.)

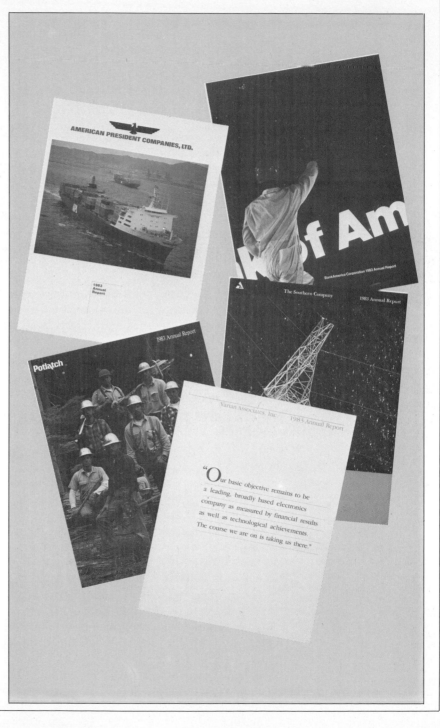

individually or in groups challenge management practices and policies. Nearly an hour was consumed at one Xerox annual meeting in debating whether the corporation should limit its operations in South Africa; in the vote that followed, management defeated the measure. Opponents of nuclear power often submit resolutions at utility company annual meetings. Although anti-management resolutions of this nature rarely pass, they obtain publicity and at times gather enough votes to influence management thinking. Training in speech skills and in the techniques of conducting a meeting is especially valuable to the presiding executive when controversy arises.

Corporate presentations to security analysts, whose opinions influence the price performance and sales volume of company securities, are more technical in nature than annual meetings. Printed and sometimes audiovisual material is prepared by public relations specialists to explain company goals, financial achievements, and projections. Since analysts are experts, their questions are searching. Skillful preparation of material by the public relations department helps the chief executive officer make an effective presentation to this critical audience.

A Department in Operation

An examination of the public relations department of a middle-size corporation in operation reveals the department's double role—as a communicator within the company and as an interpreter of the company to the public. Because it takes an innovative approach to a severe public relations problem, and is relatively typical in size and responsibilities, we shall examine the public relations department of the San Diego Gas & Electric Company. The utility has 5,000 employees and 800,000 customers in Southern California.

THE PROBLEM Like all public utility companies, San Diego Gas & Electric is consumer-intensive. It sells natural gas and electricity to homes, companies, and institutions in an urban, mountain, and desert area of 4,400 square miles. The company's customers have no choice. Since the utility holds exclusive franchises from local governments to provide service to this territory, consumers must purchase their electricity and gas from it. Such exclusivity is standard among American utilities, based on time-tested economic realities. Yet it creates a feeling among some customers that they are exploited victims of a monopoly. The rates a utility company may charge are set by the state public utilities commission after intricate hearings. The commission's role is to balance customers' rights against the company's need to earn a fair profit.

Customers are quick to criticize poor service and to condemn what they perceive to be unreasonably high rates. Although every public utility faces the problem of disgruntled consumers to some degree, San Diego Gas &

Electric's public relations problem is especially intense. The company's electric rates are among the highest in the United States, and during the 1970s a combination of soaring rates and perceived decline in service severely damaged its reputation.

San Diego G & E's troubles stemmed from the Arab oil embargo of the early 1970s. The company had depended heavily upon oil to generate its electricity; when the crisis shortage sent oil prices skyrocketing, the company's rates to its consumers rose correspondingly. Customers complained vociferously. At the same time, the company fell into financial difficulties because of the oil problem. It neglected customer relations at a moment when the need for friendly, competent service was especially intense. The morale of employees deteriorated; many believed that the widespread criticisms of their company reflected upon them personally.

THE COUNTERATTACK   A new, youthful management team took command at San Diego Gas & Electric. The chief executive officer, Thomas A. Page, adopted a fresh, candid approach to the public by frankly admitting the company's shortcomings. A new public relations director was brought in to change the company's image. Instead of taking a defensive posture, the company began to meet criticism head-on. In advertising and publicity it stressed cooperation and emphasized the community of interest between public and company (see Figure 14.5).

Typifying the company's new approach was a series of newspaper advertisements, the first of which was headlined:

YOU'RE RIGHT.
UTILITY BILLS ARE
RISING TOO FAST.
SOMETHING HAS TO CHANGE.

Under this attention-getting headline, Page said in an open letter to customers:

> You're an SDG&E customer and you're angry.
>
> The price of electricity and natural gas has shot up dramatically. Every rate increase bites deeper into your budget, leaving less money for those things you need and want.
>
> You're fed up with skyrocketing utility bills, and we don't blame you. You're calling for someone to do something about it, and you're absolutely right.
>
> At SDG&E we hear your anger and frustration every day—from our crews and meter readers in the street and our customer service personnel, right up to the executive offices and the boardroom. We don't like the situation one bit, either.
>
> So this company's top priority is to stabilize utility rates. . . .
>
> We need your help. SDG&E cannot single-handedly meet energy challenges in today's social and economic environment. Everyone who depends on utility service

FIGURE 14.5

This was one in a series of advertisements published by San Diego Gas & Electric Company in its campaign to regain public confidence. (Courtesy of San Diego Gas & Electric Company.)

must now share that responsibility. The problem of rapidly escalating utility rates demands a community of interest. . . .

In a series of messages to follow, we will inform you of each step in our effort to stabilize rates. We will also ask for your support, and let you know what specific things you can do to help achieve more stable utility rates in the future. Because today, we *all* must take part in the solution to energy problems.

Another advertisement in the series offered readers a booklet, "How to Take Charge of Your Energy Bill."

THE DEPARTMENT'S STAFF

The public relations and advertising department responsible for carrying out the corporation's aggressive campaign has a staff of 23 men and women, led by Richard L. Manning. As a vice-president, he answers directly to the president and chief executive officer.

Under Manning are the directors of three sections within the department—*public relations/corporate communication,* which includes employee communications, finance, and advertising; *public policy,* which includes policy and communication research and the news bureau under a news manager; and *community relations,* which also handles energy education and consumer affairs. The community relations staff includes a community affairs manager in each of the company's seven districts. These managers attend civic functions in their districts, tell the company's story discreetly, and as listening posts give management feedback about public attitudes and issues. For younger staff members these are excellent positions in which to learn the details of the utility business and to see the workings of public opinion at close range.

PUBLICATIONS

The department produces publications for both internal and external use. The basic *internal* publication is a monthly tabloid-size newspaper, *News Meter,* containing news stories and pictures of company affairs and employee activities. Supplementing this is a single-sheet newsletter, *FYI* (for your information), distributed to employees on an irregular basis to report important company developments quickly. Each Monday morning a factsheet, *Management Bulletin,* listing scheduled events for the week, is placed on the desks of all middle-management and upper-level executives. These copies are for public posting within the company.

In addition to these written communications, the department each day produces *Dial 2001,* a 3-minute recorded message. Employees are invited to dial this number on the internal telephone system to hear the day's company news.

External publications include a wide variety of materials. A pamphlet called *Lite Lines,* emphasizing conservation methods and similar consumer-oriented information, is inserted with the monthly bills to customers. A management-oriented mailing, *Perspectives,* is sent to selected opinion leaders among the public. Newsletters are distributed at the district level. As a public service, booklets such as "10 Fool-Proof Ways to Save Gas" are available free of charge. Much of the corporation's annual report is written by the public relations staff; graphic design and printing are handled by outside suppliers on contract. Shareholders also receive quarterly financial reports and other information.

SPEAKERS' BUREAU

The department operates a speakers' bureau consisting of 30 to 35 company employees who volunteer to address organizations and public meetings. In addition, specialists are on call when their fields of expertise are involved. Speakers receive professional training and meet at a monthly breakfast briefing. The department arranges five to seven public speeches a week. Tom Page, the chief executive officer, makes numerous speeches.

FILMS AND VIDEOTAPES

As part of its new, candid approach, the department produced a 20-minute motion picture about company operations, "The Heartbeat of the City," for indoctrination of new employees. Angry customers are shown in one segment, denouncing the company for high rates and poor service. The purpose of including this unfriendly material is to show employees what to expect. This unusual frankness helped the film win the Best of Show award at the 1982 Public Relations Society of America convention. Later it was shown to the public on cable television in San Diego.

The department videotapes the corporation's annual meeting, for later showing to employees. It also distributes videotapes on other company matters to departments.

Each district office has a video machine on which it can play tapes for selected audiences. The department uses a video recorder to make air checks of material broadcast about the company.

NEWS BUREAU

The department's news bureau operates on a beat system, under which staff members are assigned to cover specified areas of the company. The bureau handles an average of 35 inquiries a day from the news media. Reporters are put into contact with relevant company officials through the news bureau. The department's policy on news releases is conservative; it avoids overloading editors with releases of little value, electing instead to issue releases only on significant news. The news bureau prepares special feature stories for such target audience publications as *Senior World* and *La Prensa,* the latter circulating among the area's large Hispanic population.

In addition to these regularly scheduled functions, the department conducts plant tours, works with school officials on energy education programs, stages press conferences for high company executives, provides scripts for company speakers, and produces radio and television commercials.

THE RESULTS OF THE EFFORT

Public awareness of the company's new approach began to be apparent after a few months. The Public Relations Society of San Diego gave Page its Diogenes award. The award cited him for giving "leadership to his company when it had a singularly poor public relations standing in the community and for his reversal of a policy to stand silent as practiced by the former management of SDG&E to one that is open and frank." Similarly, the Press Club of San Diego gave the firm a special award for its efforts in personnel communications.

In the first winter after the new policy took effect, the number of customer complaints about high bills dropped 60 percent.

Further evidence of sharp improvement in the public's attitude toward the company is found in a comparison of opinion surveys taken in March 1982 and July 1983. When asked to state their feelings about San Diego Gas & Electric, 50 percent of those questioned in 1982 replied, "very unfavorable." Sixteen months later the number of persons replying "very unfavorable" was 26 percent—a reduction of almost half. The public relations program clearly was achieving results.

Case Studies: Public Relations Crises—A Contrast

When a corporation finds itself caught in a major crisis that threatens its reputation, its management and public relations department are put under severe stress. The way in which they handle the bad news demonstrates company philosophy and their state of preparedness. One company reacts with candor, open communication, and obvious concern for the public good. Another company tries to ride out the storm by brushing aside media and public questions, belligerently denying the existence of trouble, and creating the impression that it puts self-interest above public safety and welfare.

The forthright company emerges stronger in the public eye than before the crisis. The cover-up company harms its reputation so badly that it is damaged for years to come.

Two leading American corporations—Johnson & Johnson, health product manufacturers, and Firestone Tire & Rubber Company—endured major crises within a relatively short time of each other. The former earned praise for its handling of the problem, a public relations victory. The other suffered a public relations disaster. These two case studies explain why.

THE WRONG WAY— FIRESTONE'S DEFECTIVE RADIAL TIRES

A year after Firestone began manufacture and sale of its Radial 500 tires— highly advertised and heavily publicized—the company's director of development sent a memo to top management in which he stated, "We are making an inferior quality radial tire, which will subject us to belt-edge separation at high mileage."

Other internal warnings followed. Dissatisfied customers in exceptionally high numbers returned their 500s to dealers. Retail and oil companies for which Firestone made versions of the 500 under their firms' brand names complained about reports from customers that the tire tread separated from the steel-belt inner layer. Reports of many accidents pointed to Radial 500 tire defects as the cause.

Prompted by these warnings, Firestone might have withdrawn the tire from the market because of the indicated peril to motorists using it. The company did just the opposite. During the next 5 years, Firestone made and sold nearly 24 million Radial 500s at about $50 each. Despite growing evidence to the contrary, the company praised the tire as a good product.

BEGINNING OF A MORASS   Then, slowly at first, the truth began to emerge. The Firestone denial of its product's dangerous shortcomings crumbled, piece by piece. Making a series of public relations blunders, the company was drawn deeper and deeper into a morass. Finally, after months of damaging revelations about its cavalier attitude and lack of candor, Firestone was forced by government and public pressure into a massive product recall of the Radial 500s, the largest recall in tire history. This cost the company $140 million. No one can calculate how much long-term damage was done to the oldtime company's reputation, but clearly it was enormous.

Four years after Firestone began marketing the Radial 500, complaints about it accumulated at the Center for Auto Safety, a consumer organization in Washington, D.C. After challenging Firestone by letter about these complaints, the center turned its research materials over to the National Highway Traffic Safety Administration. This federal agency, which Firestone claimed had a grudge against it from previous episodes, investigated. Survey cards were mailed to 87,000 purchasers of new cars equipped with radial tires, asking them to indicate the brand of tires and list complaints about their performance. Only 5,400 purchasers responded, a small percentage. Firestone came off much the worst of the tire companies in these responses.

Here, Firestone made its most costly public relations error. Learning that the federal agency was about to make the survey public, the company asked the United States District Court in Cleveland for a restraining order to prevent publication of the results. The company contended that the survey was flawed and would improperly harm its reputation. The court granted the order. Instead of quieting the dispute, however, this attempt to suppress the findings had the opposite effect. People who had never heard of the survey were alerted by news stories about the legal move. The public's curiosity and suspicion were aroused. Why, many asked, was Firestone trying to conceal the information?

CONGRESSIONAL HEARINGS   News of the suppression had repercussions in Congress. The House Subcommittee on Oversight and Investigations decided to hold public hearings on the safety of the Radial 500. Piles of Firestone documents obtained by the National Highway Traffic Safety Administration yielded information harmful to the company.

Firestone made another move that heightened public suspicion. The Traffic Safety Administration sent it a special order listing 27 questions, with a request for a full, prompt response. Instead of being cooperative, the company sent a belligerent legalistic reply objecting to most of the questions. Throughout the maneuvering Firestone projected an image of greater concern for its financial self-interest than for the public safety.

The company compounded its difficulties still further by blaming owners of the Radial 500s for problems with the tires. Firestone claimed that most of the blowouts and tread separations reported on Radial 500s resulted from neglect and misuse by motorists. It contended that owners had damaged the tires by overloading them, hitting them against the curb, not keeping enough air in them, and driving too fast. This buck-passing by the manufacturer angered purchasers who had paid high prices for the tires, only to find them defective. The firm forgot the maxim that a company can prosper only when it has satisfied customers.

Despite Firestone's court action, results of the Traffic Safety Administration survey reached the public anyway. The private Center for Auto Safety requested and received the survey through the Freedom of Information Act, then gave it to the news media.

The four days of congressional subcommittee hearings, heavily covered by the news media, were extremely harmful to the company. Serving as the corporation's spokesman, its combative chief counsel was caught by committee members in misstatements and contradictions. Other witnesses told grim stories of accidents in which the tires were involved. Evidence showed conclusively that Firestone had prior knowledge of the unusually high number of complaints and of the tire's defects.

Although the company had stated that manufacture of the Radial 500 had ended 18 months earlier, the subcommittee learned that in fact production had continued until shortly before the hearings. The company had complained about a news story indicating that 8 percent of the 500s had been returned to dealers by dissatisfied customers. Evidence brought out during the investigation disclosed that actually the average return rate of the tires over a 6-year period was 17.5 percent, far higher than that encountered by any other radial tire.

LAWSUITS   According to the evidence submitted by the prosecution, the defective tires contributed to 41 deaths and 65 injuries. Lawsuits by accident victims or their survivors piled up against the company; more than 250 were pending at one time. Firestone settled out of court for $1.4 million in one case involving two deaths and a survivor who became a quadraplegic.

Finally, the cumulative disclosures, public anger, and government pres-

COLOR—AN EXTRA DIMENSION IN PUBLIC RELATIONS

An upsurge in publication of color photographs and graphics in newspapers, stimulated by appearance of the national daily *USA Today*, has accelerated an already growing trend toward use of color in public relations work.

Ways in which color can be applied effectively in addressing both external and internal audiences are illustrated with examples from contemporary public relations practice in this 16-page color section.

Color printing consists of two types. In the simpler, cheaper form known as *spot color*, colored inks—usually one or two—are applied separately to paper. Black ink often is used in combination with colors. The more complex form, *process color*, involves photographic reproduction from a slide, transparency, motion picture film, or videotape. Most color advertising is of the process type.

Application of color to achieve psychological effects and to obtain easy identification of sponsoring organizations is among the techniques demonstrated in these pages.

The Impact of Color

The impact of color is vividly apparent when a picture is printed in black and white, then in full color. This photograph of a petroleum geologist by Manuel Chavez, which appeared on the cover of *Texaco Times*, demonstrates the power of color to attract attention and stimulate interest. (Courtesy of Texaco, Inc.)

Certain colors can be used to achieve psychological effects. At the high end of the spectrum, red attracts attention and stimulates the visual sense. It is a "hot" color, suggesting excitement. This photograph of Lars Tate carrying the football for the University of Georgia suggests the power of red. (Courtesy of University of Georgia.)

	Before	After
Kodak Corporate Symbol		
Kodak Seller's Insignia		
Kodak Film Packaging		
Kodak Processing Labs Emblem		

Yellow is less vehement than red, warm rather than hot. When the two colors are used in combination, as in this Kodak insignia, the effect is lively and friendly. (Courtesy of Selame Design.)

Soothing and peaceful, green symbolizes the balance and normality of nature, as illustrated by this pastoral scene put out by the National Live Stock and Meat Board to publicize its products. Green is often combined with tan, as in this picture, to create an aura of tranquility. (© National Live Stock and Meat Board.)

Photographs in which blue dominates create a mood of relaxation and serenity. The color is particularly appropriate for generating tourism, as in this view of the Wailea beach on the Hawaiian island of Maui. A "cool" color, blue can be used to suggest deliberation and security. (Courtesy of Maui Inter-Continental Wailea.)

FULL SPEED AHEAD

• An interview with Allen Jacobson •

" I think our marketing and technical diversity represent our two greatest strengths "

Late last year, Allen Jacobson was named president, U.S. Operations. He has responsibility for 3M's four business sectors as well as the Consumer Products Group. In the following interview, he explains his priorities and comments on a variety of key 3M issues.

Editor: First, just a little bit of clarification. In your business correspondence, you sometimes sign your letters "Jake." What do you prefer to be called?

Jacobson: I guess I prefer to be called either Allen or Jake.

Editor: What is your highest priority as president of U.S. Operations?

Jacobson: To continue 3M's excellent record of profitable growth. I think we've got two main challenges in this regard: First, we need to maintain high productivity in all parts of the organization so that we can remain competitive; second, we need to come up with unique, high-quality new products that have a lot of utility for customers — those are the only kind from which you can get profitable growth.

Editor: How do you see these priorities relating to 3M employees?

Jacobson: From an employee point of view, my objective is to keep 3M a place where there are growing opportunities. That basically involves two responsibilities. On the one hand, we must maintain our profitable growth, because that creates the climate necessary for career opportunities. On the other hand, we have a great responsibility to develop people so that they can make the most of these opportunities. You have to do both.

Editor: You mentioned a need for continuing high productivity. On a scale of one to 10, with 10 representing the highest possible level of productivity, where would you place 3M right now?

Jacobson: I'd say we are possibly a strong seven.

Editor: Does that mean the greater need for attention today is in the area of new product development, rather than in the area of productivity?

Jacobson: No. I don't think you can really separate the two considerations. You can't make one statement that will be entirely true for every aspect of a highly diversified company like 3M. Remember, we've got more than $7 billion of established business out there. In relation to this, we've got to be responsive to the market, we've got to provide quality, and we've got to maintain high productivity. At the same time, each year, we have to generate almost a billion dollars worth of new business to grow the way we want to; that's where new products have to be the emphasis.

Editor: What do you regard as 3M's greatest strengths?

Jacobson: Our diversity is probably our main strength. We have many strong technologies, and our ability to combine many of these

6   3M Today

The use of one or two colored inks applied separately on printed materials such as brochures or posters can achieve attractive results at relatively low cost. The addition of blue to this page of *3M Today*, employee magazine of the 3M Corporation, gives it extra vigor. (Courtesy of Public Relations Department/3M.)

Red and blue inks on white paper produce an eye-catching effect that carries a patriotic overtone. Black ink was unnecessary on this piece of printing. (Courtesy of American Cancer Society, California Division, Inc.)

The clever silhouette adds a dramatic note to the cover of this one-color-and-black community service pamphlet. By using yellow paper, the designer obtains the impact of an additional color. The pamphlet, issued jointly by Home Savings of America and KABC-TV, Los Angeles, lists addresses of health-care, legal, nutritional, and similar services for older citizens. (Courtesy of KABC-TV, Los Angeles.)

Although this Army recruiting bumper sticker has only one color, with words in white reverse lettering, it delivers its message emphatically in short words and large block letters.

News releases sometimes include color illustrations with the text when they contain feature stories or material intended for editors of special sections. This poolside scene at the Maui Inter-Continental Wailea hotel in Hawaii was sent to travel editors as a color transparency. (Courtesy of Maui Inter-Continental Wailea.)

Color photographs for publication in food sections of newspapers and magazines are provided by product manufacturers and their public relations firms. This picture, distributed by Ketchum Public Relations, features Chambord French liquor. Products of other Ketchum clients also are shown. Note the international motif with French and American flags and French newspaper. (Courtesy of Ketchum Public Relations.)

Photographs such as this fantasy-like scene at Disneyland, distributed to entertainment and travel editors, increase the viewers' interest in attending such recreational centers. Calling itself the Magic Kingdom, Disneyland has used color pictures extensively in publicizing its attractions.

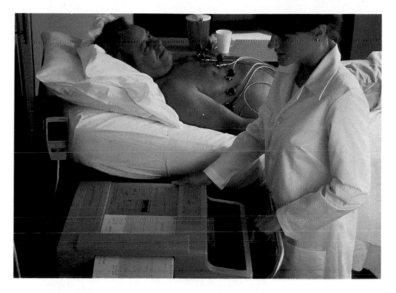

Announcements of new products sent to the trade press have greater impact when the text is accompanied by a color picture of the item. This photograph, distributed in slide form, shows a family of three new Hewlett-Packard PageWriter cardiographs in use. (Photograph provided by Hewlett-Packard.)

HEWLETT PACKARD

NEW PRODUCT
I N F O R M A T I O N

PUBLIC RELATIONS DEPARTMENT • 3000 HANOVER STREET, PALO ALTO, CALIFORNIA 94304

EDITORIAL CONTACTS   PR2903413
Scott Marber
(617) 687-1501, Ext. 2028

Mark Low   RELEASE DATE
(617) 687-1501, Ext. 2409   October 1, 1984

HEWLETT-PACKARD INTRODUCES FAMILY OF CARDIOGRAPHS

WITH ALPHANUMERIC, MEASUREMENTS AND ANALYSIS CAPABILITIES

Hewlett-Packard Company has introduced a family of

three new PageWriter cardiographs, each designed to meet the

Direct on-screen drawing is made possible by the Gibson Light Pen from Koala Technologies.

Readers of trade press and specialty publications can get an idea of the capabilities of graphic-art software programs in color-positive news releases such as this one, in which the caption is included on the photograph. (Courtesy of Koala Technologies.)

Procter & Gamble celebrated the sixtieth anniversary of its Spic 'n' Span cleaner by giving away fake diamonds called Cubic Zirconia. For each 4000 fake diamonds placed in Spic 'n' Span boxes, the company included one real diamond. A video news clip of the process, created by the Hill & Knowlton public relations firm, was shown on TV news programs nationwide. This is a frame from the release. (Courtesy of Hill & Knowlton.)

Publication of colorful brochures about university athletic teams—including schedules, statistics, and descriptions of players—is an important function of sports publicity departments. Bright covers attract the attention of sports reporters. (Courtesy of University of Georgia.)

It is commonplace for computer software programs to convert graphs and charts into slides, prints, and overhead transparencies to make the content more accessible and appealing. These examples of computer-generated designs, created by imedia, emphasize the vivid patterns of color. (Courtesy of imedia, Cupertino, California.)

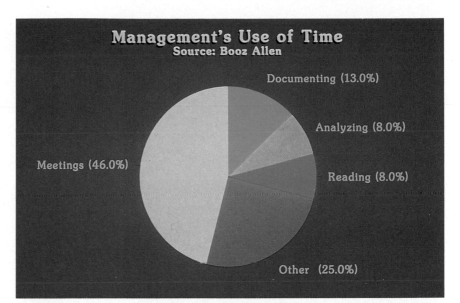

Management's Use of Time
Source: Booz Allen

- Documenting (13.0%)
- Analyzing (8.0%)
- Reading (8.0%)
- Meetings (46.0%)
- Other (25.0%)

How Visual Aids Affect Meeting Results
Wharton Study, Univ. of Pa.

	With Visuals	Without Visuals
Speaker's Goal Achieved	67%	33%
Group Consensus Reached	79%	58%
Information Retained	50%	10%
Average Meeting Length	19 min	28 min

Slide shows are a convenient, economical method of telling an organization's story. Universities, for example, use them in work with alumni, student recruitment, and fund-raising. This slide from a DePauw University presentation shows President Richard F. Rosser holding a news conference. (Courtesy of DePauw University.)

The National Live Stock and Meat Board uses filmstrips to explain the history and operation of its industry. Shown here are frames from one of the board's productions, *Shaping a Nation*. The 61-frame strip, lasting 10½ minutes, can be played with synchronized voices on cassette or live voice reading a script. A teacher's manual accompanies the filmstrip. (© 1984, National Live Stock and Meat Board.)

Drawings are an attractive way to deliver a message, especially to children. This filmstrip, distributed to schools by the National Live Stock and Meat Board and titled *Family Hero*, shows how a boy applies his classroom instruction about meat when buying and cooking for his family. (© National Live Stock and Meat Board.)

Public relations firms arrange for representatives of their clients to appear on television talk shows, during which they demonstrate their products. Here a TV guest participates in a homemaking program. (Courtesy of Ketchum Public Relations.)

Public relations departments sometimes use magazine advertising to portray the community service work of their companies. This advertisement by the Sun Company, which appeared in several national magazines, shows corporate involvement in a hometown activity. (Courtesy of Sun Company.)

This poster publicizing a Hall of Fame television drama, "Camille," creates an aura of culture and quality. The effect is achieved by use of a photograph in soft focus, surrounded by black with lettering in white. Areas of light blue, a restful color, emphasize the introspective mood of the man and woman. (Copyright 1984 Hallmark Cards, Inc.)

Dramatic color photographs are used on covers of corporate annual reports to create a perception of the companies as vigorous and innovative. This cover from an Alcoa report captures that feeling. (Courtesy of Alcoa.)

A harbor scene featuring an American President Lines container ship is an example of the striking photography that corporations publish in their annual reports and public relations brochures to illustrate their equipment at work. (Courtesy of American President Companies, Ltd.)

Trade associations find color advertising an effective method for explaining their goals and achievements. In this advertisement, the Association of American Railroads emphasizes the growing attractiveness of railroads as an investment. (Reprinted by permission of the Association of American Railroads.)

CENSORSHIP IN A FREE SOCIETY.
IT'S A BAD MATCH.

Censorship is the greatest tragedy in American literature. It constricts the mind, teaches fear and leaves only ignorance and ashes.

Today, all over the country, books are being banned, burned and censored. Teachers, students, librarians, and book and magazine publishers are being harassed.

The attacks of these self-appointed censors are endorsed by our silence.

The freedom to read is one of our most precious rights. Do something to protect it.

Contact:
People For The American Way, P.O. Box 19900 Washington, D.C. 20036 or call 202/462-4777.

Advocates of a policy or cause sometimes turn to magazine advertising to publicize their message. This strong appeal for the freedom to read, sponsored by People for the American Way, appeared in more than 25 magazines as a public service at no cost to the organization. (Courtesy of People for the American Way.)

Color plays a crucial role in design of corporate identification insignia. The bold single graphic of the fruit is the corporate symbol for the Apple Bank for Savings in New York. Selame Design borrowed the nickname of the bank's hometown, the Big Apple, for the new name, using the symbol to coordinate signs, passbooks, letterheads, and brochures. (Courtesy of Selame Design.)

Large corporations consider their identifying insignias so important that they publish manuals specifying how the symbols should be used. The Pacific Telesis Group manual from which this example was taken is nearly 50 pages long. (Courtesy of Pacific Telesis.)

Color-coded stationery creates a cohesive image for an organization. Based on an eye-catching master symbol, color variations are created for each division of a corporation or for each type of printed material an organization distributes. This illustration shows how colors identify the categories of information issued by a television station. (Courtesy of Selame Design.)

Subdued use of color suggests excellence in this rather formal invitation by the French Industrial Development Agency for American corporations to invest in France. The success-story appeal exemplifies one form of public relations effort in the United States by foreign governments. Published in *The Economist*, the advertisement was carefully crafted for a target audience, executives of the international business community. (Courtesy of the French Industrial Development Agency.)

sure forced Firestone into the huge recall. It agreed to replace free some 7.5 million radial tires purchased after September 1975 and to replace at half-price up to 6 million older ones.

As a final irony a group of Firestone stockholders successfully filed a class action suit against the company, alleging that they had lost money because of the company's behavior in the Radial 500 dispute. They contended that Firestone had failed to disclose information about the tire's defects and had not told stockholders about other alleged shortcomings in company operations. A federal judge approved a $3.2 million settlement that Firestone must pay to stockholders.

LESSONS OF THE FIRESTONE CASE   Throughout the controversy, Firestone's public relations approach reminds the observer of putting out a fire by pouring gasoline on it.

By seeking a court order to suppress the Traffic Safety Administration report, Firestone cast itself in the role of self-serving censor with something to hide. A much better course would have been to await publication, then respond with a well-prepared rebuttal pointing out the report's statistical weaknesses. Publicity about the court order led directly to the damaging congressional hearings.

Another foolish blunder was the attempt to blame customers for the product's defects. Customers antagonized in this manner often refuse to become repeat buyers.

Lack of candor and factual honesty, a belligerent attitude toward questions and criticism, a history of resistance to media inquiries, use of a spokesman lacking in public relations finesse, and an effort to blame its customers—all these created a public perception of Firestone as a selfish corporation determined to protect its profits even at the price of public safety.

THE RIGHT WAY— THE TYLENOL CYANIDE DEATHS

Johnson & Johnson had reason to be pleased with its pain-reliever product, Tylenol. Medically endorsed and vigorously publicized, the packaged aspirin-free medication was sold over the counter in pharmacies, groceries, and other stores in substantially greater amounts than its competitors. With $400 million in annual sales, Tylenol controlled 37 percent of the market and earned handsome profits. Manufacture of Tylenol was done by a Johnson & Johnson subsidiary, McNeil Consumer Products Company.

A SUDDEN CRISIS   Then, one morning, the telephone rang in the office of Lawrence G. Foster, Johnson & Johnson's vice-president for public relations in New Brunswick, New Jersey. The news that phone call brought was startling. A staff member of the Chicago *Sun-Times* reported that cyanide contained in Extra-Strength Tylenol capsules apparently had caused the deaths of some individuals in that city. The reporter requested information about the manufacture of the medication.

Eventually doctors determined that seven persons in Chicago had been killed by cyanide contained in Tylenol capsules. The news created fear in millions of other Tylenol users.

As news of the mysterious poison deaths spread during early October 1982, millions of Americans with Tylenol on their medicine shelves wondered, "If I take a capsule, will it kill me?"

The corporate crisis caused by the frightening news was unpredictable and intense, with the company's reputation and financial well-being at stake. Events of the next 10 days subjected top management and the public relations department of Johnson & Johnson to an extreme test of communication skills and company philosophy. A few weeks later, when time permitted an appraisal, media executives and public relations experts alike gave the corporation high marks for the way it conducted itself.

The unanswered questions about the incident were bewildering. Had the poison been placed in the capsules during the manufacturing process, either by error or on purpose? Had a killer slipped the cyanide into Tylenol bottles during shipping or on store shelves? If the poison had been inserted intentionally, why? Did the killer have a grudge against Johnson & Johnson or against certain stores? Or was the poisoner a random killer proud of the power to destroy unknown humans? How many of the millions of Tylenol bottles on store shelves contained the fatal poison?

Johnson & Johnson was as mystified as the public was. Management sensed immediately that it faced an overpowering demand from the public for guidance and protection.

As public relations director, Foster plunged into the baffling case with two strong assets: a plan for emergency action and a written set of corporate principles to guide him.

Almost the first thing Foster did was send an associate to Chicago aboard a company jet to collect first-hand information. "I learned long ago in the news business there's no substitute for having someone on the scene whose information you can trust," he explained later. He set up a large bank of telephones to handle the mass of media inquiries he knew would come. To answer the phones, he brought to headquarters 50 public relations staff members from the corporation's subsidiaries. This quick action enabled reporters to reach the company without frustrating delays.

OPEN POLICY Without hesitation, during the first hours of the crisis, top management put into operation an open information policy. This was in keeping with the long-established written corporate credo, which declared that the company's first responsibility is to "those who use our products and services." The credo stated, "In a business society, every act of business has social consequences and may arouse public interest. Every time business hires, builds, sells, or buys, it is acting for the . . . people as well as for itself, and it must be prepared to accept full responsibility."

The company's most urgent task was to get Tylenol capsules off store shelves and out of purchasers' homes. It halted Tylenol production, stopped distribution, and recalled supplies from retailers. To recover the capsules from consumers' homes, the company issued coupons with which consumers could exchange containers of capsules for an equal amount of Tylenol tablets, which were not subject to cyanide tampering. This exchange was publicized by full-page newspaper advertisements and news stories. Later, the company announced a toll-free number individuals could telephone to request a $2.50 coupon for purchase of safe replacement Tylenol. Consumers were encouraged to call the toll-free number for information about the safety of Tylenol. Altogether, the company recalled 22 million bottles of Tylenol capsules.

As Foster anticipated, the public relations department was besieged with inquiries from the media—1,411 telephone calls during the first 10 days, a figure that rose to 2,500 before the story died down. Johnson & Johnson received 120,000 clippings of news stories about the crisis from its clipping service.

A seven-member management committee, of which the public relations director was a member, met twice daily at the height of the crisis to evaluate the situation. To unify management's response to the public, the president of the McNeil subsidiary served as the principal spokesman.

From the first, the company cooperated fully with federal investigators, never waiting for them to pressure it to act. It offered a $100,000 reward for capture of the perpetrator.

After testing 8 million recalled capsules, investigators determined that the cyanide had not entered the fatal capsules during the manufacturing process, but on the store shelves. In fact, the exhaustive and costly testing found only eight tampered-with bottles, in which 75 capsules contained cyanide. Two of those eight containers were discovered after publication of the first news stories about the tragedy.

While conducting the recall and debating a future course, Johnson & Johnson took numerous public opinion surveys. These showed, among other things, that because of the intensive news coverage more than 90 percent of the public knew after the first week not to take Tylenol capsules. By the second week, more than 90 percent knew that Johnson & Johnson was not to blame. Another survey indicated that 35 percent of those who had Tylenol capsules in their homes threw them away.

Although the company was absolved of blame, the image of Tylenol was so critically damaged that its share of the market dropped from 37 percent to a mere 6 percent within days after the news broke. Numerous marketing experts asserted that Tylenol as a brand name was dead; that if the company decided to resume selling such a medication, it must change the brand name and image. Johnson & Johnson took a severe financial beating during the recall period—an after-tax loss of $50 million for the recall and testing, as well as development of a new tamper-resistant package.

Ignoring the doomsayers, Johnson & Johnson decided to gamble on restoring Tylenol to public acceptance. Polling and press reaction showed that widespread, friendly news coverage had convinced much of the public that the product was safe and the tampering had been an isolated incident. Nevertheless, the connection between Tylenol and sudden death lingered, subconsciously in many instances.

RECOVERY CAMPAIGN   Thus began the second phase of the Tylenol story, the comeback campaign.

To prevent a recurrence, Johnson & Johnson designed a tamper-proof container for Tylenol capsules. It strongly endorsed federal legislation making tampering a felony and regulations requiring tamper-proof packaging for a wide range of over-the-counter drugs. The company was the first to get such packaging onto store shelves. Company representatives visited the offices of more than 160 members of Congress to gain support for the regulations and legislation.

The public phase of Tylenol's recovery campaign opened with a 30-city video teleconference from New York 6 weeks after the deaths occurred. The corporation's public relations consultant firm set up this conference in three weeks, remarkably fast work for such an intricate event. The 30 cities had to be selected for convenience to the press nationally, suitable meeting rooms booked, press kits prepared, satellite transmission arrangements made, and invitations issued. Twenty-five hundred mailgram invitations were sent out; more than 500 media representatives attended. Two-way audio arrangements were made at Philadelphia, Chicago, Los Angeles, and Washington so that reporters there could ask questions of company executives in New York. Reporters in the other 25 cities could hear the questions and answers.

During the 90-minute teleconference, James E. Burke, chief executive officer, and other company officials spoke, the new packaging was shown, and the audience heard a videotaped statement by the head of the Food and Drug Administration. Samples of the safety packaging were distributed.

To induce the public to overcome its lingering psychological resistance, Burke announced two attractive offers. Former users who had thrown away their capsules were invited to call a toll-free number and request a free bottle in the new packaging. No proof of previous ownership was required. Advertisements in Sunday newspapers with 40 million combined circulation contained coupons entitling the bearer to a $2.50 discount on the purchase of any Tylenol product. This permitted consumers to obtain smaller Tylenol packages free. The headline of the advertisement was "Thank you, America."

The company also sent about 50 million capsules to physicians for free distribution to their patients, thus in effect demonstrating medical confidence in the safety of the product.

Use of the toll-free numbers by the public to obtain information and free bottles was immense; more than 325,000 calls were made.

Burke also used the teleconference to thank the news media for the fair, responsible way in which they reported the cyanide deaths— the kind of public compliments reporters and editors rarely hear.

"We were very much aware that the public welfare was at stake," Burke said, "and that the news media were the means by which we could rapidly disseminate warnings, allay mounting fears, and put the crisis in perspective. Good reporting helped to reduce those tensions. . . .

"You, the media, were the first to make the evaluation that our company and our product were also victims of this tragedy. You have treated us accordingly and we are appreciative."

Johnson & Johnson followed up the teleconference with an intensive advertising and marketing campaign. Restoration of public confidence was so successful that 6 months after the death story broke, Tylenol had recaptured about 32 of the 37 percent of the market it had previously held, despite vigorous efforts by its competitors. As the months passed, nobody had been arrested and charged with implanting the poison.

THE LESSONS OF THE TYLENOL STORY   Open communication was one key to Johnson & Johnson's success. It treated the news media as invaluable assets in warning the public and conducting the recall. The other key was the company's adherence to its longtime policy that the safety of its customers comes first.

Several specific steps were especially helpful. Establishment of additional telephone lines and expansion of the public relations staff gave reporters quick access to company representatives. Selection of a skillful principal spokesman provided the firm's statements with consistency.

The company's close cooperation with government investigators encouraged public confidence, a notable contrast with Firestone's fight against the government about the company's defective tires.

Another less tangible but significant factor was evident in Johnson & Johnson's previous record of friendly dealing with the media. No memories of adversarial clashes lingered among editors and reporters that might cause them to suspect a company cover-up when the cyanide story broke, or subconsciously inject a negative tilt into their stories. Even in the earliest days of the crisis, when the company's innocence had not yet been established, press coverage was fair and even-handed. When the crunch came, Johnson & Johnson benefited from its adherence to a longtime constructive relationship with the media.

A Case Study

INTRODUCING A PRODUCT—KODAK'S DISC CAMERA

When an international corporation launches a new product whose development cost millions of dollars and required years, the public introduction requires a campaign that is dramatic, innovative, and intensive. Eastman Kodak Company's presentation of its revolutionary disc camera in many countries around the world simultaneously was a spectacular public relations feat.

The Kodak disc camera was a radical departure in photography. Instead of advancing a roll of film another frame each time the shutter clicks, the camera records images on a revolving disc. Kodak needed to show the world that the new camera was desirable, simple to operate, and able to produce excellent photographs.

In planning the introduction, Kodak's corporate communications department had five principal objectives:

1. Preserve secrecy about the disc camera until the formal unveiling on February 3, 1982. Protection of the camera's technical secrets was extremely important, to prevent leakage of information to competitors.

2. Provide advance knowledge of the camera to selected groups of Kodak employees in order to build their enthusiasm and to brief the marketing and sales forces. The balance between this need and the secrecy requirement was delicate but was achieved successfully.

3. Prepare an elaborate press kit, create eye-catching audiovisuals, and train company executives in order to present the camera impressively on introduction day.

4. Organize simultaneous worldwide unveiling of the disc camera on the chosen date in multiple presentations in which all company representatives speak "with one voice."

5. Reach Kodak's special target audiences in addition to the general public. These include dealers and photofinishers, the financial community, shareholders, employees, opinion leaders, and the scientific and technical community.

This is how the assignment was accomplished, with impressive results:

1. *Secrecy.* Six years before the disc camera was introduced, only 25 of Kodak's 130,000 employees knew about the project. David Metz, vice-president for corporate communications, was brought into the disc development project at an early stage. For more than a year before the announcement, a corporate communications committee met biweekly to develop plans. Media inquiries based on rumors that something new was forthcoming were answered politely with statements that Kodak did not comment on development of new products.

2. *Advance knowledge.* By a few weeks before the announcement, more than 15,000 Kodak employees knew about the project, yet no significant details of the camera leaked out. Fifteen different audiovisual and filmed presentations were created to give necessary information to various internal audiences. During the year before the announcement, these were shown to company groups 110 times.

3. *Preparation of materials.* Kodak's corporate communications staff of 135 persons produced voluminous explanatory material for distribution on and after announcement day, including the following:

a. A press kit weighing 3 1/2 pounds. The kit contained 17 stories, 25 photographs, and a disc camera. Aware of contemporary sensitivity within the news media about being "bought off" with gifts, Kodak included a card stating that recipients who wished to return the camera after testing it could send it to a specified address.

b. A spectacular multimedia presentation of the new camera involving a broad-screen film that often split into three side-by-side sections. The presentation explained the optics and theory, construction techniques, and operation of the disc camera. A version of this presentation was shown to employees.

c. Television film clips and radio tapes. Photo experts were booked onto talk shows.

d. A special edition of the employee newsletter, *Kodakery,* devoted entirely to the disc. Stories were prepared as well for other Kodak publications.

4. *Announcement day.* The fanfare began with a news release and four business-page photographs delivered to the major press services for world-wide publication at 8 A.M. EST. A few minutes later, a Kodak vice-president was interviewed on ABC-TV's "Good Morning America" program, showing the disc camera for the first time.

Later in the morning, Kodak held simultaneous news conferences in New York and seven other American cities, and at Kodak locations in 40 foreign countries.

The principal conference in New York drew about 370 news media representatives. After hearing Kodak chairman Walter A. Fallon present a 50-minute multimedia show, guests were invited to try the disc camera themselves, photographing professional models. After processing, the pictures the guests took were sent to them as souvenirs. In separate rooms, Kodak executives gave interviews to reporters from especially influential general and trade media.

News conferences in the other seven American cities were led by Kodak regional directors. They had been brought to national headquarters for training that included mock television interviews.

5. *Special audiences.* A few hours after the general announcement, Kodak executives repeated the presentation to an audience of financial analysts and portfolio managers. The executives had studied a list of 100 possible questions and suitable answers prepared by the corporate communications department. That evening an investment advisory firm gave a Kodak dinner for representatives of 60 institutions that own about one-fourth of Kodak shares.

Other target-audience approaches:

a. Material about the disc was mailed to shareholders, and the annual report included an eight-page section on the camera.

b. Two weeks after the announcement, Kodak appealed directly to dealers and photofinishers with an elaborate display at the Photo Marketing Association convention.

c. Kodak scientists and engineers were made available for technical interviews.

d. In cities in which Kodak has plants, special presentations were prepared for business and civic audiences, schools, and Kodak retirees.

e. Kodak executives explained the camera to local, state, and federal officials and opinion leaders in briefings and personal visits.

This intricate public relations effort cost approximately $750,000. From it came enormous publicity and fast, tangible results—sale of an estimated 8 million disc cameras during the last 8 months of the introduction year.

QUESTIONS FOR REVIEW AND DISCUSSION

1. Why is the public's perception of a corporation so important to its success?

2. What caused the growth of the consumer movement between 1960 and 1980 in the United States? Who was its best-known leader?

3. Explain the double role of public relations practitioners in the relationship between companies and the news media.

4. What are some measures corporate executives can take to achieve better reporting of business?

5. At a time of crisis, why is an open communication policy more effective than a corporate effort to "manage" the news?

6. List the important elements that should be included in a corporate plan for emergency action.

7. What is a corporation's social contract?

8. Issues management is a growing aspect of corporate public relations work. Precisely what is it?

9. Why did the San Diego Gas & Electric Company suffer from such a bad public image?

10. Name Firestone's public relations mistakes in the controversy over its Radial 500 tires.

CHAPTER FIFTEEN

Public Affairs and Government

The term *public affairs* increasingly is used to describe a specialty area of public relations that deals with community relations and government affairs.

Although some companies incorrectly use the term as a euphemism for the full range of their public relations activities, it should be more narrowly defined as "corporate citizenship." Activities included in the term range from a donation to a local charity to the monitoring of social and political issues and lobbying for passage of favorable legislation.

On the other hand, *public affairs* is used in a much broader context by state legislatures, Congress, and various government agencies. The term is employed, as will be explained in this chapter, as a euphemism for the public relations activities of government to inform citizens about programs and policies. All military bases, for example, have a public affairs officer who regularly mails hometown news releases, arranges tours and special events, and answers inquiries from the taxpaying public.

This chapter describes public affairs activities from the standpoint of business and industry and explains how public affairs is used in government information efforts. In both cases, public affairs plays a vital role in a democratic society.

Business Public Affairs

"Corporate citizenship" is a basic tenet of American business and industry for two reasons.

First, many business leaders have realized that the only way to combat the tide of government regulation is to take the initiative and voluntarily exercise a sense of social responsibility. A great many company managers now recognize that if they don't treat employees fairly, give consumers quality products, and make efforts to solve some of society's problems, then government—reacting to public pressure—will saddle business with more regulations.

Indeed, history shows that business has been regulated in direct proportion to its social abuses. The so-called robber barons of the late nineteenth century exploited labor and resources, generating considerable regulation of railway, utility, oil, and other companies (see Chapter 3). In more recent times industry's failure to solve many of the environmental problems caused by manufacturing gave rise to increased government regulation including creation of the Environmental Protection Agency. And today the disposition of many companies to lay off workers with insufficient notice has aroused public pressure for legislation that would require firms to give employees three- to six-month notice before doing so.

The second reason for the rise of corporate citizenship and the emphasis on public affairs is realization by business and industry that they can survive and prosper only in a sound society. Thus it is to the advantage of business to help find solutions to a number of societal problems. Such assistance not only improves the quality of life but creates a reservoir of public support.

With this thought in mind, companies in recent years have performed a number of projects under the rubric of public affairs. Some examples are the following:

The Shell Oil Company distributed millions of pamphlets to motorists advising them how to get better mileage, drive in rush-hour traffic, and buy a new car.

The Carnation Company sent musical kits to inner-city schools titled "The Many Sides of Black Music." Each kit contained an album of five records and a 16-page lesson guide for teachers.

Texaco has sponsored Metropolitan Opera performances on radio on Saturday afternoons since 1940. It is the longest continuous underwriting of a program by the same sponsor in the history of radio.

The International Paper Company ran a series of institutional advertisements in magazines that focused on such topics as, "How to Write a Business Letter," "How to Improve Your Vocabulary," "How to Write Clearly," "How to Write a Resume," and "How to Use a Library." Millions of reprints were requested by schools and educational organizations.

But such endeavors are just the tip of the iceberg. Corporate public affairs specialists are engaged in a wide range of projects that foster cooperation and interaction at the community and various government levels. A survey of corporations by the Public Affairs Research Group in the Boston University School of Management, for example, indicated that the top four activities of corporate public affairs departments are (1) community relations; (2) government relations, including grassroots lobbying and political action committees; (3) corporate contributions; and (4) media relations.

To put it another way, corporate public affairs usually includes the following: government relations, lobbying, community relations, and philanthropy. The following sections describe in detail the role corporations and trade associations play in all these areas. In the first two—government relations and lobbying—other types of organizations, including labor unions and public interest groups, are also actively involved.

Government Relations

THE ROLE OF PUBLIC AFFAIRS SPECIALISTS In the field of government relations, practitioners have a number of functions: they gather information, disseminate management's views, cooperate with government on projects of mutual benefit, and motivate employees to participate in the political process.

As the eyes and ears of a business or industry, corporate public affairs specialists spend a great deal of time processing information. Because what happens in Washington or at the state and local level may have a great impact on business, corporations constantly monitor the activities of many government units. Monitoring may consist of simply keeping track of proposed legislation or of finding out what issues may be coming up for debate and possible vote. Such intelligence-gathering enables a corporation or an industry to plan ahead and, if necessary, adjust policies or provide information that may influence the nature of government decision-making.

Public affairs specialists are responsible for communicating an organization's viewpoint to elected officials and regulatory agencies—either informally, through an office visit to a government official, or formally, through testimony at a public hearing. Public affairs specialists also convey management's viewpoints by writing letters, position papers, and speeches. They may use issue advertising, plant tours, and employee publications to make sure that several publics—employees, taxpayers, elected officials, government employees—know how the company or industry stands on a particular issue.

Indeed, public affairs and public policy seem to go hand in hand today as corporations become more interested in issues management and grass-roots coalition-building (issues management is discussed in Chapter 14). A New York *Times* writer emphasized the importance of having a presence in Washington, through either a public relations firm that represents the company or the company's own staff:

Public relations executives can rightly point out that with the cacophony of interests clamoring for attention in Washington, there is a role for professional advice on how to insure that one's message is heard. With the expanding role of Congress and the increasing complexity of government, this probably is true now more than ever. There are undoubtedly times that public relations firms can help journalists, politicians and clients.

Probably the most active presence in Washington and many state capitals is the trade association that represents a particular industry. The Boston University survey previously mentioned showed that 67 percent of the responding companies monitored government activity in Washington through their trade associations. Second on the list were frequent trips to Washington by senior executives of a company, with 58 percent of the respondents saying they engaged in this activity. Almost 45 percent of the responding firms reported that they also had a company office in the nation's capital.

This high interest in public affairs paralleled the growth of government regulations and scrutiny in the 1970s as most major companies responded by expanding the number of their personnel in Washington or in state capitals.

Corporations have also cooperated with government on a number of projects. For example, an association of business and civic leaders in New York City formed the Youth Employment Task Force, which worked with government agencies to create 14,000 summer jobs for young people. The program was such a success that it received a Silver Anvil award from the Public Relations Society of America. On another level AT&T loaned its computers to the state of New Jersey to compile the results of a statewide survey on education.

The public affairs specialist frequently considers company employees a significant public. It is important that employees regularly receive information regarding the company's position on economic and political issues that could have an impact on the organization in some way. Because of this, many corporations provide educational programs to encourage employees to participate in the political process.

The Western Electric Company in Sunnyvale, California, for example, regularly conducts a "candidate day" at its plant so that employees may meet local and state nominees for office. All those on the ballot, regardless of political party affiliation, are invited to visit.

The United Life Insurance Company of Indianapolis will pay the postage if an employee wants to write to his or her elected representative. An AT&T

policy allows an employee to take a leave of absence to run for political office. Corporations such as Pan American Airlines, Chrysler, and Lockheed also have found employees to be a potent lobbying force when government aid was needed to bail the companies out of financial difficulty.

POLITICAL ACTION COMMITTEES

In certain areas of government affairs, as noted earlier, corporations and trade associations are not the only actively involved groups. Labor unions also play a significant role. One aspect of government relations that is particularly important to both business and labor is the *political action committee,* or *PAC*—a group set up by an organization to support or oppose candidates for public office. These committees were authorized by Congress after corporate money was secretly funneled to Richard M. Nixon's 1972 reelection fund. Since it remains illegal for corporations and unions to make political contributions, the PAC constitutes one way in which corporations, trade associations, and labor unions can, under strict guidelines, indirectly support various political candidates.

Businesses and unions encourage employees and members to make contributions to their PACs. The organizations are allowed to cover the administrative costs of running a PAC, but funds must come from individual pledges. Funds usually are collected through payroll deductions, or employees may simply write an annual check. Executives, managers, and certain supervisory employees normally provide the bulk of pledges, since organized blue-collar workers generally contribute through their unions. Many corporations suggest that employees contribute about 1 percent of gross salary.

The Grumman Company is one of over a thousand companies in the United States that have PACs. In 1980, this major defense and space contractor gave $280,000 to a number of political candidates. A substantial $5000 contribution was made to each of the major presidential contenders, Jimmy Carter and Ronald Reagan, and $1000 was given to independent candidate John Anderson. The Grumman PAC also gave funds to a number of members of Congress, whose names read like a Who's Who list of the House and Senate Armed Services and Appropriations committees. Because Grumman has also become a transportation company, campaign funds were provided for the chairman of the National Transportation Policy Study Committee. On a local level, the PAC contributed to all candidates in cities in which Grumman has a major facility.

Corporate PACs, of course, are not without controversy. Many citizens' groups feel that vested interests exercise undue influence on legislation and elected representatives by collectively making substantial political contributions. An example, according to some critics, is the political action committee of the National Rural Electric Cooperative Association. In a five-year period, the PAC distributed more than $500,000 to members of Congress. And,

Potlatch
Corporation's
PAC

The purpose and mechanics of a corporate PAC are best expressed on the pages of a brochure that describes the Potlatch Employees' Political Fund.

PURPOSE OF THE FUND

Selecting the best qualified political officials to lead the nation is an important individual civic responsibility. But worthy people cannot be expected to run for office—much less win—without the financial support it takes to mount a respectable campaign.

Your help is needed.

The Potlatch Employees' Political Fund is a registered political action committee sponsored by the company and designed to give financial assistance to candidates who support the free enterprise system, recognize the importance of the forest products industry, and know the need for economic growth.

The fund depends entirely on individual voluntary contributions from Potlatch employees. It is nonpartisan, supporting candidates from both major political parties, with the vast majority of the funds going to help candidates for the U.S. Congress.

HOW IT WORKS

You may contribute to PEPF in either or both of two ways:

Through a check or money order made out to the "Potlatch Employees' Political Fund."

Through a pledge. Simply indicate on the attached contribution card the total amount you wish to contribute annually, and PEPF will send you a statement on a quarterly basis. For example, if you pledge an annual contribution of $100, you will be sent a statement for $25 each quarter.

You may, or course, change the amount of your pledge at any time.

In either case, please complete the contribution card and forward to: L. Pendleton Siegel, Treasurer, Potlatch Employees' Political Fund, P.O. Box 3591, San Francisco, CA 94119.

The PEPF administrative committee has the responsibility under the fund's constitution and bylaws for disbursing money to selected candidates for elective office who are believed to be in general agreement with PEPF objectives. All contributors to PEPF are encouraged to make recommendations to the administrative committee.

Decisions of the committee will be based on a variety of factors, including contributor recommendations, the candidate's understanding and appreciation of the interests of Potlatch and the forest products industry, and the candidate's support of free enterprise and proper U.S. forestland management.

The PEPF administrative committee sends all contributors a complete financial report detailing receipts and expenditures at least once a year. The fund also publishes periodic newsletters on political developments and PEPF activities.

KEY FEATURES

PEPF is voluntary.

It is your own decision how much to give to the Potlatch Employees' Political Fund, or whether to give at all. Many business firms with similar political fundraising programs use a range of ½ of 1 percent to 1½ percent of gross salary. However, this is merely a guideline. . . .

It's confidential.

By law, PEPF's treasurer must keep detailed records of contributing individuals and their respective amounts. Periodic reports of these contributions must be filed with the Federal Election Commission, and PEPF records also may be made available to an authorized auditor. However, no information concerning employees' contributions will be disclosed by the administrative committee for any other reason.

It's tax deductible.

Any individual filing a separate federal return may take a direct tax credit of an amount equal to one-half of total annual political contributions up to a maximum credit of $50. A couple filing a joint return may take a direct tax credit of an amount equal to one-half of total annual political contributions up to a maximum credit of $100.

Tax deductions and credits also are permitted in the filing of many state returns, although the applicable laws may vary from state to state.

Employees with any questions regarding the Potlatch Employees' Political Fund are encouraged to contact a member of the administrative committee, listed on the back cover.

A copy of our report is filed with and available for purchase from the Federal Election Commission, Washington, D.C. 20463.

according to the *Wall Street Journal* (March 29, 1984), "Now the overwhelming majority of recipients are supporting the trade group's bill to keep deeply subsidized loans flowing to customer-owned rural electric and telephone utilities." Advocates, however, said that rural electric cooperatives are essential and every effort had to be made to block the Reagan administration's threat to veto any subsidies.

According to the Federal Election Commission, PACs operated by labor unions, trade associations, and corporations distribute millions of dollars to political candidates every year. In the 21 months ended September 30, 1984, for example, PAC giving totaled $72.1 million. Democratic candidates for the United States Senate and House of Representatives received $43 million and Republican candidates received $29.1 million.

The top PAC donors to federal candidates in the 1984 elections, according to unofficial tallies by the Federal Election Commission, were: National Association of Realtors, $2.56 million; American Medical Association, $2.04 million; National Education Association, $1.91 million; National Association of Home Builders, $1.75 million; United Auto Workers, $1.69 million; Machinists Union, $1.57 million; Letter Carriers Union, $1.47 million; Seafarers Union, $1.44 million; United Food & Commercial Workers Union, $1.38 million; and Associated Milk Producers, Inc., $1.18 million.

In 1984, the citizens' organization, Common Cause, began a major lobbying effort to have Congress put new restrictions on PACs. The Common Cause proposal called for a ceiling of $90,000 that a congressional candidate could receive from PACs. Part of Common Cause's concern was the fact that PACs (labor, trade groups, business) accounted for 44 percent of the contributions raised by the winning House candidates in the 1984 elections.

Lobbying

Lobbying—that is, the efforts by individuals or groups to influence the way legislators and government administrators make their decisions—is an integral and legitimate part of the democratic system; it is an activity in which almost every kind of organization engages. Although the public stereotype is that of a fast-talking person twisting the arm of an elected official to get special concessions for some monolithic corporation or powerful trade association, in reality lobbyists work for unions, political groups, ethnic societies, peace and environmental activists, consumer groups—and a host of other special-interest organizations, as well as for businesses of all sizes. A hearing of the Senate Judiciary Committee on President Reagan's nominees for the Civil Rights Commission, for example, received news releases and statements from such diverse groups as the National Association of Social Workers, League of United Latin American Citizens, American Civil Liberties Union, People for the American Way, and Americans for Democratic Action.

Lobbying takes place at the state and local level too. In California, for instance, almost $30 million was spent one year on legislative advocacy by business, local governments, labor unions, and other organizations. Those that spent the most for lobbying were, in order of expenditures, as follows:

California Medical Association

Southern California Gas Company

California Teamsters Public Affairs Council

Chevron USA

California State Employees Association

Southern California Edison

County Supervisors Association

San Diego Gas & Electric Company

California Dental Association

EXPENDITURES FOR LOBBYING

According to reports filed with Congress, the various groups that have lobbyists in Washington, D. C., spent $43 million in 1983 attempting to influence legislation. The bulk of the expenditure was for salaries, office expenses, publications, and direct mail campaigns.

Heading the list was the Natural Gas Supply Association, funded primarily by large oil companies, which spent $2.4 million seeking legislation to decontrol the price of natural gas. Second on the list was Common Cause, with lobbying expenditures of $1.95 million. Anti–gun control forces—National Rifle Association, Gun Owners of America, and Citizens Committee for the Right to Keep and Bear Arms—collectively spent $1.8 million, while Handgun Control Inc., an anti–gun group, spent $337,000. Another big spender in 1983 was Free the Eagle National Citizens Lobby, a conservative group advocating deregulation of the economy; it laid out $1.68 million. The Committee for Fair Insurance Rates, an industry group battling legislation that would outlaw gender discrimination in insurance rates, spent $1.5 million.

Despite such large expenditures, it isn't always the group with the most money that wins. Redwood National Park came into existence as a result of intensive lobbying by environmental groups such as the Sierra Club, while lumber companies vigorously lobbied against the plan. These companies were joined by a number of area citizens and local governments convinced that creation of the park would deprive the region of an employment base in the logging industry.

**"PUBLIC INTEREST"
A MISNOMER**

The average citizen should realize that self-styled "public interest" groups are really a misnomer, since all groups have vested interests, just as the National Rifle Association or General Motors does. In fact, a national survey of public interest group members by researchers Stanley Rothman and Robert Lichter showed that 90 percent of the respondents viewed themselves as "left of center" and 94 percent believed that government ought to redistribute income. It was also found that the overwhelming majority always vote for a Democratic (or a liberal) presidential candidate—having voted 96 percent for George McGovern in 1972, 93 percent for Carter in 1976, and 92 percent for Carter or Anderson in 1980. All this led the *Wall Street Journal* to conclude editorially that although "the public interest" sounds rather high-minded, most of these groups do not represent the mainstream of American public opinion. Lobbying, in other words, is conducted by all types of individuals or groups that have an interest in a particular piece of legislation.

When Congress was considering cutbacks in Social Security benefits, truckloads of mail served notice that senior citizens would not tolerate major adjustments in old-age benefits. The mail campaign, coordinated by several national organizations of elderly people, convinced members of Congress that such a formidable voting bloc should not be antagonized. As a result, no major cutbacks were made in Social Security benefits. As one observer noted, "No Congressman wants to write back to thousands of constituents that he doesn't agree with them."

In Texas a bill to regulate electrolysists—practitioners who remove hair electrically—brought dozens of people to a hearing to testify for and against the measure. Another bill that would have outlawed dogfighting didn't attract much public interest, but many raisers of pit bulldogs showed up to testify against it. Lobbyists for the Texas State Teachers' Association were on hand to fight a bill that would have permitted small school districts with no qualified mathematics or science teachers to hire noncertified teachers on a temporary basis from private industry.

**LOBBYING BY
TRADE GROUPS**

Much lobbying takes place on an industrywide basis, as noted already. The trade group representing rubber manufacturers, for example, lobbied against a proposed regulatory change for baby-bottle nipples on the basis that such a policy shift would hurt the product's "bite, durability, and shelf-life." On another front, the Association of General Merchandise Chains, representing discount stores such as K-Mart, is making sure that Congress doesn't repeal laws that bar manufacturers from setting retail prices. The trade group argues that repeal of such laws would be detrimental to the consumer and put discount stores out of business.

Competition from foreign imports usually stirs efforts to restrict them in some way. An industry group called Machine Tool Builders petitioned the Department of Commerce to limit the importation of tools. A public relations

344

firm retained by the group prepared a pamphlet for all association members that explained how to write letters to Congress. (Trade group activities are discussed in more detail in Chapter 17.)

MAIL CAMPAIGNS

Mail campaigns, as indicated, have become an important tactic in lobbying by all types of organizations. Greenpeace, the environmental group, and AT&T are among those that have been highly successful in getting citizens to send postcards and letters to elected officials. Figure 15.1 shows the ready-to-mail cards that AT&T prepared, to make it easy for consumers to send the company's message to Washington.

"You're going to see more and more nationwide organizations undertaking massive mail campaigns," said Senator Bob Packwood, Republican from Oregon. "There's no question that people in Congress are impressed with great volumes of mail."

Mail campaigns, as a form of lobbying, have been practiced for years by a major interest group, the National Rifle Association (NRA). J. Warren Cassidy, chief lobbyist for the NRA, once said, "That's been the basis of our existence—getting people to their typewriters."

FIGURE 15.1

AT&T encourages customers to oppose legislation that would permit a government surcharge on telephone rates. The postcards, already stamped and addressed, are directed by name to senators of the state in which they are distributed.

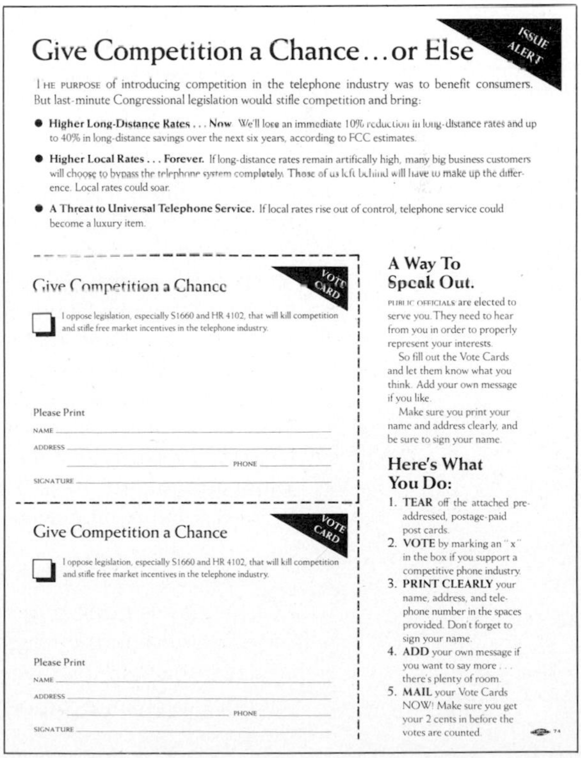

Give Competition a Chance...or Else

ISSUE ALERT

THE PURPOSE of introducing competition in the telephone industry was to benefit consumers. But last-minute Congressional legislation would stifle competition and bring:

- **Higher Long-Distance Rates...Now.** We'll lose an immediate 10% reduction in long-distance rates and up to 40% in long-distance savings over the next six years, according to FCC estimates.

- **Higher Local Rates...Forever.** If long-distance rates remain artifically high, many big business customers will choose to bypass the telephone system completely. Those of us left behind will have to make up the difference. Local rates could soar.

- **A Threat to Universal Telephone Service.** If local rates rise out of control, telephone service could become a luxury item.

Give Competition a Chance

VOTE CARD

☐ I oppose legislation, especially S1660 and HR 4102, that will kill competition and stifle free market incentives in the telephone industry.

Please Print

NAME _____

ADDRESS _____

_____ PHONE _____

SIGNATURE _____

Give Competition a Chance

VOTE CARD

☐ I oppose legislation, especially S1660 and HR 4102, that will kill competition and stifle free market incentives in the telephone industry.

Please Print

NAME _____

ADDRESS _____

_____ PHONE _____

SIGNATURE _____

A Way To Speak Out.

PUBLIC OFFICIALS are elected to serve you. They need to hear from you in order to properly represent your interests.

So fill out the Vote Cards and let them know what you think. Add your own message if you like.

Make sure you print your name and address clearly, and be sure to sign your name.

Here's What You Do:

1. **TEAR** off the attached pre-addressed, postage-paid post cards.
2. **VOTE** by marking an "x" in the box if you support a competitive phone industry.
3. **PRINT CLEARLY** your name, address, and telephone number in the spaces provided. Don't forget to sign your name.
4. **ADD** your own message if you want to say more... there's plenty of room.
5. **MAIL** your Vote Cards NOW! Make sure you get your 2 cents in before the votes are counted.

LOBBYING BY INDIVIDUAL CORPORATIONS

Individual corporations usually lobby by personally presenting information to legislators or government officials. Robert K. Gray, formerly head of Hill & Knowlton's office in Washington, and now owner of a public relations firm, uses a network of friends and contacts to get access for his clients.

One client, Republic Airlines, was faced with losing its federal subsidy for serving some small cities in its system. Gray's staff arranged for lawyers representing Republic to gain access to key members of the House Transportation Subcommittee. They explained their case and, as a result, Republic kept its subsidy.

Franklin Mint engaged Gray's firm to help convince Congress that it should be selected to design and produce special commemorative coins for the 1984 Olympics. The lobbying effort centered on demonstrating that Franklin Mint had the background and capability to do the job. The lobbyist's most effective tool is providing credible information.

THE LOBBYIST AS INFORMATION SOURCE

The lobbyist as a valuable source of information is best described by the late David W. Evans, founder-chairman of a public relations firm in Salt Lake City. He wrote in a PRSA monograph:

... [a] prime lobbying function is to be a credible and reliable source of information. Regardless of criticism by newspaper and television editorialists and many politicians—especially those whose point of view did not prevail in a legislative fight—both politicians and bureaucrats depend heavily on lobbyists for information.

Most legislators are concerned with doing a good job. They want balanced legislation that serves the interests of the people they represent as well as the citizens of the entire state. In order to frame and enact intelligent, balanced, effective legislation, every legislator needs information. If an industry is going to be adversely affected by some impending legislation, legislators, in most cases, want to know about those effects and their extent. The steel industry, for example, is subjected to about 5000 regulations and dozens of federal agency bureaucracies.

The tools of the trade for today's effective lobbying are information and a thorough knowledge of the legislative process. Today's legislative system is not confined to those who debate on the floor of a state Senate or House of Representatives. Any number of administrative rule-making agencies, budget offices, and legislative research groups provide legislative input. The effective lobbyist must know who they all are, what their information requirements are, and be prepared to meet those requirements.

Robert K. Gray adds: "Lobbying is no longer a booze and buddies business. It's presenting honest facts and convincing Congress that your side has more merit than the other."

Lobbying can also take the form of a public information campaign that attempts to change public perceptions, and result in more favorable government policies.

A good example is the work of the Committee for Energy Awareness, a group of about 100 companies including the electric utility industry, that spent about $30 million in 1983–1984 on a public information campaign showing the advantages of nuclear power. A national print and television advertising campaign buttressed the industry's arguments on the advantages, efficiency, and safety of nuclear energy.

The purpose, said the president of Georgia Power Company Robert W. Scherer, chairman of the committee, is "to bring some perspective to the nuclear question. It was the conclusion of the industry that we needed a program of public awareness. And it is not entirely advertising. The basic thrust will be the need for electric power."

One of the committee's first double-page advertisements in *Time* magazine was titled, "Nuclear Electricity: Who Stands Where?" The opening paragraph stated: "At a time of intense criticism of nuclear-generated electricity, an independent academic study found surprisingly strong support among persons considered well informed on the subject."

The Committee for Energy Awareness, of course, does not have the field to itself. The Safety Energy Committee Communications Council, a coalition of 17 energy and environmental groups, allocated $100,000 to combat the nuclear power industry. Its aim was to "increase public awareness of the serious environmental, health, and safety consequences of nuclear technology."

One of the most effective lobbying groups in Washington is the Tobacco Institute, the research and information arm of the cigarette industry. The institute, with about 40 employees, wages a constant battle with antismoking groups for the hearts and minds of elected representatives and government officials at the local, state, and federal level. Of particular concern to the tobacco industry are increasing numbers of local initiatives that seek to ban smoking in offices, restaurants, and other public places. The institute seeks to tell its side of the story through the following activities:

1. Talking to influential members of Congress and to local government officials.

2. Issuing news releases rebutting studies that link smoking with cancer and publicizing the institute's own research findings.

3. Arranging media tours in which institute representatives are sent around the country to appear on radio and television talk shows. In one 3-year period, representatives appeared on more than 1300 radio and television programs in 400 cities and 48 states.

4. Publishing newsletters six times a year that are sent to opinion leaders and government leaders.

5. Arranging letter-writing campaigns. The institute, for example, regularly encourages police chiefs to send letters to elected officials pointing out the difficulty of enforcing antismoking laws. The letter-writers say that such laws would prevent police from pursuing "real criminals." Another theme of letter-writers is the concept of "free choice."

6. Conducting massive advertising campaigns. Individual tobacco companies are major purchasers of advertising space in the print media.

A CHECKLIST FOR LOBBYISTS

A checklist for an effective lobbyist, according to David Evans, is as follows:

Is the client's or the company's position defensible? If not, what must be done to make the position acceptable?

Do both the client or the company and the lobbyist have credibility? Are both trusted as reliable and reputable sources of information, arguments, and statistics?

Have the key people been identified? Who are the people most likely to influence decisions?

To what extent is the general public affected? Are the public impacts reasonable and acceptable?

Has a strategy, including timing, been clarified? Does the plan include the necessary elements for both offense and defense?

What can the opposition do? Have they answered the same basic questions we are asking? What is their strategy and plan?

"The accuracy and thoroughness with which these few questions are answered can spell the difference in victory or defeat for the legislative lobbyist," Evans said.

In summary, lobbying is an important part of the public affairs function. An intimate knowledge of the issues and governmental procedures, and the ability effectively to communicate the organization's viewpoint, are required.

Community Relations

Not all public affairs activity takes place in Washington or the state capital. An important part consists of community relations, particularly in those towns and cities in which the company maintains an office or a manufacturing facility.

Because a corporation relies heavily on local governments for construction permits, changes in zoning laws, and even tax concessions, it is important that there be a good working relationship among the corporation, city hall, and the various community groups.

Public affairs specialists serve primarily in a liaison capacity, and, like their counterparts at the national level, they continually monitor emerging issues that may affect the corporation. These specialists are the eyes and ears of corporate management in a community, but they also spend much time interpreting the organization to the community. Telephone companies, for example, encourage executives to join civic clubs for this purpose.

A public affairs specialist may engage in a number of activities at the local level, including the following:

Attending city council meetings

Presenting information to various government advisory groups

Serving on city or county citizen boards

Joining civic clubs

Serving on the board of directors of the American Red Cross, United Way, and the like

Screening applicants for corporate contributions

Volunteering corporate facilities for meetings and production of materials

Coordinating joint projects by area businesses to hire minorities, provide summer jobs for youths, or even clean up toxic wastes

Sponsoring festivals and other special events

Here are several examples of corporate citizenship at the local level:

Syntex Corporation, in Palo Alto, California, maintains an art gallery for the enjoyment of the community.

Allis-Chalmers provides construction equipment to help build nonprofit youth and community centers.

Ralston-Purina, in St. Louis, pays high school youths to work for volunteer agencies during the summer.

Equitable Insurance Company invests in inner-city improvement projects in Chicago.

Merrill Lynch supports local productions of operas and other fine arts events.

First Interstate Bank of California conducts free financial planning seminars for senior citizens.

Philip Morris, Inc., sponsors traveling exhibits of fine art (the Vatican Collections) to assist local museums.

In 32 cities American Express has a program in which 5 to 25 cents is donated to a local cultural institution on every card transaction.

Corporate sponsorships totaling $130 million funded about 25 percent of the $515 million budget for the 1984 Olympic Games in Los Angeles.

An elite group of 29 companies, including McDonald's Corporation, International Business Machines, American Express Company, Levi Strauss & Company, and General Motors, each gave a minimum of $4 million in cash or the equivalent in products and services to become sponsors.

In return for their support, the companies earned the right to use the Olympic logo in advertising, on packaging, and even on the sides of company trucks. The Games also became a showcase for products and services. Motorola, for example, supplied all the telephones and switching equipment. ARA Services, Inc., hoped that the Olympics demonstrated the company's talents as a provider of institutional food and transportation.

Sponsoring companies also reaped a degree of public good will and increased employee morale by being good corporate citizens. "You're buying an intangible," said Dan Greenwood, vice-president of corporate relations for the Los Angeles Olympic Organizing Committee, which was in charge of the event. "It's an image thing; a great deal is image."

Corporate Philanthropy

Another area of public affairs, which often overlaps community relations, is corporate philanthropy.

In 1983, American companies contributed more than $3 billion to charitable organizations, according to statistics compiled by the American Association of Fund-Raising Counsel.[1] Contributions to education ($1.3 billion), the largest recipient, accounted for 43 percent of all corporate donations, and contributions to health and human services came in second. Culture and art, as well as civic and community activities, each received about 11 percent of the total given. Another 5 percent went to other organizations such as those aiding foreign nations and religious and women's groups.

Unfortunately, 50 percent of all corporate philanthropy comes from just 1 percent of American companies, despite the fact that corporations can now

[1] Americans donated $64.93 billion to some 300,000 charitable organizations in 1983. Of this amount, $53.85 billion was contributed by individuals. Religious organizations received 47.5 percent of the total given, followed by health and hospitals, 14.1 percent; education, 13.9 percent; social welfare, 10.7 percent; and arts and humanities, 6.3 percent.

deduct up to 10 percent of their taxable income for charitable gifts. Only a few corporations give more than 1 percent.

The rationale for giving has been summarized by Frank Saunders, vice-president for corporate relations of Philip Morris, Inc. He stated:

. . . [C]orporate executives speak of putting something back into the community, improving the quality of life for employees, attracting prospective employees, practicing corporate citizenship—what boils down to enlightened self-interest. Business doesn't get anything tangible or real that you can put in your pocket and walk away with. This is a way that corporations make friends.

Paul H. Elicker, president of SCM Corporation, stated:

We have not sponsored the Treasures of Early Irish Art at the Metropolitan or any of the other eight exhibitions over the past four years out of the goodness of our hearts. We do it because it's good for the arts, it's good for the millions of people who get pleasure viewing great works of art, and—not least—it's good for SCM Corp."

There is even some evidence that corporate philanthropy is good for the financial bottom line. A 1983 study by Professor Ritchie Lowery of Boston College showed a relationship between social responsibility and profitability. He examined the financial performance of 30 socially responsive companies and found that they performed 106 percent better in capital gain on the Dow Jones business averages than did a similar list of companies with lackluster philanthropic and social responsibility programs.

There are any number of worthwhile causes competing for the corporate philanthropic dollar, and it is not unusual for a major corporation to receive more than 5000 requests annually. Consequently, most corporations formulate specific policies regarding the kinds of charitable organizations they will support. Syntex, a pharmaceutical company, tends to support medical research and community health-care facilities. Apple Computer, on the other hand, has an active program of donating equipment to educational institutions. DuPont makes major contributions to the arts. Irving Shapiro, president of the company, said, "We look for some connection between the artistic venture and our corporate interest, which means we usually contribute in communities where we have our headquarters, offices, or a plant."

Some corporations also contribute heavily to major charities and the arts in Washington, D.C. From the corporate viewpoint, supporting a gala event at the Kennedy Center for the Performing Arts is an excellent way for its executives to meet government leaders, influential politicians, and nationally syndicated columnists.

Another form of corporate philanthropy with political overtones is support of national political party conventions. Atlantic Richfield, Bank of America, Bechtel Group, Chevron, Crocker Bank, and Diamond Shamrock contributed $100,000 each to various San Francisco committees serving as hosts for the 1984 Democratic National Convention. Most of the corporate sponsors justified the financial support on the basis of good corporate citizenship or name and product recognition.

Although corporate philanthropy is an integral part of public affairs, it does have its limitations. Contributions can help generate a reservoir of public support, but they are not a substitute for corporate performance in other areas.

David Finn, chairman of the public relations firm of Ruder & Finn (now Ruder Finn & Rotman), once said in a speech at Columbia University:

The practical risk of being dishonest or deceptive in [public affairs] programs can be considerable. A consumer advocate who believes that non-returnable containers should be banned for environmental reasons is not likely to change his mind because a major company in one of these industries subsidizes a series of marvelous films on the history of civilization or a related subject. If the advocate believes that such an expenditure is made in the hope of changing his mind, he is likely to be more vigorous than ever in his attack on the company.

Further discussion of corporate giving appears in Chapter 18.

Public Affairs in Government

Since the time of the ancient Egyptians 5000 years ago, governments have always engaged in what is known in the twentieth century as public information, public relations, and public affairs.

The Rosetta Stone, discovered by Napoleon's troops and used by scholars as the key to understanding Egyptian hieroglyphics, turned out to be a publicity release for the reign of Ptolemy V. Julius Caesar was known in his day as a master of staged events in which entrances to Rome after a successful battle were highly orchestrated.

There has always been a need for government communications, if for no other reason than to inform citizens of the services available and the manner in which they may be used. In a democracy public information is crucial if citizens are to make intelligent judgments about the policies and activities of their elected representatives. Through information it is hoped that citizens will have the necessary background to participate fully in the formation of government policies.

In the United States today, there is an increasingly strong trend toward the organized dissemination of government information. The employment of government information officers, despite efforts to reduce the federal bureaucracy, keeps expanding. Several factors have led to the growth of the government information effort. Among them are the following:

Ethical Guidelines
for Business Public
Affairs Professionals

A. The Public Affairs Professional maintains professional relationships based on honesty and reliable information, and therefore:

1. Represents accurately his or her organization's policies on economic and political matters to government, employees, shareholders, community interests, and others.

2. Serves always as a source of reliable information, discussing the varied aspects of complex public issues within the context and constraints of the advocacy role.

3. Recognizes diverse viewpoints within the public policy process, knowing that disagreement on issues is both inevitable and healthy.

B. The Public Affairs Professional seeks to protect the integrity of the public policy process and the political system, and therefore:

1. Publicly acknowledges his or her role as a legitimate participant in the public policy process and discloses whatever work-related information the law requires.

2. Knows, respects and abides by federal and state laws that apply to lobbying and related public affairs activities.

3. Knows and respects the laws governing campaign finance and other political activities, and abides by the letter and intent of those laws.

C. The Public Affairs Professional understands the interrelation of business interests with the larger public interests, and therefore:

1. Endeavors to ensure that responsible and diverse external interests and views concerning the needs of society are considered within the corporate decision-making process.

2. Bears the responsibility for management review of public policies which may bring corporate interests into conflict with other interests.

3. Acknowledges dual obligations—to advocate the interests of his or her employer, and to preserve the openness and integrity of the democratic process.

4. Presents to his or her employer an accurate assessment of the political and social realities that may affect corporate operations.

SOURCE: Public Affairs Council, a Washington-based organization of public affairs executives for major corporations.

1. *Increasing urban population.* The nation now has more than 240 million people, and the traditional New England "town hall" meeting plan in which townspeople made decisions is no longer feasible, except in very small communities. Thus more systematic lines of communication must be established to reach residents in a metropolitan area.

2. *Increasing complexity of society.* The cliché that today's society is more complex than it was 20 years ago means that government is more complex as well. There has been a proliferation of specialized agencies along with thousands of laws and regulations. Ordinary citizens increasingly find it difficult to understand what the law is, let alone to know the proper agency to which an inquiry can be directed.

3. *Increasing mobility.* City and county populations are constantly changing, and newcomers must be regularly informed about local laws and regulations, including property taxes and even something as mundane as the days of garbage pickups.

4. *Increasing citizen demands.* Sociologists call this "the age of entitlement"; citizens are demanding more services than ever from their local, state, and national governments. At the same time, there is considerable public resistance to higher taxes to pay for these services.

5. *Increasing public scrutiny.* People today are scrutinizing the costs and programs of government more than ever. There is considerable public debate on how to spend limited resources, and special interest groups are more active and vocal than in previous years. In addition, citizens now have greater access to the deliberations of government bodies through state and federal freedom of information, or "sunshine," laws.

All these factors contribute to the trend whereby government units are providing extensive public information in order to develop public understanding of programs and policies. Commonplace today are news releases, press conferences, reports, information bulletins, posters, special events, exhibits, broadcast public service announcements, brochures, and even paid advertising by government bodies.

The objectives of government information efforts have been summarized by William Ragan, director of public affairs for the United States Civil Service Commission. They are as follows:

1. Inform the public about the public's business. In other words, communicate the work of government agencies.

2. Improve the effectiveness of agency operations through appropriate public information techniques. In other words, explain agency programs so that citizens understand and can take actions necessary to benefit from them.

3. Provide feedback to government administrators so that programs and policies can be modified, amended, or continued.

4. Advise management on how best to communicate a decision or a program to the widest number of citizens.

5. Serve as an ombudsman. Represent the public and listen to its representations. Make sure that individual problems of the taxpayer are satisfactorily solved.

6. Educate administrators and bureaucrats about the role of the mass media and how to work with media representatives.

"PUBLIC INFORMATION" VERSUS "PUBLIC RELATIONS"

Although many of the objectives described by Ragan would be considered appropriate goals in almost any field of public relations, in government such activities are never referred to as "public relations." Instead, various euphemisms are used. The most common titles are (1) *public information officer,* (2) *director of public affairs,* (3) *press secretary,* and (4) *administrative aide.*

In addition, government agencies do not have departments of public relations. Instead, the FBI has an External Affairs Division; the Interstate Commerce Commission has an Office of Communications and Consumer Affairs; and the Environmental Protection Agency has an Office of Public Awareness. The military services usually have Offices of Public Affairs.

Such euphemisms serve to reconcile two essentially contradictory facts: (1) government need to inform its citizens and (2) it is against the law to use appropriated money for the employment of "publicity experts."

Congress, as early as 1913, saw a potential danger in executive branch agencies spending taxpayer dollars to sway the American public to support programs of various administrations. Consequently, the Gillett Amendment (Section 3107 of Title V of the United States Code) was passed; it stated, "Appropriated funds may not be used to pay a publicity expert unless specifically appropriated for that purpose." The law was reinforced in 1919 with prohibition of the use of any appropriations for services, messages, or publications designed to influence a member of Congress. Another law that year required executive agencies to utilize the U.S. Government Printing Office so that publications could be more closely monitored than in the past. Restrictions also prohibit executive departments from mailing any material to the public without a specific request.

Congress clearly was attempting to limit the authority of the executive branch to spend taxpayer money on public relations efforts to gain support for pet projects of the president. Some presidents chafed at this, but others thought it was entirely proper that the government should not be in the business of propagandizing the taxpayers. President Eisenhower, for example, ordered all executive branch agencies to dispense with field office information activity. The only problem was the great number of public and press requests for information. Consequently, information offices lost their titles but continued their dissemination functions under such titles as "technical liaison officers" for the Corps of Engineers and "assistant to the director" in the Bureau of Reclamation.

In 1972, alarmed by Richard Nixon's expansion of the White House communications staff, Congress reaffirmed prior legislation by stating that no part of any appropriation bill could be used for publicity or propaganda purposes designed to support or defeat legislation before Congress.

Although most citizens would agree that government should not use tax money to persuade the public of the merits or demerits of a particular bill or program, there is a thin line between merely providing information and using information as a lobbying tool.

If a public affairs officer for the Pentagon testifies about the number of MIRVs deployed by the Soviet Union, does this constitute information or an attempt to influence congressional appropriations? Or, to use another example, is a speech by the secretary of the interior about America's large coal reserves on federal land information or an attempt to lobby for the opening of wilderness areas to mining?

While ascertaining the difference between "public relations" and "public information" may be an interesting semantic game, the fact remains that the terms *public relations* and *publicity* are seldom used by a government agency—not even by the National Aeronautics and Space Administration, which is mandated by law to provide the American public with full information about its program.

Effective public relations, of course, consists of giving full and accurate information—but the expression *public relations* has the connotation in government of being just image-building and manipulation. The term *public information,* on the other hand, sounds neutral and objective.

SCOPE OF FEDERAL GOVERNMENT INFORMATION

It is often said that the United States government is the world's premier collector of information. It is also maintained, without much counterargument, that the federal government is one of the world's great disseminators of information.

The "Consumer Information Catalog," whose cover appears in Figure 15.2, lists material of interest to the general public.

The official guide to government periodicals and other publications is a much longer document. It contains almost 1,200 pages and lists at least 12,000 government publications. They range from a monthly law enforcement magazine published by the FBI to a pamphlet issued by the Department of Agriculture titled "Making Pickles and Relishes at Home." The armed forces have so many magazines and pamphlets that, says one media reporter, it would take a truck to deliver a single copy of everything on the list.

FIGURE 15.2

This 16-page catalog lists booklets issued by more than 30 United States government agencies, available from the Consumer Information Center, Pueblo, Colorado 81009.

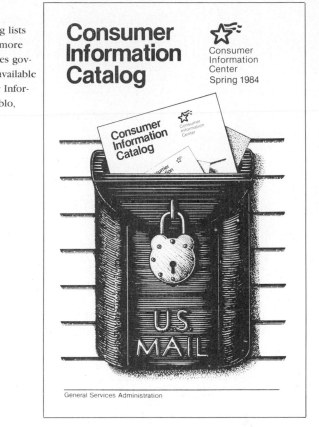

Consumer Information Catalog

Consumer Information Center
Spring 1984

Consumer Information Catalog

U.S. MAIL

General Services Administration

Another writer, somewhat critical of the federal government's production of news releases, newsletters, reports, brochures, and the like, says that all this material would fill four Washington Monuments each year.

The federal government is also one of the nation's largest advertisers. *Time* magazine estimated that 1983 expenditures for this purpose were about $200 million—still only one-third of the advertising budget of Procter & Gamble, the nation's No. 1 advertiser. In 1980 the U.S. government ranked twenty-sixth in this respect among all advertisers. This position was just behind Ralston Purina (pet foods) and Unilever (detergents and toiletries). The bulk of advertising, about three-fourths of the total, is spent by the armed forces for military recruiting. The U.S. Postal Service is also a heavy user of advertising. Its attempts to promote Express Mail and a new Electronic Mail Service has lured many customers away from private carriers such as Federal Express, Emery Freight, and Airborne.

The government has become, as well, one of the world's largest film producers, spending about $600 million for this purpose in 1983. In contrast,

Twentieth Century-Fox spent about $90 million that same year. Motion pictures are provided to schools, television stations, and civic groups. Most of the films, however, are made for the Department of Defense and used extensively in training. In a recent year the Pentagon produced 1141 motion pictures, 3560 television films, and 3412 audio and mixed-media presentations.

Although it is difficult to get an accurate count of the people employed who write, produce, and distribute all these informational and educational materials, the Associated Press in 1983 estimated that 4,100 people were employed full-time in government information and publicity activities. The federal Office of Personnel Management, however, in a breakdown of job descriptions in 1980, found a total of more than 12,000 persons. The breakdown showed the following:

3,033 specialists in public information

2,272 in writing and editing

1,722 in technical writing and editing

1,659 in visual communication

1,090 in foreign information

2,199 in editorial assistance

  182 in foreign language broadcasting

The Pentagon has the most people assigned to public information. The Associated Press reported in 1983 that 1194 people were involved in Department of Defense "public relations" activities. Although some are based in Washington, most are scattered at military bases around the world. These directors of public affairs, as they are called in the military, have a number of functions, including (1) handling hometown news releases, (2) conducting base open houses, (3) publicizing special events such as precision-flying teams, (4) briefing the media and legislators on new weapons and the like, and (5) engaging in community liaison work. All this activity on behalf of the military arouses criticism. In 1971 CBS produced a documentary titled, "The Selling of the Pentagon," in which military efforts at public information were taken to task as crossing that thin line between the dissemination of information and lobbying for increased budgets. (Press criticism of government information services is discussed in more detail later in the chapter.)

Other cabinet-level departments have large numbers of information officers, and often the heads of these agencies are criticized for promoting themselves instead of government programs. A *Wall Street Journal* reporter, Robert Greenberger, for example, wrote a story about former Secretary of Labor Raymond Donovan which stated, in part:

While all cabinet officers have public relations people, it would be hard to match the Donovan publicity machine. The Labor Department issues flurries of press releases crediting the labor secretary for even the most routine actions. Letters received praising him immediately are reproduced and sent to labor reporters across the country. Interviews are granted for stories in dozens of publications. . . .

The Environmental Protection Agency (EPA), at the height of concern about energy in the mid-1970s, had the most extensive publicity program in Washington. In all, 112 public information employees were cranking out 1000 news releases a year. In addition, the agency distributed coloring books with energy information tips to 1.7 million third graders. Columns describing how to save energy were sent to thousands of small-town newspapers. The EPA finally got into trouble with Congress for putting out a pamphlet discussing supplies of natural gas and explaining why Congress should lift price controls. Congressional critics said that publication of the leaflet no longer constituted dissemination of information but had become lobbying.

One of the smaller budgets for public information in government is allocated to the National Aeronautics and Space Administration. Its 1983 budget of $16.4 million was spent in the following ways:

$4.6 million for public information

$3.5 million for public services, such as handling two million visitors annually at nine centers

$3.1 million for publications, films, and exhibits

$3.5 million for educational programs

$1.7 million for replies to mail inquiries from the public

The size of the government's public affairs budget can be viewed from another perspective. The Associated Press estimated that the annual salaries of information officers in the executive branch of government total about $165 million. This amount, however, seems relatively insignificant compared to the $725 million price tag for a nuclear-powered submarine. Or, to put it another way, the $165 million represents the cost of only six F-15 fighter planes.

The federal government also spent $673 million on printing in 1980. Of this, $100 million was used to publish such legislative items as the *Congressional Record*. As one critic noted, "The *Congressional Record* is bloated with remarks never even uttered on the floor of the House or Senate."

Congress, although suspicious of public information expenditures by the executive branch of government, seems less critical of its own expenditures. Members of Congress, for example, use the franking privilege (free postage) to mail a barrage of newsletters, recordings, brochures, radio interviews, videotapes, and the like, to their constituents to inform them about operations of Congress. Critics complain that most of these materials are designed for self-promotion. Republican John Heinz of Pennsylvania, for example, sent out 15 million pieces of mail financed by taxpayers in 1982, a year in which he handily won reelection. Public criticism of congressional newsletters reached the point several years ago that a law was passed stating that a member of Congress could not mention himself or herself more than five times on a page!

STATE INFORMATION SERVICES

Every state provides organized public information services. In California, for example, there are 250 information officers in about 70 state agencies. Here are some examples of their activities:

The Department of Health Services distributed news releases about outbreaks of rabies and black plague—two communicable diseases that could cause epidemics.

FIGURE 15.3

A campaign to reduce highway fatalities through use of seat belts, conducted by the State of California's Office of Traffic Safety, included distribution of pictorial material to newspapers.

If you can run through a brick wall... you don't need safety belts.

CALIFORNIA TRAFFIC SAFETY

The Solid Waste Management Board conducted an extensive information program on the theme "Untrash California," designed to make citizens aware of littering and the need to recycle materials.

The Department of Commerce launched a $6.5 million campaign to lure business and tourists to California. Part of the effort was a 28-page brochure that described the state, according to one newspaper writer, as "the largest, the greatest, the richest—the place to achieve success."

The Office of Traffic Safety sent out a series of newspaper advertisements—some with catchy photographs, like the one in Figure 15.3—to remind riders to buckle up.

Most states spend a good deal of money to stimulate business and tourism. Arizona funds the monthly magazine *Arizona Highways,* while other states, including Vermont, Florida, and North Carolina, place advertising in publications such as *Time* asking readers to send for four-color brochures.

MUNICIPAL INFORMATION SERVICES

Cities also employ information specialists to generate tourism and lure and retain business. Baltimore advertises itself with a 90-foot replica of a nineteenth-century clipper ship. St. Louis invested in a replica of Lindbergh's *Spirit of St. Louis* aircraft, and flight crews and publicity people barnstormed 102 cities to hail the city as a destination for tourists and a good business site. Since 1960 Atlanta's "Forward Atlanta" campaign is reported to have brought 300,000 jobs to the area.

The city of Dallas, in preparation for the 1984 Republican National Convention, hired a public relations firm to establish what were termed "friendships" with the media. According to the Associated Press, the public relations firm met with a number of press representatives in an effort to anticipate the needs of the several thousand media visitors. City officials wanted to make sure that the image of Dallas as a "great place to live" was projected through the national media covering the convention.

Municipal information services also are manifested in a number of smaller ways. The city librarian publicizes a list of current best-sellers; an airport administrator sets up an exhibit showing the future growth needs of the airport; and a local film council works with community leaders in an effort to lure movie production companies for location shots.

City council members and administrators also pay attention to public relations strategies. They engage in such activities as the following:

Conducting city council meetings at night to increase attendance

Consulting with citizens before policy is formulated

Holding neighborhood meetings

Appearing on radio and TV talk shows, particularly those that allow audience call-ins

Implementing information and complaint telephone lines and publicizing the numbers

Using citizen advisory committees

The importance of public information and public relations at the municipal level is best described by the International City Managers' Association:

Public relations is one of many important variables which affect the ability of an administrator to accomplish program objectives. It involves cooperation between the agency (its personnel, decisions and programs) and the attitudes and desires of persons and groups in the agency's external environment. It imposes on administrators the necessity for dealing with public relations as an inherent and continuing element in the managerial process. The administrator must be mindful of public relations considerations at every stage of the administrative process, from making the decision to the final point of its execution.

CRITICISMS OF GOVERNMENT INFORMATION SERVICES

Although the need for government to inform citizens and publicize programs is generally accepted in principle, many members of the public and news media still express suspicion and even disdain for the activity, as mentioned earlier in this chapter.

The media periodically attack government information efforts. A headline on a *Wall Street Journal* story several years ago read: "Federal Flacks: Washington PR Staffs Dream Up Ways to Get Agencies' Stories Out." A headline in the San Francisco *Chronicle* on California's public information officers read: "Flock of Flacks in California." And even national columnist Jack Anderson got into the act with a piece titled, "Government Puff Artists." *Time* magazine printed an essay on government information efforts and headlined it: "Pitchmen on the Potomac."

As some of these headlines indicate, news stories sometimes show a bias against government information activity by referring to public information officers (PIOs) as "flacks." As previously mentioned, one writer for the San Jose *Mercury-News* composed a story about the invitation of an 11-year-old Maine girl to the Soviet Union by former Chairman Yuri Andropov and described it as an event staged by Soviet "flacks." He added: "If Russia's flacks can't cash in on this one, Red Square might as well be blue. . . ." The newspaper previously had carried a story about American government information activity under the headline, "The Great American Propaganda Machine."

The word *flack* probably comes from the German words *Flieger abwehrkanone,* used in World War II to mean antiaircraft defense. By the end of the war, American service people were using *flak* or *flack* as a slang word for any barrage of lies, complaints, and the like, that often came as thick and fast as antiaircraft fire.

All this verbal abuse by the press rankles dedicated PIOs, who work very hard to keep the public informed of government activities. One PIO complains: "I'm not a flack, and I resent getting stereotyped as one. It makes me wonder about the objectivity and fairness of the media, which depend on me for much of their information." His complaint is echoed by an information officer for a California agency who said that she was tired of those who complain about information officers. She added: "I'd like to see the press find out what's going on in state government without us. The press would be frustrated. People are not going to be informed unless you have people like us bending over backward for them."

Indeed, a degree of press hostility toward government information efforts seems to stem from resentment of the fact that reporters must rely heavily upon them. Columnist Joseph Kraft complains:

In the typical Washington situation, news is not nosed out by keen reporters and then purveyed to the public. It is manufactured inside the government, by various interested parties for purposes of their own, and then put out to the press in ways and at times that suit the sources. That is how it happens that when the President prepares a message on crime, all the leading columnists suddenly become concerned with crime. That is how it happens when the Air Force budget comes up for consideration, some new plane will streak across the continent in record time.

Admittedly Kraft has a point. Potential exists for abuse in the federal government's efforts, but public information officers and public affairs directors will always be an integral and valuable part of the government. The reason is that there are simply not enough press representatives in Washington to cover adequately the hundreds of federal offices. Although the White House, Congress, and even the Pentagon probably have more than enough reporters covering their activities, a wire service reporter still may be assigned to cover three or four cabinet-level agencies that have staffs in the thousands and budgets in the billions. Even a White House correspondent must rely on news releases most of the time rather than chat with the president or senior staff aides.

The result is a major dependency on the handouts of federal agencies. One text, *Media: An Introductory Analysis of American Mass Communications* by Peter M. Sandman, David M. Rubin, and David B. Sachsman, puts it bluntly: "If a newspaper were to quit relying on press releases, but continued covering news it now covers, it would need at least two or three times as many reporters." One study shows that 22 percent of all news emanating from Washington during a certain period was traced to handouts from executive agencies.

Newspaper editorials often criticize the expense of government information efforts, but defenders say such contentions are not well grounded. When media questioned the $10.7 million spent on the salaries of 250 PIOs in state agencies in California, an administrative aide to Governor Jerry Brown retorted: "The amount spent is reasonable. We're running a $20 billion business here. It seems like a modest investment to keep the shareholders [taxpayers] of the state informed."

At the federal level the money spent by the Department of Transportation on public information and public affairs is less than 0.0004 percent of the department's budget and involves 0.0008 percent of the department's 114,000 employees.

And although there is much congressional and media criticism of the government's extensive publications, these are defended on the basis of cost efficiency. A deputy director of the Department of Agriculture publications branch, for example, reported that his office alone receives about 350,000 inquiries a year. Two-thirds of the requests, he says, can be answered with pamphlets that cost between half a cent and 12 cents each, whereas individual responses could cost up to $20 each when personnel costs are included. In other words, the sheer volume of public requests requires a large array of printed materials.

An Associated Press reporter acknowledged in a story that government information does have value. He wrote:

> While some of the money and manpower goes for self-promotion, by far the greater amount is committed to an indispensable function of a democratic government—informing the people.
>
> What good would it serve for the Consumer Product Safety Commission to recall a faulty kerosene heater and not go to the expense of alerting the public to its action? An informed citizenry needs the government to distribute its economic statistics, announce its antitrust suits, tell about the health of the president, give crop forecasts.

Indeed, public affairs officers in government contend that their work is vital because the best-planned programs will do little good if the public does not know about them. The Department of Housing and Urban Development, for example, wanted to inform the public about a graduated payment mortgage program. To this end, the department produced three public service announcements (PSAs) for television and a press kit for all print media, and distributed eight million brochures to lenders and bankers. The total cost of the program, $256,000, was thought to be inexpensive compared to the estimated $5 million that advertising experts consider necessary to introduce a new product nationally.

In sum, defenders of government information efforts argue two points. First, if billions are spent on government programs, it makes sense to spend some money on publicizing those programs so that citizens can take advantage of them. Second, it is often more cost-efficient to publicize a cause than to pay for the problems that might result if no campaign had been waged. A good example is the promotion of Smokey the Bear, perhaps the most recognized symbol in America. The government information campaign about preventing forest fires has helped preserve woodlands, and it has been much more cost-effective than fighting forest fires. By the same token, a county antilitter campaign to make the public more conscious of trash might be more cost-effective than setting up crews to police roadways.

It should be kept in mind that the purpose of government information programs, despite some abuse, is to let the public know about programs that can benefit them. Explaining aspects of Medicare with 60-second television spots, for instance, or even organizing an automobile show of fuel-efficient cars developed by inventors is a valid part of governmental activities.

Public Relations and Political Candidates

The chapter so far has dealt with business public affairs and government information efforts. Another area of widespread public relations activity is in behalf of political candidates.

In America political public relations is a multimillion-dollar industry; it has come a long way since the first distribution of campaign literature on a

| A Press Secretary on the Campaign Trail | Kathy Buskin, 34, served as Senator Gary Hart's press secretary through the presidential primaries of 1984 as Hart fought an uphill battle against Walter Mondale for the Democratic Party nomination.

Buskin was not only Hart's press secretary but also a trusted adviser who helped formulate campaign strategy and positions on issues. Members of the press described her as "unflappable" and the "bionic woman" because of her ability to cope with the pressure-cooker environment of constant media and public scrutiny of her boss.

In an interview with the *Wall Street Journal*, Buskin said: "There is no way to prepare for something like this. It is impossible to understand what happens when you travel with 100 reporters. The sheer demands—lost luggage, phones for filing, information—are just enormous. It's like taking a tour of 100 high school students to Europe."

Being a press secretary to a presidential hopeful meant a 24-hour day for Buskin, even to the point of getting calls in the middle of the night from an Australian TV crew in a time zone far away from the snows of New Hampshire. But, she said, life on the road taught her a few things. "You can't give tips, and you can't play favorites. You have to be honest, but you don't have to answer every question." |

massive scale in the 1880 presidential elections. It now consists of computer mailing lists that can send a candidate's tailored letter to millions of homes, extensive use of radio and television advertising, and any number of staged events designed to give a candidate visibility. It also involves speechwriting, press kits, and news releases.

A director of public relations (often called a press secretary or administrative aide) performs a number of duties for a political candidate, including the following:

Preparation of news releases concerning the candidate's political philosophy, stands on specific issues, and campaign schedule.

Press briefings and background sessions for reporters.

Preparation of position papers.

Speechwriting.

Polling, or the commissioning of surveys, to determine the candidate's popularity.

Coordination of the candidate's schedule, and liaison with citizens' groups.

Advance work to scout potential speech sites or media "photo opportunities."

Research on the issues and recommendations to the candidate.

Maximization of press coverage. As one public relations director said: "You can go to a factory and shake hands and be seen by perhaps 100 workers. But do it on TV and you're seen by thousands—or by millions, if the national networks pick it up."

Public relations personnel expend much effort coordinating logistics and schedules, and timing public statements. Attention to detail is extremely important, and the best staffs leave nothing to chance (see Figure 15.4). Missing a plane or failing to check a microphone system can be a disaster for a candidate.

There are also frustrations. Patricia A. Bario, press secretary to Democratic vice-presidential candidate Geraldine Ferraro, abruptly resigned in the first months of the 1984 campaign because of conflicts with Ferraro's campaign manager. Bario, a vice-president on leave from the Burson-Marstteller public relations firm, complained that she had not been given access to the candidate's inner circle during the tax-return controversy. Left without answers for scores of demanding reporters, Bario told the Associated Press that she felt her credibility had been undermined.

A large number of political public relations firms are well paid for giving candidates advice and managing campaigns, but there is also a legion of volunteer workers who derive personal satisfaction in helping a candidate.

FIGURE 15.4

National political conventions involve public relations representatives for various candidates and causes, as well as corporate public relations representatives working in public affairs and product publicity. This picture was distributed by Hewlett-Packard Company, showing how a British reporter used one of its portable computers to record notes at the 1984 Democratic National Convention in San Francisco.

The only possible payoff occurs if the candidate is elected and then taps the volunteer to be a press aide on the government payroll. For example, President Carter's press secretary, Jody Powell, was a volunteer in the 1976 campaign who went from a $15,000 job on the Atlanta *Constitution* to a $55,000 annual salary at the White House.

There are several ethical guidelines for people working in political public relations. Here are some of them, as formulated by the Public Relations Society of America:

1. It is the responsibility of professionals practicing political public relations to be conversant with the various statutes, local, state and federal, governing such activities and to adhere to them strictly. This includes laws and regulations governing lobbying, political contributions, disclosure, elections, libel, slander and the like.

2. Members shall represent clients or employers in good faith, and while partisan advocacy on behalf of a candidate or public issue is expected, members shall act in accord with the public interest and adhere to truth and accuracy and to generally accepted standards or good taste.

3. Members shall not issue descriptive material or any advertising or publicity information or participate in the preparation or use thereof which is not signed by responsible persons or is false, misleading or unlabeled as to its source, and are obligated to use care to avoid dissemination of any such material.

4. In avoiding practices which might tend to corrupt the processes of government, members shall not make undisclosed gifts of cash or other valuables which are designed to influence specific decisions of voters, legislators or public officials.

5. Members shall not, through the use of information known to be false or misleading, conveyed directly or through a third party, intentionally injure the public reputation of an opposing candidate.

QUESTIONS FOR REVIEW AND DISCUSSION

1. Give two reasons why companies should engage in corporate citizenship.

2. Name the four major activities of a corporate public affairs department.

3. Explain how a corporate political action committee (PAC) works. What are the pros and cons?

4. Discuss lobbying as part of the democratic process. What kinds of groups engage in lobbying?

5. In what ways can corporate philanthropy be beneficial to the company?

6. List ten ethical guidelines for corporate public affairs specialists.

7. What societal and environmental factors have led to the growth of government information programs?

8. What are the objectives of government information efforts? What are the criticisms of such activities?

9. In what way is the press dependent upon government information programs?

10. List at least five guidelines for the conduct of political public relations.

CHAPTER SIXTEEN

International Public Relations

American corporations that operate in other countries do so in a kaleidoscope of laws, languages, and value systems often markedly different from those in the United States. In such circumstances public relations can make the critical difference between success and failure. So it is also with governments and industries that seek to influence the publics of the United States: professional public relations counseling becomes a necessity.

Public relations on a global scale and within individual countries largely is a post-World War II phenomenon. It is spreading rapidly as international trade increases, more nations seek industrial and technological development, and all governments endeavor to improve their status in the world community.

This chapter examines the phenomenon and identifies many of the methods employed and the problems encountered by those who engage in international public relations.

A Definition

International public relations may be defined as the planned and organized effort of a company, institution, or government to establish mutually beneficial relations with the publics of other nations. These publics, in turn, may be defined as the various groups of people who are affected by, or who can affect, the operations of a particular firm, institution, or government. Each public is united by a common interest vis-à-vis the entity seeking acceptance of its products or programs.

International public relations also may be viewed from the standpoint of its practice in individual countries. Although public relations is commonly regarded as a concept developed in the United States at the beginning of the twentieth century, some of its elements, such as countering unfavorable public attitudes by means of disclosure of operations through publicity and annual reports, were practiced by railroad companies and at least one shareholding corporation in Germany as far back as the mid–nineteenth century, to mention only one such country.

Even so, it is largely American techniques that have been adapted to national and regional public relations practices throughout the world, including many totalitarian nations. Today, although in some languages there is no term comparable to *public relations,* the practice has spread to more than 100 countries. This is primarily the result of worldwide technological, social, economic, and political changes and the growing understanding that public relations is an essential component of advertising, marketing, and diplomacy.

International Corporate Public Relations

GROWTH Hundreds of corporations based in the United States and other, mostly industrialized nations have been engaged in international public relations and advertising for decades. Despite the worldwide recession of the 1970s and early 1980s, their participation in the international marketplace has been steadily and dramatically growing, and they have been challenged during the last decade or so by industries in some of the less-developed nations, most of them aided by government subsidies.

Standards of living in much of the world, such as Europe, the Far East, Latin America, and other heretofore relatively untapped marketing regions, have been rising. Literacy rates have been improving, and the growth of both print and broadcast media in many countries, aided by satellite transmission, has provided an effective marketing and communication base. American and Japanese wares in particular are in great demand. The United States is exporting billions of dollars worth of products each year. These join the flow of goods produced by plants in other countries in which Americans have invested well over $60 billion.

As a consequence, United States corporations such as IBM World Trade, General Motors, Exxon, and Coca-Cola, and foreign corporations such as Philips, Sony, and Nestlé, long in the international field, have been joined by countless other companies seeking their share of the world market. IBM is an excellent example of the size and scope of these multinational corporations. IBM conducts business in more than 120 countries and receives more than one-half of its corporate gross income from sources outside the United States. The IBM payroll in 1979 supported approximately 147,000 employees engaged in non–United States operations.

Scores of United States public relations firms assist these companies in their overseas marketing and production activities. The largest in the field is Burson-Marsteller, closely followed by Hill & Knowlton. Other top agencies include Carl Byoir & Associates, Ruder Finn & Rotman, Daniel J. Edelman, Doremus & Company, Ketchum Public Relations, Gray & Company, and Sydney S. Baron & Company. The companies' own public relations, advertising, and marketing departments work closely with these agencies.

LANGUAGE, CULTURAL, AND OTHER PROBLEMS

Fundamentally, companies operating in foreign countries are confronted with essentially the same public relations challenges as those in the United States. These include (1) the formation and maintenance of favorable climates for their operations, involving relationships with local and national government officials, consumer groups, the financial community, and employees; (2) the monitoring and assessment of potentially adverse situations and the establishment of ways to counteract them; and (3) the containment of crises before serious damage is done.

These problems, however, may be aggravated by conditions such as the following:

Differences in languages and the multiplicity of languages in some countries

Longer chains of command, stretching back to the home country

Evident and subtle differences in customs

The varying levels of development of the media and public relations

Antipathy expressed toward "multinationals," a pejorative word in many countries

A dislike grounded in such factors as national pride, past relationships, envy, and apprehension, especially in regard to the United States, concerning foreign cultural, economic, political, and military influence

Image Problems
in China

With American business beginning to grow in the People's Republic of China and to develop still further in Hong Kong and the Republic of China on Taiwan, company representatives are learning all they can about Chinese customs and preferences. For example:

The Pepsi-Cola company found that its slogan, "Come alive with Pepsi!" translates literally in Mandarin Chinese as, "Pepsi brings your ancestors back from the dead!" The slogan was quickly dropped.

An American cleansing product manufacturer changed a television commercial in Hong Kong showing a green hat landing on a man's head, after it was pointed out that among Chinese a green hat signifies that the male wearing it is a cuckold.

Affluent Hong Kong residents didn't respond to advertisements showing the Marlboro man as a cowboy riding a horse tirelessly in the hot sun. So the company substituted advertisements with a younger, better-dressed man, obviously owning a truck as well as a horse, suggesting that he, unlike his American version, *owns* a piece of Marlboro country.

When Avon discovered that servants wouldn't admit just any women to their mistresses' homes in Hong Kong, the company hired well-to-do homemakers and professional women to sell to their acquaintances and gain access to their neighbors' homes.

Guinness Stout has a virile image in most parts of the world, but in Hong Kong stout was known chiefly as a beverage that women drank during pregnancy or during their menstrual periods, when they thought they needed extra strength. Now Guinness advertisements, in Chinese, emphasize that a bottle of the stout can revive a *man's* strength at the end of a working day.

McDonald's hamburger clown, Ronald McDonald, has done quite well in China, and so has the bull that is the worldwide trademark of Merrill Lynch Pierce Fenner & Smith. American and European products and services, it seems, are in high demand—for those companies that have learned not to offend or be laughed at.

The following are some examples of the types of language problems encountered:

Chevrolet executives could not figure out why the Chevy Nova was not selling well in Latin America. Then they learned that, although *Nova* means "new" in Spanish, *No va* means "It doesn't go."

A Deere & Company marketing manager, addressing a group of German dealers, chose the German word for *mouth* to describe the feeder opening of a forage harvester, inadvertently declaring that "John Deere is the biggest braggart."

Spanish customs officials delayed forwarding a badly needed Deere part because the Spanish description in shipping documents did not agree with that in the parts catalogue needed to clear the shipment. The translations had been done by different persons.

An interpreter assigned during former President Jimmy Carter's visit to Poland was fired for saying in Polish that the President "has a lust for Polish women" rather than "admired Polish women."

Corporations take steps to overcome some of the problems encountered in working in more than one language. Figure 16.1 shows the covers of a glossary Phillips Petroleum put out in three languages.

FIGURE 16.1

Phillips Petroleum publishes its glossary of oil industry terms in Norwegian, French, and English-language editions for distribution in Europe. The company has a large drilling operation in the North Sea. (Courtesy of Phillips Petroleum Company Europe-Africa.)

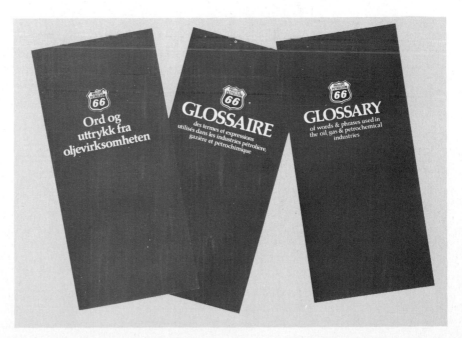

Cultural differences provide additional pitfalls, as shown by the following examples:

An American circles the thumb and forefinger to signify "OK." This gesture, however, is an offensive vulgarism to most Brazilians, who project affirmation by raising the thumb. However, that same gesture, so common with American hitchhikers, is considered rude in Scotland and Australia.

In the Middle East, the color white signifies mourning, so no executive should be pictured in white. In that same region care also must be taken in portraying or photographing women.

If an American executive lacks time to have a negotiating proposal typed and submits a handwritten version, Arabs may consider the gesture so bizarre that they will analyze the proposal intensely, seeking significant messages, or conclude that the American considers the contract unimportant.

Unlike Americans, Germans do not smile casually at almost everyone, but tend to reserve their smiles as signs of affection for close friends. So non-Germans should not take the lack of a smile as a sign of stuffiness.

When Americans make a business proposal, Japanese executives generally react with silence, giving themselves time to reflect—a sign of interest. Americans unfamiliar with this custom may be offended.

When Japanese executives suck in air through their teeth and exclaim, "Sa! That will be *very* difficult," they really mean just plain "No." The Japanese consider an absolute "no" offensive and try to respond euphemistically.

When an Asian business executive changes the date of a projected meeting, the American executive should not be offended; the Asian may simply have consulted with a religious adviser who urged a more auspicious date for the visit.

In some countries, such as Japan and those in Latin America, it is almost impossible to get a news story published or a television interview aired unless it has been prepared by a local unionized journalist.

Americans, generally punctual, must learn not to be offended when people in many other countries arrive a half-hour or more late for an appointment. Time traditionally has a different meaning in those nations.

Americans tend to separate their business and social lives. In many countries, however, business is an indirect outcome of a lengthy personal relationship; one does business with a friend, or only after a long social evening.

Americans often disregard the order in which a group of people walk through a doorway; in many rigidly hierarchical societies, however, that order may be a dead giveaway to the pecking order among them.

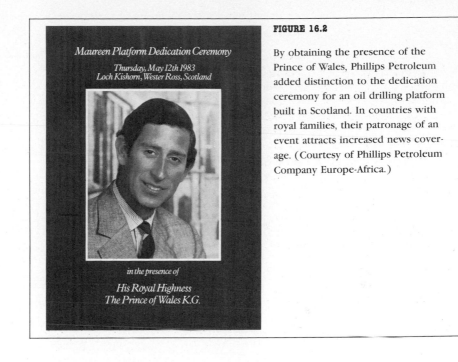

FIGURE 16.2

By obtaining the presence of the Prince of Wales, Phillips Petroleum added distinction to the dedication ceremony for an oil drilling platform built in Scotland. In countries with royal families, their patronage of an event attracts increased news coverage. (Courtesy of Phillips Petroleum Company Europe-Africa.)

All of these illustrations indicate that Americans not only must learn the customs of the country to which they are assigned but should rely upon native professionals to guide their paths. And, although they should study the language both before and after their arrival, they must realize that only by residing in the country for many years—if ever—will they be free of language problems.

Courses of study to prepare Americans to conduct business in other countries have been developed at a number of universities. Since 1970 the business school at New York University has nearly tripled its international business faculty. The University of South Carolina and the University of Denver, among others, have greatly expanded their international business programs. The American Graduate School of International Management in Glendale, Arizona, is devoted entirely to preparing students for world business careers. The nonprofit Business Council for International Understanding produces films that help Americans learn about practices in other countries. The Language and Intercultural Research Center at Brigham Young University publishes a variety of booklets which, though intended primarily for missionaries of the Church of Latter Day Saints, are useful for international business purposes.

Corporations, too, have done their homework. Their public relations experts overseas have helped them establish good rapport with the people in countries where they do business. Figures 16.2 and 16.3 illustrate two ways in which Phillips Petroleum endeavored to make itself a welcome visitor in Great Britain.

FIGURE 16.3

To counteract worries of environmentalists that oil drilling in the North Sea might damage wildlife, Phillips Petroleum produced classroom wall posters in Great Britain showing how birds and fish use the drilling platforms as resting and feeding places. An advertisement offered the posters to the public. (Courtesy of Phillips Petroleum Company Europe-Africa.)

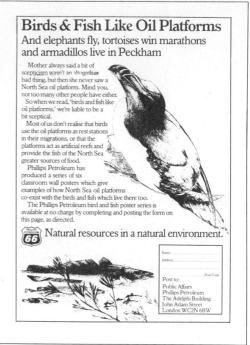

Birds & Fish Like Oil Platforms
And elephants fly, tortoises win marathons and armadillos live in Peckham

Mother always said a bit of scepticism wasn't an altogether bad thing, but then she never saw a North Sea oil platform. Mind you, not too many other people have either.

So when we read, 'birds and fish like oil platforms,' we're liable to be a bit sceptical.

Most of us don't realise that birds use the oil platforms as rest stations in their migrations, or that the platforms act as artificial reefs and provide the fish of the North Sea greater sources of food.

Phillips Petroleum has produced a series of six classroom wall posters which give examples of how North Sea oil platforms co-exist with the birds and fish which live there too.

The Phillips Petroleum bird and fish poster series is available at no charge by completing and posting the form on this page, as directed.

66 Natural resources in a natural environment.

Name
Address
Post Code
Post to:
Public Affairs
Phillips Petroleum
The Adelphi Building
John Adam Street
London WC2N 6BW

International Institutional Public Relations

Hundreds of noncorporate groups depend upon international support for their undertakings. Such organizations as the International Red Cross, the World Council of Churches, the International Council of B'nai B'rith, and the International Chamber of Commerce, along with numerous foundations, educational enterprises, labor unions, and government-support agencies, maintain vigorous public relations programs. For effective operation, their image must be kept as spotless as possible; like corporations, they must constantly monitor their environments, maintain proper relationships with the governments and publics of the countries in which they operate, and be prepared to handle crises.

The International Red Cross often is plagued with reports that relief goods and services are diverted into private hands or that aid has not been forthcoming as quickly as it might have been in major disasters around the world. Rumors that Red Cross representatives sold rather than gave cigarettes to troops in past wars still provide people who heard those reports years ago with an alibi for not giving.

Jewish groups in a number of countries mounted public relations campaigns in response to charges of Israeli complicity with the Lebanon massacre in 1982. Citizen groups supporting other Middle East countries raised funds for similar campaigns.

UNICEF, a United Nations agency that provides food, medical supplies, and other aid for millions of children on three continents, constantly must respond to charges, leveled mainly by those who dislike the United Nations, that too many of the dollars raised through card and gift sales and Halloween door-to-door solicitations are used improperly, in part through heavy administrative expenses.

The World Council of Churches, long a target on grounds that it is pro-Communist or proleftist in some of its activities, faced its most serious crisis in many years in 1982. An article by associate editor Joseph A. Harris, published in the August issue of the conservative *Reader's Digest,* the most widely circulated magazine in the world, accused the church body of anti-Western, pro-Soviet leanings, primarily through its Third World viewpoint and its support of the black revolutionary movement. The article was titled, "Karl Marx or Jesus Christ?" Soon thereafter the charges were repeated in the CBS program "60 Minutes." The council took great pains to combat the allegations. Although 28 United States Christian denominations make up 9 percent of the body's 302 members, they donate 18 percent of the funds, which in 1982 amounted to more than $10 million. Two hundred World Council members represent churches based in nonaligned nations. One council response was the publication of a five-page, paragraph-to-paragraph rebuttal to the *Digest* article. Here are excerpts from the article and the response by the council:

READER'S DIGEST

Countless World Council supporters were shocked in August 1978 when the WCC announced that its Program to Combat Racism had given $85,000 to the Patriotic Front, a Marxist guerilla organization then fighting the white-dominated regime in Rhodesia. At the time of the grant, the Patriotic Front had murdered 207 white civilians and 1712 blacks, and only weeks before had slaughtered nine white missionaries and their children.

WORLD COUNCIL

[The money] was used for education, health, and agricultural programs for Zimbabwean refugees in Botswana, Mozambique, and Zambia. There never had been any evidence that the grant, or any other grant for that matter, was used for the purchase of arms or military equipment.

Allegations that the Front was responsible for the murder of missionaries have never been substantiated. In fact, accounts of former soldiers demonstrate that the murders were the work of the Selous Scouts, an elite band of Rhodesian soldiers masquerading as guerillas.

Little attention has been given to the fact that the WCC gave $35,000 to help bring the Front to the negotiating table arranged in London by Prime Minister Margaret Thatcher.

International Government Public Relations

The governments of virtually every country have one or more departments involved in international communications. Almost all oversee broadcast operations, and many exercise direct or indirect control over the print media, including fields such as news and opinion content, acquisition of newsprint and equipment, collection and dissemination of news by foreign correspondents in their countries, news agencies that receive and transmit information, and the nations' international information and propaganda activities.

UNITED STATES

The United States Information Agency (USIA) administers a wide variety of information, educational, and cultural exchange programs around the world. The agency reports to the president and receives policy guidance from the secretary of state.

USIA employs approximately 8600 persons, of whom about 4200 are non-Americans serving abroad. About one-half of the USIA's 3400 employees in the United States are engaged in the broadcasting operations of the Voice of America. Many of the others provide support services for 600 Foreign Service information and cultural affairs officers working abroad alongside colleagues from the Department of State and other United States operations, including embassies, consulates, and other missions, in 125 countries. Among other activities, USIA operates regional libraries, plans exhibits and tours of performing groups, produces radio and television programs and research reports, and provides opportunities for foreign residents to learn English.

The Office of International Communication Policy of the Department of State performs various functions such as preparing the United States position for World Administrative Radio Conferences. As do the Soviet Union's KGB and the intelligence agencies of other countries, the Central Intelligence Agency (CIA) engages in numerous clandestine communication activities abroad in behalf of American interests.

Although commercial shortwave broadcasting in the United States began in the 1920s, it was not until Pearl Harbor that the United States government was convinced that it could not rely solely on commercial broadcasters for an international service. The Voice of America was created in 1942 as part of the Department of State. By 1946 it was broadcasting in shortwave in 24 languages. During the cold war era the American effort was increased with the establishment in Munich, Germany, of Radio Free Europe and Radio Liberation (now Radio Liberty), both financed by the CIA. Radio Free Europe broadcasts in Bulgarian, Czech and Slovak, Hungarian, Polish, and Romanian. Radio Liberty sends its broadcasts to the USSR in Russian and 15 other languages. The stations are now financed by the United States government and managed by the Board for International Broadcasting. They are not, however, part of the Voice of America.

The Voice of America prides itself upon the integrity of its news in its round-the-clock broadcasts heard by an estimated 75 million adults. Maintaining high credibility is regarded as one of the most effective public relations efforts this country can mount. Editorial opinion is limited to commentaries, always labeled as such. The commentaries increased during the Reagan administration, which also established in Florida a medium-wave station, Radio Martí, with signals directed to Cuba—an action that angered Fidel Castro, the Cuban president.

Why do the United States and other countries broadcast internationally? The answer takes many forms, including (1) to foster national interests and national prestige, (2) to keep in touch with nationals abroad, (3) to increase understanding among nations, (4) to disseminate news with accuracy and objectivity, (5) to attempt to influence the internal affairs of another country, (6) to foster the national culture including the teaching of the national language, and (7) to reserve a place in the broadcasting spectrum (controlled by the International Telecommunications Union) against a future need.

During the last decade or so, Department of State officials have been aided materially by American news media organizations, operating mainly through the World Press Freedom Committee, to respond to complaints of Third World countries. These nations seek, among other goals, independence and equity in access to global communication resources in order that their own views, values, and developmental efforts might be reported more fully and fairly. United States media leaders have counseled government representatives during debates on a proposed New World Order of Communication, conducted at UNESCO general assemblies and countless other conferences. Nonmedia representatives have joined them in lending counsel through the U.S. National Commission for UNESCO and other such bodies.

After a year's warning, the United States withdrew from membership in UNESCO at the end of 1984. It charged UNESCO with mismanagement, politicization, and "endemic hostility" toward a free press, free markets, and individual human rights. A State Department announcement stated that the United States would continue to support educational, scientific, cultural, and communications activities through other global agencies.

Also aiding the government in spreading American values around the world are innumerable films, television programs, newspapers, press association dispatches, magazines, and books. So tremendous has been the outpouring that many countries have charged "cultural invasion" and have sought ways to curtail what they consider neocolonialism.

THIRD WORLD COUNTRIES

Amid charges that the Western news agencies—Associated Press (AP), United Press International (UPI), Reuters, and Agence France-Presse—were not providing adequate and fair coverage of their developmental efforts, 85 less-developed countries in 1976 founded the Pool of News Agencies of Non-Aligned Countries. Transmission, initially provided by Tanjug, the Yugoslavian news agency, now is performed by Tunis Afrique Presse (known as

TAP), the Tunisian news agency. Using leased circuits, telex, and radioteletype channels, the agency daily distributes approximately 40,000 words of copy provided by the governments of about 40 countries. Far from being a news pool, however, the association primarily exchanges official information or government news handouts. Even so, the agency has enabled these countries to learn about each other's developmental progress, at least from the respective governments' points of view.

GREAT BRITAIN The government of Great Britain enjoyed a close working relationship with the Reuters news agency for almost 100 years beginning in the mid–nineteenth century. Paul Julius Reuter, agency owner, was granted use of cables linking the empire's outposts; in return, agency dispatches did much to further the nation's commercial and political interests, and there is little doubt that the news service was careful to say at crucial points what the British government wished it to say. With such an arrangement, historians have noted, government propaganda was particularly effective in bringing the United States to its side in World War I. Today, Reuters operates with scant if any government influence.

In 1911 the first government public relations campaign was carried out when, at the instigation of Prime Minister David Lloyd George, the Insurance Commission explained the benefits of the National Insurance Act, an unpopular measure that had attracted much adverse publicity. The Air Ministry appointed the first government press officer in 1919, and a year later the Ministry of Health selected Sir Basil Clarke, a former Reuters correspondent, as director of information.

Government public relations was substantially enlarged after World War II. The offices now are organized into three sections: press relations, publicity and inquiry, and intelligence. During recent extended freedom of information debates, however, the system was labeled the most secretive in the world (an obvious exaggeration), and demands were made that the service be disbanded and its work turned over to regular administrators.

Via shortwave, the British Broadcasting Company (BBC), chartered in 1922, carries a British point of view in its news dispatches and commentary to an estimated 75 million adults around the world each week.

As in some other countries, British politicians employ public opinion polling and public relations counseling to great advantage. Prime Minister Margaret Thatcher relied once again upon a veteran public relations counsel, Gordon Reece, to help achieve a landslide victory in her 1983 reelection campaign. The New York *Times* reported that, during her 1979 campaign, Reece "helped Mrs. Thatcher to learn to communicate on television by changing her clothes and modulating her previously strident tone of voice." Returning to England for a month after working in Los Angeles for Armand Hammer, the oil magnate, Reece helped produce innovative election broadcasts and was credited with providing only the light touch needed, and no more, in noting Mrs. Thatcher's leadership in the 1982 Falklands war.

SOVIET UNION The Soviet Union has an extensive government public relations program. During the mid-1920s the Soviet Union became the first country to produce foreign-language broadcasts via shortwave, and today its powerful stations envelop the world while incoming Western signals frequently are jammed. Its global satellite system Intersputnik, established mainly to exchange programming among countries in Eastern Europe, Cuba, Mongolia, and the USSR, is available for purchased use by anyone.

Its news agency TASS is ranked fifth in volume of dispatches, behind the AP, UPI, Reuters, and Agence France-Presse; however, media in non-Communist countries have learned to accept its dispatches for what they are—Communist propaganda disguised as news. TASS has correspondents in almost every country, but they never write a news story; they simply transmit information to the Kremlin, which processes it into TASS dispatches.

The Soviet Union's two major newspapers—*Pravda* (Truth) and *Izvestia* (News)—are read by millions of Russians, and tissue-thin copies are airmailed to subscribers around the world. *Pravda* primarily conveys government policies, but *Izvestia* encourages its readers to write letters, which are published, complaining about inadequate services and products (but *never* about government policy).

The Soviet Union participates in cultural, scholarly, and sports exchanges with most other countries; spends millions of dollars in providing training programs in countries it seeks to influence; and brings hundreds of students and others, mainly to Moscow, to engage in seminars, conferences, and university study. A pictorial magazine describing Russian life is mailed to many countries and made available in embassy study centers around the world.

Because the Soviet Union includes so many racial and ethnic groups, the government regularly sends dance and other performing groups from one region to another in an effort to promote mutual understanding and national unity among its varying cultures.

In addition to latent and obvious propaganda in its news dispatches and literature sent to other countries, one ingredient in the government's public relations program, "disinformation," runs contrary to accepted public relations practice. Disinformation is the planting by KGB agents of erroneous "news" stories with media around the world, calculated to harm countries that are its political adversaries. The late-1970s best-selling novel, *The Spike,* by Arnaud de Borchgrave and Robert Moss, describes the practice.

Public Relations in Behalf of Foreign Governments

For fees ranging upward of $1 million or more per year, American public relations firms work in this country for more than 50 nations. In recent years, for example, Hill & Knowlton has represented Indonesia and Morocco; Burson-Marsteller, Argentina, Costa Rica, Hungary, and the USSR (the latter mainly in trade fairs); and Ruder Finn & Rotman, El Salvador, Israel, and Japan. Especially active in representing foreign countries is Doremus & Company, whose clients have included Egypt, Iran, Jordan, the Philippines, Saudi Arabia, and Tunisia.

THE COUNTRIES' GOALS

What do these countries seek to accomplish? Carl Levin, vice-president and senior consultant, Burson-Marsteller, Washington, D.C., says that, among other things, the countries seek the following:

To advance political objectives

To be counseled on the United States' probable reaction to the client government's projected action

To advance the country's commercial interests—for example, sales in the United States, increased U.S. private investment, and tourism

To assist in communications in English

To counsel and help win understanding and support on a specific issue undermining the client's standing in the United States and the world community

To help modify laws and regulations inhibiting the client's activities in the United States

Under the Foreign Agents Registration Act of 1938, all legal, political, fund-raising, public relations, and lobbying consultants hired by foreign governments to work in the United States must register with the Department of Justice. They are required to file reports with the attorney general listing all activities on behalf of a foreign principal, compensation received, and expenses incurred.

ACTION PROGRAMS

Normally hired by an embassy after open bidding for the account, the firm first gathers detailed information about the client country, including past media coverage. Attitudes toward the country are ascertained both informally and through surveys conducted by a political pollster such as Pat Caddell or Daniel Yankelovich.

The action program decided upon likely will include the establishment of a national information bureau to provide facts and published statements of favorable opinion about the country. Appointments are made with key media people and other influential citizens, including educators, business leaders, and government officials. These people often are invited to visit the client country on expense-paid trips, although some news media people decline on ethical grounds. (Ethical questions are discussed in more detail shortly.)

Gradually, through expert and persistent methods of persuasion and the expenditure of what may run into millions of dollars, critical public attitudes may be changed or reinforced. Success is difficult to judge. So high are the stakes that, although the nations may change agencies from time to time, the image-polishing and fact-dissemination operation generally is made permanent.

PROBLEMS AND REWARDS

The toughest problems confronting the firm often are as follows:

Deciding to represent a country, such as Argentina, whose human rights violations may reflect adversely on the agency itself

Persuading the heads of such a nation to alter some of its practices so that the favorable public image sought may reflect reality

Convincing officials of a client country, which may totally control the flow of news internally, that the American press is independent from government control and that they should never expect coverage that is 100 percent favorable

Amnesty International, the Nobel Prize–winning human rights monitor, picketed Burson-Marsteller's offices because of the Argentine account. The

Council on Hemispheric Affairs criticized Ruder Finn & Rotman for working for the government of El Salvador. Norman Wolfson, chairman of Norman, Lawrence, Patterson & Farrell, fled Nicaragua with would-be assassins close on his heels after serving as the public relations counselor for the late dictator General Anastasio Somoza, during most of 1978. A Doremus & Company executive working for the economic development of the Philippines, whose government had placed the country under military law, also was threatened with death.

Why then do these firms work for unpopular governments? Wolfson put it this way: "I felt that I was performing a better service for my country by trying to help Americans understand Somoza than I did even by serving my country in the Navy during the Second World War." Said Burson-Marsteller's Carl Levin: "I do not think it is overreaching to state that in helping friendly foreign clients we also advance our national interests. And we help in ways that our government cannot." And, of course, retainers are large: Wolfson earned $20,000 to $30,000 per month, including expenses; Sydney S. Baron & Company was paid $650,000 annually plus expenses to promote investment opportunities in South Africa; and Burson-Marsteller received more than $800,000 a year to improve Argentina's reputation.

PUBLICITY FOR ANTIGOVERNMENT GROUPS

Although public relations counsel is usually retained by foreign governments, groups opposed to a foreign government also use public relations. The *Wall Street Journal,* in an editorial titled "Guerrilla P.R." (March 22, 1984), thought it interesting that the guerrillas battling the government in El Salvador had their own press kit. The editorial said, in part: " A few days ago, U.S. editors received a slick-looking press packet bearing the imprint of 'Fenton Communications' on behalf of something called the 'El Salvador Education Project.' It was a job any Madison Avenue house would have been proud of. What it said was that the Salvadoran guerrillas aren't participating in the elections because they are afraid of the 'death squads.' "

THE ETHICAL QUESTIONS

Entertaining lawmakers, media people, and others who influence public opinion is a long-established practice of firms representing foreign governments, either in the name of the government itself or that of organizations that share its interests. Those who attend these parties or junkets, often receiving valuable gifts as well, do so advisedly, for there is a thin line between hospitality and bribery.

Magazine writer Nicholas Burnett was one of several observers who raised the question of whether some members of the Washington press corps were being "bought" by attending the lavish Washington and New York City parties staged by Ardeshir Zahedi, ambassador to the United States of the late Shah of Iran, during the mid-1970s. The presents offered guests included cases of caviar and champagne, Persian carpets, diamond earrings, and cash (not all accepted these gifts, of course). The parties were attended by reporters, columnists, and publishers, as well as by White House staff people, members of Congress, Supreme Court justices, socialites, and film and television celebrities. Burnett cited a number of instances of favorable publicity that followed. However, most entertainment provided by organizations and individuals seeking approval of a government, industry, or a cause consists of receptions and poses no ethical problems for those participating.

HOW TO HANDLE A CRISIS

Placing full-page advertisements in the Washington *Post* and New York *Times* is almost invariably the first action taken by agents of foreign governments in seeking to influence American public opinion during a crisis. Surveys have shown that a high percentage of the nation's lawmakers and administrators read the *Post* before or soon after arriving in their offices each weekday morning. The *Times,* in particular, is read by opinion leaders not only in the East but throughout the country, and the advertisements gain important visibility, influencing editorial writers and others. Members of Congress often use these political statements in addresses to their colleagues and obtain permission to insert their remarks in the *Congressional Record.* The advertisements generally are followed by personal visits and telephone calls by foreign government agency people and their key supporters. Arrangements are made to place representatives on broadcast network programs. Press conferences are arranged, and newsletters are hastily dispatched to media, government, and other leaders.

For example, after the Israeli invasion of Lebanon in 1982, the Gray & Company public relations firm—hired by the Arab Women's Council and using contributions received from various Arab embassies—placed full-page advertisements in the New York *Times* calling attention to allegations of Israeli violations of human rights in Lebanon. The Arab League and representatives of other Middle East countries mounted similar campaigns. On the other side, the Hannaford Company—retained by the Lebanese Informational and Research Center, which represented conservative Lebanese militia who generally share Israel's goals—countered with its own campaign, joined by the United Jewish Appeal and other groups.

Another important example is the case of South Africa. Because of its apartheid policies, the Republic of South Africa for some years has engaged in an extensive information campaign in the United States. Opinion leaders in politics, government, industry, mass media, and education regularly receive a weekly publication, *South African Digest,* that summarizes a variety of news items about the country. Stories cover the fields of business, industry, sports, communications, religion, the arts, and agriculture. Reprinted are columns and editorials from the world press, as well as the South African press, about political issues facing South Africa. For example, one issue contained an opinion piece from the Washington *Post* headed, "Hypocrisy

International Crisis
Communications

Union Carbide faced an international public relations nightmare in December 1984 when a tragic gas leak at its plant in India killed more than 2500 residents of Bhopal and caused another 50,000 to be treated for gas poisoning.

This was the worst industrial disaster in history. *Time* magazine reported, "There is no way to put a price tag on the damage done to Union Carbide's image in 38 countries, from Nigeria to New Zealand, where it has factories, and the 130 nations in which it sells products."

But Union Carbide was able to generate a level of public respect in the days immediately following the disaster by implementing a crisis communication plan that portrayed genuine company concern for the victims.

The corporation chairman, Warren M. Anderson, flew to India within hours of the accident. Serving as the company's chief spokesman on the disaster, he made himself available to hundreds of reporters clamoring for information. Reporters were impressed with his open manner and found him believable when he said the disaster was Union Carbide's "highest priority."

To back up his statements, Anderson pledged $1 million in immediate relief funds for victims and their families. In addition, he offered a team of technical experts to the Indian government probing the disaster and volunteered to close the company's methyl isocyanate plants around the world. Operations at a similar plant in West Virginia were immediately suspended until the cause of the gas leak was determined.

Contributing to Union Carbide's credibility in the crisis was the company's reputation for safety concerns. The *Wall Street Journal*, for example, reported, "A study by the not-for-profit Council on Economic Priorities, which monitors corporate activities, rated Union Carbide first among the nation's eight largest chemical concerns in compliance with Occupational Safety and Health Administration standards between 1972 and 1979." Other third-party testimonials in the press also referred to Union Carbide's voluntary efforts to make its plants safer and less polluting than legislation required.

All this activity—quick action, genuine concern, openness with the press, Anderson as a central spokesperson, and the company's past record of corporate responsibility—illustrated the basic concepts of effective crisis communications on an international level.

of the Disinvestment Campaign Against South Africa." It was not noted whether the article was a letter to the editor or had been written by a *Post* staff member.

South African Digest and other publications, say South African officials, constitute one way the government can tell its side of the story. They complain that the United States news media report only the unfavorable side of their country, concentrating on the injustices of apartheid or labor strife. Consequently, the *Digest* helps provide "balance" by reporting stories with such headings as "SA Blacks Praised," "Coloured Leader Meets Premier," and "Black Home Ownership Plan."

The government also produces a number of background bulletins with titles such as "South Africa: Good Neighbor in Africa," "The Magic of Gold," and "Multiracial Sport in South Africa." Other programs include the distribution of films, placement of full-page advertisements in prestigious publications, and invitations to key American opinion leaders to take short, government-sponsored tours of the country.

These South African programs are in direct proportion to efforts by various activist groups in the United States to put pressure on American companies to withdraw from doing business in South Africa or not to initiate any investments. Activists, claiming that American money is supporting a racist system, work on four levels: (1) stockholder resolutions to change corporate investment policies in South Africa, (2) petitions to institutional investors—such as universities and religious groups—to sell stock in American companies dealing with South Africa, (3) lobbying for legislation that would restrict trade between the two nations, and (4) picketing.

Representing Foreign Industries in the United States

Industries in other countries also frequently employ American public relations firms to advance their needs in this country. Burson-Marsteller's Carl Levin tells why:

To hold off protectionist moves threatening their company or industry.

To defeat legislation affecting the sale of a client's product.

To support expansion of the client's markets in the United States.

To provide ongoing information on political, sociological, and commercial developments in the United States that could bear on the client's business interests, not only here but worldwide. In the well-organized foreign company, this information is factored into day-to-day policy decisions as well as periodic strategic plans.

One example is the public relations campaign mounted by the Japan Automobile Manufacturers Association, beginning in 1980, to counteract rising public sentiment in America for curbs on the sale of imported cars. The campaign began with a series of full-page advertisements in leading United States newspapers. The advertisements contained interviews with American economists and consumer-group leaders who defended auto imports and free-trade policies. The advertisements were headlined: "In the Consumer's Interest, Dialogues on the Open Market for Automobiles." Said a Japanese auto maker: "We wanted to start communicating with the American public." Concern for American public opinion also was represented in later decisions to build some Japanese vehicles in the United States, with American labor.

Examples of Industry Public Relations in Foreign Countries

On a global basis, public relations as an occupation has achieved highest development in the industrialized nations of the world—United States, Canada, Western Europe, and parts of Asia. It emerges more readily in nations that have multiple-party systems, considerable private ownership of business and industry, large-scale urbanization, and relatively high per capita income levels—which also relate to literacy and educational opportunities.

By the same token, public relations as a specialized activity is less developed in Third World nations in which the vast majority of the citizens are still rural villagers—a situation often accompanied by little industrialization, low levels of personal income, government ownership of major industries, and political activity limited to one official party or a military government.

SOUTH AFRICA On the continent of Africa, South Africa is the only nation that has a sufficient industrial base to support an extensive number of public relations professionals. Although media relations and product publicity were their main concerns in the past, South African practitioners are increasingly getting involved in employee communications, issues management, community relations, and investor relations.

The new orientation of South African practitioners, of couse, is related to factors in the environment of that nation. More than one million South African workers, predominantly black, have joined trade unions since the right to organize was granted in 1979. Now, for the first time, South African industry must deal with large organized groups that want more pay and better employment opportunities. At the same time, the nation is running out of skilled workers to fuel its robust economy. This means increased competition among companies for the available pool of skilled workers.

Productivity is another aspect. South Africa, like many other nations, must raise productivity to compete with foreign markets. One way to do this is to motivate workers through effective communications. Consequently, there is considerable interest in newsletters for the rank-and-file, increased training programs, and even pressure to alter government apartheid policies that restrict the recruitment of black workers.

GREAT BRITAIN

Although its industrial and communication systems were already well developed, it was not until 1910 that public relations in the modern sense was first practiced in Great Britain. In that year the Marconi Company established a department to distribute news releases about its achievements in wireless telegraphy.

Professional public relations counseling was introduced in the country in 1924, when Sir Basil Clarke, a former government press officer, established Editorial Services Ltd. in London. For his first client, a dairy group, he promoted the idea of milk pasteurization, an innovation that had met with some resistance from the public.

The first public relations officer so styled in Britain was Sir John Elliott, appointed in 1925 by the Southern Railway Company.

Today, the British Isles are honeycombed with public relations activities of every nature. For example: it is 9:50 A.M. on a Saturday in August 1982, and Barclays is about to open 54 branches for Saturday banking, an unheard-of practice in the tradition-bound country. A senior manager who has not handled over-the-counter cash for years serves the first customer. As *The Times* of London reported disparagingly, he is "surrounded by a collection of nubile young Barclays cashiers in white dresses with sashbands or printed red T-shirts, clutching balloons and leaflets while a host of public relations staff from head office herd reporters, cameramen and television crews through the doors. . . ." This, of course, was only the press agentry aspect of a sophisticated public relations campaign that included print advertisements, broadcast commercials, letters to customers, news stories, and contacts with editorial writers and columnists.

FEDERAL REPUBLIC OF GERMANY

As noted near the beginning of the chapter, some of the modern elements of public relations, such as countering unfavorable public attitudes through disclosure of operations with publicity and annual reports, were practiced by railroad companies and at least one share-holding corporation in Germany as far back as the mid–nineteenth century. Also, the Krupp Company, which became the premier industrial firm in Germany and the base of the Nazi war power, began considering the value of public relations activities. Its founder, Alfred Krupp, wrote to a financial adviser in 1866:

> We think . . . it is time that authoritative reports concerning factory matters in accordance with the facts should be propagated on a regular basis through newspapers which serve the enlightened public. We can supply the material for this purpose and should qualified experts at times be unavailable, it is our wish to contact respectable newspaper editors ourselves.

Company documents reveal that Krupp was unable to find a qualified person to assist him in the effort. However, his son, Friedrich Alfred Krupp, hired Adolf Lauter in 1893 to establish a news bureau, and the department was integrated into the firm's operations in 1901.

As the Krupp public relations efforts expanded on an international basis, other major industries followed suit. It was the German Dye Trust, controlled by the I. G. Farben cartel, that hired America's first public relations counsel, Ivy Lee, to represent its interests in the United States in 1933, soon after Adolf Hitler had come to power.

Public relations practices in Germany today are progressive and extensive, using many of the techniques employed in the United States.

International Teleconferencing

Conducting conferences in various parts of the world via satellite broadcasting rapidly is becoming an important international public relations tool. Both governments and private industries are using the new technology to advantage.

The Hewlett-Packard Company of Palo Alto, California, for example, in 1983 introduced its HP 9000 computer to 12,000 company representatives and 250 trade editors in two international video conferences: an in-house presentation that was followed two weeks later by a video teleconference for the editors in New York City, Paris, and Frankfurt.

Another teleconference allowed Michael Weiser & Associates, marketing and public relations counsel for the International Monetary Market, a division of the Chicago Mercantile Exchange, to conduct a combination presentation and press conference. Via satellite, Weiser explained the exchange's trading of Eurodollar time deposit future contracts to the press in London and Chicago. Questions from media people in both cities were fielded on the two-way audio, one-way video circuit. The London participants could see and hear everything that went on in Chicago, and could talk to officials in that city. The Chicago press could hear but not see their European colleagues. Raymond D. Minkus, Weiser senior vice-president, termed the teleconference "the most exciting communication event I've ever been involved in . . . and overwhelmingly successful."

A new electronic door-locking system for hotels and motels, called Yale-tronics, was introduced via satellite to approximately 1000 hotel and motel executives, reporters, and sales representatives, by wire and television, in Toronto, Caracas, and London, and, via radio, to the People's Republic of China. The videoconference originated at the Charlotte, North Carolina, headquarters of the Security Products Division of the Scoville Corporation, the former Yale Lock Company.

With Walter Cronkite as moderator in New York and Bill Beutel of WABC-TV as moderator in Cairo, the Overseas Private Investment Corporation, a United States government agency, and the United Nations Development Organization/United Nations Development Program, in 1981 sponsored what was termed a "telemission" to allow several hundred American investors to speak directly with high-ranking Egyptian officials. Hill & Knowlton helped to produce and publicize the videoconference, which originated in Cairo and was viewed in five United States cities.

Because the sponsors' products and services can be fully explained to participants in almost any part of the world, such teleconferences, although ranging in cost from $40,000 to $100,000 or more, are regarded as highly cost-effective and likely to increase substantially in the future.

Domestic use of teleconferencing is discussed in Chapter 21.

Foreign and International Public Relations Organizations

In virtually every country where public relations has become an economic and social force, practitioners have organized to exchange information, maintain and improve standards of professional performance, and aid in the development of international public relations. Codes of conduct are commonplace, and many organizations seek to enhance the standing of their members through certification and accreditation programs. Journals or newsletters are published, awards recognize outstanding performance, and scholarships and other assistance are provided to educational centers.

Public relations associations have been formed in well over 50 countries. In Great Britain more than 2500 practitioners belong to the British Institute of Public Relations, founded in London in 1948. Other European groups include the Association Française des Relations Publiques (France), Deutsche Public Relations Gesellschaft (West Germany), and Associazione Italiana per le Relazioni Pubbliche (Italy). The Public Relations Society of Japan includes well over 1000 members. Other examples are the Public Relations Institute of South Africa and the Zimbabwe Institute of Public Relations.

The International Public Relations Association (IPRA), an individual membership society for professionals with overseas interests, was founded in 1955. IPRA has well over 700 members in more than 60 countries and is seeking further expansion, primarily in much of Latin America, the Middle East, and Asia. Every third year IPRA sponsors a World Congress of Public Relations, which often attracts 600 or more practitioners. Additional regional meetings and seminars are planned.

The International Association of Business Communicators, which was discussed in Chapter 5, maintains an office in London that provides member services, answers inquiries, publicizes events, encourages association development, and maintains liaison with IABC's San Francisco headquarters office.

In Great Britain, IABC competes with the long-established British Association of Industrial Editors. BAIE, however, is composed mainly of people involved in internal, print-oriented communication. Much of the success of the British IABC chapter is attributed to its emphasis on solid programming, broad-based communication efforts with the business community, and members' professional development. In short, the chapter has taken the "umbrella" view of the communication profession rather than the more limited view of print-based or public relations-oriented groups. A high proportion of its members are officers and managing directors of their firms—top-level people with management responsibility for communication.

A thin-tissued, four-page newsletter, *IABC International Update,* is air-mailed monthly to association members outside the United States and Canada. In 1983 these members included 140 in Mexico, 134 in Great Britain, 65 in Australia, 21 in the Philippines, 16 in Sweden, and 10 in South Africa. Extending the IABC accreditation program to these countries is a primary goal.

In addition to the various associations that have been noted, numerous networks of public relations agencies provide clients with services almost anywhere in the world. One of the largest is IPR, which links 90 agencies in 42 countries.

Opportunities and Qualifications for International Work

Because an extensive knowledge of national history, customs, laws, and language is highly desirable, most personnel representing American companies abroad are natives of the countries or regions in which they work. Richard C. Christian, president of Burson-Marsteller, has observed that a new breed of marketing executive is emerging in Europe who is "multinational in attitude and multilingual and young."

Nevertheless, as world markets grow, U.S. companies increasingly will seek out and train executives to fill positions calling for international expertise. They will turn mainly to employees well grounded in the domestic operations of their firms, but who also have obtained substantive knowledge in international aspects of the social sciences, humanities, business, law, or other areas related to their talents and preferences, as well as in public relations. Expertise in one or more foreign languages holds high priority. For orientation, course work in international communications is highly desirable, and graduate study undoubtedly would be an asset. Consequently, the decision to seek an international career should be made during the early academic years. Many students with such ambitions serve internships and gain employment with the news media as desirable starting points.

Taking the United States Foreign Officers' examinations is the first requirement for international government careers. Foreign service work with the innumerable federal agencies often requires a substantial period of government or mass media service in this country before foreign assignments are received.

Most of the USIA's foreign service information officers begin their careers via the Career Candidate Program. Applicants take a written examination offered each December at many locations in this country and abroad. The examination tests general knowledge, English expression, and aptitude for information, cultural, economic, political, administrative, and consular work. To qualify for the USIA, candidates must receive passing grades in all areas and show particular strength in their knowledge of American culture, history, government, and society and current affairs. Other evaluations follow this examination.

After orientation and training in Washington, including geographic area studies and language instruction, a career candidate is assigned to a USIA post abroad for about a year. This training assignment is followed by a tour of duty in positions such as assistant cultural affairs officer, assistant information officer, program assistant, or, occasionally, public affairs officer at a branch of a USIA post in a large country such as Brazil or India. Permanent tenure then may be awarded in the form of a presidential commission. A foreign service information officer usually spends about two-thirds of his or her career abroad. Inquiries about various USIA positions may be made to the agency at 1776 Pennsylvania Avenue, N.W., Washington, D.C., 20547.

Two Case Studies

REPUBLIC OF CHINA ON TAIWAN

In 1971 the United States abrogated its diplomatic relations with the Republic of China on Taiwan and transferred them to the People's Republic of China. The United Nations and most other countries followed suit. The Republic of China, with its 18 million people, suddenly was confronted with the unique and delicate problem of maintaining its independence and its remarkable economic growth as an Asian bastion of the free world.

Certain that unification with Communist China would bring only disaster, the ROC government renewed its commitment to the goal of eventually reuniting all of China under a non-Communist government. It embarked upon a campaign to increase its trade and political ties with other countries and to sway world—and particularly United States—public opinion again to its side.

The public relations effort was enormous. The Republic of China's embassy and consulates in the United States were converted into regional offices forming the Coordination Council for North American Affairs, and the China External Trade Development Council began gaining maximum publicity from its successive economic missions to purchase U.S. products. During one such mission, for example, former Senator Charles Percy of Illinois accepted an invitation to speak at a major press conference in Chicago, which attracted heavy media participation.

The Government Information Office in Taipei stepped up its efforts to convince American opinion leaders, and the public at large, that Free China should not be abandoned. Key political, industrial, and educational leaders were invited, at government expense, to visit Taiwan and view for themselves such evidence of the country's relative political freedom and economic development as they could ascertain during arranged tours. During these visits, slide presentations told the Taiwan story, and the opinion leaders were given slide sets in both English and Chinese for use in presentations which they might choose to make to colleagues and civic groups back home.

Publications were widely distributed, ranging from the handsome, four-color monthly magazine, *Free China Review*, to letter-size pamphlets and a newspaper, *Free China Weekly*, reporting developments on the island.

Within the United States, the Hannaford Company, which numbers General Motors and Trans World Airlines among its almost 50 clients, was engaged to help with the public relations campaign (see Figure 16.4). Among Hannaford's numerous activities were arrangements for ROC officials to visit media editorial boards. A press kit contained basic information about the Republic of China and such pamphlets as those reproducing a *Reader's Digest* article titled, "China—Really Revealed"; a *Wall Street Journal* editorial titled, "China Illusion"; and the reprint of an impassioned Taipei address by famed writer Aleksandr Solzhenitsyn, translated from Russian, titled, "To Free China."

Public relations representatives from the ROC's regional council offices visited scores of U.S. universities, where in 1982 Taiwan students ranked second in number only to those from Iran among the approximately 325,000 international students in this country. There, they spoke to classes and at public meetings, and, in numerous other localities as well, arranged for the showing of ROC films on public and commercial television stations.

The passing by Congress of the Taiwan Relations Act, effective January 1, 1979, reiterating United States determination to continue strong support of Free China, undoubtedly resulted in part from this public relations campaign, the continuing growth of U.S. investments in Taiwan, and commerce between the two countries totaling nearly $13 billion by 1982.

Communist China, of course, has developed its own program designed to influence American public opinion, most notably in visits to the People's Republic arranged for thousands of American media people and others during the last decade.

The future of the Mainland China–Free China struggle is unknown, of

FIGURE 16.4

A graph distributed in a press kit in the United States by the Hannaford Company in behalf of its client carries the required notice for a firm representing a foreign government in this country.

Living Standards in the ROC and Mainland China

Items \ Area	Mainland China	ROC	Items \ Area	Mainland China	ROC
Living Space	3.6 m^2 per person	21.5 m^2 per person	Stereos	Not Available	One per 21.3 persons
Calories	2130 daily	2845 daily	Cameras	One per 1627 persons	One per 20.4 persons
Textiles	10 m per person	28.2 m per person	Sewing machines	One per 21 persons	One per 9.4 persons
Radios	One per 10 persons	Not Available	Bicycles	One per 10.1 persons	Not Available
Tape Recorders	One per 485 persons	One per 11.6 persons	Motorcycles	Not Available	One per 5.2 persons
B & W TVs	One per 110 persons	One per 4.8 persons	Motorvehicles	Not Available	One per 31 persons
Color TVs	Not Available	One per 7.2 persons	Newspapers	One per 25 persons	One per 9 persons

Source: Chung Hua Institution for Economic Research, Taipei, Taiwan, ROC.

THIS MATERIAL IS PREPARED BY THE HANNAFORD COMPANY, INC., 1225 19TH STREET, N.W., WASHINGTON, D.C. 20036, WHICH IS REGISTERED UNDER THE FOREIGN AGENTS REGISTRATION ACT OF 1938, AS AMENDED, AS AN AGENT OF THE REPUBLIC OF CHINA (COORDINATION COUNCIL FOR NORTH AMERICAN AFFAIRS, 159 LEXINGTON AVENUE, NEW YORK, N.Y. 10016). THIS MATERIAL IS FILED WITH THE DEPARTMENT OF JUSTICE WHERE THE REQUIRED REGISTRATION STATEMENT IS AVAILABLE FOR PUBLIC INSPECTION. REGISTRATION DOES NOT INDICATE APPROVAL OF THE MATERIAL BY THE U.S. GOVERNMENT.

course, but some opinion polls reveal strong public sentiment in favor of the Republic of China. In addition, direct investment on Taiwan by U.S. firms now totaling in excess of $547 million—including $186 million in new money in 1982 alone—represents, according to a November 1982 story in *U.S. News & World Report,* "solid proof of their conviction that the island will remain under the Nationalist Chinese flag into the indefinite future."

THE NESTLÉ INFANT FORMULA CONTROVERSY

"Thousands of babies in Third World nations have died or suffered malnutrition due to the marketing and advertising practices of Nestlé."

This was the opening sentence of a widely circulated flyer showing a skull crossed by baby bottles and bearing the legend, "Crunch Nestlé Quick—Boycott Nestlé."

The flyer was only one part of a worldwide campaign begun in the early 1970s against Nestlé, S.A. The Swiss company, founded in 1867, sells nutritive foods, instant coffee and tea, chocolates, and soup in approximately 150 countries.

Nestlé was ill-prepared to meet the onslaught and the boycott that followed: "It had virtually no public relations programs, and felt no need for anything resembling issues management," an official later reported.

So Nestlé made mistakes. The first was to treat the matter as a nutrition issue, but its defense was dismissed as self-serving and simply was not believed. The second was to sue for libel a Swiss activist group that accused Nestlé of "killing babies." The long-drawn-out trial was a public relations disaster that led directly to the boycott, which began in 1977 and ended in 1984.

Church and charitable groups, concerned scientists, consumer advocates, labor organizations, leftist activists, and other groups were drawn into the boycott, initiated by the Minnesota-based Infant Formula Action Coalition (INFACT).

The scientific case against Nestlé and other infant formula companies (although Nestlé was the sole target of the boycott) was based on five major assumptions, according to Carol Adelman, writing in the *Policy Review* publication of the Heritage Foundation:

(1) There had been a dramatic decline in breastfeeding in developing countries; (2) bottlefed infants came largely from the poorest families in developing countries; (3) bottlefed babies in both developing and developed countries had higher disease and death rates than those breastfed; (4) mother's milk was the "perfect" food; and finally (5) corporate promotional practices contributed significantly to a mother's decision to bottlefeed.

None of these assumptions had been proved, but emotions ran high as INFACT supporters angrily charged that "one million babies a year" were dying because, in their opinion, Nestlé's publicity and advertising tactics were causing infant malnutrition and disease from nonsterile bottle-feeding. Activists joined in on the wave of Third World protests against multinational corporations and the institution of advertising itself.

Stunned by the highly organized protests, Nestlé in 1980 hired Rafael D. Pagan, Jr., to formulate a public relations campaign to resolve the dispute. Pagan embarked upon what he termed a *social action management* program designed, as he put it, "to listen with political antennae to the concerns of others . . . to bridge the gap between opposing perceptions involving the corporation and the public." The following steps were taken:

1. The issues were defined and a diagnosis made of the nature of the criticizing groups—"ideologues . . . trendy clergy and lay persons . . . and [those] who were sincerely and morally concerned regarding the problems of poverty and hunger," according to Pagan.

2. A strategy was developed to deal with perceptions, not with facts alone, in the highly emotional environment. "Bold new approaches and flexibility were required to seize the initiative," Pagan told the Public Relations Society of America at its national conference in November 1982. "High levels of risk in terms of market share losses and a high corporate visibility had to be accepted by management."

3. A decision was made to "stick to the issue" at all costs and "not be distracted by the obviously preposterous claims of some critics"—essential to avoid counterproductive confrontation.

4. The social base of the controversy was expanded. "A good number of highly credible church leaders, scientists and opinion makers, who were not in agreement with the critics' questionable tactics and arguments, had remained silent for too long. They now had to be encouraged to speak out."

Two key decisions helped shift the initiative to Nestlé:

1. The company organized the Nestlé Coordination Center for Nutrition, Inc., with Pagan as president. The aim was to focus Nestlé's activities "on the positive task of performing its nutrition work so as to benefit the mothers and babies of the world—especially the Third World. . . ."

2. In addition to steps previously taken to change its marketing policy, Nestlé in 1981 accepted the aims of the recommended code for marketing breast-milk substitutes of the World Health Organization, adopted in Geneva. Detailed instructions enforcing the code were sent to all field managers.

In order to gain complete credibility, the company created an independent audit commission, with former U.S. Secretary of State Edmund Muskie as chairman. The commission met with successive groups of critics and dispatched members to countries throughout the world to monitor Nestlé's implementation of the code and to suggest changes in practices on the basis of new interpretations of the code provisions.

In 1982 the American Federation of Teachers recommended withdrawal from the boycott. Several months later the National Council of the United Methodist Church recommended that, in light of Nestlé's changed attitudes and actions, the church not join the boycott and that Methodist units already involved discontinue their activity. Several other groups reached the same conclusion. All except hard-line activists, it seemed, were being won over.

"We discovered that because business is viewed as aloof, smug, and happiest when left alone to make money," Pagan said, "people are willing to believe the most ridiculous charges against us.

"But once we became aware of the world around us and opened up to human political give-and-take, we were listened to. More important, we were ourselves changed by the process, and we feel better off for it."

The final chapter of the Nestlé case was written in January 1984 when the International Nestlé Boycott Commission (INBC), citing Nestlé's progress with the World Health Organization Code of Marketing and Breastmilk Substitutes, called upon all its member organizations to end their boycott of Nestlé products. The end of the boycott was announced in a joint press conference held by the president of Nestlé and the head of INBC.

Pagan's recommendations to other corporations faced with the need of adopting a program of social action through creative understanding may be summarized as follows:

1. Avoid the imitation of models. Once you understand the nature of the problem, tailor a task force of experienced professionals, in-house if possible, and, as needed, consultants on an ongoing basis. The unit should concentrate on political issues and devise strategies to resolve the immediate conflicts and to head off future ones.

2. Gain a commitment from the company's top executives. Direct access to those officials is equally necessary.

3. Give direct participation to prominent leaders such as those in science, ethics, church, and politics. This will "open a window" to corporate operations. Such an action is fraught with danger but the risk must be taken. Such an audit (as done by Nestlé), to be truly effective, must concern itself with the company's spirit, sensitivity, and attitudes, as well as with its tangible actions.

Pagan closed his PRSA address with a homily, stating in part:

What we in public relations must do . . . is to go back to our roots, to our historic function as the political and human face of business—only this time we must not keep political savvy and humanness to ourselves, but instill it in our clients.

For I believe . . . that the world desperately needs the know-how of business. We have so much more to offer than do our critics. But know-how is not enough.

I believe that, if business prospers in the 1980s, it will be in large measure because business changes its attitudes, opens its spirit, and admits its humanity. It must also acknowledge that its presence in a community where it is welcome and where it is given the privilege to create wealth and profits implies acceptance of a broad array of responsibilities to that community and to the larger world outside our offices.

I know that the overwhelming majority of the people of the world would respond warmly to such a higher level of concern from us.

To me, that is the best kind of public relations, and represents the highest calling of our profession.

QUESTIONS FOR REVIEW AND DISCUSSION

1. What is meant by international public relations? What are some of the reasons for its growth in recent decades?

2. What are some of the difficulties that a corporation is likely to encounter when it conducts business in another country? Enumerate some of the pitfalls that may await its public relations, advertising, and marketing personnel in such enterprises. How may these be partially or fully overcome?

3. What public information activities on an international scale does the United States government conduct?

4. Name four reasons why the United States and many other countries engage in shortwave broadcasting.

5. The United States has been accused by critics in some countries of engaging in a form of "cultural invasion." To what activities are the critics referring?

6. The Pool of News Agencies of Non-Aligned Countries provides information to about 50 countries. Is the nature of this information similar to that provided by the global news agencies? Explain your answer.

7. What are some of the public information activities of the Soviet Union? What role does TASS, the Soviet news agency, play in this regard?

8. List several objectives that foreign governments may have in conducting public relations programs in the United States. How do they seek to achieve their goals? What legal step is involved?

9. By what means is the International Association of Business Communicators enlarging its membership in foreign countries?

10. Enumerate some of the ways in which the Republic of China on Taiwan seeks to influence American public opinion.

CHAPTER SEVENTEEN

Membership Organizations

Corporations often pursue their goals not only individually but in groups called *trade associations.* Similarly, workers band together in labor unions; doctors, lawyers, and so on form professional societies; and business firms within cities join forces in chambers of commerce. Although their membership may be diverse, these organizations have in common the fact that they spend a high percentage of their budgets on public relations and communications.

Indeed, communications—to create unity of action—is the principal purpose for which most of these groups are established. They circulate and share information among their members, speak for them in public forums, educate the public about their members' work, and seek to influence government policies and legislation.

These associations legally are nonprofit organizations. They differ from most nonprofit bodies, however, because they seek to enhance the financial well-being of their members, whether they be individuals or companies. There are thousands of membership organizations in the United States, and their activities constitute an important area of public relations practice.

This chapter will examine public relations work in trade associations, labor unions, professional societies, and chambers of commerce.

Trade Associations

At last count, there were about 2000 trade associations in the United States. Because federal laws and regulations often can affect the fortunes of an entire industry, about 30 percent of these groups are based in the Washington, D.C., area. There, association staffs can monitor congressional activity, lobby for or against legislation, communicate late-breaking developments to the membership, and see government officials on a daily basis.

The membership of a trade association usually consists of manufacturers, wholesalers, retailers, or distributors in the same field. The following is a sampling of trade groups:

National Restaurant Association

Edison Electric Institute (utilities)

National Association of Manufacturers

American Newspaper Publishers Association

American Hotel & Motel Association

Retail Tobacco Dealers of America

Mobile Home Manufacturers Association

Automotive Parts and Accessories Association

Semiconductor Industry Association

American Quarter Horse Association

National Shoe Retailers Association

Printing Industries of America

Lace and Embroidery Manufacturers' Association

Although individual members may be direct rivals in the marketplace, they work together to promote the entire industry, generate public support, and share information of general interest to the entire membership. The Wine Council of California, for example, is made up of various wineries that compete with each other on the store shelf. At the same time, however, the entire membership cooperates to stimulate greater consumption of California wine and even lobby for legislation restricting foreign imports.

A TYPICAL PROGRAM To understand how a trade association uses public relations, let us examine the program of one large organization, the Council of California Growers.

Like similar bodies, the council is financed by dues from members. It is guided by an elected board of governors and a voluntary advisory council of agricultural technicians who analyze issues and assist the board. The council states its purpose clearly:

The mission of the Council of California Growers shall be to help shape favorable public opinion about California agriculture and its major issues of concern to ensure a healthy operating environment for the state's No. 1 industry.

A seven-member staff conducts the public relations program. One member specializes in pesticides, stressing their importance to agriculture and showing how they can be used safely. Other staff members enunciate the council's position on water issues. On both of these major topics, the council at times finds itself at odds with environmental groups. The council also publicizes the growers' point of view on farm labor issues.

Additionally in its external role, the public relations department explains farm issues to urban audiences, takes positions on impending legislation, conducts educational campaigns on campuses of agricultural institutions, and circulates the council's films. It works intensively with the news media. Internally, the department seeks to enlarge council membership and provides services to members.

A VARIETY OF APPROACHES   Trade associations, speaking on behalf of an entire industry, communicate to the public in a number of ways. One way is the preparation of news stories and features for newspapers. Thus, the Air Conditioning and Refrigeration Institute prepares consumer tips on how to use an air conditioner economically in the home, while the Distilled Spirits Council of the U.S. distributes a recipe for cheese fondue that calls for two ounces of Scotch or bourbon. The California Strawberry Advisory Board, using another method, sends a home economist to television talk shows to explain how much vitamin C is in a strawberry and, of course, how to make an easy dessert using the berries.

Trade groups of food growers are particularly adept at getting information in the food sections of newspapers and magazines. They send to editors a steady stream of recipes, features, and photographs of products arranged in mouth-watering servings. Typical is the following, published in a newspaper food section:

Men and women in their sixties and seventies need about one-third less calories than they did in their twenties. However, the need for nutrients apparently does not decline but may actually increase. The National Broiler Council notes that chicken is an ideal protein source for the elderly because it contains fewer calories and has a lower fat content than most red meat. . . .

An extensive multimedia campaign was launched by the California Pistachio Commission in 1984. The purpose was to sell more nuts. Public relations activities included (1) production of a 7 1/2-minute film on how pistachio nuts are grown, for students in junior and senior high schools; (2) distribution of recipe books and articles about using pistachio nuts in salads, pasta, and microwave fudge; (3) dissemination of information to restaurant chains on use of the nut in menus; and (4) appearance of commission representatives on radio and television talk shows. The slogan for the campaign was "You can't say no to a Pistachio." Another slogan under consideration was "Pistachio: Not Just Another California Nut," but the commission thought it might be misinterpreted.

Another kind of public information campaign was launched by the National Institute of Infant Services, a rather grandiose name for a trade association of diaper supply companies. After its business had been devastated by the highly advertised use of disposable plastic and paper diapers, the institute began a public relations campaign to bring young parents back to using professionally laundered cotton diapers.

The institute's approach was to employ a child-care writer to prepare recorded radio spots and newspaper columns in which the virtues of the reusable diaper are emphasized. The writer talked about such problems as comforting a teething child and hiring babysitters, while working in her suggestions about diapers. Newspapers and radio stations used these advice items without charge. The writer also prepared a booklet, "The ABCs of Diaper Rash," distributed by members of the trade association. As a result of this campaign, the companies stopped the trend toward exclusive use of disposable diapers and increased business. This is a good example of how individual companies, banding together in a common activity through a trade group, can strengthen the industry and also benefit as individual suppliers.

Other trade groups may spend the bulk of their money on advertising campaigns. To combat the perception that the chemical industry is an air polluter, the Chemical Manufacturers Association prepared a full-page magazine advertisement dominated by the photograph of a young man holding his small daughter in a swing. The headline stated, "I'm a chemical industry engineer in charge of my plant's air quality. We breathe that air. You can be sure I keep it clean."

Growers of avocados, risking possible charges of sexism, injected sex appeal into an advertising campaign for the fruit. The California Avocado Commission placed half-page advertisements in which slim actress Angie Dickinson appeared in a white leotard. She was quoted as saying that a slice of avocado contains only 17 calories. Near Dickinson's photograph was the question "Would this body lie to you?"

WORKING TO REPEAL A LAW

So far, the discussion has focused on the way trade groups publicize services and products. A vivid example of how trade associations can rally public opinion and influence legislation occurred when the American Bankers Association and the U.S. League of Savings Institutions led a campaign to repeal the federal law requiring financial institutions to withhold 10 percent of interest and dividend payments made to their investors.

The money withheld would go into the federal Treasury as advance payments on the investors' annual income tax. The law was designed to catch cheaters who failed to report dividend and interest income on their returns. An estimated 400 million interest-bearing accounts exist in the United States, most of which would be affected by the withholding law.

The banks and other financial institutions disliked the law because it required additional paperwork for them, and they would lose use of money that ordinarily would stay on account until tax time. Consequently, banks and savings and loans, traditionally strong competitors, banded together through their national trade groups, to seek repeal of the law.

The American Bankers Association provided members with protest post-cards and form letters demanding repeal, for their customers to send to Congress. Form letters-to-the-editor also were distributed. In addition, the association supplied a series of advertisements that member banks could place over their own signatures in local newspapers. The headline on one of these advertisements read:

CONGRESS WANTS A PIECE OF YOUR SAVINGS
WHAT THEY NEED IS A PIECE OF YOUR MIND

The impact of the campaign on Congress was potent. More than 11 million protest letters and postcards deluged Capitol Hill. The same Congress that had passed the law in 1982 succumbed to the pressure and repealed it in 1983. Leaders of the campaign believed that their efforts drew such a huge response because the law hit a raw public nerve—that citizens hated to give the government 10 percent of their investment income months before the annual April 15 tax deadline. This was an instance in which individual self-interest coincided with an industry's self-interest. (Letter-writing campaigns are also discussed in Chapter 15.)

A LOCAL CAMPAIGN

The small city of Blooming Prairie, Minnesota—population 2500—was the site of a week-long demonstration of energy-saving, conducted by the Natural Gas Council of Minnesota in conjunction with the local Lions Club, supported by numerous other civic organizations.

By making a single community the focus of its conservation program, the Natural Gas Council dramatized the fact that a concerted campaign can reduce individual energy bills. The council is a nonprofit group composed of representatives from various investor-owned utility companies. Its sole purpose is energy conservation education. This educational effort is intended to show that the utility companies care for the public welfare and don't coax customers into using unnecessary gas.

By working with them on this money-saving community project, the Natural Gas Council sought to establish good long-range relationships with civic leaders as well as regional and state government officials.

Called "Less-Energy Days," the Blooming Prairie project was publicized by multiple stories in the local newspaper, prepared by the council, and by news releases to regional newspapers, television, and radio stations. Articles prepared by the council described the various events and listed tips for saving energy.

Other methods used included the following:

Formation of a local energy committee, through which a special publication on money-saving methods was issued and participation encouraged.

Publication of endorsements from state and federal energy authorities, making local residents feel "special."

Provision of free home energy audit services to residents and distribution of a home energy audit questionnaire.

Construction of a large thermometer in the center of the city that indicated daily energy usage. This injected a competitive spirit into the week.

Distribution of packets on energy saving to the local schools for students to read.

Although it identified itself and its function in all material, the Natural Gas Council referred media inquiries to the local committee representative. This directed attention to the community leadership. Aided by local enthusiasm, the campaign achieved an 11.5 percent reduction in natural gas consumption and a 7.1 percent reduction in usage of electricity. Blooming Prairie received the President's Award for Energy Efficiency, a national distinction that created pride in the community.

Labor Unions

An estimated 20 million men and women are members of U.S. labor unions and employee associations. Although the vast majority of American workers are not union members (only 17.9 percent of the 110 million employed in the United States), labor unions are very much part of the American scene. This was not always the case. As pointed out in Chapter 3, unions had early confrontations with the Rockefeller family in 1913–1914 at a Colorado coal mine and with Henry Ford in the 1930s when he became the last auto maker to accept unionization of his plants.

Since that time, the purpose of labor unions has not really changed. Members band together to improve their collective financial situation and working conditions through group action. Often the union is a source of social benefits and recreation as well. Members pay monthly dues in return for union representation at the bargaining table with management, pension benefits, and a loud, collective voice in national affairs. Labor union political action committees (PACs) donated $35 million to political candidates in 1982; and union leaders regularly lobby for foreign trade restrictions to preserve jobs for members.

And, as president of the AFL-CIO, with its 14.4 million affiliated members, Lane Kirkland was among the most forceful speakers against President Reagan's policies during the early 1980s. Preparation and staging of Kirkland's speeches required the skill of the labor organization's public relations specialists. Similarly, after the AFL-CIO endorsed Walter Mondale for the 1984 Democratic presidential nomination, its public relations machinery provided Mondale with friendly audiences, banks of telephones for soliciting votes, volunteer campaign workers, and banners and other paraphernalia.

The three largest unions in the United States, in rank order, are the International Brotherhood of Teamsters, United Auto Workers, and the National Education Association. A sampling of other unions could include:

International Brotherhood of Electrical Workers

National Association of Government Employees

International Brotherhood of Police Officers

United Paperworkers International Union

Traditionally, labor unions did not have extensive or comprehensive public relations programs. About the only time an average citizen was aware of a labor union was when there was a contract dispute or a strike. Then, through the mass media, the public saw news stories and television coverage of pickets and often violent confrontations. Media coverage often showed union members in negative, adversarial positions that sometimes inconvenienced the public.

The 1980s, however, are changing union attitudes about public relations and the vital need for it. The president of the United Farm Workers, Cesar Chavez, said in a memo to union leadership: "We cannot continue to battle our opponents in the 1980s with the strategies and technologies of the 1930s . . . or even the 1960s." And picking up a cue from the traditionally better organized trade groups and corporations, Mike Dowling, public affairs director of the American Federation of State, County and Municipal Employees, stated: "I'm running this operation like a corporate communications department."

The increasing emphasis on public relations in the union movement is the result of many problems that the unions face in the 1980s and 1990s. Among them are the following:

1. Loss of public confidence as a result of (a) the conviction and imprisonment of some union officials for embezzlement and misappropriation of union funds for personal gain, (b) a general public perception that union members are overpaid and produce shoddy goods, and (c) a public perception that unions have become too powerful and often take actions that are not in the public interest.

2. Recent court cases affirming the right of employers to break union contracts if the company contends that union wages are a source of financial difficulty. Continental Airlines, as well as the San Jose (California) Unified School District, were allowed to cancel a union contract by claiming that union demands would cause bankruptcy.

3. A steady decline in union membership. Between 1974 and 1984, union membership dropped nearly 16 percent, from 23 million to 19.8 million. One reason is that membership is heavily concentrated in mature if not declining industries like autos and steel, while few inroads are being made to unionize workers in the information and technology industries. Peter F. Drucker, the management expert, wrote in the *Wall Street Journal:* "Some of the gloomier AFL-CIO staffers predict that by 1990 union membership in the private sector will be back where it was before the tremendous unionization wave of the 1930s."

4. Replacement of union workers by automation in industry and agriculture. *Newsweek* magazine estimates that "50 to 75 percent of all U.S. factory workers could be displaced by smart robots before the end of the century."

5. Failure of unions to adapt to the environment of the 1980s. Instead of planning for the future and negotiating with management for the retraining of workers in smokestack industries, they have insisted on preservation of jobs and even higher wages. John Naisbitt, author of *Megatrends,* said: "Labor unions are now entirely preoccupied with survival. All of their actions are short term and defensive in nature. Unless labor unions reconceptualize their role in society, they will continue on their dramatic downhill slide."

Unions are now beginning to respond to some of these problem areas, particularly by improving their public image and recruiting new members. They are also using more sophisticated methods of communication to tell their story to the public. Here are some examples:

The Communication Workers of America ran television commercials nationwide showing its members at work, then doing community service in their free time—for example, a telephone switchman working as a volunteer coach of a neighborhood baseball team. Another advertising campaign, launched in the fall of 1984, was a $2 million effort to persuade phone callers to use long-distance services that employ members of the Communication Workers of America.

The United Brotherhood of Carpenters and Joiners ran a commercial in which a carpenter cut out a union emblem with a jigsaw and placed it on a wooden map of North America. The message read: "We're building the 20th century." The union also publicized a toll-free telephone number that provided information about membership.

The American Federation of State, County and Municipal Employees, when it undertook organizing campaigns in Tucson and Salt Lake City, employed professional polltakers to determine the views of potential members. The union also computerized its mailing list, a practice followed increasingly by unions and trade associations.

The United Farm Workers sent a slick brochure by direct mail that urged citizens to boycott a supermarket chain because, the union charged, the stores sold nonunion lettuce. In another situation, the UFW included in the direct mail packet a handwritten facsimile letter from a young woman farm worker who allegedly had suffered sexual harassment at the hands of a grower. The strategy, according to union leader Cesar Chavez, was: "Polls show that women are more sensitive to social issues than men. This works to our advantage since women do most of the shopping and because each piece in our mail program features an appeal to women on the sexual harassment issue."

The United Steelworkers of America used advocacy advertising to protest a plan by U.S. Steel Corporation to import semifinished steel slabs from Great Britain (see Figure 17.1). The union feared that this would take away jobs from American steelworkers, but the advertisements were directed to the self-interests of stockholders in other American steel companies who, it was asserted, would be harmed by the proposed U.S. Steel–British agreement.

The International Ladies' Garment Workers Union uses national television spots that encourage consumers to "look for the union label" as a symbol of quality. The slogan dates back to the 1930s, when the phrase was used in a union-produced musical revue that ran for 1108 performances on Broadway. On another front, 17 trade unions and associations awarded a $400,000 contract to Burson-Marsteller public relations for the purpose of raising consumer consciousness with an information campaign titled, "Crafted with Pride in America."

The AFL-CIO has produced a series of television programs aimed at winning public support for its point of view on such topics as job creation, labor laws, plant closings, and workers' rights. The programs are designed to counteract the television shows of its archrival, the U.S. Chamber of Commerce, called "It's Your Business."

The Teamsters Central States Pension Fund, rocked by scandal, sought credibility by tripling the fund's accounting staff and hiring a well-regarded

FIGURE 17.1

Use of colonial-style headline type gives extra impact
to this advertisement by
United Steelworkers of
America protesting a pro-
posal by the U.S. Steel Corporation to import British
steel.

"The British Are Coming, The British Are Coming"

AND AMERICA'S STEEL INDEPENDENCE IS GOING

**A Message Especially for Stockholders
Of American Steel Companies**

As Independence Day approaches this year, Paul Revere's warning takes on a new and dangerous meaning.

It a deal struck by the U.S. Steel Corporation and the government-owned British Steel Corporation goes through as planned it could be the beginning of the end for America's steel independence. As the union representing America's steelworkers, we find that prospect extremely disturbing. and for reasons that go beyond our self-interest. It is, for example, contrary to the best interests of stockholders of other American steel companies.

Here's what is involved.

U.S. Steel wants to quit making steel at its Fairless Hills plant in Pennsylvania, but continue to operate the Fairless finishing facilities. It wants to accomplish this by importing millions of tons of semi-finished steel "slabs" from the British Steel Corporation's Ravenscraig plant in Scotland.

U.S. Steel says it would be cheaper to do this than to modernize the steel-making facilities at Fairless. To make the deal more palatable for Americans, the British say they will create a so-called "private corporation" just to operate Ravenscraig.

That's supposed to take the sting out of U.S. Steel's importation of subsidized foreign steel. Of course it ignores the fact that the Ravenscraig technology is a direct result of subsidized investment. The same is true for the entire money-losing British steel operation.

The fact is that Ravenscraig would not exist but for this subsidy.

It is indeed ironic that in the past, even U.S. Steel has charged that government subsidies saved British steel from bankruptcy and allowed it to install new technology while encountering huge operating losses.

The logical, fair and reasonable thing for U.S. Steel to do is to forget the British deal and modernize Fairless. Earlier this year our union negotiated a new contract that will save the steel industry some $3 billion. As the largest steel company, U.S. Steel will realize the largest share of those savings. Our one condition was that these savings be plowed back into existing facilities.

Certainly this is consistent with the industry's long-stated objective of modernizing its facilities to sharpen its competitive edge.

If U.S. Steel is allowed to consummate this unlikely match, it can make other deals with the Europeans, Brazilians, Nigerians, Taiwanese and others who have the capacity to flood the American market with subsidized steel. Then, one by one, other American steel companies will be forced to follow suit to remain competitive. If they don't, they'll be priced out of the marketplace.

The losers in such a scenario would be the thousands of new unemployed American steelworkers, the stockholders of other smaller American steel companies, and the American people, who would find themselves dependent on foreign producers for our steel needs, including steel for defense purposes.

Smaller steel companies are especially vulnerable. One half or more of their investment in steel properties is tied up in iron and coal mines, and the ovens and furnaces that produce steel. If those facilities are made useless by a national shift to imported raw steel, all of that will have to be written off. The effect on balance sheets and the market value of investments is obvious.

The United Steelworkers of America is determined that this will not happen. We have committed the resources of our union to this total effort. We will employ every legal means at our disposal to block this dangerous precedent.

★ Within recent days, we have engaged counsel to file on our behalf a petition charging that the proposed transaction is illegal under U.S. trade laws.

★ We will press fully our rights under existing collective bargaining agreements with U.S. Steel, as well as our rights under the National Labor Relations Act.

★ We will call for a Congressional investigation of the entire proposed U.S. Steel–British Steel arrangement—including the issuance of subpoenas to examine all documents and notes exchanged by the parties and the relative costs of producing steel at Ravenscraig and the extent of subsidization.

★ We will carry out an extensive information program to provide the public with the facts about this important case.

On April 28, the President of our union, Lloyd McBride, testified before the Steel Caucus of the U.S. House of Representatives about this matter. He closed with these words.

"We may be witnessing here the beginning—for the U.S.—of the internationalization of American steel production. And when steel companies engage in what is essentially unfair trade for the purpose of shifting their production base out of steel for the advantage of their shareholders, then our union and its members are being severely injured and sorely used. Our steel communities are severely impacted. And, I submit to you, our nation is the worse for it. When private decisions have such widespread, devastating consequences on the private and public sectors, those decisions should not be made unilaterally without a thorough investigation of the consequences.

The consequences of U.S. Steel's proposed joint venture with the British Steel Corporation are indeed great. An entire industry as we have come to know it is at stake. U.S. Steel is single-handedly attempting to forge a new national steel policy for America.

The Steelworkers of America are prepared to fight this dangerous proposal at every juncture. And we want your help.

We invite others who share our views on this important matter—especially steel company stockholders—to join us. We'll be glad to provide you with additional information.

United Steelworkers of America
Lloyd McBride, President
Five Gateway Center
Pittsburgh, Pennsylvania 15222

financial institution as the fund's money manager. In addition, the new executive director of the fund made himself readily available for media interviews.

The American Federation of Teachers hired comedian Steve Allen to host a series of programs on public and cable television titled, "Inside Your Schools." Another labor group, the National Education Association, paid $1.5 million for a television advertising campaign to illustrate teachers' good works.

It is too early to tell if increased communication activity will help solve the challenges facing labor unions today. Public relations and advertising campaigns can focus the spotlight on the positive functions that unions are undertaking, but real success will depend on how the public perceives the various messages and how the unions are able to reconceptualize themselves in the coming years.

Professional Associations

Members of a profession or skilled craft organize for mutual benefit. In many ways, their goals resemble those of labor unions in that they seek improved earning power, better working conditions, and public acceptance of their role in society. Unlike their labor union counterparts, however, members of professional organizations place emphasis on setting standards for professional performance, establishing codes of ethics, determining requirements for admission to the field, and encouraging members to upgrade skills through continuing education.

In some cases, professional organizations have quasi-legal power to license and censure members. This is true of organizations such as the American Medical Association and the American Bar Association. In most cases, however, professional groups use the techniques of peer pressure and persuasion to police the particular profession or skilled craft.

In general, professional associations are national in scope with district, state, or local chapters. Many scientific and scholarly associations, however, are international, with chapters in many nations. A good example is the International Communication Association (ICA), a group of academics and communication experts. Another is the International Communications Executives Association. There is even an international association of executives who specialize in managing trade groups and professional societies.

Organizations such as the Public Relations Society of America and the International Association of Business Communicators are classified as professional associations. Here is a sampling of other organizations:

Society of Automotive Engineers

American Library Association

American Nuclear Society

American Public Health Association

National Association of Life Underwriters

American Surgical Association

Public relations specialists for these organizations use the same techniques as their colleagues in other branches of practice. They address both internal and external audiences through a variety of communication tools, including newsletters, brochures, videotapes, slide presentations, radio and television spots, news releases, and direct mail packets.

Like their counterparts in trade groups and labor unions, professional associations are responsible for monitoring legislation that may affect the status or earning power of members. Many professional associations maintain a Washington office or one in the state capital and employ lobbyists to advocate positions. One of the most politically active groups is the American Medical Association, which is sensitive to any legislation that affects Medicare payments, malpractice liability, hospital funding, and medical research.

Public service is the hallmark of many professional associations, and a number of programs make pertinent information available to the public.

The Philadelphia Bar Association, for example, offers Dial-Law, which answers common legal questions over the telephone with taped messages on more than 70 topics. It informs callers about the association's Lawyer Referral and Information Service. More than 30,000 calls a year are received. To publicize the service, the bar association prepared radio and television announcements featuring Joseph A. Wapner, a white-haired retired judge widely known to viewers for his judicial role on "The People's Court." The number of annual calls doubled when the Wapner announcements were aired. Several other local bar associations have produced simple brochures on how to write a will, establish a trust fund, or file a grievance in small claims court. A number of local medical societies also offer advice and referral by phone.

Both the Public Relations Society of America and the International Association of Business Communicators maintain a reference library available to the public or to answer queries by telephone. Another method of public service is a speakers' bureau directory, listing members who are willing to talk at meetings of civic and business groups. Such a directory was published, for instance, by the Society of Die Casting Engineers.

Public relations activity on behalf of individual professionals is a relatively new development in the 1980s. Traditionally, lawyers and medical doctors did not advertise or seek to publicize themselves in any way. The taboo arose in part from the rules and regulations of the professional societies. Until recently, many medical societies prohibited their members from hiring public relations firms. But the Supreme Court, in several cases, said that such regulations infringed on free speech. And the Federal Trade Commission ruled in 1980 that the American Medical Association couldn't tell its members not to advertise.

Professionals such as lawyers and doctors still feel uncomfortable about advertising their services, but they are less reserved about using a public relations firm to publicize their talents. Consequently, public relations specialists are working to get lawyers, doctors, and dentists on radio and television talk shows, sending out press kits about their specialties, and even arranging speeches before targeted audiences. Figure 17.2 shows the cover of a pamphlet put out by the dental association.

One New York firm, Lobsenz-Stevens Inc., turns its physicians into authors, developing a book idea, outlining it, finding a ghost writer, and obtaining a contract. According to the *Wall Street Journal,* one plastic surgeon even went on " . . . a national publicity tour, discussing his book on talk shows and in newspapers. He signed autographs in book stores. He appeared on the Today show."

FIGURE 17.2

Clever graphics draw attention to an American Dental Association publication that urges readers to use good dental-care practices. (Copyright by the American Dental Association. Reprinted with permission.)

keep
your teeth
all your
life!

The newspaper observed another trend: "Medical associations are also hiring public relations firms to publicize new or controversial techniques. 'Fat suctioning' was the focus of a press briefing publicized by Doremus & Co. recently for the American Society of Plastic and Reconstructive Surgeons." As the *Journal* article suggests, such factors as the increased competition among medical doctors in urban areas, and the national craze for physical fitness, have stimulated physicians' reliance on public relations specialists. Both as individual professionals and as members of professional societies, doctors, like their counterparts at the bar or in the dentist's office, find it useful to let the public know what they have to offer.

Chambers of Commerce

A *chamber* is an association of business persons, often joined by professional men and women, working to improve their city's commercial climate and to publicize its attractions. State chambers of commerce and, nationally, the Chamber of Commerce of the United States provide guidance to local chambers and speak for business interests before state legislatures and the federal government. The primary interest of most chamber of commerce members, however, is focused on local affairs.

The local interest is manifested in many ways. In many cities, the chamber of commerce is the public relations arm of city government. The chamber staff often produces the brochures and maps that are sent to individuals who seek information about visiting the city or are considering moving to the area. Chambers also conduct polls and compile statistics about the economic health of the city, including data on major industries, employment rates, availability of schools and hospitals, housing costs, and the like.

Other activities that a public relations specialist might do for a chamber include the following:

1. Write and edit a monthly newsletter for members

2. Write and disseminate news releases about economic developments

3. Arrange receptions and tours for visiting business people who are considering building a new plant in the city

4. Prepare background information for chamber officials who are testifying at city council meetings

5. Contact membership organizations about the possibility of selecting the city for a convention

Chambers of commerce play the role of community booster: they spotlight the unique characteristics of a city and sing its praises to anyone who will listen. Chambers often coin a slogan for a city, such as "Furniture Capital of Indiana" or "Artichoke Capital of the World." Ironically, the small city of Coalinga, California, whose downtown was devastated by a severe earthquake in 1983, has as its slogan, "Coalinga—A City Going Places!" To which columnist Herb Caen in the San Francisco *Chronicle* added, "Right. In all directions."

Because of the nature of their membership, chambers of commerce tend to be conservative politically and to support business growth actively. Generally, they campaign for expansion of their cities in the belief that "bigger is better." This attitude at times places chambers in opposition to other community groups, who want slower, more controlled growth that will reduce the impact of massive urbanization.

A Case Study

GIVING THE POTATO A BOOST

The problem. According to an attitude-and-usage study for the Potato Board, Americans generally believed that the potato contains too many calories and little nutritional value. It was widely thought to be fattening.

The attack. The Potato Board, a nonprofit organization representing 18,000 potato growers, hired Ketchum Public Relations recently to correct the misconceptions. Coordinating its efforts with a campaign by an advertising agency, the firm sought to convince people that the potato is nutritious and can be eaten without causing weight gain.

How the public relations campaign was conducted. Major magazines including *Good Housekeeping* and *Reader's Digest* published articles praising the food value of potatoes. These articles were arranged through personal contact with the editors. Ketchum's test kitchens developed low-calorie, nutritious recipe ideas involving the potato, for distribution with photographs to newspaper food editors. A syndicated food columnist, Barbara Gibbons, was commissioned by Ketchum to write *The Potato Lover's Diet Cookbook*. To publicize the book, she made television and radio appearances nationwide. Nearly a half million requests for the book were filled by the Potato Board. Other writers about food also were placed on the air.

To reach the youth audience, Ketchum prepared an educational program. For high schools, where young people generally become weight-conscious, the program included a *Teaching Guide on Potatoes and Weight Control* and a home economics education film. In elementary schools, distribution of menu puzzles helped to get potatoes onto school menus. The puzzles taught a nutrition lesson in the classroom.

Special effort was aimed at food service outlets, to increase use of potatoes in menus. This included a Special Gourmet Program, built around the idea of putting potatoes on diet plates. Marriott Hotels successfully tested two Slender Gourmet Plates—Omelette O'Brien and Sole of Discretion—and the program then was taken to other food outlets.

Results. A survey taken before the program began showed that 35 percent of consumers believed potatoes are too fattening; only 53 percent thought them to be nutritious. In a follow-up survey two years later, 25 percent thought potatoes were too fattening; and 84 percent considered potatoes nutritious—a striking change in attitude. Four years later, a slightly different survey showed that consumers believed potatoes to be the most nutritious of the starches and not the highest in calories. Quite correctly, 73 percent believed that potatoes contain no fat. Over the 6-year period, per capita consumption of potatoes rose 4 percent.

Analysis shows that this program was aimed at several target audiences—those who prepare food at home, commercial food services, individuals worried about weight control, and students learning about nutrition. Among the principal methods of information used were newspapers, magazines, books, radio and television, films, teachers, and personal appearances.

QUESTIONS FOR REVIEW AND DISCUSSION

1. Trade associations, like other membership organizations, often have headquarters in Washington, D.C., or a state capital. Why?

2. Describe how the Council of California Growers seeks to influence public opinion about the role of agriculture.

3. In what ways do organizations of food growers try to influence home-makers through newspapers and on the broadcast media?

4. How did the diaper industry increase the public demand for professionally laundered cotton diapers?

5. What did the American Bankers Association do to generate public support for the repeal of a federal law?

6. Labor unions often get a "bad" press. Why?

7. What challenges do labor unions face in the 1980s?

8. What are the differences and similarities among trade groups, labor unions, and professional associations?

9. What decisions stimulated the trend for members of the professions to use public relations counsel?

10. Chambers of commerce often are described as the public relations arm of city government. Why?

CHAPTER EIGHTEEN

Social and Cultural Agencies

Much of society's effort to enrich contemporary life and to improve each individual's well-being is carried on by nonprofit organizations that depend heavily upon volunteer help and financing. Skillful public relations is crucial to the success of these organizations.

This chapter examines the role of public relations in this field, whose motivating forces are service, charity, and education. The diverse categories of organizations grouped under this broad heading are analyzed. The public relations goals of nonprofit agencies are listed and the methods are studied on how practitioners achieve them.

Without donations to finance their work, nonprofit social, cultural, health-care, educational, and religious agencies would collapse. Raising money is a constant challenge in which public relations representatives are directly or indirectly involved. This chapter explains fund-raising principles and methods. It closes with an examination of hospital public relations as an example of how practitioners employed by social agencies carry out their tasks.

The Challenges of Public Relations
for Philanthropic Organizations

Social service, cultural, medical, educational, and religious organizations exist to improve the human condition. Communication is essential to the success of these organizations. Since these groups are not profit-oriented, the practice of public relations in their behalf differs somewhat from that in the business world.

As discussed in Chapter 14, public relations in business life includes a defensive element, to protect the company or client from attack, as well as an assertive element, to improve the company's reputation with both external and internal audiences. Significant political, economic, and social forces are at work against the corporate community as a whole and portions of it in particular. Suspicion exists among many individuals and groups that companies, especially large corporations, make excessive profits and gouge the public. More specifically, to cite one example, the antinuclear movement applies heavy pressure against utility companies that hope to open or expand nuclear power plants.

Most social agencies are not seriously troubled by such negative image problems. Usually the agencies are regarded as "good guys" of society. This is not universally true, though. The causes some of them espouse generate emotional opposition from persons who hold conflicting views. Also, tax-exempt organizations that maintain a high profile with mass-market fund-raising operations such as telethons and direct mail sweepstakes offering huge prizes stir doubts among many members of the public concerning their credibility. Suspicious citizens ask, "Is most of the money raised really going to the cause? Or is it being eaten up by administrative costs or diverted for someone's private benefit?" Occasional news stories reporting misuse of nonprofit funds give some substance to these concerns. Fortunately, such suspicions do not rub off on most of the many thousands of well-motivated, carefully operated nonprofit social agencies. Their public relations representatives, however, should prevent trouble by emphasizing the open nature of their financing and operations. A good approach is, "If you have any questions, ask us. We will show you precisely how we work."

The word *nonprofit* should not be construed to mean that these agencies are free from money worries. Quite the opposite is true. For many of these groups, obtaining operating funds is a necessity that dominates much of their effort. Without generous contributions from companies and individuals whose money is earned in the marketplace, nonprofit organizations could not exist. As an indication of the scope of philanthropy in the United States, and of the money needed to keep voluntary service agencies operating, American contributions to charity are estimated at $65 billion annually, according to the American Association of Fund-Raising Counsel (see Figure

FIGURE 18.1

This pie chart shows percentage of total charitable giving in the United States in 1983, totaling $64.9 billion.
(*Source:* American Association of Fund-Raising Counsel, New York.)

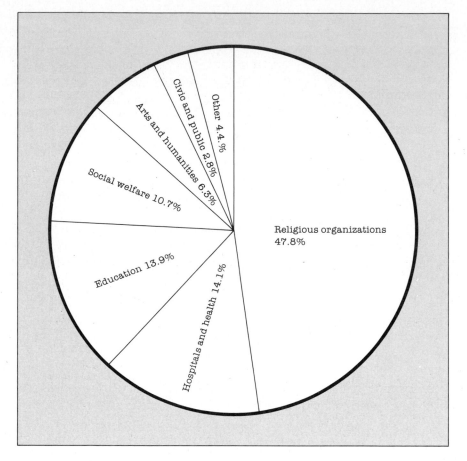

18.1). Additional funds are donated to specialized nonprofit organizations that do not fall under the "charity" mantle, and still more are contributed by federal, state, and local governments. Competition among nonprofit agencies for their share of donations is intense.

In general terms, nonprofit organizations are of two types—*service,* typified nationally by the Visiting Nurse Association and the Boys Clubs of America, and *cause,* whose advocacy role is exemplified by the National Safety Council, the National Rifle Association, and the National Association for the Advancement of Colored People (NAACP). Frequently organizations have dual roles, both service and advocacy.

Demands upon volunteer service agencies to enlarge their programs of aid to the needy are growing, in part because of efforts in recent years to reduce federal welfare services and shift increased responsibility for humanitarian work to service organizations.

The Seven Categories of Social Agencies

For purposes of identification, nonprofit organizations and their functions may be grouped into seven categories.

1. *Social service agencies.* These serve the social needs of individuals and families in many forms. Among prominent national organizations of this type are Goodwill Industries, the American Red Cross, Boy Scouts and Girl Scouts of America, and the YMCA. Local and regional chapters of these organizations carry out national programs at the community level.

2. *Health agencies.* Many of these combat a specific illness through education, research, and treatment, while others deliver generalized health services in communities. Typical national organizations include the American Heart Association, the American Cancer Society, the National Multiple Sclerosis Society, and the March of Dimes.

3. *Hospitals.* Public relations work for hospitals is a large and expanding field. The role of a hospital has taken on new dimensions. In addition to caring for ill and injured patients, hospitals conduct preventive health programs and provide other health-related social services that go well beyond the traditional institutional concept. Hospitals may be tax-supported institutions, nonprofit organizations, or profit-making corporations.

4. *Religious organizations.* The mission of organized religion, as perceived by many faiths today, includes much more than holding weekly worship services. Churches distribute charity, conduct personal guidance programs, provide leadership on moral and ethical issues in their communities, and operate social centers where diverse groups gather. Some denominations operate retirement homes and nursing facilities for the elderly. At times, religious organizations assume political roles to further their goals. The nondenominational Salvation Army provides the needy with shelter, food, and clothing. It has a vigorous public relations program to generate support and raise funds.

Churches in particular feel the pressure for increased private agency participation in welfare work. President Reagan's cutback in federal humanitarian services coincided with the recession of the early 1980s. In some cities churches operated food lines and provided emergency shelter for the homeless. Funds from local governments helped to pay the bill in certain instances.

A recent study by the Brookings Institution, *Fiscal Capacity of the Voluntary Sector,* stated in this regard: "Because religion occupies a stable, central role in American life, religious institutions will be looked to as a backup finance and delivery mechanism by other subsectors . . . particularly . . . in the human service field."

Commenting on these developments in a speech to the Baptist Public Relations Association, Don Bates, a prominent New York public relations counselor, pointed out: "Certainly the shift from government to private initiative provides more opportunities to serve people in need and to prove a case in the process for what your organization does and how it benefits the community."

5. *Welfare agencies.* Most continuing welfare payments to persons in need are made by government agencies, using tax-generated funds. Public information officers of these agencies have an important function, to make certain that those entitled to the services know about them and to improve public understanding of how the services function.

6. *Cultural organizations.* Development of interest and participation in the cultural aspects of life falls heavily into the hands of nonprofit organizations. So, in many instances, does operation of art, history, and natural science museums; libraries; and musical organizations such as symphony orchestras. Such institutions frequently receive at least part of their income from government sources; many are operated by city, state, and federal governments. Even government-operated cultural institutions depend upon private-support organizations such as Friends of the Museum to raise supplementary funds and help operate their facilities.

Regardless of their ownership and management, government or private, cultural institutions require vigorous public relations activity. Creation and publicizing of programs, formation of support groups, development of a volunteer staff, and fund-raising involve the public relations staff either directly or on a consulting basis.

7. *Foundations.* The hundreds of tax-free foundations in the United States constitute a major source of funding for nonprofit organizations. Money to establish a foundation is provided by a wealthy individual or family, a group of contributors, an organization, or a corporation. The foundation's capital is invested, and earnings from the investments are distributed as grants to qualified applicants in the field for which the foundation was established. Often foundations offer matching grants, in which recipient organizations are given money equal to the amount they raise from other sources. A variation is the challenge grant, in which the foundation offers a gift of a specified amount if the recipient organization can raise an identical sum.

The public knows about such mammoth national organizations as the Ford Foundation, the Rockefeller Foundation, and the National Science Foundation. It is probably not aware, however, of many smaller foundations, some of them extremely important in their specialized fields, that distribute funds for research, education, public performances, displays, and similar purposes.

Giving away money constructively is more difficult than most people realize. Again, public relations representation has a significant role. The requirements of a foundation must be made known to potential applicants for grants. Inquiries must be handled and announcements of grants made. In the case of the very large national foundations, at least, general information explaining the organization's work and its social value needs to be circulated. This is necessary, among other reasons, to allay uneasiness among some persons who suspect that the tax-exempt status of foundations is a device to avoid paying a fair share of the tax burden. In small foundations, public relations work is handled by the executive secretary, but most larger foundations have a public relations staff of one or more persons.

From this summary, the student can see what diverse, personally satisfying opportunities are available to public relations practitioners in the social agency fields.

Public Relations Goals

Every voluntary agency should establish a set of public relations goals. In doing so, its management should heed the advice of its public relations staff members, for they are trained to sense public moods and are responsible for achieving the goals. Emphasis on goals will vary, depending upon the purpose of each organization. In general, however, nonprofit organizations should design their public relations to achieve these objectives:

1. Develop public awareness of the organization's purpose and activities

2. Induce individuals to use the services the organization provides

3. Create educational materials—especially important for health-oriented agencies

4. Recruit and train volunteer workers

5. Obtain funds to operate the organization

The sections that follow discuss ways in which each of these goals can be pursued.

PUBLIC AWARENESS The news media provide well-organized channels for stimulating public interest in nonprofit organizations and are receptive to newsworthy material from them. Newspapers usually publish advance stories about meetings, training sessions, and similar routine activities. Beyond that, much depends upon the ingenuity of the public relations practitioner in proposing feature articles and photographs. Television and radio stations will broadcast important news items about organizations and are receptive to feature stories and guest appearances by organization representatives who have something interesting to tell. *Stories about activities are best told in terms of individuals, rather than in high-flown abstractions*. Practitioners should look for unusual or appealing personal stories—a retired teacher helping Asian refugee children to learn English, a group of Girl Scouts assisting crippled elderly women with their shopping, a volunteer sorting donated books for a Friends of the

Library booksale who discovers a rare volume. A physician who speaks to the American Heart Association and explains warning signs for a certain heart ailment in an unusually graphic manner perhaps would be willing to give the same lecture on a local magazine-type television show.

Creation of events that make news and attract crowds is another way to increase public awareness. Such activities might include an open house in a new hospital wing, a concert by members of the local symphony orchestra for an audience of blind children, or a Run-for-Your-Life race to publicize jogging as a protection against heart trouble. A museum of history may sponsor a history fair for high school students with cash prizes for the best papers and projects.

Novelty stunts sometimes draw attention to a cause greater than their intrinsic value seems to justify. For example, a bed race around the parking lot of a shopping center by teams of students at the local university who are conducting a campus fund drive for the March of Dimes could be fun. It would draw almost certain local television coverage and raise money, too. Each team would have a banner over the bed it pushed, and a streamer across the finish line would proclaim the cause. The possibilities of event publicity are countless.

Publication and distribution of brochures explaining an organization's objectives, operation of a speakers' bureau, showings of films provided by general headquarters of national nonprofit organizations, and periodic news bulletins distributed to opinion leaders are quiet but effective ways of telling an organization's story. Fund-raising, which will be discussed later, always stimulates public awareness.

USE OF SERVICES Closely tied to creation of public awareness is the problem of inducing individuals and families to use an organization's services. Free medical examinations, free clothing and food to the urgently needy, family counseling, nursing service for shut-ins, cultural programs at museums and libraries, offers of scholarships—all these and many other services provided by nonprofit organizations cannot achieve their full value unless potential users know about them.

The news media are valuable in this work. So is word of mouth. Boys and girls become interested in joining the Scouting organizations when they hear about the good times their friends are having in them. Awareness of Planned Parenthood's counseling services and Meals on Wheels food delivery to shut-ins is spread in neighborhood conversations.

Because of shyness or embarrassment, persons who would benefit from available services sometimes hesitate to use them. Written and spoken material designed to attract these persons should emphasize the ease of participation and, in matters of health, family, and financial aid, the privacy of the consultations. A health organization attracts clients with material describing the symptoms of a disease and urging those who suspect such symptoms in themselves to see a physician or to inquire at the organization's office. The American Cancer Society's widely publicized warning list of cancer danger signals is an example of this approach.

CREATION OF EDUCATIONAL MATERIALS

Public relations representatives of nonprofit organizations spend a substantial portion of their time preparing written and audiovisual materials. These are basic to almost any organization's program.

The quickest way to inform a person about an organization is to hand out a brochure. Brochures provide a first impression. They should be visually appealing and contain basic information, simply written. The writer should answer a reader's obvious questions: What does the organization do? What are its facilities? What services does it offer me? How do I go about participating in its activities and services? The brochure should contain a concise history of the organization and attractive illustrations. When appropriate, it may include a membership application form or a coupon to accompany a donation.

Organizations may design logos, or symbols, that help them keep their activities in the public eye. Figure 18.2 shows two graphics the American Heart Association uses as reminders of its message.

FIGURE 18.2

The American Heart Association supports its campaign to increase public awareness of the value of exercise with a broad range of posters and pamphlets, of which these are samples. (Reprinted with permission of The American Heart Association.)

Another basic piece of printed material is a news bulletin, usually monthly or quarterly, mailed to members, the news media, and perhaps to a carefully composed list of other interested parties. This bulletin may range from a single duplicated sheet to an elaborately printed magazine. Tax-exempt organizations that meet Postal Service standards as religious, educational, scientific, philanthropic, agricultural, labor, veterans', or fraternal groups may be able to obtain special bulk third-class nonprofit rates that let them mail their bulletins at approximately one-fourth the first-class rate.

A source of public relations support for national philanthropic organizations is the Advertising Council. This is a not-for-profit association of advertising professionals who volunteer their creative and technical skills for organizations such as the American Red Cross, the National Alliance of Business, and the National Committee for the Prevention of Child Abuse. The council creates public service advertising campaigns in the public interest. Through its efforts Smokey the Bear became a household figure in the fight against forest fires.

The council handles more than 30 public service campaigns a year for nonsectarian, nonpartisan organizations, chosen from 300 to 500 annual requests. Newspapers and radio and television stations publish or broadcast free of charge the advertisements the council sends them. The sponsoring agency reimburses the council for the cost of campaign materials.

One of the best ways to tell an organization's story succinctly and impressively is with an audiovisual package. This may be a slide show or a videotape, usually lasting about 20 minutes, to be shown to community audiences and/or on a continuing basis in the organization's building. As described earlier, an organization can create its own slide show and perhaps make its own videotape program, or specialists may be hired to do the work. Local chapters of national organizations usually are able to obtain audiovisual materials from their national headquarters.

VOLUNTEER WORKERS

A corps of volunteer workers is essential to the success of almost every philanthropic enterprise. Far more work needs to be done than a necessarily small professional staff can accomplish. Recruiting and training volunteers, and maintaining their enthusiasm so they will be dependable long-term workers, is an important public relations function. Organizations usually have a chairperson of volunteers, who either answers to the public relations (often called community relations) director or depends upon the director for assistance.

What motivates men and women to volunteer? The sense of making a personal contribution to society is a primary factor. Volunteer work can fill a void in the life of an individual who no longer has business or family responsibilities. It also provides social contacts. Why does a former business leader living in a retirement community join a squad of ex-corporate executives who patrol its streets and public places each Monday, picking up wastepaper? The answer is twofold: pride in making a contribution to local well-being and satisfaction in having a structured activity that partially replaces his former business routine. For the same reasons, the retired executive spends another day each week as a hospital volunteer, working in the supply room. Those motives are basic to much volunteerism.

Social prestige plays a role, too. Appearing as a model in a fashion show that raises funds for scholarships carries a social cachet. So does selling tickets for a debutante ball, the profits from which go to the American Cancer Society. Serving as a docent, or guide, at a historical museum also attracts individuals who enjoy being seen in a prestigious setting. Yet persons who do well at these valuable jobs might be unwilling to stuff envelopes for a charity solicitation or spend hours in a back room sorting and mending used clothing for resale in a community thrift shop—jobs that are equally important. Such tasks can be assigned to those volunteers who enjoy working inconspicuously but dread meeting the public.

Recruiters of volunteers should make clear to potential workers what the proposed jobs entail and, if possible, offer a selection of tasks suitable to differing tastes. A volunteer who has been fast-talked into undertaking an assignment he or she dislikes will probably quit after a short time.

The public relations practitioner can help in recruiting by supplying pamphlets, slide shows, speakers, and other information resources to explain the organization's purpose, to show the essential role its volunteers play, and to stress the sense of achievement and social satisfaction that volunteers find in their work. Testimony from successful, satisfied volunteers is an excellent recruiting tool. Instruction materials and speakers should be provided to train new volunteers. Those who meet the public may receive small badges with their names and the word *Volunteer* printed on them.

Like all persons, volunteers enjoy recognition, and they should receive it. Certificates of commendation and luncheons at which their work is praised are just two ways of expressing appreciation. Hospital auxiliaries in particular keep charts showing how many hours of service each volunteer has contributed. Service pins or similar tokens are awarded for certain high totals of hours worked. Whatever form of recognition it chooses, every organization using volunteers should make certain that it says, "Thank you!"

The extent to which volunteerism contributes to community life is demonstrated by a survey in a Midwestern city of 140,000 inhabitants. The study found that 200 local organizations and local chapters of national organizations used volunteers. To celebrate National Volunteer Recognition Month, a committee working through the Voluntary Action Center obtained nominations of 30 volunteers for outstanding work. The city's newspaper printed their names and published profile articles about the four mentioned most frequently. This illustrates what can be done at the community level to publicize the work of social agencies.

Thus, active, satisfied volunteers do more than provide a work force for an organization. They also form a channel of communication into the community.

FUND-RAISING At board meetings of voluntary agencies, large and small, from coast to coast, the most frequently asked question is, "Where will we get the money?" Discussion of ways to maintain present programs and to add new ones revolves around that inevitable query. Obtaining operating funds is a never-ending problem for organizations, except for a few blessed with endowments sufficient for their needs.

Although some voluntary organizations receive funds from government sources, many depend entirely upon money they raise in contributions. Because agencies receiving government funds frequently find the subsidies inadequate, they must join in the scramble for donations.

Fund-raising has been elevated to a highly developed art involving sales psychology, financial skill, ingenuity, and persistence. It may be as simple as sale of raffle tickets to neighbors, or as complex as intricate forms of accounting that provide donors with cherished tax shelters. The largest donations usually are made by corporations and foundations. Of the approximately $65 billion that Americans donate to philanthropic causes each year, however, nearly 90 percent comes from individuals. Depending upon their needs, voluntary organizations may try to catch minnows—hundreds of small contributions—or angle for the huge marlin—large gifts from big-money sources.

Public relations representatives participate directly in fund-raising by organizing and conducting solicitation programs, or they may serve as consultants to specialized development departments of their organizations. If their needs are substantial, organizations often employ professional firms to conduct their campaigns on a fee basis. In that case, the organization's public relations representatives usually have a liaison function.

Fund-raising on a major scale requires high-level planning and organization. Various departments and divisions, each with a particular area of responsibility, may be set up. An organizational chart for a typical fund-raising campaign is shown in Figure 18.3.

THE RISKS OF FUND-RAISING Fund-raising involves risks as well as benefits. Adherence to high ethical standards of solicitation and close control of money-raising costs, so that expenses constitute only a reasonable percentage of the funds collected, are essential if an organization is to maintain public credibility. Numerous groups have suffered severe damage to their reputations from disclosures that only a small portion of the money they raised was applied to the cause they advocated. The rest was consumed in solicitation expenses and administrative overhead.

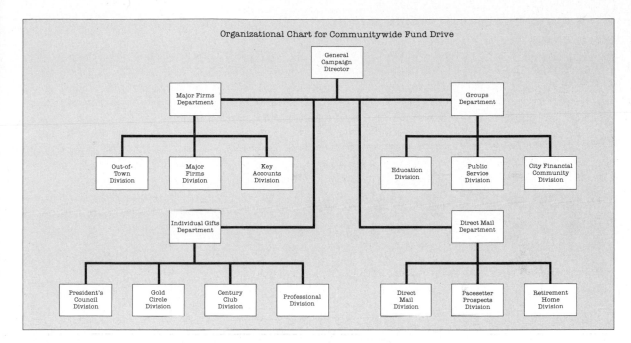

Organizational Chart for Communitywide Fund Drive

FIGURE 18.3

This chart shows the basic structure of a fund drive. Specialized groups should be added in each division as desirable to meet local geographical and organizational needs.

These fund-raising and administrative costs fluctuate widely among organizations, depending upon circumstances, and it is difficult to establish absolute percentage standards for acceptable costs. New organizations, for example, have special start-up expenses. In general, an organization is in trouble if its fund-raising costs are more than 25 percent of what it takes in, or if fund-raising and "administrative overhead" exceed 40 to 50 percent.

Some examples among respected national organizations include the following: the American Cancer Society applies 78.2 cents of every dollar it raises to its anticancer work; solicitation costs are 12.1 cents and administrative overhead 9.7 cents. The American Heart Association applies 75 cents to its work, with 14 cents for solicitation and 11 cents for administration. The Girl Scouts of America applies 71 cents to its work; 1.9 cents go to solicitation and 27.1 cents to administration. The United Way of America averages about 13 percent for fund-raising and overhead costs.

In contrast are incidents such as these: the Asthmatic Children's Foundation collected $9.9 million during several years, but only $1.4 million went to research and treatment of sick children. An Indianapolis civic club raised $32,000 for a charitable cause by selling tickets to a benefit circus but netted less than $3,000 after the promoter took his fee and expenses. A promoter who sold tickets for a fund-raising game involving a California wheelchair basketball team kept 70 percent of the gross.

To protect its reputation, a social agency should publish an annual report that specifies expenses as well as income. It should encourage its solicitors to know the financial facts so they can answer questions. Reputable agencies do this.

Charitable groups should be extremely cautious about lending their names to promoters who sell merchandise or conduct events on their behalf, using their names. Such promoters usually use paid solicitors, whose compensation eats up much of the revenue, and load on heavy administrative costs. The net income received by the group often is small, and its credibility may be damaged by deceptive, high-pressure methods the promoter employs.

MOTIVATIONS FOR GIVING An understanding of what motivates individuals and companies to give money is important to anyone involved in fundraising. An *intrinsic desire to share* a portion of one's resources, however small, with the needy and others served by philanthropic agencies is a primary factor—the inherent generosity possessed in some degree by almost everyone. Another urge, also very human if less laudable, is *ego satisfaction.* Those who are motivated by it range from donors to large institutions who insist that the buildings they give be named for them, down to the individuals who are influenced to help a cause by the knowledge that their names will be published in a list of contributors. *Peer pressure* is a third factor; saying "no" to a request from a friend is difficult. The cliché about "keeping up with the Joneses" applies here, openly or subtly. Some organizations exploit this pressure almost ruthlessly by holding dinner meetings at which those present are urged to announce their pledges publicly before their fellow guests.

While many companies are truly desirous of contributing a share of their profits to the community well-being, they also are aware that news of their generosity improves their images as good corporate citizens. Individuals and corporations alike may receive income tax deductions from their donations, a fact that is less of a motivating factor in many instances than the cynical believe.

Fund-raisers know that while many contributors desire nothing more than the personal satisfaction of giving, others like to receive something tangible—a plastic poppy from a veterans' organization, for example. This fact influences the sale of items for philanthropic purposes. When a neighbor high school girl rings the doorbell, selling candy to raise a fund for a stricken classmate, multiple forces are at work—instinctive generosity, peer pressure (not to be known in the neighborhood as a tightwad), and the desire to receive something for the money given. Even when householders are on a strict diet, they almost always will accept the candy in return for their contribution rather than merely give the money. The son of one of this book's authors once tried to sell a school benefit candy bar to a wealthy retired motion picture and television star but was turned down for the 50-cent purchase because the ex-star said he was dieting. Word of this refusal spread among the junior high crowd in the town and, almost inevitably, to their parents.

THE COMPETITIVE FACTOR   The soliciting organization also should analyze the competition it faces from other fund-raising efforts. The competitive factor is important. The public becomes resentful and uncooperative if approached too frequently for contributions. Deserving causes may fail in their campaigns if other organizations have been vigorously in the field ahead of them. That is why the United Way of America exists, to consolidate solicitations of numerous important local service agencies into a single unified annual campaign.

The voluntary United Way management in a community, with professional guidance, announces a campaign goal. Pledges are collected from corporation managements, from their employees through voluntary payroll deduction, from other individuals, and from any additional available sources during a specified campaign period. The money is distributed among participating agencies according to a percentage formula determined by the United Way budget committee.

TYPES OF FUND-RAISING   These are the principal types of fund-raising used by philanthropic organizations:

Corporate and foundation donations

Structured capital campaigns

Direct mail

Sponsorship of events

Telephone solicitations

Entrepreneurship

1. *Corporate and foundation donations.* Organizations seeking donations from major corporations normally should do so through the local corporate offices or sales outlets. Some corporations give local offices a free hand to make donations up to a certain amount. Even when the decisions are made at corporate headquarters, local recommendation is important. Requests to foundations generally should be made to the main office, which will send application forms if the organization's request falls within the scope of the foundation's purpose.

Corporations make donations estimated at more than $3 billion a year to all causes, of which roughly 40 percent goes to education. Much of this is distributed in large sums for major projects, but an increasing amount is going to smaller local programs. A directory, *Guide to Corporate Giving,* published by the American Council for the Arts in New York, describes the contribution programs of 711 leading corporations, which provide about $1 billion of the $3 billion total. As an example, in a typical recent year the largest contributor was Exxon, with $45.1 million; Atlantic Richfield was second with $28.3 million. Corporations often fix the amount they will contribute each year as a certain percentage of pretax profits. This ranges from less than 1 percent to more than 2.5 percent.

Increasingly, corporations make donations on a matching basis with gifts by their employees. The matching most commonly is done on a dollar-for-dollar basis; if an employee gives $1 to a philanthropic cause, the employer does the same. Some corporations match at a 2-to-1 rate or higher. This system tends to spread corporate gifts on a wider basis in a community to smaller, less prominent, voluntary agencies in which individual employees take an interest. By the mid-1980s, nearly 900 companies had matching-gift programs, although some were limited to higher education.

2. *Structured capital campaigns.* The effort to raise major amounts of money for a new wing of a hospital, for an engineering building on a campus, or even for the reconstruction and renovation of San Francisco's famed cable car system is often called a capital campaign.

Because of the significant amounts involved, campaign organization and fund-raising techniques become much more sophisticated than soliciting funds through bulk direct mail or selling candy and cookies from door to door. In a capital campaign, emphasis is placed on substantial gifts from corporations and individuals. One key concept of a capital campaign, in fact, is that 90 percent of the total amount raised will come from only 10 percent of the contributors. In a $10 million campaign to add a wing to an art museum, for example, it is not unusual that the lead gift will be one or two million dollars.

Capital campaigns require considerable expertise and, for this reason, many organizations retain professional fund-raising counsel. There are a number of firms in the country that offer these services, but the most reputable are those belonging to the American Association of Fund-Raising Counsel. Member firms adhere to a strict code of ethics and serve clients as management consultants. In other words, they charge on the basis of staffing required and do not take a percentage of the funds raised.

The preparation for a capital campaign, whether managed by a professional counseling firm or by the institution's own development staff, is almost as important as the campaign itself.

The first step often is a survey among community leaders and influential people to determine if there is support for the proposed campaign. Do community leaders, particularly those who will be asked to make major donations, think the cause is just and needed by the community? Is this the right time for a capital campaign? Do the proposed plans make sense? In many cases, this kind of feedback causes revision in plans and cost of the

| Writing Direct Mail Letters | A large percentage of fund-raising for charitable institutions is conducted through the direct mail letter. The purpose of the letter, of course, is to produce a response—that is, a donation. Writers of fund-raising letters have learned the best approaches: |

1. Make use of an attention-getting headline.

2. Follow with an inspirational lead-in on why and how a donation will benefit clients of the charitable agency.

3. Give a clear definition of the charitable agency's purpose and objectives.

4. Humanize the cause by giving an example of a child or family that benefited.

5. Include testimonials and endorsements from credible individuals.

6. Ask for specific action, and provide an easy method for the recipient to respond. Self-addressed stamped envelopes and pledge cards often are included.

7. Close with a postscript that gives the strongest reason for reader response.

project. A finding that community leaders are not sold on the idea signals the need for an intensive cultivation program to brief potential backers thoroughly on the project and to get their support. Cultivation programs also (1) encourage community leaders to participate in the project at an early stage and (2) identify major donor prospects.

The next step is to compile a list of companies and wealthy individuals who will personally be approached for a major contribution. It is common practice for campaign organizers to establish a specific amount of money they will request from each leading potential donor. It is also an axiom of capital fund-raising that prospective donors are asked to contribute by someone who is their peer. Thus the president of one major company will solicit the president of another leading firm. It is also a principle of effective fundraising that those who ask for gifts have already made their own pledge.

The fund campaign usually is organized on quasi-military lines, with division leaders and team captains. An advance gifts division concentrates on anticipated large donors, so that when the campaign is formally kicked off the leadership can announce that a substantial amount already has been pledged toward the goal. This provides impetus and inspiration to the bulk of the volunteer solicitors, and it creates a bandwagon effect for community support.

Donors often are recognized by the size of their gifts—and terms such as *patron, contributor,* or *founder* are used. In addition, major donors may be given the opportunity to have rooms or public places in the building named after them. Hospitals, for example, prepare "memorial" brochures that show floor plans and the cost of endowing certain facilities.

3. *Direct mail.* This is an expensive form of solicitation because of the costs of developing or renting mailing lists, preparation of the printed matter, and postage. An organization can conduct an effective local, limited direct mail campaign on its own if it develops an up-to-date mailing list of "good" names known to be potential donors and can provide enough volunteers to stuff and address the solicitation envelopes. Regional and national organizations, and some large local ones, either employ direct mail specialists or rent carefully chosen mailing lists from list brokers.

The old days when direct mailing pieces came addressed to "Occupant" are largely gone, thanks to the wonders of computers. Now the letters arrive individually addressed. Inside, the appeal letter may bear a personalized salutation and include personal allusions within the text, such as: "So you see, Mr. Smith, that this opportunity. . . ."

The abundance and diversity of mailing lists for rent is astounding. One company offers more than 8000 different mailing lists. A common rental price is $30 per thousand names. Other lists cost more, depending upon their special value. A random selection gives an idea of the targeted audiences a direct-mail solicitation can reach: 9,500 women accountants; 34,930 fertilizer dealers; 29,000 corporation attorneys; 14,700 family and marriage counselors; 49,000 parent-teacher associations; and 2.5 million college students.

In direct mail campaigns, economic success depends upon getting the mailing pieces into the hands of potential donors while not wasting postage in mailing to those who probably are not. Marketing research firms feed demographic, geographic, and psychographic information into computers; the computers then produce mailing lists focused on the desired audience. Such targeting greatly increases the predictable percentage of successful contacts from the mailing.

One marketing research firm, for example, identified 34 human factors such as age, sex, education, and levels of economic well-being. It fed these factors into computers along with a list of 36,000 zip code markets and produced 40 neighborhood types. An organization interested in reaching one of these types—the supereducated top income level, for example— could use suitable mailing lists broken down to postal area routes.

Attractive, informative mailing pieces that stimulate recipients to donate are keys to successful solicitation. The classic direct mail format consists of a mailing envelope, letter, brochure, and response device for making a contribution, often with a postage-paid return envelope.

Another essential factor in direct mail solicitation is getting recipients to open the mailing piece. This need has resulted in development of many

FIGURE 18.4

The March of Dimes annual WalkAmerica fund-raising event distributes forms on which participants list names of their sponsors and the amount pledged. (Reproduced by courtesy of the March of Dimes.)

attention-getting graphic and psychological devices. One attention-getting device that generates curiosity is to omit the name of the organization on the envelope. An address will be given, but the receiver must open the envelope to determine who sent the letter. Once a well-chosen recipient has been induced to open the envelope and begin reading the message, much of the selling work has been done. After that, the appeal of the message and the degree of ease with which the recipient can respond to it will determine the result.

The *Direct Mail List,* published semiannually by Standard Rate & Data Service, Inc., is a basic reference book for direct mail lists.

4. *Sponsorship of events.* The range of events a philanthropic organization can sponsor to raise funds is limited only by the imagination of its members.

Participation contests are a popular method. Walkathons and jogathons appeal to the current American emphasis on using the legs for exercise. Nationally, the March of Dimes holds an annual 32-kilometer WalkAmerica in 1100 cities on the same day (see Figure 18.4). Local organizations do the same in their own communities. Bikeathons are popular, too. The money-raising device is the same in all such events: each entrant signs up sponsors who promise to pay a specified amount to the fund for each mile or kilometer the entrant walks, jogs, runs, or cycles. If an entrant obtains several sponsors, at rates from a few cents up to $1 a mile, the contributions mount up.

Staging of parties, charity balls, concerts, and similar events in which tickets are sold is another widely used approach. Often, however, big parties create more publicity than profit. Other methods include sponsorship of a motion picture opening, a theater night, or a sporting event. Barbecues flourish as money-raisers in Western cities. Used-book sales can be excellent profit-makers. Raffles, either on their own or in connection with a staged event, are profitable. So are home tours. This is only a sampling of methods popular with smaller organizations, which normally do the work themselves without professional assistance.

Sale of a product, in which the organization keeps a portion of the selling price, ranges from the church baked-goods stand, which yields almost 100 percent profit because members contribute homemade products, to the massive national Girl Scout cookie sale, which grosses about $150 million annually. Light bulbs, candy, grapefruit, Christmas fruitcake, and magazine subscriptions are other commodities sold in this manner.

A key to success in all charity-fund sales is abundant publicity in the local news media. Posters, movable-letter signs, and announcements at organization meetings also help. Use of paid advertising rarely is worthwhile because its cost eats seriously into the profit margin.

Direct solicitation of funds over television by *telethons* is used primarily in large cities. A television station sets aside a block of air time for the telethon, sponsored by a philanthropic organization. During the telethon, the host and a parade of well-known guests take turns making on-the-air appeals for contributions. Donors telephone an announced number, where a battery of volunteers record the pledges. Mixed in with the appeals are bits of entertainment by the guests and prearranged on-camera presentation of large checks by corporations and other givers. Best known of the national telethons is the one conducted annually by comedian Jerry Lewis for muscular dystrophy. Telethons are expensive to stage and usually suitable only for organizations that can command entertainment talent. Collection of the telephoned pledges also may be a problem.

5. *Telephone solicitations.* Solicitation of donations by telephone is a relatively inexpensive way to seek funds but of uncertain effectiveness. Many groups hold down their cost of solicitation by using a WATS (Wide Area Telephone Service) line that provides unlimited calls for a flat fee, without individual toll charges. Some people resent receiving telephone solicitations. If the recipient of the call is unfamiliar with the cause, it must be explained clearly and concisely—not always easy for a volunteer solicitor to do. The problem of converting verbal promises by telephone into confirmed written

pledges also arises. The normal method is for the sponsoring organization to send a filled-in pledge form to the donor for signature as soon as possible after the call, reminding him or her of the promise to contribute and enclosing a reply envelope.

6. *Entrepreneurship.* Operation of gift shops, bookstores, coffee shops, and similar businesses is another source of revenue for nonprofit organizations. Museums, hospitals, and institutions of learning often use this method. Some large nonprofit organizations carry this approach much further by participating in real estate syndicates, publishing magazines that carry paid advertising, and entering the cable television business. Volunteer help often staffs the service businesses, enabling them to be profitable. However, many voluntary organizations lack the experience required to enter more complicated ventures than the gift shop level and may lose money if they do so. Another problem is opposition from commercial firms if the nonprofit organization's project impinges substantially on their fields of livelihood.

Any nonprofit organization contemplating operation of a business should check the tax laws, which require that the enterprise be "substantially related" to the purpose of the nonprofit group.

Muscular Dystrophy Is a Top Fund-Raiser

One of the most successful nonprofit organizations is the Muscular Dystrophy Association. Its primary special event fund-raiser is the Jerry Lewis Annual Labor Day Weekend telethon, which raised $30.7 million in 1983.

Although the telethon is the most visible of MDA's fund-raisers, it is only part of the story. The organization gets the bulk of its money ($76 million total in 1982, with only $28.5 million from the telethon) through direct-mail appeals, local solicitations by its two million volunteers, corporate sponsorship by such firms as Budweiser and 7-Eleven Stores, and income from the money it has been able to bank and invest over the years.

MDA's success is attributed to several factors. First, the organization has been around for more than 30 years and has had the services of Jerry Lewis for almost as long. During this period, the Labor Day Telethon has become practically a national institution that gives high visibility to MDA. Second, MDA is a centralized, tightly run organization that approaches its tasks in a coordinated, unified way. Other health-care agencies tend to be federations of more-or-less autonomous local chapters. Third, the appeal is on behalf of children struck by a serious disease; this tends to generate significant public response.

An Example: Hospital Public Relations

The expanding field of hospital service provides a blueprint of how public relations can work effectively in the nonprofit institutional field. Even relatively small hospitals employ professionally trained practitioners. Hospital public relations serves several distinct audiences, external and internal, and uses a wide variety of techniques to accomplish its multiple goals.

In addition to their traditional role, most hospitals now function as community health centers, providing a range of social services, preventive medicine, and counseling for the community. Although the great majority of privately owned hospitals are established as nonprofit institutions, competition between hospitals within a city often is strong. Like hotels, each must keep its occupancy high to offset its heavy operating expenses. Frequently this economic fact leads hospital managements into vigorous marketing practices. These require an energetic, innovative public relations program.

A glance at the annual reports of a few typical hospitals, often published as tabloid sections of their local newspapers, shows the proliferation of hospital services. In addition to the increasingly complex medical treatments hospitals provide, supplemental services include alcoholism rehabilitation, babysitter training, childbirth and parenting education, patient and family counseling, home care, hospices for the terminally ill, pastoral care, sexual dysfunction treatment, senior citizen living centers, a smokers' hotline giving advice on how to quit, speech pathology, a physician referral service, hospital tours for children, a discount hotel room booking service for families of seriously ill patients, rental of infant car seats for safety, and Tel-Med, which informs telephone callers on scores of health topics, such as "Understanding Headaches" and "Are Old-Age Freckles Dangerous?" (see Figure 18.5).

Hospital public relations programs have four basic audiences: the patients, the staff, the media, and the community as a whole. The four audiences overlap, but each should receive a special focus. This is accomplished by using the spoken, written, and visual techniques discussed in Part Five.

Although hospitals exist for humanitarian purposes, they face two significant public relations problems: extremely high charges that have risen much faster than the cost of living, and a widely held perception of some hospitals as cold institutions that don't care enough about individual patients.

Moreover, the expansion of supplemental hospital services has not won universal applause. Some physicians look upon it uneasily. In a Northern city, for instance, proliferation of services by two major hospitals prompted a group of prominent physicians to send a letter of protest to the county medical society. A copy of the letter published in the local newspaper created lively public discussion. The doctors attributed part of the higher patient charges to diversification into "wellness centers, satellite clinics, unnecessary equipment, grandiose expansion and marketing plans, excessive administrative overhead, and unsettling competition." They asserted: "These increased costs have a detrimental social and economic impact on the community."

FIGURE 18.5

Hospitals have enlarged their role in community life with illness-prevention programs such as free taped health information and advice messages. (Reprinted by permission of Marian Medical Center, Santa Maria, Calif.)

CounseLine
Parent Talk
Tel-Med®

TEL-ED

Free Health Education by Telephone!

SANTA MARIA VALLEY
928-7721
LOMPOC
734-2881

Sponsored by:
Marian Medical Center
and
The Mental Health Association

TEL-ED: A FREE COMMUNITY SERVICE

The managements of the hospitals responded with vigorous defenses of the importance of their supplementary services, but the doctors' complaint made an impact on citizens already disturbed by their high hospital and medical insurance bills.

Here are specific steps the public relations departments of typical U.S. hospitals have taken to explain the work of their institutions and to defuse criticism. Other hospitals use the same or similar methods.

A "Direct Line" telephone extension within the Sutter Community Hospitals, Sacramento, California, allows patients and community members to register complaints and suggestions to the administration 24 hours a day.

A market research survey for the North Mississippi Medical Center at Tupelo disclosed that 25 percent of the respondents believed the hospital to be less concerned with its patients' well-being than other area hospitals were. In response, the administration began a public relations program called "Close enough to care." An advisory committee of employees was formed. Staff members were asked to sign a "caring pledge" and were given a daily checklist and lapel care pin. An audiovisual presentation, shown to all employees and 3000 community members, depicted how healing is enhanced when caring and compassion are evident. Ratings on the "caring" question were high in later patient surveys. Simultaneously, monthly employee turnover decreased, indicating improved staff morale.

Hermann Hospital, Houston, Texas, has four internal television channels. Three of these provide information for patients about such topics as diet and exercise. One is an educational channel for medical staff, showing lectures, tapes, and films.

Patients at Mercy Hospital, Cedar Rapids, Iowa, pay a small fee to play bingo twice a week over a closed-circuit television system. Cash prizes are awarded. These games brighten the patients' days.

Like many other hospitals, the Baptist Medical Center–Montclair, in Birmingham, Alabama, offers classes and programs to meet community health-care needs, including an exercise class for senior citizens, a class in cardiopulmonary resuscitation, and training in learning to live with stress.

To improve staff communication, the Lankenau Hospital in Philadelphia has a confidential Dial-A-Tip internal telephone service, on which employees may ask questions about personnel policies and similar issues. Questions are sent anonymously to an administrator for answers. The service is especially popular among night-shift workers.

Eager to obtain as much television coverage as possible, the public relations staff of St. Joseph Medical Center, Burbank, California, organized a team of health-care representatives ready to provide local television stations with immediate comments on health-oriented news stories. The staff also proposes medical story ideas to the stations. Assignment editors find the group such a quick, authentic, and willing source that the hospital has appeared on local television an average of 225 times a year—a splendid way to build public awareness, especially considering that Southern California has 278 other hospitals.

Bethesda Hospital, Zanesville, Ohio, installed a mile-long fitness trail to implement its Human Energy Fitness Program. At regular intervals along the 1-mile jogging trail are exercise stations for stretching, bending, and other forms of muscular development. Each day about 350 patients, hospital employees, and area citizens use the trail.

Three Case Studies

THE BRAILLE INSTITUTE: QUIET, EFFECTIVE

Public relations work for voluntary social service agencies is largely devoid of the emergencies and negative perceptions often encountered in other areas. Many practitioners, including recent graduates, hold jobs in organizations of this type; the Braille Institute of Los Angeles provides a good example of how the public relations department of a rather large, mostly privately financed social service agency functions.

The Braille Institute serves 22,000 legally blind persons in Southern California. The legally blind are persons who may have up to 10 percent of normal vision in the better eye. Only a small portion of its $6 million annual income is obtained from government sources. The agency is widely recognized as a socially valuable, effective organization. Its public relations staff consists of seven persons.

At the Braille Institute, the public relations department serves three clearly defined audiences: *the general public, the legally blind users of the institute's services,* and *the internal audience of staff members and volunteer workers.*

The first, external, objective is to show the public how the Braille Institute's services can assist the blind to become more independent. This includes educating the public about the nature of blindness. External public relations material is carefully selected to present blind persons as normal human beings of widely diverse backgrounds who share a common affliction, not as "freaks." Success stories of accomplishments by the blind are emphasized. For the second audience, the clientele—or students, as the institute calls them—the public relations objective is to help the legally blind function as well as possible in the world. This is done through training programs and provision of informative material, in raised Braille characters, in large print, and on tape cassettes, about the world they cannot see (Figure 18.6). To serve the third audience, staff members and volunteer workers, the department provides materials about the professional field and news about developments within the institute.

FIGURE 18.6

To increase public understanding, Braille Institute issues cards showing the alphabet in print, with the Braille equivalent in raised dots below each letter. (Reprinted by permission of Braille Institute.)

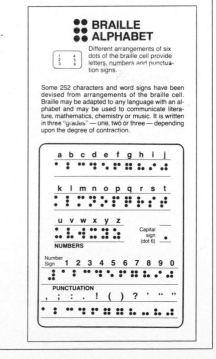

The department is organized in the following way:

Director of communications.

The *assistant director* serves as editor of *Light,* the institute's 32-page annual report, and *Scene,* its 8-page quarterly news bulletin, both intended to further public education about blindness (see Figure 18.7). Creates brochures and programs; handles publicity for special events; and prepares television and radio material.

The *communications assistant* edits the *Librarian,* distributed quarterly to patrons of the institute library, with information about new books, cassettes, records, and library events; aids the assistant director in editing *Scene;* handles audiovisual equipment; and works on general assignment.

The *coordinator of community activities* directs the institute's speakers' bureau and tours. Two 13-minute films, one describing the institute's work and the other explaining blindness to children, are available for speakers to show. The speakers are institute professionals and blind students. In a typical month, they appeared before 15 audiences of service clubs, church groups, women's clubs, and schools, and made professional presentations to seven seminars and training sessions. Contacts developed in this way sometimes induce community organizations to sponsor institute events for its students, such as a deep-sea fishing trip, a snow trip, and the Braille Institute Optimist Olympics.

The *communications assistant* helps the coordinator of community services; edits *Inter-View,* a monthly internal publication; and handles general assignments.

The *Braille publication editor* edits the *Braille Mirror,* a monthly general-interest magazine printed in Braille, partially funded by the Library of Congress and supplied free to blind readers, and *Expectations,* an annual anthology in Braille for children. Articles in the *Braille Mirror* cover the latest trends in social, cultural, political, and economic aspects of life. They are reprinted by permission from national magazines without charge.

The *assistant to the Braille publications editor* works on *Outlook,* a publication for students, in large print, Braille, and tape cassettes.

The department also has an office manager and a typist.

Radio and television public service announcements created by the department further public education and help to publicize institute events. The institute staff prepares its own slides and has done videotape production. Growth of cable television, especially the channels showing movies, has opened a new public relations medium. Since movies run varying lengths,

FIGURE 18.7

Shown here is a part of a page from *Scene,* the quarterly newsletter of Braille Institute, in which the organization emphasizes the importance of recruiting volunteer workers. (Reprinted by permission of Braille Institute.)

BRAILLE INSTITUTE

Scene

Volume 11, Number 1
Spring, 1983

Volunteers Are the Heartbeat of Braille Institute

Someone once said, "Volunteers are the heartbeat of Braille Institute." That someone is right. They are.

But volunteers are even more than Braille Institute's "heartbeat," they are part of its spirit as well.

Volunteers do willingly, for no one forces them or pays them, all kinds of unusual and ordinary, thanked for and thankless, boring or exciting, routine and last-minute work.

Hard work, satisfying work, unselfish work, important work. They record for those who are blind, drive students to and from classes, help in the press and library, visit those without sight in their homes and give of themselves in countless other ways.

One of those important other ways is volunteering to teach at Braille Institute.

Mildred Heredeen is a volunteer teacher. So is George Austin. And Betty Crotts and Jim Pearlman — and 55 more at Braille Institute in Los Angeles. There are many, many others in each of Braille Institute's centers.

What's so important about being a volunteer teacher?

Jacqueline Shahzadi, director of Student Training, puts it this way. "Volunteers are absolutely vital to our educational program," she says. "If it weren't for volunteers, our program wouldn't be of the quality it is now."

Jane O'Connor, director of Volunteer Services, states, "We receive a wealth of new ideas and enthusiasm from our volunteer teachers. They give us a spectrum of information that would be almost impossible to duplicate any place else."

How do the volunteer teachers themselves feel about teaching Braille Institute's blind students?

Mildred Heredeen teaches "Our Town" a discussion class which has guest speakers such as Vince Scully, Charles Champlin and the consuls general from the United Kingdom and Sweden. Mildred has a great feeling of love and respect for those in her class. She feels the class gives a spark to her life and that, she says, is very very satisfying.

George Austin, who teaches in-house orientation and mobility, is dedicated to Braille Institute and its people. George likes to teach. "I get more out of it than anyone," he says.

Betty Crotts, who also teaches in-house orientation and mobility, and Jim Pearlman, who conducts the "People and Places" class, have the same feelings of gratification.

As do the other volunteer teachers. The benefits derived are more than mutually appreciated — by Braille

(Continued on page 6)

Volunteer teacher Mildred Heredeen and guest speaker Scott Bornstein answer students' questions during class session of "Our Town."

Student Bernice Clark, left, and volunteer orientation and mobility teacher Betty Crotts demonstrate one of the uses of the white cane.

as contrasted to the rigid half-hour format on television networks, cable channels often have short schedule gaps that must be filled. Brief segments about blindness and success stories about what blind persons can do, packaged to fill these time gaps, are distributed to the cable channels by the department. They are well used. The institute's hour long film, "Beyond Blindness," has been shown over the Public Broadcasting System.

Although the communications department does not have direct responsibility for fund-raising and recruitment of volunteer workers, it is consulted by those staff departments and helps in preparation of their materials.

USING PUBLIC SERVICE RADIO

The problem. The Texas Real Estate Research Center at Texas A & M University was committed to provide the public with unbiased, accurate real estate news. It had little money for the purpose.

The solution. Creation of 1-minute radio spots researched, written, and recorded by the center's staff. Each 1-minute recording presents a piece of information to assist homeowners, renters, small investors, and others concerned with real estate matters.

These brief program items are aired daily or weekly by about 85 Texas radio stations as free public service announcements. Cost to the center is less than $100 per month. Each month the center mails cassette tapes containing 20 1-minute spots to the stations on the list. As a spinoff, the staff rewrites the scripts into newspaper style and assembles them as a column, "The Real Estate Consumer." The column is supplied free to newspapers in Texas; about 75 of them publish it.

For examples of effective uses of public service announcements, over radio and over television, see Figures 18.8 and 18.9.

STAGING A COMMUNITY HEALTH FAIR

Purpose. A nonprofit hospital in a relatively small city desires to promote preventive medicine and to strengthen its image as a community institution.

Method. The hospital will conduct a community health fair.

What is offered. A screening examination to detect many common health problems is given free to everyone attending the fair during an 8-hour period on a Saturday. A laboratory report on a battery of 20 diagnostic blood tests is provided for $5, far below what the tests would cost if done through a doctor's office.

How it is done. Each spring the Marian Medical Center at Santa Maria, California, a city of 40,000, conducts a health fair. Booths are set up in a large community building, each offering a specific health test. They are staffed by physicians, nurses, technicians, and hospital volunteers, all donating their services. This fair exemplifies similar programs offered by hospitals in many cities but provides a wider range of services than some do. The hospital has 125 beds and a staff of 600.

FIGURE 18.8

Public service announce-
ments (PSAs) are used by
voluntary agencies to distribute information over radio
and television. This one, prepared for radio, has 30 seconds of copy. Other PSAs
may be 10, 20, or 60 sec-
onds. The broadcast media
often air these messages
without charge as a public
service.

GOODWILL of santa clara county

helping handicapped people create new futures

CONTACT: Jim Christensen   DATE: April 12, 1984
           Karen Davidson
           (408) 998-5774

PSA TIME: 30 Seconds   RELEASE: May 6-12, 1984

ANNCR: May sixth through twelfth is National Goodwill

          Week...a week honoring Goodwill for over 80 years

          of helping people create new futures. Goodwill of

          Santa Clara County is dedicated to improving the

          lives of disabled people through vocational

          training programs.

              Goodwill offers skill training as an electronic

          technician, electronic assembler, electro/mechanical

          draftsperson, accounting or general office clerk,

          secretary or word processing operator.

              For more information call Goodwill at

          (408) 998-5774, that's 998-5774.

                                # # #

1080 north seventh street•san jose. ca 95112•(408)998-5774

FIGURE 18.9

Public service announcements for television require a visual aid. This 10-second announcement, distributed by Goodwill Industries of Santa Clara County, included a color slide with the slogan "Goodwill Industries, Inc. Our Business Works. So People Can."

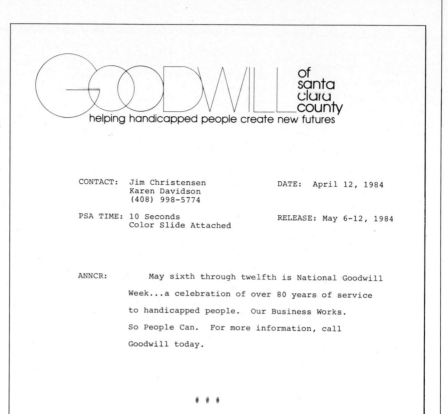

GOODWILL of santa clara county

helping handicapped people create new futures

CONTACT: Jim Christensen   DATE: April 12, 1984
            Karen Davidson
            (408) 998-5774

PSA TIME: 10 Seconds   RELEASE: May 6-12, 1984
          Color Slide Attached

ANNCR: May sixth through twelfth is National Goodwill

              Week...a celebration of over 80 years of service

              to handicapped people. Our Business Works.

              So People Can. For more information, call

              Goodwill today.

                         # # #

1080 north seventh street•san jose, ca 95112•(408)998-5774

Goodwill Industries, Inc.
Our business works.
So people can.

Visitors receive a map of the route to follow and a report form on which results of the tests are marked. At the end of the route, a registered nurse checks and interprets results for the participant. If any test result is abnormal, possibly indicating a significant health problem, the participant is advised to see a private physician. Blood test samples are sent to a commercial laboratory, which mails a report to the participant.

The free screening includes tests for glaucoma and anemia; urinalysis; measurement of height, weight, blood pressure, pulmonary function, and visual acuity; cancer checkup and education; oral and dermatological examinations. Additional educational booths cover paramedics, emergencies, pediatrics, nutrition and exercise, and pharmacy.

The result. Annual attendance is approximately 1000 persons. More women than men take the tests. Participation is heavier among persons over 50 years, including some in their 80s. A significant number of health danger signals are detected, especially involving high blood pressure, pulmonary functions, and anemia.

Behind the scenes. Conducting this health fair requires participation by approximately 200 persons and 4 months of planning and preparation. The hospital's director of development and community relations is in charge. She appoints a coordinator for each booth, who in turn selects an operations manager responsible for recruiting booth personnel and assembling supplies. Participating physicians usually work 4-hour shifts. The fair is held in late April, with the first planning meeting in early January. Adequate staffing is especially important at the blood testing booth, always very popular, to prevent long waiting lines.

Efforts are made to give the fair a festive atmosphere. Entertainment and refreshments are provided without charge, and decorative touches brighten the scene. Child-care facilities are available.

To thank the health fair volunteers, the hospital holds a barbecue for them after the event.

Abundant publicity is essential to attract large participation. The community relations department sends news releases to print and electronic media and distributes flyers to churches, organizations, and hospital employees. It describes the event in the hospital's quarterly bulletin. Word-of-mouth is valuable. Persons who attended a previous fair tell family members and friends about their good experience and urge them to attend the next one.

A poster contest among fourth, fifth, and sixth graders is effective in generating interest. Children may enter any piece of artwork of specified size depicting good health, healthful activities, or nutrition. Announcement of this contest justifies distribution of flyers about the health fair to the three grades in local schools. Many of these flyers reach the children's homes. First prize is a bicycle, and second and third prizes are roller skates. Entries are judged by the local Artists Guild and displayed at the hospital.

The cost. A health fair of this scope may cost $10,000 or more to put on, even with all the help donated. Medical supplies and printing are two substantial expenses. However, a fair of minimum proportions may be staged for as little as $1,000 or $2,000, and a good job can be done for $5,000 to $7,000. Donations may be solicited if the hospital's budget cannot cover the full cost of a fair. Chevron U.S.A. is one commercial source of funds for health fairs.

QUESTIONS FOR REVIEW AND DISCUSSION

1. Give an example of a service-oriented nonprofit organization and of a cause-oriented nonprofit organization.

2. How has President Reagan's campaign to cut back on federal welfare programs affected the role of churches?

3. What is a challenge grant?

4. Why do large foundations need public relations representatives? List some of the tasks these practitioners handle.

5. Social agencies depend heavily upon volunteer help. What motivates individuals to volunteer?

6. Why is it important for a nonprofit organization that solicits money from the public to put out a detailed annual financial report?

7. How do many corporations determine the amount of money they will contribute each year?

8. In what ways do capital campaigns differ from routine fund-raising for an organization's operating expenses?

9. List several types of fund-raising events often staged by smaller organizations using volunteer help.

10. What are the basic audiences of a hospital public relations program?

CHAPTER NINETEEN

Education

To inform a wide variety of publics, to interpret programs, and to cultivate support—that is the mission of public relations specialists on college campuses and in public school systems. This chapter discusses both types of operations.

The college public relations office provides news and publications services, coordinates special events including tours and exhibits, and performs a multitude of other tasks such as writing speeches and reports and responding to requests for information. These are the main functions of public school communication specialists as well, although generally on a much smaller scale. In addition, a university development staff works with alumni and other groups, and raises money; both are extremely important tasks, because every institution needs increased financial support.

Members of a college public relations office interact with a number of publics: students, faculty and staff, parents, alumni, the community, boards of control, foundations and other research and support agencies, government bodies, business executives, secondary schools, and other colleges, to name the principal ones. The public schools have their own set of publics—teachers, students, parents, staff, and the community. The chapter describes some school systems that have been especially successful in creating good relations with these groups.

Colleges and Universities

DEVELOPMENT AND PUBLIC RELATIONS OFFICES

The president (or chancellor) is the chief public relations officer of a college or university, he or she sets policy and is responsible for all operations, under the guidance of the institution's governing board.

In large universities the vice-president for development and university relations (that person may have some other title) supervises the office of development, which includes a division for alumni relations, and also the office of public relations; these functions are combined in smaller institutions. Development and alumni personnel seek to enhance the prestige and financial support of the institution. Among other activities, they conduct meetings and seminars, publish newsletters and magazines, and arrange tours. Their primary responsibilities are to build alumni loyalty and raise funds from private sources.

The public relations director, generally aided by one or more chief assistants, supervises the information news service, publications, and special events. Depending upon the size of the institution, perhaps a dozen or more employees will carry out these functions, including writing, photography, graphics design, and broadcasting.

Figure 19.1 shows the organization of a public relations staff at a typical middle-size university.

FIGURE 19.1

The diagram is an organizational chart of the Office of Public Relations at the University of Georgia.

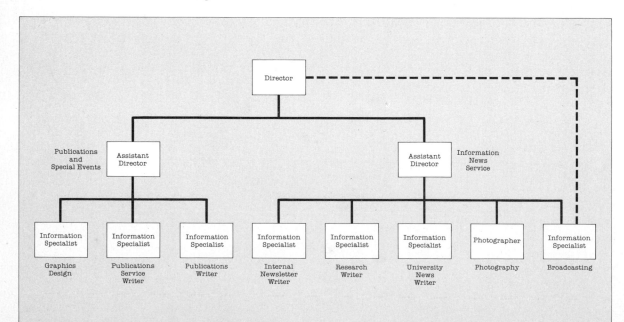

In addition, scores of specialists at a large university perform diverse information activities in agricultural, medical, engineering, extension, continuing education, and other such units.

NEWS BUREAU The most visible aspect of a university public relations program is its news bureau. Among other things, an active bureau produces hundreds of news releases, photographs, and special columns and articles for the print media. It prepares programs of news and features about faculty activities and personalities for broadcast stations. It provides assistance and information for reporters, editors, and broadcasters affiliated with state, regional, and national media. The staff responds to hundreds of telephone calls from members of the news media and the public seeking information.

SERVING THE PUBLICS In order to carry out their complex functions, top development and public relations specialists must be a part of the management team of the college or university. At some institutions this is not so, and the public relations program suffers. Ideally, these leaders should attend all top-level meetings involving the president and other administrators, learning the whys and wherefores of decisions made and lending counsel. Only then can they satisfactorily develop action programs and respond to questions from the publics those programs concern. They are indeed the arms and voice of the administration.

FACULTY AND STAFF As noted in previous chapters, every sound public relations program begins with the internal constituency. Able college presidents involve their faculty in decision-making to the fullest extent possible, given the complexities of running a major institution. It is a maxim that the employees of a company or institution serve as its major public relations representatives because they come into contact with so many people. Good morale, a necessity, is achieved in large measure through communication.

Colleges communicate with their faculty and staff members through in-house newsletters and newspapers; journals describing research, service, and other accomplishments (which also are sent to outside constituencies); periodic meetings at which policies are explained and questions answered; and numerous other ways.

Faculty and staff members who fully understand the college's philosophy, operations, and needs generally will respond with heightened performance. For example, when the University of Georgia in 1983 sought to obtain $2.5 million in contributions from its faculty members as part of an $80 million bicentennial enrichment campaign, they responded with a generous outpouring of nearly $6 million—a signal to outside contributors that helped ensure the success of the program.

STUDENTS Because of their large numbers and the many families which they represent, students comprise the largest public relations arm—for good or bad—that a university has. The quality of the teaching which they receive is the greatest determinant of their allegiance to the institution. However, a sound administrative attitude toward students, involving them as much as possible in decisions that affect their campus lives, is extremely important.

College public relations is the same in that we do some of the same things . . . news releases, publications, displays . . . and in that we have the same principles of operation:

1. Identify our constituents, our publics.

2. Locate them and determine how best to reach them.

3. Reach them with a clear message.

4. Monitor the results and measure effectiveness.

University public relations is interesting work but there are no magic formulas to being successful at it.

* * *

Two-way communication leads to an *acceptable* level of understanding. Two truths are contained here:

1. You have to listen as well as talk so you know if you are doing something that works and so you can tell your institution what is good and what is not so good.

2. You can't solve all problems and achieve total understanding and support through public relations. It takes other tools and programs and then you only achieve an acceptable level.

* * *

What are we in UGA public relations?
We deal in facts and the truth.
We don't gloss over, obfuscate, or hide information.
We don't build false images. We reflect the image, the true reality that is UGA.
We work with management in an advisory and support capacity.
We are the administration.
We try to explain policy fully after advising on that policy.
We try to anticipate the results of action taken by policy-makers and try to measure the results.

(Continued on next page)

So are other forms of communication, achieved through support of student publications and broadcast stations and numerous other ways. When, upon graduation, they are inducted en masse into the university's alumni society, chances are good that, if they are pleased with their collegiate experience, many will support the university in its future undertakings. Public relations effort directed at students is thus essential.

We try to influence sound decisions and proper directions by presenting the facts and our professional assessment of situations.

My staff and I are not the total public relations effort of the University of Georgia.

Every student, staff member, faculty member is a part of it and greatly determines if UGA is perceived to have good public relations or not so good.

Every speech made, every contact with the public including your friends and relatives, affects the public relations of the university.

We are all ambassadors of good (or bad) news about UGA.

*   *   *

To do the job well, we must:

1. Have access to information and the inner thinking of policy-makers.

2. Have good journalism skills.

3. Know our audience and how to reach them.

4. Understand the issues, the policies, the situations, if we are to explain.

5. Be creative, inventive, and professional.

6. Be able to deal with emergencies and bad news as professionally and quickly as we deal with good news.

7. Deal with inclement weather conditions affecting UGA operations with the speed of a regular news room.

8. Deal with death, disruption, etc., when they occur, as readily as we deal with a research breakthrough or a student honored nationally.

9. Plan ahead and have a plan rather than doing remedial public relations, acting rather than reacting as often as we can.

THE COMMUNITY   As in the case of industry, a college or university must maintain a good relationship with the members of the community in which it is situated. The greatest supporters that an institution may have are the people within its immediate sphere of influence, many of whom mingle with its faculty, staff members, and students. Tax dollars also are an immense benefit, although the fact that university property is tax-exempt may impose a strain unless the institution voluntarily agrees to some form of compensation for services such as fire and police protection.

The amicable "town–gown" relationship so avidly sought by city leaders

Our problems are:

1. More ideas than budget to do them with.

2. More to do than our staff or budget can do.

3. Keeping up with a fast-changing subject—higher education.

4. Dealing with issues that arise with no warning.

5. Dealing with issues that were anticipated but are complex.

6. Meeting deadlines and overcoming printing problems, technical difficulties, postal problems, etc.

7. Trying to be the public relations office for a university of 25,000 students, 7,000 employees, 130,000 alumni, and a constituency in the millions.

Career preparation best includes writing, speaking, working with people, knowledge of the news media, and specialized journalism skills including broadcasting, graphics design, editing, etc., but not all of these.

A primary qualification is to believe in what you are doing. I expect my staff to believe in the University of Georgia, to learn the facts and tell the truth.

We try to know everything we can about higher education, including trends and issues.

We try to understand the news media and know the people who work in them.

We try to be accessible.

We try to be cooperative and useful.

We try, in every way we can, to use our skills as journalists and public relations professionals, to encourage public understanding and support of the University of Georgia.

and university officials alike generally is tested in other ways as well, including students' loud parties and careless driving. University and local officials cope with these problems as well as they can.

In order to bridge the town–gown gap often evident, faculty and staff members are encouraged to achieve community visibility through work with civic and other organizations. Business groups often take the lead. The Chamber of Commerce in Lawrence, Kansas, for example, for many years sponsored an annual barbecue, including various other activities, to give faculty and townspeople an opportunity to get to know each other better.

UCSB AFFILIATES
The Best Buy In Town!

As I enter my sixth year as Chancellor at UCSB, I am mindful of the friendships I have made and the substantial support the campus has enjoyed in that time from the UCSB Affiliates, our vital liaison with the communities around us. These have been good years in which the organization has grown in size and strength and in which we have found our interests in the goals of higher education mutually satisfying.

Our expectation is that the coming year will be even more stimulating intellectually and socially, for we anticipate broadening the scope of Affiliates activities and increasing the opportunities for the members' fulfillment. There will be occasions to meet and talk with scholars who are at the cutting edge of knowledge in their respective disciplines, to exchange views with top flight students, and to learn from campus officials of the critical issues confronting UCSB and institutions like it around the country.

I sincerely hope you will take advantage of the opportunities which accompany Affiliates membership and that I can look forward to seeing you as the 1982-83 calendar unfolds.

Robert A. Huttenback
Chancellor

An attractive brochure put out by a branch of the University of California lists the university-sponsored or -arranged activities in which local residents who enroll in the "Affiliates" program can participate (see Figure 19.2).

ALUMNI   Besieged by letters and telephone calls soliciting contributions, many alumni must feel that development officers perceive them as simply dollar signs or names on a computer printout. "In the past, schools hoped to attract gifts for specific purposes—to start programs or expand facilities,"

CALENDAR
PROGRAMS AND EVENTS
1982-83

Fall Quarter 1982
- New members orientation social (G)
- Young professionals 1-day cruise to Channel Islands (G)
- 2-day cruise to Channel Islands including meals and lectures (G)
- Downtown luncheon/panel discussion (G)
- International Christmas Event (G)
- Jack Daniel's Original Silver Cornet Band (G)
- "Leonardo's Return to Vinci" opening reception and tour (A)
- "Fine Wines for the Fine Arts" sale (A)
- "The Creation of a New Spain" opening reception and tour (A)
- Bus tour to Los Angeles designer houses (A)
- "The Caretaker" and English pub party (D)
- "Leonardo" world premiere (D)
- "Love of Life"—Academy Award winning film about the life of Arthur Rubinstein (M)
- Home Musicale (M)
- UCSB Symphony Concert Orchestra Concert (M)
- Bus tour to Los Angeles for Lena Horne show (M)

Winter Quarter 1983
- Downtown luncheon/panel discussion (G)
- American Ballet Theatre II (G)
- University Art Museum opening receptions and tours (A)
- Repertory West Dance Company (D)
- "Mimania" (D)
- Fundraising brunch and auction (M)
- Home Musicale (M)
- UCSB Symphony Orchestra Concert (M)

Spring Quarter 1983
- Downtown luncheon/panel discussion (G)
- "An Evening with Queen Victoria" (G)
- Annual Dinner and Awards Ceremony (G)
- University Art Museum opening receptions and tours (A)
- Annual meeting and scholarship ceremony (A)
- "The Good Woman of Setzuan" (D)
- Home Musicale (M)
- Annual Dinner Meeting and Symphony Concert (M)

(Complete calendar to be announced)
(G) General Affiliates
(A) Art Affiliates
(D) Drama and Dance Affiliates
(M) Music Affiliates

ENJOY SPECIAL BENEFITS!

Free:
- UCSB Events Calendar
- Affiliates Newsletter
- Evening and weekend parking on campus
- UCSB Library Card
- Auditing of selected courses
- Use of the language and photo lab facilities
- Use of Recreational Facilities during open-rec hours: pool, gym, track, and weight room.

Discounts:
- Selected Extension classes each quarter
- UCSB Season Basketball Tickets
- Selected UC Press Publications
- Major purchases through United Buying Service
- Annual membership in the YMCA
- Group travel programs through the Alumni Association

---

the New York *Times* reported. "Now, faced with soaring costs and inflation-battered endowment incomes, many colleges are fund-raising to balance budgets. The result has been larger, more aggressive and increasingly sophisticated efforts at schools that can no longer sit back and hope for gifts to come their way."

Total voluntary support for education reached more than $9 billion in 1983, an all-time high, according to a report by the American Association of Fund-Raising Counsel. Some colleges employ students to telephone alumni;

Alumni solicitation letters take many forms. One of the most unusual, shown here, was written by Dan Jenkins, a 1953 journalism graduate of Texas Christian University and longtime *Sports Illustrated* writer and editor. Billy Clyde Puckett is a character in Jenkins's novel *Semi-Tough*.

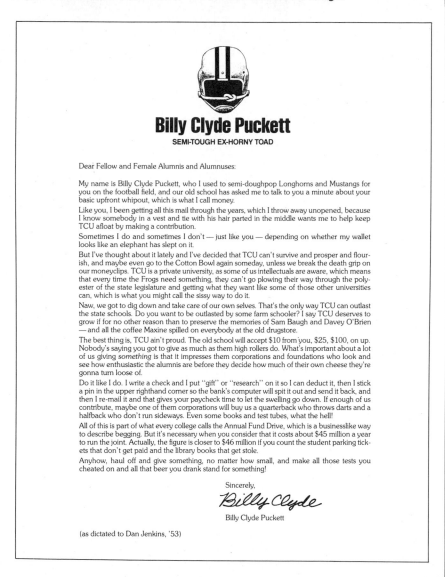

Billy Clyde Puckett

SEMI-TOUGH EX-HORNY TOAD

Dear Fellow and Female Alumnis and Alumnuses:

My name is Billy Clyde Puckett, who I used to semi-doughpop Longhorns and Mustangs for you on the football field, and our old school has asked me to talk to you a minute about your basic upfront whipout, which is what I call money.

Like you, I been getting all this mail through the years, which I throw away unopened, because I know somebody in a vest and tie with his hair parted in the middle wants me to help keep TCU afloat by making a contribution.

Sometimes I do and sometimes I don't — just like you — depending on whether my wallet looks like an elephant has slept on it.

But I've thought about it lately and I've decided that TCU can't survive and prosper and flourish, and maybe even go to the Cotton Bowl again someday, unless we break the death grip on our moneyclips. TCU is a private university, as some of us intellectuals are aware, which means that every time the Frogs need something, they can't go plowing their way through the polyester of the state legislature and getting what they want like some of those other universities can, which is what you might call the sissy way to do it.

Naw, we got to dig down and take care of our own selves. That's the only way TCU can outlast the state schools. Do you want to be outlasted by some farm schooler? I say TCU deserves to grow if for no other reason than to preserve the memories of Sam Baugh and Davey O'Brien — and all the coffee Maxine spilled on everybody at the old drugstore.

The best thing is, TCU ain't proud. The old school will accept $10 from you, $25, $100, on up. Nobody's saying you got to give as much as them high rollers do. What's important about a lot of us giving *something* is that it impresses them corporations and foundations who look and see how enthusiastic the alumnis are before they decide how much of their own cheese they're gonna turn loose of.

Do it like I do. I write a check and I put "gift" or "research" on it so I can deduct it, then I stick a pin in the upper righthand corner so the bank's computer will spit it out and send it back, and then I re-mail it and that gives your paycheck time to let the swelling go down. If enough of us contribute, maybe one of them corporations will buy us a quarterback who throws darts and a halfback who don't run sideways. Even some books and test tubes, what the hell!

All of this is part of what every college calls the Annual Fund Drive, which is a businesslike way to describe begging. But it's necessary when you consider that it costs about $45 million a year to run the joint. Actually, the figure is closer to $46 million if you count the student parking tickets that don't get paid and the library books that get stole.

Anyhow, haul off and give something, no matter how small, and make all those tests you cheated on and all that beer you drank stand for something!

Sincerely,

Billy Clyde

Billy Clyde Puckett

(as dictated to Dan Jenkins, '53)

many mail letters to specific graduating classes over the names of members who have agreed to be class agents for that purpose. Sought are not only year-by-year contributions but bequests and annuities as well. In return, the colleges publish honor rolls listing donors, invite contributors to join honorary clubs (the President's Club, for example), and name rooms and buildings for the largest givers. Educational events and special tours to foreign countries often are arranged to build and sustain alumni interest.

Universities often use matching grants to make a donor's contribution go further—and thus make giving more attractive. For instance, in 1984 a donor in Dallas, who wanted to remain anonymous, contributed $8 million toward the establishment of faculty enrichment chairs at the University of Texas at Austin. The sum was matched by foundations, and the entire $16 million, in turn, was matched by the university, making possible the establishment of 32 new chairs. Such support is essential in order for good universities to become great universities.

Influential alumni and other important friends of colleges and universities also are encouraged, through personal contact and correspondence, to provide political clout with legislative bodies and boards of regents, in support of the institutions' financial and other objectives. Such support also is important in the recruitment of students with outstanding academic or athletic achievement.

GOVERNMENT   State legislatures often hold the vital key to whether public universities receive sufficient monies to maintain facilities, faculty, and programs. Consequently, legislators constitute a vital public for any state university. They must be educated to understand the complex problems of higher education and the financial resources needed to maintain any degree of teaching quality. There is much competition for public tax monies, and university representatives must be skillful communicators to present their case in the most effective manner possible.

PROSPECTIVE STUDENTS   Suffering from declining revenues, increased costs of operation, and a dwindling pool of prospective students occasioned by lower birth rates, many colleges have turned to highly competitive recruiting methods. Some, in the "hard-sell" classification, use extensive advertising in print and broadcast media and on billboards. Other colleges and universities have replaced their catalogs and brochures with four-color, slick materials that use bright graphics and catchy headlines to lure students.

As competition for students has increased, so have the costs of recruiting them. John Minter Associates, a Denver firm that researches issues in higher education, estimates that the average per school spending on admission and recruitment in 1983–1984 exceeded $700,000 for private universities and $600,000 for public universities. This high level of activity creates many opportunities for employment in public relations and development.

The purchase of mailing lists is now a common tool of student recruit-

FIGURE 19.3

The wheel shows most of the publics with which college public relations offices endeavor to maintain two-way communication.

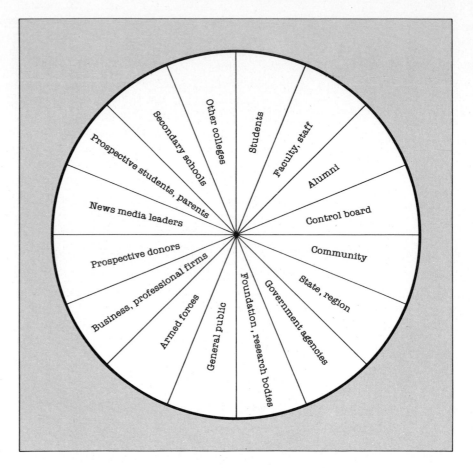

Students

Faculty, staff

Alumni

Control board

Community

State, region

Government agencies

Foundation, research bodies

General public

Armed forces

Business, professional firms

Prospective donors

News media leaders

Prospective students, parents

Secondary schools

Other colleges

ment. Approximately 900 colleges annually buy from 10,000 to 15,000 names and addresses each of high school students who have taken College Board examinations. The most sought-after prospects are National Merit Scholarship winners, and it is not uncommon for competing universities to shower a prospect with such lures as free tuition for four years, a private dorm room, guarantees of priority registration, and the like.

OTHER PUBLICS   Examples of other groups requiring special attention are shown in Figure 19.3.

SUPPORT FOR ADVANCEMENT OFFICERS

Most public relations, alumni, and development leaders—known euphemistically as *advancement officers*—enjoy the many services of the Council for Advancement and Support of Education (CASE), with headquarters in Washington, D.C. The aims of CASE are described as building public under-

458

standing, stepping up the level of alumni involvement and support, strengthening communication with internal and external audiences, improving government relations, and increasing private financial support. Among CASE current objectives are (1) helping leaders at historically black institutions advance in their careers, (2) publicizing a code of ethics, (3) developing gift and expenditure reporting standards, (4) improving the communication of university research to the public, and (5) studying the impact of new technologies.

Representing more than 2400 institutional members, CASE serves nationally as a principal public affairs arm for education, monitoring federal legislation and regulations and working with the American Council on Education and other associations on education-related issues. The organization provides district conferences and institutes, evaluation and critique services, a certification program, awards, reference materials, and placement opportunities. Thousands each summer attend its four-day assembly, replete with workshops.

QUALIFICATIONS FOR CAREERS

Journalism, public relations, advertising, speech communication, graphic design, photography, business, or a combination of these fields provides the educational background for most college advancement officers. Knowledge of the news media and strong writing skills are necessary.

The following classified advertisement, published in the newspaper trade magazine *Editor & Publisher* in January 1983, indicates the type of background needed by a director of public relations at one institution:

DIRECTOR OF PUBLIC RELATIONS

Plan, develop, and implement a variety of marketing-advertising and public and college relations programs designed to (1) increase enrollment through a team approach; (2) increase community awareness of the programs, courses, and services offered by the college; (3) oversee all college publications; and (4) establish an alumni organization to help support the college. Previous successful experience in a leadership position in marketing and/or public relations. Bachelor's or master's degree in these areas preferred. Salary negotiable. Starting date, March 1983. Deadline for receipt of application: February 18, 1983. . . . An affirmative action, equal opportunity employer.

Elementary and Secondary Schools

RESPONSE TO CONTEMPORARY ISSUES

When in 1983 the National Commission on Excellence in Education, citing "a nation at risk," called for massive educational reform, the resulting nationwide debate represented the latest in a series of public examinations that education in America has undergone during the last several decades. Integration, busing, accountability, book censorship, sex education, discipline, drugs, and vandalism—all these issues have commanded continuing public attention.

The 18-member commission made recommendations in five major areas, based on the belief that everyone can learn, that everyone is born with an urge to learn that can be nurtured, that a solid high school education is within the reach of virtually all, and that life-long learning will equip people with the skills required for new careers and for citizenship. Among the recommendations were the following:

1. *Content.* State and local high school graduation should be strengthened, and all students seeking a diploma should be required to take four years of English, three years of mathematics, three years of science, three years of social studies, and one-half year of computer science. Two years of foreign language were strongly recommended for the college-bound.

2. *Standards and expectations.* Schools, colleges, and universities should adopt more rigorous and measurable standards, and higher expectations, for academic performance and student conduct, and four-year colleges and universities should raise their admission requirements.

3. *Time.* Significantly more time should be devoted to learning the New Basics. This would require more effective use of the existing school day, a longer school day, or a lengthened school year.

4. *Teaching.* Teacher candidates should be required to meet high educational standards, and demonstrate an aptitude for teaching and competence in an academic discipline. Salaries should be made more competitive and market-sensitive, with promotion, tenure, and retention tied to teacher evaluation. Teachers should be under 11-month contract. Career ladders should be developed. Substantial nonschool personnel resources should be used to help overcome the shortage of math and science teachers. Incentives should be developed to attract outstanding students to teaching. Master teachers should help design teacher preparation programs and supervise beginning teachers.

5. *Leadership and fiscal.* Citizens should hold educators and elected officials responsible for providing the leadership necessary to achieve these reforms, and citizens should provide the fiscal support and stability required to bring about the reforms.

Although stung by the commission's indictments, school officials welcomed the nationwide interest aroused. They were hopeful that the spotlight thrown on educational needs would result in another post-Sputnik-type wave of support, which indeed followed.

News of the commission's recommendations reached the offices of thousands of school superintendents almost immediately over the Education U.S.A. Newsline and Information Network, an electronic news and advisory service of the National School Public Relations Association (NSPRA). When local media people called shortly thereafter, many of the more alert superintendents and their communication coordinators were prepared to offer reactions.

NSPRA followed its newsline alert with a special bulletin to members describing the recommendations more fully. The bulletin contained a statement by its president, William J. Banach, urging educators to " . . . initiate the movement toward better educational programming by matching the commission's recommendations against what exists in local districts. Then they should take their findings to the people, explain the value of a well educated society, and work with citizens, business people, governmental leaders, and others to generate support for the kinds of schools America needs and deserves."

Also enclosed was a telephone survey questionnaire prepared by Banach for use by school public relations people to ascertain community attitudes toward the recommendations—a necessary first step in the coordination of local school response with anticipated state and federal legislation and recommendations.

These actions, and others taken throughout the nation, provided a striking example of the vastly increased appreciation of the role of public relations that has swept many school districts and state and federal school offices in recent years.

And it has come none too soon. Questions had steadily mounted over the teaching of basic reading, writing, and computation skills; the requirements for graduation; the toughness of courses; and more. California's Proposition 13 had been preceded and followed by taxpayer revolts elsewhere in the nation that brought tightened purse strings for school maintenance and the defeat of one capital improvement bond issue after another. Busing and integration—the major problems of the 1960s and 1970s—remained key issues. The campaign seeking tax credits for parents of children enrolled in private schools was troublesome. There were fewer students, more citizens without school-age children, more one-parent families. School-building closings and boundary shifts brought protests.

The larger, more progressive school systems and thousands of smaller ones had long maintained public relations programs in an effort to deal with these issues and to prepare for them in advance when possible. Budgetary squeezes, however, had constricted most of these programs. But the necessity of sound community relations—at the heart of both management and public relations—was more apparent now than ever. If funds were not available or the system too small to warrant a full-fledged public relations program, then a sole information specialist was employed, full- or part-time. School public

FIGURE 19.4

Here is a sampling of the locally produced news releases
and pamphlets, as well as idea-
stimulating, instructional publications of state and national
school public relations associations, that cross the desk of
the public relations coordinator of the Clarke County
School District in Athens,
Georgia.

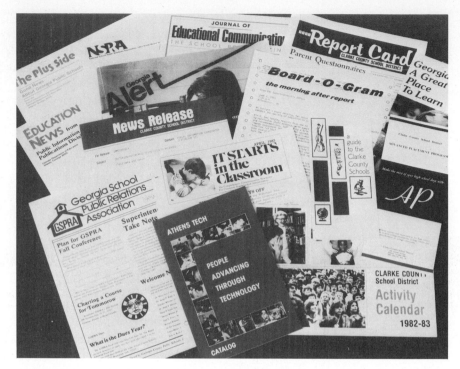

relations had come into its own. Figures 19.4 and 19.5 indicate the types of
communication that take place at the elementary and secondary school level.
Public relations specialists keep in touch with each other (Figure 19.4), and
PTAs reach out to the community (Figure 19.5).

**REACHING THE
PUBLICS**

The primary publics of a school system are teachers, children, parents, staff,
and the community. As in all public relations, research, planning, action, and
evaluation comprise the essential steps with which to reach these publics.
On the desks of information directors, communication coordinators, and
school–community relations specialists (or whatever the title may be, and it
varies widely) are booklets prepared by national and state offices detailing
hundreds of ways in which they may carry out their mission. Perhaps the
best way to describe school public relations in its major aspects is to examine
some of the outstanding programs accorded the Gold Medallion award of
the National School Public Relations Association.

THE MOST EXTENSIVE PUBLIC RELATIONS PROGRAM   The Dallas Independent
School District is said to have the most extensive communication program
in the United States. The school board has set a number of "targets for the

80s": (1) to improve student achievement, (2) to increase employee performance, (3) to provide accountability, (4) to promote school-community relationships, (5) to maintain an effective governance system, and (6) to ensure adequate funding.

The board's mandate calls for the appointment of a communication contact person in every school. Principals are charged with using the talents of parents and other members of the community "in a decision-making capacity." Not only the Parent-Teachers Association but also business and industrial firms and other educational systems are involved in volunteer and adopt-a-school programs.

School communication personnel have set their own goals: (1) to obtain comprehensive, accurate, and fair coverage of school activities; (2) to provide employees with timely and accurate information; (3) to provide other citizens with such information; and (4) to assist the general superintendent and board of education in their efforts to communicate with employees and other systems.

ANALYSIS OF PUBLIC OPINION   Formal opinion surveys for schools often cost from $7,500 to $15,000, but the Utica (Michigan) Community Schools system since 1971 has been conducting Project HEAR (Householder Educational

Attitude Reactions) at a cost of only about $250 per year. The system uses volunteers to telephone a random sample of approximately 300 persons and ask questions for about 15 minutes.

Many of the questions are borrowed from the annual Gallup poll of the Public's Attitudes Toward the Public Schools and from a countywide survey conducted by the Macomb (Michigan) Intermediate School District; other questions reflect local school district issues. A computer generates the phone numbers from names on a voter registration list, and the questions are pretested for proper phrasing. The persistent but courteous callers have achieved a remarkable 100 percent response rate, thus ensuring the reliability of the random-selection method, even though it is restricted to registered voters and does not include the community at large. The responses are used to readjust school programs each year.

FACE-TO-FACE COMMUNICATION   Supplementing the newsletters and brochures distributed by all systems, the Fairfax County (Virginia) Public Schools, a large district in suburban Washington, emphasizes face-to-face communication. The superintendent meets monthly with advisory councils representing all categories of employees, bimonthly with a planning council representing citizen organizations, and regularly with a countywide student advisory council.

Members of the office of community relations (1) help the PTA county council conduct semiannual school-community nights, (2) maintain regular contact with other local groups, (3) operate a speakers' bureau equipped with a slide-tape presentation, (4) conduct administration building tours for school staffs, and (5) arrange student award ceremonies at school board meetings with accompanying publicity.

Confronted with the potential defection of parents of preschool children to private schools, the system conducted "kindergarten roundup" programs and tours in all elementary schools. The invitations to parents were accompanied by a brochure describing five preschool classes as well as free vision and hearing tests. Slide-tape shows were screened at the open houses and questions answered. The result? A record kindergarten enrollment the following fall.

The Fairfax County system won a Gold Medallion for its total public relations program because of, among other achievements, its good relationship with the news media, including service to 100 media outlets—suburban weeklies as well as metropolitan dailies and dozens of radio and television stations.

The system's winning techniques included (1) close personal daily contact with news people; (2) special orientations for new press representatives; (3) distribution of systemwide news stories, feature story tips, and memoranda concerning future events; (4) public service announcements for radio and television; (5) weekly taped radio programs about the school system;

(6) press packets for board meetings; (7) distribution of photographs; and (8) interviews with board and key staff people.

PUBLIC FORUMS   For only $35 each, the New Jersey School Board Association prepared a kit containing a 33-minute filmstrip, introductory comments, instructions on how to guide a discussion period, and an in-depth questionnaire with which to obtain valuable feedback at public and in-school meetings, as well as a take-home brochure. It was designed so that any volunteer could conduct such a forum. The filmstrip stars students, teachers, and others, and relates how public education seeks to respond to social change.

MARKETING OF PUBLIC SCHOOL EDUCATION   A pioneer in public opinion surveying in education, William J. Banach, administrative director at the Macomb Intermediate School District in Mount Clemens, Michigan, developed a 2-year plan designed to discover what the public wants in its schools and how to respond to those desires, and to educate citizens about actions the school can and cannot take. Banach based the campaign on what he termed "the 90-7-3 concept of school communication":

Ninety percent of the school's image is who we are and what we do 24 hours a day. How school people think, act, and appear and what they say are key factors in marketing. This is why staff training is an integral part of a marketing program— to help people understand their communication roles and how important they are.

Seven percent of the marketing effort is listening—tuning in to find out what people like, don't like, want, don't want. Anything we do to know more about our "customers" is worth doing.

Three percent of marketing is outbound communication—publications, posters, news releases, and other visible and tangible items.

In successive phases, the marketing plan was targeted at (1) elementary parents, with a focus on reading, writing, and arithmetic; (2) secondary students and their parents, emphasizing "the basics and beyond" and beginning with specific objectives based on survey results and meetings with student leaders; and (3) citizens without children in school.

Arrangements were made for teachers to apply "No. 1 apple" stickers to outstanding student papers, and all classroom papers were sent home each Friday. Posters welcoming visitors were placed at each school. The slogan "Your public schools . . . There's no better place to learn" was displayed on billboards, calendars, bookmarks, bumper stickers, T-shirt transfers, and thank-you cards.

A survey made a year after the campaign began revealed enhanced public confidence in the schools. The Macomb Plan, as it is called, has attracted national attention.

CAMPAIGNS TO FINANCE THE SCHOOLS   When schools opened in Springfield, Oregon, in 1980, there was money enough for only three or four months of classes. Unemployment was high, and the district had already lost two finance campaigns in a row. Nevertheless, school leaders decided to seek a $12.6 million operating levy at an election in September and a new tax base guaranteeing up to $16.9 million in annual funding at the November general election.

Because state law prohibited the use of public funds to advocate any election issue, the system's communication officer could only issue appeals through publications already authorized, make talks, and enlist volunteer help. Private sources provided a budget of about $1000 for each election. Past campaigns were analyzed and a new strategy was devised, built around two main points:

Instead of emphasizing the money needed and aiming messages at male heads of households, all advertising was directed at women and stressed children rather than budgets. One advertisement showed a child's smiling face and the words, "Vote Yes! For Kids. District 19 Tax Base Nov. 4."

Volunteers gained insight into voter preferences through a barrage of telephone calls. Persons indicating a negative response were ignored, while those favorable or undecided were sent pamphlets and contacted personally in an effort to sway or reinforce their decisions.

Elements of the campaigns also included paid media spots, a speakers' bureau with slide presentation, broadcast public affairs programs, internal communication among the district's 7000 employees, a focus on the black community, yard signs, endorsements by the board of realtors and other civic leaders, news media conferences, announcements on marquees, and T-shirts.

Both measures passed in surprisingly large voter turnouts. In evaluating the campaigns, system leaders concluded that the person-to-person element was the most effective of all. And the combined cost of both campaigns was only $900.

CRISIS COMMUNICATION   For emergencies such as earthquakes, sudden loss of utilities, severe storms, hazardous material spills, explosions, fires, tornadoes, nuclear warnings, plane crashes, bomb threats—for all such crises a communication plan should be in readiness. For the Great Falls (Montana) Public Schools, situated in a city near an Air Force base and missile sites, Audrey Olson, the school district's information consultant, embarked on a project of integrating all emergency procedures into one comprehensive crisis procedure manual.

Communication procedures were provided in checklist form. In an attached envelope were important documents addressing unique situations facing individual schools. Copies of the manual were placed near every telephone in the district, and checklist instructions were made available in every classroom without a phone. A special alert radio was installed in the schools and the administration building.

Procedures were included for pupil dismissal, transportation, and media relations. The manual also contains policy statements by top officials and a letter with which explanations may be provided for parents.

A Case Study

Although school integration controversies have largely subsided, shifts in population and declining enrollments are causing communication problems for schools throughout the country. The following case study of how the Pittsburgh School District gained peaceful acceptance of an extensive desegregation plan is reproduced in its entirety from a booklet published by the National School Public Relations Association, from which the preceding case studies have been digested.

"KNOWING MAKES IT EASIER"[1] It was September 1980, and the Pittsburgh (Pa.) School District was about to begin another school year. Even at the last minute nobody was quite sure how it would go, because on the first day of this school year the most extensive desegregation plan in the city's history was to be implemented.

The district had been almost entirely reorganized. The heart of the plan was a network of 10 integrated middle schools for all children in grades 6, 7 and 8. The proportion of elementary students in racially balanced schools was increased from 29 percent to 50 percent, and a magnet program was expanded to serve more than 5000 students.

Everybody in the district held their breath. But they had done their work well. The quiet and uneventful school opening was in direct contrast to the preceding months of uncertainty and confusion, demonstrations and boycotts, legal actions and counteractions that prevailed until the last week in August, when the final barrier was removed. After months of negotiations the district reached a three-year agreement with the teachers association, and a new superintendent, Richard C. Wallace, arrived from Massachusetts to take the helm.

The public relations program, which won a Gold Medallion Award in the special topic category, had two central goals, according to public information director Pat Crawford: (1) to disseminate accurate information and thus control rumors and misinformation, and (2) to gain widespread community support for a smooth school opening.

[1] This case study appeared in "Learn from the Winners: School PR Programs That Work," published by the National School Public Relations Association, 1801 North Moore St., Arlington, VA 22209.

The difficulties were compounded by the fact that the desegregation plan adopted by the school board was under attack in the courts even as the schools were opening. "It was difficult to make a statement in the indicative mood," Crawford wrote.

"*If* clauses prefaced our pronouncements and publications."

Recognizing the critical role of the local media in a scenario like this one, Pittsburgh launched a model program to encourage good media relations. It trained staff people on how to deal with the inevitable crush of reporters, and set up facilities and ground out information to make it as easy as possible for newspeople to get what they were looking for. The district encouraged news and public affairs programming throughout the desegregation crisis to deemphasize the emotional busing issue in favor of factual information. As a result, the issue stayed in the public eye all summer.

The public information office developed a handbook for parents on school district transportation, and devoted its community newsletter to information about the plan. But there remained a need for a single and accurate source of information in the city, and that's what inspired the campaign promoting the Information Center based on the theme, *"Knowing makes it easier."*

Television and radio spots featuring original music and lyrics, newspaper ads, billboards and bus cards were just some of the ways the district spread the center's number far and wide. "You can find out about scheduling transportation, and more," a TV spot said. "We can even help arrange for you to visit your school first hand, or talk with students or the parents of students who attended there last year. So call the Pittsburgh Schools Information Center at 622-3575. Knowing *does* make it easier . . . That's what education's all about."

But while the information effort was moving straight ahead on all cylinders, the quest for community support had to change direction in midstream. At the start, the goal had been to secure support for the board's plan. But now, since nobody knew what plan would actually be in effect until the court ruled, the goal was modified to read *"support for a smooth opening."* It was a goal, the district felt, that nobody could dispute, at least publicly.

The original Coalition for Integrated Schools, which had brought together representatives of community organizations to help the school district in earlier days, had been disbanded because of an internal split over the merits of the case. So Crawford joined forces with the City Commission on Human Relations to coordinate the activities of all groups expressing an interest in a "smooth opening." This included the clergy, who through an interfaith committee pleaded in their churches for peace, and political and civic leaders, including the mayor, who urged citizens to live up to Pittsburgh's reputation as "City of Champions." The county bar association agreed to participate in a speakers bureau, and local corporations and foundations came up with money to help finance the efforts.

Even the news media charted a course parallel to their traditional news-gathering function. They agreed with school officials that if the public thoroughly understood the facts there would be no trouble on opening day and their programming reflected that belief.

One television station produced a five-part series on what the district was doing to prepare students, staff and parents for the new organization.

Another TV station aired a one-hour live show discussing the plan, the process, and what it might mean to students in the classroom.

A third TV station produced a series of five children's newsbreaks, featuring young people telling children what the desegregation plan was all about, what they could expect, and where they could find out more about it.

Newspapers chipped in with coverage of activities designed to prepare for the opening, including articles on summer camp activities, inservice programs and parent orientation sessions.

Most important, the tone was optimistic throughout.

At the same time, as a byproduct of the effort with community groups, the district was able to put together a "key communicator" network as a two-way pipeline into various sections of the city. That network was to remain in place long after opening day as a way to counteract rumors and get feedback from the community.

Did it all succeed? Even though the eventual shape of the desegregation plan was still bouncing around the courts, school opened September 2 to this headline in the *Post-Gazette:*

INTEGRATION STARTS CALMLY IN CITY SCHOOLS

The first day under the city school board's desegregation plan bore little resemblance to the 12 years of rancor and controversy that led up to it.

And the new superintendent, on his first day on the job, was quoted this way: "It's been a great day for Pittsburgh schools. The general feeling of the administrative staff was that this was a much smoother opening than one would have expected even a year ago."

QUESTIONS FOR REVIEW AND DISCUSSION

1. Who is the chief public relations officer on a college or university campus? Why?

2. A college news bureau is involved in a vast array of day-to-day public relations operations. Name five or six of these functions.

3. With what primary public does a sound university public relations program begin? Why? List eight other constituencies that must be addressed in such a program.

4. In what ways may powerful alumni and other friends provide support for an institution of higher learning? What is the role of the development office in gaining this support? What is CASE and what support does it provide for public relations and alumni officers?

5. The National Commission on Excellence in Education in 1983 called for massive educational reform. What were its main concerns and how did school officials respond?

6. The Dallas Independent School District has one of the most extensive communication programs in the country. What are some of the objectives of the Dallas school board?

7. If you were to conduct a formal opinion survey, could you improve on the procedures followed by the Utica (Michigan) Community Schools system? Explain your answer.

8. Tell how the Fairfax County (Virginia) Public Schools system maintains effective community relations.

9. Do you agree with the marketing concept used by public relations people in the Macomb Intermediate School District in Mount Clemens, Michigan? Describe the key points of this plan in explaining your answer.

10. What public relations problems may be evident when a community turns down a bond issue to improve school financing? What public relations actions do you consider important in building and maintaining strong support of schools?

CHAPTER TWENTY

Entertainment and Sports

Use of promotional techniques to publicize individuals, entertainments, and sporting events is another facet of public relations work. Although occupying only a small segment of the public relations spectrum, personality buildup and entertainment "drum-beating" attract public attention because of their highly visible and sometimes gaudy nature. Men and women engaged in what is known colloquially as "hype" need ample technical skills and an energetic approach because the work is highly competitive and subject to unpredictable changes in public mood.

Personal and entertainment publicity dates back to the early days of traveling theatrical troupes and circuses. Practitioners became known as press agents. Today's version of the craft is more complex and sophisticated, especially in its heavy use of television. This chapter examines how publicity methods are used to create awareness of personalities and to generate interest in shows and athletics. After discussing the concepts of the "personality" and "celebrity," it explores the question of ethics in this highly charged field. The steps in an entertainment publicity campaign are listed. The last part of the chapter takes a close look at sports publicity, examining the Super Bowl as the most extravagant example of this area of public relations.

The Use and Abuse of Publicity

Why did the mayor of Los Angeles proclaim World Laugh Day and dedicate the occasion to Bob Hope on the very day the comedian starred in a television special titled, "Who Makes the World Laugh?" Why did a national magazine publish a list of "10 Most Watchable Men," issued by an organization called Man Watchers, Inc.? In fact, why would anybody incorporate such an organization? Included on the list were such names as Tom Selleck, Marcus Allen, and Paul Newman. Why did an almost unknown actress-model named Victoria Principal suddenly blossom forth on national magazine covers after appearing in the television series "Dallas"?

These publicity events, like thousands of similar personality exposures, didn't just happen. They were carefully arranged by men and women whose job is to create "personalities" that, for a short time at least, may become household words (see Figure 20.1). The work these specialists do represents the publicity aspect of public relations in its most intensive form.

The publicity buildup of individuals and events is an integral part of the American fabric, and those who engage in it must be creative and extremely hard-working. This area is outside the mainstream of public relations, however, and professional public relations practitioners often are embarrassed by the tactics of press agents and publicity experts. Although only a relatively small number of men and women are engaged in the promotion of entertainers, politicians, and "beautiful people," the exaggerations and "little white lies"—not so little, at times—that some of them use are wrongly viewed by

FIGURE 20.1

Publicity campaigns for shows and personalities, while only a minor aspect of public relations, require the skills and perseverance of specialists such as Eddie Jaffe, a Broadway press agent for nearly 50 years. His clients ranged from famous stage personalities to Zorita the Snake Charmer. He is shown here covered by a portion of his clippings. Creating headline "angles" is vital in this work. (Courtesy AP/Wide World Photos.)

472

uninformed people as representative of the public relations industry as a whole.

Nevertheless, all students of public relations should learn how the publicity trade functions. At some point in their careers, they may find a knowledge of its techniques useful—for example, if they are engaged to guide the career of a political aspirant or advise an ambitious professional person or business executive. When applied discreetly and honestly, the techniques of publicity can be useful in many situations. They fall into disrepute when employed to create false images and to substitute deceit for truth.

The Cult of Personality

In contemporary society, the cult of personality has attained enormous stature. Newspapers run daily columns of short items about people by whom their readers supposedly are fascinated. The magazine *People* achieved very large circulation quickly after its appearance. The same personalities turn up on television and radio talk shows all over the United States. Weekly gossip tabloids such as *National Enquirer* and *Star* peddle sensational revelations about the private lives of individuals.

Celebrity worship isn't new. A hundred years ago, press agents touring the small cities of the country ahead of traveling theatrical parties showered local editors with publicity stories—and often with gossipy, unprintable asides—about the stars of their shows. Their purpose was to stir public interest in the performers and create an audience for the forthcoming shows. The flamboyant P. T. Barnum was the first highly acclaimed press agent in the United States. His success in stirring public excitement about his performers, ranging from a giant elephant to the Swedish singer Jenny Lind, was immense because he knew how to tap the public's desire for entertainment (see Chapter 3).

The objective is the same today, but the methods for achieving it have expanded greatly, especially through television. And the electronic medium has become vital in politics as well as in entertainment. Increasingly, Americans are learning about their candidates through exposure on nightly newscasts and paid TV and radio advertisements. In the presidential election of 1984, TV played as essential a role as the traditional open-air rallies and whistle-stop campaigns.

The Mystique of "Celebrity"

WHAT MAKES A STAR? What constitutes being a celebrity? In some instances fame is based on solid achievement that has won recognition on its own merits, perhaps with an assist from professional publicists. In his time, Henry Ford was a celebrity, as were Charles Lindbergh and Admiral Richard Byrd, the polar explorer.

Today, people such as Bob Hope, Barbra Streisand, and even Henry Kissinger are considered celebrities because of their talents and staying power in the public eye.

In many instances, however, celebrity status is somewhat fragile and fleeting. After Mark Spitz, a ruggedly handsome young man, won an unprecedented seven gold medals for swimming in the 1972 Olympic Games, he sought, with professional guidance, to capitalize on his international recognition with television acting engagements, public appearances, and advertising endorsements. The attempt failed to gather much momentum, largely because Spitz was not very talented or credible out of a swimming pool. Transference of fame from one field to another did not succeed.

Someone involved in an incident that catches the media's attention may become a celebrity practically overnight. John Z. DeLorean, the maverick car manufacturer, was already highly visible when he was arrested in Los Angeles on charges of cocaine dealing. Because of this, he achieved one of his goals in life, though not in the way he had expected: to appear on the cover of *Time* magazine.

This kind of celebrity status has led Barbara Goldsmith, author and social historian, to write in the New York *Times* magazine (December 4, 1983):

The line between fame and notoriety has been erased. Today we are faced with a vast confusing jumble of celebrities: the talented and the untalented, heroes and villains, people of accomplishment and those who have accomplished nothing at all, the criteria of their celebrity being that their images encapsulate some form of the American dream, that they give enough of an appearance of leadership, heroism, wealth, success, danger, glamour and excitement to feed our fantasies. We no longer demand reality, only that which is real-seeming.

Goldsmith adds, "The public appetite for celebrity and pseudo-event has grown to Pantagruelian proportions, and for the first time in history, the machinery of communications is able to keep up with these demands, even to outrun them, creating new needs we never knew existed. To one extent or another, all the branches of the media have become complicitous to this pursuit. . . ."

What she means is that the publicist and the press agent have a ready market for the materials, staged events, and hype that they constantly peddle to mass media outlets. A place on the "Johnny Carson Show" is the most sought-after publicity appearance on television because of the large audience—estimated at 20 million Americans nightly. Its host entertains a stream of guests who take advantage of the exposure to hype their latest book, song, or movie.

If a client is lucky, the publicity on the "Johnny Carson Show," in *People* magazine, or in the Hollywood gossip columns becomes self-multiplying. A press mention confers celebrity status and this, in turn, generates even more publicity and invitations to the right events. Through the efforts of a publicist, an aspiring actress may be invited to celebrity parties escorted by a celebrity male. A great deal of media exposure was generated, for example, by having Michael Jackson escort Brooke Shields to a Hollywood gathering. It is not certain which one of them got more publicity mileage from the photographs taken of the two together.

Eventually, the publicist's news releases begin to refer to the person as a celebrity. Presto, the client is a celebrity. Nobody officially proclaims the celebrity status, any more than some mysteriously remote Solomon on a high pinnacle sends down official word that a sports "star" has become a "superstar."

Barbara Goldsmith, in her New York *Times* magazine article, points out the importance of image to an aspiring celebrity:

> **Image is essential to the celebrity because the public judges him by what it sees—his public posture as distinguished from his private person. Entertainers are particularly adept at perfecting their images, learning to refine the nuances of personality. Indeed, the words "celebrity" and "personality" have become interchangeable in our language. Public relations people, who are paid to manufacture celebrities for public consumption, are often referred to as image makers.**

Indicative of the commercialization of personality is the success of a company called Celebrity Service, which keeps files on approximately 300,000 individuals and publishes up-to-date information about them in a daily *Celebrity Bulletin*, available for a high subscription fee. It also issues an annual celebrity *Contact Book*. Much of the information is supplied by public relations representatives, whose clients are pleased to be on the service's list. No one pays to be listed: "celebrity" importance is the criterion.

A PRESS AGENT'S REVELATIONS

An entertaining source book on the activities of a Hollywood press agent is *Walking the Tightrope* by Henry Rogers, (of Rogers & Cowan Public Relations). In the book, the author recounts how he attracted media attention to an aspiring actress named Rita Hayworth. The news angle was her fabulous wardrobe—even though he spent a week before the *Look* magazine interview borrowing clothes all over town for Hayworth's closet.

In more recent years, Rogers had Cheryl Tiegs, the famous model, as a client. The publicity campaign was to reposition her as a beauty and physical fitness expert, since she had reached the golden age of 30 and could no longer generate high modeling fees in a culture that emphasizes youth. Part of the firm's work involved (1) getting her on television talk shows to speak about beauty care and physical fitness, (2) convincing *Time* magazine that she would make an excellent cover story—which appeared, and (3) sending her on a multicity tour to publicize her book.

PSYCHOLOGICAL EXPLANATIONS

Psychologists offer varied explanations of why the public becomes impressed—often *fascinated* is the more accurate word—by highly publicized individuals. In pretelevision days, the publicity departments of the motion picture studios promoted their male and female stars as glamour figures who lived in a special world of privilege and wealth. Dreaming of achieving such glory for themselves, young people with and without talent came to Hollywood to crash the magical gates, almost always in vain. Thousands more back home spun fantasies about being Marilyn Monroe or Clark Gable. They cherished machine-autographed pictures of their favorites and read with relish inflated stories about the stars in fan magazines, visualizing themselves in the glamour figures' places.

In the earlier days of personality buildup, *wish-fulfillment* was a compelling force. It still is. Their exposure on television in the intimacy of the family living room, however, makes personalities seem much closer to admiring viewers today than the remote gods and goddesses were in the glory days of the major motion picture studios. Such is the power of television, in fact, that reporters and anchorpersons who talk on camera about the activities of celebrities attain celebrity status themselves.

Many ordinary people leading routine lives yearn for heroes. Professional and big-time college sports provide personalities for *hero worship*. Publicists emphasize the performances of certain players, and television game announcers often build up the stars' roles out of proportion to their achievements; this emphasis creates hero figures for youthful sports enthusiasts to emulate.

In addition to admiration for individual performers, members of the public develop a *vicarious sense of belonging* that creates support for athletic teams. Sports publicists exploit this feeling in numerous ways. A winning baseball team becomes "our" team in conversations among patrons of a bar. To signify their loyalty, children and adults alike wear baseball caps bearing the insignia of their favorite major league teams. Enthusiasts decorate their automobiles with bumper stickers and license-plate holders bearing the name of their favorite team. It isn't surprising that alumni of a university gnaw their fingernails while watching their school basketball team in a tight game, but the same intensity of support is found among fans who have no direct tie to the school. For many years, the vehement rooting from afar for Notre Dame's football team by its so-called sidewalk alumni has been notorious. A championship professional sports team stirs widespread community support.

Still another factor is the *desire for entertainment* most people feel. Reading fan magazines, or watching their favorite stars being interviewed, or lining up in front of a box office hours before it opens, to be sure of getting a ticket—these are ways to bring variety and a little excitement into the daily routine of life.

A public relations practitioner assigned to build up the public image of an individual, either to increase the client's ego satisfaction or to stimulate sale of tickets to an event involving the individual, should analyze the ways in which these psychological factors can be applied. Since the client's co-operation is vital in promotional work, a wise publicist explains this background and tells the client why various actions are planned.

The Practitioner's Responsibility

DAMAGE CONTROL

A practitioner handling an individual client is responsible for protecting the client from bad publicity as well as generating positive news. When the client appears in a bad light because of misbehavior or an irresponsible public statement, the publicist must try to minimize the harm done to the client's public image. To use a naval term, the objective is damage control.

Often politicians who say something controversial in public, then wish later that they hadn't, try to squirm out of the predicament by claiming they were misquoted. This is a foolish defense unless the politician can prove conclusively that he or she was indeed quoted incorrectly. Reporters resent accusations of inaccuracy and may hold a grudge against the accuser. If the accused reporter has the politician's statement on tape, the politician looks even worse. A better defense is for the politician to explain what he or she intended and to express regret for the slip of the tongue.

THE QUESTION OF ETHICS

Personal misconduct by a client, or the appearance of misconduct, strains a practitioner's ingenuity and at times his or her ethical principles. Some practitioners will lie outright to protect a client, a dishonest practice that looks even worse if the media show the statement to be a lie. On occasion, a practitioner acting in good faith may be victimized because the client has lied. As a cynical old-time Hollywood publicist put it, while describing how he helped cover up for a famous film hero (married) who found his actress girlfriend dead in her bedroom under strange circumstances, "We told him that before we could lie for him, he had to tell us the truth." Generally, experienced publicists advise their clients in trouble to remain out of sight and talk to as few persons as possible during the critical period.

Issuing a prepared statement to explain the client's conduct, while leaving reporters and their editors dissatisfied, is regarded as safer than having the client call a news conference, unless the client is a victim of circumstances and is best served by talking fully and openly. The decision about holding a news conference also is influenced by how articulate and self-controlled the client is. Under questioning, a person on the defensive may say something that compounds the problem. Guiding a personality through a period of trouble is an unpleasant, difficult aspect of a practitioner's job and may test his or her standards of good professional behavior. (*Defensive* news conferences are discussed more fully in Chapter 23.)

Conducting a Personality Campaign

A campaign to generate public awareness of an individual should be planned just as meticulously as any other public relations project. This is the fundamental process, step by step, for the practitioner to follow.

INTERVIEW THE CLIENT

He or she should answer a detailed personal questionnaire. The practitioner should be a dogged, probing interviewer, digging for interesting and possibly newsworthy facts about the person's life, activities, and beliefs. In talking about themselves, individuals frequently fail to realize that certain elements of their experiences have publicity value under the right circumstances.

Perhaps, for example, the client is a little-known actress who has won a role as a Midwestern farmer's young wife in a motion picture. During her get-acquainted talks with the publicist, she happens to mention in passing that while growing up in a small town she belonged to the 4-H Club. The feature angle can be the realism she brings to the movie role: when she was a member of the youth organization, she actually did the farm jobs she will perform in the film.

Not only must practitioners draw out such details from their clients; they must have the ingenuity to develop these facts as story angles. When the actress is placed as a guest on a television talk show, the publicist should prompt her in advance to recall incidents from her 4-H experience. Two or three humorous anecdotes about mishaps with pigs and chickens, tossed into the TV interview, give it verve. The audience will remember her. The television show host should be tipped off to lead the interview in this direction.

PREPARE A BIOGRAPHY OF THE CLIENT

This basic document should be limited to four typed pages, perhaps less. News and feature angles should be placed high in the *bio,* as it is termed, so an editor or producer can find them quickly. The biography, a portrait and other photographs of the client, and, if possible, additional personal background items should be assembled in a press kit for extensive distribution. Usually the kit is a cardboard folder with inside pockets to hold the contents.

PLAN A MARKETING STRATEGY

The practitioner should determine precisely what is to be sold. Is the purpose only to increase public awareness of the individual, or also to publicize the client's product, such as a new television series, motion picture, or book? Next, the practitioner should decide which types of audience are the most important to reach. For instance, an interview with a romantic operatic tenor on a rock-and-roll radio station would be inappropriate. But an appearance by the singer on a public television station's talk show would be right on target. A politician trying to project himself as a representative of minority groups should be scheduled to speak before audiences in minority neighborhoods and placed on radio stations whose demographic reports show that they attract minority listeners.

CONDUCT THE CAMPAIGN

The best course normally is to project the client on multiple media simultaneously. Radio and television appearances create an awareness and often make newspaper feature stories easier to obtain. The process works in reverse, as well. Using telephone calls and "pitch" letters to editors and program directors, the publicist should propose print and on-air interviews with the client. Every such approach should include a news or feature angle for the interviewer to develop. Since magazine articles require longer to reach print, the publicist should begin efforts to obtain them as early as feasible, once the exposure process has begun to gain momentum.

NEWS RELEASES   News releases are an important avenue of publicity, but the practitioner should avoid too much puffery. *Bulldog,* a West Coast public relations newsletter, once gave a "fireplug" award to a press agent who wrote a release about a Frank Sinatra concert in the Dominican Republic. The release said, in part:

The Sinatra concert represented the first time a legendary star has ever performed for a subscription pay television service. The historical event, in a balmy night that could only rival, not surpass, the audience's decibel level for enthusiasm, should overshadow any in-person star appearance ever offered on subscription television. The Sinatra and Santana/Heart doubleheaders may well be recorded as pay TV milestones.

PHOTOGRAPHS   Photographs of the client should be submitted to the print media as often as justifiable. The standard head-and-shoulders portrait, often called a "mug shot," in the press kit is basic. Photographs of the client doing something interesting or appearing in a newsworthy group may be published merely with a caption, without accompanying story. If the client seeks national attention, such pictures should be submitted to the press associations so that, if deemed newsworthy, they will be distributed to hundreds of newspapers. (Newspaper and magazine requirements for photographs are discussed in Chapter 24.)

The practitioner and the photographer should be inventive, putting the client into unusual situations. The justification for a successful submission may be thin if the picture is colorful and/or timely. Typically, the Associated Press distributed a photograph of actor Larry Hagman, villain of the television show "Dallas," and his Swedish-born wife, Maj, posing with three young women and a young man in Scandinavian national costumes. Two of the Scandinavians held small Swedish and Norwegian flags. Everyone was smiling. The pose resembled those found in hundreds of amateur snapshot albums. Although of little significance from either news or photographic points of view, the picture was published in newspapers a few days before Christmas because it was seasonal. The caption stated: "Actor Larry Hagman and his Swedish-born wife Maj pose with representatives of the Scandinavian community in Los Angeles Wednesday after the group presented Hagman and his wife with traditional holiday ornaments from their native countries." Obviously this was a contrived situation, but a pleasant one; it contributed to the desired image of Hagman as a nice fellow off-screen.

Some cliché situations produce publishable photographs year after year because editors desire a visual representation of an event. What a galaxy of pulchritude it would be if someone assembled in one place all the aspiring young actresses who have ever been photographed turning the hands of a clock forward or backward an hour to signify the daylight-savings time change each spring and fall! Editors know the situation is trite. Yet many publish the pictures as reminders to readers and incidentally as a relatively lame excuse to use the picture of a pretty young woman.

Sharply increased awareness among editors of women's concern about sexual exploitation has largely eliminated "cheesecake" pictures—photo-

480

graphs of nubile young women in which the news angle often is as skimpy as their attire—from newspaper pages. At one time such pictures were published frequently as editors tried to spice up their pages. Occasionally such a picture shows up in print today, blatantly contrived and perhaps in bad taste, such as the one of a smiling man pointing to the replica of a check painted on the bare stomach of a belly dancer. The caption read: "Julian Caruso, an entertainment manager, arrived in court in Stafford, England, yesterday to pay a parking fine. He didn't want to pay the fine, the equivalent of $17, because, he said, Stafford lacks adequate parking. To emphasize his displeasure, he presented the court a check written on the stomach of a belly dancer, Sandrina. Court officials took a look at her—real name, Sandra Audley— and decided they couldn't handle the check in that form."

Stunts like this are a throwback to old-time gimmick press agentry, yet sometimes they succeed. The picture was distributed by the Associated Press and published large size in at least one metropolitan newspaper.

Cheesecake photographs still are printed in the trade press, even though they are seldom seen in daily newspapers. Some practitioners persist in having bikini-clad models appear at trade shows and shopping center openings, but in doing so they risk having the events picketed by irate women— and men, too.

PUBLIC APPEARANCES   Another way to intensify awareness of individual clients is to arrange for them to appear frequently in public places. The appearances may be as lowly as cutting the ribbon at a new supermarket or attending opening ceremonies at a county fair. Pictures are taken at the event and possibly published. Anyone with name recognition may be introduced to the audience if he or she attends a local charity event or similar good cause and also may be photographed chatting with prominent guests.

Commercial organizations at times hire celebrities of various calibers to dress up dinner meetings, conventions, and even store openings. A major savings and loan association employs a group of early-day television performers to appear at openings of branch offices. Each day for a week, for two hours, an entertainer stands in a guest booth, signing autographs and chatting with visitors, who receive a paperback book of pictures recalling television's pioneer period. Refreshments are served. A company photographer takes pictures of the celebrity talking to guests. Later, visitors who appear in the pictures receive them as a souvenir. These appearances benefit the commercial sponsor by attracting crowds and help the entertainers stay in the public eye.

AWARDS   A much-used device, but still successful, is to have a client receive an award. The practitioner should be alert for news of awards to be given and nominate the client for appropriate ones. Follow-up contacts with persuasive material by the practitioner may convince the sponsor to make the award to the client. In some instances, the idea of an award is proposed to an organization by a practitioner, whose client then conveniently is declared the first recipient. The entertainment business generates immense amounts of publicity for individuals and shows with its Oscar and Emmy awards. Winning an Academy Award greatly strengthens a performer's career and means much additional box office revenue for a film. There are myriads of lesser accolades, such as the Person of the Year, Humanitarian, Friend of Animals, and similar presentations.

QUESTION-AND-ANSWER COLUMNS   Another source of exposure in print is the question-and-answer column in newspapers and magazines. The format is for well-known persons to answer questions that readers have submitted to the columnist. Some of the questions published are legitimate; the columnist often asks public relations representatives of the personalities involved to supply answers. However, less legitimately, practitioners sometimes submit questions about their clients along with the answers, and the columnist publishes both—an easy way for the writer to fill a column. In some instances, a columnist may even invite practitioners to send in such question-and-answer sets.

NICKNAMES AND LABELS   Creating catchy nicknames for clients, especially sports and entertainment figures, helps the practitioner get their names into print. Celebrity-worshipers like to call their heroes and heroines by nicknames, as though the practice denotes a personal relationship. Thus we see and hear such familiarities for professional basketball players as "Doctor J" and "Magic," and "Old Blue Eyes" and "Elvis the Pelvis" for entertainers. Cliché-prone reporters and columnists help to perpetuate these appellations.

A questionable variation of the nickname consists of adding a descriptive word to the name of a person being publicized, to create a desirable image or career association. Sometimes this is done to provide a respectable veneer for a person of dubious background. In the Palm Springs resort area, to cite an instance, a socially active figure named Ray Ryan hired a practitioner whose task was to build up the image of Ryan as a well-to-do oilman. In every news release about Ryan and every telegram inviting social, business, and media individuals to Ryan's elaborate parties, the practitioner referred to his client as "oilman Ray Ryan." Publications in the area consistently printed "oilman Ray Ryan," giving the publicist the effect he desired. Actually, Ryan also was involved in big-time professional gambling—an involvement apparently responsible for the fact that when he stepped on the starter of his automobile one day a murderer's bomb planted in the car killed him.

RECORD THE RESULTS   Those who employ practitioners want tangible results in return for their fees. The practitioner also needs to compile and analyze the results of a personality campaign in order to determine the effectiveness of the various methods used. Tearsheets, photographs, copies of news releases, and, when possible, videotape clips of the client's public appearances should be given to the client. Clipping services help the practitioner assemble this material. At the end of the campaign, or at intervals in a long-term program, summaries of what has been accomplished should be submitted. Estimates of the audiences reached, based on circulation figures of publications, audience estimates of radio and television stations, and similar statistical criteria often impress clients, although their value as indicators of a campaign's true effectiveness is doubtful (see Chapter 10).

Promoting an Entertainment

**PUBLICITY
TO STIMULATE
TICKET SALES**

The primary goal of any campaign for an entertainment is to sell tickets. An advance publicity buildup informs listeners, readers, and viewers that an event will occur and stimulates their desire to attend it. Rarely, except for community events publicized in smaller cities, do newspaper stories and broadcasts about an entertainment include detailed information on ticket prices and availability. Those facts usually are deemed too commercial by editors and should be announced in paid advertising. Even pop singer Michael Jackson's managers found the press uncooperative when they requested newspapers to publish ticket application coupons free of charge for his "Victory" tour in 1984. However, some newspapers may include prices, times, and so on in tabular listings of scheduled entertainments. Performance dates usually are included in publicity stories.

Stories about a forthcoming theatrical event, motion picture, rock concert, or similar commercial performance should concentrate on the personalities, style, and history of the show. Every time the show is mentioned, public awareness grows. Thus, astute practitioners search for fresh news angles to produce as many stories as possible. Even two-paragraph items are valuable if they mention the names of the show and its stars. Newspaper entertainment pages frequently use such short pieces.

**AN EXAMPLE:
PUBLICIZING A PLAY**

Let us look at the way a new play can be publicized. The methods are the same, whether the work will be performed on Broadway by professionals or in the local municipal auditorium by a little-theater group.

Stories include an announcement that the play will be presented, followed by releases reporting the casting of lead characters, start of rehearsals, and opening date. Feature stories, or "readers," discuss the play's theme and background, with quotations from the playwright and director inserted to emphasize an important point. In print, radio, and television interviews the play's star can tell why he or she finds the role significant or amusing.

Photographs of show scenes, taken in costume during rehearsal, should be distributed to the media, to give potential customers a preview glimpse.

As a reminder, a brief "opening tonight" story may be distributed. If a newspaper lists theatrical events in tabular form, the practitioner might submit an entry about the show, to make the editor's work easier and increase the likelihood that the listing will appear correctly.

THE "DRIP-DRIP-DRIP" TECHNIQUE OF PUBLICITY

Motion pictures studios, television production firms, and networks apply the principle of "drip-drip-drip" publicity when a show is being shot. In other words, there is a steady output of information about the production. A public relations specialist, called a unit man or woman, assigned to a film during production turns out a flow of stories for the general and trade press and plays host to media visitors to the set. The television networks mail out daily news bulletins about their shows to media television editors. They assemble the editors annually to preview new programs and interview their stars. The heaviest barrage of publicity is released shortly before the show openings.

Such an outpouring of publicity, for instance, drew exceptionally high ratings for the final episode of the long-running television weekly show "M*A*S*H*." After the announcement that the series about a military hospital in the Korean War would end, the buildup for the final episode began. Reporters were invited onto the set when the episode was filmed. Their stories added to the anticipation. When the episode was shown several weeks later, the event was treated as national news, receiving spot coverage in electronic and print media. The "hype" not only enlarged the audience substantially but promoted the reruns of the series.

One danger of excessive promotion of an event, however, is that audience expectation may become too high, so that the performance proves to be a disappointment. A skilled practitioner will be judicious in his or her use of publicity, and stay away from "hype" that can lead to a sense of anticlimax.

A LOOK AT THE MOTION PICTURE INDUSTRY

By market research and interpretation of demographics and psychographics, motion picture public relations departments define target audiences they seek to reach. Most motion picture publicity is aimed at the 18-to-24-year-olds, where the largest audience lies. Seventy-five percent of the film audience is under age 39.

Professional entertainment publicity work is concentrated in New York and Los Angeles, the former as the nation's theatrical center and the latter as the motion picture center. (American television production is divided primarily between those two cities, with the larger portion in Los Angeles.)

A typical Los Angeles–area public relations firm specializing in personalities and entertainment has two staffs: one staff of "planters," who deliver to media offices publicity stories about individual clients and the projects in which they are engaged, and another staff of "bookers," whose job is to place clients on talk shows and in other public appearances. Some publicity stories are for general release; others are prepared especially for a single media outlet such as a syndicated Hollywood columnist or a major newspaper. The latter type is marked "exclusive," permitting the publication or station that uses it to claim credit for "breaking" the story.

A cardinal sin of "exclusive" publicity is to give a story to two media outlets simultaneously, in the hope that one or the other will use it. This practice is called "double planting." Anyone caught doing this risks falling into disfavor at both outlets, which may punish the practitioner by refusing to use other material he or she provides.

Another device is to provide supplies of tickets for a new movie or show to radio stations, whose disc jockeys award them to listeners as prizes in on-the air contests. In the process, these announcers mention the name of the show dozens of times. Glamorous premieres and trips for media guests to distant points so they can watch the filming or attend an opening are used occasionally, too.

For such services to individual or corporate entertainment clients, major Hollywood publicists charge at least $3000 a month, with a 3-month minimum. The major studios and networks have their own public relations staffs.

Sports Publicity

Professional and big time college sports, especially football and basketball, are entertainment that must be sold like other shows. They compete for the consumer's time and dollars just as motion pictures, fairs, rock concerts, and plays do. Sports has a highly exploited star system in which colorful individual athletes are publicized as energetically as contract film stars of the major motion picture studios once were. As a result, a special field of sports public relations has developed, using the same principles as other entertainment publicity, but with angles all its own.

COLLEGE AND UNIVERSITY SPORTS

In universities, the sports publicity director usually is an athletically inclined practitioner whose task is to build crowds for games, maintain alumni enthusiasm for the old school's teams, and assist in enticing high school athletic stars to enroll in the school. Among the standard tools of the sports publicity director are press kits, news releases, publicity photographs, interviews with coaches and sometimes with players, and press box tickets for games. At the start of each football practice season, a press day is held during which photographers take on-field pictures of the players in uniform and reporters talk with coaches and players.

Emphasis on individual stardom in college football and basketball is heavy because stars sell tickets, and college football is big-dollar business. Star-studded winning teams fill the seats, earn money and public attention

Hyping the Heisman Trophy	Doug Flutie of Boston College received the 1984 Heisman Trophy as the year's best collegiate football player. Although the award, voted by U.S. sportswriters, was based on his performance, effective publicity was also a factor.

Each week during the season, Boston College mailed "The Flutie Watch," which detailed the activities of its star quarterback, to sportswriters. Reid Oslin, assistant athletic director for sports publicity at Boston College, told the *Chronicle of Higher Education*, " . . . We want Doug to win the Heisman on the field . . . but we do let the writers know what he has accomplished."

And such publicity seems to have an effect. In the same article, Michael Wilson of the Washington *Post* said, "It makes the writers aware of athletes that they would not be aware of. Most writers cover one team, so they don't see all the people so they need to know about them."

Other institutions, of course, were also promoting their top prospects for the Heisman Trophy. The U.S. Naval Academy, for example, took Napoleon McCallum to Baltimore, dressed him like John Paul Jones, and posed him in front of the U.S.S. *Constellation*, an early American warship, with a football in one hand and a sword in the other. The resulting poster carried the caption, "I have not yet begun to run."

from postseason games, and encourage alumni to make contributions. Thus the campaigns by sports practitioners to get college players named to all-American teams are intense, often employing attention-getting techniques that have little direct bearing on the games themselves.

An example: sports editors coast to coast received, from the Clemson University publicity department, cereal boxes resembling those of the "Special K" brand. On the boxes were printed statistics about Terry Kinard, the Clemson free safety, and praise for him as all-American material—the implication being that Kinard (the "K") was something special.

Letting its imagination soar even further, in publicizing another player, Clemson later sent out a card whose cover carried a back view of a pretty young woman, with the headline "Most Gentlemen Prefer Blondes. . . ." Turning to the inside, the recipient saw a photograph of a husky young man in a tuxedo, holding a football and standing near the young woman. At the top was the headline, "Most Clemson Fans Prefer the Strong, Silent Type." The facing page contained a photograph of Dan Benish, a defensive tackle, in action and listed statistics on his career. The copy announced that he was an all-American candidate. The back page showed Benish walking away with his arm around the young woman, whose face was never seen.

Both the Kinard and Benish publicity devices were efforts to gain name recognition for them so that sports editors would remember them among the hundreds of college players in the same positions.

When a university has a football player believed capable of winning the Heisman Trophy, the annual award to the man selected as the best college player, its publicity department outdoes itself. During running back Hershel Walker's last year at the University of Georgia, the university's media football guide featured a large photograph of Walker holding a helmet, on which a replica of the Heisman Trophy was reflected. Suggestive photography, indeed! He won the award, too.

PROFESSIONAL SPORTS   Public relations departments of professional football and baseball teams strive to create images for their clubs that will catch the fans' attention. The Los Angeles Dodgers feature Dodger Blue, the predominant color of their uniforms. When the aggressive, belligerent Billy Martin managed the Oakland Athletics, the management promoted "Billy Ball" to suggest excitement. Even after Martin moved back to the New York Yankees, the term *Billy Ball* remained alive in the San Francisco Bay area as the name of a successful race horse. Bumper stickers, license-plate holders, posters, and buttons are distributed, publicizing team names and images.

The San Francisco Giants, who play in windswept, chilly Candlestick Park, decided to capitalize on what is regarded as a negative factor. They spent $900,000 in publicity and advertising one season after a marketing survey identified the ball park's atmospheric conditions as the team's greatest disadvantage. Adopting a humorous approach, the publicity department designed a logotype showing the letters *SF* encrusted in ice. Each fan who stayed for an extra-inning night game received a button on which the words *Croix de Candlestick* appeared above the frigid lettering. This was described as a "badge of courage." The theme of the campaign was that a fan who attends a night game at Candlestick Park is tough and tenacious—a clever attempt to get positive value out of a disadvantage.

SUPERSPORTS: THE SUPER BOWL   The ultimate in sports hype is the National Football League's championship playoff game, the Super Bowl. A football game, frequently no more exciting and often less so than many regular season games, has been turned into a weeklong spectacular. To suggest stature and great importance, each year's game is known by a Roman numeral—not just Super Bowl 20 but Super Bowl XX.

More than 2500 media credentials are issued, and print and electronic reporters fall over each other during the week, hunting story angles. Raucous parties mark the week as free-spending ticketholders swarm into the host city. The telecast of the game itself is seen by more than 100 million viewers, according to the ratings. The network whose turn it is to broadcast the game uses more than 20 cameras, a dozen or so videotape machines for replays, and about 100 microphones to inundate viewers with pictures and commentary. ABC, which televised the 1985 Super Bowl, recovered its investment, plus, by charging $525,000 for a 30-second commercial. During the game, one ABC announcer noted that the cost of a commercial was about the same as the entire cost of the Stanford University stadium (site of the game) when it was built in the 1920s.

Anyone responsible for staging a sports event, in fact, can benefit from studying the public relations effort at a Super Bowl, then reducing it in scope to fit the particular need.

At the 1985 Super Bowl XIX between the San Francisco 49ers and the Miami Dolphins, for example, the NFL issued 2700 sets of media credentials. To offer adequate press service, the NFL public relations department supplemented its staff by bringing in the publicity directors of several league teams. During the week preceding the game, the league ran buses for the

FIGURE 20.2

Distribution to the media of detailed statistics about games and players is an essential element of sports publicity. This is the cover of a 44-page media guide issued by the National Football League to reporters covering Super Bowl XVIII at Tampa, Florida, in January 1984.

media from hotels to the practice fields, arranged news conferences and photographic sessions, organized parties, and operated a central media headquarters in a hotel.

Each representative received an artificial leather briefcase containing a game ticket, direction guide, brochure about the competing teams, a pen, and a clipboard. To assist sports writers, publicity departments compiled sets of facts about teams, as Figure 20.2 illustrates. At the stadium on game day, the league provided a four-tiered main press box, an auxiliary press section, and extra workrooms below the stands. After the Sunday afternoon game, the department opened a large dining room at the headquarters hotel, to which news people were invited as NFL guests. On Monday morning, media coverage ended with a news conference given by the winning 49ers coach, Bill Walsh.

By paying close attention to detail, providing ample staff personnel, and arranging adequate working space, the NFL kept the media throng satisfied in a situation that, poorly handled, could have become chaos.

QUESTIONS FOR REVIEW AND DISCUSSION

1. Why do public relations students need to understand how the personal publicity trade functions, even if they do not plan to handle theatrical or sports clients?

2. What is the most sought-after publicity appearance on American television?

3. Name two psychological factors underlying the American obsession with celebrities.

4. When politicians say something they wish they hadn't and it is published, they often claim that they were misquoted. Why is this poor policy?

5. What is the first step in preparing a campaign to increase the public's awareness of an individual client?

6. What is a *bio?* What should it contain?

7. "Cheesecake" photographs once were commonplace in American newspapers, but few are published now. Why is this so?

8. A professional blunder committed by some entertainment practitioners is called "double planting." What does this mean?

9. Why do practitioners put emphasis on certain players on sports teams?

10. What is one device the promoters of the annual professional football Super Bowl use to suggest that the event has great stature?

Part five

TACTICS

CHAPTER TWENTY-ONE

Public Relations and New Technologies

Enormous changes are occurring in the mechanics of communication. The technology available to public relations practitioners has expanded spectacularly. Therefore, this chapter begins by explaining these recently developed electronic methods.

The chapter focuses primarily on three major developments: (1) the computer, (2) satellite transmission, and (3) videotape. It explains how they operate and tells how they are used in public relations work.

Within a public relations office, uses of the computer include preparation of news releases, dispatch of electronic mail, and maintenance of mailing lists and lists of contacts. The computer also is valuable in gathering information from outside sources, especially from data bases.

Public relations organizations use satellite transmission for distribution of news releases and for conducting teleconferences. Videotape has innumerable applications; some examples are given in the chapter. Other new technologies described include teletext, videotex, and fiber optics.

The Communications Explosion

Fortunately for public relations people, the communications explosion of recent years gives them an array of new tools with which to communicate their messages more rapidly, attractively, and precisely. The electronic revolution has added zest to their work. It challenges the ingenuity of practitioners to find new ways of applying technology to their jobs.

An earlier generation worked primarily with telephone, typewriter, pencil, and mimeograph machine. The telephone remains vital. Imagine trying to work for a day without it! But the new technology has produced equipment that, if not entirely replacing the old standbys, works faster and more flexibly than they do. The word processor supplants the typewriter at desks, and the high-speed duplicating machine produces sleek printlike copies, sometimes in color, that are far superior to the output of the traditional mimeograph machine.

The Computer

By definition, a computer is a machine that accepts and processes information and supplies the results in a desired form. The digital computer processes the information with figures, using binary or decimal notation to solve mathematical problems at high speed. Development of the microcomputer has added flexibility and convenience for users.

FIGURE 21.1

The versatility of the personal computer, such as this Hewlett Packard 150, has created new ways for public relations practitioners to communicate.

Since a computer can store, codify, analyze, and search out information at speeds far beyond human capability, its applications are enormous. When we add its ability to transmit this information over long distances at fantastically high speeds, its potential becomes even greater. Still more astounding is the anticipated development of the "thinking" computer. This machine, designed to diagnose and solve problems, in addition to calculating and processing data as present computers do, is in the experimental stages in Japanese and American laboratories.

It is easy to become bewildered by all the fascinating applications of the computer, which has entered almost every phase of daily life (see Figure 21.1). The text will concentrate on the way public relations practitioners can make effective use of this new equipment.

WORD PROCESSING

As a tool for writers, the computer has two striking advantages over the typewriter: (1) the capacity to store created material in its memory system for instant recall, and (2) the ability to make corrections, insert fresh material, and move material from one portion of a document to another. Typewritten copy must be retyped to incorporate changes; in word processing, alterations are made by the push of keys and movement of the little cursor light to the indicated position.

Material written on a computer can be transferred electronically to another person's computer for review, correction, and approval. By using a printer attachment, the writer can obtain a "hard copy" version printed on paper. Here are a few specific examples of how computer word processing can be used in public relations practice.

BUSINESS LETTERS   The word processor can produce professional-quality business letters from material typed into the computer. If a counseling firm wishes to send an identical letter, except for a few personalized touches, to 10 prospective clients, some taps on a keyboard will produce a different salutation on each plus individualized copy changes aimed specifically at each recipient. On the typewriter, this special attention would require the time-consuming typing of 10 letters. With word processing, the result can be obtained with a small amount of keyboard punching. This instance is merely a sample of how business-letter writing can be speeded up with a computer.

PROCESSING OF NEWS RELEASES   Word processing is valuable in preparation of news releases. Like letters, releases can be reworded by computer for different types of publications, such as trade magazines, daily newspapers, and the business press. The draft of a news release can be placed in computer storage while the client makes revisions on a printout copy. These changes can then be made without the time-consuming process of retyping the entire release. Also, the draft of a news release can be entered in storage by its writer and later called up on another screen by the supervisor who must review and approve it.

CORRECTION OF SPELLING AND GRAMMAR   Special software programs—sets of instructions telling the computer what to do—can improve the public relations writer's work by correcting spelling and grammatical mistakes.

ELECTRONIC MAIL   A piece of writing delivered from the originator's computer into the recipient's computer, instead of being sent by mail or messenger service, often is called *electronic mail*. When a writer is creating copy for a brochure, the edited text can be recorded on a disk for delivery to the printing company. Or, if the printing company has suitable computer connections, the brochure copy can be transmitted electronically from the writer's computer into the printing company's computer. No paper is used. That computer in turn can feed the copy into a phototypesetting system, from which it will emerge as type on paper ready to be reproduced, with headlines included.

MAILING LISTS   Up-to-date mailing lists are vital in public relations work. The old method was to have a separate metal plate for each person, with relevant information punched onto the plate. These plates were kept in trays and fed through a machine to stamp the addresses onto mailing pieces. Today, lists of names are typed into a computer and stored in its memory. Changes of address or other alterations can be made by calling up a name and using a few keystrokes. When a mailing is to be made, the desired names on the master list can be activated and printed on adhesive labels or on the individual envelopes.

The capability to select groups of names from the master list assists the practitioner in reaching target audiences. Typically, Edward Reed, vice-president of Claire Harrison Associates, wrote in *Public Relations Journal* that his firm maintains a mailing list of about 3500 names in its computer system. He explained, "We have divided our list into 175 homogenous groups, and we can pick specific groups for a specific mailing. Requesting this from the computer takes no time at all, and we can print on labels, envelopes, or even generate personalized letters."

LISTS OF CONTACTS   In a related application, public relations offices use the storage and call-up facilities of computers to maintain ready-reference lists of individuals with their telephone numbers and addresses, job titles, and other personal data, which can be listed by category.

By keeping names and addresses on a computerized list, the public relations practitioner can easily add new names and make corrections—and the computer keeps everything in alphabetical order. This eliminates the traditional address card file.

With certain software programs, a person can summon a desired telephone number onto the screen and, with a single command, have the computer automatically dial the number.

DATA BASES   The sampling of computer applications just described is essentially in-house, involving material created and stored within the public relations office. The computer also is invaluable as a collector of information from outside sources. As a research tool, the computer's importance is growing swiftly because the number and size of the data bases from which it can extract information are multiplying.

In the past, doing research involved poring through books, reports, and similar printed matter in search of desired information. Although this traditional method remains basic, it has been supplemented enormously by creation of computer storage systems. These hold masses of diverse information, ranging from remote statistical data to current news stories, that may be tapped by computer users.

The researcher gains access to a desired data base by telephoning a publicly listed number or a private number, depending upon the nature of the base. Users often are assigned a password that when typed into a computer opens a data base to them. For use of some bases, the researcher pays an hourly fee; for others, a subscription fee plus time charges. Still other data bases are available free because their proprietors operate a public service or desire distribution of the stored information to the public for commercial or professional reasons. Data bases assist users by showing indexes on the computer screen that direct them to desired categories of material.

In order to enter a data base, a computer must be equipped with a *modem* (short for *modulator/demodulator*), an attachment that converts the computer's electrical signals into signals that can move along the telephone line.

Approximately 1500 data bases were in operation by the mid-1980s, and the number is growing. They range from the so-called commercial "supermarkets" that offer a broad assortment of information categories to specialized technical services. Local bulletin board data bases operate in large cities, and interlocking regional networks have been created.

Here are some of the best-known data bases:

Dow Jones News/Retrieval. A source of business information, it provides stock prices and other financial news, along with the content of the *Wall Street Journal* and transcripts of the Public Broadcasting System's "Wall Street Week" television program. It also covers sports, weather, and movie reviews.

Gems from Data Base Research

Data bases contain masses of information available to assist public relations practitioners on difficult assignments who need answers to obscure questions. Specialists trained in data base research usually can find the answers, often in a surprisingly short time.

Writing in *Communication World*, Hank Bachrach gave this sampling of questions data base researchers have been requested to answer:

What is the state-by-state tally of sheep slaughtered in the past year?

How much underwear is produced in Malaysia?

What is the heartbeat of an elephant? of a mouse?

How many bottle caps are produced in the United States?

What are the thermodynamic properties of potassium?

How is a wife in a harem defined for tax purposes?

Drawing by Curt Hopkins, in *Communication World.* (Reprinted by courtesy of *Communication World.*)

NEXIS. This includes the text of leading newspapers, press association reports, business magazines, and newsletters. It also has a law data base, LEXIS.

Dialog Information Retrieval Service. This has more than 180 data bases, many of them deriving from the space program, from which the user may choose. Newspaper and magazine indexes are included in its 80 million entries.

The Source. Services include news, games, numerous categories of information, and electronic mail.

CompuServe. This offers services similar to those provided by The Source.

VU/TEXT. Operated by Knight-Ridder Newspapers, Inc., this includes the contents and electronic libraries of numerous newspapers. A researcher can call up the entire text of the Washington *Post* on either VU/TEXT or NEXIS.

Several reference books provide lists of available data base services. Two important sources for a listing of services are *The Computer Phone Book,* by Mike Cane, published by the New American Library, New York, and *The Directory of Online Databases,* put out by Cuadra Associates, Santa Monica, California.

Some public libraries offer computer search service for relatively small fees, to assist individuals who do not have computers or prefer to have a trained librarian conduct the search. Typically, a person can hunt through a magazine index to find listings of articles on desired topics, information on specified medical problems, and government reports—types of information a public relations practitioner often needs in formulating programs.

HOW ONE PUBLIC RELATIONS FIRM USES DATA BASE RESEARCH There are a number of ways in which public relations firms use on-line data base research. Regis McKenna Public Relations, headquartered in Palo Alto, California, and specializing in high technology clients, provides a good example.

David M. Schneer, head of secondary research services at Regis McKenna, explains that about half his time is devoted to conducting information searches for clients. A software manufacturer wanted to learn about the customer service and support policies of other software firms. Using NEXIS and Dialog, Schneer rapidly compiled a list of pertinent information that had appeared in business and trade magazines. The information helped the client develop its own customer support plans and position its services against the competition.

On another occasion, a microprocessor manufacturer, monitoring its entry into a relatively new market, wanted to learn if anything had been written about the use of its product in industrial robots. And a manufacturer of microcomputer software used on-line data base research to determine the product publicity activities of its competition. Clients also use data base research to check dissemination of their own messages. What publications, for example, have mentioned the company? in what context?

Regis McKenna also uses on-line data bases to research new clients. Retrieval of information about a company's products, sales, competition, management, and reputation enables account executives to be highly knowledgeable about the client in first meetings and also to recommend appropriate public relations programs.

A third use of on-line research at Regis McKenna is staff education. An account executive, just assigned a new account, can rapidly gain information about the client and its products by using a data base. For example, an account executive wanted information about CAD/CAM systems (computer-aided design and computer-aided manufacturing) in preparation for a meeting with a client. Regis McKenna also maintains a library that subscribes to 250 newsletters and magazines in the electronic and business field so that the staff can easily find complete articles from a bibliography provided by on-line data bases. Says Schneer:

In an information society, research from on-line data bases is rapidly becoming a valuable service that public relations firms can provide clients. Public relations firms and corporate communication departments will find it extremely difficult to monitor today's marketplace without using state-of-the-art on-line research techniques.

GOVERNMENT DATA BASES   Although their data bases sometimes are not directly available to public users, many government departments and private organizations such as trade associations retain large amounts of information in computer storage for use in answering inquiries.

Here is just one example of how such computerized information is handled. The Environmental Protection Agency operates an issues information file, open to the public. The file contains material on the background, current status, impact, and implications of 72 key environmental and regulatory issues. Statements by agency representatives are in the file, including key paragraphs from the speeches of EPA officials. A public relations practitioner assigned to write a speech for a client on an environmental topic—acid rain, perhaps—can quickly obtain the pertinent information, including EPA's policy position, by tapping into this accumulation of information.

GRAPHICS   Use of computers to design eye-catching colored graphics—drawings, graphs and charts, and text—for publications is emerging as a new technology in public relations practice. Recent developments in computer software make such graphics possible, although they remain expensive.

Attractive graphics give visual impact to annual reports and employee publications, as well as to video programs and slide presentations. The techniques of computer graphics are still evolving and somewhat complicated, but the imaginative visual effects that experts can obtain are astonishing.

Slide presentations in particular can be enhanced dramatically with computer-generated graphics. Representations of people, designs, and charts add visual zest that stimulates audiences. Increasingly public relations departments and firms employ such graphics to dress up transparencies used in presentations to gain management approval for their ideas. Still another application of computer graphics is in news releases, especially those reporting on corporate sales and earnings. (Preparation of slide shows is discussed in Chapter 24, "Visual Tactics.")

Satellite Transmission

Text messages and pictures can be flashed around the world in seconds by using satellite transmission, a fact of enormous significance to public relations communicators.

Satellite transmission on a reliable 24-hour basis became possible when a satellite was shot aloft to the precise altitude of 22,300 miles above the equator. There a satellite has an orbital period of 24 hours. It thus remains stationary above a fixed point on the earth's surface, available for relaying back to receiving dishes on earth the transmissions beamed up to it from originating points on the ground. So valuable is satellite transmission that a constantly growing number of satellites are being parked above the equator in what scientists call the *geostationary belt*.

When information is dispatched by computer through a ground "uplink" station to a transponder pad on a satellite, then bounced back to a receiving dish on the ground and into a receiving computer, enormous amounts of material can be transmitted over great distances at breathtaking speeds. One computer can "talk" to another via satellite about 160 times faster than can be done over landlines, and at much lower cost. For instance, transmission of a long novel by this method requires only a few seconds.

The *Wall Street Journal* and *USA Today* use satellites to transmit entire page layouts to regional printing plants. The Associated Press, United Press International, and other news services transmit their stories and pictures by satellite. The television and radio networks deliver programs in the same manner.

In public relations practice, satellite transmission has become a tool of impressive dimensions in several ways.

NEWS RELEASE DELIVERY
More than a dozen American companies deliver news releases electronically to large newspapers and other major news media offices. In the receiving newsrooms these releases are fed into computers, to be examined by editors on video display terminals for possible publication or broadcast.

The difference between news release delivery firms and the traditional news services such as the Associated Press is this: Newspapers, radio, and television stations pay large fees to receive the reports of the news services, which maintain staffs of editors and reporters to gather, analyze, select, and write the news in a neutral style. On the other hand, the news release delivery companies are paid by the creators of news releases to distribute those releases to the media, which pay nothing to receive them. These delivery services are prepaid transmission belts, not selectors of material. They do enforce editing standards and occasionally reject releases as unsuitable.

Electronically delivered news releases have an advantage over the conventional variety. Releases transmitted by satellite tend to receive closer, faster attention from media editors than those arriving by mail.

The largest of the news release delivery companies, PR Newswire, was the first to distribute its releases by satellite. Using time on the SATNET satellite system of the Associated Press, PR Newswire's computers distribute releases and official statements from more than 7500 organizations directly into the newsroom computers of the media. Each day it transmits approximately 150 such releases. The releases by PR Newswire go into several commercial data bases. Satellite delivery of public relations news material undoubtedly will increase as other distributors adopt the method.

VIDEO AND AUDIO NEWS RELEASE DISTRIBUTION

Transmission by satellite also makes fast distribution of video news releases possible. The picture-and-voice releases are sent primarily to cable television networks, local television stations, and cable systems that operate local-origin channels. The video releases may be short commercials, sponsored films, or original works such as "The Home Shopping Show" on Modern Satellite Network, in which new products and services are demonstrated on the air.

Voice-and-sound news releases for use on radio also are distributed by satellite. Business Wire, second largest of the news release distribution services, in affiliation with Audio Features Inc., sends these ready-to-broadcast releases over the satellite/audio circuits operated by the Associated Press and United Press International. So does Washington Broadcast News.

GLOBAL TRANSMISSION OF MESSAGES

Still another use of satellite communication is found in *global electronic mail*. For example, Apple Computer of California regularly communicates with its foreign offices through a Tym-Net system that allows a public relations manager to type a message into an Apple computer in California and, through a modem, electronically transmit that message via satellite anywhere in the world within seconds.

Some American corporations send facsimile pages of annual reports by satellite to printing firms in Japan and Korea. These corporations find that the cost of overseas transmission, printing, and air shipment back to the United States is lower than if the printing were done by American companies.

TELECONFERENCING

The most spectacular use of satellite transmission for public relations purposes is *teleconferencing,* also called *videoconferencing.* Through it, groups of conferees separated by thousands of miles can interact instantaneously

Southwestern Bell, in what was billed as the "largest employee special event ever broadcast," used satellite transmission to reach its employees at 57 locations with a theatrical show to celebrate the company's divestiture from AT&T.

A 33-piece orchestra, 10-member dance company, 5 professional actors, 100-member chorus, and a score of company and community officials used entertainment and information to tell an estimated 57,000 employee viewers about the company's future as an independent company. Art Hoffman, manager of employee information, told *PR Reporter*, a weekly newsletter: "We saw an opportunity to change a potential negative into a positive by creating a special event where employees could vent those divestiture-related negative feelings. At the same time we could give them reasons to feel good about their top management and about prospects for future business."

with strong visual impact. By 1990, videoconferencing will be a sizable industry, according to John F. Budd, Jr., vice-president of external relations for Emhart Corporation. Budd, who was one of the first public relations practitioners to use videoconferencing for corporate annual meetings, predicts " . . . it will be a $360 million industry, which is 40 percent greater than 1985's expected volume. . . ."

A traditional conference consists of a group of men and women assembled at a central location for discussion, exchange of information, and inspiration. Participants frequently come from distant points. Their travel costs and hotel bills often are high, they may be plagued by the nuisances of flight reservations and connections, and they may be away from their offices for days.

Satellite-relayed television has changed this concept radically. Now the conferees can remain at their home offices, or gather in groups in nearby cities, and hold their conferences by television. Travel time and costs are reduced or eliminated entirely.

The practice of long-distance discussions among widely separated groups began in the 1930s when the telephone company created conference calls that enabled three or more parties to talk among themselves. When the visual element was added, the impact increased dramatically.

The most widely used form of teleconferencing blends one-way video and two-way audio. The principal performers make their presentations—introduction of a new product, for example—before television cameras in a studio or auditorium. The guests assembled at distant locations watch the televised presentation on large screens. In order to keep the transmission private, the signals can be scrambled at the uplink and unscrambled at the

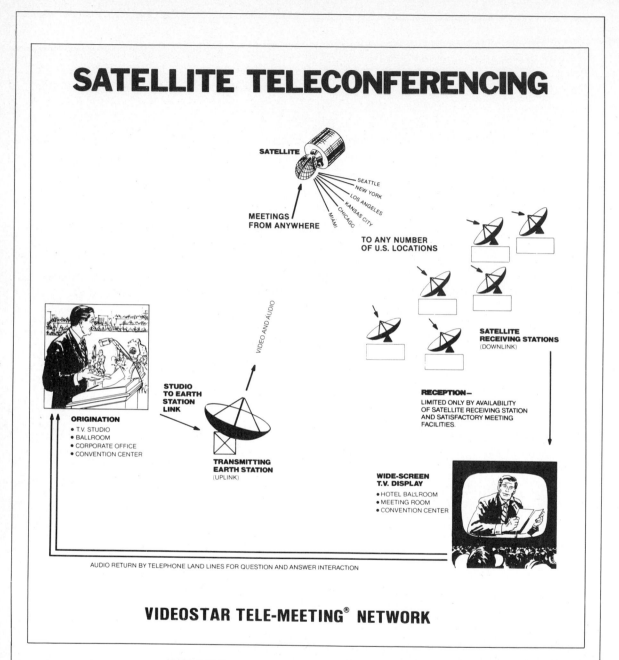

SATELLITE TELECONFERENCING

SATELLITE

SEATTLE
NEW YORK
LOS ANGELES
KANSAS CITY
CHICAGO
MIAMI

MEETINGS FROM ANYWHERE

TO ANY NUMBER OF U.S. LOCATIONS

SATELLITE RECEIVING STATIONS (DOWNLINK)

VIDEO AND AUDIO

STUDIO TO EARTH STATION LINK

ORIGINATION
• T.V. STUDIO
• BALLROOM
• CORPORATE OFFICE
• CONVENTION CENTER

TRANSMITTING EARTH STATION (UPLINK)

RECEPTION— LIMITED ONLY BY AVAILABILITY OF SATELLITE RECEIVING STATION AND SATISFACTORY MEETING FACILITIES.

WIDE-SCREEN T.V. DISPLAY
• HOTEL BALLROOM
• MEETING ROOM
• CONVENTION CENTER

AUDIO RETURN BY TELEPHONE LAND LINES FOR QUESTION AND ANSWER INTERACTION

VIDEOSTAR TELE-MEETING® NETWORK

FIGURE 21.2

The graph explains how satellite teleconferencing operates. (Reprinted by courtesy of VideoStar Connections, Inc.)

downlink when they reach earth again. Figure 21.2 shows, in schematic form, how the satellite transmission works.

Telephone circuits can be arranged from the receiving points back to the place where the presentation originated. Guests can phone in their questions, then see and hear their queries answered by the sponsors. Teleconferences may be videotaped for showing to other groups later.

In a more elaborate and expensive form, video transmission can be simultaneous in both directions, enabling direct two-way visual and spoken communication.

Here are examples of the video teleconference in operation:

In Las Vegas, Chrysler Corporation introduced its new models to dealers with a live show, which included pretaped sequences showing the new models in dramatic settings. Other dealer groups that were assembled in 22 cities across the country watched the show simultaneously by teleconference. This method replaced the earlier practice of taking a traveling show of new models from city to city at high cost.

General Electric announced a major reorganization of its sales force to 1600 employees assembled at 23 locations. After watching a 30-minute teleconference presentation by top company executives, the employees in each of the 23 locations were invited to call in questions over a telephone circuit. Answers by the executives to the 52 questions received were seen and heard by all groups.

To provide its 16,000 employees worldwide with an annual report on company affairs, the Holiday Inn organization held a teleconference that reached three continents. Originating at Memphis, Tennessee, the conference was beamed to employees and associates assembled at 140 Holiday Inns in the United States, and at sites in Hong Kong, England, and Germany. Telephone circuits from each receiving site back to Memphis enabled viewers to ask questions, the most significant of which were answered on the telecast by company executives. The questions primarily concerned employee benefits and company expansion plans.

Using satellite transmission from the United States, a panel of public relations executives, including an author of this textbook, discussed trends in the business for members of the Australian Public Relations Association assembled at a meeting in that country.

Johnson & Johnson used a national teleconference to announce that the company was bringing Tylenol back on the market in new tamper-proof packaging after seven persons died in Chicago from taking poisoned capsules of the painkiller. The New York news conference was relayed by satellite to

FIGURE 21.3

The Johnson & Johnson tele-conference reintroducing Tylenol capsules in new tamper-proof packaging was relayed by satellite to 30 cities. In Chicago, reporters crowd around the television screens while the corporation president, James E. Burke, thanks the media for even-handed coverage of the crisis. (Courtesy of *Communication World.*)

500 journalists in 30 cities—see Figure 21.3. (The Tylenol case is discussed in Chapter 14.)

To introduce a newly developed hepatitis B vaccine, Merck Sharp & Dohme used a teleconference beamed to more than 400 locations where doctors, health care workers, and reporters had gathered. After watching the presentation, the invited guests telephoned questions to a panel of experts.

Atlantic Richfield Company created its own teleconferencing network for internal corporate use. Company groups in distant cities can confer and examine such material as blueprints and documents.

Technical refinements of teleconferencing are still being developed. Voice-activated cameras can focus on participants in conference for closeups as each speaks. Hard (printed) copies of documents under discussion can be transmitted from one conference point to another. A more economical system is the "slow scan" conference. This provides for transmission of still pictures or slides over a telephone circuit between conference points, with voice transmission over a separate line.

Commercial firms provide teleconference facilities for a fee, and consultants may be hired to handle the details of presenting a teleconference.

Costs are high but are expected to fall as rental expenses for satellite transmission space decreases. To decide whether a teleconference will be cost-effective, a potential user should obtain quotations on all expenses involved, and should then compare these figures to the price of travel, lodging, and entertainment if all employees or invited guests were brought to a central conference location. To these travel costs should be added the intangible one of work time lost by employees away from their offices. International teleconferencing is especially attractive for multinational corporations because of the high cost of overseas travel. (For additional information, see Chapter 16.)

Those who use teleconferencing emphasize that it is most effective for reaching large audiences for such purposes as introduction of a product, sales meetings, and announcement of new corporate policies. Like other electronic methods of communication, though, it lacks the personal warmth that comes from a handshake and a face-to-face conversation.

Videotape

The third major tool not available to earlier generations of public relations people, but invaluable in contemporary practice, is videotape. It has replaced motion picture film under most circumstances because it is less expensive and more convenient. Furthermore, these desirable attributes make videotape useful in situations where motion picture film could not be considered.

Videotape is a plastic tape coated with iron oxide on which visual and audio signals are recorded in magnetic patterns. The tape is small, easily edited, and ready for quick playback after a scene has been shot. Television news programs use videotape, often in combination with satellite transmission. A war incident filmed on videotape in a distant country and transmitted to the United States by satellite can be shown to American viewers nationwide within a few minutes. The home viewer can record the scene from the family television set with a videocassette for later replay.

The uses of videotape in public relations work are limited only by the imagination of the practitioner. A few examples: for its distributors, Coors Brewery in Golden, Colorado, produces a monthly half-hour videotaped show in magazine format that presents new sales plans and shows departments of the company at work. Also, the brewery supplies television stations with unedited half-hour videotapes of brewery operations, from which the news departments can use footage as desired to illustrate stories. In still a third use, the company shows videotapes to employees in training programs. Similarly, Levi Strauss & Company produced several news features on videotape about its sponsorship role in the Olympic Games at Los Angeles. One described the dress of the American team members, all wearing Levi Strauss clothing. Atari, the electronic game manufacturer, issued a video news release to announce a new game.

Numerous other uses of videotape are mentioned in this book, especially in Chapters 23 and 24.

Other Tools

Electronic methods of communication are expanding rapidly as new techniques become available. Any attempt to name them all is futile, since new developments make the list out-of-date almost instantly. Even so, it is useful to examine a few of the recent additions that are of particular interest to public relations people.

TELETEXT This is one form of the recently developed concept of *information on demand*. By pushing a few keys, viewers can summon onto the screen indexes of material stored in a computer. From these indexes, the viewers call up what they wish to see. In addition to news, a major component in teletext, the viewer may wish to look at entertainment guides, community service listings, or capsule reviews of restaurants, all of which are targets for public relations practitioners publicizing their clients' services. Teletext is a one-way information service, sender to viewer.

VIDEOTEX This more complex form of on-demand service is a two-way, or interactive, system. On videotex, viewers call up on the screen what they wish to watch, then by using telephone circuits can respond to what they have seen.

Videotex usage is still developing as the systems come into commercial service. Among the applications are conducting two-way banking operations, ordering goods displayed on the screen, and having viewers answer poll questions put to them.

In the area of corporate information, videotex has a significant potential. Reporting the ideas of Perry Jaffe, director of the Pratt Center for Computer Graphics and Design, Bill Hunter tells in *Communication World* how videotex can be applied in this sphere:

> If an employee wants to see the latest company newsletter, he or she might simply hit a button on a computer terminal and get the information, supplemented by computer graphics or video strips of the company president delivering a speech to shareholders.
>
> At the end of a segment, the employee might be invited to press a button to see portions repeated or to hear additional comments about some specific issue. Or employees might be asked to communicate back about whether they understand the points the president was trying to make. Press Y for "yes" and N for "no."

FIGURE 21.4

As part of its press kit for the Olympic Games in Los Angeles, Pacific Bell provided a striking illustration of new communication technology. A fiber optics cable the size of a finger (right) can carry 100 times more telephone calls than the standard 3½-inch copper cable. (Courtesy of Pacific Bell.)

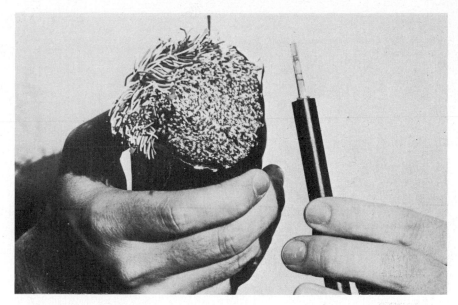

FIBER OPTICS

Transmission of messages is being revolutionized by use of *fiber optics.* Instead of sending signals by wire, this system uses highly transparent strands of glass thinner than human hair. Replacing electronic signals, pulses of light flash along these glass strands at the rate of 90 million per second. So fine are these strands that 240,000 telephone calls can be transmitted at one time through a single fiber optics cable (see Figure 21.4).

QUESTIONS FOR REVIEW AND DISCUSSION

1. What are two principal advantages of the word processor over the typewriter?

2. Define the term *electronic mail.*

3. What is a data base and how does a researcher use it?

4. At what height do communications satellites orbit the earth? Why are they placed at that altitude?

5. What is the difference between a news release delivery service such as PR Newswire and a news service such as the Associated Press?

6. Teleconferencing is growing in popularity. Explain how it operates.

7. What are the advantages of videotape over motion picture film?

8. Explain the difference between teletext and videotex.

9. As a corporate public relations director, how might you employ videotex to improve internal communication?

10. How fast do pulses of light travel through fiber optics?

CHAPTER TWENTY-TWO

Written Tactics

Of all the tools a public relations practitioner uses, the news release is the most common. It is the primary written method of conveying news to the media for publication or broadcast. As such, the news release requires careful preparation and judicious distribution so that its information will be delivered to the right places in an accurate, timely, easily usable, and attractive manner.

This chapter begins with a discussion of the techniques of the news release. Then it examines other types of written communications used in public relations. It explains the purpose of each kind, the methods employed in developing it, and its relative value in campaigns to reach specified audiences. The materials described include factsheets, newsletters, company magazines and newspapers, publications such as brochures and handbooks, information distributed within organizations (staff bulletins and employee home mailing pieces, for example), annual reports, and corporate advertising. Many, indeed, are the ways to use the written word!

The News Release

Basically, a *news release* is a simple document whose purpose is the dissemination of information in ready-to-publish form. Editors of print and broadcast media to whom news releases are sent judge them on the basis of news interest for their audience and timeliness, and in some instances on their adaptability to the medium's form. Releases should be prepared so that the media can relay their news content to audiences easily, with confidence in their accuracy. Editors want the main facts stated succinctly in the opening paragraph of a release, for quick recognition. A news release is a purveyor of information, not an exercise in writing style, except in those cases of longer releases that are clearly intended to be feature stories. The writer of a basic news release should leave the clever writing to staff members of the media.

A news release faces intense competition when it arrives on an editor's desk, against scores or even hundreds of other releases. As they scan the releases, editors make almost instant decisions, assigning each release to one of three categories:

1. *Obvious news.* Copy that is certain to be used.

2. *Maybe.* Stories possibly worth developing if a reporter has the time. A sharp news angle in a release may put it in the "obvious-news" category instead of the risky "maybe" pile. Potentially good stories placed in the "maybe" pile face the danger of being thrown away after a second reading if the key information is poorly developed.

3. *Discard.* Releases of insufficient interest to the receiving editor's audience and those of marginal value that would require too much effort to develop. These go into the wastebasket.

News releases that are prepared according to the criteria described in the following sections have the best chance of being accepted for publication, assuming that their content is newsworthy.

PHYSICAL APPEARANCE There is a standard format for news releases:

Use plain white 8 1/2-by-11-inch paper.

Identify the sender in the upper-left-hand corner of the page, listing name, address, and telephone number. Especially if the sender is a large organization, also give the name of an individual within the organization as a point of contact.

Below the identification state *For Immediate Release* if the material is intended for immediate publication, as most news releases are. If a time restriction is necessary, as with an advance copy of a speech to be delivered at a specified hour, indicate the desired publication time—for example: *For Release at 6 p.m. EST Feb. 12.* This is called an *embargo.* Media recipients of embargoed material have no legal obligation to obey its restrictions, but they normally do so out of courtesy and mutual convenience unless they believe that the embargo is an obvious effort to manipulate the news. Embargoes should be used only when genuinely necessary.

The standard form for the heading looks like this:

```
Jane L. Haber
Williams & Johnson, Inc.
3156 Woodlake Avenue
Somerset, Oregon 97986
Telephone 805-937-0042

     FOR IMMEDIATE RELEASE
```

Leave 2 inches of space for editing convenience before starting the text.

The text starts here with a clearly stated summary lead.

Leave wide margins. Double-space the copy to give editors room in which to edit the material.

Never split a paragraph from one page to the next. Put (*more*) at the bottom of each unfinished page.

Place an identifying slugline and page number at the top of each page after the first.

Some public relations practitioners place a summary headline above the text, for quick identification and possible use by the editor. Others use no headline, in the belief that headline-writing is entirely the editor's business.

CONTENT There are a few essential rules for content:

Begin the news release with a tightly written summary lead and state the fundamentals—who, what, when, where, and why—early in the copy. The first sentence should state the most important point in the story. *Do not bury the lead.*

Be concise. Edit the copy to remove excess words and "puff" terminology. A competent editor would cut them out, anyway. Few news releases need to be more than two pages long; most can be written in a single page. A reporter may obtain additional details by telephoning the number listed at the beginning.

Be absolutely certain that every fact in the release is correct and every name spelled properly. Check the copy closely for grammatical and spelling errors.

For protection against errors and misunderstandings, a public relations counselor is wise to have the client initial a file copy of each news release before its distribution. In company public relations departments, similar initialing by a superior is desirable and in some cases mandatory.

In most instances, those who issue news releases welcome follow-up inquiries from reporters and are happy to provide additional information about the news situation. They desire the fullest exposure possible for their stories.

When a story is controversial, and the organization or individual issuing the news release is in a defensive position, this openness sometimes diminishes or even vanishes. The attitude of some upper-management executives toward the media in controversial situations is, "Tell them only what we want the public to know. Let them find out the rest for themselves, if they can." This attitude on the part of management may persist even to the point of having the public relations department omit relatively simple information from routine releases. One major financial firm with scores of branches, for example, puts out news releases announcing appointment of new branch managers without mentioning the name of the person whom the appointee replaces—an obvious question every good reporter should want answered.

This management attitude of playing it close to the chest is a source of mistrust among the media toward companies that follow the practice. A survey by a unit of the J. Walter Thompson advertising agency showed that 55 percent of the business editors who responded criticized corporate press releases for burying important information. Astute reporters try to read between the lines of a news release and frequently apply pressure on the public relations source either to provide more background or to put them in touch with someone who will. When an obviously incomplete news release is put out, the individual who issues it must be prepared for such difficult moments, especially if management orders are, "Don't tell them another thing!"

Frequently, as news-oriented persons, public relations practitioners wish they could be more informative in their releases than management policy permits. As the influence of upper-level public relations executives on corporate policy-making increases, which it is doing gradually, many firms are adopting a more forthright approach. A company has no reason to wash its dirty linen in public in a voluntary outburst of confession. Yet greater frank-

ness in news releases and willingness to volunteer answers to reasonable questions that good reporters will ask anyway help to build a company's credibility in the eyes of media and public.

This advice is given to the management of newspapers as well. When a reporter on the *Wall Street Journal* was fired for giving advance information to stock trader friends, a New York *Times* reporter got the run-around from the managing editor of the financial daily. His published story carried the sentence, "Norman Pearlstine, managing editor of the *Wall Street Journal,* which has not been charged with any wrongdoing, could not be reached for comment, said a company spokesman, Lawrence Armour." *Bulldog,* a public relations newsletter, gave the *Wall Street Journal* a "fireplug" award for doing the same thing that it often criticizes other organizations for doing.

DELIVERY OF NEWS RELEASES

News releases should be conveyed to the media in a timely and effective manner. As pointed out in Chapter 12, releases should be addressed to recipients by name whenever possible. Releases may be sent in a broadside manner to large numbers of recipients, in an approach called *macro-distribution,* or to carefully selected target media sources, in the *micro-distribution* technique. The high cost of postage and of specialized delivery services causes most public relations practitioners to select recipients of their news releases with care, not sending to those unlikely to use the material. Therefore, practitioners should familiarize themselves with the appropriate media sources for their firm or their clients. Figure 22.1 shows covers of a variety of trade journals that would be suitable targets in the high-technology field.

Locally, releases should be sent by first-class mail, or delivered by hand if they contain urgent material. Use of bulk mail to save postage is unwise. Delivery is subject to delay, and recipients of bulk mail tend to dismiss it as of little importance.

Delivery of releases regionally or nationally is more complicated because of timing problems and the need to reach the proper outlets and individuals in areas where the sender lacks knowledge of local situations. Accurate, current mailing lists substantially influence the amount of exposure a news release obtains. For this reason, many organizations employ distribution firms to handle their mailings.

Recent developments in computer techniques give the creator of a release numerous options for its delivery, depending upon the importance of the release and budget allocations. Distribution by mail still is the cheapest, most common, and least attention-getting method. Mailgrams and regular telegrams are more expensive but have an aura of importance; they are a popular way of delivering invitations to meetings and events.

FIGURE 22.1

Practitioners who work in product publicity and marketing communication need knowledge of the trade press. Shown here is a sampling of specialized magazines serving the computer and electronics industry. Editors of these publications are interested in new product, technical, and application articles as well as case histories.

ELECTRONIC DELIVERY As pointed out in Chapter 21, distribution of news releases electronically is one result of the satellite and computer revolution.

Companies whose services are based on computer programming offer various types of news release delivery, usually aimed at carefully targeted lists of recipients. The public relations practitioner writes a news release and turns over the copy to one of these distribution companies. Depending upon the type of distribution the practitioner chooses, the commercial firm either prints and mails it to a selected mailing list or distributes it electronically.

One company advertises that its computers contain an up-to-date list of more than 100,000 editors, broadcasters, and syndicated columnists by name. It will print and mail a release to whatever segment of this mailing list the author of the release wishes to reach, putting the copies into the mail on the specific day requested.

Instead of using the mail, another firm distributes the releases more rapidly, dramatically, and expensively by electronic methods. The author turns in the release copy to the company, which dispatches it by high-speed private wire to outlets chosen by the author. The release arrives in newsrooms on special public relations printers in the same ready-to-publish form as if it had been mailed. Recognizing the growing dependence upon computers in newsrooms, this company also will dispatch a news release from its computers directly into the computers of newsrooms, just as press associations send copy to many newspapers.

In the growing number of instances in which the public relations practitioner has suitable word processing equipment, the release can be composed on the writer's video screen, transmitted into the distribution firm's computer, checked there, and dispatched into the computers of designated recipients. Not a word has appeared on paper from the originator to the ultimate recipient. Such electronic distribution is much more expensive than the traditional mailings. However, distribution firms offering the service claim better usage of a release sent electronically. Recipients include commercial data bases, whose clients such as stockbrokers and banks may call up the information.

EDITORIAL PROMOTION SERVICES   Still another way of distributing news about products, services, and events nationally is through an editorial promotion service. A company or firm sends a featurized news release about its project or product to the promotion service (see Figure 22.2). If the service's editors deem the content to be newsworthy and written in competent news story style, they include the release in one of their periodic mailings to newspaper editors. Photographs and appropriate drawings may be included to illustrate the releases. Brand names are permitted in such releases, although they usually are placed inconspicuously well down in the stories. Smaller newspapers in particular use editorial promotion service copy as textual matter in special advertising sections on such themes as gardening, home repair, Mother's Day, auto repair, and fashions. To win acceptance by an editorial

With eye safety practices and protective eyewear, 90 percent of eye injuries can be avoided, reports the National Society to Prevent Blindness. The appropriate protection can shield the eyes from most potential hazards.

To learn about eye safety and your eyes, write for a free booklet. Send a stamped, self-addressed, business-size envelope to your state Society to Prevent Blindness or the National Society to Prevent Blindness, 79 Madison Avenue, New York, N.Y. 10016.

FIGURE 22.2

Clipsheets distributed free to daily and weekly newspapers by editorial promotion services deliver feature material such as this example. Source of the material pays the cost.

promotion service, copy must be free of hard-sell "puffery," concentrating instead upon an informational approach.

An example of the material distributed is this story excerpt from a Stamps-Conhaim mailing:

> Anyone who is trying to finance an education today cannot be too happy with the budget cut news coming from Washington. With cutbacks in student aid, one thing is for sure—federal money for a college education is a lot harder to come by and the competition is nothing short of fierce.
>
> Certainly budget cuts will hurt the traditionally aged college students, but the effect will be that much more devastating on the older students who have been flocking back to the classroom in record numbers these past few years to train for new careers. Finding established funding has always been difficult for this group, who today comprise over 40 percent of all college enrollment.
>
> One good source of aid for female students over 30 is the Clairol Loving Care Scholarship Program. Established in 1974 as part of Clairol's policy to support the efforts of women, the scholarship program awards scholarships of up to $1000 to qualified women over 30 for studies leading to a career goal on the undergraduate and master's levels, in the professional schools and for vocational training. . . .

At the end of the story, readers are told where to write for information about scholarship applications. While publicizing the Clairol name and hair-coloring product, which is sold heavily to women over 30, the story has legitimate news interest. A good likelihood exists that it will be published in numerous newspapers. By arriving on editors' desks under the auspices of the editorial promotion service, rather than as a mailed news release, its chances of receiving attention are enhanced. Clairol's scholarship program is a good example of how a manufacturer can publicize a product in a socially significant manner.

LOCALIZING A NEWS RELEASE

National corporations realize that when the releases they send out are localized, usage of them by the media will be substantially higher. The local angle should be placed in the lead if possible. Inclusion of local names or statistics attracts editors; they know it interests readers. For example, a corporation with offices and plants in 20 cities sends out a release reporting that it currently has 30,000 employees systemwide, who last year received total wages and health benefits of stated amounts. The release might be published rather inconspicuously in the newspapers of some company cities but would receive little or no broadcast attention because it is too general. Even company employees would have difficulty relating to it. However, if the releases sent to the media in each company city told how many employees the company had in that locality, and how much these workers received in payroll and health benefits last year, likelihood of widespread use would be high.

Despite their desirability, localized releases traditionally have been expensive to prepare and send out. Computerization has changed this somewhat. Now a corporation can prepare a standard national news release giving general information for use by all recipients. It also can prepare paragraphs containing the local information for each company city. These paragraphs are inserted by computer appropriately into the releases intended for each specific city. The media outlets in that city receive only the releases especially tailored for them.

GETTING EXTRA MILEAGE FROM NEWS RELEASES

Shrewd practitioners find ways to get extra value from published news releases. Clipping services they employ send them stories in newspapers and magazines based on their releases. Some distribution firms also offer clipping services. By sending photocopies of these clippings appropriately to sales representatives and company officials in each territory, practitioners keep the field force informed about what is being published concerning the company and its products. The same system is useful for trade and professional associations. When an individual is mentioned favorably in a news story based on a release, the practitioner can please the individual by sending a copy of the story to him or her with a note of congratulation. This bit of mild flattery is effective both with employees, who may display the clipping on an office wall, and with nonemployees, who are pleased to know that the company recognizes them.

A discussion of television news releases appears in Chapter 24.

The Factsheet

Although factsheets are distributed by public relations practitioners to the same media outlets as news releases are, and somewhat resemble releases physically, they serve a different purpose. As described previously, the news release is written in news story form, ready for publication. A *factsheet* tells editors in advance about an event that will occur and provides information reporters will need to cover the event. It is a brief, staccato listing of essential facts, not a ready-to-print story. Figure 22.3 shows both a news release and a factsheet publicizing the same event—the opening of a new restaurant.

Distribution of a factsheet should be done several days or a week in advance of the event, under normal circumstances, so that editors may enter the event on their assignment sheets and may schedule coverage. A factsheet can serve as the basis of an advance story written about an event, but its more important purpose is to attract reporters for on-the-scene coverage and to help them plan their work.

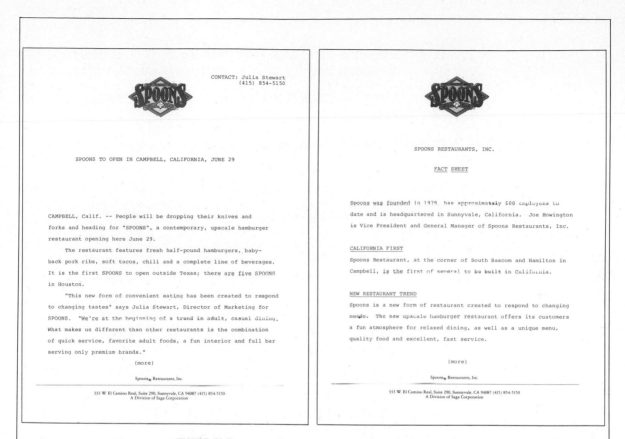

CONTACT: Julia Stewart
(415) 854-5150

SPOONS TO OPEN IN CAMPBELL, CALIFORNIA, JUNE 29

CAMPBELL, Calif. -- People will be dropping their knives and
forks and heading for "SPOONS", a contemporary, upscale hamburger
restaurant opening here June 29.

The restaurant features fresh half-pound hamburgers, baby-
back pork ribs, soft tacos, chili and a complete line of beverages.
It is the first SPOONS to open outside Texas; there are five SPOONS
in Houston.

"This new form of convenient eating has been created to respond
to changing tastes" says Julia Stewart, Director of Marketing for
SPOONS. "We're at the beginning of a trend in adult, casual dining.
What makes us different than other restaurants is the combination
of quick service, favorite adult foods, a fun interior and full bar
serving only premium brands."

(more)

Spoons Restaurants, Inc.

333 W. El Camino Real, Suite 290, Sunnyvale, CA 94087 (415) 854-5150
A Division of Saga Corporation

SPOONS RESTAURANTS, INC.

FACT SHEET

Spoons was founded in 1979, has approximately 600 employees to
date and is headquartered in Sunnyvale, California. Joe Howington
is Vice President and General Manager of Spoons Restaurants, Inc.

CALIFORNIA FIRST
Spoons Restaurant, at the corner of South Bascom and Hamilton in
Campbell, is the first of several to be built in California.

NEW RESTAURANT TREND
Spoons is a new form of restaurant created to respond to changing
needs. The new upscale hamburger restaurant offers its customers
a fun atmosphere for relaxed dining, as well as a unique menu,
quality food and excellent, fast service.

(more)

Spoons Restaurants, Inc.

333 W. El Camino Real, Suite 290, Sunnyvale, CA 94087 (415) 854-5150
A Division of Saga Corporation

FIGURE 22.3

To announce the opening of a restaurant in California, Saga Corporation distributed to
news media both a news release and a factsheet, as shown, along with two pictures of
the restaurant's interior, a factsheet on the restaurant chain, and a copy of the restaurant's menu.

Here is an example of the factsheet form that editors like to receive:

TO: All news media in central Illinois.

FROM: Santa Rosa County Fair.
John Thornburg, PR director.
2600 N. Spring Avenue, Santa Rosa, IL
(Phone 213-937-2045).

WHO: Santa Rosa County Fair Association.

WHAT: 37th annual county fair.

WHEN: July 24–28, 1985.

WHERE: County fairgrounds, W. Main Street, Santa Rosa.

WHY: To provide educational exhibits, encourage agriculture, display homemaking and craft skills, and offer entertainment.

ALL EVENTS AND EXHIBITS WILL BE OPEN TO REPORTERS AND PHOTOGRAPHERS.

Attention is called to these special events:

WEDNESDAY, July 24. Horse show arena, 3 p.m. Mule races. Jockey categories include boys and girls age 12 and under, men weighing 250 lbs. or more, and grandmothers. An opportunity for humorous pictures and stories.

THURSDAY, July 25. Main stage, 8 p.m. Performance by country singing star Wilma Waverly. Miss Waverly will be available for interviews and photographs backstage at 5 p.m. Thursday.

FRIDAY, July 26. Homemaking building, 2 p.m. Awarding of prizes for best cakes and pies. After the presentation a group of boys and girls will be invited to sample the winning entries and choose their favorites. Feature picture possibility.

SATURDAY, July 27. Horse show arena, 9 a.m. Livestock auction of animals entered by 4-H Club members.

SUNDAY, July 28. Main stage, 2 p.m. Ethnic dance program and closing ceremonies.

NOTE: Enclosed find complete fair program and general advance news release. Call Thornburg for further information.

NEWSROOM: Typewriters and paper, lists of prize winners and contest entrants, phones, etc., will be available at the pressroom in the administration building.

The Newsletter

Designed as an informal publication to deliver information to a target audience at regular intervals, the newsletter is precisely what the two portions of its name indicate: *news* transmitted in the chatty, brisk style of a *letter*. Newsletters are used frequently by corporations to communicate with employees and stockholders, by nonprofit agencies and associations to reach members and friends, and by sales organizations to deliver information and personnel chitchat to representatives in the field. Expert opinion and inside advice in specialized fields also are sold to subscribers in newsletter form by commercial publishing firms. The covers shown in Figure 22.4 indicate the variety of organizations that put out newsletters.

FIGURE 22.4

Many organizations publish newsletters to inform employees and the public about their activities. This is a cost-effective method of reporting events that might not be covered by the mass media. Practitioners often begin their public relations careers by writing and editing newsletters.

The typical newsletter is a four-page folder of 8 1/2-by-11-inch pages, set in typewriter-style type rather than regular printer's fonts. This style projects an air of informality and urgency. Ragged right-edge margins, typewriter style, add to the impression. Ample use of white space increases readability.

The newsletter can be double-folded into a No. 10 business envelope, or it can be a self-mailer—that is, when folded, it has space on an outside surface for the address and stamp. A piece of tape sometimes is used to hold the self-mailer shut. While envelope mailing generally is considered to have greater impact, the self-mailer is more economical. The choice is a question of budget. Some newsletters have three holes punched along the fold, so they can be filed in ring binders.

Newsletters for internal audiences typically report to employees on trends in their field of work, forthcoming events, personnel changes and policy announcements within the organization, news from field offices, introduction of new products, unusual achievements by employees, results of surveys, and new publications. The goal is to make employees feel that they are informed about company affairs, right up to the minute.

A newsletter aimed at an outside audience, members of an organization, or both, may contain items about political trends that could affect the organization or field of interest, announcements of new programs and policies, brief human interest stories about personnel or recipients of organization services, promotions and retirements—whatever news the editor believes of interest to readers that can be told succinctly. On complicated stories, the newsletter should give the basic facts and indicate where readers can write or telephone for additional details. A newsletter is a brisk compilation of highlights and tidbits, not a place for contemplative essays or detailed professional discussion.

Punchiness in writing style is essential for a successful newsletter. Sentences are short and direct. The writing is authoritative and no-nonsense in tone, from a busy writer to a busy reader. Another secret of the successful newsletter is to cover several topics that will appeal to a wide variety of readers. The single-topic edition should be avoided as too limited in interest.

For internal use among departments and branches of large corporations with extensive word processing facilities, the electronic newsletter has made its appearance. The editor composes the letter in the usual way. The copy then is coded into the computer system, dispatched, and delivered to everyone on the receiving list on hard copy from the recipients' printout machines.

Company Periodicals

Hundreds of well-edited, well-written, and attractive periodicals published in the United States never are seen by the general public. They are produced by public relations departments of companies or their counseling firms and distributed free to carefully selected audiences. Whether designed to be read by employees, stockholders, customers, or combinations of these audiences, periodicals are among the most effective channels of continuing communication that a company can use. Like any publication issued at regular intervals, the company magazine or newspaper creates a sense of anticipation of its arrival. This helps to strengthen the ties between management and the groups it seeks to inform and influence.

Experts emphasize the importance of four elements in maintaining a good relationship between management and employees—employee recognition, communication, a sense of belonging, and emotional security. When all of these elements function well, productivity tends to rise. Workers who believe that their jobs are secure and their personal worth recognized will contribute more than disgruntled ones.

Along with other forms of internal communication—including company brochures, staff–management meetings, audiovisual presentations, and memoranda—company periodicals help substantially in the development of all four elements. The periodicals communicate information and decisions from management to employees. They increase the workers' feeling that they know what is going on in the company, and why. Management can use the periodicals to influence the attitudes of employees. However, this purpose must be accomplished with caution and finesse. If employees sense that management is talking down to them and using the periodical merely as a propaganda vehicle, the publication may become an object of derision rather than a tool for achieving the two-way communication management desires. Periodicals also can serve as channels for communication from employees to management through letters to the editor, question-and-answer features, and similar editorial devices.

Company magazines take many forms. Some are printed in several colors, with dramatic graphics, on slick coated paper. From this elaborate and expensive format, they range down to four-page folders in black and white that resemble a small tabloid newspaper. The publication interval may be weekly, biweekly, monthly, or quarterly. Decisions on format and frequency depend upon the size of the public relations budget and the audience management seeks to reach. Some companies have found that their blue-collar employees get more satisfaction from a periodical which is simple in design and presentation than from an elaborate, multicolored, sophisticated-looking magazine such as those distributed to stockholders and others the company seeks to impress.

Large corporations frequently publish several periodicals, each designed for a different audience. Usually the objective of a publication is stated in small type in its masthead. Typically, *Chevron World,* published quarterly by Standard Oil Company of California, states, "The *Chevron World* is published and distributed by the company's Public Affairs organization for the information of shareholders, employees, and other interested parties." Knowledge of this stated purpose helps a student to scrutinize the content of a periodical and analyze why various elements were included. (*Chevron World* is described in detail later in the chapter.)

Nonprofit organizations publish periodicals for much the same purposes that corporations publish theirs. Instead of trying to please stockholders and customers, nonprofit organizations must seek the support of contributors. Their product is service. Therefore, periodicals aimed at contributors and possible donors emphasize the quality and social value of the service the organization delivers. Internal periodicals fill the same role in management-employee relations that company periodicals do. In the discussion of company periodicals that follows, therefore, those of nonprofit organizations are included for simplicity.

Company magazines fall into four major categories, grouped by the audience they serve. To illustrate how the various types function, the following sections analyze the contents of typical magazines in each category.

MAGAZINES FOR EMPLOYEES AND RETIREES

The employee magazine is a means by which management can inject a personal touch into company affairs. As a humanizing tool, it helps to offset the feelings of some employees, especially in large corporations, that they have little significance as individuals to management. Through its pages, the company can recognize the achievements and personal milestones of those who work for it. A well-edited employee periodical helps to instill an attitude among employees that they are part of the company. At the same time, the magazine offers management an opportunity to report its policies and explain why they were made. When the publication is in newspaper format, the appearance is different but the goals are the same.

For example, *NSP news* is a 24-page, slick-paper, black-and-white magazine issued monthly by the Northern States Power Company of Minneapolis. Heavy emphasis is given to photographs of employees at work and sites of company operations. A typical issue has a dramatic full-page cover photograph of a lineman repairing snow-covered wires atop a pole after a storm.

The table of contents lists the articles and features in the periodical. Each item is summarized here briefly:

Day-care survey. Employees disapprove of the prospect of company day care; they like the idea of job-sharing.

Union women. They tackle some of the roughest, dirtiest jobs NSP has to offer. The overwhelming reason: money.

PCB burn. The company gets ready to burn PCB-contaminated oil at the High Bridge plant. NSP believes burning is cheaper and cleaner than other disposal methods.

St. Anthony Hydro. History abounds at the falls that gave birth to Minneapolis. The article contains photographs and text about the site of early-day power facilities.

Year-end review. NSP board chairman Don McCarthy looks back over the past year and offers his assessment in an interview.

French Island. An old oil-burning plant resumes operation, burning waste wood as its main fuel.

Briefly. This section consists of two pages of concise news items about events involving the company and its employees. Typical headlines: "Heavy Snow Douses Power to Thousands"; "Welders Retested After Cheating Allegations"; "Employee Dies En Route to Work."

Retirements. A paragraph is included about each recent retiree, describing NSP job, family, plans, and the like.

Promotions. This feature lists individuals who have been promoted and their new assignments.

Classified. A full page of classified advertisements placed by employees lists items for sale (everything from a player piano to a set of barbells), houses for rent, and wanted items.

Deaths. Brief obituaries of employees and retirees appear.

Anniversaries. This feature presents a list of employees, with job description, who have completed 25 years or more of service, compiled in 5-year segments.

People. This is a text-and-photo feature on the back cover about an NSP telephone operator who won $25,000 in a McDonald's contest.

Analysis of this table of contents shows how skillfully the editor aimed the magazine directly at the interests of employee readers. *NSP news* exemplifies the ably edited company periodical aimed at a single-target audience. Individual workers receive recognition for career milestones and achievements. Employee opinion is sought and reported in the survey on day care. The illustrated article headlined "Blue-Collar Women" describes female workers loading trucks, working on underground cables, repairing and servicing vehicles, and operating coal conveyors. A paragraph summarizes the company's employment situation on such outdoor work:

At the entry level, women fill 16 percent of NSP's service jobs and 7.4 percent of the laborer jobs. At the apprentice and craft levels they account for only 2.1 and 1 percent. And their presence in the union workforce is aided by the company's policy "to use them in all positions."

Management's point of view on overall issues is included through the interview with the chairman of the board. In it he admits candidly that the company does not communicate well enough with its employees and announces formation of task forces to study pay, benefits, and job postings.

Another approach to the employee periodical is to emphasize a special topic in each edition. *Between Branches,* the bimonthly publication of Avco Financial Services, in a typical issue has a large cover photograph of a woman talking to a robed judge, captioned, "Keeping us honest. See page 1." The periodical unfolds into a four-page tabloid newspaper size. The woman on the cover proves to be an Avco auditor whose job is to search out thievery within the organization—not only an interesting feature but a warning to employees of the international financing company that those who steal from their employer probably will be caught.

The largest portion of the tabloid, however, is devoted to three related items telling employees about college costs and outlining ways to obtain scholarships. One article is headed, "Doing Your Homework on Scholarships." A long box accompanying this story lists places to write for information about scholarships. The third item, headed "Avco Gets A+ in Student Loans," describes the company's low-interest Education Financing Plan for children of employees. Not only does this article give employees useful information but it implicitly reminds them that the company has a policy of assisting its employees.

Effective employee communication can be achieved even when the editor of a periodical must operate with a modest budget, a limitation that occurs frequently with nonprofit organizations in particular. An example is *insight,* published monthly for personnel of Parkview Memorial Hospital, Fort Wayne, Indiana. The format is a single long horizontal sheet that, with two vertical folds, becomes a six-page publication. Like the others, but in briefer form, it contains reports of employee achievements and milestones, news items about hospital activities, and illustrated feature stories about departments. Under the headline, "Rub-a-Dub-Dub, Millions of Pounds in the Tub," one story describes how the hospital laundry washes and sometimes irons 78,000 pounds of linens each week, more than 4 million pounds a year. One December issue, headlined "Christmas Is for Sharing," was built around nine signed articles by staff members describing personal holiday experiences.

MAGAZINES FOR STOCKHOLDERS AND EMPLOYEES

Because a magazine of this type is aimed at two audiences, its approach must be broader. Although stockholders and employees share concern about the success of their company, their interests are not identical. News about the activities and milestones of individual employees does not interest stockholders. The magazine's focus needs to be more on technical and economic developments in the corporation's field and on the company's strategy to take advantage of them. A magazine distributed to stockholders as well as to employees usually is more visibly management-oriented than one for employees only. It must be kept in mind that many employees also are stockholders, often as participants in company-sponsored stock purchase programs.

An example of the company periodical distributed to both stockholders and employees is *Chevron World,* published quarterly by Standard Oil of California as a colorfully printed, 30-page, slick-paper magazine. The items appearing in a typical issue are summarized here:

Cover. The illustration depicts a multicolored horizontal pattern on which ships in silhouette are shown with long lines running out from them, captioned, "Searching for the sound of oil." A note inside explains that the cover is a computer-generated, colored seismic section plot.

Inside of cover. A policy statement by the chairman of the board discusses the company's heavy involvement in oil development in Indonesia.

NewsFront. This is a two-page summary of petroleum industry developments in newsletter form.

Natural Gas. A long article about natural gas reserves and price control, illustrated with colored bar charts and other graphic devices, is accompanied by a shorter piece about crude-oil price decontrol. The two articles emphasize the industry's case for decontrol.

Chevron's TV School. The story describes the school in which Chevron instructs its executives on how to appear on television programs and undergo questioning. Each executive goes through a course lasting two and a half days. After citing the harshness of questioning by Mike Wallace on "60 Minutes," the article states, "Of course, not all media questions are adversarial or aimed at the jugular. Most inquiries and requests for interviews are in the best interest of the industry—which has a story to tell—*and* the public, which should know what is going on in the business."

Destination: Bering Sea. A seismic ship's journey into Arctic waters to find possible oil-bearing formations is described. Brilliantly illustrated, with a full-page aerial photograph of the vessel, this article is the magazine's cover story.

New Taxes—Discriminating Against Oil? This is a discussion of the heavy tax bills oil companies must pay.

The Heritage of Islam. The item presents a page of color photographs of the Islamic cultural and scientific exhibition touring the United States. This article reflects the company's commercial involvement in the Islamic world.

North Sea Oases. Illustrated in watercolor, the article explains how birds use Chevron's North Sea oil platforms as landing points; it is a relatively subtle response to environmentalist concerns about the damage oil spills do to birdlife.

Tar Sands. This is a one-page article about Chevron's investment in an exploratory project in Utah.

Spectrum. The feature contains a collection of brief news stories about Chevron oil explorations, leasing projects, and pipeline plans around the world.

Back cover. A nature photograph of birds resting on a North Sea oil platform is shown.

The difference in approach between *Chevron World* and the magazines edited exclusively for employees is obvious. In this publication, employees are given a carefully crafted picture of their company's ambitious search for new energy sources. Their pride in the company's size and ingenuity is stimulated. They receive strong exposure to management's views on taxation and legislation. Corporate image-building is the dominant theme. (Another company periodical, *Standard Oiler,* is distributed only to employees and retirees. A 34-page slick-paper bimonthly, it contains individual milestone information, queries from readers, and information about company operations that is of direct value to employees. Each issue includes two or three more broadly based oil-oriented feature stories. Thus the two magazines give employees differing perspectives on their employer, global in one and personal in the other.)

MAGAZINES FOR MARKETING STAFF MEMBERS AND WHOLESALERS OF COMPANY PRODUCTS

These periodicals are unabashedly promotional, edited to encourage sales through inspirational essays and how-to-do-it articles.

An excellent example of these direct sales-booster periodicals is *Team Talk,* published by Anheuser-Busch of St. Louis to promote its group of beers. Articles contain cheerleader sentences of a type the reader would be unlikely to find in the magazines previously analyzed. These quotations from wholesalers are included in articles about their activities:

> Everybody loves a winner and wants to be associated with a class organization . . . our retailers and the general public know we are proud of our products. Anheuser-Busch is a winner, and we want to be one, too.

Team Talk is a 24-page bimonthly magazine illustrated with large color photographs and striking drawings. See Figure 22.5, which shows the cover of one issue. The contents of another issue not only show the editorial approach but provide intriguing insight into the way a successful company sells its products in an intensely competitive market:

FIGURE 22.5

Team Talk is a marketing link between Anheuser-Busch and its beer wholesalers. This cover emphasizes the international aspect of the company's operations. (Reprinted by permission of Anheuser-Busch, Inc.)

Cover. The single word *IMAGE* in bright blue on a black background is reflected upside down, as in a mirror. A subtitle at the bottom of the cover states, "A Reflection of Quality," and refers to a story on page 2.

The Look of the Leader. This mirror-image device on the cover is duplicated in smaller type as a headline. This article tells how beer wholesalers can enhance their image as the purveyors of quality products by placing company-specified signs on their warehouses and trucks and by having their drivers and other employees wear clean, well-tailored uniforms.

A-B Gets High Marks on College Campuses. A pair of articles describe how Anheuser-Busch wholesalers promote the sale of their beers in universities, one on a large campus and the other at a smaller university. The articles carefully point out how the sellers obey state laws against selling beer to students under the minimum age in each state.

Wholesalers employ students to visit campus activity centers and dormitories to talk up the drinking of Budweiser; these representatives report to the wholesalers about forthcoming campus events where beer sales might be successful. At the Phi Psi 500, a 1.5 mile run at Cornell University, there were Budweiser start and finish banners, all 1800 contestants received Budweiser T-shirts, and all race staff members were given golf shirts with brand identification. At the Cortland State University picnic, attended by 9000 students, the wholesaler gave away 3000 Budweiser Light frisbees. Student workers at five pouring stations received Budweiser Light hats.

Such high volume distribution of gifts shows the importance the company places on brand-name exposure. Another method is distribution of Budweiser posters at dormitories and fraternity and sorority houses on the opening days of school, when students are moving in and looking for room decorations. Distributors have placed recycling containers on campuses. The proceeds from the recycled aluminum cans are donated to charity or to a student organization.

For the company and its wholesalers, the payoff for these campus promotions is the sale of beer. *Team Talk* articles are sprinkled with sentences such as, "More than 312 half barrels of Budweiser were consumed during the day, and 560 cases of Budweiser and Budweiser Light were consumed that evening during a concert."

Another issue of *Team Talk* reported jubilantly on the success of the Budweiser/Tufts University Kiss-Off. Male and female winners of the "Hottest Lips on Campus" awards received trophies, then demonstrated their techniques in an impromptu Kiss-Off between them. The five male judges kissed the five female judges while the crowd cheered and Budweiser sales soared. Other items in that issue include the following:

IWITOT. These initials stand for "I Wish I'd Thought of That," a two-page layout of reports from Anheuser-Busch wholesalers about sales methods they had used successfully.

I'm Back! This feature presents a cartoon-type layout about the return of Bud Man, a hooded, caped character resembling Superman and used in company promotions.

Headlines. This is a two-page layout of news stories about Budweiser publicity and advertising campaigns, from which other wholesalers can draw ideas.

Who's News. Two pages of brief stories about the activities and promotional efforts of Budweiser wholesalers are offered.

In summary, the content of *Team Talk* urges marketing people to exploit established events by pushing exposure of their products and to create special events for the same purpose. Its goal is stimulation of its readers. In *Team Talk,* the corporate communications department functions as a clearinghouse through which sales ideas are disseminated.

MAGAZINES FOR CUSTOMERS AND MEMBERS

As a psychological link to their customers, to remind them of company products and services, some firms publish magazines addressed exclusively to this group. Magazines published by national organizations for their members are similar in purpose and character, although in some instances somewhat wider in editorial range. The cost of a membership magazine normally is included in the annual dues.

The customer magazine is not a catalog, although it may contain pages offering services or products, often packaged in special offers. Primarily its objective is to present a favorable image of the company, rather than direct selling.

A colorful example of the customer magazine is *Silver Circle,* a 48-page quarterly published by Home Savings of America and distributed free to members of its Silver Circle. The Circle is a device designed to increase deposits in this very large savings and loan association. Home Savings depositors who have at least $5000 in their accounts, or have an Individual Retirement Account or a Keogh retirement account with the company, become Silver Circle members. They receive the magazine and a membership card entitling them to discounts on numerous travel and entertainment items.

The editors of *Silver Circle* can make several important assumptions about their audience: (1) those who receive the magazine have at least a moderate amount of spare money; (2) members holding retirement accounts in particular may be expected to have substantial interest in travel; (3) all probably have at least a fundamental understanding of financial matters. Relative affluence, money awareness, interest in travel: those three attributes of the *Silver Circle* audience are the framework upon which the magazine is built. Examination of a typical issue shows how the contents are tailored to these factors:

Cover. A large color photograph shows two mature couples standing by the rail of a white cruise ship at sailing time. Smiling happily, they hold glasses aloft in a toast while a balloon and streamers add a festive touch. Below is a caption, "Win a Princess Cruise . . . Discover the Most Exciting New Savings Investment in Years. Details page 4."

The Money Market Account. An article outlines the plan offered by Home Savings (and in various forms by its competitors). Tied in with the article is a description of Home's Money Market Sweepstakes.

Financial Planning. Illustrated by a full-page color photograph of surgeons, this article is summarized by its subtitle, "Checkpoints for Supplemental Medical Insurance."

Astrology—Prophetic Science or Bunk? This is a change-of-pace story with no financial overtones.

Legal Matters. A description of the expanding law of product liability is presented.

Other financial articles discuss so-called Sweep Accounts, the Individual Retirement Accounts, taxes, and bargain-hunting. Mixed with them are a profile of a square-dancing couple, an article on arthritis, and a heavily illustrated one on selecting pets. The remaining third of *Silver Circle* includes travel articles, lists of cruises, a hotel and resort guide listing places that offer Silver Circle discounts, and discount coupons from amusement centers.

The interlocking tie-ins between the magazine and the hotels, restaurants, and amusement parks offering discounts in it illuminate the techniques of entertainment sales promotion. Those who give discounts know they are reaching an audience with money to spend. Home Savings in turn earns good will from magazine recipients by offering such bargains. When presented in the context of a sleek magazine, the discounts avoid the look of being gimmicks that may have a catch in them somewhere.

Brochures and Handbooks

Writing informational publications to fill innumerable needs is among the most common duties of public relations practitioners. Some printed pieces are issued at stated intervals, such as quarterly reports to stockholders and college catalogs. The majority, however, are designed to last for indefinite periods, subject to updating as required. Most of this material is distributed free, although price tags may be placed on more elaborate and expensive items such as museum catalogs.

Whatever their purpose, these publications share clearly defined writing requirements. Clarity is essential. Frequently the writer must explain technical material or simplify complex issues for a reader who knows little about the topic. This calls for explanations that are straightforward, shorn of jargon, and stated in terms of reference that a casual reader can comprehend quickly. Paired with clarity is conciseness. Informational writing should be tightly done. Elaborate literary devices should be left to the fiction writer. The person who delivers information needs to pare excess verbiage from sentences and paragraphs.

Every brochure, handbook, or other form of printed information should be organized on a firm outline that moves the reader forward comfortably through unfamiliar territory. Frequent subheads and typographical breaks are desirable. The writer often operates under budget restrictions that dictate the size of the publication—perhaps a 4-page folder, perhaps a large-format brochure of 30 pages consisting primarily of illustrations with short blocks of type. Space limitations should be regarded as a challenge to the writer's skill at condensation.

The following are the types of publications in this category that a public relations writer is most frequently called upon to create.

INFORMATIONAL BROCHURES   These describe the purposes, policies, and functions of an organization. Tour-guide folders given out at museums are an example of this form. So is the 12-page pamphlet "Foundation for Public Relations Research & Education," in which that organization explains its role and the services it offers.

HANDBOOKS   More elaborate than basic brochures, these usually include policy statements, statistical information, and listings of significant facts about the issuing organization and its field of operation. Handbooks often are designed for distribution primarily to news media sources as handy references for a writer or broadcaster in a hurry. Trade associations and large corporations are among the most frequent users of the handbook as a public relations tool.

Typical examples of the handbook are the following:

"Sharing the Risk," published by the Insurance Information Institute. Nearly 200 pages describe property and casualty insurance concepts, regulations, and policies, ranging from homeowners' losses to nuclear risks.

"Oil & Gas Pocket Reference," published by Phillips Petroleum Company. This is a 60-page small-format booklet of statistics about the oil industry. Included are such lists as the top 10 U.S. oil-producing states; the top 15 oil-producing nations, with amounts; oil and gas imports by year; and significant reference dates.

CORPORATE BROCHURES FOR EXTERNAL USE   Frequently aimed at specific audiences rather than at the general public, these may be such items as the inserts utility companies include with their bills, financial documents such as quarterly reports to stockholders and proxy statements for potential stock purchasers, owners' manuals, and teaching materials that help students learn about the issuing industries.

CORPORATE BROCHURES FOR INTERNAL USE

To inform and train their employees, companies issue a broad range of brochures and handbooks. These may be distributed at in-plant meetings or to individuals at work, or mailed to the employees' homes. In simplest form, information sheets may be posted on company bulletin boards. Readership of these boards is high; anything posted there will be noticed and probably will become a topic of conversation on the job.

Examples of in-company brochures and manuals include the following:

Atlantic Richfield Company's 12-page booklet to assist older employees make the transition from work to retirement. It answers questions that concern every employee approaching retirement, such as financial planning, use of leisure time, and health benefits.

A manual describing proper telephone techniques, given to employees of Washington Federal Savings and Loan Association in Seattle. Employees discuss the manual in seminars during which they see a 25-minute film depicting "telephone traps" in which they might find themselves.

GLOSSARIES

Trade associations and corporations in technical fields often issue pamphlets defining terms, including jargon as well as standard words, commonly used in their work. Like handbooks, glossaries are distributed extensively to the news media, to help writers understand the special language and use it accurately. Glossaries sometimes are included in other corporate publications.

An oil industry glossary, for example, includes words and terms such as *desiccation, dispersant, huff-and-puff,* and *wrinkle chaser*—hardly the language that a nonspecialist writer runs across in daily life. (*Huff-and-puff* is descriptive of techniques to recover oils by steam injection. A *wrinkle chaser* is a geologist.) Figure 22.6 presents some highlights from the glossary put out by Phillips Petroleum, from which the examples here were also taken.

The Annual Report

Preparation of a corporation's annual report is a major function of the firm's public relations department or counseling firm—the company's most significant and expensive written contact with its stockholders and the financial community.

Annual reports of many large corporations are works of graphic beauty. Printed on slick, heavy magazine paper and brightened with abundant color photography, a report puts the company's best foot forward as strongly as the past year's performance will permit. Some companies state the bad news in a report as inconspicuously as possible, perhaps in a footnote. This practice

FIGURE 22.6

Phillips Petroleum Company compiled and distributed a glossary of energy and petrochemical terms. The cover and excerpts are shown here. Figure 16.1 shows how the company handles the same material in European editions. (Reprinted by permission of Phillips Petroleum Company.)

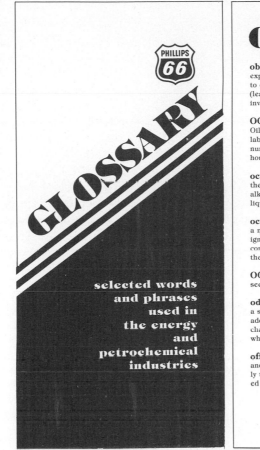

obligatory wells:
exploratory wells that an operator undertakes to drill as a condition of the agreement (lease, license, farm in) covering the acreage involved in an exploration program.

OCAW:
Oil, Chemical and Atomic Workers Union, a labor organization representing a large number of the industry's refinery and other hourly workers.

octane:
the eighth member of the paraffinic (or alkane) family of hydrocarbons; a petroleum liquid under almost all conditions.

octane number:
a measure of a fuel's resistance to pre-ignition (knock) when fired in an internal combustion engine; the higher the number, the more antiknock quality.

OCS:
see **Outer Continental Shelf.**

odorant:
a substance, such as a mercaptan, that is added to odorless gases to give them a characteristic smell so they can be detected when there is a leak.

offloading:
another name for unloading; refers specifically to liquid cargo such as crude oil and refined products.

96

is deceptive and creates a bad impression of the corporation on reporters and other astute readers, who will find the bad news anyway.

Technically, the corporate annual report is an informational document filed with the Securities and Exchange Commission. In practice it has grown into much more than that. It is a handsomely printed vehicle used by management to impress stockholders with its stewardship of their money and, through its impact on security analysts and brokerage houses, to encourage others to purchase the company's stocks and bonds. The report also is used as a showpiece in recruiting new employees. The cost of a report often exceeds $2 a copy. The Southern Company, a large public-utility holding corporation, rather typically spent $413,000 to produce its annual report in a recent year.

A corporate annual report is divided into two general sections:

1. *Detailed financial information about the company's condition and performance during the past year.* A consolidated balance sheet and management's discussion of the financial condition are essential elements. A letter from the corporation's auditing firm attesting to the validity of the figures is included, along with separate breakdowns of certain financial aspects. The statistical material in this section is prepared by the financial department of the corporation and approved by top management. This material is coldly objective, not promotional in tone except in the sense that favorable figures encourage potential purchasers of the stock.

Other relevant information about the corporation usually is published in this section for reference. This may include lists of the board of directors, with information about their career backgrounds, and company officers; principal office address; name of the transfer agent handling the stock; stock exchange listing; and overseas connections. Specific financial data are required by the Securities and Exchange Commission in an annual report. It is for this reason that a specialist in financial public relations should be given the assignment to compile these reports.

2. *Management's presentation of accomplishments during the past year, its goals, and outstanding problems.* This material, appearing in the first portion of the report just after a one-page summary of financial highlights, is designed to give a good impression of management's work. While the prose is restrained, use of striking color photography and other graphics, often in full-page size, helps to suggest corporate vigor and achievement.

Centerpiece of this front section is a report to stockholders by the chairman of the board. Sometimes, a joint report is signed by the chairman and the president. This is the "message." The top executive reviews basic developments of the year, mentions earnings per share, outlines corporate strategy, describes problems encountered and steps taken to overcome them, speaks proudly of achievements, includes words of praise for the workforce, and perhaps makes a plea to stockholders for support of the company in its efforts to pass or defeat legislation affecting it. Utility company chief executive officers almost invariably report the need for higher rates.

The report traditionally closes with an optimistic summary of the outlook for the coming year. Even when the prospect is poor, the report to stockholders finds reason for hope, coupled with staunch words about management's commitment to their interests and its determination to overcome obstacles. What management would dare to say otherwise and expect to stay in office?

Concise articles about construction projects, new products, environmental efforts, research programs, employee accomplishments, and planned expansions often are included. Photographs show employees on their jobs and company equipment in operation.

A look through a stack of typical reports shows increasing emphasis on company efforts to make a favorable impact not only on stockholders but on the communities in which plants are situated, on customers, and on employees. Recurring references to a corporation's social responsibilities and environmental concerns are evident. This sampling of headlines over articles in recent annual reports illustrates the trend:

"Community Outreach Program"

"Consumer Advisory Panel Formed"

"Customer Service Important"

"Conservation Emphasized"

"Equal Employment Opportunities"

"Vehicle Accident Rate Improves"

Those who prepare annual reports serve two kinds of readers—(1) the financial community and financially oriented investors who study the statistics in detail and (2) stockholders with little financial sophistication who may be unable to read a balance sheet but desire to know in a general way how the company is faring. Some stockholders do little more than read what they regard as the most important sentence in the report—the amount of dividends each share of stock paid—and look at the photographs. Thus the report must be meticulously accurate to satisfy expert readers and, at the same time, written in easily comprehended style for casual readers.

Occasionally a company breaks out of the mold with an ingenious or humorous approach, to give an impression of being a place in which creativity is admired. The H. J. Heinz Company of Pittsburgh in its 1982 report featured 10 winners of a worldwide poetry contest for Heinz employees that drew 700 entries. Each poem was illustrated by a full-page reproduction of a painting commissioned for the report and was accompanied by comments from the poet-employee and the artist. Heinz conceived the report as a tool to be used in recruiting, marketing, and image-building in addition to its financial purpose. Emphasis on employees' literary ability generated staff morale.

A furniture designer and manufacturer, Herman Miller, Inc., supplemented a recent annual report with a packet of 10 four-color postcards attached to the front cover. The cards, showing employees at work, contained brightly written commercial messages.

Resembling magazines, annual reports usually vary in size between 36 and 80 pages. They are mailed bulk rate to stockholders, the financial community, business editors, libraries, and special lists of persons whom the company wishes to cultivate. Copies are available upon request at corporate public relations offices. Some corporations offer cassette recordings of their reports to persons with impaired vision.

As supplements to printed annual reports, but never as replacements for them, some companies issue videotaped annual reports for showing to employees, stockholders, and financial groups. Teleconferencing an annual meeting is an increasingly common practice. Exposure of videotaped reports on cable television is another possibility. Most frequently, these visual presentations are directed to employees. In certain companies, after a visual presentation is made to assembled employees, a senior management official discusses the printed report and encourages the group to ask questions. When a company produces both printed and videotaped annual reports, emphasis in the printed version is on the financial facts and in the videotape on the way the company and its employees do things. Thus duplication is held to a minimum.

Corporate Advertising

Traditionally, *advertising* is defined as purchased space or time used to sell goods or services, while public relations space in the media is obtained free. The line of demarcation becomes fuzzy when a company engages in *corporate advertising,* also called *institutional advertising.* Such advertising is processed and purchased in the regular manner. Its purpose, however, is not to sell the company's products or services directly but to enhance public conception of the company or to advocate a company policy (see Figure 22.7).

Corporate advertising is space or broadcast time purchased for the benefit of the company rather than for its products or services. The corporate communications department and public relations counseling firm have a role in formulation of corporate advertising programs, as part of their function to protect and shape the company's reputation.

A substantial majority of corporate advertising is done in magazines, approximately 60 percent of it in consumer magazines. Network and spot television commercials are used extensively, along with Sunday magazines, radio, and outdoor advertising. Relatively little of it goes into newspapers.

Corporate advertising may be divided into three basic types: (1) *general corporate image-building,* (2) *investor and financial relations programs,* and (3) *advocacy.*

IMAGE-BUILDING   Image-building advertising is intended primarily to strengthen a company's identity in the eyes of the public and/or the financial community. Conglomerates whose divisions market unrelated products seek through such advertising to project a unified, readily recognized image. Others use it to coun-

FIGURE 22.7

International Paper Company enhances its reputation as a caring corporation with corporate advertisements urging an increase in reading. In this advertisement in *Editor & Publisher,* it concedes frankly, "We figure the more people read . . . the more paper you'll buy from us." (Reprinted by permission of International Paper Company.)

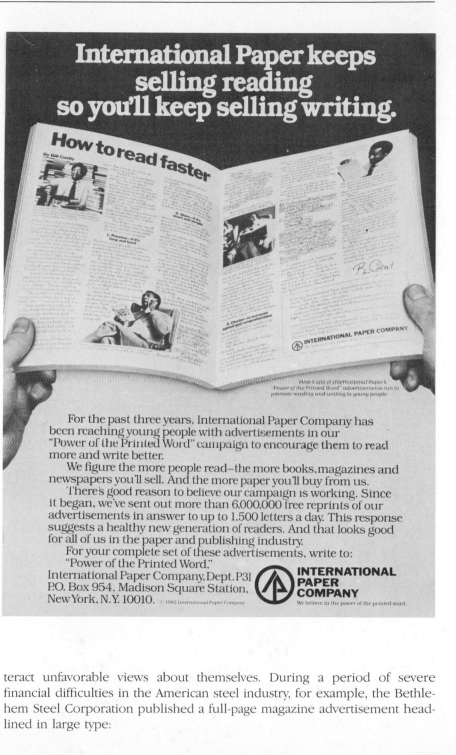

teract unfavorable views about themselves. During a period of severe financial difficulties in the American steel industry, for example, the Bethlehem Steel Corporation published a full-page magazine advertisement headlined in large type:

10 actions
Bethlehem has taken
to help improve future
profitability

The text listed the 10 actions, among them the following:

We've streamlined our organization from top to bottom, eliminating layers of management and supervision.
We've reduced our salaried work forces by about 30% in two years.
We've shut down a number of facilities, and we're disposing of others, that were unprofitable or did not fit Bethlehem's long-range strategic plan....

The advertisement closed with a strong boldface final paragraph:

Some of these actions were painful, but necessary to make Bethlehem the tougher, more competitive company we are today.

In other words, "Look at us now!" The purpose was to emphasize that Bethlehem had acted vigorously to correct its faults. Now its task was to make the public, and especially investors, recognize the change.

Other corporations use institutional advertising to demonstrate what good corporate citizens they are. General Motors, for example, published a full-page advertisement headed, "How to Stop Drunk Driving." The subhead said, "Tough laws may help, but we also need to change our attitudes." This discussion of the effect of alcohol on drivers made no attempt to sell new cars but portrayed General Motors as being concerned with increasing the safety of all automobile drivers.

Users of such advertising hope also that by portraying a company favorably, the advertisements will improve employee morale, thus helping to retain the workforce, and simultaneously aid in recruiting new employees.

FINANCIAL RELATIONS PROGRAMS

The second form of corporate advertising is aimed straight at the financial community. The advertiser tries to depict its financial strength and prospects so favorably that security analysts will advise their clients to purchase its stock. When a corporation has millions of shares outstanding, even a fractional improvement in their price is beneficial.

ADVOCACY

The third, sometimes controversial, form of corporate advertising is advocacy. In such advertisements, a corporation or association tries to influence public opinion on a political or social issue. Only a small portion of corporate advertising expenditure goes into advocacy advertising, but because these

540

How TV reports the recovery

Malice in wonderland

Ever get the queasy feeling watching the three TV networks' news programs that you're peering through the looking glass, like Alice? We do, especially when watching news reports on the economy. Television news seems to turn most of the positive indicators of a healthy economic recovery into negatives. It's like Humpty Dumpty telling Alice: "When I use a word…it means just what I choose it to mean—neither more nor less."

Our own queasiness has now been documented. The non-profit Institute for Applied Economics monitored and recorded network TV news programs seven days a week for six months during 1983. The Institute found that while factory output, auto sales and personal income were all up, and inflation and unemployment were down, "the coverage on network television was still in recession." Indeed, according to the report, about 85% of all "in-depth" or interpretative economic stories aired during this period were <u>negative</u>— giving viewers the impression that the economy was moribund, when in reality it was rebounding sharply.

Numerous examples of network news distortion are listed in the Institute's report. Here are some of the most flagrant:

• On July 8, the Department of Labor announced a significant <u>drop</u> in unemployment. It also noted that 1.6 million more people were working in June 1983 than in December 1982. But CBS reporter Ray Brady, according to the Institute, placed the "whole emphasis…on those who remained out of work—not on those who were rejoining the work force." ABC News on the same date focused on just <u>one</u> unemployed steelworker, who said: "There's an upturn in the economy but it hasn't affected us yet." The clear implication was that the recovery was spotty, at best.

• On July 28, Dan Rather said on CBS that "Many people argue that anytime inflation stays down, that's good news. Some others argue, yes, but the way you get it down matters, and if it stays down too much for too long, the wealthy benefit disproportionately." The clear implication here: Bringing inflation under control could be less than positive and might even be a negative.

• On August 6, on NBC, the Institute noted that "good economic news was presented within the worst possible context"— the town of Renovo, Pennsylvania, one of the most depressed areas in the nation with 800 of 1,100 workers unemployed. "Although Renovo didn't reflect the whole country, the impression was given that the recovery was making a small dent in a very bad national problem."

• On September 2, the Labor Department reported another drop in unemployment. But on September 8, both CBS and ABC focused on 40 job openings at the Magic Chef Company in Galesburg, Illinois, where there were 2,000 applicants. "The good news about hiring was reported but the context (2,000 job-seekers in line) was negative."

• On December 2, "ABC located two upper middle-class men who had been unemployed for at least one and a half years and focused on their experiences." Result? "A story that began with a 0.4% drop in unemployment ended in complete despair and talk of suicide."

These distortions turn economic facts into drama—and occasionally into soap opera. And that's a pity, because millions of Americans rely principally on network television news for information on complex public issues.

We do wish the networks would more carefully segregate opinion from news. When one masquerades as the other, the harm is not just to the viewers, but to the nation as a whole.

Alice's make believe world belongs on the bookshelf, where it's clearly labeled fiction. TV news should deal in facts.

Mobil

© 1984 Mobil Corporation

advertisements sometimes touch public sensibilities, they receive considerable attention.

Mobil has been among the most vehement corporations in its advocacy advertising, emphasizing its aggressive positions on matters of energy control and chiding the media for what Mobil's advertising has called "irresponsible reporting." The tone of this advertising brought criticism against the giant oil corporation. One of Mobil's advertisements is shown in Figure 22.8.

Chase Manhattan Bank also encountered criticism for some of its advocacy advertising, as it conceded frankly in a full-page newspaper advertisement.

This advertisement was dominated by a drawing of several of the Founding Fathers, above the headline:

In accordance with the wishes of our founding fathers, we'll continue to speak out.

The text stated, in part:

> In the past year, Chase has been running a series of advertisements which expressed our views on some of today's important economic issues. These included the need for greater productivity . . . the need to stimulate research and development . . . tax incentives to spur investment, generate capital and modernize our industrial plant . . . government overregulation . . . inflation. And the spurious rhetoric about "excessive" corporate profits.
>
> Since then, these topics have become central issues in this critical election year. For that we're grateful, because the American public surely deserves a full and open debate as to how best these pressing national problems can be solved.
>
> On the other hand, it's caused us to go through some soul-searching in recent weeks. We've frankly asked ourselves whether an institution such as ours should continue to speak out on important and sometimes sensitive issues in the middle of a national election.
>
> So we went back to the First Amendment to our Constitution and took a long and thoughtful look. As a result, we've decided to go right on speaking out, even though we obviously risk causing controversy or alienating a constituency. . . .

EVALUATING CORPORATE ADVERTISING

How effective is corporate advertising? Because of its abstract nature, measurement of results is difficult. In this sense it resembles public relations programs more than it does traditional advertising, which can be evaluated in terms of units sold.

Ogilvy & Mather, a major advertising agency, studied corporate advertising. It announced these conclusions:

> We have learned that good corporate advertising can:

Build awareness of a company.

Make a favorable impression on investors and security analysts.

Motivate employees and attract recruits.

Influence public opinion.

Strengthen relations with dealers.

Influence legislation.

> We have learned that corporate advertising cannot:

Gloss over a poor record or a weak competitive position.

Boost the price of your stock next month.

Swiftly turn the tide of public opinion.

There are no quick fixes. Advertising can spread the truth about your company but cannot *conceal* it.

Thomas F. Garbett, a recognized authority on the subject, offered this justification for corporate advertising, in an article published in the *Harvard Business Review:*

Although many companies assume that the safest course is to keep a low profile, this may in fact be a dangerous tack. If some inadvertent disclosure brings high visibility or even incidental exposure, an unknown company maintains little cred ibility as it moves to counter public criticism. . . . When people first get acquainted with a company through an unfortunate disclosure, they often distort what little they know and make generalizations about missing information. The less filled out a company's image is, the more subject that image is to wild distortions.

QUESTIONS FOR REVIEW AND DISCUSSION

1. What is an *embargo* on a news release? Does it have any legal standing?

2. What are the physical requirements for an attractive news release?

3. A public relations counselor should have a client initial a file copy of each news release before distribution. Why?

4. Describe the difference between a news release and a factsheet.

5. To what audiences might a corporate public relations department send a newsletter?

6. As editor of a company magazine intended for employees and retirees, what would be your objectives?

7. Handbooks are issued frequently by corporations and trade associations. What types of material do they usually contain?

8. To what federal agency must corporate annual reports be submitted?

9. Corporate or institutional advertising differs in purpose from ordinary advertising. Explain this difference.

10. What risk does a corporation take when it uses aggressive advocacy advertising?

CHAPTER TWENTY-THREE

Spoken Tactics

Long before prehistoric men and women scratched picture messages on rocks, they communicated with each other by voice. The words may have been little more expressive than the "ughs" cartoonists put into the mouths of cave dwellers, but they delivered information and expressed feelings.

The spoken word is humanity's most ancient form of communication, except perhaps for hand gestures and facial expressions. Under many circumstances it is still the most powerful form. Speech is a basic tool for the public relations practitioner; this chapter examines ways to use it.

The text provides down-to-earth advice on ways to carry out assignments that practitioners face every day: how to write and stage a speech, help a management representative hold a news conference, give a press party, assist a client in preparing for an interview, and run an effective meeting.

At the close, word-of-mouth publicity and ways to combat the often insidious effects of rumors are discussed.

Face-to-Face Discussion

A conversation face-to-face between two persons is widely regarded as the most effective form of interpersonal communication. This is certainly true in the world of work. The chemistry of personality that can develop during a business call is not easily defined but can be tremendously valuable.

Visualize these typical situations: a salesperson soliciting an order from a customer at lunch, a public relations representative at an editor's desk explaining the reasons for her hospital client's fund drive, a corporate vice-president for public affairs calling on a city council member to urge the opening of a new street to reduce traffic congestion outside the company's manufacturing plant. In each case, the logic of the persuader's arguments is reinforced by the impact of the individual's personality. Sincerity impresses the listener. An aggressive, demanding approach arouses irritation. A smile, perhaps a casual quip, and a friendly but respectful manner help immeasurably in putting across the message.

The personal call is among the most potent methods a public relations practitioner can use. It may fail, however, no matter how good the cause, if the caller arrives ill-prepared and handles the presentation clumsily. Here, from a veteran newspaper editor who has listened to hundreds of across-the-desk public relations presentations, is advice on how to present a case effectively:

1. *Telephone in advance for an appointment.* Then be on time. Don't walk in "cold" and expect a hearing.

2. *Identify yourself and your purpose immediately.* Present a business card if possible, so the recipient has your name and affiliation at hand during the discussion and for filing later.

3. *Be concise.* Editors, program directors, and other opinion-makers on whom you call are busy. Even those who appear relaxed and casual have other work waiting to be done. Make your presentation succinctly. Describe what your client plans to do, explain the purpose of the program, tell how it will help the public, and state specifically what support you hope to receive from the person you are addressing. Respond to your host's questions without meandering up side conversational paths, politely seek a commitment if that seems appropriate, then leave. Unless the listener judges your proposal to be excessively commercial or self-serving, you can expect a sympathetic hearing in most instances.

4. *Don't oversell.* Don't plead. Persons who receive presentations dislike being pressured and instinctively build defense mechanisms against excessively emotional "pitches." Never say, "You must help us!" Persons whose aid you seek resent being told that they "must" do anything.

5. *Express appreciation for your host's time and for anything he or she can do to assist your cause.*

6. *Leave behind written material—a brochure, a news release, a factsheet—for your host to study later.* Be certain that the material includes a telephone number at which you can be reached for further information. Asking your host to read the material while you sit there is a poor tactic, unless it is very short; the result may be a hasty, reluctant scanning rather than the thoughtful reading you desire.

If the presentation can be made at lunch, over coffee or perhaps over a drink, outside the office setting, its impact may be stronger—assuming that the person being solicited will spare the necessary time.

7. *Follow up with a note of appreciation for the reception, expressing hope that the recipient can use the information you left.* It subtly reminds the person to read the material, if that hasn't happened, and to do something about it.

If the presentation can be made at lunch, over coffee or perhaps over a drink, outside the office setting, its impact may be stronger—assuming that the person being solicited will spare the necessary time.

If you are working with an editor or program director in a small community, or with a person you know well, the approach can be more informal. However, conciseness, restraint, and the delivery of printed information are important in every situation.

Face-to-face discussion also is an essential tool for open communication within business organizations. Such conversations between management representatives and supervisors, supervisors and foremen, management and union officers, spread understanding of a company policy or a new product among the employees. Slightly less intimate, but almost as effective if well done, is the small-group discussion directed toward the same goal. Internal communication through staff study meetings, employee training sessions, and department meetings creates a more competent, motivated workforce and identifies areas of employee dissatisfaction. (A discussion on how to conduct an effective meeting appears later in this chapter.)

A blind spot in company management, in small firms as well as large ones, is the too-frequent assumption that employees down the line know the reasons for company policies. The cynical wisecrack "There's no reason for it, it's just company policy" shows a weakness of management that need not exist if verbal channels of internal communication are used frequently and intelligently. Explaining *why* something is done is just as important as explaining *how* it should be done.

Vital as they are in reaching opinion leaders, person-to-person conversations form only one segment of a campaign to inform the public and mold opinion through the spoken word. A public relations campaign usually must reach many persons at the same time. This can be done orally through speeches, news conferences, and appearances of representatives on radio and television. Although the impact of a speaker's personality on individual listeners may diminish when the message is delivered in a large meeting hall or filtered through a receiving set, the sheer abundance of simultaneous contacts speeds up distribution of the message.

Each of these spoken methods will be discussed in detail. The text will first examine the speech: how to plan it, how to write it, and how to assist the speaker who delivers it.

Assignment: Speechwriting

Public relations practitioners frequently are called upon to write speeches for their employers or clients. As speechwriters, their role is a hidden one. They labor silently to produce the words that may sparkle like champagne when poured forth by their employers from the lecterns of convention halls. In the White House, the wraps of anonymity are drawn around the writers who churn out speeches and statements for the president of the United States. A president who utters a memorable phrase gets the credit, but some unknown writer in a back office probably created it. There is nothing discreditable about this. Presidents have more urgent tasks than to think up catchy quotations. Although speechwriters receive no ego-building recognition, they find personal satisfaction in creating competent speeches for someone else. Speechwriting is a highly skilled craft.

Turning loose a speaker, especially an inexperienced one, before an audience without a text, or at least a careful outline, may be an invitation to boredom. The "and . . . uhs" and "as I was sayings" will proliferate like rabbits. The audience will squirm, inwardly at first and then conspicuously in their chairs, as the speaker stumbles along. The opportunity to deliver a message that informs, persuades, and entertains listeners has been thrown out the window. That is why speakers who lack the time or the skill to do their own preparation need able speechwriters.

Some speakers prefer to work from notes rather than read a text. In that event, the writer should prepare a full speech for the speaker to study, then reduce the main elements of it to note cards arranged in proper sequence. Talking from notes increases the air of spontaneity, if the speaker is experienced and comfortable before an audience. It also magnifies the risk that the speaker will meander and lose control of the time.

A written speech should reflect the personality and voice patterns of the speaker, not those of the writer.

Speeches come in many sizes and serve many purposes. The writer may be called upon to prepare a light 20-minute talk for the service club luncheon circuit, a provocative 10-minute statement to open a panel discussion, or a scholarly 45-minute lecture for delivery before a university audience. Possibly the assignment may be for "just a few remarks" to welcome foreign visitors on a plant tour. Or it could be for a hard-sell pitch to raise money for a local charity campaign.

THE BASIC POINTS OF SPEECHWRITING

Whatever the assignment, here are basic points for the speechwriter to keep in mind:

1. *A speech should say something of lasting value.* Even a talk intended to entertain, full of fluffy humor, should be built around a significant point. A speech needs both content and style; without the former, the latter is empty.

One veteran speechwriter for a large corporation and an influential trade organization applies what he calls the "Door Test" to the speeches he writes. After hearing a dinner speaker, the listeners go out the door of the banquet room and on entering the doors of their homes are greeted by their spouses and asked what the dinner speaker said. In reply, the listeners give the essence of the speech as they remember it. Was there a message clear and concise enough to remember? Did the speech pass the Door Test?

2. *A speech should concentrate on one, or at most two, main themes.*

3. *A speech needs facts.* The information must be accurate. The writer's skill as a researcher is put to the test, to dig up information that will illustrate and emphasize the speaker's theme. Before a speaker makes a statement, the information in it should be verified beyond any doubt.

4. *The type of audience should influence the style and content of the speech.* When a company celebrates its fiftieth anniversary with a reception and dinner dance for its employees, they don't want to hear the president drone on for 30 minutes about the corporate financial structure. The setting calls for some joking, a few nostalgic stories, references to some individuals by name, words of appreciation for what the employees have contributed, and a few upbeat words about the future. On the other hand, the president may ask the writer for a speech about the company for delivery at a meeting of security analysts. That is not the place for droll stories. The audience wants facts on which to base investment decisions, not entertainment.

5. *Clarity in speechwriting is essential.* If the listeners don't understand what the speaker is saying, everyone's time is wasted. This happens when the speech contains complicated sentences, technical information that the speaker fails to explain in terms the audience can comprehend, and excessive jargon or "inside" talk. The speechwriter's challenge is to simplify and clarify the speaker's message without destroying its significance.

AN EXAMPLE OF SPEECHWRITING

To determine how the speechwriting process works, consider how a specific assignment could be handled. The assistant public relations director of a large regional restaurant chain is assigned to prepare a speech for the general manager to deliver at a chamber of commerce banquet in a middle-size city where the company has recently opened a luxury restaurant. What does the practitioner do?

First, she must know what the speaker desires to emphasize. The management has heard extensive word-of-mouth criticism about the high dinner prices the new restaurant charges. Some business has been lost because of this. The general manager sees the speech invitation as an opportunity to explain why the restaurant must charge these prices and to stress what good values the dinners really are. To do so, he must give the audience a frank behind-the-scenes look at the restaurant business—an opening for the speechwriter to spice up the necessary financial information with whimsical backstage anecdotes.

Twenty minutes of such material, brightly presented, will entertain and inform this business-oriented audience. It will demonstrate that the restaurant organization is efficiently run and does its best to provide residents with a distinctive place to dine at the lowest feasible cost. Indeed, here is an excellent public relations moment.

The speechwriter rarely talks with the general manager. So she must use her speech-planning appointment with him not only to learn what he wants to say but to study his style. Does he speak intensely or in a casual, wry manner? Is his speech staccato or a bit fulsome? The words she writes should be shaped to his natural style. Probably he can provide her with one or two of his favorite restaurant anecdotes. She can talk later with other officials of the company to obtain additional stories.

With this guidance in hand, how does the practitioner organize and write the speech?

A speech is built in blocks, joined by transitions. The following pattern for assembling the blocks provides an all-purpose outline on which most speeches can be built:

Introduction. Establishment of contact with audience.

Statement of main purpose of speech.

Development of theme with examples, facts, and anecdotes. Enumeration of points in 1, 2, 3 order is valuable here. It gives a sense of structure and controlled use of time.

Statement of secondary theme, if there is one.

Enunciation of prinicipal point to which speaker has been building, the heart of the speech.

A pause at this plateau, with an anecdote or two: a soft place while audience absorbs principal point just made.

Restatement of theme in summary form.

Brief, brisk conclusion.

This plan of speech organization is *deductive;* that is, the central theme is stated almost at the beginning, and the points that follow support and illustrate the theme. A less common type of organization is *inductive*. In it the speaker presents points of information and arguments leading up to a statement of the principal theme near the end of the speech.

Following the preceding deductive outline, the speechwriter uses the first 2 minutes of the allotted 20 to build rapport between the general manager and the audience. The manager explains that when his company first considered coming to this city, he doubted that the area would support the luxury type of restaurant it operates. But the chamber of commerce convinced him that it would, and he is delighted that he had the good sense to listen. (A light, slightly self-disparaging touch.) He congratulates the chamber on the excellent statistical material it provided, thanks the membership for the organization's aid in solving the problems of setting up business, and mentions by name a few individuals who were especially helpful.

Then come these building blocks:

Statement of main purpose. The speaker says he wants to tell the audience about how a luxury restaurant operates, what its problems are, and why the customer sees things done a certain way. A summary of purpose in a single theme sentence at this point gives the speech a solid foundation. Almost as an aside he remarks, "Perhaps this will help you understand why our dinners cost as much as they do."

Development. The manager states his company's total investment in opening this restaurant and reveals the number of people needed to run it, mentions kitchen jobs the diners never know about . . . lists how many potatoes, steaks, heads of lettuce, and pounds of coffee are consumed in a week . . . relates a story about the night when the maitre d' had a full book of reservations and the salad chef walked out in a huff after a quarrel with his waitress girlfriend . . . describes how the chain's bill for pork and beef has soared.

Statement of secondary theme. The speaker explains how the restaurant chooses its menus. He describes research into which entrees sell well or poorly, nutritional factors, and the difficulties in finding reasonable prices for the high-quality foodstuffs that will maintain the restaurant's standards of excellence.

Enunciation of principal point. Operation of a first-line restaurant in a time of high labor costs and rising food prices is a risky business, subject to the vagaries of weather, the economy, and the largely unpredictable turns of public fancy. By its steady growth, his organization has proved that a significant percentage of the public, "including here in this city," will patronize a restaurant that serves fine food with alert service in a distinctive setting. "Our challenge is to provide these things at the lowest prices we can offer while earning a legitimate profit from our investment."

Pause on plateau. The manager relates two anecdotes, one about what happened in the kitchen when a cook tried to fry rotten eggs and the other about a diner who tried to steal some silverware, only to have it drop out of his pocket near the front door. Both stories illustrate problems of operating a restaurant.

Restatement of theme. The speaker's summary emphasizes his pride in the way local diners have patronized the new restaurant, proving his belief that the establishment provides the city with a type of high-quality dining that its citizens want and appreciate.

Brief conclusion. The audience hears a bit of news: the speaker announces that the restaurant has arranged to receive ample supplies of a popular but relatively rare fish. Next week the restaurant will add the fish, prepared in an unusual manner, to the menu at a special low introductory price. He invites everyone to come and try it.

One more step remains to make this a thoroughly successful public relations appearance. The speaker knows that the audience will be invited to ask questions; he has had the speechwriter give him a list of antagonistic queries he may receive. These include such challenges as, "Why do you hold people with dinner reservations in the bar so long before seating them—to make more money on liquor?" and "Is it true that you require waitresses to surrender a percentage of their tips to management?" His ability in answering the tough ones will improve or detract from the good impression his speech has made.

Speechwriting Techniques

THE DIFFERENCE BETWEEN THE WRITTEN AND SPOKEN WORD

The first principle in writing words to be spoken is to make them flow in the way a person actually talks. Writing intended for the ear must be simpler in construction and more casual in form than writing meant for the eye. Instead of saying, "the Chicago man," make it "the man from Chicago"; it sounds more natural. Contractions such as *don't* and *won't* increase the sense of informality.

Short, straightforward sentences are best. To provide variety, an occasional long sentence is acceptable if its structure is simple. So is a scattering of sentences beginning with brief dependent clauses. Often the ear fails to comprehend as fully and quickly as the eye does because the listener is easily distracted or may not hear clearly. The audio channel becomes clogged. Complex grammatical constructions should be avoided. A person can read a complicated sentence again and again until its meaning is clear. A listener who hears that same sentence spoken has no opportunity to hear it again because the speaker has moved ahead to new material. Thus a speaker, especially when handling difficult information, should repeat key points of the speech, couching them if possible in slightly different form.

Studies indicate that the average person listens four times as rapidly as the average person speaks. Thus the listener may be thinking about other matters while hearing the speaker. Even for a skillful speaker, holding the listener's undivided attention is extremely difficult; recapitulation of main points helps the listener retain at least the main thrust of the speech.

Here, for example, is a sentence from a published news story that would be unacceptable in a speech text because of its intricate structure:

Wright, who has agreed to pay the fine, said she believes the commission's action, which comes three weeks before the Nov. 2 election, will have no effect on her reelection campaign against Democrat C. D. (Dick) Stine.

If the material were written as follows, listeners could comprehend it far more easily:

Wright has agreed to pay the fine. The commission's action comes only three weeks before the November 2nd election. But Wright believes that it will not affect her campaign for reelection against Democrat Dick Stine.

An excellent way to grasp the concept of writing for speech is to close your eyes and listen to people around you talk. Do the same thing while hearing a radio newscast, which has been written especially for the ear. Visualize how the words you are hearing would appear on paper. Notice how often people use fragments of sentences. The words that would complete the sentences are implied, a kind of verbal shorthand. Such fragments in a speech increase the feeling of naturalness.

The incomplete sentence is used quite effectively in this excerpt from a speech by John C. Bedrosian, president of the American Federation of Hospitals. His topic, the high cost of medical care, was complex, and he dealt with the problem in depth. A brisk text, however, kept the speech from bogging down. Brief sentences, sentence fragments, and short words are used to offset such necessary long ones as *catastrophic* and *ambulatory;*

Hospital care is expensive. There is no denying that. It is essentially designed to provide care to the critically ill. Catastrophic illnesses. Major surgeries. Serious injuries. Any institution that is equipped and staffed to provide the highest level of care is by its very nature not economically appropriate for low-level care.

That's why we are witnessing the growth of alternative care and treatment sources. Satellite clinics, for example, surgi-centers, and other ambulatory care facilities. Skilled nursing homes for recuperation from illness or surgery. Home health care, a concept that has really only gotten started.

All of these are approaches that match the level of care to the need, and at a significant reduction in cost.

A speaker normally delivers a text at the rate of about 150 words a minute. A standard page of pica-sized typewriter copy contains about 250 words. So, when preparing a 20-minute speech, the writer must produce about 3000 words, approximately 12 typewritten pages. If the speaker is an

Pro Athletes Give
Speaking Hints

Articulate professional athletes are popular public speakers. Audiences like to see them in person and hear behind-the-scenes stories of sports. Many are scheduled through the *Sports Illustrated* Speakers Bureau.

Three famous sports speakers handled by *Sports Illustrated* describe how they organize their talks and establish personal contact with audiences.

BILLY CASPER, golfer: I have found that most people like to hear me talk about some behind-the-scenes aspects of golf. I try to relate the humorous side of the game and give my audience some insight into what we go through in a normal working day. I would suggest that unless a person is extremely experienced in speaking before large audiences, he avoid telling jokes. But, as any athlete knows, there are enough situations in sports that are funny by themselves and do not need forced attempts at humor. If I feel that my audience will appreciate and respond to a more serious subject, I cut down on the humor and talk on the role of sport in our society.

HARMON KILLEBREW, former major league baseball star: I usually begin by some reference to people in the audience and try to keep my whole talk on as much a personal level as possible. Since my main function as a speaker is to entertain the listeners, I stay away from a complicated approach. I try to keep the subject of my talk to one point and build up that point in various ways. For example, if my main point is the difficulties faced by an athlete in professional sports, I would begin by telling an anecdote that points this out. I would then establish my own point of view and follow this up with some further stories which illustrate my premise. I try to maintain interest by relating humorous or generally little-known stories and then end my speech by restating the original premise.

BART STARR, professional football coach: I try to cement as strong relationships as possible with the people to whom I talk. After my talk I try to stay around as long as possible and talk with people from the audience. I've found that doing this establishes a personal rapport with the people, and often leads to further assignments. *I always send the chairman of the group a short note thanking him for his hospitality.*

especially fast talker, this wordage might be increased a bit. Pauses for emphasis and laughter, however, tend to make a speaker's delivery before an audience slower than during practice run-throughs.

SOME TIPS FROM PROFESSIONALS

Here are tips on writing from professional speechwriters:

Read aloud the words you have written, to be certain that they sound natural to the ear.

Avoid clauses that complicate sentences. Instead of writing, "John Williams, chairman of the State Highway Commission, said, etc.," eliminate the clause by writing, "Chairman John Williams of the State Highway Department said, etc."

Use smooth transitions to move from one section of the speech to the next, as in these examples:

> "And while discussing the fine art of communications, Japanese style, I would like to mention the role of the press." (K. M. Chrysler of *U.S. News & World Report.*)

> "Now I'd like to move to a second major challenge facing us—crime." (James B. Jacobson of Prudential Insurance Company of America in a speech on "Challenges and Choice—Inflation and Crime.")

Use rhetorical questions. They provide change of pace and are a good device to introduce new ideas. An example:

> "Is it too difficult to develop a curriculum whereby students can be fully educated? I think not. It has been done before and quite well." (Benjamin H. Alexander, president of the University of the District of Columbia.)

Draw verbal pictures. Help the audience to visualize scenes, color, movement.

Be wary of jokes. Some speakers tell them well, others fumble. Never let your speaker use that bromide, "That reminds me of a story." If used, jokes should be woven into the text, not telegraphed in advance. Those involving racial and religious topics are likely to offend some members of the audience. Don't use them. The light touch desired in a speech can be obtained by anecdotes or quips that provoke a smile or a chuckle.

Quote statistics sparingly. Provide them in graphic terms when possible. Dixy Lee Ray, former chairperson of the Atomic Energy Commission, did it this way: the amount of energy being used in the United States today is equivalent to what could be produced by the human muscle of approximately 300 slaves per person working 24 hours a day, 365 days a year, consuming no energy themselves.

554

ESTABLISHING A BOND WITH THE AUDIENCE

Use of the second-person form of direct address is a clever tool for speakers trying to establish a personal bond with the audience. A physicist delivering a university lecture would avoid such a device; it might subtly lower the intellectual level of his speech. Politicians use it frequently.

Writing in *Speechwriters' Newsletter,* Stephen R. Maloney pointed out how skillfully President Ronald Reagan used the "you and I together" approach in his broadcast speech in August 1982 promoting a tax increase bill. A year earlier he had pushed through a major tax reduction bill. Reagan's task was to explain and justify his reversal of tax policy in a period of national recession. This was the opening paragraph of the Reagan speech:

There is an old saying we've all heard a thousand times about the weather and how everyone talks about it but no one does anything about it. Well, many of you must be feeling that way about the present state of our economy. Certainly there's a lot of talk about it, but I want you to know that we are doing something about it. And the reason I wanted to talk to you is because you can help us do something about it.

Maloney wrote:

What the President does in his introduction is to plant a powerful suggestion— one that he reinforces throughout the speech—in the mind of his listeners that the tax increase was somehow *their* idea.

Through a repeated use of the words "we" and "ours" the President stresses the bond of commonality—not *his* economic program but "*our* economy." The repetition of the word "you" also serves to involve the audience, drawing them into the discussion, breaking down their resistance, and enlisting them in the cause.

Late in the speech Reagan returned to the direct-address style he used in the opening paragraph. He said, "You helped us to start this economic recovery program last year, when you told your representatives you wanted it. You can help again. . . ."

Analyzing this statement, Maloney pointed out, "The implication is: This isn't *my* tax increase; it's part of *our* (yours and mine) economic program."

Of such niceties of language are successful speeches of persuasion made.

Visual Aids for a Speech

A speech often can be strengthened by use of visual devices. Graphs and charts, a common kind of visual aid, are only as good as their visibility to the audience. A chart too complicated for easy comprehension or too small to be read from the rear of the room is almost useless. Slides projected onto a screen are frequently used. They must be simple in content; holding a slide on the screen long enough for the audience to study involved information creates restlessness. (Audiovisual aids are discussed in Chapter 24.)

Use of objects is still another form of visual aid for a speaker. The model of a new company product displayed near the lectern is an example. A blown-up reproduction of a United Way fund drive emblem hung behind the head table is another. President Jimmy Carter tried a similar technique by wearing a cardigan on camera, instead of the usual presidential suitcoat, during a nationally telecast speech urging energy conservation. The device was so obvious, however, that criticism of the presidential image-building effort severely weakened its effect.

Staging a Speech

Effective speeches don't just happen. They have to be rehearsed and prepared—or, in the language of the theater, "staged." Organizations frequently rely upon a practitioner's understanding of potential audiences to ensure that a speaking engagement helps the organization get a positive message across. And to create a pool of talented speakers, some organizations establish training programs.

THE PRACTITIONER'S ROLE

Public relations practitioners who write speeches are frequently called upon by management to give their opinion about whether the company should accept an invitation to speak and, if so, how the firm should use such a forum to present its views and policies in the most favorable light.

When an invitation arrives, the first decision to be made is whether a speech should be delivered at all. This is where the practitioner's advice may be sought by company management. Thought should be given as to whether the occasion provides a suitable opportunity to further the speaker's cause, and whether the size and significance of the audience justify the time and effort involved. Although this may sound a little arrogant, it is only a matter of practicality.

On the other hand, a public relations representative whose employer desires to make speeches can create ample opportunities. Waiting for invitations is unnecessary. Offers to make a speaker available to organizations without charge may be made discreetly by letter, telephone, or word-of-mouth. The approach is to suggest that the speaker has an unusual message that should be of special interest to the group being solicited. If the speaker is a corporation executive, the hosts should be assured that they will not be subjected to a heavy sales pitch.

Management also is likely to seek out the practitioner's opinion when a speaker must appear before a hostile audience—a real test of public relations skill. While not always pleasant, the experience can pay dividends. A utility company president who proposes construction of a nuclear power plant in the neighborhood cannot expect a cordial welcome when addressing an antinuclear alliance. If the official can command respect by a pleasant, frank manner, however, some in the audience may realize that the company president is not the ogre they had imagined. Having achieved this, the speaker can lay out the pronuclear arguments before the opponents and at least make them aware of the utility's reasoning.

George Graff, former president of McDonnell Douglas, a manufacturer of aircraft, often found himself before hostile audiences who regarded him as a leader in the armaments race. He met this antagonism head-on by opening his speeches thus: "I'd rather have an industry making toasters, but we're in the real world. I'd like to talk to you about that real world." Surprised by this approach, his listeners would give him their attention. People usually respect frankness in others and, while not always admitting it, may grudgingly admire a person for voluntarily facing up to enemies.

Members of the public are not the only audiences an organization's speaker may be called upon to address. Management representatives—including public relations staff members—frequently make speeches within the organization, as part of an employee relations program. Although the atmosphere normally is friendly, the speaker still must maintain good rapport with the audience. Practitioners themselves may address a group, or they may offer guidance to other speakers in presenting the message. During times of internal hostility such as labor disputes, public relations expertise may be essential.

SPEECH TRAINING PROGRAMS

Even a brilliantly written speech can fail if it is delivered poorly. Upper-echelon executives for whom speeches are a required part of the job should be offered training by professionals in the techniques of public speaking. Progressive organizations also search among their employees for men and women who can be trained to speak effectively.

Employees selected may be assigned to attend on-the-job training sessions in speechmaking. They are instructed in such basics as diction, stage presence, voice projection, reading audience reaction, and handling questions. Videocassette tapes and other teaching aids enhance the instruction.

When a company needs to explain its policy to employees and seek their cooperation, top-echelon officials aren't always the best ones to do it. A well-trained fellow worker in a department may succeed better in convincing his or her colleagues to authorize automatic payroll deduction for United Way contributions than a speaker sent out from the executive offices. When management trains speakers from various work levels, provides them with well-written speeches appropriate for their need, and gives them a suitable setting, they can fill a valuable role in the internal communication chain. What's more, they can give management enlightening feedback from their colleagues.

Helping the Speaker
Polish and Present the Speech

After writing a draft of a speech, the writer should go over it with the speaker, who may request changes. By listening to the speaker read the material aloud, the writer can detect clumsy portions and smooth them out. The more frequently a speaker reads the text aloud in practice, the better the on-stage performance will be. A videotape made of a practice session will show the speaker where improvement is needed.

The finished version of a speech should be typed on 8 1/2-by-11-inch pages in easily read type, without excessive crowding. Some speakers prefer that the typescript cover only the upper two-thirds of a page, to prevent them from dropping their heads too low as they read. If the bottoms of the typed pages are crimped a bit, the speaker can turn them without having two stick together.

Writing an introduction and sending it to the person who will present the speaker is a good tactic. This assures that the information about the speaker will be correct. Although the introducer may alter the material, the content probably will be approximately what the public relations representative desires.

At the scene of the speech, these are actions the public relations representative should take:

The microphone should be tested. The audiovisual equipment should be set up and checked and the slide projector focused. Charts or flipcards should be arranged in correct order on an easel.

Extra copies of the speech should be brought along. These are for distribution to the news media and to listeners who request a copy.

The speech should be recorded on tape. The tape can be used to settle any disputes over what the speaker said, to provide "actuality" excerpts for local radio stations, and to assemble material for a postmortem session between speaker and writer analyzing the performance. If the speaker is well known, especially if he or she is from out of town, the public relations representative may arrange for radio, television, and newspaper interviews as well as provide tape excerpts to the stations.

Two other steps can be taken to obtain additional exposure for an important speech: (1) copies can be mailed to a selected list of opinion leaders and (2) the speech can be rewritten as an article for a company publication or submitted to a suitable trade magazine (see Figure 23.1).

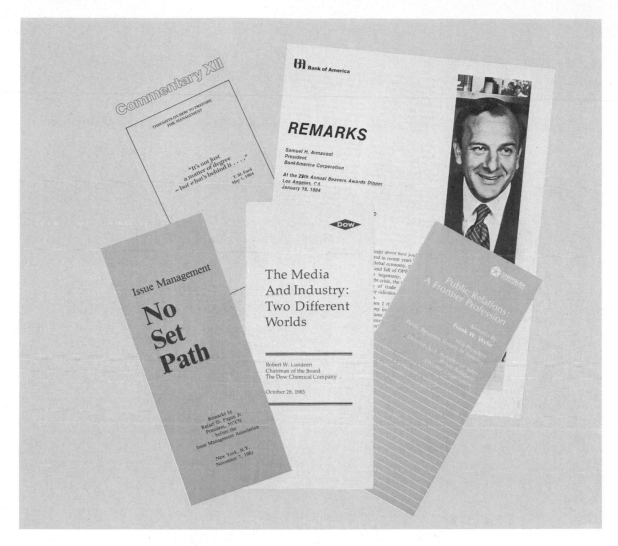

FIGURE 23.1

A spoken communication can reach an important additional audience when printed and sent to opinion-makers such as newspaper editors, government officials, academicians, and persons who speak for industry. A popular format is pocket-sized, but 8½-by-11-inch sheets also are used.

Speakers' Bureaus and Hotlines

Speakers' bureaus operated by trade associations, social agencies, and corporations constitute an important instrument for bringing speakers and audiences together (see Figure 23.2). They function something like a company's

Club need a speaker? Give us a call.

If you're looking for a speaker to stimulate, educate or just plain entertain your club or organization, the Indiana & Michigan Electric Company Speakers Service can provide just that person.

The I&M speakers pictured above are people who live and work in your community and who are available to meet your specific program needs. They have been trained in public speaking and are eager to share their knowledge and special talents with your group.

Talks range from home energy management to future energy alternatives, and electrical safety to environmental concerns. If your organization would like to emphasize energy concerns, why not have an I&M speaker conduct a "Conserve With Comfort" workshop for you?

I&M also has a variety of films and slide presentations on energy subjects. If you would prefer a film, a speaker will introduce it and then answer questions following its showing.

Many I&M speakers present topics of personal interest to them. Some of the subjects include "Our Fair Lady" which is an interesting look at the Indiana State Fair, "Mind Your Manners" which is a humorous look at eating in public, and "The $500 Business Suit" that explains how transmission lines are maintained with the "live line" method.

If your club or organization is looking for an interesting program call your local I&M office and ask for information on the Speakers Service. All programs are provided free of charge.

I&M Indiana & Michigan Electric Company

pool of internal speakers, but on a more elaborate scale. Speakers developed within an organization are made available by the bureaus upon request. The bureaus also seek to place speakers before attractive, influential audiences. Utility companies, which have a constant need to build friendly community relations, are especially heavy users of the speakers' bureau concept. Typically, a telephone company in Illinois has a bureau with 42 trained speakers who talk before all types of clubs and civic organizations. Before being sent out to represent the company, the speakers receive professional training and must pass auditions.

Talent-booking agencies that place professional speakers for a fee sometimes also call themselves speakers' bureaus. The roles of these two types of speakers' bureaus are quite unalike: one provides speakers without charge, to promote the cause of the corporation or organization that operates it, while the other does so on a direct profit-making basis. It is important to distinguish between the two.

Somewhat related to the organizational speakers' bureau is the telephone *hotline* service operated by some trade associations and companies to provide quick answers, especially to the news media (see Figure 23.3). This

FIGURE 23.3

Trade associations place advertisements in media journals, such as this one in *Editor & Publisher*, to stimulate use of their telephone hotlines. (Reprinted by permission of Association of American Railroads.)

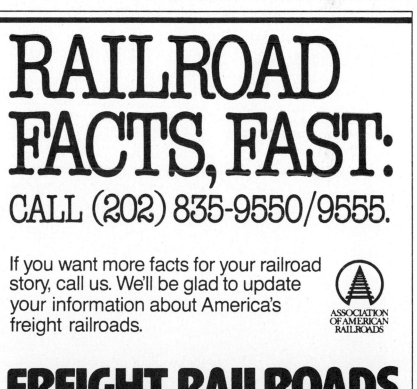

RAILROAD FACTS, FAST: CALL (202) 835-9550/9555.

If you want more facts for your railroad story, call us. We'll be glad to update your information about America's freight railroads.

ASSOCIATION OF AMERICAN RAILROADS

FREIGHT RAILROADS ARE ON THE MOVE.

facility generally offers toll-free telephone service using the 800 prefix. The following advertisement by the Edison Electric Institute Information Service in *Editor & Publisher,* the newspaper trade journal, illustrates how the hot line functions:

You don't need a press conference to get the energy story

Let's have a conference right now.

And it won't even cost you a dime.

One of our experts is ready to help you with your newsbreak, feature, or editorial.

Ask for facts, background, and the national perspective on electric energy.

Ask about energy sources, economics, and the environment.

Because energy is one of the crucial issues in American life today, there's someone on the hotline, 24 hours a day, 7 days a week.

Just think. By using the phone, you"ll be saving energy while writing about it.

Call toll-free 800-424-8897

Special Types of Speaking Opportunities

THE NEWS CONFERENCE

A speaker addressing an audience represents one-way communication. Listeners receive the message, either accepting or rejecting it, but do not engage in a dialog during which they can challenge the speaker's statements. The speaker commands the situation. The only exception occurs when a speaker agrees to accept questions from the floor—a practice that some speakers relish but others avoid either because they realize that they do not perform well spontaneously or they desire to avoid embarrassing questions.

At a news conference, communication is two-way. The person speaking for a company or a cause submits to questioning by reporters, usually after a brief opening statement. A news conference makes possible quick, widespread dissemination of the sponsor's information and opinions through the news media. It avoids the time-consuming task of presenting the information to the news outlets individually and assures that the intensely competitive newspapers and electronic media hear the news simultaneously. From a public relations point of view, these are the principal advantages of the news conference. Against these important pluses must be weighed the fact that the person holding the conference is open to severe and potentially antagonistic questioning.

In public relations strategy, the news conference can be either an offensive or a defensive device, depending upon the client's need.

Most news conferences—or press conferences, as they frequently are called—are *positive* in intent; they are affirmative actions to project the host's plans or point of view. A governor may hold a news conference to announce major personnel changes in the state administration; a land developer, to disclose plans for a huge construction project in a city; a corporation, to unveil a new product whose manufacture will create many new jobs; a civic leader, to reveal the goals and plans for a countywide charity fund drive she will head; a police chief, to explain his program for reducing drug traffic. Such news conferences should be carefully planned and scheduled well in advance under the most favorable circumstances.

Public relations specialists also must deal frequently with unanticipated, controversial situations. A business firm, an association, or a politician becomes embroiled in difficulty that is at best embarrassing, possibly incriminating. Press and public demand an explanation. A barebones printed statement is not enough to satisfy the clamor. This is the moment for a press conference that is *defensive* in nature, an effort to put out the fire with the least damage possible. The person who holds the conference will face uncomfortable minutes under sharp questioning. However, the alternative of "stonewalling" silence is worse. It leaves public and press with a feeling of evasion and a suspicion that the truth is even worse than it actually is. A well-prepared spokesperson may be able to achieve a measure of understanding and sympathy by issuing a carefully composed printed statement when the news conference opens. This should be as frank as possible, explaining how the controversial situation arose. If the company or person involved was the victim of circumstances, this should be emphasized.

Knowing that the reporters will ask harsh questions—that is their job—the spokesperson should prepare answers in advance for all the tough questions that can be anticipated. This is how presidents of the United States get ready for their news conferences. No matter how trying the circumstances, the person holding the news conference should create an atmosphere of cooperation and sincere intent to be helpful. The worst thing he or she can do is to appear resentful of the questioning. The person never should succumb to a display of bad temper. A good posture is to admit that the situation is bad and that the organization is doing everything in its power to correct it. (Further discussion of crisis public relations appears in Chapter 14.)

Rarely, an organization or public person caught in an embarrassing situation foolishly attempts to quiet public concern by holding a news conference that really isn't a news conference. The host reads a brief, inadequate statement, then refuses to answer questions from reporters. This practice alienates the press, which feels cheated. Suspicions of the host's conduct are increased, not minimized. If, for a valid reason, only a brief statement can be issued at the time, this should be done by distribution of a news release rather than by summoning reporters to a nonproductive conference.

Two more types of news conferences are held occasionally. One is the spontaneous conference arising out of a news event: the winner of a Nobel Prize meets the press to explain the award-winning work . . . a runner who has just set a world's record breathlessly describes his feelings . . . a woman appointed to a high-court judgeship tells reporters about her legal philosophy . . . a candidate for mayor makes an election night claim of victory. The other type is the regularly scheduled conference held by a public official at stated times, even when there is nothing special to announce. Usually this is called a briefing—the daily State Department briefing, for example.

PLANNING AND CONDUCTING A NEWS CONFERENCE   First comes the question, "Should we hold a news conference or not?" Frequently the answer should be "No!" The essential element of a news conference is *news.* If reporters and camera crews summoned to a conference hear propaganda instead of facts, or information of minor interest to a limited group, they go away disgusted. Their valuable time has been wasted—and it *is* valuable. Editors complain that they never have enough staff hours available to cover everything they would like to cover; if they send reporters to a conference that has been called merely to satisfy the host's sense of self-importance, they resent the fact. The next time, they probably won't send reporters.

If the material involved fails to meet the criteria of significant news, a wise public relations representative will distribute it through a press release. The information has a chance of being published based on its degree of merit without irritating editors and reporters.

A successful news conference needs as much planning as time permits. If possible, written notices should be sent to the news media at least a week in advance. Usually this is done by mail, but some organizations use telegrams or mailgrams for major conferences in the belief that the extra impact justifies the additional cost. Every news outlet that might be interested in the material should be invited. An ignored media outlet may become an enemy, like a person who isn't asked to a party. The invitation should include a factsheet listing the general nature of the material to be discussed (so an editor will know what type of reporter to assign), the person who will hold the conference, time, and place.

What hour is best? This depends upon the local media situation. If the city has only an afternoon newspaper, 9:30 or 10 A.M. is good, because this gives a reporter time to write a story before a midday deadline. If the city's newspaper publishes in the morning, 2 P.M. is a suitable hour.

Another prime goal of news conference sponsors is the early evening newscasts on local television stations, or even network TV newscasts if the information is important enough. A conference at 2 P.M. is about the latest that a television crew can cover and still get the material processed at a comfortable pace for inclusion in a dinner-hour show. This time period can be shortened in an emergency, but the chances of getting on a show diminish as the processing time dwindles.

A warning: a public relations representative in a city with only an after-noon newspaper who schedules a news conference after that paper's dead-line, yet in time for the news to appear on the early evening television newscasts, makes a grave blunder. Newspaper editors resent such favoritism to television and have long memories. Knowledge of, and sensitivity to, local news media deadlines are necessary elements of a public relations repre-sentative's work.

Deadlines for radio news reporters are less confining than those for newspapers and television, because radio newscasts are aired many times a day. The conference hours suggested for newspapers and television are suitable for radio as well, though.

If a person holding a news conference plans an opening statement, distribution of printed copies to the reporters present is desirable. This accomplishes three objectives: (1) it assures that the content of the an-nouncement will be quoted accurately, (2) it gives reporters time to digest the material, and (3) it reduces the amount of hurried scribbling reporters must do to record an oral pronouncement. The spokesperson should read the statement aloud if it is brief, for the benefit of television and radio; or if it is long, the person can say, "You all have copies of my statement. Now I am happy to answer your questions about it." The speaker can read excerpts from a long statement to the radio and television microphones at the end of the conference. Some public relations practitioners deliver copies of an important statement to the reporters' offices at about the same hour as the news conference, so editors will know what kind of story to expect and allocate space for it.

When a public relations representative playing devil's advocate tests the speaker in advance with tricky questions, the danger of unpleasant surprises is reduced. If answers to some anticipated questions are judged to be too negative or too revealing for public disclosure, the spokesperson should devise in advance ways to turn them aside as gracefully as possible. For instance, if an answer might divulge too much information to a business competitor, the host may say quite frankly, "That is a trade secret we simply cannot reveal. I'm sure you will understand."

It is important to remember that the reporters are present at the host's invitation. As the price for having an opportunity to make a presentation to the media, the host must submit to questioning. If the spokesperson becomes antagonistic to the reporters, they will become the same in return. The bitter verbal duels between President Richard Nixon and White House reporters in his nationally televised news conferences during the Watergate scandal are a famous example of this.

Here are two pieces of advice from longtime public relations specialists to persons who hold news conferences:

1. *The speaker should never attempt to talk off-the-record at a news confer-*

ence. If the information is so secret that it should not be published, then the speaker shouldn't tell it to reporters. Many editors forbid their reporters to honor off-the-record statements, because too often the person making them is merely attempting to prevent publication of material that is legitimate news but might be embarrassing. Any statement made before a group will not stay secret long, anyway. If one reporter present ignores the request and publishes the material, those who honored it are placed at an unfair competitive disadvantage.

2. *The speaker should never lie!* If he or she is pushed into a corner and believes that answering a specific question would be unwise, it is far better to say, "No comment" in some form than to answer falsely. A person caught in a lie to the media suffers a critical loss of credibility.

PREPARING THE SCENE   At a news conference, public relations representatives should stay in the background. The show belongs to the spokesperson and to whatever specialized assistants that person may invite to answer technical questions. The job of the public relations staff is to make things run smoothly.
Here is a checklist of housekeeping tasks to be performed:

Microphones should be tested in advance and adjusted if necessary.

An ample supply of the news releases to be handed out should be brought, and the practitioner should make certain that everyone receives one.

Sufficient chairs, arranged so the reporters can see and hear the speaker easily, should be provided.

A slightly raised platform and a table at which the speaker may sit should be set up. A lectern is used sometimes but adds an air of formality. Having something to sit or stand behind, however, often relaxes a speaker. It also provides a place for notes.

The room should be brightly lighted.

Writing material should be available in case a reporter needs it.

If the news to be released is major and urgent, telephones should be provided. Press association and electronic media reporters in particular often need to phone highlights of the news conferences to their offices. Newspaper reporters do, too, if the conference is close to their deadlines.

Adequate electrical outlets for television and radio equipment should be provided. If the meeting is in a hotel, the practitioner should check to see what union regulations, if any, apply to plug-in procedures.

The conference should be tape-recorded.

If possible, a list of the reporters who attend and the organizations they represent should be kept for future reference.

Some organizations provide coffee and possibly sweet rolls for their media guests as a courtesy. Others find this gesture unnecessary because most of the newspeople are in a hurry, more concerned with getting the story than with enjoying social amenities. Liquor should not be served at a regular news conference. Such socializing should be reserved for the press party, discussed in the next section.

At some news conferences, still photographers are given two or three minutes to take their pictures before questioning begins. Some photographers complain that, thus restricted, they cannot obtain candid shots. If free shooting is permitted, as usually is the best practice, the physical arrangements should give the photographers operating space without allowing them to obstruct the view of reporters.

Relationships between print and television reporters sometimes become strained at news conferences. Print reporters complain at times that the television reporters, with their equipment and support crews, get in the way and prevent them from questioning the speaker effectively. They also accuse some newsmakers of playing to the cameras so blatantly that they partially ignore the efforts of print reporters to obtain a detailed story.

A practitioner should take particular care to arrange the room in such a way that the electronic equipment does not impede the print reporters. Some find it good policy for the speaker to remain after the news conference ends and make brief on-camera statements for individual TV stations, if their reporters request this attention. Such statements should not go beyond anything the speaker has said to the entire body of reporters.

A final problem in managing a news conference is knowing when to end it. The public relations representative serving as backstage timekeeper and watchdog should avoid cutting off the questioning prematurely. To do so creates antagonism from the reporters. Letting a conference run down like a tired clock is almost as bad. At every conference there comes a moment when the reporters run out of questions and the danger of dull repetition arises. A speaker may, or may not, recognize this. If not, the practitioner may step forward and say something like, "I'm sorry, but I know some of you have deadlines to make. So we have time for just two more questions."

Presidential press conferences do not have this problem. Long-standing custom limits these conferences to 30 minutes. At that point, the senior press association reporter present calls out, "Thank you, Mr. President!" and the conference ends. Everyone concerned with public relations should study a presidential press conference on television. The kinds of questions asked, the manner in which the president answers them, the nature of any opening announcements, and the physical facilities—all of these provide clues for organizing news conferences of a more mundane nature.

THE PRESS PARTY AND THE PRESS TRIP

In the straightaway news conference, the purpose is to transmit information and opinion from the conference speaker to the news media in a business-like, time-efficient manner. Neither side wishes to turn the meeting into a social event. It is part of the day's work. Often, however, a corporation, an association, or a political figure wishes to deliver a message or build rapport with the media on a more personal basis; then a social setting is desirable. Thus is born the press party or the press trip.

THE PRESS PARTY This gathering may be a luncheon, a dinner, or a reception. Whatever form the party takes, standard practice is for the host to arise at the end of the socializing period and make the "pitch." This may be a hard-news announcement, a brief policy statement followed by a question-and-answer period, or merely a soft-sell thank-you to the guests for coming and giving the host an opportunity to know them better. Guests usually are given press packets of information, either when they arrive or as they leave.

The press party is a softening-up process, and both sides know it.

The advantages of a press party to its host can be substantial under the proper circumstances. During chitchat over food or drink, officials of the host organization become acquainted with media people who write, edit, or broadcast material about them. The company president with a public image of cold austerity and a reporter who described him thus in print may find that as baseball fans they share a sense of pain over the perennial lowly standing of the Cleveland Indians. Or the director of marketing may discover that she and a television reporter attended the same small university a few years apart. Although the benefit from the host's point of view is difficult to measure immediately, opening the channels of communication with the media at multiple informal levels may prove highly advantageous in the future.

Also, if the host has an important policy position to present, the assumption—not necessarily correct—is that editors and reporters will be more receptive after a social hour. The host who expects that food and drink will buy favorable press coverage may receive an unpleasant surprise. Conscientious reporters and editors will not be swayed by a free drink and a plate of prime ribs followed by baked Alaska. In their view, they have already given something to the host by setting aside a part of their day for the party. They accept invitations to press parties because they wish to develop potential news contacts within the host's organization and to learn more about its officials.

Until a few years ago, though, *free-loading* by news people at parties was widespread and accepted as normal practice. Often press guests were given expensive gifts. In large cities, the expectations of certain reporters, especially those covering business and entertainment, became absurdly high. One co-author of this book recalls attending a new-model announcement dinner for the press given some years ago by the Chevrolet division of General Motors. During dinner, the public relations director announced that there would be gifts for the guests when they went home. Each guest was asked to fill out a color preference card—blue, green, or tan.

One guest at the author's table asked another, quite seriously, "Do you think they are going to give us cars?" The other responded, with equal gravity, that perhaps they might. The actual gift proved to be an expensive blanket of the preferred color, packed in an individualized cedar chest. This type of payoff for attending the presentation became known as "loot." None of the media guests refused to accept the gift. (Present practice concerning gifts will be described shortly.)

Here are two actual examples of press parties:

1. Officials of Blue Cross in a Midwestern state regularly hold a series of dinners in major cities for invited members of the local media. The guest lists include men and women who cover the health field, have a role in editing stories about it, or comment on it editorially. During a cocktail party before dinner, Blue Cross officials mingle with the guests. The public relations consultant accompanying them helps with introductions. During dinner, the host group spreads itself around to sit with guests.

After dinner, the chief executive speaks briefly, explaining what Blue Cross regards as the significant trends and problems in health care. Then he opens the meeting to questions. Inevitably, queries center on why medical costs are so high and what Blue Cross is doing to control them. Some questions are friendly, some barbed. The public relations consultant distributes packets of news releases, factsheets, and charts. No gifts are offered to the guests.

2. A land developer invited local media guests and civic leaders to a luncheon at which he disclosed plans for a major shopping center at the edge of the city. Printed invitations announced a reception at noon and lunch at 12:30. Acceptances by phone were requested by a certain date. Arriving guests received paste-on tags imprinted with their names, large folders containing news releases, photographs of the developer and of an artist's rendering of the project's exterior and interior, and a factsheet giving the developer's biography and a list of projects he had built. The artist's renderings stood on easels around the room; a scale model of the project was displayed on a table. Drinks were served, followed by a large luncheon. After the meal, the developer spoke about the project and answered questions. Although most of the queries were friendly, some probed intensely into the financing, the construction schedule, and the number of tenants signed up.

The normal adjournment hour for luncheon sessions is 1:30 P.M. This one ran a few minutes past that hour because of the number of questions. No press luncheon ever should run past 2 P.M.

THE PRESS TRIP   A journey that may last for several days is an expensive elaboration of the press party; it is known as a "junket." Typically, selected editors and reporters are invited to inspect manufacturing facilities in several cities, to ride on the inaugural flight of a new air route, or to watch previews of the television network programs for the fall season.

THE ETHICS OF GIFT-GIVING   Severe self-searching by media members in recent years concerning acceptance of gifts, entertainment, and free travel has led to curtailment of these costly gestures. Some publishers, editors, and station managers forbid their employees to accept such favors, in order to protect their editorial integrity. Others believe that an absolute ban is unrealistic. Instead, they have rules that in essence forbid employees from accepting any gift or entertainment that has substantial value or that might be interpreted as tending to influence their news judgment. When press trips of obvious news significance are involved, some media managers insist upon repaying the host for transportation, food, and lodging costs incurred by their employees.

This application of higher ethical standards by the media has reduced the frequency and lavishness of press parties and trips but has not eliminated them. Many editors see value in having staff members attend such gatherings because, as described earlier, they provide access to the host's operations, thinking, and personnel that might not be available otherwise. Such information can be important in developing news stories and assessing company actions. Those news managers may allow the host to pay the bill if the cost is relatively small. Big gifts are forbidden. A token remembrance such as a felt-tipped pen and notepad with the host's name printed on them usually is acceptable as a bit of routine hospitality.

A public relations representative who organizes a press party or trip should determine in advance the rules enforced by local media managements and design the event to stay within them. A media guest never should be placed in the embarrassing position of having to refuse a too-large gift in public, or, equally embarrassing, of accepting one as other media guests with stricter rules look on. If a news organization insists upon paying its employee's expenses before it will let the person attend, the host should accept the payment without protest. (For further discussion of ethical standards, see Chapter 6.)

ORGANIZING A PRESS PARTY OR PRESS TRIP   The key to a successful event is detailed organization. Every step of the process should be checked out meticulously. Even then, things may go wrong, as the following example illustrates.

The public relations director of a large water district took metropolitan media leaders on a three-day tour of irrigation projects. The first leg of the trip was by commercial airliner to a city 400 miles away, with one stop en route. When the public relations man had everyone checked into a hotel (he had preregistered them to speed up the process), the editor of a major newspaper reported that the airline had failed to deliver his suitcase. Even worse, the suitcase contained medicine he needed to take every four hours. The public relations man spent a frantic period on the phone, until the airline found the case at the stopover airport and arranged to deliver it. Most leaders of press tours have similar tales of crises to tell.

In planning the press event, the practitioner has to consider a variety of details. Menus for a luncheon or dinner should be chosen carefully. Do any of the guests have dietary restrictions? Has the exact hour of serving been arranged with the restaurant or caterer, to allow sufficient time for the program? The ususal check on microphone and physical facilities is essential.

Even such a seemingly trivial item as a name tag requires the practitioner's careful attention. Paste-on tags written in advance are lined up on a check-in table at the entrance to the room. A host or hostess hands the tags to the arriving guests. A guest who can be welcomed by name, without having to state it, feels subtly flattered. Almost inevitably, though, some name tags will be unclaimed because individuals who accepted fail to show up. In a perfect world, absentees would telephone to cancel their acceptances, but public relations life doesn't work that way. Occasionally, an invited person who failed to answer the invitation will arrive unexpectedly; blank name tags should be kept available for such a situation. (Arrangements with the restaurant should include agreement on the percentage of meals ordered that can be cancelled at the last moment without charge. Press kits should be sent to the absentees.)

Fouled-up transportation is perhaps the worst grief for a person conducting a press tour. Buses that fail to arrive at the departure point on time and incorrect booking on airliners irritate the guests and give tour managers gray hairs. Some guests may be prima donnas with inflated egos who will be dissatisfied with almost any hotel room assigned to them. None of the tour guests should be allowed to feel that others are receiving favored treatment. Booking and maintaining a firm tour schedule is essential. When stops are made, the host should specify their length, then begin to round up the strays a few minutes before departure time. Otherwise, the trip may bog down in confusion.

As much as possible, the tour host should "walk through" the entire route to confirm arrangements and look for hidden troubles. A practitioner who invited Southern California media people to the opening of a gambling casino in a small Nevada town found this out to his sorrow. He chartered an airplane to fly the guests from the Palm Springs area to an airfield near the casino. The guests were entertained at dinner in the casino dining room, then were given packages of chips and coins to start off their evening of gambling. Soon, as anticipated, they were spending their own money. The return flight was to take off at midnight, and they were to be back at their point of departure by 1 A.M. After arriving at the casino, however, the public relations man learned bad news: because the airfield had no lights, the plane could not take off until dawn. The press guests were stuck for the night. No sleeping accommodations were available, the fun of gambling had palled, most of the guests had lost their money, and the desert night was long. When the party finally reached home at 8 o'clock the next morning, the guests were broke, exhausted, and furious with the host. A relatively good publicity idea had turned into a fiasco.

THE INTERVIEW   Another widely used spoken method of publicizing an individual or a cause is the interview, which may appear in print form in newspapers and magazines or be transmitted electronically via television and radio. In both versions, the ability of the person being interviewed to communicate easily is essential to success. Although required to stay in the background during a client's interview, with fingers crossed that all goes well, a public relations specialist can do much to prepare the interviewee for the experience.

Techniques for arranging interview appearances by clients are discussed in Chapter 12. This section will examine the steps the public relations representative can take to increase the odds for an effective performance.

In all interviews, the person being questioned should say something that will inform or entertain the audience. Otherwise, the public exposure is wasted. The practitioner should prepare the interviewee to meet this need. An adroit interviewer attempts to develop a theme in the conversation— to draw out comments that make a discernible point or illuminate the character of the person being interviewed. The latter can help the interviewer—and his or her own cause as well—by being ready to volunteer specific information, personal data, or opinions about the cause under discussion as soon as the conversational opportunity arises.

In setting up an interview, the public relations person should obtain from the interviewer an understanding as to its purpose. Armed with this information, the practitioner can assemble facts and data for the client to use in the discussion. The practitioner also can aid the client by providing tips about the interviewer's style and approach.

A significant difference exists between interviews in print and those on radio and television. In a print interview, the information and character impressions the public receives about the interviewee have been filtered through the mind of the writer. The man or woman interviewed is interpreted by the reporter, not projected directly to the audience. On radio and television, however, listeners hear the interviewee's voice without intervention by a third party. During a television interview, where personality has the strongest impact of all, the speaker is both seen and heard by the audience. Because of the intimacy of television, a person with a weak message who projects charm or authority on the air may influence an audience more than one with a strong message who does not project well. When a charismatic speaker is armed with a strong message, the impact can be enormous.

The following sections describe these two types of interview in detail.

When an organization or individual is advocating a particular cause or policy, opportunities to give newspaper interviews are welcomed, indeed sought after. Situations arise, however, when the better part of public relations wisdom is to reject a request for an interview, either print or electronic. Such rejection need not imply that an organization has a sinister secret or fails to understand the need for public contact.

For example, a corporation may be planning a fundamental operational change involving an increase in production at some plants and the closing of another, outdated facility. Details are incomplete and company employees have not been told. A reporter, perhaps suspecting a change or by sheer chance, requests an interview with the company's chief executive officer.

Normally, the interview request would be welcomed, to give the executive public exposure and an opportunity to enunciate company philosophy. At this moment, however, public relations advisers fear that the reporter's questions might uncover the changes prematurely, or at least force the executive into evasive answers that might hurt the firm's credibility. So the interview request is declined, as politely as possible. The next week, when all is in place, the chief executive announces the changes at a news conference. *Avoiding trouble is a hidden but vital part of a public relations adviser's role.* At a later time, the public relations representative might make a special effort to do the would-be interviewer a favor on a story, to remove any lingering feeling of having been slighted.

An alternative approach would be for the chief executive officer to grant the interview, with the understanding that only topics specified in advance would be discussed. Very rarely is such an approach acceptable, however, because reporters usually resent any restrictions and try to uncover the reasons for them.

THE PRINT INTERVIEW   An interview with a newspaper reporter may last about an hour, perhaps at lunch or over coffee in an informal setting. The result of this person-to-person talk may be a published story of perhaps 400 to 600 words. The interviewer chooses bits from the conversation, weaves them together in direct and indirect quotation form, works in background material, and perhaps injects personal observations about the interviewee. The latter has no control over what is published, beyond the self-control he or she exercises in answering the interviewer's questions. Neither the person being interviewed nor a public relations representative should ask to approve an interview story before it is published. Such requests are rebuffed automatically by newspapers as a form of censorship.

A talk with an entertainment personality is among the most common forms of newspaper interview. Many personality interview stories carrying

Hollywood or New York datelines are proposed by practitioners endeavoring to build up a performer's image or to publicize a new motion picture or television series. In the following example, the writer uses the star's quotations to build a theme; his mention of the star's forthcoming television special is worked into the text as part of that theme.

Burns at 86

By Vernon Scott

HOLLYWOOD (UPI)—The question was asked forthrightly:

"George Burns, at 86 do you honestly consider yourself a sex symbol?"

"Absolutely!" came the reply.

"Of course I'm a sex symbol. I've been at it longer than anyone else. If I don't know what to do about sex at my age, it's too late to learn."

Ensconced in iron-bound self-confidence—or delusion as the case may be—Burns put the finishing touches on his new hour-long television special, "George Burns and Other Sex Symbols," on NBC Monday.

The other sex symbols are guest stars Bernadette Peters, Linda Evans and John Schneider, all young enough to be his grandchildren.

George, however, is supremely confident his own charm, talent and allure are all that are necessary. After all, his third record album in three years is currently in release. It's titled "Young at Heart. . . ."

What more could a practitioner ask from a newspaper interview? It contains a plug for the Burns TV show and one for his new record album, inserted casually into a news story with a catchy headline angle.

Similar elements are found in the following excerpt from a business-page interview with a grower of Kiwis. Most readers, uncertain what Kiwis are, would never guess that a man could become a millionaire by growing them. Notice how well prepared the grower was with quotable comments and pertinent facts about his unusual business. Publication of this San Francisco *Chronicle* interview was timed to the Kiwi harvesting season; interest it created could be translated readily into purchases at the food store.

Kiwi Pioneers Have Last Laugh

When the three Tanimoto brothers planted their first acre of Kiwi fruit 17 years ago, "we put it in back of our peach groves so people wouldn't laugh at us," recalled George Tanimoto.

"Everybody laughed anyway, and we laughed too," Tanimoto said last week. "Now they say he's laughing all the way to the bank and it's true."

Year after year, the Tanimoto brothers waited for a crop. Finally, in 1970—after 5 years of fruitless ridicule—the first fuzzy brown egg-shaped pods of Kiwi appeared on their vines.

Tanimoto sold his maiden Kiwi crop to Frieda Kaplan, a Los Angeles fruit dealer who happened to be allergic to Kiwi. At first, he shipped the fruit south in three wooden boxes that looked suspiciously like coffins, then individually wrapped them in packages called "flats," because Kiwis are very sensitive and will shrivel and shrink when exposed to gas fumes or other ripening fruit.

Today, the 56-year-old Tanimoto is a millionaire because he didn't quit on what he affectionately calls the "Ugly Fruit"....

Neither of these interview stories is a direct hard-sell job, nor can it be described as outright "puffery." The purpose from the newspaper's point of view was to tell readers something interesting. From a public relations point of view, both stories distribute knowledge of the product involved, with the possibility that this knowledge will stimulate purchases of the product.

Magazine interviews usually explore the subject in greater depth than those in newspapers, because the writer may have more space available. Most magazine interviews have the same format as those in newspapers. Others, such as those published in *Penthouse* and *U.S. News & World Report,* appear in question-and-answer form. These require prolonged questioning of the interviewee, sometimes at several tape-recorded sessions, by one or more writers and editors. During in-depth interviews, the person interviewed must be alert against letting down his or her guard and saying something that has unfortunate repercussions.

Such an instance occurred in 1976 when Jimmy Carter was running for president against President Gerald Ford. Carter was a deeply religious man, a fact his public relations advisers emphasized by publicizing his work as a Sunday School teacher and lay preacher in a Southern Baptist church. When they sensed that these pursuits made Carter appear too sanctimonious to voters less religiously inclined, his advisers sought to have him offset this image by being interviewed in *Playboy.*

In the published interview Carter, although happily married, admitted that he had "looked upon a lot of women with lust" and "committed adultery in my heart many times." Angry reactions from his conservative followers were swift. He had besmirched their perceived image of him. Although this frank admission of a common enough male trait made Carter seem more "human" to some voters, overall the interview statements damaged his campaign. He was, of course, elected anyway.

A third, even more elaborate, form of magazine interview story is the long profile, such as those published in the *New Yorker.* Reporters doing profiles usually travel with the interviewee, observing the subject at close range over extended periods. Before trying to interest a magazine in doing such a profile on a client or employer, the public relations adviser should be satisfied that the intended subject of the profile is willing to accept the interviewer on an intimate basis for long periods and will wear well under close scrutiny. Outbursts of anger, a dictatorial manner toward assistants, excessive drinking, and similar private habits produce a bad effect when revealed in print. The profile when published might have a negative result instead of a positive one.

RADIO AND TELEVISION INTERVIEWS   With more than 9000 AM and FM radio stations operating in the United States, the possibilities for public relations people to have their clients interviewed on the air are immense. Although most radio time is devoted to music and advertising, stations need voices and ideas to fill their public service hours and newscasts. Chapter 12 discussed the public relations opportunities radio and television provide. This discussion will be concerned with the preparation and techniques of on-the-air appearances.

Three principal requirements for a successful radio or television broadcast interview appearance are the following:

1. *Preparation.* Guests should know what they want to say.

2. *Concise speech.* Guests should answer questions and make statements precisely and briefly. They shouldn't hold forth in excessive detail or drag in extraneous material. Responses should be kept to 30 seconds or less, because seconds count on the air. The interviewer must conduct the program under severe time restrictions.

3. *Relaxation.* "Mike fright" is a common ailment for which no automatic cure exists. It will diminish, however, if the guest concentrates on talking to the interviewer in a casual person-to-person manner, forgetting the audience as much as possible. Guests should speak up firmly; the control room can cut down their volume if necessary. (Personal appearances on television are discussed in more detail in Chapter 24.)

A public relations adviser can help an interview guest on all of these points. Answers to anticipated questions may be worked out and polished during a mock interview in which the practitioner plays the role of broadcaster. If a tape recording or videotape can be made of a practice session, the guest-to-be will have an opportunity to correct weaknesses in manner and content that may be revealed. The more confidence an interviewee can develop before going to the studio, the easier the performance will be.

All too often, the hosts on talk shows know little about their guests for the day's broadcast. They haven't read the author's book or have barely heard of a social welfare program the guest is advocating. The public relations adviser can overcome this difficulty by sending the host in advance a factsheet summarizing the important information and listing questions the broadcaster might wish to ask. On network shows like Johnny Carson's, nationally syndicated talk shows like Merv Griffin's, and local programs on metropolitan stations, support staffs do the preliminary work with guests. Interviewers on hundreds of smaller local television and radio stations, however, lack such staffs. They may go on the air almost "cold" unless provided with volunteered information.

Training business executives in speaking techniques, described earlier in the section on speechmaking, also helps to prepare them for broadcast appearances.

CONDUCTING A MEETING   Meetings are a major public relations tool in contemporary American life. They can be an extremely effective form of communication, or they can be incredible bores. Speakers who drone on too long and discussions that degenerate into petty quibbling act as soporifics on the audience. The hardness of chairs seems to increase by geometrical progression as the presiding officer introduces speaker after speaker. Collective attempts at mental telepathy by audience members urging the chairperson, "Please, please, let us go home," never seem to work. Far from accomplishing a worthwhile purpose, such meetings alienate their audiences. Everyone's time is wasted.

Meetings held for public relations purposes take many forms and vary greatly in size. Sessions may be informational and friendly, they may be heated and controversial, or they may be largely formalized gatherings such as banquets and dedications. Within a company or an organization, they are held to explain and discuss policy, to plan programs, and to train employees. Half a dozen persons may participate, or more than a hundred. Whatever the size and form of a meeting, good planning and an alert presiding officer can assure that the meeting accomplishes its purpose without leaving participants glassy-eyed with fatigue.

GUIDELINES FOR MEETINGS   Preparation and firmness discreetly applied can control the dynamics of a meeting. The program should move briskly toward a goal. Few people have ever been heard to complain that a meeting was too short. Participants should have a feeling of movement without the appearance of hurry. By following these 12 guidelines, the organizers and presiding officer can create an effective session:

1. If the meeting is open to the public, an audience should be built through distribution of news releases and through other forms of publicity such as posters and announcements at clubs.

2. An agenda should be made and followed.

3. The meeting should start promptly at the announced hour.

4. Speakers should be allotted specified amounts of time and urged to cooperate.

5. Physical arrangements of the hall should be checked in advance—acoustics, seating of the audience so that it is centered in front of the speakers, adequate lighting and fresh air, advance placement of visual aids, and the like.

6. If possible, the reading of minutes and reports should be avoided. Distribution of these documents in printed form is one way to solve this time-consuming problem.

7. Printed material should be distributed to an audience at the start or the close of a meeting, not while the session is in progress. The latter is distract-ing.

8. Discussion should be controlled even-handedly so that the audience has adequate opportunity to express itself but isn't allowed to wander from the theme. In a controversial situation, a time limit should be set on each speaker from the floor—5 minutes, perhaps—and enforced. When the discussion lags, it should be cut off. One or two verbose individuals should not be permitted to dominate a discussion.

9. In a panel discussion, the presiding officer should give all panel mem-bers equal opportunity to be heard. The moderator should try to distribute questions from the floor equitably among the panelists.

10. In long meetings such as a seminar or a training session, periodic recesses should be called; the meeting should resume promptly after the allotted time. A recess should be at least 10 minutes, 15 or 20 if the crowd is large.

11. The meeting should be brought to a constructive conclusion. If there are several speakers, the best one should be scheduled last, if possible. At the end of a discussion, the presiding officer should summarize for the audience what was said. If a motion for action will be needed, arrangements may be made in advance for someone to offer it.

12. A closing time should be set and strictly adhered to, especially if it has been announced in advance.

Word-of-Mouth

The most ephemeral form of spoken communication is word-of-mouth. Its impact, both favorable and unfavorable, can be potent, yet attempts to harness and measure it have yielded few tangible results.

In its heyday as an American luxury automobile, the Packard was adver-tised around the slogan "Ask the man who owns one." Similarly, a large Midwestern men's clothier used the slogan "One man tells another." One man certainly *does* tell another about things he likes or dislikes. So do women. In these two cases, the effort to generate word-of-mouth support for a product was based on quality—the assumption that the Packard owner and the clothing shopper would tell others how satisfied they were and encourage them to make similar purchases.

Nowhere is word-of-mouth influence greater than in the entertainment field. A motion picture may receive splendid reviews from the critics and enjoy heavy advertising support, yet prove to be a box-office disaster. Another film at which the critics sneer, and which has only a minor advertising budget, may become a runaway moneymaker. The deciding factor: word-of-mouth.

Where's the Beef?

Word-of-mouth, featuring a line from a fast food chain's television commercial belittling the size of the meat patties in a rival's hamburgers, gave the beef industry a splendid, unexpected boost.

In the Wendy's commercial, three elderly women were shown peering suspiciously at a large bun containing a tiny hamburger patty. One of them exclaimed in a raucous voice, "Where's the beef?"

The commercial was aired in early 1984, during the campaign between Walter Mondale and Gary Hart for the Democratic presidential nomination. Hart maintained that he offered new ideas. Mondale charged that Hart's claim was mere talk without substance.

To emphasize his point, in a televised news conference Mondale borrowed the commercial's punchline and asked Hart, "Where's the beef?" The crowd laughed. The political jibe flashed from coast to coast. "Where's the beef?" became an even more widely known national catch phrase, applied by speakers in dozens of usages. Soon T-shirts and sweatshirts appeared with the question printed on front.

The beef industry was delighted by this bonus. To keep the publicity rolling, it staged an award ceremony for Clara Peller, the 82-year-old woman who asked the question in the commercial. The National Cattlemen's Association presented her with a 25-pound hamburger topped by a little regular-sized bun and other gifts, including a branding iron with her initials, a cowboy hat, an apron with the words "Beef Gives Strength," and a pink hat on which was printed, "Beef Builds Beautiful Bodies. See Below."

Mrs. Peller also was given a plaque for "all she has done to make Americans aware of the value of beef." The ceremony received national news coverage. The cattleowners' association voted a thank-you resolution to Wendy's as well.

As for the commercial itself, Wendy's reported a sales increase of more than 17 percent in the second month after the advertisement began appearing.

This incident illustrates the mercurial and unpredictable nature of word-of-mouth communication. Circumstances, not planning, made the national phenomenon happen. The cattleowners' association, however, did an effective job of capitalizing upon it.

People who heed the critics' praise and see the first film tell their friends, "It's a bore. Don't waste your money." so the friends go instead to the other movie, remembering that someone had said that it was "*really* funny" or "wait until you see the shower scene."

Producers of formula movies aimed at the upper-teenage audience, loaded with nudity, suggestive sex, and bawdy humor, know that locker-room talk among high school and university youths will sell as many tickets as good reviews. The filmmakers play to the tastes of these young men because they usually decide which movie they and their dates will see.

When word-of-mouth functions to endorse or condemn products, it operates as a legitimate channel for expressing public taste. The manufacturer takes the risks of the marketplace, for better or worse. If a product is poor or fails to satisfy public desires, the unstructured verbal reaction that flows from person to person will stimulate customer rejection. Conversely, national fads are spawned in the same way.

THE INSIDIOUS PROBLEM OF RUMORS

Phrased negatively, word-of-mouth becomes gossip or even worse, a whispering campaign. Such campaigns, often inspired by persons with malicious motives, can be destructive in the extreme and bitterly unfair. Bad news travels faster than good news. Even when nasty rumors about individuals or products are shown to be baseless, to the satisfaction of fair-minded individuals, they stay alive in the minds of suspicious persons who get a petty thrill from believing that they are in the know.

Political leaders are especially vulnerable to malicious whispering. During election campaigns, a whisper begins to circulate mysteriously that a candidate is concealing an unsavory secret in his or her personal life. Usually these rumors are financial, criminal, sexual, or racial in nature. Rarely can such stories be traced to their sources. It must be assumed, however, that many are started deliberately for partisan purposes—a disturbing debasement of the right of free speech. A particularly vicious form of rumor is that a prominent person has cancer, or that a product causes cancer.

The person or company victimized by a whispering campaign is placed in a precarious position. The victim may choose to ignore the calumny, hoping that it will die out yet fearing that it will spread even further. Or the victim may decide to fight back with a strong denial, supported by as much tangible evidence as can be mustered. The difficulty with a public denial is that it brings the rumor to the attention of those who had not heard it but fails to convince those who contend without evidence that the rebuttal is a cover-up. Before deciding to strike back, a victim must weigh how much damage the rumor is doing and how effectively the denial can be stated.

When a rumor spreads within a corporation or organization, certain steps can be taken to combat it. Management, working through the public relations and/or personnel department, first should try to determine who is spreading the rumor and for what motive. Sometimes rumors are born not from evil

Procter & Gamble Fights a Rumor

Malicious gossipers spread a rumor that Procter & Gamble's man-in-the-moon trademark symbolized devil worship. (Reprinted by permission of the Procter & Gamble Company.)

A ridiculous rumor that Procter & Gamble, the maker of soap and food products, promoted devil worship harassed the huge corporation so badly that it mounted a major public relations campaign to quash the malicious tale.

The company's circular trademark shows a man-in-the-moon face in profile, looking at a field of 13 stars representing the original American colonies. The trademark was registered with the U.S. Patent Office in 1882.

A hundred years later, in the early 1980s, a whispering campaign began, maintaining that the trademark is a symbol of satanism, or devil worship. One word-of-mouth version said that a P & G executive had discussed satanism on a nationally televised talk show. Another rumor claimed that Procter & Gamble was being taken over by the "Moonies," followers of the Reverend Sun Myung Moon and his Unification Church.

The rumors were supported by printed material demanding a boycott against Procter & Gamble. They became so intense in the spring of 1982 that the company received 15,000 telephone calls about the matter in one month. It decided to strike back.

The company obtained public statements from producers of the Merv Griffin and Phil Donahue talk shows, the programs most frequently mentioned in the rumor, that no P & G executive had ever appeared on them. Next, the public relations department released statements from several prominent ministers denouncing the rumor and urging their followers to ignore it. Among those quoted were Billy Graham; Jerry Falwell, leader of the Moral Majority; and Donald E. Wildmon, director of the National Federation for Decency.

Then the company took even stronger action. It filed suit in the federal district courts of four Southern and Southwestern states against seven men and women whom it charged with circulating "false and malicious" statements about the company and calling for a boycott of P & G products. The defendants were accused of "libeling the character" of the company. P & G asked the courts to stop the individuals from circulating the rumor and to impose unspecified monetary damages.

The company's counterattack, widely publicized, was effective. The telephone calls to the company diminished slowly, although still coming in at a rate of 200 to 300 a day three months after the peak of the rumor.

The rumor unexpectedly resumed in 1985, causing 12,000 telephone inquiries to the company in two months. Hoping to check its spread, Procter & Gamble decided to remove the trademark from its products; however, the company emphasized that it would continue to use the insignia on letterheads and publications.

intent but spontaneously from employee anxiety and lack of accurate information.

Because rumors are spawned in a vacuum, distribution of accurate information to show the rumor to be false is the quickest, most effective way to quash it. Meetings with opinion leaders among employees to give the facts and enlist their support are an efficient way to start a counterattack. If circumstances justify, meetings of departments or other large employee groups may be summoned for the same purpose.

When conducting a rebuttal operation, management should accentuate the positive. Management should avoid referring directly to the rumor while disseminating the truth, if possible, lest it accidentally be spread further. Borrowing from the techniques of military counterintelligence, some managements plant counterrumors through trusted employees as an offsetting force. This practice has its dangers, however, and may confuse the situation even more. When a detrimental rumor circulates through a community, much the same methods of fighting it can be employed.

MEASURING THE EFFECTS OF WORD-OF-MOUTH COMMUNICATION

Although efforts to measure the specific effects of word-of-mouth communication have been relatively few, and of minor value, the Coca-Cola Company did obtain enlightening information from a study it sponsored concerning public reaction to its handling of consumer complaints.

Questionnaires were sent to hundreds of persons who had filed complaints with Coca-Cola's consumer affairs department. Responses showed that individuals who felt that their complaints had not been resolved satisfactorily told a median of 9 to 10 persons about their negative experience. Those who were completely satisifed told a median of 4 to 5 persons about their good results—a word-of-mouth distribution of bad news over good by a ratio of approximately 2 to 1. Nearly 30 percent of those who felt that their complaints had not been resolved satisfactorily said they no longer bought Coca-Cola products. On the other hand, nearly 10 percent of the satisfied complainers reported that they now bought more Coca-Cola products as a result of the good treatment. Two lessons for companies trying to preserve a favorable image with customers emerge from this survey:

1. The best service possible should be given, so that complaints are held to a minimum.

2. Complaints should be handled promptly and thoroughly, so that customers feel the company really cares about them. Not only may unhappy customers become noncustomers but their word-of-mouth criticism may drive away other potential purchasers—how many, no one ever knows. As an example, an eight-year-old girl sued the makers of Crackerjack because she didn't find a prize in a box she purchased. She had written to the company about the mistake, but it failed to answer the letter. The lawsuit she brought gave the company bad nationwide publicity.

QUESTIONS FOR REVIEW AND DISCUSSION

1. List three tasks a public relations representative should perform when preparing for and making a face-to-face presentation to an editor.

2. How many themes should a speech have?

3. What are some key building blocks a writer uses in constructing a speech?

4. Which type of sentence structure should a speechwriter use? Explain your answer.

5. Why do companies sometimes use fellow workers rather than high executives to address audiences of employees?

6. How should a company executive prepare to hold a news conference?

7. Should a spokesperson speak off the record at a news conference? Why or why not?

8. What might a corporate host hope to accomplish by holding a press luncheon instead of a morning news conference?

9. How can a public relations representative help a client prepare for a television interview?

10. A company may be harassed by malicious rumors about its policies. If it decided to strike back, how might it do so?

CHAPTER TWENTY-FOUR

Visual Tactics

The third major form of public relations communication is *visual*, in which the message is delivered to the recipient through the eye by fixed or moving images. Frequently, the form is *audiovisual*, when sound accompanies the visual message.

This chapter examines the visual and audiovisual methods. Television is the most pervasive, because virtually every home in the United States and Canada has at least one television set. With the swift growth of cable television and transmission by satellite, the possibilities of television as a public relations tool are proliferating.

Motion pictures are another method with many applications; so are videotapes. Generally grouped under the term *audiovisual aids*—still images for projection—are slides and film-strips, usually with live or recorded narration. Still photography delivers public relations messages in the print media. Outdoor displays and corporate design are other forms of visual but silent communication.

Television

The human eye is a magnificent channel for communication, carrying messages to the brain at astounding speeds, often so subtly that the recipient is not consciously aware of absorbing them. These images are stored in the brain, combining with the intake of audible and tactile impressions to help form opinions, trigger decisions, and generate actions. Since these are the goals of public relations, the role of visual communication in public relations practice obviously is vital.

Television is the dominant form of visual communication in contemporary life. As stated in Chapter 12, the Nielsen survey for 1985 showed that television sets in United States households were turned on an average of 7 hours and 8 minutes a day.

Chapter 12 examined how the television industry is organized and listed ways in which public relations practitioners can use television to advance their causes. This chapter will look more closely at techniques employed for this purpose and will discuss the growing use of television for internal corporate communication.

NEWS RELEASES

Practitioners can provide news releases to television stations in several ways, ranging from a simple sheet of paper to an expensively produced videotaped story ready to go on the air. The type of news material, the time factor, and the originator's budget will determine which method is best for each story.

THE PRINTED NEWS RELEASE   Identical to that sent to newspapers, the so-called handout frequently is sufficient (see Chapter 22). If the news director or assignment editor at a station judges the material to be newsworthy, a staff member is assigned to handle the story, rewriting it briefly in television style or, if the material justifies, going to the scene with a camera crew to obtain visual support for the facts. When a television reporter and crew come on assignment in reponse to a news release, the public relations practitioner who sent out the release should do everything possible to assist them, such as providing an authoritative spokesperson who will appear on camera to state the facts and answer questions, and helping to arrange other shots the reporter and photographer may request.

A fundamental difference between a news story on television and one in a newspaper is *motion*. Stories that can be illustrated easily and effectively often will receive more air time than ones that cannot. The rule for a practitioner trying to place a news story on television is: *think pictures!* The representative never should tell a reporter and photographer what pictures to shoot or what questions to ask but may discreetly suggest possible picture and story angles.

The other primary factor in television news coverage is *brevity*. A story that runs 400 words in a newspaper may be reported in only two or three sentences in a newscast. If a television crew spends an hour shooting a story with a practitioner's help, and the story then receives 30 seconds or less of air time, the inexperienced public relations representative may feel let down. All that work, with such a brief result! As any veteran will advise, however, there is no reason for disappointment. The impact of even a very brief item on a popular newscast can be heavy.

THE PREPARED SCRIPT   This second, more elaborate, form of television news release is accompanied by one to four slides to illustrate the text. In this method, the public relations representative does most of the television news department's work on the story. Smaller stations with limited news staffs may be especially willing to air such ready-to-use material if it is newsworthy, perhaps even if only marginally so. In preparing scripted news releases, the writer should avoid terminology that sounds like advertising or "puff" publicity. Graphics created by computers can be used effectively in news releases. (See Figure 24.1.)

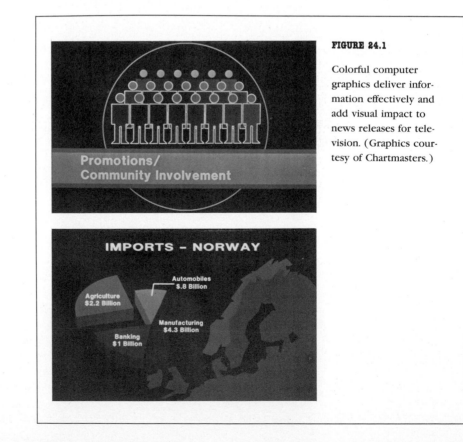

FIGURE 24.1

Colorful computer graphics deliver information effectively and add visual impact to news releases for television. (Graphics courtesy of Chartmasters.)

For a fee, specialist commercial firms will prepare a news release script with slides from a practitioner's material, send the script to television stations, and report on the use they made of it.

Videotaped excerpts from local speeches made by the practitioner's client, delivered to a television station along with a written news release explaining the circumstances in which the speech was made, may be used in the station's newscasts if the content is significant or provocative. Prospects for use of the material are improved if it is delivered quickly after the event for same-day use.

THE VIDEOTAPED NEWS RELEASE   The most elaborate and expensive form of news delivery to television stations is the videotaped news release. This ready-to-use report prepared by a public relations organization presents news about a product, a service, or an idea, usually in featurized style (see Figure 24.2). In its most highly developed form, the videotaped news release may cost $10,000 or more to produce and distribute. Location shots by film crews and other production work resemble that done for television commercials.

Several factors should be considered before an organization commits that much money to a news release. Is the story sufficiently newsworthy, so that many of the stations receiving the release probably will put it on the air? Can the story be told well visually? Does the producer have sufficient time to prepare the release? As much as six weeks may be needed to create an outline, shoot the videotape, edit the release, and distribute it. Visual footage for use in videotaped releases often may be obtained from government and commercial archives to supplement freshly shot footage.

If the topic is strong enough, the release might be divided into two or three parts, for use in newscasts as a mini-series. Health, scientific, and social-problem topics are especially suited for this treatment.

The Canadian government, for example, prepared a three-part videotaped news release for Canadian and American stations and networks describing the contribution to the U.S. space program made by Canadian engineers, who developed the remote-arm manipulator used on space shuttle flights. This release had strong news value and excellent visual elements. *Public Relations Journal* reported that the Canadarm videotaped news release was put on the air by 100 network affiliates and independent stations, reaching an audience estimated at six million.

In producing videotaped news releases, the sponsoring organizations must present the material as *news*. Advertising sales-pitch techniques should be scrupulously avoided; so should glorifying adjectives. The benefit to the producing organization is indirect, by making known to the public the existence of the service, the idea, or the product. Sales efforts must be handled separately. If stations receiving the release view it as an obvious attempt to obtain free advertising, they will throw it away.

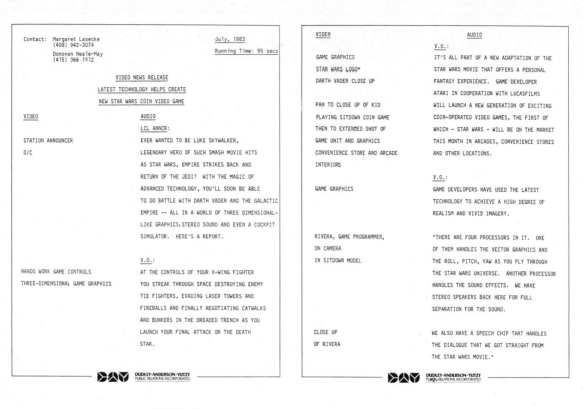

FIGURE 24.2

A public relations firm prepared this video news release script to publicize a coin game. As the opening page indicates, the left side provides video instructions; the right side presents the spoken copy.

NEWS ON CABLE TELEVISION

Expanding swiftly during a period of experimentation in the 1980s, newscasts on cable television provide fresh opportunities for public relations exposure. Innovative practitioners can find ways to place their news stories before cable-viewing audiences in addition to viewers of the over-the-air television stations and networks.

Numerous newspapers have obtained local cable channels on which they produce newscasts, using their own staff-gathered material as resources. Videotaped news releases, as described above, have an excellent possibility of receiving air time on these newscasts. Using satellite distribution, nationwide superstations such as WTBS-TV in Atlanta and WGN-TV in Chicago, and networks such as Cable News Network, reach large numbers of cable viewers from coast to coast. These outlets are worthwhile targets for the public relations practitioner.

PERSONAL APPEARANCES ON TELEVISION

Anyone invited to appear on television in a talk show or for an interview should prepare for the occasion. The beaming red light of a television camera aimed at a guest, indicating that he or she is on the air, can have a terrifying effect on an inexperienced performer. The throat goes dry. The words won't come out. The guest projects discomfort and uncertainty to thousands of viewers, precisely the opposite of the effect desired. A valuable opportunity is wasted.

Public relations practitioners can help their clients avoid this unpleasantness by coaching them in what to say and how to behave. Playing the role of interviewer in practice sessions, the coach can rehearse the guest by asking anticipated questions. If the subject matter is controversial, the practitioner should fire antagonistic questions to test the guest's mettle. As much as possible, the guest's prepared responses should be honed down to 30 seconds or less. (Preparation for appearances on television is discussed in Chapter 23.)

In general, guests on television should dress conservatively. On most shows a business suit is appropriate for men; for women, a suit or dress of simple pattern without conspicuous ornamentation. White clothing, including shirts, should be avoided, as should metallic decorations—all might reflect studio lights. On shows featuring entertainers and sports figures, dress is more informal, to the point of conspicuous casualness. By watching a show in advance or asking production personnel, the public relations person can advise a client how to dress suitably for the appearance.

Professional coaches who prepare guests for television appearances make these suggestions for their personal conduct:

Use of gestures. The guest should create movement for the camera, even though seated, by changing facial expressions and by moving the hands, arms, head, and shoulders to emphasize points. Potential guests can observe these tricks by watching professional actors on talk shows.

Use of eye contact. The guest should look at the interviewer, as in a private conversation. If the camera is focused directly at the guest, he or she should talk to it. The trick is to think of the camera eye not as an electronic device but as another person whom the speaker is trying to inform or convince.

Proper placement of the body. Persons being interviewed should not cross their legs; the position is awkward. It is better to sit with one foot in front of the other. Leaning forward in the chair makes a person appear more aggressive. Keeping the hands apart allows the guest to use them for gesturing. Guests also should be coached to mention key points about the event or product several times.

TELEVISION FOR RESTRICTED AUDIENCES

Television can be utilized to tell a story to the general public through news releases and personal on-the-air appearances. This is the external face of the medium, aimed at viewers who choose their programs by flicking the dial from channel to channel. Less well known, but growing enormously, is use of television to reach controlled private audiences in selected locations without having the program content seen by the general public.

The uses of *closed-circuit television,* tremendously enlarged by development of satellite transmission, are multiplying. Corporations employ it to deliver information and training material to their employees, to conduct sales meetings, to present financial information to security analysts and shareholders, to show the proceedings of their annual meetings, and to hold long-distance news conferences. Surgeons, engineers, and other professional groups employ television to discuss technical developments and to solve problems.

Uses of Videotape

As described in Chapter 21, videotape has become a communication method of great importance. Its flexibility and low cost enable organizations to deliver their messages visually to internal and external audiences in ways that never were feasible before the tape technique was created.

Following are descriptions of several videotape techniques used by corporations for sales and informational purposes.

VIDEOTAPED FINANCIAL REPORTS

Corporations increasingly are putting their financial information onto videotape for showing to shareholders and security analysts. Videotaping of annual meetings is one aspect of this trend. Especially prepared reports with graphs and other visual aids also are taped.

Distribution of videotaped material needs as much attention as preparation of the content. Videocassettes may be mailed to brokers and other financial specialists for their individual viewing, if they have access to playback machines. Perhaps more effective is a personal showing of the videotaped material by a company executive to groups of invited guests, who can ask questions after viewing the tape. Another method is to invite interested investors and brokers to request a loan copy of the videotape.

INTERNAL CORPORATE TV NEWS PROGRAMS

Large corporations with thousands of employees scattered in many locations keep hunting for ways to give their employees a sense of company pride and common purpose. Among the print media, company newspapers and magazines have that goal. The audiovisual equivalent is the corporate television news program.

Such programs need a strong professional touch in production; hence, they are expensive to create. They should have a well-defined formula for content. Management-oriented material should be presented discreetly in news style. The techniques of brevity, visual story-telling, human interest, and touches of humor that mark a successful commercial television newscast need to be applied to a corporate news program—not an easy task. Television consultant firms may be employed to produce the program or to provide technical assistance.

Showing of these programs to employees on a voluntary basis is done at lunch hours or other convenient times. Videotape cassettes of the shows can be distributed to sales and other employees working in the field. Playing the programs on cable television in cities where corporate plants are located is another possibility.

VIDEOTAPED TRAINING AND MARKETING PROGRAMS
Companies often prepare videotapes to train employees in technical skills. Tapes instructing sales personnel on methods of selling and explaining the firm's products are widely used. The flexibility and economy of videotape, compared to motion picture film, make it especially valuable in presentations of this type.

VIDEOTAPED SALES MESSAGES
A recent development as the electronic revolution changes publicity methods is distribution of sales messages on tape to selected potential customers. *Videocassettes* are mailed upon request to prospective buyers who can play these illustrated sales messages on home recorders. A stamped, self-addressed envelope for return of the cassettes to the firm is included. Because of the costs involved, this method is used primarily for higher-priced items, by companies selling direct to the consumer rather than through retail outlets.

Looking into the future, some electronics enthusiasts predict that a prospective purchaser, after seeing an item advertised, will be able to dial a toll-free number on a home telecomputer, watch the sales demonstration on the home televison screen, and order the item by pushing the proper button on the computer terminal. Payment for the item will be drawn by computer from the customer's bank account. Whether or not future sales methods follow this precise line, the use of electronic demonstration and selling inevitably will grow.

Motion Pictures

Hollywood commercial feature films viewed by millions of customers in theaters constitute only a fraction of the films produced in the United States and Canada every year. Hundreds of motion pictures, often equal in quality to theatrical films, are made annually by sponsors for showing to selected audiences. Only a handful of these ever will appear on commercial theater screens, and then only as supporting films on programs of mass market entertainment.

Sponsored films have a major role in public relations work, as noted in Chapter 12. Designed to inform, instruct, and persuade, often subtly, they play to a huge cumulative audience. Unlike commercial films, most of them are shown to viewers without charge. The makers of these films, and in some instances the organizations showing them, bear the cost in order to further their purposes directly or indirectly.

Public relations practitioners can make use of mass market entertainment motion pictures, and more important, of sponsored nontheatrical films.

HOLLYWOOD ENTERTAINMENT FILMS

When that lonesome waif from outer space, E.T., discovered that Reese's Pieces, a chocolate and peanut butter candy, were an earthly delight, he not only pleased his palate but demonstrated the publicity value of a motion picture tie-in for a manufacturer. The Hershey Food Company, their maker, reported a 65-percent increase in sales for Reese's Pieces after theatergoers saw that they were the extra-terrestrial character's favorite candy. Since *E.T., The Extra-Terrestrial,* quickly became the all-time box office champion motion picture, Hershey cashed in handsomely.

This is how the arrangement worked: MCA, the picture's production company, asked Hershey if it would be interested in a publicity tie-in. After determining that the movie was a suitable family production, Hershey agreed. It placed special displays in the lobbies of the hundreds of theaters showing the movie. Purchasers of Reese's Pieces at theater candy counters received special E.T. stickers. Hershey also provided supermarket displays and premiums such as T-shirts, stickers, and posters. Hershey's extensive efforts helped to publicize the movie without cost to the film's producers. The tie-in was mutually beneficial to candymaker and filmmaker.

Placement of brand-name products in motion pictures, either as background or for use by a character in the story, is a highly developed public relations specialty. When moviegoers see a character swinging a tennis racket whose brand name is visible, or climbing aboard an airliner whose company logotype appears in large letters in front of the wing, they probably are watching a tie-in deal in operation. (Tie-ins on television are discussed in Chapter 12.)

Motion picture companies like tie-ins because they often save money on location sites and props. A tie-in with an airline may give the producer free use of an airplane's interior for a key scene. The use of real-life props adds realism to a scene, as well.

Some public relations experts specialize in creating such tie-ins. They represent scores, or hundreds, of clients who would like to see their products shown in a movie. By analyzing scripts to be filmed, the specialists find product-display opportunities that their clients might be able to fill.

One representative, typically, charges up to $10,000 for arranging a product appearance. Many manufacturers consider this price reasonable compared to the cost of making and showing a television commercial for the product. Although the product's appearance is incidental to the story, unsupported by "selling" words, they believe that the visual impact and implied endorsement of the product are worth the cost.

SPONSORED FILMS The range of films made to be shown free of charge, or to be rented or purchased for showing to private audiences, is immense. Most sponsored films are loaned without charge to audiences whom the makers wish to reach with their messages. Others are made by corporations specifically for showing to their internal audiences for education and training. Prints of certain sponsored films may be purchased by organizations and schools for repeated showings to changing audiences. For example, schools often buy prints of a film on schoolbus safety, "The Big Yellow Fellow," sponsored by Charms Candy.

Churches, schools, social and cultural organizations, athletic teams, business and industry, agricultural groups: all are among the audiences for sponsored films. Their interests are diverse; so are the kinds of films made to be shown to them. Some are openly promotional; some are vehicles for advocacy. In others the filmmakers keep their messages so subtle that only the incidental appearance of equipment bearing the manufacturer's name gives a clue to the sponsors. Many films made to enhance the public's knowledge of an industry or field of service avoid reference to sponsoring companies, except for credit lines at the opening or close.

Cable television has opened a new outlet for sponsored films. Consumer education pictures in which the sponsor's commercial message is subdued appear on many cable channels. These stations use the films, at little or no cost, to fill broadcast time with material different from what regular television stations and networks show.

Production of nontheatrical films is a substantial industry, involving an estimated 600 established producing and marketing firms around the world. Their filming techniques and equipment in many instances are highly advanced. When they can convince managements of sponsoring firms to take a chance on being "different," filmmakers do innovative and ingenious work to break out of the traditional success-story mold that makes some industrial films in particular a bit dull.

Motion pictures are produced in four sizes. The Hollywood-type entertainment picture usually is made on 35-millimeter film for large-screen projection in theaters. A few elaborate ones use 70-millimeter film; some sponsored films are made on 35 millimeter or, rarely, on 70 millimeter.

However, the majority of sponsored films are issued in 16-millimeter width, the most widely used for school and small-auditorium showing. A few are available in 8 millimeter, a size that won popularity for home movies. Some sponsored pictures are issued on videotape. The type of use anticipated and the projection equipment most likely to be employed influence the film size selected.

A limiting factor on use of videotape is lack of standardization in tape size and equipment. Some players take 1/2-inch tape, other take 3/4-inch. Some take reel-to-reel, others take cassettes. Availability of playback equipment, while growing, is somewhat limited. The standard movie projector is still the workhorse. However, more and more schools and organizations will acquire videotape equipment in coming years.

The length of sponsored films varies greatly, again depending upon anticipated use. The National Association of Secondary School Principals made an effective film, *Education: An American Essential,* only 7 minutes long. It was designed as an opening for community meetings and as a public service filler for television stations. However, most sponsored films are substantially longer. A survey of adult groups and educators by the Modern Talking Picture Service, a large distributor that has 6900 active titles in circulation, showed a strong preference for films 21 to 30 minutes in length.

Filmmaking is a highly skilled craft. Unless an organization or corporation happens to have experienced filmmakers on its staff, it should employ one of the many companies that produce sponsored films. In this area do-it-yourself efforts are treacherous and frequently wasteful, with amateurish results.

The documentary approach is most common in free-loan films. Producers may inject substantial entertainment values to hold audience interest while delivering the facts and may employ humor, such as cartoon-like drawings, to brighten the tone. Often a well-known personality serves as narrator. In the film produced by the secondary school principals, actor Jack Lemmon did the narration, pictured in various classes at the high school his daughter attended at the time.

Here is a sampling of sponsored films, providing some indication of the wide variety of subject matter covered:

An advocacy film. Ridin' the Edge was issued by Allstate Insurance Company to publicize the use of air-cushion safety devices in automobiles. Allstate urges adoption of this equipment as a life-saving device that would, incidentally, reduce its payout of death benefits. The film is built around dramatic footage of an automobile-crash stunt in which the driver smashed into a wall at 30 miles an hour but escaped injury because he was protected by an inflatable air cushion. The short film was shown at Radio City Music Hall in New York; on television; to civic, industrial, and political groups; and to schools. Within 3 years after its release, it had been shown 125,000 times to an estimated 46 million people.

A corporate film for internal communication. Desiring to explain its benefit program for employees in a manner that they would remember, United Technologies Corporation hired comedian Jonathan Winters to star in a 17-minute picture, *Count On It* (see Figure 8.1, Chapter 8). Winters created six off-beat characterizations. In each role he ad-libbed information about an aspect of the program, such as retirement and dental care. UTC employees performed in the scenes with him. Surveys showed that the humorous yet accurate film stimulated much positive discussion among employees. Production cost was approximately $51,000.

An industrial documentary film. The World's Favorite Raisin tells the story of the Sun-Maid product. The 20-minute film shows production of raisins from the grape on the vine to their appearance on store shelves. Interwoven is the history of the Sun-Maid company. Visitors to Sun-Maid's plant at Kingsburg, California, see the film as part of their tour. It also is shown to schools, community groups, and special-interest organizations. In the first 6 months after its release, the picture had more than 1000 showings in 27 states.

A corporate training picture. The Levi's Fit Test and how it should be conducted is explained in a 90-minute training program by Levi Strauss & Company for international showing. The Fit Test is a marketing research tool used by Levi's staffs in various locations to determine how their particular publics define a good fit and how Levi's jeans compare to competitive garments sold in that area. In this training picture, objectives and criteria of the test are explained and the step-by-step process of an actual test is shown. Test results are displayed, after which Levi's marketing experts discuss the techniques used. The program has been used by Levi's branches in 10 foreign countries, accompanied by a 40-page sample report.

A government social-problem film. The Utah Department of Health produced a frank film about a serious social problem. *If You Want to Dance . . .* concerns an unwed teenage couple faced with the consequences of an unplanned pregnancy (see Figure 24.3). Candid but constructive, the 14-minute film opens with a locker room scene in which three high school boys are talking about sex, then shifts to a hospital room where two pregnant unwed teenage girls discuss their problems. Much praised, the film has been widely shown to high school classes, church groups, and community organizations. A discussion guide is distributed with the film, which is available for loan or purchase on both 16-millimeter film and 3/4-inch videocassette.

A soft-sell corporate film in which the sponsor's role is held to a minimum. The motion picture *Big Wyoming: The Awakening Giant* tells about that Western state and its huge, barely tapped resources. The film was made by Union Pacific, whose tracks run through the state, but no attention is focused on the railroad. Pictures of its trains are shown incidentally, as part of a collective effort to develop the state.

FIGURE 24.3

This print shows a locker room scene from a film about teenage pregnancy, *If you Want to Dance . . .*, produced by the Utah Department of Health. The film has been widely shown in school, church, and community meetings. (Copyright © by Peter C. van Dyck, courtesy of Utah Department of Health.)

A film made specifically as an educational tool. Made for showing in schools, *Nuclear Weapons: Can Man Survive?* is a 24-minute film by Screen News Digest, a commercial company, exploring humanity's prospects for controlling the nuclear weapons it has created. Historical footage depicts development of the atomic bomb and the results of its use at Hiroshima and Nagasaki. Other shots show test·firings of various contemporary nuclear missiles. Prominent personalities discuss the proposed bilateral freeze on nuclear weapons production, pro and con. The film is dramatic but objective, intended to stimulate student thinking and discussion.

Still Images for Projection

Slides, filmstrips, and transparencies—all of them methods for projecting still images onto a screen—often are referred to as audiovisual aids. Properly, the word *audiovisual* encompasses all forms of sound-and-picture projection, including motion pictures, but in practice it frequently is applied only to these simpler forms. Inclusion of such visual aids in programs stimulates audiences.

Audiovisual aids are much cheaper than motion pictures and videotapes and have simple projection requirements. All that is needed are a relatively inexpensive slide projector, an electrical outlet, and a small screen. A presentation of still images accompanied by live or recorded narration often is the most efficient method for bringing a message to a small audience. Public relations practitioners find scores of uses for such presentations.

SLIDE SHOWS Slide presentations range upward from Uncle Chester showing the dinner guests slides he made during his trip to Europe—usually too many and occasionally upside-down—to the projection of intricate triple-screen, three-dimensional productions issued by some corporations.

For his performance before the captive audience in the living room, Uncle Chester selects the slides he likes best and delivers a rambling ad-lib narration about them as they flash on the screen. This is exactly opposite from the way a professional slide show should be constructed.

A slide show should be built on a well-defined theme, to tell a story and deliver a message. The script should be written and approved first, then the visual elements should be developed to illustrate and emphasize points in the script. Standard technique is for a visually oriented person to study the script, marking places in it that lend themselves to illustration by photograph or drawing. An artist then creates rough storyboards, indicating the illustration perceived for each point. More detailed and refined storyboards may be developed in subsequent story conferences. Photographer and artist go to work, producing 35-millimeter slides that meet the requirements of the storyboards. Slides and motion picture film can be coordinated.

Depending upon its purpose, a slide show might consist of photographs, as in a program made by a state tourist board to publicize the scenic attractions of the state. Or, if intended to explain retirement benefits to an internal audience of employees, it might be made entirely with drawings and explanatory text slides. A combination of photographs, drawings, and text also can be effective. Leasing of stock shots of scenery, people, and events from commercial firms specializing in this work is a convenient way to fill out the picture requirements of a show. Some large picture firms have from two to five million still photos and slides on file to fill requests.

Whatever form the slide show takes, inclusion of humorous bits creates audience interest. These might be cartoons or candid photographs in which individuals are caught in laughable situations.

Text-only slides often help to give a presentation cohesion and to emphasize key points. The content of each text slide should be brief, making a single clear statement in a maximum of 25 to 30 words. A slide containing 10 words or fewer can be powerfully effective. Color slides containing text and/or drawings need strong contrast, usually a dark background of blue, black, or brown with letters and pictures in white, yellow, or red.

A narrator may deliver the script of a slide show live, or it may be accompanied by a taped voice synchronized with the progression of slides. Slides can be shown on an automatic projector controlled by a button the speaker presses to change them.

If a company or organization has competent writing, photographic, or graphic talent on its staff, it may be able to produce an attractive slide show using its own resources. Outside graphic talent may be hired, or the sponsor may employ a firm specializing in audiovisual work to handle the entire production. Specialist organizations are able to produce elaborate slide shows with dramatic graphic effects. Animation and masking that reveals only part of a picture at a time add visual zest, and use of multiple screens and projectors provides dramatic impact.

FILMSTRIPS

A filmstrip consists of a series of 35-millimeter or 16-millimeter slides reproduced in sequence on a short piece of film. The strip can be advanced slowly, one frame at a time, in an inexpensive projector, with each frame held on the screen as long as desired. Filmstrips are economical, small, and easily transported. They are especially useful as instructional tools for single concepts. If a recorded narration accompanies the filmstrip, the frames must be advanced at a coordinated speed.

OVERHEAD TRANSPARENCIES

A simple, economical form of audiovisual aid is a sheet of transparent acetate or similar material on which illustrations and/or lettering have been placed. When this sheet is laid on a flat glass surface in the projector, the images are reproduced on a screen behind the speaker by light transmitted by mirrors and lenses. Overhead transparencies are especially good in classrooms and small discussion groups because of their flexibility.

Masking a transparency permits a speaker to show several steps in a process with only one transparency. If the same series of steps were shown by slides, a separate slide would be necessary for each step.

When a speaker wishes to show the operation of a piece of machinery, for example, masking can be done in the following way: The transparency contains a diagram of the entire machine. A piece of onionskin or white opalescent plastic is laid over each portion of the diagram and taped lightly into place. As the blanked-out transparency appears on the screen, the speaker removes each sectional overlay progressively and explains the revealed portion of the diagram, until the entire diagram is visible. The speaker can draw or write on a transparency while it is being displayed on the screen.

Still Photography

A story in the print media, especially newspapers and magazines, may, and frequently should, be told in pictures as well as words. Still photography is an essential tool for every practitioner who works with publications.

NEWSPAPER REQUIREMENTS

Newspaper editors like to receive black-and-white photographs of persons mentioned in news releases. The presence of a photograph with a release sometimes increases the likelihood that the story will be published. Or, as frequently happens, a photograph of a newsworthy individual or group will be published without an accompanying story, the necessary information having been condensed into the photo caption.

The type of photograph most easily placed in a newspaper by a practitioner is the head-and-shoulders portrait of a client. These portraits, known in the trade as *mug shots,* frequently are published in one-column or half-column size to illustrate textual material. Group shots are published less often than individual pictures because they require multiple-column space. Practitioners submitting group photographs should keep the number of persons in a picture small and have them tightly grouped—a maximum of five persons unless the picture is a highly unusual one.

Photographs on the main news pages of a newspaper usually are taken by staff photographers or are provided by the news picture services. They stress spot-news action. The chances for a public relations practitioner to have a submitted photograph published in these up-front pages are relatively small, except for one-column portraits. When spot news is involved, the practitioner is better advised to telephone the photo editor of a newspaper and call attention to a picture possibility that a staff photographer can cover. Staff photographers know their editors' requirements, space limitations, and deadlines. They can respond very quickly to fast-breaking news situations.

Other sections of a newspaper provide abundant opportunities for publication of photographs submitted by practitioners.

The business pages regularly include photographs of meetings, new products, and individuals appointed to new positions. Sports editors welcome photographs of athletes and coaches in various poses. Entertainment editors need pictures of performers, individually and in groups, and publish still photos taken from scenes in locally playing motion pictures and television shows. Travel editors desire photographs of interesting scenes and modes of transportation.

An expecially broad target for the practitioner is the section of a newspaper called Family Living, Life Styles, Today's Scene, or something similar. For many years these sections were referred to as "women's," "society," or, in newspaper slang, "sock." They concentrated on engagements and weddings, parties and club meetings, food, beauty, and fashion. Now their appeal is greatly enlarged, aimed at men as well as women.

While retaining the traditional elements, these sections have added material about family life and problems, personal finances, careers, and contemporary life styles. This broadened appeal has multiplied the photographic possibilities for the public relations practitioner, both to submit photographs and to query editors with ideas for illustrated feature stories by staff members about activities of their clients.

Family-Living sections often publish pictures of groups planning charity events, civic affairs, and social organization parties. These pictures generate interest in the event, help to sell tickets, and incidentally serve as an ego payoff to workers who appear in them. Unfortunately, far too many such pictures belong to the waxworks school of photography—stilted, self-conscious poses in which the participants appear ramrod-stiff and painfully artificial. A photographer's ingenuity is challenged to invent an interesting piece of business for the participants to do, and to coax them to relax.

When shooting a publicity shot, a clever photographer will include, if possible, a prop that helps to carry the message. A picture promoting a Red Cross blood drive, for example, would be strengthened by inclusion of a Red Cross poster or similar symbol.

Publicity shots may be submitted by the practitioner, or arrangements may be made with an editor for a staff photographer to handle the assignment. If a staff photographer is assigned, the practitioner must make certain that all participants in the picture assemble at the appointed place on time, appropriately dressed. The photographer is busy and, in a sense, the editor is doing the organization a favor.

Creativity also should be applied to news pictures submitted for publication. Groundbreakings, installations of officers, delivery of donation checks—routine events that frequently fall within the domain of the public relations worker—are notorious sources of cliché photos. Some newspapers refuse to publish photographs of these events for that reason. A practitioner taking a picture of such an event, or a commercial photographer hired to do so, should use every ounce of innovative skill to find a new camera angle or piece of action.

Photographs submitted to newspapers normally are 8 by 10 inches in black and white, with caption material attached either to the back or bottom of the picture. *The practitioner should be absolutely certain that the names in the caption are spelled correctly and match up in left-to-right sequence with the photograph itself.* An added precaution is to count the number of persons in the picture and the number of names in the caption, to be sure that they correspond. Smaller prints usually are acceptable for head-and-shoulders portraits. Newspapers are publishing a growing number of color photographs, most of them feature pictures arranged in advance or news action pictures taken by staff members. The practitioner should submit color slides, not color prints.

Since newspapers maintain large files of published and unpublished photographs, it is not unusual for a "mug shot" of a newsworthy personality to be published more than once—a bonus for the practitioner who submitted it. Individuals change in appearance as they age, and occasionally an editor will reach into the files in a hurry and publish an obviously outdated picture of a news figure. The public relations person handling a prominent individual can avoid this embarrassment by submitting an up-to-date photograph from time to time, with a request that it replace the old one.

The importance of including a selection of photographs in a press kit introducing such projects as a new shopping center, a sales program, a political campaign, or a fund drive is obvious. The kit should contain pictures of the key persons involved and of physical aspects of the projects.

On a national or regional basis, the alert practitioner may obtain space by appealing to newspaper editors' interest in hometown angles. At a national convention of, say, automobile dealers, the public relations staff can run a "production line" in which individual dealers are photographed in company with a celebrity. These captioned photographs are sent appropriately to hometown newspapers. Smaller dailies and weekly newspapers are the most likely to use them. Similarly, public relations representatives for cruise lines take shipboard photographs of vacationing couples standing before a background showing the ship's name, for hometown publication.

At least rudimentary knowledge of photographic techniques is an important asset for all men and women working in public relations. The best way to obtain this is to take a college course in news photography. If this cannot be done, courses in photography are available in many adult education programs. Membership in a camera club is another way.

MAGAZINE REQUIREMENTS

These resemble those of newspapers, although emphasis is primarily on feature photographs. Some magazines use only color photographs, some only black and white, some both. The practitioner should study each magazine before submitting pictures to it. Color slides rather than prints should be sent.

Trade and professional magazines frequently use submitted photographs of individuals, new products, and industrial installations. When sending in a proposal for a feature story about a client, the practitioner should offer to provide photographs to accompany the text, regardless of whether the story is written by the practitioner, by a free-lance writer, or by a magazine staff member. Many magazines do not have photographic staffs, or budgets and facilities for acquiring pictures, and so depend upon submitted pictures. Attractive photographs accompanying a manuscript enhance the possibility that it will be accepted for publication.

Public relations departments and counseling firms should include in their annual budgets a substantial amount for photographic service. In addition to submitting pictures to the media, representatives often find it effective to send souvenir prints of these pictures to persons appearing in them and to important persons such as dealers and customers. Such small gestures have a flattering effect.

COMIC BOOKS AND CARTOONS

Another eye-catching way to deliver visual messages in print is to use comic books and cartoons. The artwork must be of professional quality, however, or the effect is diminished. Drawings are especially good for illustrating steps in a process, as in an owner's instruction manual. If an artist can create a whimsical cartoon character that symbolizes the service or objective, entire campaigns can be built around it.

Outdoor Displays

Although billboards, building signs, and other forms of outdoor announcements are erected primarily for advertising and identification, they have potential uses as public relations tools. Billboards may remind motorists and pedestrians of a citywide charity fund drive in progress. A changing electric sign outside a bank showing time and temperature performs a public service and creates good will for the bank; so does a signboard on which annoucements of forthcoming civic events are placed. An ingenious practitioner working for a nonprofit organization may be able to find numerous outlets of this type to deliver a message, at little or no cost.

A public relations specialist should know the fundamentals of billboard design and economics, in case a situation arises in which outdoor displays will fit into a publicity program. The standard billboard of the type seen along streets and on buildings is 12 by 25 feet. The colorful paper posters pasted onto it are slightly smaller, leaving a white frame around them. The standard poster is called a 24-sheet, because at one time 24 sheets of paper were needed to cover the space on a full-sized billboard. Modern printing processes do it with 10 sheets. Small posters called 3-sheets are designed to attract pedestrian readers at sidewalk level.

Outdoor advertising companies rent display space on their billboards on the basis of what they call a *100-showing*—that is, the number of boards in a market area calculated to expose the advertiser's message to approximately 100 percent of the people at some time during the 30 days it is posted. The number of boards that constitute a 100-showing fluctuates from market to market, based on traffic studies.

When messages are painted onto the billboards instead of being pasted on, their effective life is longer and the space rental price higher.

Successful billboard copy must be short and illustrations simple, because the duration of viewing time as motorists pass is brief. Eye-catching impact is the goal. That requires powerful design and strong colors. Perhaps the greatest advantage of billboards is their reminder value in support of a program using other methods as well. Design and preparation of billboard posters is handled by advertising agencies, while physical placement is done by the billboard companies.

Corporate Design

The need to present a unified visual image to the world is becoming increasingly evident to corporations and nonprofit organizations. Especially among corporations that have grown rapidly by acquiring many subsidiaries, the uncoordinated proliferation of letterheads, signs, publication symbols,

FIGURE 24.4

When General Telephone and Electronics Corporation changed its stock market symbol from GEN to GTE, it alerted investors with this newspaper advertisement. Later the company shortened its official name to GTE Corporation. (Reprinted by permission of GTE.)

news release sheets, packages, and other visual public representations of the organization gives a jumbled, unfocused appearance.

Creation of a simple, powerful logotype for use on all printed matter and signs projects an image of the company as a tightly knit contemporary operation. An impressive logo suggests quality and strength.

In the acquisition-minded climate of corporate life today, companies often add so many subsidiaries that the original names of the parent firms become inadequate to describe their overall function. So these corporations adopt generalized names, usually of one or two words. Standard Oil of New Jersey renamed itself Exxon Corporation, American Machinery & Foundry Company became AMF Incorporated, and General Telephone and Electronics Corporation officially became GTE Corporation (see Figure 24.4).

When the huge American Telephone & Telegraph Company was broken up by court agreement in 1984, a fascinating example of corporate name selection took place. The 22 Bell Telephone System operating subsidiaries were reorganized into seven independent corporations. Each needed a name as the focal point for corporate identity.

Three stayed with tradition by choosing names that incorporated the word *Bell* and geographic identification—*Bell Atlantic, Bell South,* and *Southwestern Bell.* A fourth dropped *Bell* but emphasized geography—*US West.* Trying to establish completely new images, the other three selected *Ameritech, Pacific Telesis,* and *Nynex.* Years will pass before the wisdom of these conflicting approaches can be determined.

Corporate redesign usually involves coordinated effort by the public relations and marketing departments. First, management must define the objectives to be sought in the new design. Should the graphic style be ultramodern, formal and conservative, or perhaps old-fashioned to suggest historical continuity? A counseling firm and graphics specialist usually are brought into the discussion. A detailed audit of existing printed materials and signs is necessary, to establish the areas where the new design will be used. In a corporation with numerous divisions, the logotype may be color-

FIGURE 24.5

These are examples of corporate symbol redesign—the old (left) and the new (right). (Courtesy of Selame Design.)

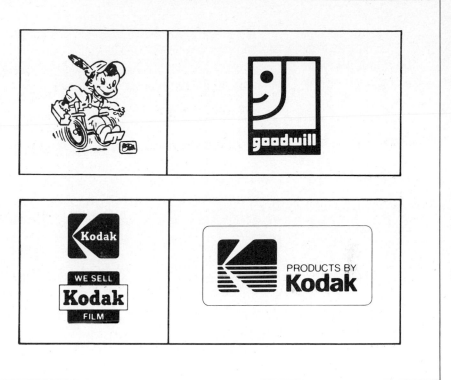

coded—a different color for each division, with identification of the division in type below.

Practitioners working with smaller companies and nonprofit organizations can achieve visual unity and focus public attention, just as the huge corporations do.

Goodwill Industries, for example, formerly had as its symbol a cartoon character, a smiling young man with a feather in his hat and a lunch box in his hand rolling along in a wheelchair. The national help-the-handicapped organization found that the symbol, while clever, did not print well and lacked sales appeal on signs outside its retail outlets. The design consultant Goodwill employed replaced the symbol with a rectangular logo in which a large lower-case g in the upper-left corner looks like half of a smiling face (see Figure 24.5).

In another piece of clever public relations and marketing, Goodwill put a "Morgie" label on the used jeans it sells, thereby spoofing the current fad for designer jeans that bear high-fashion labels. Sales of the used jeans rose, and Goodwill received excellent national press coverage.

Creation of a graphics standards manual helps a large organization to enforce its unified designs throughout all its operations.

**QUESTIONS
FOR REVIEW
AND DISCUSSION**

1. What is the fundamental difference between a news story in a newspaper and one on television?

2. Under what conditions might a public relations adviser recommend distribution of a videotaped news release?

3. In what ways can a corporation make use of videotaped presentations?

4. If you were handling public relations for an airline, what types of publicity tie-ins might you develop with a Hollywood motion picture producer?

5. A food manufacturer plans to produce a sponsored film about a new corn-based cereal. What elements might it include in the film? To what target audiences might it show the film?

6. Why is it desirable to write the script of a slide show before the pictures are taken?

7. What is a storyboard?

8. Why is a "mug shot" a useful photographic tool in public relations practice?

9. Billboard companies rent display space on the basis of a *100-showing*. What does this mean?

10. How can graphics design help to strengthen a corporation's public image?

by Loet A. Velmans

THE FUTURE OF PUBLIC RELATIONS

Public relations has changed dramatically during my nearly 40 years in the business of communications—this textbook is evidence of that—but the changes have been in scope and means, not in its basic purpose. As one of the founders of public relations and the founder of my company, John W. Hill, wrote some 20 years ago, "The roots of public relations are fixed in the basic fact that public opinion, confused, obscure, unpredictable as it may often seem, is the ultimate ruling force in the free world. A fundamental function of public relations is to help public opinion reach conclusions by providing it facts and interpretations of facts. . . . Only with the understanding and support of public opinion can business flourish and grow."

This is the mission of public relations, and it has not changed substantially since the industry's beginnings in the 1920s. And I don't believe that mission will change substantially in the next 60 years either. What will change, however, are the kinds of projects public relations practitioners do, the means by which they do them, the expanding international scope of communications and communications problems, and the way business approaches the task of communications.

I have observed in recent years that more and more business leaders are acknowledging the integral importance of communications to corporate goals. Recently, the Conference Board (a group of prominent business executives) conducted a survey and found that chief executive officers (CEOs) spend more than 50 percent of their time on matters of communication such as lobbying and public relations. Increasingly, business is turning to communications to address the problems wrought by a volatile economy and new competition in the United States and from abroad.

At the same time, new communications technologies and techniques are providing public relations professionals with the means to communicate more information to more audiences. Indeed, it is the combination of the exploding *means* of communications technology and the exploding *availability* of that technologically available communications that is rapidly changing the face of public relations. Coping with these changes means far more than merely a working knowledge of how to use communications and communications technology; it also means a responsibility for using it well. Simplistic messages, after all, work very well on many of these technologies, but that way can lead to societal destruction. The Nazis knew well that the simplistic sells well; they also knew that dramatic presentation sells the simplistic.

An important distinction must be made here: Simple is not the same as simplistic. Messages often have to be made simple—to appeal to a particular audience, to conform to the demands of a specific medium, or to isolate distinct parts of a complicated argument. But messages must never be made simplistic—that is, distorted in their essential nature in order to appeal to often base, popular motives.

Our continuing professional challenge is to find ways to communicate tailored messages simply and effectively without being simplistic and distorting.

And we have to do so very quickly. Technology is changing far more rapidly, in many cases, than we are. Indeed, one of the most fascinating things about the new communications technologies is that they allow a whole culture to "skip" stages of cultural growth. A number of nations are supplying remote towns and villages with television sets and with television programming by means of satellite transmission. These countries are, to a large degree, bypassing the print media stage amd moving directly into electronic media.

Corporate and Financial Relations

Traditionally, corporate and financial relations have been limited to two things: maintaining a good corporate image and complying with the requirements of the Securities and Exchange Commission concerning release of information, earnings results, and other financial data. In fact, in the early days of public relations, many corporations tried to keep their names out of the paper. Now, however, businesses are working to create and establish a corporate identity—the word *image* is not accurate any more, if it ever really was. In addition, corporations are going beyond the mere requirements for information disclosure and are actively communicating with the financial community and shareholders. To fulfill both these goals, corporations are turning to public relations.

The biggest change in this area is one we are seeing somewhat today: corporate strategy and corporate communications working together. There was a time when the board of directors of a company met, made decisions, and then told a public relations person to make sure the newspaper published the necessary information. But now, chief executive officers and high-ranking corporate officials are including public relations professionals in policy-making meetings for counsel, to evaluate strategic decisions in terms of the impact on the world at large, and to design communications strategies to deal with that impact. In short, public relations in the arena of the corporation is moving from a reactive, defensive stance to an active one, seeking to create a place for a company in the complex world marketplace.

In terms of investor relations, two factors are changing the way a corporation approaches the financial community and shareholders. One is, of course, the wave of merger and acquisition activity. The other is the changing makeup of shareholders.

Public relations will continue to increase in importance with respect to mergers and acquisitions, both to help companies soften the threat of a takeover and to help them effect one. Already, this activity has earned public relations a place beside investment banking and legal professions as outside expertise to help a corporation achieve a particular goal.

The rise in financial relations can be attributed in large part to the fundamental change in stock ownership. It was not so long ago that 70 percent of the market was owned by individuals and 30 percent by institutions such as insurance companies and pension funds. Now the ratio is completely reversed: 70 percent of the nation's stock is held by institutions, whose investment goals are often considerably different from those of the private investor. This changing market mix will continue to spawn new developments in financial relations as we look for new ways to communicate a company's performance to a decreasing number of portfolio managers and investment analysts.

Marketing Communications

Product marketing was one of the earliest public relations disciplines, and it has continued to grow throughout the field's history. And it is here that technology has had the greatest effect on the public relations business for two reasons. First, the great variety of new media such as cable television and new products such as video cassette recorders have made it increasingly difficult to reach a mass audience effectively. Advertisers and marketers are thus turning to public relations and marketing communications to assist them in their missions. The second reason is that those same technologies have provided the public relations professional with new channels of communication. The sheer volume of media space and time available has increased greatly, and the communications possibilities have increased accordingly.

Marketing communications will continue to change because of these phenomena. Instead of simply working to get as much exposure as possible, product marketers will work to get the right kind of exposure. Survey research, already an important tool for public relations, will be used more and more to help marketers find out who is buying their product—as well as what they read, watch, and listen to. The increasing sophistication of communications tools will mean, as it has meant, an increasing ability to target messages narrowly, allowing product marketers to speak with just those people they wish to reach.

Public Affairs and Lobbying

Despite the recent trend to deregulation, business and government are inextricably linked, and this will continue to present new opportunities for the public relations professional. More and more, public relations will work to support the lobbying function through such tasks as issues monitoring or generating grass roots support. Since the 1960s, the public has become more skilled and more interested in making companies responsible to the public at large. As issues arise, corporations must become involved with the communications process in order to protect their interests and inform the public of their own concerns.

Businesses are increasing their involvement with the community, and public relations will be called upon not only to inform the world about the programs and plans companies develop to be "good citizens," but to assist in their development.

International Public Relations

As the economic and political world is global in scope, so is public relations. Issues that affect business and government cross national boundaries with increasing speed and in any direction. Public relations professionals must not only be adept at understanding and communicating complex messages within a single nation and a single culture, but more and more we must be adept at carrying out this job internationally. To be able to do this, in addition to mastering the tools and intellectual constructs of the profession, is a challenge indeed that each professional entering the field must meet.

Success in accomplishing this goal and mastering any of the public relations fields depends a good deal on education. While public relations practitioners should be generalists—a wide-ranging education is important—they should also receive the kind of training people get for law and business. We must constantly strive to improve the level of professionals in the public relations industry if we are to achieve the goal of becoming integral to the corporation. This text is a valuable step in that direction.

LOET A. VELMANS
Chairman, President, and Chief Executive Officer
Hill and Knowlton, Inc.

A PUBLIC RELATIONS GLOSSARY

Account executive   A person in a public relations firm or advertising agency who works with a client on a program.

Accreditation   In public relations, the designation *APR* given to members of the Public Relations Society of America with at least five years of experience who have passed written and oral examinations. The International Association of Business Communicators has a designation, ABC, standing for Accredited Business Communicator, based on experience and testing.

Actuality   A brief on-the-scene report, live or on tape, inserted into a radio news show.

Agenda-setter   A term often applied to the mass media, whose choice of news stories and headlines suggests to the public what to think about.

Annual report   A corporate information document filed each year with the Securities and Exchange Commission. Many companies expand their reports with illustrations and text for distribution to stockholders, employees, and other interested persons.

Benchmark study   A measurement of audience attitudes before and after a public relations campaign.

Bill stuffer   Company information or sales material placed in an envelope containing a customer's bill.

Bio   Slang abbreviation for the detailed biography a practitioner prepares for a client.

Booker   Publicist whose assignment is to place clients on talk shows and in other public events.

Bottom line   Popular usage indicating the most important fact; derived from the bottom line of a financial statement, showing net profit or loss.

CEO   Chief executive officer of a corporation.

Channeling   The technique of tapping a group's attitudes with salient messages that propose a course of action.

Cheesecake   Photograph of a scantily clad young woman used as a publicity device.

Communication audit   A review to determine what public relations material the target audience is receiving and what it desires to receive.

Copyright   The protection of a creative work from unauthorized use.

Copy testing   The technique of trying out material on a small group before distributing it to an entire audience.

Corporate advertising   Advertising intended to enhance public conception of a company or to advocate a company policy. (See *Institutional advertising.*)

Corporate communications   Term covering all types of communication by a company to both external and internal audiences.

Courtesy bias Tendency of some survey respondents to give a socially "correct" answer rather than one disclosing their true opinions.

Crisis communications Methods and policies a corporation uses in distributing information when its operations become involved in an emergency situation affecting the public.

Data base Indexed information held in computer storage, from which a computer user can summon selected material, usually for a fee.

Decoder In communication theory, one who receives a message. (See *Encoder.*)

Demographics The characteristics of a human population, including size, density, growth, distribution, and vital statistics.

Editor Director of a newspaper's news and editorial department; may be subordinate to the publisher or on an equal footing, depending upon the newspaper's organization.

> **Associate editor** Director of the editorial and commentary pages.
>
> **Managing editor** Manager of news operations, to whom the city editor answers.
>
> **City editor** Director of the local news staff; the person to whom most news releases are addressed.

Electronic mail Textual messages transmitted from one computer terminal to another, rather than delivered by a mail carrier or messenger.

Embargo Statement of the day and hour set by the creator of a news release for use by the news media.

Encoder In communication theory, one who sends a message. (See *Decoder.*)

External publication One designed to be read by persons not employed by the sponsoring organization. (See *Internal publication.*)

Factsheet An advisory information sheet about a forthcoming event.

Feedback Reaction from those affected by an activity or public relations material about the situation.

Fiber optics Transmission of signals through highly transparent strands of extremely thin glass, instead of by wire.

Filmstrip Sequence of film frames which, when advanced one by one in a projector, present a topic on a screen; used as a training tool.

Flack Derogatory term applied primarily to a person who publicizes entertainment events and personalities. (See *Press agentry.*)

Focus group Panel of persons, representative of the audience a public relations practitioner desires to reach, who are asked to give their opinions of proposed programs.

Free-loading The practice of some reporters and editors to accept gifts, entertainment, and travel from organizations seeking to influence them.

Gatekeeper Editor, reporter, or news director who decides what material is printed and broadcast.

Gross impressions Total circulation and listening audience of the print and broadcast media which use a news release.

Hierarchy of needs   Abraham Maslow's definition of an individual's five levels of needs, a basis for planning appeals to self-interest.

Hotline   In public relations, a toll-free telephone number set up by a trade association or corporation to provide quick answers, especially to the news media.

Hype   The promotion of movie and television stars, books, magazines, and the like, through shrewd use of the media; used as both noun and verb. (See *Press agentry.*)

Hypodermic needle theory   The belief that people receive information directly without any intervening variable, as in a vacuum.

Image-building   Protection and enhancement of the reputation of an organization or individual.

Information on demand   Computerized information on requested topics called up on a television or computer screen by the user.

Information retrieval   Act of obtaining desired pieces of information from material stored in a computer.

Institutional advertising   Advertising intended to strengthen a company's image, rather than to stimulate immediate sales of its products or services. (See *Corporate advertising.*)

Internal publication   One designed for distribution primarily to employees. (See *External publication.*)

Internship   Temporary employment by a student to obtain professional work experience.

Interpersonal communication   Exchange between two or more persons in close proximity using conversation and gestures.

Issues management   Program of identifying and addressing issues of public concern in which a company is, or should be, involved.

Libel   Mainly defamation by written or printed words. (See *Slander.*)

Line function   Pursuit of management objectives through supervision, delegation of authority, and work assignments. (See *Staff function.*)

Literary agent   Person who represents an author in dealings with publishers.

Lobbyist   Person who presents an organization's point of view to Congress or other government bodies.

Marketing communications   Product publicity and promotion.

Message entropy   Tendency for a message to dissipate, or lose information, as it is disseminated.

Muckrakers   Writers who seek to expose corrupt and immoral conduct by companies, institutions, and governments; specifically, a group of early 1900s writers in America.

Mug shot   Slang term for a head-and-shoulders photograph of an individual for newspaper publication.

News conference   Meeting at which the spokesperson for an organization delivers information to reporters and answers their questions; often called a *press conference.*

News release Timely information about an activity of a public relations practitioner's client or organization, distributed in ready-to-use form.

Off-the-record Practice of giving reporters confidential information with the demand that it not be published.

100-showing Number of billboards needed to expose a message to approximately 100 percent of the population in a designated area within 30 days.

Opinion leader Articulate person knowledgeable about specific issues whose opinions influence others.

Pattern speech Basic speech written so that several speakers can deliver it to different audiences with only minor variations.

Pilot test Tryout of a public relations message and key copy points on a small audience before general distribution.

Planter Publicist who delivers news releases to media offices and urges their use.

Positioning The practice of creating corporate identity programs that establish a place in the market for a company and its products. Also, the effort to get ahead by doing something first.

Press agentry Term applied primarily to the publicizing of entertainers and shows; often used in a derogatory sense.

Press kit Folder containing news releases, photographs, and background information, distributed to media representatives.

Preventive public relations Efforts to maintain good will for an organization or individual through reinforcing messages.

Probability sample Survey in which every member of the targeted audience has a chance of being selected for questioning.

Product recall Act of calling back from consumers a company's product found to be defective, for repair or replacement.

Public affairs Term used primarily to describe work in the areas of government and community relations.

Public information Term used primarily by government agencies, social service organizations, and universities to describe their public relations activities.

Publisher Chief official of a newspaper who directs financial, mechanical, and administrative operations, and sometimes news and editorial operations as well.

Purposive sampling Selection of opinion leaders to be interviewed; usually used when approval of the group is necessary for success of a public relations campaign.

Quota sampling Selection of a group to be polled that matches the characteristics of the entire audience.

Royalty fee Amount of money received by an author for each copy of a book sold, usually 10 or 15 percent of the retail price.

Satellite transmission The method of transmitting text, pictures, and sound by beaming an electronic signal to a transponder on a satellite orbiting 22,300 miles above the earth, from which it bounces back to receiving dishes on the ground.

Semantics Study of words and their use and interpretation.

Semantic noise   Inept language usage that impedes the receiver's ability to comprehend a message; for example, use of trade jargon to a general audience.

Slander   Oral defamation of character. (See *Libel.*)

Social contract   Popular term for a corporation's set of responsibilities to the public.

Source credibility   Use of representatives who have expertise, sincerity, and charisma to win acceptance from an audience.

Split message   Exposure of two or three different appeals to separate audiences, to determine which is most effective.

Sponsored film   Motion picture paid for by an organization to deliver information or a message, usually shown without charge.

Staff function   Pursuit of management objectives through suggestions, recommendations, and advice. In corporate organization, public relations is a staff function. (See *Line function.*)

Talk show   Television or radio program on which a host or hostess chats with guests.

Teleconference   Presentation or discussion by television involving groups assembled at scattered receiving points, usually with telephone or television channels that permit distant viewers to ask questions or express reactions.

Teletext   System of delivering news and other information to a television screen, in which the viewer can select certain portions of the material to watch.

Telethon   Fund raising program on television lasting several hours, in which appeals for donations are mixed with entertainment.

Trade journal   Magazine designed and edited for a special-interest commercial or professional group.

Trademark   Name, symbol, or other device identifying a product, officially registered and legally restricted to the use of the owner or manufacturer.

Transfer   Technique of associating a person, product, or organization with individuals or situations of high or low credibility, depending on the intention of the message.

Transparency   Sheet of transparent acetate or similar material on which text or graphic material is placed, for showing on an overhead projector.

Videocassette   Small container of videotape that can be inserted in a playback machine for projection.

Videoconference   See *Teleconference.*

Videotape   A recording of moving images and sound on magnetic tape.

Videotex   Two-way communication system in which a viewer receives information on a screen and sends messages by keyboard.

BIBLIOGRAPHY

This bibliography was compiled by the Information Center of the Public Relations Society of America and is intended for reference only. Books should be obtained from their publishers.

General Books

ARONOFF, CRAIG, and BASKIN, OTIS W. *Public Relations: Profession and Practice*. St. Paul, Minn.: West, 1983.

BENN, ALEC *The 23 Most Common Mistakes in PR*. New York: AMACOM, 1982.

BERNAYS, EDWARD L. *Public Relations*. Norman: University of Oklahoma Press, 1977.

BITTLESTON, JOHN, and SHORTER, BARBARA. *Book of Business Communications Checklists*. New York: Wiley, 1982.

BLACK, SAM, and SHARPE, MELVIN. *Practical Public Relations*. Englewood Cliffs, N.J.: Prentice-Hall, 1983.

CENTER, ALLEN H., and WALSH, FRANK E. *Public Relations Practices: Case Studies*. Englewood Cliffs, N.J.: Prentice-Hall, 1985.

COLE, R. *Practical Handbook of Public Relations*. Englewood Cliffs, N.J.: Prentice-Hall, 1981.

CONNER, DEE, et al. *Hitting Your Target with PR and Publicity*. Boise, Idaho: PR Enterprises, 1981.

Critical Issues in Public Relations. New York: Hill and Knowlton, 1976. (420 Lexington Avenue, New York, N.Y. 10017)

CULLIGAN, MATTHEW J., and GREENE, DOLPH. *Getting Back to the Basics of Public Relations*. New York: Crown, 1982.

CUTLIP, SCOTT M., CENTER, ALLEN H., and BROOM, GLEN M. *Effective Public Relations*. 6th ed. Englewood Cliffs, N.J.: Prentice-Hall, 1985.

Dartnell Public Relations Handbook. Chicago: Dartnell, 1980.

EHRENKRANZ, LOIS B., and KAHN, GILBERT R. *Public Relations/Publicity*. New York: Fairchild, 1983.

GRUNING, JAMES, and HUNT, TODD. *Managing Public Relations*. New York: Holt, Rinehart and Winston, 1984.

HELM, LEWIS, and HIEBERT, RAY. *Informing the People: A Public Affairs Handbook*. New York: Longman, 1981.

KADON, A. *Successful Public Relations Techniques*. Scottsdale, Ariz.: Modern Schools, 1976.

LESLY, PHILIP. *Lesly's Public Relations Handbook*. Englewood Cliffs, N.J.: Prentice-Hall, 1983.

LEWIS, H. G. *How to Handle Your Own Public Relations*. Chicago: Nelson-Hall, 1976.

LONDGREN, R. *Communication by Objectives: A Guide to Productive and Cost-Effective Public Relations and Marketing*. Englewood Cliffs, N.J.: Prentice-Hall, 1983.

LOVELL, RONALD. *Inside Public Relations*. Boston: Allyn & Bacon, 1982.

MARSTON, JOHN. *Modern Public Relations*. New York: McGraw-Hill, 1979.

————. *The Nature of Public Relations*. New York: McGraw-Hill, 1983.

MOORE, H. FRAZIER, and FRANK KALUPA. *Public Relations: Principles, Cases, Problems*. 9th ed. Homewood, Ill.: Irwin, 1984.

NAGER, NORMAN R., and ALLEN, T. HARRELL. *Public Relations Management by Objectives*. New York: Longman, 1983.

NEWSOM, DOUG, and SCOTT, ALAN. *This Is PR: Realities of Public Relations*. Belmont, Calif.: Wadsworth, 1985.

NOLTE, L. W. *Fundamentals of Public Relations*. Elmsford, N.Y.: Pergamon Press, 1979.

NORRIS, JAMES. *Public Relations*. Englewood Cliffs, N.J.: Prentice-Hall, 1984.

REILLY, R. *Public Relations in Action*. Englewood Cliffs, N.J.: Prentice-Hall, 1981.

ROSS, R. D. *Management of Public Relations*. New York: Wiley, 1979.

SEITEL, FRASER. *The Practice of Public Relations*. Columbus, Ohio: Merrill, 1984.

SIMON, RAYMOND *Public Relations: Concepts and Practice*. New York: Wiley, 1984.

————. *Publicity and Public Relations Worktext*. New York: Wiley, 1983.

SPERBER, NATHANIEL H., and LERBINGER, OTTO. *Manager's Public Relations Handbook*. Reading, Mass.: Addison-Wesley, 1983.

STEINBERG, C. *Creation of Consent: Public Relations in Practice*. New York: Hastings House, 1975.

VOROS, GERALD J., and ALVAREZ, PAUL H. *What Happens in Public Relations*. New York: AMACOM, 1981.

Special Interest

BIOGRAPHY/MEMOIRS

BARMASH, I. *Always Live Better Than Your Clients: The Fabulous Life and Times of Benjamin Sonnenberg*. New York: Dodd, Mead, 1983.

Biographies of the FORTUNE 100 PR Department Heads. New York: O'Dwyer, 1981. (271 Madison Avenue, New York, N.Y. 10016)

HIEBERT, RAY. *Courtier to the Crowd*. Ames: Iowa State University Press, 1966. (Biography of Ivy Lee)

ROGERS, HENRY C. *Walking the Tightrope*. New York: Morrow, 1980.

BUSINESS/CORPORATE/ MANAGEMENT

BRADSHAW, THORNTON, and VOGEL, DAVID. *Corporations and Their Critics: Problems of Corporate Social Responsibilities*. New York: McGraw-Hill, 1982.

BUCHHOLZ, R. *Business Environment and Public Policy: Implications for Management*. Englewood Cliffs, N.J.: Prentice-Hall, 1982.

BUDD, J. *Corporate Video in Focus: A Management Guide to Private TV*. Englewood Cliffs, N.J.: Prentice-Hall, 1983.

BURGER, CHESTER. *The Chief Executive: Realities of Corporate Leadership*. Boston: CBI Publishing, 1978. (51 Sleeper Street, Boston, Mass. 02210)

CHASE, HOWARD. *Issues Management: Origins of the Future*. Stamford, Conn.: Issues Action Publications, 1984. (105 Old Long Ridge Road, Stamford, Conn. 06903)

Corporate Economic Education Programs. New York: FERP, 1979. (633 Third Avenue, New York, N.Y. 10017)

CURTISS, ELLEN T., and UNTERSEE, PHILIP A. *Corporate Responsibilities/Opportunities to 1990*. Lexington, Mass.: Heath, 1979.

D'APRIX, ROGER. *The Believable Corporation*. New York: AMACOM, 1977.

DEAL, TERRENCE, and KENNEDY, ALLAN A. *Corporate Cultures*. Reading, Mass.: Addison-Wesley, 1982.

DRUCKER, PETER. *Management: Tasks, Responsibilities, Practices*. New York: Harper & Row, 1974.

FALLON, W. *AMA Management Handbook*. New York: AMACOM, 1983.

GREFE, E. *Fighting to Win: Business Political Power*. San Diego: Harcourt Brace Jovanovich, 1981.

HENRY, K. *Defenders/Shapers of Corporate Image*. New Haven: College and University Press, 1972.

LESLY, PHILIP. *Overcoming Opposition: A Survival Manual for Executives*. Englewood Cliffs, N.J.: Prentice-Hall, 1984.

MARLOW, E. *Managing the Corporate Media Center*. White Plains, N.Y.: Knowledge Industry Publications, 1981.

MARSTELLER, WILLIAM A. *Creative Managment*. Chicago: Crain Books, 1981.

NEAL, ALFRED. *Business Power and Public Policy*. New York: Praeger, 1982.

PALUSZEK. J. *Business and Society: 1976-2000*. New York: AMACOM, 1976.

———. *Will the Corporation Survive?* Englewood Cliffs, N.J.: Prentice-Hall, 1977.

PETERS, THOMAS J., and WATERMAN, ROBERT R. JR. *In Search of Excellence*. New York: Harper & Row, 1982.

RUCH, RICHARD, and GOODMAN, RONALD. *Image at the Top: Crisis and Renaissance in American Corporate Leadership*. New York: Macmillan, 1983.

SETHI, S. PRAKASH, and SWANSON, CARL L. *Private Enterprise and Public Purpose*. New York: Wiley, 1981.

SPITZER, CARLTON. *Raising the Bottom Line: Business Leadership in a Changing Society*. New York: Longman, 1982.

STECKMEST, F. *Corporate Performance: The Key to Public Trust*. New York: McGraw-Hill, 1982.

WAYS, MAX. *The Future of Business: Global Issues in the 80s and 90s*. Elmsford, N.Y.: Pergamon Press, 1980.

COMMUNICATION/ PERSUASION/SOCIAL SCIENCE

ABELSON, HERBERT, and KARLINS, MARVIN. *Persuasion*. New York: Springer, 1970.

AGEE, WARREN K., AULT, PHILLIP H., and EMERY, EDWIN. *Introduction to Mass Communications*. 8th ed. New York: Harper & Row, 1985.

BITTNER, JOHN R. *Mass Communication: An Introduction*. Englewood Cliffs, N.J.: Prentice-Hall, 1983.

BLAKE, REED H. and HAROLDSON, EDWIN O. *Taxonomy of Concepts in Communication*. New York: Hastings House, 1975.

BOETTINGER, H. *Moving Mountains*. New York: Macmillan, 1975.

D'APRIX, ROGER. *Communicating for Productivity*. New York: Harper & Row, 1982.

DEMARE, G. *Communicating at the Top*. New York: Wiley, 1979.

DIDSBURY, HOWARD. *Communications and the Future*. Bethesda, Md.: World Future Society, 1984.

GOLDHABER, G. *Organizational Communication*. Dubuque, Iowa: Brown, 1979.

HAIGH, ROBERT, et al. *Communications in the Twenty-First Century*. New York: Wiley, 1981.

HIEBERT, RAY, UNGURAIT, DONALD F., and BOHN, THOMAS. *Mass Media III*. New York: Longman, 1982.

LARSON, CHARLES U. *Persuasion*. Belmont, Calif.: Wadsworth, 1983.

LESLY, PHILIP. *How We Discommunicate*. New York: AMACOM, 1979.

————. *Selections from Managing the Human Climate*. Chicago: Philip Lesly, 1979. (130 E. Randolph Street, Chicago, Ill. 60601)

NAISBITT, JOHN. *Megatrends*. New York: Warner Books, 1982.

REARDON, K. *Persuasion: Theory and Context*. Beverly Hills, Calif.: Sage, 1981.

COMMUNITY RELATIONS YARRINGTON, R. *Community Relations Handbook*. New York: Longman, 1983.

CRISIS/EMERGENCY BERNSTEIN, ALAN. *Emergency Public Relations Manual*. Highland Park, N.J.: Pase, 1982.

NEWTON, C. *Coming to Grips with Crisis*. New York: AMACOM, 1981.

DESIGN SERVICES JONES, GERRE. *How to Market Professional Design Services*. New York: McGraw-Hill, 1983.

————. *How to Prepare Professional Design Brochures*. New York: McGraw-Hill, 1976.

————. *Public Relations for the Design Professional*. New York: McGraw-Hill, 1980.

EDUCATION/CAREERS BONUS, T. *Improving Internal Communications* (college). Washington, D.C.: CASE. (11 DuPont Circle, 20036)

BORTNER, D. *Public Relations for Public Schools*. Cambridge, Mass.: Schenkman, 1983.

Building Public Confidence in Your Schools. Arlington, Va.: NSPRA, 1978. (1801 N. Moore Street, Arlington, Va. 22209)

Careers in Public Relations. New York: Public Relations Society of America, 19——.

Design for Public Relations Education. New York: Status/Trends of Public Relations Education, 1975. (Foundation for Public Relations, 415 Lexington Avenue, New York, N.Y. 10017)

Effective Public Relations for Colleges. Washington, D.C.: CASE, 1979. (11 DuPont Circle, 20036)

FARLOW, HELEN. *Publicizing/Promoting Programs.* New York: McGraw-Hill, 1979. (Education programs)

KINDRED, LESLIE W., et al. *The School and Community Relations.* Englewood Cliffs, N.J.: Prentice-Hall, 1976.

KOBRE, SIDNEY. *Successful Public Relations for Colleges/Universities.* New York: Hastings House, 1974.

Public Relations in the Community College. Washington, D.C.: CASE, 1981. (11 Dupont Circle, 20036)

Public Relations Job Finder. Englewood Cliffs, N.J.: Prentice-Hall, 1981.

RECK, W. EMERSON. *Changing World of College Relations.* Washington, D.C.: CASE, 1976. (11 DuPont Circle, 20036)

ROTMAN, M. *Opportunities in Public Relations.* Lincolnwood, Ill.: National Textbook Company, 1983.

ROWLAND, A. WESTLEY. *Handbook of Institutional Advancement.* San Francisco: Jossey-Bass, 1977.

Small College Advancement Program. Washington, D.C.: CASE, 1981. (11 DuPont Circle, 20036)

WALLING, D. *Complete Book of School Public Relations.* Englewood Cliffs, N.J.: Prentice-Hall, 1982.

WOODRESS, FRED A. *Public Relations for Junior Colleges.* Danville, Ill.: Interstate, 1976.

EMPLOYEE RELATIONS (FOR EMPLOYEE PUBLICATIONS, SEE SECTION "WRITING/ SPEAKING/STYLEBOOKS/ NEWSLETTERS")

BURKETT, D. *Very Good Management: Guide to Management by Communicating.* Englewood Cliffs, N.J.: Prentice-Hall, 1983.

D'APRIX, ROGER. *Communicating for Productivity.* New York: Harper & Row, 1982.

DEUTSCH, ARNOLD. *Human Resources Revolution.* New York: McGraw-Hill, 1979.

DUNHAM, RANDALL, and SMITH, FRANK J. *Organizational Surveys.* Glenview, Ill.: Scott, Foresman, 1979.

Employee Annual Report: Purpose, Format, Content. Chicago: Ragan Communications, 1984. (407 S. Dearborn St., 60605)

How to Prepare and Write Your Employee Handbook. New York: AMACOM, 1984.

Inside Organizational Communications. San Francisco: International Association of Business Communicators, 1981. (870 Market Street, San Francisco, Calif. 94102)

ETHICS

CHRISTIANS, CLIFFORD, et al. *Media Ethics.* New York: Longman, 1983.

HILL, IVAN. *Ethical Basis of Economic Freedom.* New York: Praeger, 1980.

LITSCHERT, ROBERT J. et al. *The Corporate Role and Ethical Behavior.* New York: Van Nostand Reinhold, 1977.

WALTON, CLARENCE, ed. *Ethics of Corporate Conduct.* American Assembly, Columbia University. Englewood Cliffs, N.J.: Prentice-Hall, 1977.

FINANCIAL   *Effective Public Relations and Communications: A Handbook for Banks.* Washington: American Bankers Association, 1982.

GRAVES, JOSEPH.   *Managing Investor Relations.* Homewood, Ill.: Dow Jones-Irwin, 1982.

KIRSCH, DONALD.   *Financial and Economic Journalism.* New York: New York University Press, 1978.

MARCUS, BRUCE.   *Competing for Capital in the '80s: An Investor Relations Approach.* Westport, Conn.: Quorum Books, 1983.

ROALMAN, A. R.   *Investor Relations Handbook.* New York: AMACOM, 1974.

———.   *Investor Relations That Work.* New York: AMACOM, 1981.

The SEC, the Securities Market and Your Financial Communications. New York: Hill and Knowlton, 1985.

WILSON, M. H.   *Corporate Investor Relations Function.* Charlotte, N.C.: UMI Press, 1980.

GOVERNMENT/POLITICS/ PUBLIC AFFAIRS   CHASE, HOWARD.   *Issues Management: Origins of the Future.* Stamford, Conn.: Issues Action Publications, 1984. (105 Old Long Ridge Road, Stamford, Conn. 06093)

Corporation in Politics. New York: Practicing Law Institute, 1981. (810 Seventh Avenue, New York, N.Y. 10019)

GOLLNER, ANDREW.   *Social Change and Corporate Strategy: The Expanding Role of Public Affairs.* Stamford, Conn.: IAP, 1984. (105 Old Long Ridge Rd. 06903)

Government/Press Connection: Press Officers and Their Offices, Washington, D.C.: The Brookings Institution, 1984.

HELM, LEWIS, and HIEBERT, RAY.   *Informing the People: A Public Affairs Handbook.* New York: Longman, 1981.

HIEBERT, RAY.   *Political Image Merchants.* Washington: Acropolis, 1975.

Issues Management Programs: Why They Fail and How to Make Them Work. Human Resource Network, 2011 Chancellor St., Philadelphia 19305, 1984.

NAGELSCHMIDT, J.   *Public Affairs Handbook.* New York: AMACOM, 1982. (Available from Public Relations Society of America)

Public Interest Profiles. Washington: Foundation for Public Affairs, 1982. (1220 16th Street NW, Washington, D.C. 20036)

Social Change and Corporate Strategy: The Expanding Role of Public Affairs. Stamford, Conn.: Issues Action Publications, 1983.

YORKE, HARVEY, and DOHERTY, LIZ.   *Candidate's Handbook for Winning Local Elections.* Novato, Calif.: Harvey Yorke, 1982. (Box 252, Novato, Calif. 94948)

GRAPHICS/PHOTOGRAPHY   DOUGLIS, PHILIP.   *Pictures for Organizations: How and Why They Work as Communication.* Chicago: Ragan Communications, 1982.

LEFFERTS, ROBERT.   *Elements of Graphics: How to Prepare Charts/Graphics for Effective Reports.* New York: Harper & Row, 1981.

MARSH, P. *Messages That Work: Guide to Communication Design*. Englewood Cliffs, N. J.: Prentice-Hall, 1983.

SELAME, ELINOR *Developing a Corporate Identity*. Lebhar-Friedman, 1980.

WHITE, JAN. *Mastering Graphics: Design and Production Made Easy*. Ann Arbor, Mich.: Bowker, 1983.

INTERNATIONAL *Financial and Other Relations in Europe*. New York: Burson-Marsteller, 1979. (866 Third Avenue, New York, N.Y. 10022)

ROTH, ROBERT. *International Marketing Communications*. Chicago: Crain, 1982.

SHAEFFER, BRUCE. *Doing Business in America: Guide for the Foreign Investor*. Homewood, Ill.: Dow Jones-Irwin, 1984.

LEGAL *Association Legal Checklist*. Washington: Chamber of Commerce, 1983. (1615 H Street NW, Washington, D.C. 1983)

LAMB, R., et al. *Business, Media, and the Law*. New York: New York University Press, 1980.

NELSON, HAROLD L., and TEETER, DWIGHT L. JR. *Law of Mass Communications*. Mineola, N.Y.: Foundation Press, 1982.

SANFORD, BRUCE. *Synopsis of the Law of Libel and the Right of Privacy*. New York: World Almanac, 1981.

SHAPIRO, A. *Media Access*. Boston: Little, Brown, 1976. (Legal guide)

SIMON, MORTON. *Public Relations Law*. New York: Foundation for Public Relations, 1969.

ZUCKMAN, Harry, and GAYNES, MARTIN J. *Mass Communication Law in a Nutshell*. St. Paul, Minn.: West, 1977.

LIBRARIES EDSALL, M. *Library Promotion Handbook*. Phoenix, Ariz.: Oryx Press, 1980.

GARVEY, M. *Library Public Relations*. New York: Wilson, 1980.

LERBURGER, B. *Marketing the Library*. White Plains, N.Y.: Knowledge Industry Publications, 1981.

USHERWOOD, R. *The Visible Library: Practical PR for Public Libraries*. Phoenix, Ariz.: Oryx Press, 1981.

MARKETING/RESEARCH BERDIE, DOUGLAS R. *Questionnaires: Design/Use*. Metuchen, N.J.: Scarecrow Press, 1974.

BREEN, G. *Do-It-Yourself Marketing Research*. New York: McGraw-Hill, 1982.

DeLOZIER, M. WAYNE. *The Marketing Communications Process*. New York: McGraw-Hill, 1976

FINE, SEYMOUR. *Marketing of Ideas and Social Issues*. New York: Praeger, 1981.

GOLDMAN, J. *Public Relations in the Marketing Mix.* Chicago: Crain, 1984.

LOWERY, SHEARON, and DeFLEUR, MELVIN. *Milestones in Mass Communications Research.* New York: Longman, 1983.

ROBINSON, EDWARD J. *Public Relations Survey Research.* New York: Irvington, 1969.

STEMPEL, GUIDO H., and WESTLEY, BRUCE H. *Research Methods in Mass Communication.* Englewood Cliffs, N.J.: Prentice-Hall, 1979.

UDELL, JON G., and LACZNIAK, GENE R. *Marketing in an Age of Change.* New York: Wiley, 1981.

WEINRAUCH, J. DONALD, and PILAND, WILLIAM E. *Applied Marketing Principles.* Englewood Cliffs, N.J.: Prentice-Hall, 1979.

MEDIA/PRESS RELATIONS

BLAND, M. *Executive's Guide to TV/Radio Appearances.* White Plains, N.Y.: Knowledge Industry Publications, 1980.

BLYTHIN, SAMOVAR. *Communicating Effectively on Television.* Belmont, Calif.: Wadsworth, 1985.

BRUM and ANDERSON. *Having Effective Media Interviews.* 425 Lumber Exchange Building, Minneapolis, Minn. 55402.

CLIFFORD, MARTIN. *Complete Guide to Satellite TV.* Blue Ridge, Pa.: Tab Books, 1984.

CORRADO, F. *Media for Managers.* Englewood Cliffs, N.J.: Prentice-Hall, 1984.

MacDOUGALL, KENT. *Ninety Seconds to Tell It All: Big Business and the News Media.* Homewood, Ill.: Dow Jones-Irwin, 1982.

MARTIN, DICK. *Executive's Guide to Handling a Press Interview.* New York: Pilot Books, 1981.

Media Resource Guide. Foundation for American Communications, 3383 Barham Blvd., Los Angeles, Calif., 90068.

MINCER, RICHARD, and MINCER, DEANNE. *Talk Show Book.* New York: Facts on File, 1982.

ROSSIE, C. *Media Resource Guide.* Los Angeles: Foundation for American Communications, 1983.

MEETINGS

How to Run Better Business Meetings. St. Paul, Minn.: Visual Division, 3M, 1979.

Planning, Conducting, Evaluating Workshops. Larry N. Davis: Austin, Tex.: Learning Concepts, 1975.

Professional Guide to Successful Meetings. New York: Bill Communications, 1976. (633 Third Ave.)

NONPROFIT/HEALTH/FUND-RAISING

Basic Guide to Hospital Public Relations. Chicago: ASHPR, 1984. (840 N. Lake Shore, Chicago, Ill. 60611)

BATES, D. *Communicating and Moneymaking.* New York: Heladon, 1979. (Box 2827 Grand Central Station, New York, N.Y. 10017)

BROCE, THOMAS E. *Fund Raising.* Norman: University of Oklahoma Press, 1979.

CONNORS, TRACY. *Nonprofit Organization Handbook.* New York: McGraw-Hill, 1979.

GABY, P. and D. *Nonprofit Organization Handbook.* Englewood Cliffs, N.J.: Prentice-Hall, 1983.

GRASTY, WILLIAM K., and SHEINKOPF, KENNETH. *Successful Fundraising.* New York: Scribner, 1982.

KOTLER, PHILIP. *Cases and Readings for Nonprofit Organizations.* Englewood Cliffs, N.J.: Prentice-Hall, 1983.

———. *Marketing for Nonprofit Organizations.* Englewood Cliffs, N.J.: Prentice-Hall, 1982.

KURTZ, HAROLD P. *Public Relations and Fund Raising for Hospitals.* Springfield, Ill.: Thomas, 1980.

LORD, JAMES. *Philanthropy and Marketing: New Strategies for Fund Raising.* Cleveland: Third Sector Press, 1983.

McMILLAN, NORMAN. *Marketing Your Hospital.* Chicago: American Hospital Association, 1982.

MILLER, IRWIN. *Health Care Survival Curve: Competition and Cooperation in the Marketplace.* Homewood, Ill.: Dow Jones-Irwin, 1984.

OAKS, L. ROBERT. *Communication by Objective.* South Plainfield, N.J.: Groupwork, 1977.

PRAY, FRANCIS. *Handbook for Educational Fund Raising.* San Francisco: Jossey-Bass, 1982.

Public Relations Guides for Nonprofit Organizations: 1. *Planning/Setting Objectives.* 2. *Using Publicity to Best Advantage.* 3. *Working with Volunteers.* 4. *Making the Most of Special Events.* 5. *Measuring Potential/Evaluating Results.* 6. *Using Standards to Strengthen Public Relations.* New York: Foundation for Public Relations, 1977.

RADOS, D. *Marketing for Non-Profit Organizations.* Dover, MA.: Auburn House, 1981.

RIGGS, LEW. *The Health Care Facility's Public Relations Handbook.* Aspen, 1982

SNOOK, I. D. *Building a Winning Medical Staff.* Chicago: American Hospital Publishing Co., 1984.

TAYLOR, BERNARD. *Guide to Successful Fund Raising.* South Plainfield, N.J.: Groupwork, 1976.

WARNER, IRVING. *Art of Fund Raising.* New York: Harper & Row, 1975.

POLICE/FIRE DEPARTMENTS

EARLE, H. Police/Community Relations. Srpingfield, Ill.: Thomas, 1980.

GARNER, G. *The Police Meet the Press.* Springfield, Ill.: Thomas, 1984.

JOHNSON, THOMAS A., and MISNER, GORDAN. *The Police and Society.* Englewood Cliffs, N.J.: Prentice-Hall, 1982.

RADELET, L. *Police and the Community.* New York: Macmillan, 1980.

Successful Public Relations. Boston: National Fire Protection Association, 1974.

PRESENTATIONS LEECH, T. *How to Prepare, Stage, and Deliver Winning Presentations.* New York: AMACOM, 1983.

PROFESSIONALS/
CONSULTANTS/PERSONAL BETANCOURT, HAL. *The Advertising Answerbook: Guide for Business and Professional People.* Englewood Cliffs, N.J.: Prentice-Hall, 1982.

BRAUN, IRWIN. *Building a Successful Practice with Advertising.* New York: AMACOM, 1981.

GOULD, J. S. *How to Publicize Yourself, Your Family, and Your Organization.* Englewood Cliffs, N.J.: Prentice-Hall, 1983.

GRAY, JAMES. The Winning Image. New York: AMACOM, 1982.

HAMEROFF, EUGENE C., and NICHOLS, SANDRA. *How to Guarantee Professional Success.* Washington: Consultant's Library, 1982.

JOHNSON, B. *Private Consulting.* Englewood Cliffs, N.J.: Prentice-Hall, 1982.

KENNEDY, J. H. *Public Relations for Management Consultants.* Fitzwilliam, N.H.: Consultants News, 1983.

KOTLER, PHILIP, and BLOOM, PAUL. *Marketing Professional Services.* Englewood Cliffs, N.J.: Prentice-Hall, 1983.

McCAFFREY, MIKE. *Personal Marketing Strategies: How to Sell Yourself, Your Ideas, and Your Services.* Englewood Cliffs, N.J.: Prentice-Hall, 1983.

SARNOFF, D. *Making the Most of Your Best: A Complete Program for Presenting Yourself and Your Ideas with Confidence and Authority.* New York: Holt, Rinehart and Winston, 1983.

PUBLICITY KNESEL, D. *Free Publicity: A Step by Step Guide.* Sterling, 1982.

LEIDING, OSCAR. *Layman's Guide to Successful Publicity.* Salem, N.H.: Ayer Press, 1979.

NOLTE, L. W., and WILCOX, DENNIS L. *Effective Publicity: How to Reach the Public.* New York: Wiley, 1984.

QUINLAN, J. *Industrial Publicity.* New York: Van Nostrand, Reinhold, 1983.

WAGNER, GARY. *Publicity Forum.* New York: Weiner, 1977.

WEINER, R. *Professional's Guide to Publicity.* New York: Weiner, 1977.

WINSTON, M. *Getting Publicity.* New York: Wiley, 1982.

YALE, DAVID. *Publicity Handbook.* New York: Bantam, 1982.

REAL ESTATE *Home Builders Publicity Manual.* Washington, D.C.: National Association of Home Builders, 1984.

MARCUS, B. *Marketing Professional Services in Real Estate.* Chicago: National Association of Realtors, 1981.

Public Relations for Home Builders. Washington: National Association of Home Builders, 1978.

RELIGION   CRAIG, FLOYD A. *Christian Communicator's Handbook.* Nashville: Broadman Press, 1977.

Religious Public Relations Handbook. New York: Religious Public Relations Council, 1982.

SUMRALL, VELMA, and GERMANY, LUCILLE. *Religious Public Relations Handbook.* New York: Seabury Press, 1979.

RESTAURANTS/FOOD SERVICE   FISHER, WILLIAM P. *Creative Marketing for the Foodservice Industry,* New York: Wiley, 1982.

SMALL BUSINESS   BLAKE, GARY, and BLY, ROBERT W. *How to Promote Your Own Business.* New York: New American Library, 1983.

CARLSON, L. *Publicity/Promotion Handbook: Complete Guide for Small Business.* Boston: CBI Publishing, 1982.

SPECIAL EVENTS   LIEBERT, EDWIN, and SHELDON, BERNICE E. *Handbook of Special Events for Nonprofit Organizations.* Association Press, 1982.

SPORTS/TRAVEL/ RECREATION   BRONZAN, ROBERT T. *Public Relations, Promotions, Fund-Raising for Athletic Programs.* New York: Wiley, 1976.

EPPLEY, GARRETT G. *Improve Your Public Relations.* Arlington, Va.: NRPA, 1977. (Parks)

REILLY, ROBERT T. *Travel/Tourism Marketing Techniques.* Wheaton, Ill.: Merton House, 1980.

THEATER   MARSHALL, S. *Promotion for Theater.* Carmel, CA.: Creative Books, 1983.

UTILITIES   SULLIVAN, FRANK C. *Crisis of Confidence: Public Relations and Credibility.* Phoenix, Ariz., 1977.

WRITING/SPEAKING/ STYLEBOOKS/NEWSLETTERS   ARNOLD, E. C. *Editing the Organizational Publication.* Chicago: Ragan Communications, 1984.

Ayer Public Relations/Publicity Stylebook. Fort Washington, Penn.: IMS Press, 1983.

BEACH, M. *Editing Your Newsletter.* Portland, Ore.: Coast to Coast Books, 1983.

BERNSTEIN, THEODORE. *The Careful Writer.* New York: Atheneum, 1975.

Broadcast News Stylebook. New York: Associated Press, 19—.

Darrow, Richard W. *House Journal Editing.* Danville, Ill.: Interstate, 1975.

Douglas, G. *Writing for Public Relations.* Columbus, Ohio: Merrill, 1980.

Executive Speechmaker. New York: Foundation for Public Relations.

F., F., and B.: *Producing Flyers, Folders, and Brochures.* Chicago: Ragan Communications, 1984.

Guidelines for Report Writers: Complete Manual for On-the-Job Report Writing. Englewood Cliffs, N.J.: Prentice-Hall, 1982.

Hayakawa, S. I. *Language in Thought and Action,* San Diego: Harcourt Brace Jovanovich, 1978.

How to Conduct a Readership Survey. Chicago: Ragan Communications, 1982.

Hudson, Howard Penn. *Publishing Newsletters.* New York: Scribner, 1982.

Jacobi, Peter. *Writing with Style: The News Story and the Feature.* Chicago, Ragan Communications, 1982.

The New York Times Manual of Style and Usage. Rev. and edited by Lewis Jordan. New York: Times Books, 1977.

Newsom, Doug, and Siegfried, Tom. *Writing in Public Relations Practice.* Belmont, Calif.: Wadsworth, 1981.

On Graphics: Tips for Editors. Chicago: Ragan Communications, 1981. (Newsletters)

Pesman, S. *Writing for the Media.* Chicago: Crain, 1983.

Reid, Gerene. *How to Write Company Newsletters.* Deming, Wash.: Rubicon, 1980.

————. *Speaking Well.* New York: McGraw-Hill, 1982.

Roman, Kenneth, and Raphaelson, Joel. *Writing That Works.* New York: Harper & Row, 1981.

Stedman, William A. *Guide to Public Speaking.* Englewood Cliffs, N.J.: Prentice-Hall, 1981.

Stylebook/Libel Manual. New York: Associated Press, 1977.

Wales, La Rue Jr. *Practical Guide to Newsletter Editing/Design.* Iowa University Press, 1976.

Words into Type. 3rd ed., rev. Englewood Cliffs, N.J.: Prentice-Hall, 1974.

Bibliographies/Directories

BIBLIOGRAPHIES

Norton, Alice. *Public Relations: Guide to Information Sources.* Detroit: Gale Research Company, 1970.

Public Relations, the Edward Bernayses and the American Scene. Faxon, 1978.

MEDIA DIRECTORIES

Ayer Directory. IMS Press, 426 Pennsylvania Avenue, Fort Washington, Penn. 19034.

Bacon's Publicity Checker: Magazines/Newspapers. 322 S. Michigan, Chicago, Ill. 60604. (Two volumes)

Broadcasting/Cablecasting Yearbook. Broadcasting Publications, 1735 DeSales, NW, Washington, D.C. 20036.

Burrelle's Media Directories: New York State; New Jersey; Pennsylvania; New England; Connecticut; Maine; New Hampshire; Massachusetts; Rhode Island; Vermont; New England Talk Show; Greater Boston. 75 E. Northfield, Livingston, N.J. 07039.

Burrelle's Special Directories: Black Media; Hispanic Media; Women's Media.

Business/ Financial/Economic News Correspondents & Contacts. Larriston, Box 1351, New York, N.Y. 10025. 1983.

Cable Contacts Yearbook. Larimi. 151 E. 50th Street, New York, N.Y. 10022.

Cable TV Publicity Outlets—Nationwide. Box 327, Washington Depot, Conn. 06794.

College Alumni Publications. Weiner, 888 Seventh Avenue, New York, N.Y. 10106. 1980.

Editor & Publisher International Year Book. 850 Third Avenue, New York, N.Y. 10022.

Family Page Directory. Box 327, Washington Depot, Conn. 06794.

Gebbie Press All-in-One Directory. Box 100, New Paltz, N. Y. 12561.

Greater Philadelphia Publicity Guide. Box 365, Ambler, Penn. 19002. 1982.

Hudson's Washington Media Directory. 7315 Wisconsin Avenue, Bethesda, Md. 20814.

Investment Newsletters. Weiner, 888 Seventh Avenue, New York, N.Y. 10106.

Kaufman Editorial Guide. 2233 Wisconsin Avenue, NW, Washington, D.C. 20007.

Medical/Science News Correspondents. Larriston, Box 1351, New York, N.Y. 10025.

Metro California Media. Box 327, Washington Depot, Conn. 06794.

Midwest Media Directory. 176 W. Adams, Chicago, Ill. 60690.

Military Publications. Weiner, 888 Seventh Avenue, New York, N.Y. 10106.

Minnesota Publicity Handbook; Twin Cities Publicity Handbook MIS Corporation, 1536 S. Oberlin, Fridley, Minn. 55432.

National Directory of Newsletters. Gale Research Company, Book Tower. Detroit, Mich. 48226.

New England Media Directory. 5 Auburn, Framingham, Mass. 01701.

New York Publicity/Outlets. Box 327, Washington Depot, Conn. 06794.

News Bureaus in the U.S. Weiner, 888 Seventh Avenue, New York, N.Y. 10106.

Newsletter Yearbook Directory. Box 311, Rhinebeck, N.Y. 12572. 1983.

Northwest Handbook. Box 9304, Seattle, Wash. 98109. (Annual)

Oxbridge Directory of Newsletters. 183 Madison Avenue, New York, N.Y. 10016. 1983.

Standard Periodical Directory. Oxbridge, 183 Madison Avenue, New York, N.Y. 10016.

Syndicated Columnists. Weiner, 888 Seventh Avenue, New York, N.Y. 10106.

Talk Show Directory. National Research, 310 S. Michigan, Chicago, Ill. 60604. 1983.

Texas Media Guide. Ampersand Inc. 1103 S. Shepherd Drive, Houston, Tex. 77019.

TV Contacts; Radio Contacts; Cable Contacts. Larimi, 151 E. 50th Street, New York, N.Y. 10022.

TV Publicity Outlets—Nationwide. Box 327, Washington Depot, Conn. 06794.

Working Press of the Nation. National Research, 310 S. Michigan, Chicago, Ill. 60604. (Volume 5 is employee publications directory.)

INTERNATIONAL MEDIA DIRECTORIES

Bacon's International. 322 S. Michigan, Chicago, Ill. 60604.

Media Guides International: 1. *Worldwide—Newspapers/Magazines.* 2. *Worldwide—Consumer Magazines.* 3. *Europe—Business/Professional Publications.* 4. *Latin America—Business/Professional Publications.* 5. *Asia, Australia, USSR—Business/Professional Publications.* Directories International, 150 Fifth Avenue, New York, N.Y. 10011.

Ulrich's International Directory. Bowker, 1180 Sixth Avenue, New York, N.Y. 10036.

OTHER DIRECTORIES

Awards, Honors, Prizes. Gale Research Company, Book Tower, Detroit, Mich. 48226. 1982.

Chase Calendar of Annual Events. Contemporary Books, 180 N. Michigan, Chicago, Ill. 60611.

Consultants/Consulting Organizations. Gale Research Company, Book Tower, Detroit, Mich. 48226.

Encyclopedia of Associations. Gale Research Company.

Finding the Right Speaker. ASAE, 1575 I Street NW, Washington, D.C. 20005.

Fortune 500 Directory. Box 8001, Trenton, N.J. 08650.

International Directory of Special Events and Festivals. Special Events Reports, 213 W. Institute Place, Chicago, Ill. 60610.

National Directory of Speakers on Public Relations Topics. Public Relations Society of America, 845 Third Avenue, New York, N.Y. 10022. 1982.

National Trade/Professional Associations. Columbia Books, 777 14th Street NW, Washington, D. C. 20005.

O'Dwyer's Directory of Corporate Communications. 271 Madison Avenue, New York, N.Y. 10016.

O'Dwyer's Directory of Public Relations Executives.

O'Dwyer's Directory of Public Relations Firms.

Personal Image Consultants. Editorial Service, 96 State Street, New York, N.Y. 11201.

Professional's Guide to Public Relations Services. Weiner, 888 Seventh Avenue, New York, N.Y. 10106.

Public Interest Profiles. Public Affairs Foundation, 1220 16th Street NW, Washington, D.C. 20036.

Speakers and Lecturers: How to Find Them. Gale Research Company, Book Tower, Detroit, Mich. 48226.

Periodicals

Cable Hotline. Larimi, 151 E. 50th Street, New York, N.Y. 10022. (Twice monthly)

Case Currents. CASE, 11 DuPont Circle, Washington, D.C. 20036.

Channels. Box 600, Exeter, N.H. 03833. (Monthly)

Community Relations Report. Box X, Bartlesville, Okla. 74005. (Monthly)

Contacts. Larimi, 151 E. 50th Street, New York, N.Y. 10022. (Weekly)

Corporate Communications Report. 112 E. 31st Street, New York, N.Y. 10016. (Six issues a year)

Corporate Public Issues. 105 Old Long Ridge Road, Stamford, Conn. 06903. (Two issues a month)

Corporate Shareholder. 271 Madison Avenue, New York, N.Y. 10016. (22 issues a year)

Investor Relations Newsletter. 305 Madison Avenue, New York, N.Y. 10165. (Monthly)

Investor Relations Update. NIRI, 1730 K Street NW, Washington, D.C. 20006. (Monthly)

IPRA Review. 49 Wellington Street, London WC2E 8BN, England, (Quarterly)

Jack O'Dwyer's Newsletter. 271 Madison Avenue, New York, N.Y. 10016.

Media Alerts. Bacon's, 332 S. Michigan, Chicago, Ill. 60604. (Bimonthly)

PR Aids' Party Line. 330 W. 34th Street, New York, N.Y. 10001. (Weekly)

PR Casebook. 62 Derby Street, Hingham, Mass. 02043. (Monthly)

PR Reporter. Box 600, Exeter, N.H. 03833. (Weekly)

Professional Marketing Report. Box 32387, Washington, D.C. 20007. (Monthly)

Public Affairs Review. 1220 16th Street NW, Washington, D.C. 20036. (Annual)

Public Relations Journal. Public Relations Society of America, 845 Third Avenue, New York, N.Y. 10022. (Monthly)

Public Relations News. 127 E. 80th Street, New York, N.Y. 10021. (Weekly)

Public Relations Quarterly. 44 W. Market Street, Rhinebeck, N.Y. 12572.

Public Relations Review. 7100 Baltimore Boulevard, College Park, Md. 20740. (Monthly)

Ragan Report. 407 S. Dearborn, Chicago, Ill. 60605. (Weekly)

Social Science Monitor. 7100 Baltimore Boulevard, College Park, Md. 20740. (Monthly)

Special Events Report. 213 W. Institute Place, Chicago, Ill. 60610. (24 issues a year)

Speechwriter's Newsletter. Ragan, 407 S. Dearborn, Chicago, Ill. 60605. (24 issues a year)

Sports Media News. 34 Washington Road, Princeton, N.J. 08550. (Monthly)

Video Monitor. 7100 Baltimore Boulevard, College Park, Md. 20740.

[*Communication World.* International Association of Business Communicators, 870 Market St., San Francisco, Calif. 94102. (Monthly) *Communication World* is the magazine of the IABC.]